*SOCIOLOGY: AN INTRODUCTION*

# SOCIOLOGY: AN INTRODUCTION

*SECOND EDITION*

**Christopher Bates Doob**
*Southern Connecticut State University*

**HOLT, RINEHART AND WINSTON, INC.**
*New York   Chicago   San Francisco   Philadelphia*
*Montreal   Toronto   London   Sydney   Tokyo*

*Once again, to Eveline Bates (Doob)*
*and Leonard William Doob who, besides*
*being my parents, have always been my*
*best teachers.*

*Front cover collage by Joan Hall*

Printed in the United States of America

8 9 0 1     039     9 8 7 6 5 4 3 2 1

**Library of Congress Cataloging-in-Publication Data**
Doob, Christopher Bates.
  Sociology: an introduction.

  Bibliography: p.
  Includes index.
  1. Sociology.  I. Title.
HM51.D645  1988      301      87-3471

ISBN 0-03-012804-8

Holt, Rinehart and Winston, Inc.
The Dryden Press
Saunders College Publishing

# PREFACE

About halfway into the completion of this second edition, I was walking my dog when an eight-year-old neighbor approached me. He was aware that I do much of my work at home, but he knew little about it and for some reason wanted to know more that day. I told him I was revising a textbook. He asked me what revising meant, and I gave him the general idea. He paused to think for a moment and then said: "Oh, it's kind of like rewriting a paper after the teacher has corrected it."

"That's a pretty good sense of it," I replied.

He paused again. "But if it's like rewriting a paper, why's it taking you so long?" This, I admitted, was a very smart question.

Outside the circle of eight-year-olds, in fact, it's still a smart question. In many cases the revision of a text is a pretty cursory affair, but this one hasn't been. Guided by reviewers' suggestions, and those of my editors, I have introduced many changes and important features in the second edition which, I believe, make this a better, more appealing book. The most major of these changes are:

A new, streamlined 17-chapter format positions the comprehensive coverage more comfortably within an academic semester.

A new built-in study guide enables students to review the material they have just learned.

New "Research in Sociology" sections provide concrete illustrations of what sociological research involves.

New "American Controversies" boxes expose students to sociological issues which provoke different, often dissenting responses.

## ORGANIZATION

I remain convinced that a fairly traditional organization is the best for an introductory text. Thus the five parts of the first edition have been retained. Part One examines the particular features, contributions, and theories that distinguish the sociological point of view and surveys the major methods and problems of doing research. Part Two launches into the variety of influences, conditions, and pressures that help to make individuals part of the larger social environment. Part Three examines the nature of inequalities in modern society and the processes that affect specific minorities in America. Part Four brings the student to the next level of complexity in social arrangements by surveying a range of social institutions, how (and how well) they meet the collective needs of American society, and how and why they are changing. The final section of the text examines the forces and issues that have had an impact on each level of our social order, from relationships between institutions to small-group interactions.

While the overall structure of the book remains the same as in the first edition, we have developed a briefer format for this edition, reducing the number of chapters from 21 to 17. Many instructors of Introductory Sociology indicated to us that they would be more comfortable with a shorter text and that the best place to economize would be in the coverage of the social institutions. Thus the institutions are now presented in combination chapters, which illustrate the respective relationships between religion and education, the political and economic institutions, and science and medicine. In addition, material from the first-edition chapter on social change has been repositioned in the new Chapter 17 ("Collective

Behavior, Social Movements, and Social Change") to underscore the effect organized behavior can have on our attitudes, beliefs, and subsequent actions.

The new organization of the text should also be more compatible with the syllabus for a 15- or 16-week course.

## STYLE OF PRESENTATION

Many introductory sociology students, even potential majors, have little background in the social sciences and even less familiarity with the way scientists and academicians think. For this reason textbooks that make assumptions about the students' reach can easily slip beyond their grasp. In spite of a subject matter that is inherently interesting and relevant, student motivation can quickly subside when there are too many hurdles to learning. Students need to feel successful about understanding and interpreting what they read. This means that a text must spell out the implications of the material presented in straightforward language, interrelate facts and ideas so that they make sense together, and anchor concepts and theories within familiar experiences and events.

To help the student experience success—and, I hope, excitement—in learning about sociology, I have tried to provide the following:

Careful attention to vocabulary and sentence length, consistent presentation of basic terminology, and a personalized, informal style that speaks with, instead of at, the student.

An orderly presentation of topics, moving—especially in Part Four—from large-scale theoretical and substantive issues to small-group and individual experiences.

A special emphasis on contemporary issues and examples with which students already have some familiarity and personal interest.

Careful integration of all visual supplements to the text—figures, charts, tables, and photographs—through well-developed captions and in-text references and explanations.

Coverage that is comprehensive—all the major topics, research, and trends—without being overly detailed.

A balanced presentation of the major theories with careful attention to both their contributions and their limitations.

Up-to-date statistical information drawn from government and survey data with special care given to explaining the relevance of these facts and figures to the issues and trends under discussion.

Throughout the preparation of the second edition, there has been a relentless effort to supply new source material—new studies and statistics, in particular.

## SPECIAL AIDS TO TEACHING AND LEARNING

It is easy to fill a text with a range of pedagogical devices. In fact, it is sometimes difficult to know when to stop. I have, however, selectively assimilated a variety of aids that I felt would work together in the scope of an introductory text and genuinely enhance the teaching/learning effectiveness of the chapters.

### Built-in Study Guide

Study-guide materials are now included after each chapter in the text, so that students will have immediate, economical access to features that can aid their review of the text material. The sections contain:

*Summaries.* Numbered sets of paragraphs at the end of each chapter provide a framework for review and help to reinforce learning.

*Glossaries.* Terms are boldfaced and defined in the text proper and then regrouped and redefined in an end-of-chapter glossary for easy reference and review.

*Learning Objectives.* This list of major issues outlines the basic material that must be learned within the particular chapter.

*Tests.* True-false, multiple-choice, and essay tests offer opportunities to determine how well one has assimilated the material. At the end of the study-guide sections, answers to the first two tests are provided.

*Annotated Readings.* Each chapter of the study guide contains an average of ten incisively annotated readings drawn from a broad variety of categories: novels, essays, case studies, articles, critiques and theoretical analyses, biographical and autobiographical accounts, practical guides, historical and cross-cultural documents, and literature surveys.

*Student Projects.* These projects, which involve a reorganization of material in the chapter or some kind of simple study, give students a chance to apply the knowledge obtained in the chapter.

## "Research in Sociology" Sections

I believe that one of the most difficult tasks teachers of introductory sociology must face is conveying a concrete sense of the challenges and problems involved in doing sociological research.

To make this task easier, this edition includes five new sections which examine sociological research into the topics of culture, sexuality, rape, charisma, and prison riots. It is my intention that these "Research in Sociology" sections will reexamine throughout the text many of the methodological issues discussed in Chapter 2, and, most importantly, that they will bring sociological research to life for the student.

## Boxed Features

There are three types of theme boxes in this edition of the text, two of which may be found in each chapter. Each box is tied to discussions within the body of the chapter.

*Contemporary Issues.* These boxes provide recent illustrations of issues and topics discussed in the text and include such subjects as freedom of the press, black executives and corporate stress, and an original case study on the vicious cycle of poverty.

*Cross-Cultural Perspectives.* These inserts offer an invaluable counterperspective to issues and trends in American society by examining such topics as the relationship between blacks and whites in South Africa, elderly in Abkhasia, and the role of public protest in Argentinian politics.

*American Controversies.* These boxes are a new feature, providing opposing positions on such issues as sociologists' preferences for particular theories, competition in American society, and the desirability of nuclear energy. As students evaluate, discuss, and debate these issues, the stimulation they receive will undoubtedly produce insights into the related social processes.

## SUPPLEMENTS TO THE TEXT

No text can address all the particular needs of each student and instructor, and so the quality of the supplementary materials is nearly as important as the text itself. The following supplements provide a comprehensive and easy-to-use package of materials suitable for different paces and styles of teaching and geared to both the motivational and learning needs of various students.

**Instructor's Manual.** Prepared by Robert Alexander, North Hennipin Community College.

Each chapter of the Instructor's Manual contains a chapter synopsis, teaching objectives, a list of key concepts and terms, lecture ideas with references, topics for class discussion and activities, and an annotated list of films.

New to the second-edition Instructor's Manual are debate exercises in every chapter. Drawing on controversial issues discussed in the text, these exercises present opinions suitable for debate in the classroom. It is my hope that these debates will provide an exciting way for students to evaluate some of the complex—and sometimes contradictory—ideas that arise in a sociological inquiry.

**Test Bank Manual.** Prepared by Robert Thompson, Minot State College.

Each chapter of the test manual contains one hundred multiple-choice items, designed in part to test knowledge and in part to test students' ability to apply information from the text.

## Computerized Test Bank

The CTB offers all the items from the printed Test Bank on floppy disks for easy and flexible test construction using the Apple IIe or IBM systems.

## SocialScene®: Interactive Data Analysis Software

Also new to this second edition of the text is *SocialScene,* an interactive data analysis program for undergraduate sociology students. With a few simple commands, students can use *SocialScene* to run chi-square values of actual general social survey data. *SocialScene* will help students explore the

---

methods of data analysis and the interrelationships between variables affecting trends such as social and geographic mobility, racial discrimination, work satisfaction, and changing gender roles.

## ACKNOWLEDGMENTS

Once again, the professionals at Holt, Rinehart and Winston have done their work enthusiastically and well. Carol Einhorn and Lucy Rosendahl effectively launched the revision, and Ms. Einhorn proved to have the perfect combination of intelligence, toughness, and cheerful energy to guide the manuscript to its completion. At that point the project was once more placed in the capable hands of Jeanette Ninas Johnson, Special Projects Editor. I am also indebted to Robert Kopelman, Art Director; Annette Mayeski, Production Manager; and Michael D. McDonnell, Manager of Rights and Permissions. I also want to acknowledge Cheryl Mannes for her fine contributions as photo researcher.

One of the most meaningful elements in the process of writing this text has been the working relationship established with colleagues who have served as reviewers. As I begin to understand that process a bit better, I feel, if anything, more appreciation and gratitude than I did the first time. The reviewers were Robert Alexander, North Hennepin Community College; G. William Anderson, College of Lake County; Charlene Black, Georgia Southern College; Joseph Byrne, Ocean County College; Penelope Canan, University of Denver; Virginia Cleveland, Jefferson Community College; Will Cooper, Cypress College; Walter Dean, Community College of Baltimore; Warren Deley, California Polytechnical State University, San Luis Obispo; Linda Havir, St. Cloud University; Kathryn Johnson, Indiana State University, Northwest; John McKinstry, California Polytechnical State University, San Luis Obispo; Michael Miller, University of Texas, San Antonio; Ronald Neff, Mississippi State University; Marjorie Parks, St. Louis Community College; Bradford Powers, Dean Junior College; William Schwab, University of Arkansas; Robert Snow, Arizona State University; Susan Takata, University of Wisconsin, Parkside; Eugene Tashima, Victor Valley College; Robert Thompson, Minot State College; William Thompson, Emporia State University; Sharon Timmerman, Indiana State University; Dorothy Warrick, Anoka Ramsey Community College; Ira Wasserman, Eastern Michigan University.

I am also grateful to Bonny Francis, who as an employee of the Professional Development Support Program of Southern Connecticut State University, played a major role in manuscript preparation.

Teresa E. M. Carballal was there once again to help in little and big ways, my partner in this project as in everything else important.

# CONTENTS

# DETAILED CONTENTS

# FEATURE CONTENTS

## CONTEMPORARY ISSUES

## Cross-Cultural Perspectives

## American Controversies

# Research in Sociology

# PART ONE
*The Contribution of Sociology*

**1**
*Introduction*

**2**
*Doing Research in Sociology*

# 1
# INTRODUCTION

In August 1911, the last survivor of a small band of Indians (as Native Americans were then called) left his northern California homeland and started wandering aimlessly toward the south. Overcome by grief, loneliness, and exhaustion, he was found crouched against a fence in a small town about forty miles from where he started. Not knowing what to do with this apparently homeless man, the sheriff brought him to the local jail, where people tried to communicate with him in English, Spanish, and several Native American languages. But the man, who became known as Ishi, understood nothing.

This strange, mysterious man intrigued those who met him, and soon articles about Ishi appeared in newspapers throughout the state. Two social scientists from the University of California read the accounts of Ishi, and they immediately suspected that he might be a rare individual—a Native American who had somehow escaped the direct influence of American culture. Excited by the prospect of studying such a person, the two social scientists arranged for Ishi to live in San Francisco.

Gradually the social scientists and Ishi learned to communicate with each other, and it became clear that the earlier speculations were correct. Ishi, they discovered, was the last living member of his tribe—a people that had spent decades since the settlers' arrival hiding from these strangers who had driven them from their villages and had taken their land. He was the product of a true Stone-Age culture, where all tools and weapons were skillfully handmade out of stone and wood according to traditions that had been maintained for centuries.

Citizens of San Francisco were fascinated by this man who had suddenly entered their world. At appointed times each week, large crowds gathered to watch as Ishi demonstrated how to string a bow, make a fire with a wooden drill, and chip arrowheads. Ishi was equally interested in others and particularly fascinated by large numbers of people. He had belonged to a small tribal group, and the largest gatherings he could remember had involved forty or fifty people. San Francisco presented crowds of an entirely different scale. When Ishi was taken to the theater, he spent the first two acts staring at the audience, amazed at the sheer numbers of people. Once Ishi was driven to a bluff overlooking a beach where thousands of people were on the sand below him. His biographer later wrote:

> He said over and over softly, half-whisperingly, *Hansi saltu, hansi saltu*! Many white people, many white people! He had not known so many people could inhabit the earth at one time . . .

> *(Kroeber, 1963: 139)*

Ishi's story, which ends with his death in 1914, is a dramatic illustration of a fundamental sociological principle: People's outlooks and behavior are shaped by the social forces they encounter. Ishi had grown to adulthood in a social world where such social forces as values, beliefs, language, technology, and life-style patterns were radically different from those produced by the twentieth-century culture to which he was suddenly exposed. What Ishi experienced in his last few years was probably scarcely different from being magically transported to the modern era from a culture 5,000 years old.

For sociologists Ishi's story is just one of the countless examples of how people are affected by their social world. Sociology centers on the belief that a scientific analysis of these social forces is one of the most effective ways to understand human behavior. To restate this, **sociology** is the scientific study of human behavior in groups and of the social forces that influence that behavior.

In the first section of this chapter, we look at the

group settings of human behavior and describe the scientific nature of sociology. Our focus then shifts to a discussion of prominent sociologists who have contributed significantly to the development of so-ciological thought. In the final section, we survey the three most prominent contemporary theories of sociology.

# The Sociological Perspective

The sociological perspective emphasizes that people's thoughts and actions are strongly influenced by the groups to which they belong as well as by other social forces present in society. Of course, individuals often have the opportunity to choose between or among alternative courses of thought and action. But they are not entirely independent beings. From birth until death, they are imbedded within and influenced by groups. Some of these groups are small and immediate—families and friends—and others are larger and more remote—the economy and government, for instance.

The ways in which groups influence their members can be surprising, even for sociologists. In the late 1930s, a young sociologist named William Foote Whyte was conducting a lengthy study of a group of young men in Boston. One evening Whyte and a number of the men went bowling. Before they started their game, some of the group leaders predicted that they would score higher than the others. At first Whyte paid little attention to the predictions, because such an outcome made little sense. Why, for example, should Frank Bonnelli, the best athlete in the entire group, finish well down the list? Why did Frank himself say that he did not expect to score well, not when he was "playing with fellows I know like that bunch" (Whyte, 1955: 318)?

After some thought Whyte realized that he was observing the influence of a group upon each of these men. The expectations and support of the group leadership strongly affected each man's bowling scores, regardless of his ability. Even Whyte himself was affected. That evening he felt strong group support, and as he stepped up to bowl, he was confident that he would hit the pins at which he aimed. He had never felt that way before. Whyte later wrote, "It was a strange feeling, as if something larger than myself was controlling the ball as I went through my swing and released it toward the pins" (Whyte, 1955: 319). When the bowling was over, Whyte checked the scores. He was pleased to discover that the predicted order of finish was almost correct. Whyte now had evidence to support his idea that the group was influencing its individual members.

**Figure 1.1**
**Three Tests for Helpfulness and Friendliness at Different Hours**

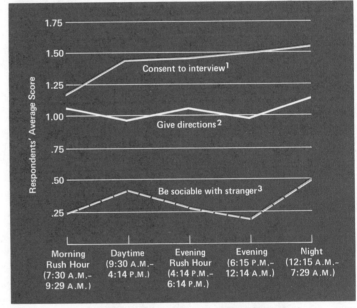

[1] Score based on zero points for nasty refusal, one point for polite refusal, and two points for consent.
[2] Score based on zero points for nasty response and no directions given, one point for directions given, and two points for giving directions and then expanding discussion to other topics.
[3] Score based on one point for smiling only, one point for chatting only, two points for both, and zero points for neither.

*The results of simple tests, which the sociologist developed to measure the three activities represented here, indicated that at night people were more likely to consent to an interview, to give directions, or to be sociable with a stranger than they were at other hours. A fourth test—the return of a lost key—did not produce greater helpfulness and friendliness at night. (Source: Adapted from Murray Melbin. "Night as Frontier."* American Sociological Review. *Vol. 43. February 1978, p. 16.)*

In Whyte's research group, influence upon individuals' behavior is obvious. That is not always the case when sociologists examine a topic. For example, consider the subject of "night." Many Americans will suggest that it is a time to sleep, to watch late movies, or to party on weekends. But how does one analyze it sociologically?

Murray Melbin (1978) began with the suggestion that although the night is a period of time, it can be occupied just like land: Those who are awake and active are the occupiers of the night. According to Melbin, the night is the modern frontier. Like people on the frontier, those who are active at night have a sense of themselves as a group; they promote helpfulness and friendliness as they face common dangers and loneliness. Melbin felt that he had an interesting idea, but was he correct? To find out, he conducted research to determine whether people were unusually helpful and friendly at night. As Figure 1.1 indicates, he learned that at night people were more willing to provide directions, to complete a brief interview, and were more sociable with strangers than they were during the day. One young man told Melbin, "At 4 a.m. if someone sees you walking the streets at the same time he does, he must think, 'gee, this guy must be part of the brethren [a kindred soul], because no one else is awake at these times' " (Melbin, 1978: 19).

Melbin concluded that once one visualizes the night as a frontier, he or she begins to understand what kind of people are awake at those hours and how their behavior differs from that of people who are active only during the day. According to Melbin, the night is the new frontier in many industrialized nations, not just in the United States.

Melbin's investigation is the first published study about the night as a frontier. If additional studies are conducted, it will be interesting to observe whether or not their findings are consistent with his.

The previous examples help to illustrate the basic meaning of the sociological perspective. The following Contemporary Issue provides a prominent sociologist's analysis of why this perspective is both important and useful.

Melbin, like William Foote Whyte, did not just state his expectations but also did research to determine whether or not they were correct. Melbin's investigation was thus rooted in the scientific

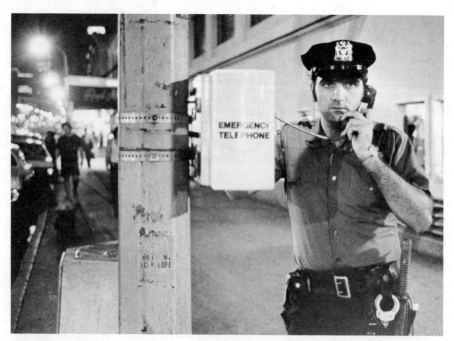

*An attribute of the police that receives little attention is that many of their members actively occupy the night. One might wonder just how occupying the night affects police officers' outlooks and behavior.*

**CONTEMPORARY ISSUE**

## C. Wright Mills on Private Troubles and Public Issues

When should the sociological perspective be applied to individuals' problems? In *The Sociological Imagination*, C. Wright Mills offered a clear answer: when the problem ceases to be what he called "a personal trouble" and becomes "a public issue."

Consider the topic of unemployment. If a small number of men and women are unemployed, that is their personal trouble. We can examine their character and skills and probably find deficiencies that make them incapable of holding a job. However, if 8.5 million people representing over 7 percent of the labor force are unemployed—this was the situation in the middle 1980s—then sociological analysis produces a different conclusion. Such a high unemployment rate represents a public issue. Sociologists, economists, and other analysts cannot focus only on individuals

and their inadequacies to understand why so many people are unemployed. They must examine the American economic system and assess the various reasons why such a substantial percentage of Americans are unable to find jobs.

Consider another topic: If few couples seek divorce, one might conclude that these individuals are suffering from personal problems. Perhaps they lack the skills and motivation necessary to make a marriage succeed. However, the current situation, in which about one-half of recent first marriages will end in divorce, represents an unprecedentedly high divorce rate. Sociologists must analyze a number of new social conditions to understand why such a high rate of divorce now exists.

Mills realized that in times of rapid social change, most people find it difficult to

look beyond personal troubles to the public issues that affect them and people they know. He emphasized, however, that the more capable one becomes in using the sociological imagination, the more insight one develops into many problems in one's own life and the more effectively one will be able to deal with them.

After more than two decades of being a sociologist, I am deeply impressed by the contribution the sociological perspective makes. Using it doesn't make life idyllically simple, but it does help people to understand more fully the problems in their personal, professional, or political life. That's a huge step, because once one understands a problem, the possibility of confronting and resolving it are greatly increased.

Source: C. Wright Mills. *The Sociological Imagination.* New York: Grove Press. 1961.

method. It is this method that distinguishes the sociological perspective from a "commonsense" interpretation of the world.

A **science** is a systematic effort to develop general principles about a particular subject matter, based on actual observations and stated in a form that can be tested by any competent person. Sciences are usually divided into two main branches: the **natural sciences**—older sciences such as astronomy, chemistry, physics, and biology that study the physical world; and the **social sciences**—the sciences that focus on various aspects of human behavior. Besides sociology, the

social sciences include anthropology, economics, history, political science, and psychology.

While social sciences have sometimes been labeled "nonsciences," sociology is just as scientific in its approach as biology or physics. Like their colleagues in the natural sciences, sociologists systematically use testable observations to develop general principles about human beings, their subject matter. For two reasons, however, sociology is less advanced as a scientific discipline than the natural sciences. First, sociology is about 150 years old—a much newer field than any of the natural sciences, which are many centuries old. Second, a

**8**

study of human beings poses some special problems. Unlike rats, rocks, or molecules, people are self-aware and capable of changing their behavior when they decide to; in fact, individuals sometimes alter their behavior when they know they are being observed. Furthermore sociologists are more limited in what they can do to their subjects than are their colleagues in chemistry, physics, and biology.

Why did sociology develop? As with all sciences, the sociological perspective suggests that certain social conditions have encouraged the birth of this field.

## The Development of Sociology

Sociology originated in France during an era of political, economic, and social disruption. Beginning with a major revolution in 1789, France went through a series of radical political upheavals. Meanwhile the Industrial Revolution was drastically changing the economic and social structure of French society. Thus it is hardly surprising that many contemporary social philosphers such as Auguste Comte (1798–1857) placed a strong emphasis on the need to reestablish order in the developing industrial society. Comte, who has often been described as "the father of sociology," coined the word "sociology" and produced a useful distinction between what he called "social dynamics" (social change) and "social statics" (social order or stability). However, the work of three other nineteenth-century European social thinkers — Karl Marx, Émile Durkheim, and Max Weber — has left a more significant impact on modern sociology.

### Karl Marx

Karl Marx (1818–1883) was born in the Rhineland district of Germany. The young Marx attended local schools and then went to the University of Bonn and later the University of Berlin, where he associated with a group of radical philosophers whose ideas influenced his later writings. In 1841 Marx received a doctorate from the University of Jena but was unable to obtain a university position because of his radical affiliations. Instead he took a position with a left-wing newspaper. When the paper was closed down by the authorities in 1843, he moved to Paris, where he became acquainted with some of the leading French socialists. While in Paris Marx met Friedrich Engels (1820–1895), with whom he frequently collaborated throughout the rest of his life. Engels, the son of a wealthy textile manufacturer, often provided financial support for Marx and his family

when no other source of income was available. Marx was expelled from France in 1845 because of his socialist activities. Later he returned to Germany, from where he was deported once again, and when he returned to France, he received the same treatment. In 1849 Marx and his family moved to London, where he spent the rest of his life.

Marx was not a sociologist, and yet his ideas have had a significant impact on sociology in several ways. First, throughout his work Marx emphasized the importance of economic factors in determining social life. In particular, he stressed that the capitalist economic system is responsible for the injustices and inequalities of the modern social-class structure. As we see in the upcoming discussion of sociological theories, many modern sociologists are sympathetic to this conclusion.

Another of Marx's key ideas was that systems of belief and thought are the products of the era in which they are located. This position asserts that even cultural and religious ideas are products of economic and social conditions and that, as these conditions change, so do the ideas. Once again, many contemporary sociologists back the Marxist position.

A third main idea that has emerged from Marx's writings is the concept of work alienation — that modern workers have lost control over their work routines as well as what happens to the products of their labor. A century after Marx wrote on the subject of work alienation, sociologists continue to explore and refine this concept.

### Émile Durkheim

Émile Durkheim (1858–1917) was born in Lorraine, on the northeastern border of France. The son of a rabbi, Durkheim received his basic education in France and then studied economics, folklore, and cultural anthropology in Germany. In 1887 he returned to France as a professor of sociology at the University of Bordeaux, where he taught the first sociology course offered at a French university. In 1896 Durkheim founded *Année Sociologique*, which was for years the leading journal of sociological thought and research in France. In 1902 he joined the faculty of the University of Paris.

In response to France's disasterous defeat in the Franco-Prussian War and the chaotic era that followed this defeat, Durkheim, like Comte, developed an overriding concern for social order. He believed that the scientific study of society could provide a sense of how to establish and maintain social order in modern industrial societies. Durkheim believed that one way to learn about social order was to study a situation in which order appeared to be absent — suicide. Durkheim's *Suicide*, which was published in 1887, was a careful investigation of suicide rates in various European countries. It was also the first prominent study conducted by a sociologist.

Durkheim's project had two goals. First, he intended to refute the popular theories that attempted to analyze the differences in group suicide rates by using biological ("racial"), genetic, climatic, or geographical factors. Second, he wanted to develop a theoretical approach that would better explain the suicide rates in different places. Durkheim's evidence supported his first goal. His data clearly invalidated the old theories about suicide rates. The evidence also suggested a new theory — that suicide was produced by three basic social conditions. One condition was the individual's lack of group support. Durkheim's investigation showed that single people were more likely to commit suicide than married people, and married individuals with children were even less likely to kill themselves. A second condition promoting suicide, according to Durkheim, was the disruption of social life. He found that depression, revolution, war, or even sudden prosperity within a society can increase that society's suicide rate. Finally Durkheim suggested that in some preindustrial societies, as well as in some modern armies, people would be called on to commit suicide for the common good. In Japan, for example, the practice of hara-kiri, ritual suicide committed by nobility when they felt they had performed a dishonorable act, assured that the family and community would be spared disgrace.

Sociologists have been critical of Durkheim's *Suicide*. Yet the book remains a significant contribution to the field because it was the first effective attempt to test sociological theories by conducting scientific research. In addition, Durkheim demonstrated that suicide, which is an individual act, can be explained by sociocultural factors. Thus the study both justifies and illustrates the utility of the sociological perspective.

## Max Weber

Max Weber (1864–1920) was a member of a wealthy German family. As a young man, Weber received training in law and economics. He earned a doctorate in law from the University of Berlin in 1889 and joined the bar a short time later. In 1891 he became a member of the law faculty of the University of Berlin, and in the following years Weber earned several full-time appointments at leading German universities. In the course of his life, Weber published a large number of books and essays. He also traveled widely, including a visit to the United States.

No sociologist has had a more profound impact on the field of sociology than Max Weber. His contributions to sociological thought will be apparent throughout this text. The areas of study to which he made extensive contributions include bureaucracy and formal organization, religion, political authority systems and political organization, caste and class, economic activity, and the city.

One of Weber's most significant contributions was the **principle of verstehen** (understanding), which describes an effort to grasp the relationship between individuals' feelings and thoughts, and their actions. To Weber the principle of *verstehen* involved the following three-step process. First, a sociologist observing a situation tries to imagine the emotions people are feeling. Second, that observer attempts to figure out the participants' motives. Third, the sociologist's explanation of any activity that occurs includes his or her interpretation of the participants' feelings and motives. Consider the following illustration: A young man and a young woman are walking arm in arm while chatting loudly and smiling at each other. Suddenly the young woman says: "I don't want to climb mountains for my vacation." The young man stops walking, pulls his arm away from hers, jams his hands into his pockets, and without a word turns and walks stiffly and quickly in the direction from

**10**

which they had come. A sociologist, who employs the principle of *verstehen*, might conclude that the young man is angry with the woman's statement; his motive is to communicate that anger; therefore he acts in a way that shows her that he is angry.

The principle of *verstehen* was an important contribution to sociology because it helped to "humanize" the field, emphasizing the fact that people's feelings and motives and not just their behavior must be studied.

## The Development of American Sociology

Although Durkheim, Marx, Weber, and other Europeans made the initial contributions to sociology, the field has been most widely accepted in the United States. Social problems arising in the early twentieth century encouraged the growth of sociology in this country. Rapid industrialization and urbanization made poverty, violence, crime, and vice painfully apparent in American cities. Like their European predecessors, the early American sociologists believed that an effective study of society could promote an understanding of major social problems and their solutions.

In 1892 Albion W. Small (1854–1926) became the head of a newly formed department of sociology at the University of Chicago. He retained this position until 1925. During that era the Chicago department was the unchallenged leader in American sociology. Until 1930, in fact, the University of Chicago produced more Ph.D.'s in sociology than all other American sociology departments combined. Among them was Lester F. Ward (1841–1913), another important early American sociologist. Like Comte, Ward believed that the discovery of the basic principles of social behavior could lead to effective social reform. In the 1920s Robert Ezra Park (1864–1944), a former journalist, organized an ambitious research program at the University of Chicago designed to promote the understanding and the elimination of such major urban problems as juvenile delinquency, crime, divorce, and social disorganization.

From the 1940s through the 1960s, leadership in sociology spread from Chicago to such universities as Harvard, Columbia, and Michigan. Also, the focus of sociology shifted. The dominant concerns were no longer specific social problems but rather the development of theory and advances in research techniques. Talcott Parsons (1902–1979), the most significant figure in the discipline from the early 1940s until the late 1960s, emphasized the need to develop a systematic general theory of social action. He believed that until such a theory was constructed, the empirical research conducted by sociologists would lack overall coherence and sociology would never become a mature science. Robert Merton (1910–     ), a student of Parsons, has also emphasized that the growth of sociology can only occur effectively if theory and research promote each other's development.

In the late 1960s, antiwar and civil-rights protests resurrected the former concern with significant social problems. During the 1970s and 1980s, however, there has been no single dominant figure or issue in sociology. Traditional topics like the family, race relations, and the cities are still being studied, and such social issues as gender roles, aging, environmental problems, energy, and nuclear power and weaponry have started to receive extensive attention.

Members of the discipline tend to be liberal politically and socially, and conservatives who recognize this trend are sometimes critical. Attacking what he considered the overabundance of liberal judges, Ronald Reagan said, "We don't need a bunch of sociology majors on the bench." Sociologist Herbert Gans disagreed, saying that the sociological perspective is far more likely than tough talk to help eliminate crime—that our "anticrime policies have to be based on understanding why America creates so many criminals, on the streets and on Wall Street." Gans added that the president's remark made him proud to be a sociologist (Gans, 1986: A26).

From the beginning American sociology has emphasized the development of effective theories.

## Contemporary Sociological Theories

A **sociological theory** is a combination of observations and insights that offers a systematic explanation of social life. We all make use of informal

theories about social behavior. Parents and educators, for instance, often support different ideas about proper child-rearing. The old saying "Spare the rod and spoil the child" is one informal theory on this topic. Americans also have different theories about the best strategy to maintain world peace. One theory favors the development of increasingly powerful nuclear weapons that will make the Soviets avoid nuclear war for fear of massive retaliation. Opponents of nuclear weaponry consider this theory insane, emphasizing that a continuing nuclear-weapons buildup increases the possibility of accidental nuclear war. They offer a contrasting theory that proposes bilateral nuclear disarmament as the best way to prevent such a war.

A major difference between the theories constructed by practicing sociologists and those developed by the majority of the public is that sociologists, like other scientists, are expected to subject their theories to continuous scrutiny and testing. They conduct extensive research to determine whether or not their theories provide effective explanations of social behavior, and they carefully examine their colleagues' studies published in professional journals and books to further evaluate relevant sociological theories.

Sociologists have produced a wealth of fine theories. In this section we will focus on three important theories that sociologists continue to examine and reevaluate: structural-functional theory, conflict theory, and symbolic interaction. Like all theories, those examined here differ most fundamentally in the factors that they designate the most effective in explaining human behavior.

## Structural-Functional Theory

The modern American occupational structure contains more than 20,000 types of jobs. People in each kind of job tend to be interdependent with those in many other work roles. Nurses, for instance, provide direct care for the sick and injured, act as administrators in hospitals, and in some cases teach student nurses. In turn, they depend on other workers for food, clothes, transportation, communication, entertainment, and many other needs. Farmers supply meat, poultry, vegetables, fruit, and dairy products to the American consumers, but they too depend on other occupational groups to meet their needs in a range of areas.

The interdependence of different categories of American workers illustrates **structural-functional theory.** This theory suggests that groups in interaction tend to influence and adjust to each other in a fairly stable, conflict-free pattern. In our example the groups in interaction are the various occupational groups. According to this theory, these groups are mutually supportive and interdependent, and each group contributes to the overall stability of the society. The focus of this type of theory is the concept of **function**—an adjustive or stabilizing consequence produced by an item, individual, or group and affecting a particular group or society. For example, the functions performed by nurses help restore sick and injured workers in various occupational categories to health (an "adjustive consequence"). Nurses, in short, function to maintain the stability of the American occupational system, according to structural-functional theory.

### Functions and Dysfunctions

Robert Merton (1968) has developed some important refinements of the structural-functional theory. He defined a **manifest function** as a function that is intended and openly recognized by members of the group producing it. A **latent function** is a function that is not intended and often unrecognized by members of the group producing it. A **dysfunction** is a disruptive or destabilizing consequence produced by an item, individual, or group and affecting a particular group or society. A dysfunction can be manifest or latent. The following discussion uses computer technology to illustrate the four types of functions and dysfunctions.

One manifest function of the computer is its ability to contribute directly to the effective performance of different types of workers. Computers can do such things as keep business accounts, retrieve the police records of criminal suspects, provide doctors with detailed information about drugs and diseases, and offer research sociologists lists of all studies published on a given topic. The manifest functions provided by computers have had a decisive effect upon the structure of the American work force. It is apparent, for example, that many businesses are more efficient and prosperous because of their effective use of computers.

Less obvious are the latent functions of computers. Some companies are now considering the possibility of placing computer terminals in employees' homes and letting them work there. With such an arrangement, couples might be able to maintain closer, more satisfying relationships.

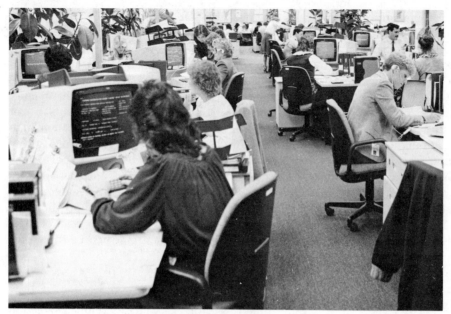

*A manifest function of computers is that with them office workers can store and retrieve information much more efficiently than they can without them.*

Children might develop a better understanding of their parents' work activities than they generally have been able to do in the recent past. In addition, if employees were permitted to perform most or all of their work tasks at home, it would be less likely that they would need to move every time they changed jobs. As a result many families would be able to develop more stable community relationships than they have at present (Toffler, 1981). All of these observations illustrate some latent functions of computers. In other words computers can have indirect effects that were not intended by those who first developed them.

Computers have also caused certain problems or dysfunctions. For example, they simplify or eliminate many work tasks that people have traditionally performed. The elimination or phasing out of certain job holders, such as filing clerks, research assistants, and factory workers, represents a manifest dysfunction for the people in those job categories.

Like many, perhaps most, new forms of technology, computers have sometimes contributed to problems that their owners and advocates never anticipated. In other words they created latent dysfunctions. For example, ingenious but dishonest individuals have learned to engage in so-called computer crimes. Stanley Mark Rifkin, a computer analyst in Los Angeles, used a computer to trick the machines at the Security Pacific National Bank into giving him $10 million. While free on bail for that crime, he was arrested for using a computer to try to steal $50 million from the Union Bank (Friedrich, 1983: 22).

Another latent dysfunction of computers could provide disastrous results for the entire planet: American nuclear weaponry is linked to computerized warning systems that could malfunction, leading to a nuclear war. Jonathan Schell wrote:

> On three occasions in the last couple of years, American nuclear forces were placed on the early stages of alert: twice because of the malfunctioning of a computer chip in the North American Air Defense Command's warning system and once when a test tape depicting a missile attack was inadvertently inserted in the system. The greatest danger in computer-generated misinformation and other mechanical errors may be that one error might start a chain reaction of escalating responses between command centers, leading, eventually, to an attack.
>
> *(Schell, 1982: 27)*

These examples suggest that the structural-functional theory makes a distinct contribution to sociological thought by emphasizing the functions and dysfunctions that promote cooperation and stability within societies. The most profound limitation of this theory, according to critics, is its failure to examine systematically conflict and change in social relations.

## Conflict Theory

Conflict theory argues that groups are inevitably organized to compete against each other. Change is a continuous element in this theory. Karl Marx's theory of class conflict is the foundation upon which modern conflict theory has been built. In Marx's view societies are structures in which a ruling class controls the means by which goods are produced and seeks to extend its wealth and power. In industrial societies workers eventually organize themselves to overthrow their oppressors. According to Marxist theory, the defeat of the ruling class and the economic system it controls would create extensive change because economic systems significantly affect all other elements within any society.

Some American sociologists have developed conflict perspectives that share Marx's focus on the centrality of both conflict and the role of the ruling class. For example, C. Wright Mills, author of *The Power Elite* (1956), argued that an upper-class group of politicians, businessmen, and military leaders effectively controls American society, placing the top priority upon their own political, economic, and military interests and subordinating those of the general citizenry. Mills's conflict analysis and the related work of Ralf Dahrendorf (1959) received little attention from American sociologists until the middle of the 1960s. At that time college- and university-centered protest groups began to analyze the basic social and political conditions in American and other Western societies. Many sociologists concluded that structural-functional theory could not supply an adequate analysis of the role of power in societies or of the conflicts and changes that occur within them. Conflict theory provides a useful perspective on the economic, political, and other major institutions. In addition, it permits us to examine smaller social systems — individual families, work units, religious organizations, and the like — by focusing on power relationships, conflict, and change within these structures.

In brief, **conflict theory** contends that the

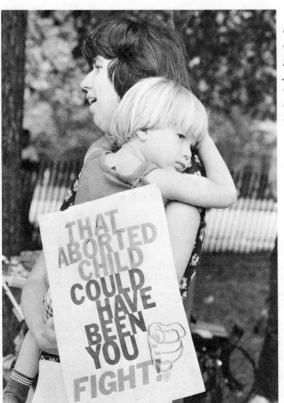

*The issue of abortion has been a focal point of heated conflict. The struggle for "pro-choice" legislation has been challenged by the struggles of "pro-life" groups to legally prohibit abortion except in strictly defined cases. The means for change — demonstrations, debates, and lobbying — have been essentially peaceful, but the goals of each side would seem to resist a tendency toward a cooperative and stable solution.*

**14**

struggle for power and wealth in society should be the central concern of sociology. Many people are restricted or controlled by limits placed upon them by the powerful, and this restriction creates or at least encourages conflict. In turn, conflict generates change. According to this theory, there is never enough wealth and power to satisfy everyone within a given society. Those who have the wealth and power, the chief beneficiaries of the existing system, will attempt to control the general citizenry in order to protect their own privileges. The wealthy, for instance, will contribute heavily to the campaigns of politicians who support legislation to protect the economic interests of the wealthy.

People with limited power often engage in conflict in order to reduce or remove restrictions placed on them by the powerful; they are seeking to obtain a full share of the benefits the society can provide. Conflicts sometimes involve physical violence, sometimes not. Arguments, debates, lawsuits, picketings, and strikes are generally nonviolent activities, but they all involve conflict.

In recent years many groups of people—in particular, racial and ethnic minorities, and women—

have begun resisting the restrictions traditionally placed on them. These groups have initiated the long and difficult process of changing social arrangements that have denied them an equal opportunity to seek wealth, power, and prestige in American society. Since the goals of these groups require the pursuit of scarce resources, conflict is usually one consequence of their efforts. Sometimes such conflict has been violent, as in the killings of black leaders and other activists during the 1960s, but more often it has been nonviolent, as in the lobbying for the Equal Rights Amendment.

The conflict perspective makes an important contribution to sociological analysis by focusing on issues of struggle and change. Like structural-functionalism, however, this theory does not examine all aspects of society. In particular, it fails to take into account the topics of cooperation and stability addressed by the structural-functional perspective.

The following American Controversy suggests the possibility that the supporters of these two theories might differ in more than their theoretical preferences.

---

## AMERICAN CONTROVERSY

## *Why Sociologists Prefer Particular Theories*

As the previous section suggests, the approaches of structural-functionalism and conflict theory are quite different. Sociologists often have a strong preference for one theory or the other. Why is that?

Let's use prominent sociologists as illustrations. Why, for example, did Talcott Parsons support structural-functional theory? Alvin Gouldner has argued that one specific condition in Parsons's upbringing most strongly supported his preference for a theory that has downplayed conflict and change. That condition was

his date of birth, the year 1902. Actually, date of birth seems to combine with several other causal factors. Born at the beginning of the twentieth century, Parsons grew up in an upper-middle-class family during an era of affluence. He attended Amherst College in Massachusetts and later Heidelberg University in Germany. Parsons was a faculty member at Harvard University before the stock-market crash of 1929 signaled the beginning of the Great Depression. The poverty, misery, and inequality that encouraged other sociologists to embrace conflict

theory were always distant from Parsons's own life.

C. Wright Mills grew up in a different time and place. He was about sixteen years younger than Parsons, and so he was a college student during the 1930s. In those depression years, brutal economic conditions encouraged sociologists to launch strong criticisms of American society. Furthermore Mills did not leave his native state of Texas until he was twenty-one. Mills himself believed that growing up outside of major urban centers made it easier for him to become a critic of the political and economic activity that was concentrated in those cities. Thus some factors in Mills's background seem to have encouraged him to become a conflict theorist.

As we read in the section on conflict theory, the protests of the 1960s convinced many sociologists that structural-functional theory did not effectively analyze the conflict and change that were widespread at that time. During that era, conflict theory gained support. What about in the 1980s? As you examine modern society, which theory seems to provide a more effective analysis? In your response you might include references to important political and economic issues currently in the news. It is often difficult to analyze our personal reasons for reaching a particular conclusion but, nonetheless, try to explain why you prefer one of the two theories. In other words, try to determine what factors in your own background encourage you to support one of these perspectives instead of the other. It also might be interesting to discuss respective preferences and the reasons for those preferences with a group of fellow students.

Sources: Alvin Gouldner. *The Coming Crisis of Western Sociology*. New York: Equinox. 1970; Irving Louis Horowitz (ed.). *The New Sociology*. New York: Oxford University Press. 1964.

## Symbolic Interaction

Julie and her husband are at a party. Julie, a private person, wants to make a point to her husband but does not want to cause a scene. Her words emerge in little more than a whisper. "Frank," she begins, "your treatment of me has been intolerable ever since we arrived. You're going to have to stop it." Julie says the word "stop" slowly and emphatically. She has not raised her voice, but Frank has received her message.

This example illustrates a type of social analysis that is the focus of a theory known as symbolic interaction. **Symbolic interaction** is a theory that emphasizes the importance of symbolic communication—the use of gestures and, above all, language—in the development of the individual, group, and society. Human beings are unique in their capacity to use symbolic communication. Knowledge of what a symbol is will help us to understand the significance of this form of communication.

A **symbol** is an object or event whose meaning is fixed not by the nature of the item to which it is attached but by the agreement of the people who use it in communication. For example, words such as "book" or "shoe" are symbols. But there is nothing inherent in the nature of the actual items we call "book" or "shoe" that requires us to use those words. We use those words because people who speak the English language have agreed to associate the particular word with the particular object. Moreover, by using words we are able to communicate with one another in a way that otherwise would be impossible. The symbolic-interactionist theory appreciates the subtlety of human communication. Julie knew that if she said the word "stop" slowly and emphatically, Frank would grasp the meaning she wanted to convey. The supporters of this theory also emphasize that communication is not entirely verbal: Gestures and body language play an important part.

Sociologists who employ symbolic interaction tend to focus on the more minute, personal aspects of social interaction occurring in small groups. In their approach to the study of society, they consider such questions as: What is the process by which children develop a sense of what is appropriate and inappropriate behavior? How do peer-group leaders influence the quality of members' performance of activities that occur within the group context? What actions do men and women take when trying to attract the interest of a member of the opposite sex at a party? What are the activities that people pursue when they join a weight-loss organization, and what factors make it more or less likely that these procedures will succeed? The symbolic-interactionist theory generally focuses on face-to-face situations, but it can also analyze other settings. For instance, people are involved in symbolic interaction when they are reading books, painting pictures, obeying (or disobeying) traffic lights, and playing video games.

This theory can illustrate how various forms of symbolic interaction, or their absence, affect peo-

**16**

**Table 1.1**
**Three Contemporary Sociological Theories**

| THE THEORY | DEFINITION |
| --- | --- |
| Structural-functional theory | A theory suggesting that groups in interaction tend to influence and adjust to each other in a fairly stable, conflict-free pattern |
| Manifest function | A function that is intended and openly recognized by members of the group producing it |
| Latent function | A function that is not intended and often unrecognized by the group producing it |
| Manifest dysfunction | An intentionally disruptive or destabilizing consequence produced by an item, individual, or group |
| Latent dysfunction | An unintentionally disruptive or destabilizing consequence produced by an item, individual, or group |
| Conflict theory | A theory contending that the struggle for power and wealth in society should be the central concern of sociology |
| Symbolic interaction | A theory that emphasizes the importance of symbolic communication in the development of the individual, group, and society |

ple's perceptions. For instance, Americans aged sixty-five and more tend to consider themselves particularly likely to become victims of crime; it turns out that the elderly are the least victimized of all age categories. Several factors associated with the process of symbolic communication contribute to their strong, if somewhat unrealistic fear. The mass media often sensationalize crime against the elderly more than crimes against younger people. In addition, the elderly frequently have fewer social supports in their neighborhood and elsewhere; they often feel there are few people with whom they communicate in a comfortable, pleasant manner. This isolation makes them feel especially vulnerable to violent crime (Yin, 1980).

Symbolic-interactionist theory provides a significant contribution by analyzing human relations in a small-group setting. Unlike structural-functionalism and the conflict approach, however, this theory does not examine larger topics such as the processes that promote stability and change in the entire society.

## Commentary

The previous discussion of contemporary sociological theories suggests that there is no such thing as the best sociological theory. As the American Controversy suggests, background factors can determine the theoretical approach a sociologist prefers. One individual might feel most comfortable focusing on how social groups provide support and continuity (structural-functional theory), while another chooses to study what appear to be the inevitable sources of conflict. Thus, no theory is inherently correct or incorrect. In some situations, a particular theory is more appropriate or is well matched with a sociologist's personal tastes. Within the field of sociology and even within individual sociology departments, people recognize that their colleagues differ in their theoretical preferences. Sometimes disagreements are sharp and well publicized. Often, however, preferences for different theories lead to useful discussions and debates. (See Table 1.1 for a summary of the three theories discussed in this section.)

## STUDY GUIDE

## Summary

1. Sociology is the scientific study of human behavior in groups and of the social forces that influence that behavior.

2. The sociological perspective emphasizes that people's thoughts and actions are strongly influenced by the groups to which they belong and by their interaction in those groups. Sociology is a science, but is has two distinct disadvantages when

compared to the natural sciences: It is a much newer discipline and its subject matter, which is human beings, poses special problems.

3. Auguste Comte has been described as "the father of sociology." Marx, Durkheim, and Weber also made major contributions to the development of the field in Europe. In the United States, the University of Chicago was the first center of sociology. Then, in the 1940s, the most prominent departments developed at Harvard, Columbia, and Michigan. During these years Talcott Parsons and Robert Merton had the strongest influence on the discipline. In the 1970s and 1980s, there have been no dominant figures or issues in sociology.

4. A sociological theory is a combination of observations and insights that offer a systematic explanation about social life. Structural-functional theory suggests that groups in interaction tend to influence and adjust to each other in a fairly stable, conflict-free pattern.

In contrast, conflict theory contends that the struggggle for power and wealth in society should be the central sociological concern.

Symbolic interaction is a theory emphasizing the importance of symbolic communication — gestures and, above all, language — in the development of the individual, group, and society.

There is no such thing as the best sociological theory. A sociologist uses a particular perspective because it seems most appropriate for a particular analysis or because it matches his or her personal tastes.

## Glossary

**conflict theory**   a theory contending that the struggle for power and wealth in society should be the central concern of sociology.

**dysfunction**   a disruptive or destabilizing consequence produced by an item, individual, or group and affecting a particular group or society.

**function**   an adjustive or stabilizing consequence produced by an item, individual, or group and affecting a particular group or society.

**latent function**   a function that is not intended and often unrecognized by members of the group producing it.

**manifest function**   a function that is intended and openly recognized by members of the group producing it.

**natural sciences**   older sciences such as astronomy, biology, chemistry, and physics that study the physical world.

**principle of verstehen**   Max Weber's concept that involves an effort to grasp the relationship between individuals' feelings and thoughts and their actions.

**science**   a systematic effort to develop general principles about a particular subject matter, based on actual observations and stated in a form that can be tested by any competent person.

**social sciences**   the sciences that focus on various aspects of human behavior.

**sociological theory**   a combination of observations and insights that offers a systematic explanation about social life.

**sociology**   the scientific study of human behavior in groups and of the social forces that influence that behavior.

**structural-functional theory**   a theory suggesting that groups in interaction tend to influence and adjust to each other in a fairly stable, conflict-free pattern.

**symbol**   an object or event whose meaning is fixed not by the nature of the item to which it is attached but by the agreement of the people who use it in communication.

**symbolic interaction**   a theory that emphasizes the importance of symbolic communication — gestures and, above all, language — in the development of the individual, group, and society.

## Learning Objectives

After studying this chapter, you should be able to:

1. Define sociology.
2. Discuss the sociological perspective.

3. Define science, distinguish between natural science and social science, and discuss two problems sociology faces in the scientific study of human beings.
4. Describe the social conditions of the era in which sociology originated and identify Auguste Comte's contributions to the field.
5. Summarize the contributions to sociology made by Karl Marx, Émile Durkheim, and Max Weber.
6. Discuss the twentieth-century development of American sociology.
7. Define sociological theory and compare and contrast it with informal theory.
8. Define structural-functional theory, conflict theory, and symbolic-interaction theory; provide examples of each; and discuss their respective strengths and weaknesses.
9. Indicate why there is no one "best" sociological theory.

## Tests

### True–false test

_____ 1. William Foote Whyte's study of young men in Boston suggests that the expectations and support of the group, especially its leaders, influence individual members.

_____ 2. Melbin's study concluded that at night people are much less friendly and helpful than during the day.

_____ 3. Sociology is less advanced as a scientific discipline than the natural sciences.

_____ 4. Durkheim found that in some preindustrial societies as well as in some modern armies, people will be called upon to commit suicide for the common good.

_____ 5. The principle of *verstehen* has helped to humanize sociology.

_____ 6. From the 1940s through the 1960s, the University of Chicago dominated the field of sociology.

_____ 7. The elimination or phasing out of workers when computers are used is an example of a latent function for those workers.

_____ 8. Conflict theory asserts that conflict inevitably leads to violence.

_____ 9. Symbolic-interactionist theory never analyzes face-to-face social situations.

_____ 10. No sociological theory is inherently correct or incorrect.

### Multiple-choice test

_____ 1. The sociological perspective:
    a. indicates that people are seldom influenced by the groups to which they belong.
    b. can be used to explain the bowling performances of the young men described in Whyte's study conducted in Boston in the 1930s.
    c. is not relevant to Melbin's research on people's behavior at night.
    d. a and b

_____ 2. Which of the following is a natural science?
    a. biology
    b. economics
    c. history
    d. sociology

_____ 3. In which of the following ways does sociology differ from the natural sciences?
   a. Sociology is an older field.
   b. Its subject matter (human beings) is less difficult to study than the subject matter in the natural sciences.
   c. Sociologists are less limited in what they can do to their subjects than their colleagues in the natural sciences.
   d. Unlike natural scientists, sociologists study human subjects who are self-aware and can alter their behavior when they so choose.

_____ 4. Karl Marx's theory was based in part on which of the following ideas?
   a. The socialist economic system is responsible for injustice and inequality in the modern social class structure.
   b. Systems of belief and thought are independent of the era in which they are located.
   c. Modern workers have more control over their work routines than did preindustrial workers.
   d. Economic conditions determine what happens in the social world.

_____ 5. Durkheim's study of suicide theorized that suicide was produced by three basic social conditions. Which of the following is NOT one of these basic conditions?
   a. the disruption of social life
   b. the individual's lack of group support
   c. certain distinct personality characteristics
   d. the individual's need to commit suicide for the common good

_____ 6. The principle of *verstehen* is a three-step process. Which of the following actions is NOT part of the process?
   a. The sociologist tries to figure out the participants' motives.
   b. The observer tries to imagine the emotions people are feeling.
   c. The sociologist makes recommendations to improve the situation.
   d. The observer's explanation includes an interpretation of the participants' feelings and motives.

_____ 7. According to structural-functional theory, a function that is intended and openly recognized by members of the group producing it is called:
   a. a manifest function.
   b. a latent function.
   c. a manifest dysfunction.
   d. a latent dysfunction.

_____ 8. Computer crime is described in the text as an example of:
   a. conflict theory.
   b. social dynamics.
   c. a latent dysfunction.
   d. a manifest dysfunction.

_____ 9. According to conflict theory, the central sociological concern should be:
   a. the legal system.
   b. politicians' bid for election.
   c. physical violence.
   d. the struggle for wealth and power.

_____ 10. Symbolic interaction affects people's perceptions. Which of the following factors associated with symbolic communication contributes to fear of crime among the elderly?
   a. mass media sensationalism about crime against the elderly
   b. the loss of effective mental powers

    c. the tendency to be living in crowded buildings
    d. widespread social supports available to the elderly

### Essay test

1. Discuss the sociological perspective, giving an example that demonstrates its usefulness.
2. Summarize the contributions to early sociology made by Marx, Durkheim, and Weber.
3. Define sociological theory. Give an example of an informal theory of social behavior and indicate how such a theory differs from the sociological type.
4. Define structural-functional theory. Describe situations that demonstrate the workings of a manifest function, a latent function, a manifest dysfunction, and a latent dysfunction.
5. What is conflict theory? Discuss a social situation where this perspective seems particularly relevant.
6. Define symbolic interaction. Describe a group context that illustrates the symbolic-interaction process.
7. Is there such a thing as the best sociological theory? Discuss.

## Suggested Readings

Bart, Pauline, and Linda Frankel. 1986. *The Student Sociologist's Handbook*. New York: Random House. Fourth edition. A source book providing valuable information to the beginning sociology student about writing a sociology paper, doing library research, examining periodical literature, following guides to research and resource material, and using computers in sociological work.

Coser, Lewis A. 1977. *Masters of Sociological Thought: Ideas in Historical and Social Context*. New York: Harcourt Brace Jovanovich. Second edition. Description of the leading classical theorists. Coser examines each writer's sociological work, his biography, the intellectual context in which his work was developed, and the social context in which each master lived. Comte, Marx, Durkheim, and Weber are included.

Finsterbusch, Kurt, and George McKenna. 1986. *Taking Sides: Clashing Views on Controversial Social Issues*. Guilford, CT: Dushkin. Fourth edition. An examination of a "pro" and "con" position on twenty different topics that are of interest to sociologists. These issues include the benefit of sociology to society, the contribution of the women's movement, the effective way to prevent nuclear war, the state of the economy, and prospects for prosperity and freedom in the future.

Kennedy, Robert E., Jr. 1986. *Life Choices: Applying Sociology*. New York: Holt, Rinehart and Winston. An examination of the social context in which modern young people are making basic life choices. Using statistical data and sociological analysis, the author demonstrates to college students how sociological thinking can be used in their own lives.

Mills, C. Wright. 1959. *The Sociological Imagination*. New York: Oxford University Press. A conflict-perspective analysis of American society that makes some thought-provoking proposals about the role that ought to be played by modern sociologists.

Theodorson, George A., and Achilles G. Theodorson. 1969. *A Modern Dictionary of Sociology*. New York: Crowell. Concise definitions of an extensive list of sociological concepts.

Turner, Jonathan H. 1985. *Sociology: A Student Handbook*. New York: Random House. A pleasant, optimistic, informative book, showing how the field of sociology can provide a wealth of insights to students about the workings of society and also offer them a variety of possible careers.

## Student Projects

1. Take a topic of interest to you that deals with human behavior (for example, the effects of war, male-female differences, or violent crime). Using books, magazines, and other media sources, dis-

cuss the social forces that produce this behavior and also the effects that this particular activity has upon different groups in American society. Share your report with other students and obtain their reactions to your conclusions.

2. Consider a current social problem (for example, unemployment, civil rights, family tensions). Indicate why this problem has occurred and continues to occur, using the three major sociological theories—structural-functional, conflict, and symbolic-interactionist theory. Does any theory seem more or less effective than the others for explaining the behavior? Does any theory do more to suggest actions that might solve the problem?

## Answers to Test Questions

### True–false test

| | | | | |
|---|---|---|---|---|
| 1. t | 3. t | 5. t | 7. f | 9. f |
| 2. f | 4. t | 6. f | 8. f | 10. t |

### Multiple-choice test

| | | | | |
|---|---|---|---|---|
| 1. b | 3. d | 5. c | 7. a | 9. d |
| 2. a | 4. d | 6. c | 8. c | 10. a |

# 2
# DOING RESEARCH IN SOCIOLOGY

The Scientific Approach of Sociological Research

Stages in the Research Process

Types of Research Design

Surveys    Experiments    Observation Studies    Secondary Analysis

Issues in Sociological Research

Objectivity in the Research Process    Ethics in the Researcher's Role

Study Guide

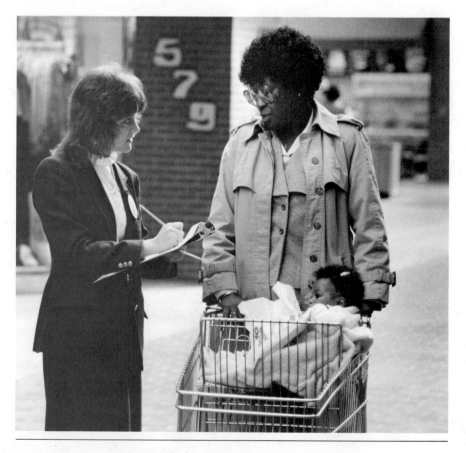

In 1986 William Darrow, Research Sociologist at the Centers for Disease Control, indicated that "[m]uch has been learned in the five years since the first cases of AIDS were reported. . ." (Berg, 1986). Darrow studied AIDS patients to learn how their sexual practices spread the disease, and his findings have served as the foundation for the development of AIDS education and prevention programs. Carole Campbell, another sociologist, has started to study prostitutes to determine whether they are a means by which the virus is transmitted from high-risk groups, like bisexual men and drug users, to the general populace. Important issues in this research concern the prevalence of AIDS among prostitutes, the extent to which the disease is obtained from sexual contact with bisexuals or drug users, and the determination of whether or not prostitutes are altering their sexual practices (such as requiring customers to use condoms).

The other major body of sociological research on AIDS involves studies seeking means of effective behavior modification. From an investigation of 133 gay men who did not have the virus, sociologists Karolynn Siegel and Laurie Bauman found that men whose reports of their behavior indicated that they were at high risk frequently underestimated their risk. A major strategy these men employed was the denial of their own anxiety. Siegel emphasized that to eliminate high-risk behavior, people's anxiety must be sufficient to motivate different sexual patterns but not so high that denial of anxiety occurs. In other behavior-modification research on AIDS victims, Samuel Friedman has studied intravenous drug users. He has concluded that because addicts' time, attention, and money are largely controlled by their addiction, they generally have fewer resources than other potential victims to learn about preventive measures. Programs to educate addicts on AIDS prevention have been developed in Holland and New York City, and Friedman indicated that the mass media and public health programs should be enlisted to support such efforts (Berg, 1986).

Whether a sociological study involves AIDS or some other topic, effective research must follow certain rules. Sociologists speak of **methodology,** the set of principles and procedures that guides sociological research. The use of methodology permits sociologists to do research that produces systematic, convincing results. One writer has observed:

A personal opinion like "I think capitalism exploits the poor" may influence your friends and even your relatives to think that there is some injustice in our society. But it probably won't make any waves with others. If, however, you can cite . . . evidence . . . , a more compelling argument results, because you relate a judgment to a measurement of reality. People who don't even like you, but who favor some kind of fairness in wealth distribution, might find such a statement a powerful cue to examine our economic system critically.

*(Hoover, 1980: 7)*

This chapter is fundamental. The substance of sociology comes from articles, monographs, and books that present research findings. This research, however, could not have been done without the principles and procedures we discuss in this chapter. In the upcoming section, the discussion focuses on sociology as a science, including the stages in the research process. Then the four principal types of social research are analyzed. The final section examines a couple of significant issues involving the researcher's role.

# The Scientific Approach of Sociological Research

In medieval Europe there was a popular belief that the devastating epidemics that occasionally swept across the continent were caused by gases or mists originating somewhere in the East. Medical research has discredited this theory, establishing that a variety of microorganisms are responsible for these diseases. In another case, however, folk wisdom proved correct. In the late eighteenth century, Edward Jenner investigated English peasants' claims that people who had contracted cowpox, a relatively mild disease, would be immune to smallpox. After determining that the peasants' claim was accurate, Jenner developed a vaccine that used cowpox bacteria to immunize people against smallpox, one of the most potent diseases ever suffered by humanity.

Scientists seek the truth systematically. A central concern in this process is **causation**—a situation in which one variable can produce the occurrence of another. A **variable** is a factor that has two or more categories or measurable conditions. Common sociological variables are social class (working class, middle class), political affiliation (Democrat, Republican), and sex (male, female). An **independent variable** is a variable that influences another variable—the dependent variable. Thus the **dependent variable** is the variable that the independent variable influences. In sociological research dependent variables are frequently attitudes and activities.

Sociologists agree that causation is present if three conditions are met (Cole, 1980). First, causation can only occur if the independent variable exists before the dependent variable. For example, people's political affiliation, which exists when they enter the polls, often strongly influences their voting behavior. In other words the affiliation, the independent variable, exists before the voting behavior, the dependent variable. Second, if causation occurs, then change in the independent variable affects the dependent variable. Thus whether voters are Democrats or Republicans strongly influences how they vote.

Finally causation cannot be established until researchers have ruled out the influence of other possible independent variables. The way to do this is to analyze the effect of each possible independent variable on the dependent variable, while keeping constant all other possible independent variables.

Suppose that a team of social scientists suspects that introductory sociology courses have a smaller proportion of participants in class discussion than more advanced sociology courses do. When other possible independent variables—such as students' age, their background, and the size of classes—are kept the same for introductory and advanced courses, no noteworthy differences in the proportion of participants emerge. Then the researchers use the same process to determine whether other factors serve as independent variables in this situation. They may find that the smaller the class, the greater the proportion of participants in discussions. Therefore the size of the class and not the subject emerges as the independent variable in this instance.

Sociologists recognize that in the situations they study, causation is difficult to determine. It is seldom possible to specify that "a" or "b" is the sole independent variable influencing "c." Sociologists generally must settle for a **correlation**—a statistical description of the relationship between variables. A positive correlation of $+1.0$ indicates the strongest possible statistical relationship. It means that an increase in an independent variable is associated with a corresponding increase in the dependent variable. A negative correlation of $-1.0$ is a perfect inverse relationship. It means that an increase in the independent variable is associated with a corresponding decrease in the dependent variable. A correlation of 0 indicates no relationship at all between the two variables.

Correlations almost always fall somewhere between the two extremes. For example, sociologists undertaking the hypothetical study just mentioned might find a correlation of $-.72$ between class size and the amount of discussion. Thus as classes become larger, class discussion tends to decrease. One more point: By squaring a correlation, one can determine how much of the total variation in the dependent variable is associated with the independent variable. If we square the figure of $-.72$, we obtain a value of nearly .52. That figure signifies that class size accounts for about 52 percent of the variation in the amount of class participation. Other independent variables, such as the professor's style and the subject matter of the course, account for the other 48 percent of the variation.

## Stages in the Research Process

The following analysis considers the major activities of sociologists in the course of their research. The stages are presented here in an ideal, logical pattern that does not necessarily summarize the sequence of events in an actual study.

It should also be emphasized that sociological theory has a powerful effect on researchers while they work. From the choice of topic to the reporting of their findings, they are likely to be influenced by the ways different theories encourage them to analyze the social world. They also tend to keep in mind the possibility that their findings can contribute to existing theories, either supporting certain theoretical positions or suggesting new ones.

1. *Choosing a Topic.* Several factors are likely to determine a sociologist's choice of a subject to study. The factors include the researcher's personal interest in the topic, its current popularity, the potential contribution such a study would make to sociological literature, and the availability of government or private funding for research in that area.

2. *Reviewing the Literature.* As sociologists start a research project, they are aware that others have done work that may help them. It is likely that a theory or set of theories can map out the questions their studies should attempt to answer. In addition, previous investigations might provide researchers with some specific aids for their own study.

3. *Formulating a Hypothesis.* Researchers are looking for answers to questions. To guide their searches, they present their expectations in a form that permits them to be researched. A **hypothesis** is a scientifically researchable suggestion about the relationship between two or more variables. Most sociological studies are devised to test hypotheses—that is, to find out whether or not they are true. Thus hypotheses are central to the development of sociological investigations. Hypotheses contain both independent and dependent variables, as the following illustrations indicate.

The higher a couple's social class, the fewer children they have. (For data related to this hypothesis, see Chapter 9.)

Protestants are more likely than Catholics to be ambitious and hard working. (See Chapter 13.)

Young people are more likely than the middle-aged or elderly to engage in crime. (See Chapter 8.)

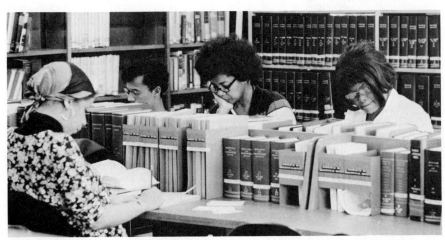

*Reviewing the literature already published on a given topic is an important part of the research process.*

**26**

Brown-eyed individuals are more intelligent and sensitive than blue-eyed people. (Obviously ridiculous but still testable.)

4. *Picking the Research Design.* In order to do research, sociologists must choose one of the four research methods that we discuss in the following section. A researcher's preference for one particular method might help determine the choice. In many situations, however, the particular hypotheses to be tested will require a certain type of design. Surveys are the most popular research method in sociology, but the other approaches are also frequently used.

5. *Gathering the Data.* Data are the substance of a study. Thus even though collecting and recording data sometimes strike those who perform the tasks as tedious work, it is essential that they do these jobs conscientiously. Researchers for large sociological projects often hire graduate students, undergraduates, or other people to conduct interviews. In training interviewers, team leaders must help their workers develop the requisite skills. In addition, they must convince them that conscientious job performance is essential for the effective completion of the study.

*One of the benefits of large studies is that the participants can engage in brainstorming sessions throughout the research process. From reviewing the literature to producing a report, many heads often produce more insight and understanding than one person working alone.*

**Figure 2.1**
**Stages in the Research Process[1]**

[1]Read this figure from the bottom to the top.

*The stages of the research process must build one upon the other in a particular order. Other sequences are possible, but any other arrangement is likely to produce a somewhat distorted result.*

6. *Analyzing the Data.* At this point sociologists examine their data, finding out whether the information supports the hypotheses or whether new hypotheses need to be developed to account for the data. Frequently sociological theories as well as the substance of related research can help complete the analysis.

7. *Producing a Report.* Funding organizations that sponsor studies require researchers to write a report summarizing their findings. In addition to such a formal requirement, researchers belong to a scientific community, and they realize that an article in a professional journal or a monograph is an effective way to make their peers aware of their research results. Sociologists are likely to emphasize implications that their findings have for sociological theory when they write up their studies. Furthermore they probably discuss the directions that future research could take. (See Figure 2.1.)

When a sociologist's peers read a report of findings, they consider validity. **Validity** is the condition where a research item accurately measures what it claims to measure. For example, a group of workers might express satisfaction with their work to a researcher, but is this investigator obtaining valid information? Perhaps not. The workers' statements might reflect their knowledge of a false rumor indicating that the investigator will pass on all dissatisfactions to their boss, who then plans to fire any discontented employees.

Besides validity, sociologists assessing their peers' work are concerned with reliability. **Reliability** is consistency in measurement. In the above example, evidence in favor of reliability would be obtained if the researcher conducted the same study in a different setting with people of similar background and those individuals expressed a comparable level of job satisfaction to those interviewed in the original study.

## Types of Research Design

Even though sociological research generally passes through the same sequence of stages, the research process can vary considerably. One major reason is that the different research methods pose particular demands and challenges. We explore these differences in the upcoming discussion of the four major techniques of social research — surveys, experiments, observation studies, and secondary analysis.

### Surveys

A **survey** is a research technique that uses carefully constructed questions to obtain a variety of facts about people's thoughts and behavior. One type of survey is an **interview** — a set of questions that are delivered face-to-face or over the telephone. The other type of survey is a **questionnaire,** in which a respondent writes the answers to a list of questions. The questions contained in a survey can either be closed-ended, requiring responses that fall into two or more categories provided by the researcher, or open-ended, permitting respondents to speak or write whatever they want. Surveys are administered in a variety of natural settings, such as in homes, offices, restaurants, and even on park benches or beaches.

Researchers conduct surveys by taking a sample from a population. A **population** is the entire category of people possessing the characteristics that interest a researcher — the female students at a certain college, male blue-collar workers in a midwestern city, or the entire American electorate, for example. A **sample** is a limited number of individuals chosen from a population for the purpose of conducting research. Researchers often use a **random sample,** which is a sample drawn from a population by a process that assures that every individual in that population has an equal probability of being included.

Why do sociologists bother with random sampling? The reason is that the information this technique elicits is more likely to produce a sample with members whose charactertistics are representative of the overall population than is a nonrandom sample. And why is it important to have a representative sample? If the informants in a random sample are representative of the population, then whatever conclusions researchers reach about the sample will apply to the entire population.

To illustrate the utility of random sampling, we might consider the surveys conducted before presidential elections — presidential polls. The naive observer might suspect that the best way to predict the outcome of a national election is to sample as many people as possible. In 1936 the staff of the *Literary Digest,* a prominent magazine, used this approach. These researchers mailed out about 10 million post-card ballots, obtaining their list of respondents from telephone directories and auto-registration records. The results of their survey indicated that Alfred Landon, the Republican candidate, would win easily, with about 56 percent of the vote.

The *Literary Digest* poll was proved dramatically wrong when Franklin Roosevelt, the Democratic candidate, obtained 56 percent of the popular vote and carried forty-six of the current forty-eight states. The problem with the *Literary Digest* poll was that it drew its sample only from people who had cars and telephones. In other words its sample consisted of relatively affluent persons in the 1930s — and the affluent tend to vote Republican. There was, in short, a distortion, or bias, built into the *Literary Digest*'s sampling procedure. A young pollster named George Gallup used a random sample to predict that Roosevelt would win the election, and he also predicted the precise outcome of the *Literary Digest* poll. Gallup's triumph in 1936 helped convince the American public that with a random sample of about 2000 people, pollsters could usually make accurate predictions about the outcome of presidential elections (Gallup, 1972).

Undoubtedly you are aware of many other modern uses of surveys. Television, radio, newspapers, and magazines frequently report the results of public-opinion polls on a range of subjects. Big businesses conduct surveys in order to learn how consumers or potential consumers react to their products. Political candidates or parties sponsor survey research in order to determine politicians' popularity or the electorate's dominant needs and interests. The principal difference between sociological surveys and other surveys is that the sociological variety involves more extensive analysis of patterns and relationships in the social world. Morton Hunt's research on sexuality in the 1970s is a case in point.

### A Study of Sexual Behavior

Was our country becoming more sexually liberated in the 1970s or was sexual activity simply becoming more publicized? Did changes in sexual behavior involve an easily visible minority or the unseen majority? Was the supposed drive for liberation producing greater satisfaction or only a frantic search for new kicks and stronger sensations? These were the kinds of questions that the Playboy Foundation, which has sponsored research on sexual behavior and sex education for many years, commissioned a survey to answer. The foundation hired the Research Guild, a prominent research company headquartered in Chicago, to design and deliver a questionnaire to a sample of adult Americans both male and female, married and unmarried. The survey contained 1000 to 1200 items of information and determined the respondent's background, complete sex history, and attitudes toward sexual practice.

In 1972 the staff of researchers obtained 2026 questionnaires from people in twenty-four cities around the country. The sample contained 982 males and 1044 females. It was 90 percent white and 10 percent black. Seventy-one percent of the people were currently married, 25 percent never married, and 4 percent once married but still unremarried. Other major social characteristics,

such as age, educational attainment, occupational status, and urban–rural residence were all found in approximately the same proportions as in the adult American population. On the other hand, the researchers did not locate illiterates, poverty-stricken individuals, inmates of prisons and other institutions, or the members of such marginal groups as communes or isolated religious cults. Overall the researchers admitted that their sample was not fully representative of the adult population—they did not use a scientifically random technique to choose their subjects—but they contended that the sample was fairly representative.

The survey provided answers to many questions, including those mentioned at the beginning of this discussion. The research suggested that Americans were becoming steadily more permissive toward premartial sexuality. Earlier studies had found no change in the public's attitudes toward premarital intercourse between 1937 and 1959. In both of those years, 22 percent of the respondents said it was all right for both men and women, 8 percent said it was all right for just men, and slightly over half concluded it was all right for neither. Survey research done during the 1960s indicated that attitudes toward premarital sexuality began to change markedly, particularly among younger people. The study done in the 1970s provided further evidence supporting such a shift. Where strong affection between the partners exists, 75 percent of males and 55 percent of females believed that premarital sex was acceptable for a male. The respective acceptability figures for females were 66 percent and 41 percent.

Another important issue that the survey addressed involved Americans' philosophical outlook on sexuality. For instance, do they tend to maintain a "recreational philosophy," emphasizing thrills and kicks, or do they widely endorse a "romantic philosophy," favoring traditional emphases on intimacy and love? The survey data largely supported the second position in the area of premarital sexuality. The majority of young Americans included in the survey wanted premarital sex to be both exciting and emotionally meaningful. They were more inclined to consider such activity thoroughly justified when it occurred within a valued relationship than when it represented only sensuous and casual indulgence.

*Commentary*

This study illustrates a strength of surveys. With surveys, researchers can easily gather a great deal of information—in this case through questionnaires. A disadvantage of surveys is that they do not directly measure what people have done but only what they say they have done. The head researcher conceded this deficiency: "Undoubtedly, the fading of memory, the magnifications of wishful thinking, the obscurations of prudery and other similar factors introduced some distortions, but there was no way to overcome this" (Hunt, 1974: 19).

## Experiments

An **experiment** is a research technique in which the investigator manipulates conditions so that the effects produced by one independent variable can be isolated and observed. Experimenters seek to establish causal connections. The most basic procedure is to select two groups of respondents whose social characteristics are similar, duplicate to the extent possible the conditions affecting the two groups, and then introduce the expected independent (experimental) variable to one group (the experimental group) and not to the other (the control group). Experiments can be conducted either in laboratories or in natural settings.

The following well-known study of aggression conducted by Albert Bandura illustrates the basic experimental model. In Bandura's study a number of children who had basically similar social characteristics were randomly divided into two groups. Both groups of children were placed in a room that contained a large plastic doll, a punching-bag toy. In the experimental group, the children observed an adult hammering the doll, and when the adult stopped doing it, the children started to hammer the doll themselves. In the control group, where no adult hammered the doll, the children were much less likely to do it themselves. Since the only difference between the two groups was the presence of the experimental variable in one group and its absence in the other, the researchers were in a strong position to assert that the presence of the experimental variable—the adult's hammering of the toy—caused the greater amount of children's hammering in the experimental group (Bandura et al., 1963).

Sometimes experimenters decide that circum-stances do not require a control group: that with two groups of subjects possessing similar backgrounds exposed to two or more experimental variables, any behavioral differences that the subjects exhibit are likely to result from the different experimental variables. The following study offers such an illustration.

*Experiment on Work Roles and Perceptions*

Americans can become heated about the topic of personal worth. "How dare you even suggest that some people in this country are better than others?" a citizen might ask angrily.

Ronald Humphrey (1985) studied this emotional subject. In a recent experiment, he hypothesized that people who are in high positions in organizational structures and do high-level tasks will be more favorably regarded than individuals of equal ability who have lower positions and are performing low-level tasks.

Humphrey used college students as his subjects—100 students in twenty experimental groups. Within each experimental group, three individuals were randomly assigned to be clerks and two to be managers. Because the members of each group had not previously known each other, there seemed no reason to suspect that before the introduction of the experimental variable, there would have been a tendency for some individuals to receive a higher evaluation than others. So there appeared to be no necessity to use a control group.

After they were assigned to be clerks or managers, the subjects were taken to an "office" where they were seated and told that the study was designed to determine how people work together in an office setting. Then the experimenter went from one subject to another explaining in a loud voice what each individual was expected to do—low-skill, repetitive jobs for the clerks and more challenging and interesting tasks for the managers. For the next two hours, the members of the groups performed their respective activities. At the end of the two-hour period, the subjects were given a brief set of questions in which they were asked to rate themselves and each other on a variety of traits such as leadership ability, intelligence, assertiveness, supportiveness, warmth, and humor. The results were generally consistent with Humphrey's hypothesis: Both clerks and managers rated managers more favorably. This pattern emerged even though the students were aware of the random assignment to the two groups and thus knew that there was no reason to believe that the "managers" actually were possessed of more desirable traits than the "clerks." Humphrey concluded that the manner in which organizations are set up—in this case with clerks having lower status and performing lower-status tasks than managers—will strongly affect participants' evaluations of each other.

### Commentary

Both of the experiments we have discussed indicate a distinct strength of the experimental method—the likelihood of establishing a causal link. The researcher sets up an experiment that seeks to eliminate the influence of other independent variables. If this is effectively done, the dependent variable—the manner in which the subjects respond—can be attributed to the influence of the experimental variable; such was the case when the research subjects provided different evaluations of "clerks" and "managers." In contrast, surveys and observation studies do not employ procedures that rigorously test the isolated impact of an independent variable.

Experiments, however, also have weaknesses. One issue is the problem of whether or not they are realistic. Would Humphrey's results have been produced in "the real world"? One possibility is that in an actual office, clerks and managers would have more information about each other. This might affect their respective perceptions and perhaps offset the tendency for individuals to be evaluated primarily on the basis of the positions they hold and the work they do. Another criticism of many experiments involves an ethical issue—whether it is right to engage in deception in the course of doing research. Does the end, which in this case is the investigator's quest for information, justify the means, the use of deceit? In Humphrey's study the subjects were told that the experimenter was attempting to determine how people work together in an office setting. This was a minor deception. As we see in the section about research ethics at the end of this chapter, sometimes experimenters engage in much larger deceptions.

## Observation Studies

To some people it might seem a bit obscene that individuals can do research simply by observing others. "All right," an individual might say, "I can understand that conducting surveys and experiments is hard work. But just people watching?!"

Actually that can be quite hard work. It is true that sociologists who conduct observation studies do not enter the research situation with a carefully developed survey or experiment, but they must be prepared to be active investigators who conscientiously observe their research subjects over a fairly long period of time (months, sometimes even several years), analyze what they observe, and relate their conclusions to concepts and theory in their field.

There are two types of observation research. Some studies use **nonparticipant observation,** a method of observation in which an investigator examines a group process without taking part in the group activities. In many instances, however, researchers believe that they will obtain a more detailed knowledge of their topic if they use **participant observation,** a method of observation in which an investigator becomes involved in the activities of the group being studied.

### Commentary

The research section at the end of Chapter 3 ("Culture") discusses the use of participant observation for studying culture. At that time the strength offered by this research method becomes apparent: the opportunity to observe individuals and groups over time in a natural setting. Neither surveys nor experiments obtain the same rich detail about research subjects. On the other hand, because of the long involvement with their subjects, observation researchers, particularly participant observers, risk the possibility of emotional involvement—attraction, dislike, or some other distinct reaction—that will distort their observations. Observation studies have another weakness: They usually involve a single or a small number of group situations. As we have observed, sociological inquiries are seeking to uncover patterns and generalizations. Researchers who study a single or small number of cases might encounter unique or unusual characteristics in the situations they are studying, and these qualities might encourage the investigators to produce misleading or incorrect generalizations.

No matter what research technique they employ, sociologists often use tables as a means of presenting their data. The following Contemporary Issue is a lesson in how to read a table.

**CONTEMPORARY ISSUE**

## *Reading a Table*

Anyone studying sociology needs to read tables. This exercise might seem confusing at first. However, it is not difficult, especially if you carefully follow the sequence of steps listed below, concentrating on each step as it is reached.

1. **Examine the title, which indicates the topic to be analyzed.** This point might seem obvious, but many people plunge into tables and other reading matter without even a glance at the title, which is a succinct summary of the information the writer is supplying. In Table 2.1 the topic is sources of satisfaction and enjoyment. The data in this table appear in percentage form. Sometimes tables present the numbers of people instead of percentages.

2. **Read captions and footnotes.** It is probably even easier to jump over these sources of information than the titles of tables—since their placement is less prominent—but such omissions are unfortunate. The caption is likely to offer a brief substantive statement about the data. In this case the caption supplies the precise wording of the question. Footnotes are likely to provide such facts as the source of the data and the means by which the information was obtained. In both cases the reader learns something about the quality of the research. The Roper Organization is a well-established commercial survey firm. As our discussion on surveys indicated, a national random sample of 2000 men and women offers an accurate representation of the entire adult American population on a given question.

3. **Identify the variables.** When researchers devise tables, they frequently put the independent variable across the top and then set the dependent variable(s) down the side. Sociologists are likely to assume this arrangement exists when they first examine a table. However, anyone reading a table must be aware that for emphasis or convenience researchers can reverse the pattern. The convention is maintained in this table. The independent variable—level of education—is across the top, and the dependent variables—the sources of satisfaction and enjoyment—produce a list down the left side.

4. **Study the labels to understand the data appearing in the table.** Researchers call each vertical list of data a "column" and each horizon-

**Table 2.1**
**People's Sources of Satisfaction and Enjoyment[1]**

| SOURCES OF SATISFACTION AND ENJOYMENT | EDUCATION LEVEL | | |
|---|---|---|---|
| | COLLEGE GRADUATE | HIGH-SCHOOL GRADUATE | LESS-THAN-HIGH-SCHOOL GRADUATE |
| Television | 33% | 50% | 65% |
| Music | 34 | 33 | 23 |
| Reading books, magazines, newspapers | 34 | 29 | 19 |
| Work | 31 | 22 | 13 |
| Radio | 16 | 22 | 27 |
| Physical exercise | 20 | 14 | 9 |

[1] The data presented here were obtained from 2000 men and women 18 years of age and over. The sample was obtained nationwide, and a complicated sampling procedure insured the randomness of the respondents chosen. Interviews were conducted face-to-face in the respondents' homes.
Source: Adapted from the Roper Organization. *Roper Reports.* May 1981.

*The following message was on a card that was shown to respondents. "Here are some things most people experience in their daily lives. Of course, they may all be important, but which three or four of those things do you find give you the most personal satisfaction or enjoyment day in and day out?"*

tal list a "row." Read the labels for each column and row and try to set them firmly in mind because you will need to consider both column and row headings simultaneously when you read the table. The variable across the top—education—has three breakdowns: college graduate, high-school graduate, and less-than-high-school graduate. Thus there are three columns of data. A set of six dependent variables—television, music, reading, work, radio, and physical exercise—runs down the side. So there are six rows of data.

5. **Analyze the information presented in the table.** Since the independent variable tends to be across the top of the table, you should examine the column headings to see whether the various categories of the independent variable establish distinct patterns in relation to the categories listed down the side. The accompanying table does indicate some distinct differences among the respondents with different levels of education. For instance, the higher the education, the less likely television is a major source of satisfaction and enjoyment: The specific figures are 33 percent for college graduates, 50 percent for high-school graduates, and 65 percent for less-than-high-school graduates. On the other hand, the higher the education, the more likely that people will feel that reading books, magazines, and newspapers is a major source of satisfaction and enjoyment: 34 percent for college graduates, 29 percent for high-school graduates, and 19 percent for less-than-high-school graduates.

6. **Consider how further analysis can expand the central conclusions.** As you study the table, you will perceive that the greater the education, the more likely that people find satisfaction and enjoyment in active pastimes—reading (mental activity), work, and physical exercise—and less likely in passive areas—television and radio. Additional research could investigate a number of issues. It would be interesting to know what independent variables besides education operate in the process of choosing one's pastimes. It is possible, for instance, that people's family background and their friends' characteristics might help determine their preferences for active or passive sources of satisfaction and enjoyment.

## Secondary Analysis

Sometimes researchers may use **secondary sources,** data banks available to researchers but produced by other individuals and organizations for their own purposes. The United States Bureau of the Census, for example, obtains large quantities of data that frequently provide a source for sociological research. In some cases researchers find that they can use earlier studies as a source of data. Other secondary sources include diaries, letters, court records, biographies, autobiographies, and novels.

Secondary sources may provide a researcher with the only information on a particular topic. Unless he had a time machine to transport him back to the last third of the nineteenth century, Richard Sennett (1974) could not have gathered direct information about Chicago families between the years 1872 and 1890. He had to rely on a variety of secondary sources—census data, novels, and historical analyses, in particular.

Using these materials, Sennett was able to learn a great deal about nineteenth-century families. For example, the census data demonstrated that in the majority of cases, husbands were at least five to ten years older than their wives. The researcher wondered why such a gap existed. The census material offered no information on this point, but Sennett was able to find a clue in another source. A novel about a middle-class Chicago household of the 1880s suggested that a young doctor would not get married until he was sufficiently well established to maintain his family at a comfortable material level.

Sennett's analysis of secondary material also revealed information about the number of children that middle-class Chicago families produced as well as some reasons for the particular family size. In Union Park, the area of Chicago on which Sen-

**Table 2.2**
**Types of Research Design**

| TYPE | VARIETIES | STRENGTHS | WEAKNESSES |
|---|---|---|---|
| Survey | Interview, questionnaire | A great deal of information can be gathered easily and efficiently | Possibility of distorted findings since data involve people's words and not their actions |
| Experiment | Laboratory or field experiment | Assessment of causality | Possible artificial influence of experimenters operating in a laboratory setting; ethical issues associated with experimenters' deception |
| Observation studies | Nonparticipant observation, participant observation | Detailed observations of groups over time in a natural setting | Danger of emotional involvement and loss of objectivity; problems of generalizing from a single case |
| Secondary sources | | Procurement of data in situations where the use of other methods is either impractical or infeasible | The diverse limitations imposed by researchers not gathering data themselves: e.g., inability of secondary sources to answer some questions of particular significance to the study at hand |

nett focused his study, the 1880 census data indicated that the average household size was 3.9 people. The researcher wondered why the families were so small. Historians' analysis of that era concluded that economic conditions supported the limited number of children. In nineteenth-century American cities, it cost a lot of money to raise and educate middle-class children in a manner that would ensure that the offspring avoided a disastrous decline in social position. Thus family financial resources usually had to remain concentrated on a few children, one or two but seldom any more.

Sennett's study illustrates that sociologists can often use secondary sources to gather information on a subject that cannot be studied by other sociological research techniques.

See Table 2.2 for summary information about the four types of research design discussed in this section.

# Issues in Sociological Research

We now turn to some general issues in research that pose major challenges to sociologists.

## Objectivity in the Research Process

**Objectivity** is the ability to evaluate reality without using personal opinions and biases. Researchers try to maintain objectivity in their work, that is, to report the facts in the situations that they study without reflecting their personal feelings. If two investigators conducted the same piece of research independently of each other and produced the same or almost the same findings, then we would have strong reason to believe that they had achieved objectivity.

The loss of objectivity can occur for several reasons. Some research areas might provoke intense personal feelings in entire groups of investigators.

**34**

As an extreme case, it would be unreasonable to expect a black or Jewish sociologist to do an objective study of the Ku Klux Klan, a group that has had a history of terrorizing both ethnic groups, especially blacks. Furthermore the majority of American sociologists are white, male, middle-class, and politically liberal, and each of these qualities could be a source of bias in a research situation.

Another reason for the loss of objectivity is a researcher's commitment to a fixed theoretical or idealogical position. As the Cross-Cultural Perspective below suggests, researchers sometimes approach their studies not as open-minded observers but as individuals selectively seeking evidence for a particular position.

A third factor endangering objectivity is the researcher's relations with his or her respondents. During a participant-observation study, an investigator might develop such a close relationship with research subjects that he or she might begin to accept their definitions of critical situations—their analyses of community events, their assessments of the "good people" and the "bad people," and more. Such a situation can endanger the objectivity of a project.

Sociologists can take several steps to avoid the loss of objectivity. First, recognizing that both their topics and their techniques are affected by their own values, they can attempt to analyze carefully how their values apply to their studies. Once they have determined the impact of their values, they are probably less likely to let them undermine the objectivity of their investigations. Second, sociologists might seek the assistance of colleagues who can visit the research site and make independent assessments of the people under study. The colleagues' assessments, though based on brief observations, might provide the investigators with clues to whether or not they are losing their objectivity.

A researcher's objectivity can also be assessed by another person's follow-up investigation. After reading a report about a particular study, a second sociologist might want to determine the accuracy of the findings. He or she will conduct a **replication**—a repetition or near repetition of an earlier study to determine the accuracy of its findings.

The loss of objectivity can occur in any social–scientific study. As the following Cross-Cultural Perspective indicates, even famous social researchers can be vulnerable to this criticism.

## CROSS-CULTURAL PERSPECTIVE

### *Margaret Mead in Samoa: Objectivity in Participant-Observation Research*

Objectivity is a priority in research, but sometimes investigators fail in this regard. This box illustrates some of the conditions that might undermine objectivity.

In 1925 Margaret Mead, a twenty-three-year-old anthropologist, arrived in Samoa. After nine months of research, she produced a book that became the first anthropological bestseller, *Coming of Age in Samoa.* Nearly sixty years later, Derek Freeman, a New Zealand anthropologist, completed a book indicating that Mead's participant-observation study lacked objec-

tivity and that its conclusions were largely incorrect.

Before Margaret Mead left for Samoa, she had been a graduate student of the anthropologist Franz Boas. At the time Boas was deeply involved in the debate about whether human development is primarily the result of biological or cultural influence. According to Freeman, Boas wholeheartedly supported the latter idea, and, to bolster the cultural position, he sought evidence to counter his opponents' contention that the turmoil of adolescence was a biological ne-

cessity. In Samoa Margaret Mead hoped to find a culture free of adolescent stress, and this discovery would have given Boas valuable ammunition in his debate with the biological determinists. Freeman contended that Boas was pleased with the study that Mead planned to undertake. Freeman wrote: "In Margaret Mead there was at hand a spirited young cultural determinist ideally suited to the project he had in mind" (Freeman, 1983: 60).

If Freeman is correct, then Margaret Mead's objectivity was already seriously tarnished before she even left the United States. Independent support for Freeman's claim does exist. Robin Fox, an English anthropologist, indicated that Mead characterized the relationship of Boas with his graduate students in the following fashion: "He told us what to look for and we went and found it" (Leo, 1983: 69).

Freeman concluded that because Mead's research lacked objectivity, she produced blatantly inaccurate findings. In *Coming of Age in Samoa*, Mead described a culture in which people had a pleasant, relaxed attitude toward sex. Before marriage, she contended, adolescents could engage in free love-making, and marriage itself was not a major hindrance to free love. Mead's overall sense of the Samoans was that they were an amiable, relaxed, peaceful people. Freeman disagreed with her on both points. His own recent study concluded that Samoan adolescents were subjected to authoritarian control. The adults did not encourage youthful sex; in fact, they explicitly prohibited it. In addi-tion, Freeman did not believe that the Samoans he observed were an amiable, peaceful people. His impression was that they were competitive, jealous, and frequently violent. While Mead reported that forcible rape was unknown to the Samoans, Freeman offered data indicating that the incidence of forcible rape was high, twice that of the United States and twenty times that of England. He claimed that all Margaret Mead had needed to do to learn about the frequency of rape among the Samoans was to read the local newspaper, which regularly reported rape cases during her stay.

Derek Freeman claimed throughout his book that biological factors have as much impact in the shaping of human development as cultural factors do. Freeman's critics, however, contended that, like Mead, he too has forsaken objectivity in an effort to convey an ideological position. Bradd Shore, a third anthropologist who has done fieldwork in Samoa, suggested that the Samoans fall somewhere between the Mead and Freeman characterizations. They are neither as amiable and peaceful as Mead described nor as competitive and violent as Freeman claimed.

The Mead–Freeman confrontation is not the first situation in which anthropologists have studied the same culture and produced different findings. Because the loss of objectivity is a danger in their studies, anthropological researchers have found an increasing number of ways to control their biases. Often they use independently developed psychological tests as a nonsubjective means of assessing respondents' thought and behavior patterns. Census data and statistical analysis can serve the same purpose. Team research can permit anthropologists to examine a wider range of groups and activities than a single investigator could. In addition, this approach provides team members an opportunity to evaluate each others' objectivity and to attempt to correct any individual biases that might distort their findings.

Sources: Derek Freeman. *Margaret Mead and Samoa.* Cambridge: Harvard University Press. 1983; John Leo. "Bursting the South Sea Bubble." *Time.*Vol. 121. February 14, 1983, pp. 68–70; Eliot Marshall. "A Controversy on Samoa Comes of Age." *Science.* Vol. 219. March 1983, pp. 1042–1045; John Noble Wilford. "Customs Check: Leave Your Ideological Baggage Behind." *New York Times.* February 6, 1983, section 4, p. 8.

## Ethics in the Researcher's Role

All sociologists will agree that research must be conducted in an ethically sound manner. Exactly what the ethical limits should be, however, is often a topic for debate. In this section we consider three possible areas where ethical problems can arise — issues of confidentiality, painful self-revelation, and use of findings.

### Problem of Confidentiality

There are different aspects to the issue of confidentiality. Occasionally sociologists publish data that prove embarrassing or irritating to informants who feel that their confidentiality has been violated. On the other hand, sociologists like Mario Brajuha sometimes find themselves acting to protect informants' confidentiality.

In 1982 Mario Brajuha, a graduate student in sociology at the State University of New York at Stony Brook, began his dissertation research, a participant-observation study of a restaurant where he was employed as a waiter. Brajuha had collected about 700 pages of notes when a suspicious fire destroyed the restaurant.

A few days later local fire and police investigators contacted Brajuha demanding his cooperation, including the release of all his records. Brajuha notified members of the sociology department, and they suggested that he meet with the University Attorney's Office, where the advice was to comply with all requests. Brajuha rejected the advice. He agreed to give oral testimony to the grand jury on information he obtained as a restaurant employee but refused to surrender his notes, believing that this move would have been a violation of the confidentiality he had promised all informants.

This course of action was unacceptable to the Assistant Attorney General, and he threatened to have Brajuha jailed for contempt. On the day that he was expected to surrender his records, Brajuha appeared before the judge presiding over the case. Upon examination of Brajuha's records, the judge agreed that the researcher's claim that people would be embarrassed if his records were revealed was realistic. Nonetheless, the judge eventually ruled that Brajuha should surrender his notes. The pressure on Brajuha increased when the Federal District Attorney issued a subpoena for the research records. Attorneys for both sides presented their cases to a federal judge who ruled that serious scholars must be permitted the same confidentiality as journalists. At the same time, the Brajuha case was sent back to the lower court for additional information. One unanswered question was whether or not as a graduate student Brajuha could claim to be a serious scholar.

This question was never answered in court. Following a reorganization of the Federal Attorney's Office, there was an out-of-court settlement with Brajuha supplying federal investigators some carefully edited information from his notes.

Because of this settlement, it remains unclear when scholars will be permitted to maintain confidentiality. However, the Brajuha case established the possibility that, in the future, sociologists and other researchers can successfully invoke such a privilege (Hallowell, 1985).

## Problem of Painful Self-Revelation

When research subjects are manipulated, painful self-revelations are sometimes produced. Stanley Milgram (1974), a psychologist, did a series of experimental studies in which his subjects believed that they were applying a sequence of increasingly powerful shocks to hypothetical subjects in a learning experiment. Milgram's elaborate "shock machine" did not actually administer any shocks to the supposed victims, who had been instructed by the researcher to express surprise, pain, and sometimes even pleas for mercy after the subject pushed one of the shock buttons. Yet for the purposes of the experiments, which focused on the subjects' willingness to obey an authority figure (the researcher), it was essential that the people who pushed the buttons on the machine believed that it was producing real shocks. The following exchange illustrates how a typical subject responded to this experimental situation.

The subject began the experiment calmly but became increasingly nervous as he proceeded. After believing that he had administered a 180-volt shock, this man pivoted in his chair and addressed the researcher in an agitated voice:

> SUBJECT: I can't stand it. I'm not going to kill that man in there. You hear him hollering?
> EXPERIMENTER: As I told you before, the shocks may be painful, but—
>
> *(Milgram, 1974: 73)*

As the voltage increased, the subject became even more agitated:

> SUBJECT: What if he's dead in there? . . . I mean, he told me he can't stand the shock, sir. I don't mean to be rude, but I think you should look in on him. All you have to do is look in on him. All you have to do is look in the door. I don't get no answer, no noise. Something might have happened to the gentleman in there, sir.
> EXPERIMENTER: We must continue. Go on, please.
>
> *(Milgram, 1974: 76)*

The subject did go on, pushing the voltage buttons until the experimenter finally indicated that the exercise was over.

Milgram explained that before subjects left, a "friendly reconciliation" occurred between them and their imagined victims. Furthermore the researcher made an effort to reduce any tensions

*In the above series of photos taken from the film* Obedience *by Stanley Milgram, one can see the "shock machine," the "victim" (seated, upper right), the researcher (in white lab coat), and the subject (bottom photos).*

that had arisen during the experiment. But could he succeed in this regard? One critic expressed strong doubts:

> It would be interesting to know what sort of procedures could dissipate the type of emotional disturbance just described. In view of the effects on subjects, traumatic to a degree which Milgram himself considers nearly unpecedented in sociopsychological experiments, his casual assurance that these tensions were dissipated before the subject left the laboratory is unconvincing.
>
> *(Baumrind, 1964: 422)*

Some psychologists and sociologists have defended Milgram's research. Several have pointed out that his experiments revealed startling, important findings about people's tendencies to obey

authority figures. But does the importance of the findings justify the emotional disruption that many subjects suffered? If researchers accept that the ends justify the means, then they have assumed a frightening ethical position.

## Use of Findings

When a team of sociologists is hired by a government agency or business to conduct a study, they are likely to undertake the project enthusiastically. "This is our chance to really let those guys in government (or the corporate world) know what is going on," the researchers might say. So they will complete their study, usually including in their report a list of recommendations on how to improve the workings of the structure investigated. The re-

**38**   port will be issued and then . . . nothing. William Freudenburg and Kenneth Keating have noted that " . . . most writers currently find little evidence to suggest that . . . policymakers commonly make direct use of social science input; by contrast, there is evidence that reports are often filed and ignored" (Freudenburg and Keating, 1985: 581).

When their findings are ignored, researchers are likely to feel frustrated — to emphasize that the policymakers who hired them probably did so because "it looked good" and made it appear that they, the policymakers, wanted more information about the subject studied, and were willing to consider changes and improvements when, in fact, they were not. At such a time researchers are likely to feel that they have been mistreated, wronged. To them the issue appears to be an ethical one.

But Freudenburg and Keating (1985) have suggested that social scientists who want their recommendations accepted by policymakers should think in political, not ethical terms. They wrote, "As the realistic politician Franklin Roosevelt is reported to have said privately to an interest group seeking his support, 'You've convinced me. Now go out there and put some pressure on me'" (Freudenburg and Keating, 1985: 595).

Freudenburg and Keating suggested that instead of using their studies to attempt to convince policymakers of changes that must be made, researchers are better advised to spend their time and energy supplying information and expertise to organizations initiating lawsuits on the public's behalf.

# STUDY GUIDE

## Summary

1.  Methodology is the set of principles and procedures that guides sociological research.

2.  The stages of the research process include choosing a topic, reviewing the literature, formulating a hypothesis, picking the research design, gathering the data, analyzing the data, and producing a report.

3.  The four principal types of sociological research design are surveys, experiments, observation studies, and secondary analysis. A survey is a research technique that uses carefully constructed questions to obtain large amounts of information about people's thoughts and behavior. The two principal types of surveys are interviews and questionnaires. An advantage of surveys is that they permit researchers to gather a great deal of information easily. A disadvantage is that they measure people's reported behavior and not their behavior, and sometimes these reports are inaccurate or incomplete indicators of individuals' actions.

An experiment is a research form in which the investigator manipulates conditions so that the effects of one variable can be observed while other variables are held constant. An advantage of experiments is that they can indicate a causal link. At the same time, they have weaknesses. Critics question whether experimental results would materialize in the "real world." Another criticism involves an ethical issue — whether it is right to engage in deception in the course of research.

Observation research, participant observation in particular, offers the special opportunity to study individuals and groups over time in a natural setting. On the other hand, participant observers can lose their emotional detachment, and such a loss might impede a full and balanced understanding of the group process under investigation.

Secondary sources are data banks available to researchers but produced by other individuals and organizations for their own purposes. The United States Bureau of the Census obtains large quantities of data that can serve as the principal or exclusive source for sociological research.

4.  Researchers are expected to be objective. A number of factors influence their success in this regard.

Research has raised serious ethical questions. Problems arising in major social-scientific studies involve confidentiality, painful self-relevation, and the use of findings.

# Glossary

**causation** a situation in which one variable can produce the occurrence of another.

**correlation** a statistical description of the relationship between variables.

**dependent variable** the variable that the independent variable influences.

**experiment** a research technique in which the investigator manipulates conditions so that the effects produced by one independent variable can be isolated and observed.

**hypothesis** a scientifically researchable suggestion about the relationship between two or more variables.

**independent variable** a variable that influences another variable—the dependent variable.

**interview** a type of survey composed of questions that are delivered face-to-face or over the telephone.

**methodology** the set of principles and procedures that guides sociological research.

**nonparticipant observation** a method of observation in which an investigator examines a group process without taking part in the group activities.

**objectivity** the ability to evaluate reality without using personal opinions and biases.

**participant observation** a method of observation in which an investigator becomes involved in the activities of the group being studied.

**population** the entire category of people possessing the characteristics that interest a researcher.

**questionnaire** a type of survey in which a respondent writes the answers to a list of questions.

**random sample** a sample drawn from a population by a process that assures that every individual in that population has an equal probability of being included.

**reliability** consistency in measurement.

**replication** a repetition or near repetition of an earlier study to determine the accuracy of its findings.

**sample** a limited number of individuals chosen from a population for the purpose of conducting research.

**secondary sources** data banks available to researchers but produced by other individuals and organizations for their own purposes.

**survey** a research technique that uses carefully constructed questions to obtain a variety of facts about people's thoughts and behavior.

**validity** the condition where a research item accurately measures what it claims to measure.

**variable** a factor that has two or more categories or measurable conditions.

# Learning Objectives

After studying this chapter, you should be able to:

1. Define methodology and explain its importance in scientific research.
2. Define causation, distinguish between an independent variable and a dependent variable, and identify the conditions necessary for causation.
3. Define correlation, indicating its relationship to causation and distinguishing between positive and negative correlations.
4. List the stages in the research process, describing the sociologist's tasks at each stage.
5. Define hypothesis and explain the contribution hypotheses make in the research process.
6. Distinguish among the following concepts—population, sample, and random sample—and explain the importance of random sampling in sociological research.
7. Define and discuss the four major types of research design—surveys, experiments, observation studies, and secondary analysis—and evaluate strengths and weaknesses of the first three types.
8. Define objectivity, explain its importance in scientific research, identify factors that may hinder objectivity, and indicate how the loss of objectivity may be prevented.
9. Identify and discuss ethical issues involved in sociological research.

Tests

## True – false test

_____ 1. In sociological research, dependent variables are frequently attitudes and activities.

_____ 2. A correlation of "0" indicates no relationship at all between two variables.

_____ 3. Surveys usually obtain samples instead of populations.

_____ 4. A strength of surveys is that they not only find out what people say they have done but also what they have done.

_____ 5. In Humphrey's experiment, he used real clerks and managers to play their respective roles.

_____ 6. The loss of objectivity is less likely to occur in an observation study than in an experiment or survey.

_____ 7. Data produced by the United States Bureau of the Census is never used by sociologists as a secondary source.

_____ 8. Mario Brajuha's effort to protect informants legally established the possibility that in the future sociologists can invoke the privilege of confidentiality.

_____ 9. Stanley Milgram's experiments illustrate the ethical principle that the ends justify the means.

_____ 10. Freudenburg and Keating have concluded that social researchers seeking to influence governmental policymakers must act independently of citizen groups working on the same issue.

## Multiple-choice test

_____ 1. Scientists' central concern is:
   a. causation.
   b. the systematic pursuit of the truth.
   c. the effective use of random samples.
   d. correlation.

_____ 2. Causation cannot be established until researchers have *ruled out* the:
   a. existence of other possible dependent variables.
   b. influence of other possible independent variables.
   c. possibility that the independent variable existed before the dependent variable.
   d. inverse relationship between variables.

_____ 3. "The higher people's social class, the fewer children they have" is an example of a[n]:
   a. theory.
   b. correlation.
   c. hypothesis.
   d. logical pattern.

_____ 4. The precise demand made of researchers by funding organizations is that they:
   a. gather data.
   b. analyze their findings.
   c. summarize their findings in a report.
   d. demonstrate the importance of their findings for sociological theory.

_____ 5. The *Literary Digest* poll of 1936 demonstrated that:
   a. random samples don't work.
   b. biases in sampling can produce disasterous research results.

      c. very large samples are necessary for predicting elections.
      d. several other types of samples work as well as random samples.

_____ 6. In Bandura's experiment with a punching-bag toy:
      a. there was no independent variable.
      b. there were no children in the experimental group.
      c. the adult's hammering of the toy occurred in the control group.
      d. the adult's hammering of the toy occurred in the experimental group.

_____ 7. Participant-observation studies:
      a. make it possible to observe individuals and groups over time in a natural setting.
      b. are usually done with surveys.
      c. require a set of no less than six hypotheses.
      d. use a control group.

_____ 8. Richard Sennett needed information on Chicago families for the period 1872–1890. Information of this sort must now be obtained from:
      a. experimental design.
      b. primary sources.
      c. secondary sources.
      d. nonparticipant observation.

_____ 9. The loss of objectivity can occur because:
      a. some researchers are not intellectually equipped for the studies they do.
      b. some topics provoke intense feelings in entire groups of investigators.
      c. researchers do not have a fixed theoretical or ideological position.
      d. investigators are too detached from their informants.

_____ 10. Milgram's "shock-machine" studies focused social scientists' attention on the ethical issue of:
      a. painful self-revelation.
      b. confidentiality.
      c. validity.
      d. replication.

## Essay test

1. Discuss the stages in the research process, indicating the major activity occurring at each stage.
2. What is a survey? Indicate a major strength and a major weakness of this approach.
3. Define experiment and indicate how the experimental process works. What are an important strength and an important weakness of this technique?
4. Discuss observation studies, defining participant observation and pointing out a significant strength and a significant weakness of this research form.
5. What are secondary sources? Under what conditions might a sociologist decide to use them?
6. Define objectivity and discuss conditions that can undermine it during research.
7. Discuss two areas in which ethical problems can arise in the course of social-scientific studies.

## Suggested Readings

Bailey, Kenneth D. 1982. *Methods of Social Research.* New York: The Free Press. Second edition. A comprehensive introduction to sociological research methods, including four chapters on the details of constructing surveys.
Cole, Stephen. 1980. *The Sociological Method: An Introduction to the Science of Sociology.* Chicago: Rand McNally. Third edition. A short, well-written analysis of the sociological research process. The author

provides a continuous flow of effective examples to illustrate the concepts or research procedures he describes.

Hammond, Phillip E. (ed.). 1964. *Sociologists at Work*. New York: Basic. Sociologists involved in eleven, methodologically varied studies candidly analyzing their research experience in detail. These accounts offer a concrete discussion of issues and problems that can arise at different steps in the research process.

Hoover, Kenneth R. 1984. *The Elements of Social Scientific Thinking*. New York: St. Martin's. Third edition. A short, nicely written introduction to the thought process that is necessary to produce effective social-scientific research. This book might prove particularly useful for students who are interested in pursuing social research as a career.

Huff, Darrell. 1954. *How to Lie with Statistics*. New York: Norton. A revealing, entertaining discussion of the problems and limitations of statistical material.

*Sociological Abstracts*. A report issued five times a year and containing summaries of the latest articles and books in sociology.

Webb, Eugene J., Donald T. Campbell, Richard D. Schwartz, and Lee Sechrest. 1966. *Unobtrusive Measures*. Chicago: Rand McNally. A discussion of a variety of ingenious ways in which social researchers can gather information about individuals and group members without directly interacting with them.

## Student Projects

1. Assume you have been hired to study a problem of job satisfaction/dissatisfaction where you work. You have recently developed the following hypothesis: The better workers are paid, the greater their job satisfaction. In your library find articles and books on job satisfaction and use these sources for developing a study to test this hypothesis. Are you able to discuss effectively all the stages in the research process? (Hint: *Sociological Abstracts* and *Psychological Abstracts* will help you find articles.)

2. In a newspaper or magazine find a questionnaire or self-test. Make a list of the variables asked about, such as age, sex, level of education, and occupation. What is the questionnaire trying to determine? Sort the variables into two categories—independent and dependent variables. Now using these variables, construct what seem to be reasonable hypotheses about the subject in the questionnaire. (See the discussion on hypotheses in the text.)

## Answers to Test Questions

### True–false test

| | | | | |
|---|---|---|---|---|
| 1. t | 3. t | 5. f | 7. f | 9. t |
| 2. t | 4. f | 6. f | 8. t | 10. f |

### Multiple-choice test

| | | | | |
|---|---|---|---|---|
| 1. b | 3. c | 5. b | 7. a | 9. b |
| 2. b | 4. c | 6. d | 8. c | 10. a |

# PART TWO

## The Individual in Society

**3**
*Culture*

**4**
*Groups*

**5**
*Social Interaction*

**6**
*Socialization*

**7**
*Gender Roles and Sexuality*

**8**
*Deviance*

# 3
# CULTURE

Is it obvious that everyone walks the same way? Perhaps it seems obvious, but it is actually not true. A recent study of human locomotion in 160 societies (Devine, 1985) has revealed that many early Western observers entering non-Western societies immediately noticed that the people displayed manners of walking that were different from their own. The researcher wrote, "Whether they describe the novel walk or trot . . . as graceful, poised, noble, peculiar, stilted, or ungainly is secondary to the fact that they were so conscious of a difference that they almost always felt compelled to comment on it . . ."(Devine, 1985: 553).

Travelers' written accounts also show that non-Western people were often aware that their styles of locomotion were different from Westerners'. In one journal a visitor to a South Pacific island indicated that the local people found Europeans' gait so humorously awkward that they would burst into uncontrolled laughter.

A cultural item — in this case, style of walking — does not simply materialize. Distinct factors encourage its development. Were we to study a variety of cultures, we would be likely to find suggestions about the development of cultures' walking or running styles indicated by apparent connections between their styles and the traditional activities performed within particular cultures. Even though modern cultures are complex, careful analysis can produce an understanding of their development, patterns, and contributions.

**Culture** consists of all the human-made products associated with a society. Basically two types of cultural products exist — the material and the nonmaterial. Material products consist of the physical objects people make and use — ranging in size from laboratory-developed microorganisms to skyscrapers, and in complexity from the crudest stone or wood tools and weapons to the most sophisticated computers. Nonmaterial products are intangible. However, these nonmaterial products are the foundations of culture, providing information essential for interpersonal behavior and for the development of material culture. Beliefs, technology, values, norms, and language are important types of nonmaterial culture that will be discussed in the next section of this chapter.

Culture is one of the most basic yet profound realities of our lives. Culture provides us with a shared framework to guide us as we solve our everyday problems. If this statement seems abstract to you, try applying it to yourself. Imagine that you are sitting alone, just thinking. Note that the process of thought involves language and that language is a shared component of culture. You feel hungry. You might think that hunger is simply a biological urge, but a person's sense of hunger is inevitably affected by cultural standards. Perhaps you find yourself looking at your watch wondering if it is "time" to be hungry. Many, perhaps most, Americans are geared to three meals a day at fairly fixed times. However, people in other cultures often follow different arrangements; and, of course, differences also exist in food preferences. Americans would probably find their culturally prescribed sense of hunger rapidly receding if they were offered a few staples of some different cultures — such delicacies as lice, lizards, snakes, ants, worms, animal eyes or brains, wasps, and beetles.

Perhaps you take culture for granted, but like air, which you might also take for granted, culture plays a fundamental part in your life. Consider politics: Americans frequently complain about the corruption and ineffectiveness of their politicians, and as a kind of impotent protest many people often fail to vote. Most of us seem to accept our existing political system most of the time with relatively little thought. But imagine how you would respond if the political leadership suddenly declared that you could never vote again and that as an ordinary citizen you could never participate at all in the political process — as often is the case in many nations.

A distinction needs to be made between "culture" and "society." Culture involves the human-made products associated with a group, and **society** consists of the interacting people who share a culture. The two concepts are closely interrelated. A culture cannot exist without a society to imple-

*The activities in which the members of different cultures engage influence walking styles. We Westerners seldom carry heavy objects for long distances. If we did, many of us would probably alter our current walking style to make the impact of weight less burdensome.*

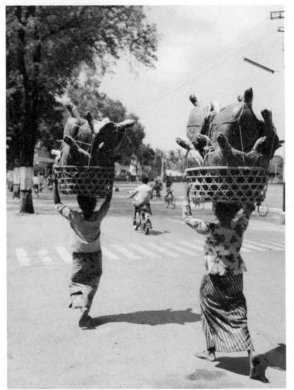

ment it, and a society cannot exist unless a culture provides guidelines for its activities. In one sense culture is like a game plan developed by a coach for an athletic team. The team needs the game plan to guide the strategy for its upcoming contest. However, without the players to put it into action, the game plan is no more than an idea. Given the close relationship between the terms "culture" and "society," it is not surprising that they are often used interchangeably. Yet you must realize that a distinction between the two can be made.

In this chapter we will examine the components of culture, the diversity and unity of culture, and American culture. One additional point: Does the following use of "culture" sound familiar? Someone says, "She's a really cultured person." Or someone else contends, "He ain't got no culture." In these instances "culture" means classy, polished, or stylish—in short a quality of someone a "cut" above the average. We are not concerned with this meaning of "culture." Whether we are classy or not, all of us have culture.

## Components of Culture

Since the arrival of modern humanity, cultural development has been rapid. About 40,000 years ago, humans started wearing clothes, constructing shelters, and learning to survive in climates ranging from the tropical to the subarctic. About 4000 years ago, the domestication of animals and the cultivation of crop plants became widespread, producing a profound effect on human life. People no longer needed to follow big game from

place to place. With improved production of crops and animals, the environment could support increasingly larger populations, permitting a growing number of people to move into specialized occupations. Towns and cities started to develop. About 200 years ago, the Industrial Revolution began, eventually producing worldwide communication systems, effective mass transportation, and a vast assortment of technological advances.

In this section we examine the following components of culture: beliefs, technology, values, norms, and language.

*An example of both the material and nonmaterial aspects of contemporary American culture is the shopping mall. These malls are specially designed physical structures containing countless physical objects (from food to clothing) which people make and use. They are also partly an expression of American values, norms, and symbols. People come not only to purchase but to share an environment and to participate in a way of life.*

### Beliefs

A **belief** is a statement about reality that people accept as true. Beliefs are based on observation, logic, tradition, other people's opinions, or faith. Thus one can speak about scientific and nonscientific beliefs.

People who share a given culture do not necessarily share beliefs. In the United States, there has been widespread disagreement about the respective intelligence of blacks and whites, with an increasingly smaller percentage of the public believing that the intelligence of blacks is inferior. In 1963, 39 percent of a national sample of whites believed that blacks were mentally inferior to whites. By 1978 the figure had slipped to 25 percent (Louis Harris and Associates *Newsweek* Poll, 1978).

Age often affects beliefs. One would be hard pressed to find any adult Americans who believe in Santa Claus, but many children do. As Table 3.1 indicates, a recent national poll concluded that 87

**Table 3.1**
**American Children's Belief in Santa Claus**

| ALL CHILDREN | AGES 3–5 | AGES 6–8 | AGES 9–10 |
|---|---|---|---|
| 87% | 96% | 88% | 69% |

Source: *New York Times Poll.* December 24, 1985.

*As children become older, they are less likely to believe in Santa Claus.*

percent of American children aged three to ten believe in Santa Claus. While few differences were found between boys and girls, whites and blacks, or Protestants and Catholics, the children's age was highly correlated with belief. The older the children, the less likely they believed in Santa. The survey demonstrated that older children were more inclined to see logical reasons not to believe in Santa. For instance, Sara Oates, aged eight, pointed out, "A bike can't come down a chimney" (Rimer, 1985).

Beliefs can produce deadly effects. For early Americans the doctrine of Manifest Destiny reflected the belief that the Europeans and their descendants were the properly dominant race in North America; thus they were supposed to be the guardians of American Indians, the land, and other natural resources. This popular nineteenth-century belief was a rationalization for the settlers' violent takeover of Indian lands and for a pattern of violating treaties once they were signed.

Beliefs supply the framework for people's perceptions. Many Americans believe that people are generally untrustworthy, that only locks, bolts, and bars can protect personal property. Thus it surprised a newsman accompanying President Nixon's tour to China to find that his camera was still sitting on the bus seat where he had forgotten it. Americans abroad can also encounter foreigners' beliefs about the United States. To the poor people of many African, Asian, and Latin American countries, all Americans seem fabulously wealthy. These poor would find it difficult to believe that poverty, malnutrition, and hunger exist in the United States. Furthermore the widespread exposure of American television programming has contributed to a glamorous, violent image of the country. To many foreigners the United States is the land of "Dallas," "Dynasty," "Knots Landing," "Miami Vice," and "Moonlighting."

## Technology

**Technology** is any repeated operation that people use to manipulate the environment to achieve some practical goals. Perhaps it is the technology of modern cultures that most dramatically sets them off from earlier cultures. Since Mark Twain wrote *A Connecticut Yankee in King Arthur's Court,* many writers and filmmakers have dramatized the tremendous power and influence time travelers could exercise if they could move backward to ancient cultures. One can argue that such a "step backward in time" was in effect made by European explorers and settlers when they used advanced weaponry, communication forms, and means of transportation to subdue or annihilate the native inhabitants of five continents.

Technology profoundly affects people's everyday lives in various ways, such as compelling the

*When beliefs or belief systems are challenged, the consequences can be dire. In the time of the astronomer Galileo (1564–1642), the dominant belief was that the earth was the fixed center of the universe. When Galileo (shown standing before a Roman Catholic Cardinal) claimed that his studies proved the earth revolved around the sun, he was branded as a heretic and forced to choose between recanting or being put to death.*

development of new occupations. A hundred years ago none of the following occupations existed: radiologist, astronaut, computer programmer, professional racing-car driver, or deep-sea diver. These occupations could not exist because the respective technologies that make them possible had not yet been invented. Technology can also influence existing occupations. Today a doctor's job is often simplified by modern equipment. Does the leg have a fracture or the brain contain a tumor? X-rays and brain scans can provide definitive answers that could not be obtained in the past.

Sometimes, however, new technologies can be dysfunctional for specific groups. From 1900 to 1902, American naval authorities steadfastly rejected a new technological device that greatly improved the accuracy of guns mounted on warships. The drawback was that the new apparatus eliminated much of the previous artistry; in particular, while the new mechanism permitted a lowly recruit to fire more shells with greater accuracy than was previously possible, the innovation required the dismissal of the coordinating officer (Freeman, 1974).

## Norms

For a moment imagine that we are small enough to fit into an anthill or a beehive. Standing out of the flow of traffic, we would observe thousands of insects unerringly moving about their tasks, each a tiny cog in a complicated organizational structure. Such behavior is a magnificent testimony to the finely tuned genetic programming of these little organisms. Human beings, however, function very differently from ants and bees. We are primarily directed or controlled not by instinctive genetic guidelines but by learned norms.

A **norm** is a standard of desirable behavior. Norms are the rules people are expected to follow in their relations with each other. Norms not only provide guidelines dictating appropriate behavior in a given situation but also supply people with expectations of how others will respond to their actions. Norms often vary widely from society to society. In many respects English and American cultures are similar, and yet numerous normative differences exist — for example, the English drive on the left-hand side of the street and they always hold their forks in the left hand while eating.

Norms also change over time. In the early twentieth century, bathing suits were ridiculously modest by current standards. Our skimpy modern models would have been viewed with horror.

Norms are often situational; that is, they are associated with certain positions people fill and not with others. It is considered appropriate to express one's problems and fears to therapists but not to bank tellers, whose embarrassment or irritation would indicate that they expect only "small talk" when transacting bank business. During a football game, the players are supposed to block and tackle each other, but they are penalized for continuing such action after the whistle has been blown to stop play. In some situations people find it difficult to forsake previously relevant norms after they have become inappropriate or even criminal. After returning to the United States, some Vietnam-War veterans found themselves diving to the ground when a car backfired. Some veterans discovered it was difficult or impossible to forsake a violent life and either got into trouble with the law or signed on as mercenaries in foreign wars.

Sociologists make some basic distinctions about norms. It should be emphasized that the following two-part classifications are simplifications of reality, which were developed to demonstrate specific qualities of norms. Actual norms often fail to fit neatly into one category or the other.

*Folkways and mores.* **Folkways** are norms that specify the way things are customarily done; they are concerned with standards of behavior that are socially approved but not considered morally significant. Violation of folkways seldom leads to punishment. Folkways leave room for eccentric or harmless behavior. Picking one's nose in public, littering, or arguing loudly with one's spouse at a party would be considered violations of folkways.

Violations of mores are much more serious. Child abuse, forcible rape, torture, murder, and cannibalism are prominent examples of violations of mores. **Mores** (pronounced "morays") are norms people consider vital; they are embedded in what members of a society believe to be morality. Unlike folkways, mores involve clear-cut distinctions between right and wrong. Punishment for the violation of mores will range from avoidance and ridicule to imprisonment and death.

*Very different norms can co-exist within the same society. The wet suit, surfboard, and "laid back" lifestyle contrast sharply with the norms of the Amish (Mennonites) who, as suggested by their "plain folk" clothing, continue to try to maintain their traditional standards within our rapidly changing American society.*

*Explicit and implicit norms.* Within a culture some norms are **explicit,** out in the open. Explicit norms are learned formally. For example, as children we were told by parents, "Don't speak with your mouth full, Sarah" or "Stop that, Frank! Don't hit your sister." Because explicit norms are formally learned, almost everyone can explain them. Other norms are **implicit,** lying beneath the surface and not easily stated. Often these norms are most easily identified when violated. In many American households, parents enforce an implicit norm about nudity. The family members are not supposed to see each other naked. In most families this norm is probably never stated, but the children learn it when mom or dad hurriedly turns around or closes the bedroom door so as not to be seen without clothes.

*Ideal norms and real norms.* **Ideal norms** are standards requiring strict obedience to the guidelines provided. In everyday life, however, some "slippage" occurs because the standards are often too lofty, impractical, or demanding. As a result **real norms** emerge: the adjustment of standards to the practical conditions of living.

Small deviations from norms are expected, even tolerated, but limits to the deviations are set.

People often fail to achieve ideal norms, even where they want to. For example, let us suppose that every day in the park a man sees a particular woman whom he would like to meet. He has watched numerous movies and television skits that suggest how this should be done: He should simply go up to her and start talking or contrive some means for meeting her, such as an apparently accidental collision in front of the grocery store. But he lacks the courage for such a ploy and constantly scolds himself for falling short of the ideal norm.

When people find it unpleasant or awkward to acknowledge that their response falls short of an ideal norm, they are likely to offer rationalizations to explain why they are not responsible for the violation of the ideal norm. The Hindu religion prohibits Indian farmers from killing cattle. Through the centuries farmers have developed means of avoiding direct slaughter. For example, to "kill" unwanted calves, owners place a triangular wooden yoke around the calves' necks so that when they try to nurse they jab the cow's udder and get kicked to death.

Farmers then rationalize that the cows, not they, were responsible for the calves' death (Harris, 1974: 28).

## Values

Fierceness is very important to the Yanomamö of the South American jungle. When a Yanomamö wife has been caught in an affair with another man, this value is reflected in universally endorsed club fights. In these duels one man holds a ten-foot club, steadies himself by leaning on the club, and then exposes his head for a blow from the opponents's club. After that the positions are reversed. The majority of duels end up as free-for-alls, with everyone clubbing everyone else. Fatalities sometimes result but not often because the headmen of the different groups stand by with bows drawn ready to kill anyone who delivers an intentionally lethal blow. The scalps of the older men often have as many as a dozen enormous, angry scars, which are fully displayed on the possessors' proudly shaved heads (Chagnon, 1977). Around the planet, Americans are considered aggressive and prone to violence, and yet they are amateurs compared to the Yanamamö who emphasize the values of fierceness and violence.

As this illustration suggests, values vary from one culture to another, but all cultures have them. A **value** is a general conviction about what is good or bad, right or wrong, appropriate or inappropriate. Values are abstract, stating broad behavioral preferences, while norms guide behavior in specific situations. Americans tend to embrace the value of patriotism. Norms associated with patriotism specify that adult citizens should vote and that they should stand up, face the flag, and sing when the national anthem is played in public. Values concern what people regard as good or desirable, while beliefs focus on what they consider true and factual.

Values are important because they influence the content of norms. If a culture such as the Yanomamö values fierceness and violence, its norms will provide such opportunities as club fights that permit members to demonstrate fierceness and engage in violence. When a culture such as the Arapesh of the South Pacific values intimate, gentle interpersonal relations, its norms will emphasize such activities as conscientious, loving child care and extreme efforts to avoid interpersonal conflict (Mead, 1963).

While values influence the development of norms, the "fit" between the two is not always a neat, one-to-one relationship. By definition, values are abstract and norms are specific. Thus it is not surprising that different norms can be derived from a given value. The American emphasis on competition is a case in point. One high-school football coach might tell his players that they should do anything to win. "The other team is the enemy out there," he explains. "They're trying to stop you from winning, and you've got to punish them for that." He teaches his players a number of illegal moves that can knock opponents out of action and yet are difficult for a referee to detect. In contrast, another coach tells the team to "play hard and clean. Win or lose, if you can say at the end of the game that you've given it your all, I'll feel I've done my job."

## Language

Alice and Bill are an elderly couple with an elderly dog. They tell people that their dog is just like a member of the family. "He listens to everything I say," Bill reports, "and I can tell by the look in his eye if he agrees with me." Alice concurs. "Ralph is nothing short of brilliant," she explains. "He must understand what I say, because he seems to know what I plan to do almost before I've made the decision myself." Undoubtedly Ralph is very sensitive to his owner's wishes and plans, but is he actually using language?

Ralph is responding to signs. A **sign** is an object or event that stands for something else. Many signs provide a fixed interpretation. The smell of smoke suggests that a fire is in the vicinity, the taste of a particular beverage indicates that it is coffee. Ralph's capacity to interpret signs is aided by hearing and a sense of smell that are well developed. Thus no matter how quietly Bill or Alice opens the refrigerator door, Ralph will dash to the kitchen, hoping for a snack.

While Ralph can detect certain signs, he has limited capacity to understand symbols. A **symbol** is a sign with a meaning that is not fixed by the nature of the item to which it is attached but by the agreement of the people who use it to communicate. In American culture, a wave of the hand stands for "hello" or "good-bye," a whistle blown by a policeman or a referee means "to stop," and the color black represents mourning.

A **language** is a system of symbolic communication that uses words, which are sound patterns that have standardized meanings. Like all symbols, words for items are not choices fixed by the nature of the items themselves. The four-legged piece of furniture on which we write papers and letters is called a "desk," but no inherent quality of the object requires it to be so labeled. The desk could just as easily be called a "glump." In this case the word is "desk" because the members of English-speaking cultures recognize and accept the word to represent the particular object. Language has two prominent traits as a communications system. First, there is its symbolic quality, which we have just discussed. Second, the symbols of language are combined in ways prescribed by a set of norms called "grammar": for instance, the grammatical norm of word order. Thus "Marilyn smiled at Frank" has a different meaning from "Frank smiled at Marilyn."

We have considered some of the qualities of language. How should we describe its purpose?

## The Social Construction of Reality

Basically language supplies meaning to cultures in a couple of ways. Language can be used to accumulate human experience. When animals die, everything they have learned from experience perishes with them. But language lets human beings develop a history. Through written or oral accounts, we can gain access to the knowledge and experience that have gone before. No matter how intelligent human beings might be, without language each generation would possess no more advantage over its ancestors than do geese, rabbits, or donkeys over their predecessors.

Second, language organizes our preception of the world. We can use language to refer to the past ("I went yesterday"), the present ("I am going now"), or the future ("I will go next week"). Language permits us to speak about single cases ("It was hot yesterday") or make general statements ("Summers are always hot around here"). Without language we would not be able to interpret the evidence of our own senses, and with language we are capable of describing subtle thoughts and perceptions.

The last point raises an interesting question. Do the people of all cultures see the world the same way, or do their respective languages organize their perceptions in different ways?

### THE LINGUISTIC-RELATIVITY HYPOTHESIS

The **linguistic-relativity hypothesis** contends that the unique grammatical forms of a language actually shape the thoughts and perceptions of its users (Sapir, 1921; Sapir, 1929; Whorf, 1956). According to this conception, therefore, language is much more than just another element of culture.

The issue of time provides an example. Americans and other Westerners tend to think of time as something that can be broken into segments—years, days, hours, minutes, and seconds—and used for one's purposes. "Time is money," says a businessperson in the best American tradition. Someone asks a friend to stay and talk. "Can't," the other replies. "I haven't got the time." To Americans time is scarce, elusive, and therefore precious. In contrast, the Hopi Indians have no words for "time," "late," "day," "hour," and "minute." They live in the present, emphasizing that all forms of life are working on their own time schedules and that things simply happen when they happen and will take as long as they take (Whorf, 1956). Inevitably these different orientations to time have created conflicts between the Hopi and whites. Table 3.2 shows how a grammatical difference between English and Spanish illustrates the linguistic-relativity hypothesis.

The more involved the members of a culture are with a particular activity or thing, the more detailed their language becomes. Children who throw snowballs, skiers, and Eskimos all make detailed linguistic references to the qualities of snow, and Eskimos have more than twenty words to distinguish different types. Arabs have hundreds of words to describe camels and camel equipment, and in societies where grazing animals are a prominent feature, one often finds a variety of terms for different textures of hay. Americans do the same thing with cars, distinguishing a number of types—station wagons, sports cars, compacts, subcompacts, and sedans—as well as companies and finally models produced by a given company: Buick's Riviera, Electra, Lesabre, Regal, Skylark, and so on.

These examples suggest that some relationship exists between language and people's thoughts and perceptions. However, the examples do not necessarily confirm the linguistic-relativity

**Table 3.2**
**The English and Spanish Use of the Pronoun "You": An Illustration of the Linguistic-Relativity Hypothesis**

| ENGLISH USE OF "YOU" | SPANISH USE OF "YOU"[1] | |
|---|---|---|
| | "TU" (INFORMAL) | "USTED" (FORMAL) |
| For all people, regardless of the type of relationship or age | Family members<br>Friends<br>Children and adolescents<br>God<br>Animals | Individuals with whom formal relations exist (one's doctor, teacher, or plumber) |

[1] Usage varies to some extent from one Spanish-speaking country to another. Furthermore there is a distinct tendency for younger people to use the informal form more readily.

*The use of the two "you" forms in Spanish affects people's perceptions and behavior. Young people know that they are considered adults when strangers begin using the formal form. On the other hand, when adults start addressing each other with the familiar form, they have crossed the boundary from acquaintance to friend. The fact that modern English has only the single "you" form means that similar perceptions are not built into the language.*

hypothesis — the idea that language shapes thought and perception. Which is it? Does language shape people's view of reality, or is it really the other way around? The problem is somewhat like the old question about the chicken or the egg — an issue that cannot be resolved by research. What seems most probable is that language develops as a means of enabling people to describe and explain their experiences. Then once a particular language has evolved, it shapes the world view of those socialized into its usage.

Thus moderate support for the linguistic-relativity hypothesis seems justified: Language does appear to influence certain perceptions and thoughts. This relationship is apparent in everyday life. For example, consider the function of a word like "un-American." Such a term establishes a clear boundary, indicating that any outlook or activity not traditionally American is traitorous. In particular, it is "un-American" to be "soft" on "Commies." These terms rigidly outline the idea that Americans are good and that they, the "Commies," are bad. Such uses of the language predispose many Americans to indiscriminately accept all

**Table 3.3**
**Culture**

| COMPONENT | BRIEF DEFINITION | EXAMPLES |
|---|---|---|
| 1. Belief | 1. A statement about reality that people accept as true | 1. "The earth is round." |
| 2. Technology | 2. Any repeated operations people use to manipulate the environment for practical goals | 2. A wooden club or a computer |
| 3. Norm<br>  a. Folkways<br><br>  b. Mores | 3. Standard of desirable behavior<br>  a. Norms that specify the way things are customarily done<br>  b. Norms people consider vital | <br>  a. Norms about public nosepicking or street littering<br>  b. Norms about murder and rape |
| 4. Value | 4. A general conviction about what is good or bad, right or wrong, appropriate or inappropriate | 4. Equality or a sense of racial superiority |
| 5. Language | 5. A system of symbolic communication using words, which are sound patterns that have standardized meanings | 5. English, Spanish, and Hottentot |

negative evaluations of the Soviet Union, Eastern Europe, and China and to ignore or at least to tolerate the U.S. government's support of anti-communist dictatorships, the injustices of the U.S. economic system, and the enormous financial emphasis the government places on defense.

Table 3.3 summarizes the discussion on culture presented in this section.

# We and They: Cultural Diversity and Conflict

From the previous discussion, you have learned that all cultures contain the same basic components. In fact, anthropologists have discovered that cultures always have a large number of **cultural universals** — traits believed to exist in all cultures. George Murdock (1965) listed over sixty cultural universals, including cooking, family, feasting, folklore, funeral rites, gift giving, greeting forms, housing, incest taboos, laws, medicine, music, sport, toilet training, and toolmaking.

A major reason that cultural universals develop is the need to resolve the issues that all human beings face in the common effort to survive and, whenever possible, to enjoy life. Thus new members must be reared; guidelines for behavior must be developed; goods and services must be produced and distributed; sick people must receive care; people must be given opportunities to escape the daily "grind."

But while cultural universals do exist, there is a great deal of variety in the ways in which different societies carry out a given universal. For instance, Americans often greet each other informally, while the Baganda of Uganda (East Africa) exchange a standardized set of questions and answers.

This section focuses on cultural differences. Within a given culture, groups will often make a "we-they" distinction — an emphasis on being culturally separate from and superior to other groups. That same distinction is sometimes made when the members of different cultures make contact.

## Diversity and Conflict within Cultures

So far we have been discussing culture as though all its elements were shared equally by everyone within the society. This is not always the case. In most societies subcultures exist. A **subculture** is the culture of a specific segment of people within a society, differing from the dominant culture in some significant respects, such as in certain norms and values or in language. When do sociologists determine that a particular segment of the population possesses its own subculture and when do they decide that a subculture does not exist but that people merely have a number of relatively unimportant differences with the dominant culture? Frankly this distinction is hard to make with actual cases. As we saw in the discussion about types of norms, concepts do simplify reality. We can learn from studying concepts but must realize that reality is usually more complicated than they suggest.

In modern, industrialized societies, many subcultures exist. They are based on such factors as occupation, racial and ethnic status, disadvantaged conditions (such as being blind, deaf, or retarded), or deviant or previously deviant life-styles (such as being a criminal, an addict, an alcoholic, an excriminal, an exaddict, or an exalcoholic).

Subcultures are usually functional for their members because they provide emotional and social support and help them to cope with their life situations. An American with a strong ethnic affiliation might say, "I was born in this country, raised here, and most of the time I feel like an American. But also, deep down, I'm Greek. And when I'm back in Baltimore having a Greek meal, surrounded by family and friends and speaking Greek, then I'm really home." Or an exaddict might explain, "After going through this drug program, I'm convinced that the only people who should work with junkies are exjunkies. After all, we've been through the whole thing ourselves. We know all the tricks, and so they won't pull anything with us."

### Subcultures and Countercultures

Subcultures are generally supportive for their members, but let us consider whether they are beneficial for the society as a whole. One might argue that a society that allows many subcultures to develop — that, in essence, lets people "do their own thing" — gives those people a chance to feel self-fulfilled. Furthermore members of such tolerated groups would probably be unlikely to rebel because they are permitted to live much as they like. However, sometimes rebellion may seem to be the only way in which members of a subculture can accomplish their most cherished goals.

A case in point involves the escalation of the protests of the 1960s. In the early years of the decade, some middle-class white students formed a subculture that worked with southern blacks to promote the racial integration of buses, restaurants, and other public facilities. Others actively sought nuclear disarmament. The number of students involved in this protest-oriented subculture was small, and their tactics were nonviolent.

By 1966, however, the situation had changed. Small but determined groups of blacks, other ethnics, and whites, both on college campuses and elsewhere, began to take a variety of measures to oppose dominant American economic and political policies. Members of the different protest groups made speeches, wrote pamphlets and articles, and participated in sit-ins and building takeovers. These and other actions were supposed to dramatize to the American public the need to oppose the Vietnam War, the capitalist economic system, civil-rights injustices, and also local economic and political issues.

The protest groups were a counterculture. A **counterculture** is a subculture whose members consciously and often proudly reject some of the most important cultural standards of the mainstream society. Countercultures require extensive, sometimes full-time, commitment of members' time and energy and tend to have relatively few members. Under certain conditions countercultural groups will receive a larger, subcultural support.

In April 1969, for instance, 120 members of the Afro-American Society took over the student union at Cornell University. The black students' action was precipitated by a cross burning on the lawn in front of the black women students' dormitory. Soon after the building takeover, 150 white students, who were members of the countercultural Students for a Democratic Society, gathered in front of the occupied building to assist the black students in case other whites broke in and tried to free the building.

In the first and second day following the occupation, most students continued their normal activities. The building takeover, however, gradually produced a growing excitement and interest, especially when it was learned that some of the students had brought in guns. Following negotiations with university administrators, the members of the Afro-American Society left the building several days after their occupation began. By then thousands of students and faculty had put aside their normal activities and were spending most of their time attending meetings. Within a week of the takeover, classes were suspended for the rest of the semester. Students and faculty started organizing at the departmental level in order to plan changes in their programs that would promote more effective learning and would increase their respective contributions to the university community and the society. In short, for the span of several weeks, members of the student subculture became involved in the kind of activities that normally occupied only individuals in the counterculture.

The countercultural activity of the 1960s created considerable disruption and conflict, and one might argue that it was harmful to the society as a whole. However, as a legacy of those protests, a number of previously unquestioned social, economic, and political conditions have been challenged, and new perspectives and, in some cases, laws have been introduced. Civil-rights legislation was passed to attack prejudice and discrimination in education, housing, jobs, public accommodations, and voter registration in the South. Legislation also established new programs to relieve the effects of poverty. In addition, the protests against the Vietnamese War contributed to the Nixon Administration's withdrawal of troops from Vietnam.

## A Look at Other Cultures

Americans are often surprised and sometimes shocked when they are introduced to some common practices of other cultures. In a number of societies, children may watch their parents engage in acts of sexual intercourse. In one culture all males must perform explicit homosexual acts before adopting heterosexual roles in adulthood. In another society all males at puberty go through a ritual where the penis is cut to the urethra and sliced the entire length of the organ. Are these people "crazy"? No, they simply have cultural patterns that differ from those of Americans.

*An ethnocentric American might say that the office is no place to exercise. Chinese citizens, however, would point out that practicing Tai Chi before work not only helps people feel good physically but also creates a sense of participation in harmonious group activity.*

When people of one culture assess the standards and practices in another, two possibilities exist. One alternative is that people view the customs of the other culture as inferior; the other possibility is that they consider them different.

*Ethnocentrism*

**Ethnocentrism** is the tendency to automatically evaluate other cultures by the standards of one's own. Ethnocentric people consider other cultures inferior to their own.

Many people spend their entire lives without ever leaving their own culture. It is hardly surprising that such persons tend to view their particular cultural standards as the only acceptable way to live. Consider Laura Bohannon's experience. Bohannon (1975), an anthropologist, attempted to tell the story of Shakespeare's *Hamlet* to a group of old men of the Tiv tribe in Nigeria. It was her chance, she felt, to make *Hamlet* "universally intelligible." However, she failed because the story aroused the old men's ethnocentrism, and they constantly interrupted Bohannon to emphasize that the cultural practices she was describing were unacceptable. For instance:

The elders could not understand why Hamlet was upset when his mother remarried quickly. After all, if she had not done so, there would have been no man to hoe the land.

The old men could not accept the claim that a ghost appeared before Hamlet and spoke to him. They explained to Bohannon that no such things as ghosts exist. It was an omen, but omens, the men contended, cannot talk.

Furthermore it was not appropriate for Hamlet to avenge his father's death. Since the killer was a generation older than he, the task should have been performed by an older man.

Like the members of many other cultures, the Tiv elders were ethnocentric because they had been immersed in their own cultural tradition from infancy, with little exposure to any other. An additional factor helps explain the occurrence of ethnocentrism: It can be functional for those who practice it. First, ethnocentrism can establish and sustain group loyalties, especially under stressful conditions. Warfare would be a case in point. If soldiers are going to fight well, they should believe that their cause is just, and ethnocentric slogans and inspirationally titled policies promote such a belief. For instance, World War I was sold as "the war to end all wars" and "the war to make the world safe for democracy." In World War II, Americans and their allies believed that they were

**58**

fighting for the "Four Freedoms" — freedom of speech and expression, freedom of worship, freedom from want, and freedom from fear. These slogans were first presented to Americans by President Roosevelt in the course of his message to Congress in January 1941, shortly after the United States entered the war. During the Korean War, ethnocentric passions centered on "stopping the spread of the Red menace," and the policy designed to accomplish this task was called "containment." In the Vietnam-War era, the target of the most prominent slogan was not the enemy but antiwar protesters. "America, your country, love it or leave it" was an outright demand that people be ethnocentric.

Ethnocentrism has another function: to help an already dominant group maintain its position of superiority. In many American cities of the 1830s, Protestant groups distributed large amounts of strongly anti-Catholic literature. The most notori-

ous of these publications was Maria Monk's *Awful Disclosures,* an account of atrocities experienced by a young woman in a Catholic convent. The book was eventually exposed as the work of anti-Catholic propagandists; yet it went into twenty printings and sold over 300,000 copies. Anti-Catholic ethnocentrism helped spur the development of a movement of native-born Protestant Americans that strongly resented the masses of newly arrived Irish immigrants. This anti-Catholic movement developed because the Protestant workers feared competition over jobs with the Irish, because they saw Catholicism as a threat to established values, and because they wished to maintain the northern European homogeneity of this nation's large cities (Shannon, 1966: 41–43).

We have seen that the Tiv of Nigeria and Americans often engage in ethnocentric behavior. The upcoming Cross-Cultural Perspective illustrates ethnocentrism among the French and Chinese.

## CROSS-CULTURAL PERSPECTIVE

### *French Wine Venture in China in a Ferment*

It seems reasonable to assume that the more closely people from different cultural traditions must interact, the more likely it becomes that ethnocentrism will surface. Certainly the history of a cooperative wine-producing effort between the French and the Chinese seems to be a case in point.

The joint venture began optimistically. France's Remy Martin Ltd., which is best known for its cognac, decided to develop an Oriental wine for Chinese restaurants in both Asia and Europe. The French firm provided $270,000 worth of winery equipment and their experience in the business. The Chinese supplied water, workers,

electricity, a factory, and land in exchange for 62 percent of the profit from sales.

Problems started almost immediately. The French firm wanted the Chinese farmers, who grew their grapes chiefly for eating, to upgrade the quality of their crop. The Remy winegrowers were astonished to learn that the art of grape cultivation had not advanced much beyond the Middle Ages in China. For one thing the farmers covered their vines with paper bags to protect them from insects, and as a result the grapes never matured in the sun — which is essential if they are to be of high quality. In addition, the farmers often brought their

grapes to market a full day after harvesting, well past the point of freshness.

Guillaume d'Avout, Remy Martin's managing director for Far East operations, expressed the French opinion of Chinese grape farming, "Their methods were, how should I say, primitive . . . We had to tell them that we wouldn't accept damaged grapes or grapes that weren't fresh enough to make a wine for export on the world market." Ju Lifan, a Chinese winery official, offered this response, "The French were so picky, you just couldn't satisfy them . . . They wouldn't buy grapes unless they had 18 percent sugar content. We had never heard of such a thing" (Weisskopf, 1982: 6).

The Frenchmen began getting their way by offering more money for top-quality grapes. This situation created another problem. Because the French had to pay more than they had originally planned for grapes, the cost of the wine rose. The French wanted to keep the cost of the wine as low as possible. Pricing, of course, is one factor in a customer's decision to buy a product. As socialists, however, the Chinese showed little concern for competitive pricing and cost cutting.

The Chinese and French also differed on another economic issue—how many workers to employ. D'Avout contended that the Chinese had "a natural tendency" to increase the number of workers as much as possible and that they were not nearly as production-minded as the French.

Overall there was a sharp, often bitter clash between cultural styles. The French considered their Chinese workers much too casual. One Remy Martin official complained that the first lesson was "to teach them . . . not to spit in the winery . . . " The Chinese, on the other hand, found the French too high strung. One Chinese winemaker said: "When the electricity fails, they fly into a rage."

In spite of the operational problems, the wine has already sold well in restaurants in Hong Kong, Singapore, and Malaysia. The French firm has been sufficiently pleased by initial sales that it plans to double its output and try to break into the European market. It will be interesting to see to what extent the French and Chinese are able to resolve their cultural differences as their uncomfortable partnership continues.

Source: Michael Weisskopf. "French Wine Venture in China in a Ferment." *International Herald Tribune*. June 1, 1982, p. 6.

## Cultural Relativism

At the beginning of this section, we noted that when people look at other cultures they are likely to view them either as inferior or different. When people are being ethnocentric, they view other cultures as inferior. On the other hand, if they practice cultural relativism, they see them as just different. **Cultural relativism** is the principle stating that a culture can only be effectively evaluated when analyzed by its own standards and not by those of any other culture. A custom is not good or bad or right or wrong in and of itself. The cultural relativistic point of view requires that any element of a culture be evaluated in relation to the entire culture. People who adopt this point of view recognize that while the life-style in another culture might make no sense at first, a careful study will reveal an understandable pattern.

The fact that Indian Hindus are often desperately poor and yet refuse to eat local cows, which wander where they wish, dumbfounds many Americans. Marvin Harris, an anthropologist, has noted that during lectures students would often ask for an explanation:

"But what about all those cows the hungry peasants in India refuse to eat?" The picture of a ragged farmer starving to death alongside a big fat cow conveys a reassuring sense of mystery to Western observers. In countless learned and popular allusions, it confirms our deepest conviction about how people with inscrutable Oriental minds ought to act.

*(Harris, 1974: 11)*

Harris studied the relationship between cows and the Hindu culture. Indeed, he did find out that in the Hindu religion the cow is the symbol of all living creatures and that there is no greater sin than killing one.

Harris also uncovered other important information. He found out that cows generally give about 500 lbs. of milk a year—an important, sometimes critical part of the family diet. In addition, the cows' manure is the only fertilizer that poor farmers can afford, and when dried it also serves as a primary cooking fuel. Furthermore the possibility exists that a cow can give birth to a male calf that, when castrated, will develop into an ox, the scarce, highly prized animal used by Indian farmers for dry-field plowing. Certainly Hindus' religion requires them to revere cattle, but a careful analysis of the culture shows that some practical reasons reinforce their conviction that cattle should not be killed.

**60**

# American Culture

As our focus shifts from the contacts between different cultures to the analysis of American culture, your first reaction might be to suspect that cultural variation and conflict will be much less prominent issues. But do not forget our discussion of counterculture! American culture has always contained conflicting elements, and that tendency is especially clear in this era of rapidly changing values.

## Traditional American Values

Robin Williams, Jr. (1970: 452–500) has produced a well-known analysis of American values. Williams has described fifteen value orientations, which have been evident in American culture. These value orientations include achievement and success, progress, equality, freedom, democracy, humanitarian goals, and racism and other themes of group superiority.

Some studies suggest that a number of these values are more strongly emphasized in American culture than in most other cultures. For instance,

research supporting the conclusion that an emphasis on achievement and success is particularly strong in our culture is offered by the fact that in the United States, men in higher occupational positions reported greater self-confidence than other men, while in Poland, where the emphasis on achievement and success is probably weaker, men in higher occupational positions actually expressed lower levels of self-confidence than other men (Slomczynski et al., 1981). In addition, in a study on gender-role ideals (to be examined at greater length in Chapter 7), a researcher learned that compared to their counterparts in six European countries, young American women and men are more likely to emphasize assertiveness and ambition as part of the gender-role ideal—qualities that generally are associated with an emphasis on achievement and success (Block, 1973).

In a society that prizes achievement and success, people are likely to be very competitive. The following American Controversy presents two positions about competition and encourages readers to think about and evaluate them.

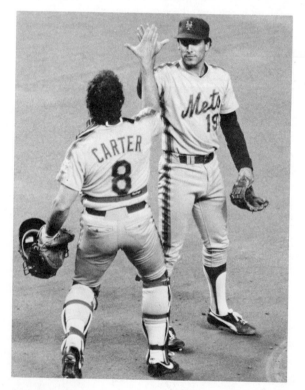

*In American culture, where competition is a prominent value, sports provide a setting for graphically displaying the glory of winning and the pain of losing. In 1986 the New York Mets, who won the World Series, had a glory-filled year.*

**AMERICAN CONTROVERSY**

## *Competition in American Society*

Whether it is in sports, business, or school, Americans stress the importance of defeating the competition. Our language is filled with expressions that make this point. "In business it's kill-or-be-killed," the husband says when he gets home from work. "Honey," his wife replies, "it's a dog-eat-dog world out there." Talking to his sister on the telephone, Betty's father says: "Yes, Judy, we're so proud of our little girl. Year after year she's at the top of her class!" An emphasis on competition exists in our society, but is it desirable? This box offers arguments for and against an emphasis on competition.

Those who strongly emphasize competition are likely to say that it is "the American way" — separating winners from losers in head-to-head competition. The proponents of competition will often contend that the process is character-building. They will argue that in the course of competition, individuals will be encouraged to do better; as the well-known phrase goes, they will "strive for excellence." Sport, many backers of competition will argue, is so popular in the United States because it is a theatre in which competition appears in a pure form. Football, in particular, is competition with a crude yet appealing style, where magnificent physical specimens use both brawn and brains to try to defeat each other in a nearly no-holds-barred situation of team-to-team combat.

The critics of an emphasis on competition might accept part of the last point. While they would probably concede the impact of spectator sport in the United States, they would be critical of its impact. There's no need to glorify violent competition, they would argue. With limited emphasis on competition, children can grow up to be intelligent, skilled, and sensitive to the needs of others. The opponents of competition might even cite research indicating that in experimentation involving physical skills, an emphasis on competition lowered performance level (Baumeister, 1984). Furthermore people de-emphasizing competition would be likely to point out that often what appears to be open competition is not. One individiual or organization starts with the advantage of better education, an emotionally healthy upbringing, more extensive work experience, or a tax break from the government. Those speaking on behalf of competition, the critics will contend, are the people most likely to have a lion's share of the advantages.

What do you think? Do you strongly favor one position or the other? Or do you find yourself somewhere in the middle, supporting competition under some circumstances and not others?

Evaluate and discuss the following statement: In many competitive circumstances, it is possible to avoid a focus on competition by, instead, striving to do one's best. While discussing the issue of competition, try to understand more fully the position of those who think differently from you. Attempt to figure out what the circumstances were that led to your respective positions on the issue. One way to analyze the topic would be to reverse positions with someone whose stance is different from your own. See if you can state that individual's outlook convincingly to him or her, and then that person should try to perform the same task.

Source: Roy F. Baumeister. "Choking under Pressure: Self-Consciousness and Paradoxical Effects of Incentives on Skillful Performance." *Journal of Personality and Social Psychology.* Vol. 46. March 1984, pp. 610–620.

## Changing American Values

How have American values been changing in recent years? Would you agree with the popular belief that about two decades ago a swing in a liberal direction took place and that recently there has been a swing back toward conservatism? Daniel

**62** Yankelovich (Keene and Yankelovich, 1984), a widely recognized specialist on public opinion, would not.

Yankelovich has suggested that changes in values cannot be characterized with unidimensional words like "liberal" and "conservative." He has concluded that as one looks at national survey data over the past two decades, two trends become apparent, particularly for young people: a period of reaction and then a period of accepting harsh economic realities.

In the 1960s and 1970s, the time of reaction occurred. There was a widespread desire to break with the conformity and the limited options imposed in the 1950s—the expectation that men would be restricted to being providers and women to being housewives, that success could only be obtained by accumulating status and wealth. In the 1960s some young people openly rebelled, joining protest groups that sought to eliminate conformity and limited options. Public protests continued in the 1970s, but frequently reaction took the form of personal efforts to improve oneself through meditation, therapy, group therapy, religion, or some other means of self-development.

According to Yankelovich, the 1980s have been a decade when young people have been forced to accept some harsh realities, recognizing that the affluent economy of the past has ceased to exist. Good jobs are hard to obtain. This is no longer perceived to be a world of unlimited growth and wealth where one can plunge into hedonism and expect to live decently. Young people have been forced to plan their lives carefully and intelligently.

When one examines survey data on modern young Americans' values, the two trends just described are apparent. First, young people today seem to have accepted some of the legacy from the 1960s. In particular, they have been emphasizing an extension of individuals' rights—those of blacks and women, in particular. For instance,

**Table 3.4**
**Young Americans' Changing Values**

| FACTORS INFLUENCING VALUE CHANGE | YOUNG PEOPLE'S CURRENT VALUES |
|---|---|
| 1. Reaction to traditional values in the 1960s and 1970s →| 1. Extension of individuals' rights |
| 2. Accepting harsh realities of the 1980s →| 2. A set of conservative tendencies |

Source: Adapted from Karlyn Keene and Daniel Yankelovich. "American Values: Change and Stability." *Public Opinion.* Vol. 6. January 1984, pp. 2–8.

when asked in the early 1970s whether one would vote for a woman if one's political party nominated her for president, 86 percent of the 18–24 age group said they would support her; in contrast, a decade later 94 percent of the same age group indicated they would provide support (National Opinion Research Center, *General Social Surveys*, 1983).

Besides this liberal tendency, young Americans' values have recently demonstrated a conservative trend. For instance, modern American youth has been more inclined to support the death penalty and oppose abortion and extramarital sex than their counterparts of a decade ago. This pattern seems to have developed because modern young people, more than those of ten or twenty years ago, have been compelled to recognize that they live in a tough world where the success and comfort they seek will be achieved only through a disciplined life-style. (See Table 3.4.)

We have been discussing young people's value changes over the past couple of decades. What value changes do you anticipate for American youth in the next twenty years?

# STUDY GUIDE

## Summary

1. Culture consists of all the human-made products associated with a society. The products of culture divide into the material and the nonmaterial.

2. The different components of a culture—beliefs, technology, norms, values, symbols, and language—are all products of their respective cul-

tural traditions, and each, in turn, affects the culture from which it develops.

3. Within cultures and between cultures, differences often exist, and sometimes these differences produce conflict. In modern societies various subcultures arise based on such factors as occupation, racial and ethnic status, disadvantaged conditions, and deviant or previously deviant life-styles. Some subcultures, namely, countercultures, reject many of the standards of the mainstream society. As the members of one culture contact those of another, ethnocentrism frequently develops. Although members of all cultures can be ethnocentric, the practice is most dominant in isolated societies. To offset ethnocentrism, one can use a cultural-relativistic approach to other cultures.

4. Sociologists have extensively studied American values. Robin Williams, Jr. has described fifteen value orientations, which have been prominently displayed in American culture. Studies have suggested that the values of achievement and success are more apparent in American culture than in most other cultures.

5. Young Americans' values have been changing in recent years. The sources of change appear to be a reaction to traditional values, beginning in the 1960s, and an acceptance of the harsh realities of the 1980s. Modern young people's values emphasize an extension of individual rights and also a set of conservative tendencies.

## Glossary

**belief** a statement about reality that people accept as true.

**counterculture** a subculture whose members consciously and often proudly reject some of the most important cultural standards of the mainstream society.

**cultural relativism** the recognition that a culture should be evaluated by its own standards and not by those of any other culture.

**cultural universals** traits believed to exist in all cultures.

**culture** all the human-made products associated with a society.

**ethnocentrism** the tendency to automatically evaluate other cultures by the standards of one's own.

**explicit norm** a standard that is out in the open.

**folkway** a norm that specifies the way things are customarily done; folkways are concerned with standards of behavior that are socially approved but not considered morally significant.

**ideal norm** a standard requiring strict obedience to the guidelines provided.

**implicit norm** a standard that lies beneath the surface and is not easily stated.

**language** a system of symbolic communication that uses words, which are sound patterns that have standardized meanings.

**linguistic-relativity hypothesis** the contention that the unique grammatical forms of a language actually shape the thoughts and perceptions of its users.

**mores** norms people consider vital.

**norm** a standard of desirable behavior. Norms are the rules people are expected to follow in their relations with each other.

**real norm** adjustment of a standard to the practical conditions of living.

**sign** an object or event that stands for something else.

**society** the interacting people who share a culture.

**subculture** the culture of a specific segment of people within a society, differing from the dominant culture in some significant respects.

**symbol** a sign with a meaning not fixed by the nature of the item to which it is attached but by the agreement of the people who use it to communicate.

**technology** any repeated operation people use to manipulate the environment to achieve some practical goals.

**value** a general conviction about what is good or bad, right or wrong, appropriate or inappropriate.

# Learning Objectives

After studying this chapter, you should be able to:

1. Define culture and describe its importance in human life.
2. Define the major components of culture—beliefs, technology, norms, values, and language—and discuss their respective functions.
3. Examine the different types of norms, defining and discussing folkways and mores, explicit and implicit norms, and ideal norms and real norms.
4. Distinguish between sign and symbol, define language, and explain how language supplies meaning to culture.
5. Define and illustrate the linguistic-relativity hypothesis.
6. Define subculture and counterculture, providing examples of each.
7. Distinguish between ethnocentrism and cultural relativism and explain two functions of ethnocentrism.
8. List several traditional American value orientations and discuss research concluding that Americans emphasize achievement and success.
9. Examine young Americans' changing values, indicating why the changes are occurring and what new commitments are emerging.

# Tests

## True–false test

_____ 1. Society cannot exist without culture, but culture exists independent of society.

_____ 2. People who share a given culture can disagree about some beliefs.

_____ 3. In modern societies real and ideal norms tend to be identical.

_____ 4. Values are important because they influence the content of norms.

_____ 5. The smell of smoke is a sign of the presence of fire; in this case smoke is a sign but not a symbol.

_____ 6. Social scientists have concluded that in the past twenty years the number of cultural universals has declined sharply.

_____ 7. Bohannon's experience in trying to bring Shakespeare's *Hamlet* to the Tiv tribe suggests that this universal story actually eliminated ethnocentrism.

_____ 8. People who take a cultural-relativistic perspective believe that the life-styles of other cultures have understandable patterns.

_____ 9. A recent study has concluded that the levels of self-confidence expressed by American and Polish men in high-status jobs are strikingly similar.

_____ 10. Daniel Yankelovich concluded that in the 1980s young Americans have become more inclined to support the death penalty and oppose abortion than young people of a decade ago.

## Multiple-choice test

_____ 1. Material culture includes:
   a. beliefs.

   b.  physical objects people make and use.
   c.  values.
   d.  b and c

_____  2.  Which of the following is NOT a component of culture?
   a.  language
   b.  value
   c.  technology
   d.  group

_____  3.  Which statement about technology is NOT true?
   a.  It has profound effects on people's everyday lives.
   b.  It can contribute significantly to the development of new occupations.
   c.  It cannot be dysfunctional for specific groups.
   d.  It involves manipulation of the environment.

_____  4.  Which of the following is (are) true about folkways?
   a.  They specify the way things are customarily done.
   b.  They are considered to be morally significant.
   c.  Violation always leads to punishment.
   d.  All of the above

_____  5.  The idea of adjustment of a standard to practical conditions of living is found in which one of the following concepts?
   a.  explicit norm
   b.  implicit norm
   c.  real norm
   d.  ideal norm

_____  6.  Values:
   a.  are abstract, stating broad behavioral preferences.
   b.  are becoming rare in modern societies.
   c.  have little or no relationship with norms.
   d.  are a type of material culture.

_____  7.  The linguistic-relativity hypothesis:
   a.  does not apply to modern languages.
   b.  indicates that some ethnic groups have a greater inborn tendency to use complex language forms than other ethnic groups.
   c.  has been used to explain body language but not spoken language.
   d.  contends that the unique grammatical forms of a language actually shape the thoughts and perceptions of its users.

_____  8.  The members of a certain occupational group develop a common set of beliefs, values, and activities that are different in significant respects from those in the general culture. These people share a
   a.  counterculture.
   b.  subculture.
   c.  cultural-relativistic approach.
   d.  ethnocentric outlook.

_____  9.  Ethnocentrism can be functional for those who practice it because it:
   a.  encourages people to become more tolerant.
   b.  helps dominant groups retain positions of superiority.

    c. establishes how much influence different mores maintain.
    d. helps make explicit norms more implicit.

_____ 10. Young Americans' values today:
    a. can most accurately be labeled conservative.
    b. have not changed significantly for twenty years.
    c. can most accurately be labeled liberal.
    d. have been affected by some harsh economic realities in the 1980s.

## Essay test

1. What is culture? Why does culture have a profound impact on people's lives?
2. Discuss five cultural components, indicating how each affects social activity.
3. Define the different types of norms and illustrate each type.
4. Discuss the linguistic-relativity hypothesis, giving examples that demonstrate its usefulness.
5. Define the concepts of subculture and counterculture, emphasizing their impact on societies.
6. Define ethnocentrism and cultural relativism and give examples of each.
7. How do young Americans' values differ from those of young people ten or fifteen years ago? Why have these changes in values occurred?

## Suggested Readings

Curry, Timothy, and Robert M. Jiobu. 1984. *Sports: A Social Perspective*. Englewood Cliffs, NJ: Prentice-Hall. An interesting, readable text on sport, an important but often analytically neglected aspect of American culture. The book includes effective discussions on cultural sources of competition and deviance in the sporting world.

Harris, Marvin. 1974. *Cows, Pigs, Wars and Witches*. New York: Random House. A captivating series of essays demonstrating how to apply the concept of cultural relativism to a variety of cultural situations where Americans' ethnocentrism is likely to be aroused.

Kohn, Alfie, 1986. *No Contest*. Boston: Houghton Mifflin. A detailed, highly critical analysis of the impact of competition on American society. Most provocative is the final chapter, which contains suggestions for deemphasizing and eventually eliminating competition from modern life.

Slater, Philip. 1976. *The Pursuit of Loneliness*. Boston: Beacon. Revised edition. A critical examination of American value conflicts: the longing for engagement, dependence, and community that is often frustrated by emphasis on individualism and competition. The family, the political structure, and the economy are examined.

Williams, Robin M., Jr. 1970. *American Society: A Sociological Interpretation*. New York: Random House. Third edition. A well-known analysis of American culture and society containing a comprehensive classification and examination of American values.

Yankelovich, Daniel. 1981. *New Rules: Searching for Self-Fulfillment in a World Turned Upside Down*. New York: Random House. Drawing on decades of survey data, the author assesses the changes occurring in American values and suggests the most beneficial adjustments Americans can make.

## Student Projects

1. Select some aspect of federal-government activity, such as military spending, foreign aid, relations with the Soviet Union, welfare programming, or civil rights. Read the editorial pages of a major

daily newspaper for two or three weeks and then list the expressed values you find related to your topic. Can you conclude that there is a consistent set of values presented in the editorials?

2. Choose a holiday celebrated in American culture, such as Halloween, Easter, Passover, Christmas, Thanksgiving, or the Fourth of July. List the norms associated with celebrating the holiday. Do the "norms of celebration" suggest any value conflicts? Find information in the library about the origins of the holiday. What value(s) seem(s) to have inspired its development?

## Answers to Test Questions

### True – false test

| | | | | |
|---|---|---|---|---|
| 1. f | 3. f | 5. t | 7. f | 9. f |
| 2. t | 4. t | 6. f | 8. t | 10. t |

### Multiple-choice test

| | | | | |
|---|---|---|---|---|
| 1. b | 3. c | 5. c | 7. d | 9. b |
| 2. d | 4. a | 6. a | 8. b | 10. d |

# RESEARCH IN SOCIOLOGY: SECTION I

## The Participant-Observation Study of Culture

Participant-observation studies, which we briefly examined in Chapter 2 ("Doing Research in Sociology"), have represented an effective technique to uncover the subtlety and complexity of individual cultures. Certainly this type of research has produced more accurate information about cultures than the earliest efforts to understand them.

To modern Americans it is clear that to understand cultures one must conduct research—careful research. But 150 years ago, such a conclusion was not obvious. In that era scholars were more inclined to read and reflect and then produce abstract conclusions. It was the era of "armchair anthropology," and one of the best-known scholars of that time was Lewis Henry Morgan. Morgan and other "armchair" anthropologists often provided interesting, logical analyses. However, the problem was that they were not scientific; little or no supportive research had been done.

Early in the twentieth century, the anthropological approach changed. It was at this time that one of the most renowned participant-observation studies of culture was done by Bronislaw Malinowski, in the Trobriand Islands of New Guinea in the South Pacific. At first Malinowski found the research difficult. He had few guidelines on how to conduct this kind of research. Furthermore he was an outsider, he did not speak the language, and there were no other Europeans around. Malinowski wrote, "I had periods of despondency, when I buried myself in the reading of novels, as a man might take to drink in a fit of tropical depression and boredom" (Malinowski, 1922: 4). Certainly Malinowski was implying that "armchair" anthropology would have been easier. In the end, however, his persistence paid off. Malinowki was able to develop several procedures for conducting participant-observation research: to have one's research goals set clearly in mind; to isolate oneself from members of one's own culture by immersing oneself in the local culture; and to develop techniques for obtaining thorough information about the entire culture.

Besides helping to refine the participant-observation technique, Malinowski uncovered some significant information about the Trobriand Island culture. Particularly interesting were his conclusions about magic. Malinowski learned that magic played an important part in the tribespeople's daily lives. They believed that magical rites and spells would insure the success of gardening and fishing throughout the society. Thus this research helped reject what was then a widely held but erroneous view that magic is used only for such personal and vicious purposes as causing harm to enemies.

### Sociologists' Use of Participant Observation

Eventually sociologists began to adopt the participant-observation technique. Their use, however, tended to occur in modern cultures, which generally are more complex and diversified than those studied by anthropologists. As a result sociologists have not studied entire cultures but focused on subcultures. Perhaps the best-known of all such sociological investigations has been William Foote Whyte's *Street Corner Society* discussed in Chapter 1 ("Introduction"). Like Malinowski, Whyte had a problem of entry into the community he studied—Cornerville, an Italian–American slum district of Boston. On the advice of a friend, he tried going to a bar and buying drinks for a woman; this, he had been told, was an effective way of obtaining a woman's life story. For his efforts, however, he almost got himself thrown down a flight of stairs. Finally Whyte met a local young man known as Doc, who became interested in the study and promised to do everything he could to advance the research.

The book that Whyte eventually wrote contained some important conclusions about American slum communities. Just as early anthropologists made unsupported generalizations about culture, some social scientists of Whyte's era produced undocumented statements about the culture and structure of slum communities. In particular, they believed that slums were completely disorganized. Whyte's three-year study compelled him to disagree:

Cornerville's problem is not lack of organization but failure of its own social organization to mesh with the structure of the society around it. This accounts for the development of the local political and racket organizations and also for the loyalty people bear toward their . . . [ethnic group] and toward Italy.

*(Whyte, 1955: 273)*

Whyte documented this point at length, showing that in spite of their involvement in local organizations, most of the young people he studied failed to succeed in the larger society.

Through the years sociologists have continued to use the participant-observation technique to clarify the workings of subcultures. In the late 1950s, Blanche Geer found that only three days of research during the orientation of freshman at the University of Kansas gave her and her coworkers new, revealing information about them. Geer wrote:

Before entering the field, I thought of them as irresponsible children. But as I listened to their voices, learned their language, witnessed gesture and expression, and accumulated the bits of information about them which bring people alive and make their problems real, I achieved a form of empathy with them and became their advocate.

*(Geer, 1964: 341)*

Geer suddenly found herself immersed in her informants' lives; she obtained information about college-student subculture, which she was able to pass on to her readers.

Recent participant-observation research has also revealed the workings of American subcultures. William Waegel examined the police subculture and the use of deadly force. As he began the study, Waegel realized that previous research had uncovered a number of factors linked to police violence: the level of violent crime in a community, occupational stress suffered by police, and the influence of the work environment. But in the tradition of participant-observation research, Waegel believed that an effective understanding of the situation would emerge only with an intensive investigation of how the relevant actors — in this case the police — behaved in the research context. Thus

he focused on the beliefs in the police subculture that rationalize the use of deadly force. One belief centered around the following idea: "I'd rather be judged by twelve than carried out by six." The argument is that police work is filled with danger and anxiety; sometimes a policeman's split-second decision to shoot will make the difference between living and dying. Another belief justifying force could be summed up with this statement: "What's another dead animal?" Widespread racism is our society is a contributing factor to this belief. In addition, this position is often supported by the pleas of victims or victims' relatives to avenge a crime.

Waegel's study points to the special contribution that participant-observation investigations can make to the understanding of culture. Cultures are often filled with subtle conflicts and inconsistencies. It is difficult to sort out the complexities. Surveys might provide some information, but often the subtleties are best revealed by painstaking, detailed observation: Waegel spent ten months as a participant observer in a police department, where he observed officers and interviewed them about shooting incidents and their use of firearms.

## Conclusion

These studies have produced important information about cultures that was not previously known. But are the results of these investigations unquestionably correct? Certainly not! As we saw in Chapter 2, one of the principal difficulties with participant-observation research is the problem of generalizing from a single case. Could Malinowski claim that in all technologically simple societies magic would be used in just the same way that it was in the Trobriand Islands? Could Waegel be certain that police personnel in another city would rationalize the use of deadly force in precisely the manner that his informants had? In both situations the answer is no. But that does not detract from the significance of these studies. They produced powerful conclusions that later researchers could investigate.

Sources: Blanche Geer. "First Days in the Field." In Phillip E. Hammond (ed.), *Sociologists at Work*. New York: Basic. 1964, pp. 322–345; Bronislaw Malinowski. *Argonauts of the Western Pacific*. London: Routledge and Kegan Paul. 1922; Lewis H. Morgan. *Ancient Society*. Cambridge, MA: Belknap. 1964. Originally published in 1877; William B. Waegel. "How Police Justify the Use of Deadly Force." *Social Problems*. Vol. 32. December 1984, pp. 144–155; William Foote Whyte. *Street Corner Society*. Chicago: University of Chicago Press. Revised edition. 1955.

# 4
# GROUPS

Imagine spending six months in a spacecraft! The view is incredible—270 miles down to earth and a sunset or sunrise every ninety minutes. But you can't leave the spacecraft, which is the size of a moderate-sized motor home, and you must live with the same companion or companions the entire time. Both the United States and the Soviet Union have had long spaceflights; the Soviets have had three lasting between six and seven months while the longest U.S. flight was the eighty-four-day Skylab mission in 1974. Valery Ryumin, who was on a pair of two-men Soviet missions, pointed out in his diary that people on long spaceflights have been compelled to solve problems together: ". . . taking into account the feelings of the other. Here we are totally alone. Each uttered word assumes added importance. One must bear in mind—constantly—the other's good and bad sides, anticipate his thinking, the ramifications of a wrong utterance blown out of proportion" (Bluth, 1985: 31). Ryumin added that after two spaceflights he completely understood the writer O. Henry's claim that a sure way to produce a murder is to lock two men in a small cabin and keep them there for two months.

While there have been no murders in space, there has been evidence of hostility and stress. Evidence to date suggests that the longer the flight, the more likely incompatibilities will appear. Cosmonaut Lenov has concluded that ". . . it is impossible to insure good compatibility on a long flight." One of the sources of tension in long spaceflights is that the individual is with the same crew all the time. Normally people's lives fluctuate between work and play, and in the latter—at home with the family, for instance—one can relax and feel that he or she is not being judged. In a spacecraft, however, one's colleague(s) is (are) always close by; the individual can never entirely escape the formality of the work situation. This source of tension is compounded by the fact that in

*Group activity can be strongly influenced by physical surroundings. Certainly the restricted quarters in which astronauts in space must live significantly affects their group behavior.*

spaceflight there is constant danger; one can never relax and entirely get away from work.

In one respect, perhaps, the American crews have had an advantage over their Soviet counterparts. The Soviets maintain two-person crews for long spaceflights, while Americans have used three people. Research on small groups has demonstrated that an odd-numbered membership means that when decision-making occurs, tension-producing deadlocks of numerically equal factions will be avoided. Evidence to date suggests Americans with their crews of three have had fewer interpersonal problems than the Soviets with their crews of two.

Whether we are in space or simply on earth, much of our time is spent in groups, and what happens in the groups to which we belong profoundly affects our lives. A **group** consists of two or more interacting people who share certain expectations and goals. When people belong to the same group, there is a feeling of unity, a set of common goals, a number of collective norms, and a direct or indirect communication among the members based on their common rights and obligations.

Everyone participates in groups. Families and school classes are groups. So are army units, baseball teams, corporate boards of directors, debating organizations, exotic dance troups, and so on. It would be easy to move through the alphabet and provide a long list of groups to which people belong.

We can distinguish groups from two closely related clusters of people—aggregates and categories. An **aggregate** consists of two or more people who share physical space but lack the interaction of group members. Aggregates can sometimes become groups. For example, a number of people might be waiting for a bus. Since they are not interacting, they do not consititute a group. However, a group might form if an approaching person fainted and several individuals rushed forward to provide assistance. A **social category** consists of a number of people who have one or more social characteristics in common, such as age, sex, marital state, income, or race. Members of a category sometimes have common values, interests, or grievances that can provide a foundation for the development of such groups as women's-rights organizations, taxpayers' associations, and ethnic support groups.

Ever since you were born, you have been involved in group activity. Most likely awareness started in the family, where even in infancy you began to have some sense of how you would fit in. You probably learned what behavior would please a parent or older sibling and what behavior would displease such people. Very quickly others' body language and words made it clear when you could get away with imposing your own will in a situation involving family or peers. As you have grown older, you have extended your range of group involvement. It should be easy to name a number of groups to which you belong—for instance, your family, a group of close friends, the classroon portion of this introductory sociology course, some extracurricular club or team, and an organization for which you work. It is also likely that within a year or two years, some of your group affiliations will change, and since all of us are strongly influenced by the groups to which we belong, you also will change.

The group is the most basic unit of sociological analysis. In the next section, we analyze several important types of groups. Then we look briefly at institutions, which are large systems that contain groups and that fulfill the basic needs of citizens within a society. The chapter concludes with an assessment of some of the prominent problems facing Americans in everyday group activity.

## Types of Groups

The group is one of the most significant concepts in sociology, and sociologists have designated many varieties. Primary and secondary groups, in-versus out-groups, membership and reference groups, and formal organizations and bureaucracies are among the most prominent types.

## Primary and Secondary Groups

The terms primary and secondary groups are not widely known in U.S. society, but we are all aware of their significance in the everyday social world. For instance, a woman comes home from work and says to her husband, "It was awful, Ted. The boss called me into his office and just spilled his guts—all the problems he's having with his wife and children. Then he started to cry. I was so embarrassed." She pauses to draw a deep breath. "This was a man I've been on formal terms with for five years. The most intimate thing I knew about him was that he'd get really excited over last year's marketing reports. And now this . . ." Obviously the woman's boss had violated a norm that had kept their relationship formal to that time. Here is another example. Jack and Judy are graduate students giving a party for a dozen of their friends. At first Jack enjoys himself, but he soon perceives that an uneasiness fills the room. It's too quiet. Eventually he realizes that the problem is Judy. She's still wrapped up in her research project and can't talk about anything else. He walks up to her, angrily pulls her aside, and whispers in her ear, "Dammit, Judy, will you lighten up? These are our friends, not your colleagues. There's a time and a place for everything!"

As members of both primary and secondary groups, we all learn what is appropriate behavior in each group setting. Generally speaking, primary-group behavior is more personal and less specialized than secondary-group behavior. Let's examine both types.

### Primary Groups

A **primary group** is a group in which relationships are stable over long periods of time, members are able to expose many facets of their personality, and a strong sense of affection and identity (a "we feeling") develops (Cooley, 1962: 23). Primary groups are small, permitting face-to-face contact. The family is the most important primary group. Other primary groups to which many Americans belong include peer groups, neighborhood circles, social clubs, and informal groups within complex organizations, such as cliques within factories or offices. Research and analysis of

*While the family is the most important primary group, other types of interrelationships also reflect several features associated with primary groups. For example, long-time neighbors can have strong expectations and can "count" on one another for help and support, sometimes as much as family members.*

primary groups have extended from early in the twentieth century to recent years (Scott and Scott, 1981).

#### PRIMARY-GROUP NORMS

Primary-group norms are sometimes consistent with the standards that exist elsewhere in society and are sometimes not. Consider the issue of disciplining children within the family. In preindustrial societies most family norms were widely shared. Modern societies are less consistent in this respect. Many modern parents are permissive, putting few limitations on their children's behavior and seldom punishing them when they break existing family rules. Children whose families have lenient primary-group norms are likely to have a difficult and confusing time if they encounter teachers who set exacting limits on their behavior. The reverse condition can be equally confusing. A. S. Neill (1960), the founder of the well-known English school Summerhill, permitted his pupils to do almost anything they pleased as long as they neither hurt anyone nor destroyed property. Neill strongly discouraged children from highly controlled fam-

**74**

ily situations from applying for admission to Summerhill—the adjustment would have been too difficult.

Since primary groups involve extensive, intimate relations, their members have ample opportunity to observe each other and assess the group's norms. "You know, Mommy," a little girl says. "Every time I talk about the money for dancing lessons, Daddy starts wrinkling his nose and sniffing. Then he hardly talks to me for the next couple of hours." With no more than a facial expression or a few words, primary-group members can let each other know whether their behavior is desirable or undesirable. Frequently people in these groups conform to each other's expectations because they value their membership and do not want to risk losing it.

### SOLIDARITY AND PRIMARY-GROUP MEMBERSHIP

Willie Stargell, a star of the Pittsburgh Pirates for two decades, was being interviewed at the beginning of his last season. It has been a marvelous experience, Stargell said, much more exciting than he ever could have imagined. He was asked what he

would miss the most. Stargell smiled. "The guys," he said. They had lived together through the long baseball seasons, struggled, and finally had won the World Series. The primary-group quality of that team was demonstrated by the fact that the members called themselves "the family."

Common activity often seems to be a principal basis of primary groups. A study of undergraduate psychology majors revealed that friends were more similar in their activities than in their attitudes and were more accurate in estimating friends' activity preferences than their attitudes. Attitudes tended to be as dissimilar between friends as they were between strangers, but activity preferences were distinctly more similar between friends than between strangers (Werner and Parmelee, 1979).

Primary groups also emerge in the course of activity—warfare, for instance. Most of us probably have seen the vintage World War II films that portray the fighting men as motivated primarily by patriotism and a fervent belief in "the American way." In contrast, research has shown that during war American soldiers are primarily motivated by loyalty to their buddies. For instance, a soldier

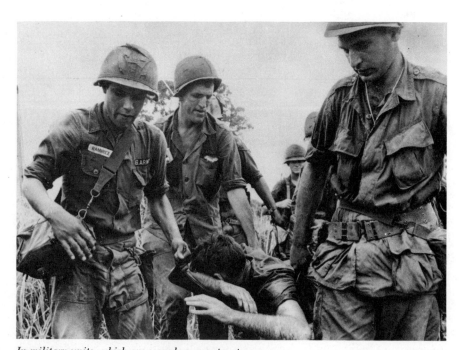

*In military units, which are secondary groups, strong primary groups are likely to develop because of the members' critical dependence on each other. In this photo, which was taken during the Vietnam War, soldiers are carrying a wounded buddy who was shot in the leg by a sniper.*

wounded while fighting in Sicily commented:

> You know the men in your outfit. You have to be loyal to them. . . . They depend on each other — wouldn't do anything to let the rest of them down. They'd rather be killed than do that. They begin to think the world of each other. It's the main thing that keeps a guy from going haywire.
>
> *(Stouffer et al., 1949: 136)*

Captain John Early, a veteran of Vietnam and a former mercenary, called the association between men in combat "a love relationship." He emphasized the importance of this relationship among professional soldiers. "And you'll find that people who pursue combat . . . are there because they're friends, the same people show up in . . . wars time and again" (Quoted in Dyer, 1985: 104). In secondary groups such strong personal commitments are less common.

### Secondary Groups

A **secondary group** is composed of people who cooperate with each other for specific, practical reasons and generally maintain few if any strong emotional ties within the group. Face-to-face contact between secondary-group members is normally limited, with the individuals relating to each other exclusively on the basis of specific roles they are playing — secretary and boss, student and teacher, or senator and constituents. However, primary relations sometimes arise within secondary groups. The members of a college class or of a work team are initially secondary-group members, but in the course of their activity together they may develop genuine friendships.

Since primary groups involve a more intimate kind of relationship than do secondary groups, one might be tempted to conclude that primary groups are "good" and secondary groups are "bad." No justification for such a judgment exists. Primary and secondary groups simply serve different functions in people's lives. In fact, in a secondary group, the strong emotions that normally accompany primary-group relations can impede effective decision-making. For example, presidents and their advisers have sometimes made poor decisions on crucial issues because of the emphasis on cohesiveness and unanimity (primary-group feelings) that have crept into their secondary group. In 1961 John Kennedy had just been elected president, and his immediate advisers were convinced that with Kennedy leading the country "the world was plastic and the future unlimited" (Janis, 1972: 36). They believed, in short, that with Kennedy in command anything could be accomplished. There was a powerful sense of united purpose, a "we feeling," shared by the circle of advisers around the president. Some of these advisers had personal misgivings about the administration's plan to overthrow the Castro regime in Cuba. However, because of the strong "we feeling" that filled this secondary group, their misgivings were mildly expressed or not expressed at all. When the Bay-of-Pigs invasion occurred, it was a humiliating failure for Kennedy and his administration.

A recent experiment emphasized that the "we feeling" within a secondary group leads to the rejection of members' opinions when they disagree with the majority. In discussions of political candidates, it was learned that when individuals offered descriptions that were unfavorable toward the most popular candidates, the participants tended not to examine the new, critical material, and the initially favored candidates retained stronger support than other candidates (Stasser and Titus, 1985).

## In-Groups versus Out-Groups

Even some nonhuman species establish group boundaries. For instance, among wolves, when a family wants to designate its territory, the members mark it off with a trail of urine (Mowat, 1965: 60). Human beings can be just as explicit about boundaries. We mark them with such things as family names, passports, team uniforms, or employee membership cards.

The idea of group boundaries is central to the distinction between in-groups and out-groups. An **in-group** is any group characterized by a strong sense of identification and loyalty and by the exclusion of nonmembers. An **out-group** is composed of nonmembers of an in-group who are viewed with hostility and even contempt by in-group members (Summer, 1906: 12–13).

In-group/out-group hostility occurs frequently in small groups. The struggle for scarce resources is one way to produce it. Some years ago Muzafer and Carolyn Sherif (1956), both social psychologists, studied friction and competition between two groups of twelve-year-old boys, with a dozen to

**76**

a group. The Sherifs conducted experiments in which the members of each group were required to cooperate with each other in order to win a tournament of competitive games. The competition was keen because the boys on each team had been promised a four-bladed jackknife if they won, and these knives were highly valued. Competition soon led to bad feelings between the two groups, and cheers like "2–4–6–8, who do we appreciate" deteriorated to "2–4–6–8, who do we appreci-*hate*." Throughout the experiment hostility between the two groups remained at a high level, and retaliatory acts occurred on both sides.

In-group/out-group friction can develop between small groups and also between nations. Many Americans have expressed a strong out-group hostility toward communist societies and governments for half-a-century, and in the 1980s the Reagan administration encouraged this tradition. In 1980 a representative sample of adult Americans was asked to indicate their feelings about communism as a form of government. One percent said it was good, 13 percent said it was all right for some countries, 27 percent said it was bad

but not the worst, and 59 percent said that it was the worst possible type of government (National Opinion Research Center, *General Social Survey*, 1980).

Is this negative outlook toward communism likely to continue? While it is impossible to give a definite answer, a recent study reached a conclusion that might offer a hint. Two researchers learned that negative feelings toward an out-group become more pronounced when in-group members have recently experienced failure (Meindl and Lerner, 1984). So it is possible that if unemployment, underemployment, and other serious economic problems become more widespread in the United States, then Americans' negative reaction to communism will increase. If affluence occurs, however, a more benign outlook might develop.

As the above material suggests, situations where the concepts in-group and out-group are applied are situations where people's feelings are strong and often conflicting. The following American Controversy provides an opportunity to address this emotional issue personally.

---

**AMERICAN CONTROVERSY**

## *In-Group Membership: Healthy or Unhealthy?*

Americans vary considerably in their feelings about in-groups and out-groups. Let us consider a number of different issues.

To begin, there are people who are strongly inclined to designate their own in-group superior. For instance, members of the American Nazi Party or of the Ku Klux Klan believe in what they call "racial superiority"; they claim that members of certain racial groups are superior to members of other racial groups. Whites, primarily whites of northern European backgrounds, are considered the in-group, and nonwhites — blacks and Asian groups as well as Jews — are members

of the out-group. This kind of in-group/out-group distinction is particularly inflexible because there is nothing people can do to move from the in-group to the out-group: They are locked in by superficial biological characteristics. While our society officially discourages using racial characteristics as a way of making an in-group/out-group distinction, such activity continues to be widespread.

Other uses of in-groups and out-groups are generally considered more acceptable —claims of patriotism, for example. Historically politicians, business leaders, and others have suggested that ours is the greatest country in

the world. In both times of war and peace, it has been claimed that anyone who opposes the interests of the United States is misguided at best and downright evil at worst.

In the past couple of decades, however, this outlook has begun to change. At the time of the Vietnam War, a large number of Americans took the position that their government was making a mistake—a tragic mistake—by involving itself in a war with a little country in southeast Asia. Slogans were the order of the day as youthful opponents of the war shouted: "Hell no! We won't go!" From the perspective offered by the in-group/out-group distinction, these protesters were turning their backs on traditionally patriotic (in-group) standards demanding that all young men be willing to serve and die for their country in its wars. Traditional patriots were horrified by such a stance, and often their reply was: "America, your country, love it or leave it!" In other words, as in-group members, traditional patriots were telling the antiwar protesters that either they played by the rules of the in-group or got out—left the country and joined the (communist) out-group.

Perhaps the contemporary issue that most significantly challenges a conventional outlook on patriotic in-groups and out-groups is the

topic of nuclear weaponry. In late 1983, 83 percent of the American public believed that both sides would be annihilated in a nuclear war. So it is widely believed that neither side could win a nuclear war; there would only be losers. Such a position represents a challenge to a traditional sense of in-group superiority; the current belief contends that no country would emerge superior from a nuclear confrontation. Furthermore an awareness of the great danger represented by nuclear war has forced Americans to recognize that in this case the normally unchallenged fear and hostility between the in-group and out-group could be precipitators of catastrophe for all.

Now comes the chance to

discuss and argue a little. Get together with a group of your friends or fellow students and examine the following questions:

1. Are you a member of any in-groups? What are they? What are their positions about their respective out-groups?
2. Do you approve of patriotic in-groups? Does the present presidential administration effectively express your patriotic views? Discuss.
3. What effect, if any, does the nuclear issue have upon traditional American perceptions of the Soviets as an out-group?

Source: Roper Organization. *Roper Reports.* December 1983.

## Reference Groups

Cal and George are sitting in the lounge an hour before their fraternity party is due to begin. Cal says enthusiastically,

"Boy, I love this place!"
"You mean the frat house?"
"Yeah, I feel awfully lucky to be a member of Alpha Beta Alpha. I just like everything about the place—the way the guys talk and dress, the kinds of things they like to do for fun . . ."
"I think you're nuts." George stands up and starts pacing nervously. "I've had it with all of them. I think they're a bunch of jerks. In fact, I'm thinking of getting out next semester."

For George the fraternity is a mere **membership group**—a group to which an individual belongs. Cal's feelings are very different. For him the fraternity is not only a membership group, but it is also a **reference group**—a group whose standards a person uses to help shape his or her own values,

beliefs, and behavior. The previous illustration suggests that the way people regard a particular group will affect their attitudes toward and behavior within that group. Research has offered some support for these conclusions (Granberg et al., 1981). Recent studies have determined that reference groups affect people's behavior in a variety of areas, including younger siblings' behavioral style (Abramovitch et al., 1986), adolescents' likelihood of smoking and drinking (Biddle et al., 1985), and young people's tendency to engage in deviant activities (Patterson and Dishion, 1985).

It is important to recognize that a group can be a reference group even if an individual does not belong to it. **Anticipatory socialization** is the acceptance of a group's standards preparatory to becoming a member of the group. When little children talk and behave like older children, they are preparing themselves for their later roles. Adolescents, college students, and older adults engage in similar, if more sophisticated, behavior. Anticipa-

*Reference groups provide standards which can deeply affect the values, beliefs, and behavior of its members. Such groups, like the West Point cadets, may also reflect some characteristics of secondary and even primary groups.*

tory socialization can provide benefits for individuals. Research conducted during World War II suggested that privates who accepted the formal army standards valued by officers were more likely to be promoted than were privates who did not accept those standards (Merton, 1968: 319).

Theodore Newcomb's analysis of the attitudes and beliefs of women at Bennington College in Vermont is a well-known investigation of reference-group behavior. The original research took place over a four-year period so that Newcomb could study changes in his informants' attitudes and beliefs during their college careers. He found that most of the freshmen reflected their well-to-do parents' conservative views on political and economic issues. As they moved through college, however, the women tended to adopt the much more liberal attitudes of their teachers. The faculty members served as a reference group for the students. The teachers did not deliberately try to change their students' values, but they did ". . . think of their students . . . as having led overprotected lives, and they included among their teaching responsibilities that of introducing students to the rest of the world" (Newcomb et al., 1967: 4). A sizable minority of the students resisted the teachers' liberal values. These students tended to be relatively isolated at college, overdependent on their parents, or rebellious toward prevailing community values. In a follow-up study, Newcomb and his associates (1967) learned that the women who were liberals when they left college in the late 1930s were still liberal in 1960, while those who were conservative in the 1930s were usually still conservative more than twenty years later. This research suggests that the impact of reference groups on a person's standards can persist over long periods of time.

Figure 4.1 represents the different kinds of groups discussed in this section.

**Figure 4.1**
**Group Members' Shared Outlooks**

*In this figure, the members of each group type share a common outlook. Thus, if we consider the groups in the numerical order shown, we see the following patterns: (1) a feeling of exclusiveness; (2) a feeling of exclusion; (3) a "we" feeling; (4) cooperation for distinct, practical reasons; (5) a recognition of belonging to a group; (6) a willingness to accept the influence of group standards to shape one's own values, beliefs, and behavior.*

## Formal Organizations and Bureaucracies

Throughout our lives all of us are in regular contact with schools, hospitals, courts, corporations, and government agencies. These are **formal organizations,** which are groups characterized by carefully stated rules, clearly defined members' roles, and distinct objectives. As formal organizations become larger and more complex, they need **bureaucracies**—formal organizations' administrative sections that have the task of controlling their operation. Students, for example, are part of the formal organization of a school, but they are not part of its bureaucracy because they have no administrative duties.

Bureaucracies often evoke a negative image in our minds. In its least negative form, our stereotype of bureaucracy includes masses of paperwork, inefficiency, and taut nerves. More negatively we might visualize mental patients or prison inmates incarcerated for years, perhaps for decades, because of some "bureaucratic slip-up," or Adolph Eichmann claiming that he was a guiltless cog in the Nazi bureaucracy when he "just followed orders" to execute millions of Jewish concentration-camp victims.

Bureaucracies did exist in preindustrial times — in ancient Egypt, China, and Rome, for instance — and the impressive monuments and buildings those ancient civilizations produced are in part a result of the organized use of men and materials that their bureaucracies helped promote. After the Industrial Revolution, profit seeking within the capitalist economic system and the necessity of paying increasingly high wages to workers were both incentives to establish large-scale bureaucratic structures that used workers efficiently and gave business owners increased control over both their employees and the work process. Eventually bureaucratic procedures came to be used in public institutions, such as government, education, the penal system, and facilities for the mentally ill and retarded.

As bureaucracies became prominent in modern societies, Max Weber produced what is now considered to be the classic analysis of this type of structure.

### Weber's Analysis of Bureaucracies

Weber developed an ideal-type model of bureaucracy. An **ideal type** is a simplified description of some phenomenon based on an analysis of concrete examples, emphasizing those characteristics that best help us to understand its essential nature. Weber analyzed bureaucracies as the most efficient means of structuring employees' time and energy. His ideal-type model emphasized the following points (Gerth and Mills, 1946: 196–198).

*Specialization.* Within a bureaucracy it is most efficient to have each worker specialize on a narrow task, thus becoming an expert in its performance. When faculty members at a college or university have questions concerning their salaries, they call the payroll office and speak to the person in charge of the faculty payroll, the specialist on this subject within the college bureaucracy.

*Formal qualifications for bureaucratic roles.* The members of bureaucracies are hired on the basis of merit, not favoritism; they have the appropriate educational credentials and/or experience. Much of the training for bureaucratic positions, of course, occurs before a person actually enters an organization. However, within many large-scale bureaucracies, training for medium-status roles is common today. Personnel are often expected to complete intensive training programs that may vary in length from a few days to many months and are sometimes carried on at special centers built by the organization. ATT, several fast food chains, and many of the major insurance companies have developed such centers. Successful completion of these programs makes employees eligible for higher salaries and promotion. In addition, graduates are provided with certificates that resemble diplomas and are meant to increase the sense of personal pride resulting from affiliation with their organization.

*Full-time employment.* In modern bureaucracies the amount of work that must be completed generally requires that staff members be hired on a full-time basis. During formally prescribed hours, they are expected to be on the job devoting their time and energy to their tasks. How employees spend their time when they are off the job is not the concern of the bureaucracy; a clear distinction is drawn between work and personal lives.

*Impersonality.* Officials remain impersonal with their clients, treating them as "cases" and not as individuals. They adopt the same formality in their relations with fellow staff members. As a result personal preferences and biases are excluded from the work process and are unlikely to affect the decisions bureaucratic officials must make.

*Files, providing written documentation of precedents.* The decisions of a bureaucratic staff are based on precedent, and so in order to make decisions, they must be sure that all prior actions of the bureaucracy are recorded and retained indefinitely for reference. Specialists receive the task of organizing and updating these files. Since Weber's era, computers, microfilm, and other types of modern technology have greatly increased the efficiency with which these records can be maintained.

*Hierarchy of authority.* Within bureaucracies people receive orders or directives from their superiors and are directly accountable to them. Majors give orders to captains in the army, just as deans issue commands to departmental chairpersons in colleges and universities. In both situations the "chain of command" is a distinct, efficient means for the transmission of orders and information.

*Elaborate formal norms.* There are clear-cut rules governing all possible contingencies. These rules tend to remain stable over time and must be learned by employees of the organization. Try to imagine what a bureaucracy would be like without such an emphasis on rules. Consider, for instance, college registration. For many students and college administrators, this is a difficult, time-consuming period at the beginning of each semester. If there were no rules covering such matters as reimbursement of funds, numerical limitations on class size, or prerequisites for entry into certain courses, administrators would need to deliberate on each case as it arose, making the long lines students sometimes must face during registration seem, in contrast, very short.

As we have noted, Weber's description of bureaucracy offers a simplified version of its structure and activities—an ideal type. Modern analysts of bureaucracies have continued to use Weber's ideas in their own work (Hammond and Miller, 1985; Langton, 1984; Sjoberg, Vaughan, and Williams, 1984). At the same time, it has been recognized that bureaucracies contain some important characteristics he did not consider.

## Informal Structure of Bureaucracies

"Things are not always what they appear to be." This well-known saying can apply to Weber's analysis of bureaucracies. He suggested that bureaucracies are formal structures, with clearly designated lines of authority and fully specified rules. In any particular organization, however, one individual frequently exercises much more influence in reality than does another occupying a comparable position in the formal organizational structure. Similarly workers frequently recognize that some rules are much more important than others, despite the fact that in the organizational handbook all rules appear equally important. As Figure 4.2 suggests, the informal organization within a bureaucracy frequently decreases the significance of the formal structure. Cliques, grapevines, and informal power alliances are among the factors contributing to this outcome.

An important set of studies demonstrating the

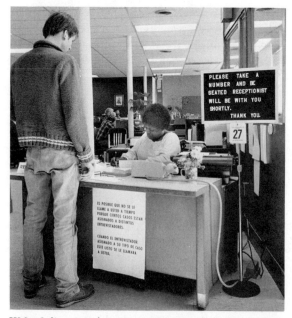

Weber believed that the clients of bureaucracies benefit from impersonal treatment because all are treated alike. Critics of bureaucracies disagree, contending that such individuals as those pictured above have their humanity diminished by being processed as numbered objects.

**Figure 4.2**
**Informal Activities of a Bureaucracy: Commentary on Weber's Model**

*Partial organizational chart. When the informal activities of a hypothetical computer company are examined, exception can arise to each of the points contained in Weber's model of bureaucracies.*

| WEBER'S CHARACTERISTICS | INFORMAL ACTIVITIES IN THE COMPUTER COMPANY PROVIDING EXCEPTIONS TO WEBER'S MODEL |
|---|---|
| 1. *Specialization* | 1. Booming domestic sales necessitates a temporary shift to sales of one-third of the advertising specialists. |
| 2. *Formal qualifications* | 2. The manager of the purchasing department has advanced rapidly because he is an expert at "playing politics;" although he has very little experience in the area of purchasing. |
| 3. *Full-time employment* | 3. A twenty-year-old computer whiz is paid a full-time salary for part-time work. |
| 4. *Impersonality* | 4. Some customers receive distinctly preferential treatment. It is well known that a number of mayors received huge discounts on high-priced models in exchange for their cities signing large contracts with the company. |
| 5. *Written documentation of precedents* | 5. The vice-president for sales has been so busy directing the hiring and training of sales staff that he has not kept records on the procedures he has used. |
| 6. *Hierarchy of authority* | 6. The president, who has a strong background in product testing, frequently bypasses the production vice-president to give orders to the testing department. |
| 7. *Elaborate formal norms* | 7. Members of the advertising department recognize that some of the rules relating to their duties are more important than others. Many members of this department, for example, break an office rule about taking office supplies for personal use. |

impact of the informal structure within bureaucracies was conducted at the Hawthorne plant of the Western Electric Company in Illinois (Roethlisberger and Dickson, 1939). One of the principal Hawthorne studies was completed by some observers sitting in a room with fourteen workers wiring telephone equipment. The researchers learned that the workers had developed group norms that were often in opposition to the official norms established by management. For instance, if someone worked more quickly than the standard, fellow workers designated that person a "ratebuster," while someone who worked more

slowly than the norm was called a "chiseler." The punishment for minor violations was often "binging"—hitting the offender on the upper arm—or ridicule. The worst violation of the informal group norms occurred when a worker "squealed" on fellow workers to the foreman. In this case the punishment was exclusion; the other workers pretended that the person did not exist.

Informal group norms defined "a fair day's work" as less than the amount of production desired by management. In order to conform to group norms, the fastest members simply stopped working earlier than did the others. These workers seemed to realize that voluntary restriction of output was functional for the group as a whole since increased production would probably have encouraged the company to initiate layoffs. In addition, if the workers had increased their production level, cut-throat competition and massive disruption of the group might well have occurred. The informal norms restricting productivity prevented the occurrence of both possibilities (Blau and Scott, 1963: 92–93).

Besides his failure to analyze the informal workings of bureaucracies, Weber also overlooked their dysfunctions.

### Dysfunctions of Bureaucracies

Weber's ideal type of bureaucracy emphasizes the positive contributions this type of structure can make. However, bureaucracies may also be dysfunctional for some of the people in contact with them (Burns, 1980).

Efficiency is one of the most obvious assets of bureaucracy, but placing an excessive emphasis on it can violate humanitarian standards. For example, in public mental hospitals, the laundering process is easier if patients are issued institutional clothes. This procedure eliminates the necessity of individually marking each piece of clothing and returning it to its owner. The emphasis on efficiency, however, overlooks the fact that wearing one's own clothes can be very meaningful, providing continuity with one's previous life and perhaps helping combat mental illness.

Another possible dysfunction of bureaucracies is their concern with self-perpetuation. Staff members are likely to stress the importance of their group operation, whether or not they are providing a demonstrably useful service; the obvious collective motive is that members' jobs are their source of livelihood. Governmental agencies are particularly notorious for finding reasons for continuing to survive after their original purpose has been accomplished or abandoned. Self-perpetuation can also develop at the individual level, with bureaucratic leaders often seeking to maintain and increase their power, usually to the detriment of both subordinates' and clients' interests (Sjoberg, Vaughan, and Williams, 1984).

Communication problems can also be a dysfunction of bureaucracies. Within the construction industry, for example, managers used to hold meetings over a cup of coffee at the work site. However, in recent years these organizations have grown larger and more complex, and the different functions have become more separate. One observer wrote:

> On our present job, our engineer–managers are paper-oriented . . . Their working styles consist of spending days and weeks studying details on plans or researching specifications before they are ready to help our people who are doing construction work. Many or most consider neat files more important than getting involved in meeting deadlines, making decisions which might be risky, and taking abuse for failures or mistakes.
>
> *(Applebaum, 1982: 231)*

This statement suggests that the growth of bureaucracies isolates managers and encourages a more aloof, less communicative style than they generally maintained when the structures were smaller.

An additional dysfunction of bureaucracies is that they encourage the development of a type of personality regarded as abnormal. The **bureaucratic personality** emphasizes rules and procedures and tends to lose track of organizational goals (Merton, 1968). This type of person enforces "rules for rules' sake." Most of us have probably encountered such an approach when dealing with certain bureaucratic personnel: The college official who never "bends" the rules to help students; the motor vehicles department clerk who makes a host of trivial corrections on a car registration application; or the hospital administrator who will not admit a patient, even one in considerable discomfort, until the proper forms are completed in triplicate. On the other hand, some evidence suggests that in reality bureaucratic personalities are not common in modern bureaucracies. For example, Melvin Kohn (1971) studied a sample of over 3000 men engaged in a wide variety of civilian occupations. He discovered that men working in bureaucracies more readily think for themselves, are more open to new experiences, place greater emphasis on self-direction, and maintain more responsible moral standards than do nonbureaucratic personnel. Kohn suggested that the fact that bureaucratic organizations often hire people with better educational qualifications than those found in many other types of jobs helps to explain the differences.

We have seen that bureaucracies often have dysfunctional tendencies, but is the modern picture primarily negative? The following Cross-Cultural Perspective provides one response to this question.

## CROSS-CULTURAL PERSPECTIVE

*The Human Factor in Bureaucracies: The Japanese Case*

William Ouchi (1981), a management specialist, has developed Theory Z: a model for organizing bureaucracies that is based on Japanese management practices and emphasizes long-term planning, decision-making by consensus, and the development of intense loyalty between workers and management. Ouchi has contended that Theory Z can help many American firms with serious problems of high employee turnover, declining productivity, and profound worker alienation. Some American corporations, including IBM, Proctor and Gamble, and Hewlett–Packard, now use Theory Z techniques.

The theory commands attention because Japanese production has become legendary in Western societies. Between 1975 and 1981, the annual sale of Japanese cars in the United States rose from 800,000 to 1.9 million; Japanese products now control 23 percent of the American car market. Japanese cameras, radios, televisions, microwave ovens, and motorcycles have also proven popular in the United States and other Western nations.

The central idea of Theory Z is the importance of establishing a powerful bond between workers and their firms. Japanese managers take a number of steps to maintain and strengthen this bond. Among them:

1. *Lifetime employment.* Over 35 percent of the Japa-nese work force is covered by this practice, which requires sacrifice by all company employees when recession or other problems threaten layoffs. Instead of dismissing workers, management will cut everyone's paychecks, including its own, or will defer payment of the large, twice-yearly bonuses all employees normally receive.

2. *Evaluation and promotion policies.* Many Japanese companies provide promotions as infrequently as once every ten years. Yet since all employees receive the same treatment, no one must fear falling behind.

3. *Nonspecialized careers.* Unlike American managers, who generally specialize in one area of company business (sales, finance, or production), Japanese executives regularly move from one corporate department to another and eventually become experts in the entire structure and activities of their firms.

4. *Collective decision-making.* In comparison with American executives, who are often expected to act quickly and decisively and to accept the consequences of their individual decisions, Japanese management makes major decisions by means of a collective compromise process that may involve sixty to eighty people. The Japanese call this process of establishing consensus *nemawashi* (root building). In the same way that a gardener carefully wraps all the roots of a tree together before planting it, Japanese business leaders must bring together all the members of a company before finalizing a decision. This process may be tedious, but when it is completed everyone is likely to feel committed to the collective goal.

Because the Japanese approach to business is different from that of the United States, one might suspect that it would be ineffective in the United States. It has, however, been fairly successful in some cases. In a Sony plant in San Diego, which employs 1800 workers, 700,000 color television sets were produced in 1981, a level of productivity that approaches the one achieved in the Japanese plants. The Japanese factory manager said: "Americans are as quality conscious as the Japanese. But the question has been how to motivate them." Management has tried to build strong ties with the workers, expecting that they will then reciprocate. During the recession of 1973–1975 when television sales dropped and production plummeted, no one was fired. Workers stayed busy working on plant maintenance and other chores. In fact, since the plant opened in 1972, no workers have been laid off. This personnel policy has been a success. Several attempts to unionize the work force have been defeated by margins as high as three to one. A parts dispatcher who was a former member of the Retail Clerks Union explained: "Union pay was better, and the benefits were probably better. But basically I'm more satisfied here."

Sony has not forced Japanese customs on its American workers. The use of lemon-colored smocks for assembly-line workers is optional, and most of the employees prefer jeans and running shoes. An attempt to establish an exercise period similar to those common in the Japanese plants was dropped when managers saw it was not popular. Inevitably differences in customs cause some misunderstandings. American workers often interpret the Japanese system of managing by consensus as reflecting an inability to make decisions. One employee complained: "There is a lot of indecision. No managers will ever say do this or do that."

In general, however, most of the workers like the Japanese management style and so do not feel it is particularly foreign. An American supervisor said, "A long time ago, Americans used to be more people-oriented, the way the Japanese are. It just got lost somewhere along the way" (Coutu, 1981). The Japanese approach to employee–management relations appears to contain some valuable lessons for Americans.

Sources: Christopher Byron. "How Japan Does It." *Time.* Vol. 117. March 30, 1981, pp. 54–60; D.L. Coutu. "Consensus in San Diego." *Time.* Vol. 117. March 30, 1981, p. 58; William Ouchi. *Theory Z: How American Business Can Meet the Japanese Challenge.* Reading, MA: Addison-Wesley. 1981

## Communities

As the young man reached the center of the park, his dog ran up to an elderly man sitting on a bench. "Here. I've got something for her," the old man said. Stiffly he reached into his pocket and took out a cookie.

"I'm sure she'll like it."

"You know, these days many people your age don't have enough time to stop and talk."

"Well, I guess I rush around too, but I'm not in that bad a hurry. Besides I'm living right over there on Court Street, and I'm interested in the community."

"The community." The old man nodded and smiled as if the phrase were the punchline to a quiet joke. "This ain't no community no more. Back in the thirties, back then it was a community. People of all ages used to be out on the street till midnight. There'd be vendors selling food and drinks. Back then you could sit in the park and watch the whole show. It was better than a Jimmy Cagney thriller." He paused to look at a man walking by. "Do you know him?"

"I don't think so."

The old man nudged his listener with an elbow. "You should. That's Barry Garcia. He's got the little factory over on Sweet Street. Right now he's paying twenty-five workers, but he's moving out to Shortland Hills into a large, new plant. That guy's really going places, and Barry's from right here—the community." He nodded proudly.

Like this man, many Americans yearn for a sense of community they once knew or perhaps they know only from hearsay, and at the same time they respond positively to the very social conditions—the emphasis on individual achievement and on industrial development—that have undermined communities in the United States and other Western countries. For many Americans it has been difficult to come to grips with their changing communities.

A **community** is a settlement of people living in a specific geographical area and maintaining a system of interrelationships that satisfies many of the people's physical and social needs. Because of the interrelationship among its inhabitants, a community is normally a source of group identification.

Early in the twentieth century, Robert Ezra Park and other members of the so-called Chicago School of Sociology undertook community studies that helped transform sociology from an armchair discipline into an empirical science. Park, a former newspaper reporter, retained his sharp curiosity for facts; when he became a professor at the University of Chicago, he outlined a program of research into the sociology of the community. Park emphasized that sociologists studying communities should analyze them as social systems, characterized by shared feelings about morality, business, the law, politics, and the future of the area (Krause, 1980). Community studies continue, with research on American communities having recently analyzed such subjects as the sources of residential satisfaction within communities (Baldassare, 1986), the relationship between people's age and their sense of closeness to other community members (McAuley and Nutty, 1985), and neighbors' support of widows who live alone (O'Bryant, 1985).

The large body of community studies that began at the University of Chicago has led to some definite conclusions about the differences between rural and urban community life.

*Goals.* In early communities people produced their own food, shelter, and other necessities. People literally had to depend upon each other for survival. With industrialization most people start working outside the communities where they live, and as a result interdependence with their neighbors begins to decline. Many Americans are pessimistic about community life. In the spring of 1980, 45 percent of a national sample thought a decline in neighborliness was likely to occur in the future. Fifty-eight percent of the people from rural areas expected such a change to take place, compared with only 40 percent of the people living in the twenty-five largest metropolitan areas (Roper Organization, *Roper Reports,* Spring 1980).

A sociological study of a small upstate New York town concluded that the residents believed that cities breed corruption, that they are unwholesome environments for children and families, that industrial workers are highly paid for doing minimal work, and that universities and urban churches are centers of atheism and have generally lost touch with the spiritual lessons taught by rural life (Vidich and Bensman, 1968: 30–33).

*Social Interaction.* When people live in highly interdependent communities, close and frequent contact with their friends, relatives, and acquaintances is common. Extensive social interaction does sometimes occur among suburban or urban residents, but it happens less frequently than in rural areas, where considerable interdependence among residents is still normal. In the upstate New York town of Springdale, neighborliness is displayed most typically during times of personal and family crisis — birth, death, illness, fire, or catastrophe. On

such occasions friends and neighbors usually pull together to help those distressed. Collections of money are taken, meals are prepared, and cards of condolence are sent. A family whose house or barn has burned down may discover that a "bee" has been organized that will raise funds to rebuild. Borrowing is perhaps the most widespread sign of neighborliness. Farmers like to feel that "in a pinch" there is always someone from whom they can get help, tools, advice, or labor. In a community where "stores don't carry everything," housewives frequently trade and borrow (Vidich and Bensman, 1968: 33–38).

*Tasks.* In preindustrial communities the family was essentially a unit of economic production, and everyone, even young children, had a part to play in this activity. With both men and women employed away from the home and children occupied all day in school, this function of the family has declined in modern times. However, farm families still amount to a unit of production in a town like Springdale. Of course, the children must go to school, and men and women living and working on farms must often take second jobs. Thus many modern Springdale residents find themselves simultaneously performing the tasks of both the past and present.

*Ranking.* The system of social ranking in communities is largely based on occupational roles. In a hunting society, a man's status is likely to be determined principally by his skill as a hunter; in an agricultural society, by ownership of land and livestock. In modern societies, which are characterized by much more varied economies, there are many criteria for evaluating people. These include power, income, wealth, family prestige, education, life-style, and material possessions. In rural communities like Springdale, the occupational structure is more homogeneous than in cities, which is one reason for the widespread claim that "we're all equal." It is a violation of folkways to act as if economic inequalities make a difference. Although they have large homes, the wealthiest inhabitants of Springdale live simply, without servants. The serviceman, the delivery boy, and the door-to-door salesman knock at the door and are asked to enter before stating their business. In general, inequalities in income and wealth do not go unnoticed, but they do not

**Figure 4.3**
**People's Satisfaction with Their Community Compared to Other Important Dimensions of Their Lives**

*This figure emphasizes that about two-thirds (67 percent) of the respondents in a national sample were highly satisfied with their community as a place to live. Seven other important dimensions of people's lives scored higher than the community issue, while five scored lower. (Source: Adapted from George Gallup.* Gallup Poll. *January 17, 1982.)*

totally determine the public evaluation of an individual (Vidich and Bensman, 1968: 39–41).

*Social Control.* In small, preindustrial societies, where people share similar attitudes, values, and standards of conduct, significant violations become matters of general community concern. To some extent the knowledge that this will occur inhibits people's misconduct, and yet major violations, requiring formal punishments, do occasionally take place. In cities, where support for norms is less universal, social control is more likely to require the threat or actual use of formal sanctioning procedures—fines and imprisonments, in particular. In Springdale the citizens almost unanimously disapprove of certain types of behavior, including holding a grudge, not getting along with others, stirring up trouble, acting better than others, trying to run everything, attempting to cheat people, and not telling the truth (Vidich and Bensman, 1968: 36–39).

Differences between urban and rural communities as well as between old and modern communities do exist. Yet a recent study suggests that people analyzing communities should maintain caution: In particular, they should recognize that highly positive images of closely knit communities in the past might be oversimplified (Lee et al., 1984).

Figure 4.3 indicates that when interviewed by a major survey firm, Americans generally expressed a positive outlook toward their communities.

## Institutions

We have just examined the principal types of groups distinguished by sociologists. All groups are visible to the naked eye; they exist in a concrete sense. The same claim, however, cannot be made about institutions, even though they contain a visible element—groups.

An **institution** is a system of statuses, roles, groups, and behavioral patterns that satisfies a basic human need and is necessary for the survival of a society. Industrial societies always contain a well-developed set of institutions, while preindustrial societies often have limited or no development in many institutional areas. The chapters in the third section of the text examine major institutions.

The family is an institution that supplies a host of functions, including sexual regulation, reproduction, child-rearing, and the provision of food, shelter, and emotional support. Religion serves such functions as the development of group cohesion (a common sense of purpose), the maintenance of social control, and the provision of an ethical design for living. The education institution offers a variety of functions, including the transmission of culture, the teaching of knowledge and skills, and the sorting of students into vocational and college-preparatory programs. The political institution maintains social order and exerts changes in the legal structure, while the economic institution controls the production, distribution, and consumption of goods and services. Medicine is concerned with the prevention and treatment of disease and the treatment of injury, and science supplies systematic knowledge that can be used to produce progress in a variety of technological and social areas. Institutions not discussed in this text include the military, which can either attack the enemies of a society or defend against them, and sport, which provides recreation, exercises, and entertainment.

Institutions tend to be stable because members of society, especially those wealthy and powerful, usually do not feel that social change supports their interests. Consider the political institution. For almost the entire history of the United States, there have been only two political parties in most elections. The majority of the citizens, especially influential people, find that their political interests are sufficiently well represented by the principal parties that they are not motivated to support third parties. Thus third parties have almost always lacked the wealth and influence to launch successful political campaigns, even at the local level.

Institutions do not change readily, but when they do, they are likely to alter one or more other institutions. The reason this happens is that institutions are intimately tied to each other. Changes in the economic institution, for instance, can affect families. In an agricultural society, children represent a source of wealth for their parents—more hands to work the land. However, in an industrial society, where people live off wages, children represent an economic liability. It makes sense, therefore, to restrict the number of children. This appears to be one important reason that families in industrial societies are smaller than families in agricultural societies.

Across time and space, the form of a particular institution and the kind of activities it produces will often vary. Recreation and sport, for instance, have changed over time in U.S. society. In the first permanent American villages, the Puritans opposed play, games, and sport for two reasons. First, they emphasized that it was a full-time task simply to survive—to wrest a living from the wilderness and to protect themselves from the Indians. Second, religious rules prohibited leisure, branding such activities as idle and wasteful. But as the frontier slowly moved westward, religious restrictions weakened. Gambling on horse races, cock fights, fist fighting, wrestling, and rifle shooting were popular activities. In the taverns, drinking (sometimes competitively), cards, billiards, bowling, and rifle and pistol shooting provided both competition and entertainment (Leonard, 1980: 23–24). As the country grew, leisure also expanded. Industrialization, transportation growth, and the expansion of mass media all contributed. Eventually leisure and spectator sports became big business.

Other societies often have institutions very different from those in the United States. As part of the U.S. sport institution, Americans have a variety of spectator sports but none like the following examples. In Merida, in western Spain, the people once walled off an enormous plain to a height of four feet, creating a small lake on which ships could engage in simulated naval battles. In less technologically advanced societies, citizens use natural structures as settings for spectator sports. In a remote island of the New Hebrides, the entire community would gather at the bottom of a cliff to watch young male villagers throw themselves headlong toward the cliff floor, confident that the vine ropes attached to their heels would bring them to a halt just before they smashed into the rocks (Michener, 1976: 11–12).

One more point about institutions: They are part of the **macro-order**—the large-scale structures and activities that exist within societies and even between one society and another. As an illustration of the last point, one can argue that an effective understanding of the American economy must analyze its extensive links to the economies of other countries. The previous section on types of groups contains some discussion of the **micro-order**—the structure and activity of small groups.

## Humanization of Group Activity

Several sections of this chapter—in particular, the discussions of bureaucracy and community—document the emphasis on efficiency and achievement pervading modern American society. But there is a second important theme in American group life—a concern with intimacy and community. Sociologist Philip Slater (1976) contended that Americans must choose between an emphasis on community, in which the wish to live in trust and cooperation in a collective setting is the chief concern, and a focus on competition, in which the advancement of the individual at the expense of others is given top priority. American culture, Slater noted, did not invent competition, but he claimed that, compared to most other societies, the United States is extraordinarily competitive.

Certainly many Americans do adopt a highly impersonal life-style in order to pursue achievement. Yet at times the reality of how depersonalized and even brutalized modern life has become still strikes Americans—for example, when they sort through the red tape after a crime or a car accident has taken place, are audited by the Internal Revenue Service, or become embroiled in a lawsuit. At such times it is quite common to ask, "Why can't I just find some reasonable guy, and the two of us can sit down over a cup of coffee and work this thing out?" But the solution is seldom that simple. Everyday life is often formal and impersonal, guided by bureaucratic rules and policies and by local, state, and federal laws. To some degree, at least, it is questionable whether it could be otherwise in a modern society.

Americans seem painfully aware that rules and laws play a significant, sometimes stifling role in shaping their lives. In addition, partially because of the importance of these rules and laws, many Americans have become increasingly inclined *not* to see issues in moral terms but instead to consider only their own personal gain. In short, this is the post-Watergate era. In February 1981, 44 percent of a national sample of respondents were pessimistic about the moral and ethical standards in the United States, and only 30 percent were optimistic about those standards (Roper Organization, *Roper Reports,* February 1981).

Yet some solutions are available to problems of modern American group life. For instance, as the Japanese example suggests, we can sometimes learn new, productive approaches and techniques from other societies. The Japanese, more than Americans, have found that worker morale and productivity will be high if there is an emphasis on effective communication and consensus. In addition to borrowing other people's ideas and approaches, Americans can take direct action. Consider the contemporary decline of community life. What can be done about this problem? Sociologist Elliot Krause (1980) has pleaded, "Join your community! Now, not later!" He urged his students to go out and get to know their town or city, mapping out the landmarks and the different districts. In addition, he suggested that students should read their community newspaper in order to discover what issues are currently controversial. Then, Krause said, they should join action groups whose values and tactics they can endorse. At the very least, such participation can help one feel less like a robot.

# STUDY GUIDE

## Summary

1. A group consists of two or more interacting people who share certain expectations and goals. Groups can be distinguished from aggregates and categories, which are related concepts.

2. Sociologists have defined many different types of groups. Primary groups entail stable, long-lasting relationships, permitting members to exercise many facets of their personality and developing strong ties of affect and identity. In contrast, secondary groups are composed of people who join a group for specific, practical reasons and generally maintain few, if any, powerful emotional ties.

Another important conceptualization involves in-groups versus out-groups. An in-group is any group characterized by a strong sense of identification and loyalty and a feeling of exclusiveness toward nonmembers. The out-group is composed of nonmembers of the in-group who are viewed with hostility and even contempt by in-group members.

Reference groups, groups that a person uses to help shape his or her own values, beliefs, and behavior, are influential in the socialization of people. The concept of "anticipatory socialization" suggests that groups can serve as reference groups even if people do not belong to them.

Another significant type of group is the bureaucracy—a formal organization's administrative section that has the task of controlling its operation. Max Weber has analyzed the bureaucracy as an ideal type, indicating the bureaucratic features that make it the most efficient structure for using employees' time and energy within an organizational structure. Later sociological analysis has emphasized the informal group activities within bureaucracies as well as their dysfunctional aspects.

The community is a settlement of people living in a specific geographical area and maintaining a system of interrelationships that satisfies many of the people's physical and social needs. Preindustrial and industrial communities differ in a number of fundamental respects.

3. An institution is a system of statuses, roles, groups, and behavioral patterns that satisfies a basic human need and is necessary for the survival of a society. Institutions examined in this text include the family, religion, education, the polity, the economy, medicine, and science.

4. In an industrial age, people often find themselves confronting two, opposing demands—one pulling them toward efficiency/achievement and the other toward intimacy/community. People can take decisive steps to offset the impersonal tendencies of modern life.

## Glossary

**aggregate** two or more people who share physical space but lack the interaction maintained by group members.

**anticipatory socialization** the acceptance of a group's standards preparatory to becoming a member of the group.

**bureaucracy** a formal organization's administrative section that has the task of controlling its operation.

**bureaucratic personality** a personality that emphasizes rules and procedures and tends to lose track of organizational goals.

**community** a settlement of people living in a specific geographical area and maintaining a system of interrelationships that satisfies many of the people's physical and social needs.

**formal organization** a group characterized by carefully stated rules, clearly defined members' roles, and distinct objectives.

**group** two or more interacting people who share certain expectations and goals.

**ideal type** a simplified description of some phenomenon based on an analysis of concrete examples, emphasizing those characteristics that best help us to understand its essential nature.

**in-group** any group characterized by a strong sense of identification and loyalty and a feeling of exclusiveness toward nonmembers.

**institution** a system of statuses, roles, groups, and behavioral patterns that satisfies a basic human need and is necessary for the survival of a society.

**macro-order** the large-scale structures and activities that exist within societies and even between one society and another.

**membership group** a group to which an individual belongs.

**micro-order** the structure and activity of small groups.

**out-group** nonmembers of the in-group who are viewed with hostility and even contempt by in-group members.

**primary group** a group in which relationships are usually stable over long periods of time, members are able to expose many facets of their personality, and a strong sense of affection and identity develops.

**reference group** a group whose standards a person uses to help shape his or her own values, beliefs, and behavior.

**secondary group** a group composed of people who cooperate with each other for specific, practical reasons and maintain few, if any, strong emotional ties within the group.

**social category** a number of people who have one or more social characteristics in common.

## Learning Objectives

After studying this chapter, you should be able to:

1. Define group and distinguish among group, aggregate, and category.
2. Compare and contrast primary and secondary groups.

3. Define in-groups and out-groups and indicate circumstances encouraging their development.
4. Distinguish between membership and reference groups and define anticipatory socialization.
5. Define formal organization, bureaucracy, and ideal type and discuss Weber's analysis of bureaucracies.
6. Describe informal activities within bureaucracies.
7. Identify dysfunctions of bureaucracies.
8. Define community and discuss rural and urban community activities.
9. Define institution and describe the functions of the major institutions.
10. Indicate major problems of group life in modern society and suggest how these problems might be solved.

## Tests

### True–false test

_____ 1. The family is an important primary group.

_____ 2. After World War II, American soldiers' primary groups failed to develop a sense of loyalty among their members.

_____ 3. The struggle for scarce resources is one way to produce in-group/out-group hostility.

_____ 4. Anticipatory socialization only occurs when people already belong to a reference group.

_____ 5. Newcomb's study of college women's political attitudes and values over time indicated that teachers' influence had little or no lasting effect on attitudes and values.

_____ 6. Bureaucracies do not exist separately from formal organizations.

_____ 7. An ideal type emphasizes those characteristics of a phenomenon that best help us to understand its essential nature.

_____ 8. In analyzing bureaucracies, Weber produced major insights about their informal structure.

_____ 9. A recent review of the evidence has concluded that in the past American communities were very closely knit.

_____ 10. Industrial societies always contain a set of well-developed institutions; while preindustrial societies often have limited or no development in many institutional areas.

### Multiple-choice test

_____ 1. A number of people who have one or more social characteristics in common, such as age, sex, or race, would be a(n):
   a. group.
   b. aggregate.
   c. social category.
   d. secondary group.

_____ 2. Compared to a primary group, a secondary group tends:
   a. to have less face-to-face contact.
   b. to have more of a "we feeling."
   c. to be inferior.
   d. to involve a more intimate kind of relationship.

_____ 3. When a person accepts a group's standards preparatory to becoming a member of the group, this behavior is called:
   a. a membership group.
   b. aggregate behavior.
   c. anticipatory socialization.
   d. an ideal type.

_____ 4. Which statement is true of bureaucracies?
   a. They have existed for less than a century.
   b. They are informal organizations.
   c. They do not exist in economic or political structures.
   d. They are found in large formal organizations.

_____ 5. Which of the following characteristics is included in Weber's analysis of bureaucracies?
   a. an informal system of authority
   b. hiring based on formal qualifications
   c. a blending of work and personal lives
   d. self-perpetuation as a goal

_____ 6. Which of these factors is an important dysfunction of bureaucracies?
   a. an excessive emphasis on efficiency
   b. the discouragement of the bureaucratic personality
   c. specialization
   d. unwritten traditions

_____ 7. Communities:
   a. have not been studied by sociologists in recent decades.
   b. tend to demonstrate stronger interdependence among neighbors in urban than in rural areas.
   c. are now revitalized in most large cities, according to a recent study.
   d. have been studied by sociologists since early in the twentieth century.

_____ 8. Which of the following statements is true of institutions?
   a. In some societies many institutions simply exist without any apparent functions.
   b. They tend to be unstable.
   c. Their structures and activities tend to be very similar across time and space.
   d. When they change, they tend to affect other institutions.

_____ 9. Institutions are part of the:
   a. micro-order.
   b. macro-order.
   c. aggregate structure.
   d. bureaucratic ideal type.

_____ 10. Solutions to the problems of modern group life discussed in the text include:
   a. joining community activities.
   b. the maintenance of an impersonal life-style.
   c. learning new ways to succeed in competitive situations.
   d. a and c

## Essay test

1. Define the following concepts—group, aggregate, and social category—and give an example of each.
2. Evaluate the following statement: Primary groups are "good" and secondary groups are "bad."

3. Describe two situations presented in the text illustrating how in-group/out-group hostility is produced.
4. Distinguish between formal organizations and bureaucracies and summarize Weber's analysis of bureaucracies. Then examine the informal structure and dysfunctions of bureaucracies, indicating why this material represents a criticism of Weber's work.
5. Define community and discuss four significant differences between rural and urban communities.

## Suggested Readings

Blau, Peter, and Marshall W. Meyer. 1971. *Bureaucracy in Modern Society.* New York: Random House. Second edition. An examination of the theory of bureaucracy and the actual activities, functions, and dysfunctions of modern bureaucratic organizations.

Fischer, Frank, and Carmen Sirianni (eds.). 1984. *Critical Studies in Organization and Bureaucracy.* Philadelphia: Temple University Press. Twenty-eight articles on organizations and bureaucracies, including classic analyses by Marx, Weber, and others; assessments of individuals' adaptations to limited power in the organizational context; and examinations of efforts to establish and maintain democratic organizations.

Gerth, H. H., and C. Wright Mills (eds.). 1946. *From Max Weber.* New York: Oxford University Press. This well-known collection contains an informative biography of Max Weber and compelling excerpts from his major works, including a chapter devoted to his analysis of bureaucracies.

Grusky, Oscar, and George A. Miller (eds.). 1981. *The Sociology of Organizations.* New York: Free Press. Second edition. A book of sociological readings composed of theoretical essays and studies about formal organizations and bureaucracies.

Kanter, Rosabeth Moss. 1977. *Men and Women of the Corporation.* New York: Basic Books. Case-study research explaining why sexism persists in modern American corporations.

Krause, Elliot. 1980. *Why Study Sociology?* New York: Random House. A short, clearly written, thought-provoking book containing two chapters especially relevant to this chapter—one entitled "Understanding Relationships" and the other "Joining a Community."

Shkilnyk, Anastasia M. 1985. *A Poison Stronger than Love: The Destruction of an Ojibwa Community.* New Haven: Yale University Press. The moving account of how a forced move to a reservation and industrial waste in the local river combined to destroy a Native-American community.

## Student Projects

1. Interview three people, preferably of different ages, who have been residents of your community for at least five years. Ask them what significant changes thay have seen in their community, why they consider these changes significant, and whether they feel optimistic or pessimistic about the impact of the community changes. Then seek information about your community in a local newspaper. (Hint: At the end of the year, many newspapers contain sections reviewing the year's events.) Did your informants highlight the same changes as those discussed in the newspaper? Does what you learned about your own community correspond with information in the text? Discuss.

2. Keep a diary for a week which logs a) your formal activities at work and school and b) your social activities. At the end of the week, use your diary to answer the following questions:
   a. How much involvement in primary and secondary groups occurred? Was one type of involvement more rewarding than the other? Explain.

b. Did you experience any in-group/out-group tensions or hostilities? From what sources?

c. Did you obtain significant support from any reference group(s)?

d. Did your contact with bureaucracies suggest that they are efficient, inefficient, or both?

e. How often did you feel your activities were affected/controlled by others? Explain.

## Answers to Test Questions

**True–false test**

| | | | | |
|---|---|---|---|---|
| 1. t | 3. t | 5. f | 7. t | 9. f |
| 2. f | 4. f | 6. t | 8. f | 10. t |

**Multiple-choice test**

| | | | | |
|---|---|---|---|---|
| 1. c | 3. c | 5. b | 7. d | 9. b |
| 2. a | 4. d | 6. a | 8. d | 10. a |

# 5
# SOCIAL INTERACTION

Mothers have an important impact on their children. What about the mothers of prominent men? Has their influence been particularly significant? Some historical evidence suggests that it has been in a number of ways.

One way these mothers have apparently asserted their influence has been by developing their sons' self-confidence. The morning of his West Point examination, Douglas MacArthur's mother accompanied him as far as the door, where she gave him advice he never forgot:

> You must believe in yourself, my son, or no one else will believe in you. Be self-confident, self-reliant, and even if you don't make it, you will know you have done your best. Now go to it.
>
> *(McCullough, 1983: 34)*

MacArthur had a brilliant academic record at West Point and later became one of the most celebrated war heroes in the history of the United States.

Perhaps these mothers' most significant influence has been the sense of mission they have emphasized. Anna Wright, whose son Frank Lloyd became a famous architect, told him the following:

> You will find goodness and truth everywhere you go. If you have to choose, choose truth. For that is closest to Earth. Keep close to Earth, my boy: In that lies strength. Simplicity of heart is just as necessary to an architect as for a farmer or a minister if the architect is going to build great buildings.
>
> *(McCullough, 1983: 38)*

Whether it is the relationship between mothers and sons or a greeting as two people pass each other on the street, human contacts involve **social interaction**—the basic process through which two or more people use language and gestures to affect each other's thoughts, expectations, and behavior. Through social interaction people obtain the knowledge and skills that make them functioning members of society. Sometimes, as in the illustration of mothers and sons, one individual has more impact than another, but a mutual impact is nearly always possible. We can even affect our parents. An additional point about social interaction is that it is essential for all organized life. No social activity could take place in the political, educational, religious, economic, or familial structures without the process.

In this chapter we explore social interaction. The first section examines three important theories in this area. Next, the major components of social interaction are considered. The chapter concludes with an analysis of what happens when social-interaction patterns are disrupted.

# Theories of Social Interaction

This section discusses three theoretical perspectives that help explain social interaction: symbolic interaction, ethnomethodology, and dramaturgic sociology.

## Symbolic Interaction

**Symbolic interaction** is a theory that emphasizes the importance of symbolic communication — gestures and, above all, language — in the development of the individual, group, and society. A variety of research related to this theory has been produced. For instance, recent studies using the perspective of symbolic interaction have included investigations about the image of the self presented in North Yemeni wedding ceremonies (Caton, 1985), the influence of individual and peer-group characteristics on the development of juveniles' police records (Morash, 1984), and the effect of spouses' evaluations on research subjects' sense of self (Schafer and Keith, 1985).

As we noted in Chapter 3 ("Culture"), signs are objects or events that stand for something else. Many signs have fixed meanings. Smoke is a sign of fire; a blush is a sign of embarrassment. Symbols are signs with meanings not fixed by the nature of the items to which they are attached but by the agreement of people who use them to communicate. A language is a system of symbolic communication that uses words, which are sound patterns that have standardized meanings. (See Figure 5.1.)

To understand symbolic interaction, researchers must study unobservable activity—people's thoughts and feelings—as well as observable activity (Rochberg-Halton, 1982). For example, one might wonder whether telephone operators enjoy their work or feel dehumanized—trapped in an inhuman occupation. Investigators could observe operators working contentedly, but they probably would not reach a definite conclusion because operators are expected to be pleasant and always

**Figure 5.1**
**A Comparison of Signs and Symbols**

Signs have fixed meanings and fixed responses. When the telephone rings, people know that a caller is on the line, and they will generally pick up the receiver. Symbols, however, have neither fixed meanings nor fixed responses. A red light, for instance, can mean to stop one's car at an intersection, to recognize danger when a jammed valve is creating a buildup of pressure that will soon produce an explosion within a furnace, or to realize that one has entered a so-called "red-light district" where houses of prostitution are located. As the figure indicates, each meaning of a symbol requires a particular response.

"up" for their customers. Interviews can be revealing in such a situation. A study of 500 veteran operators concluded that most were satisfied with their jobs. Many liked the fact that their work is highly structured and uncomplicated. One operator explained, "There will be no surprises on my job today. I have the complete freedom of doing only what is required. All I have to do is pick up the headset and plug in and the calls will come" (Singular, 1983: 22).

*Social Setting*

The symbolic-interactionist theory emphasizes that only exposure to social interaction can make people capable of distinctly human conduct, such as the ability to use symbols or to imagine how others feel in given situations. In essence, we are not born human, but we become human as we engage in interaction and develop relationships with our fellow human beings.

Certainly some situations elicit more emotional involvement than others. With lovers, family members, or close friends, we are likely to exchange fuller, deeper explanations of feelings and actions than with other people.

At the other extreme are impersonal, work-related contacts. One might wonder how the setting of telephone operators' jobs affects their emotions and thoughts. Typically operators spend six-and-a-half hours a day standing or sitting in front of computer terminals. Through earphones they receive a constant stream of unknown voices—up to two calls a minute or about 800 a shift. A researcher concluded that veteran operators

. . . are extremely occupied by their work, but remember almost nothing of what has occurred afterwards. Operators have overlearned their jobs and function at the level of peripheral [minimal] awareness. The callers' information seems to pass from their ears to their hands without ever becoming part of a cognitive [thought] process.

One operator observed:

As the voices come into my mind, I just freeze the information in one part of my brain and hold it there. Then I pull it out whenever I need it. This allows me to distance myself from my work and ignore the fact that callers treat me like a rock.

*(Singular, 1983: 22)*

While the proponents of symbolic interaction emphasize the idea that people are influenced by their settings, they also observe that the use of language as a form of symbolic communication often makes it possible to alter situations that become undesirable or oppressive. Telephone operators, for instance, are usually unionized, and if some of their working conditions are unsatisfactory, they can seek to change them during negotiations for their next contract.

## Ethnomethodology

Two mothers are sipping coffee and talking. One turns to the other and says, "Carrie, I don't know what it is. You seem to have such an effortless time with your children."

"It's really pretty straightforward, Lucy," the other replies. "I have a set of simple rules, and come hell or high water I stick to them. The kids and I really understand each other."

Carrie seems to have some grasp of the ethnomethodological perspective. **Ethnomethodology** is the study of the sometimes recognized but often unrecognized social order, the set of underlying shared norms and expectations that promote harmony in most everyday social interaction. While one can consider ethnomethodology a form of symbolic interaction, this approach focuses on the process by which the social order develops and not on social interaction itself. Compared to symbolic interaction, ethnomethodology has received limited attention in sociology. Nonetheless, its perspective interests many sociologists, as a recent exchange of viewpoints about the quality of current research on the topic suggests (Bruce and Wallis, 1983; Sharrock and Watson, 1984).

Harold Garfinkel, a sociologist, has been the leading proponent of ethnomethodology. Garfinkel's studies emphasize that an effective way of grasping the significance of shared norms and expectations is to violate them. As people express their irritation, anger, or confusion in response to the violation, the functions performed by the underlying norms will become apparent.

In one informal study, Garfinkel asked undergraduate students to violate the "seen-but-unnoticed" set of shared understandings that existed in their families. Members were horrified. The students' reports were filled with accounts of anger, astonishment, bewilderment, anxiety, and embarrassment. Parents demanded explanations. What was wrong? Was the student sick? Had he or she flunked a test at school? Garfinkel wrote, "One student acutely embarrassed his mother in front of her friends by asking if she minded if he had a snack from the refrigerator. 'Mind if you have a little snack? You've been eating little snacks around here for years without asking me. What's gotten into you?'" (Garfinkel, 1967: 47–48). Eventually the students told their families what had been happening. Most were neither amused nor intrigued by the study. To them the underlying social order was not a subject of interest. The aroused emotions of family members demonstrated, however, that they became acutely concerned when there was a disruption of the established patterns.

Garfinkel's studies all involved contrived experimental situations. Under natural circumstances people may also find themselves facing challenges to the existing social order that reveal its unstated but nonetheless great significance. In the winter of 1846, the Donner Party, a group of travelers heading westward, was trapped by a blizzard in the Sierras. Slowly the party began starving to death. Just before he died, F. W. Graves urged his weeping, grief-stricken daughters to take any measure possible to keep themselves alive. With his last breaths, Graves insisted that the living use his flesh to sustain themselves. Soon the deed was done. An historian provided the following account, "The men finally mustered up courage to approach the dead. With averted eyes and trembling hand, pieces of flesh were severed from the inanimate forms and laid upon the coals. It was the very refinement of torture to taste such food, yet those who tasted lived." But the eating of human flesh was not the only horror of the situation. The historian explained:

> Although no person partook of kindred flesh, sights were often witnessed that were blood curdling. Mrs. Foster . . . fairly worshipped her brother Lemuel. Has human pen power to express the shock of horror this sister received when she saw her brother's heart thrust through with a stick, and boiling upon the coals?
>
> *(McGlashan, 1879: 69–70)*

It is obvious that cannibalism represents a serious violation of cultural standards. However, why this is true is not immediately self-evident. After all, few if any of us receive parental advice urging us to refrain from eating human flesh. However, we do encounter an unrelenting if often implicit emphasis on the spiritual value of human beings.

**98**    To eat people is to unspeakably violate underlying normative standards: to reduce human beings to something repulsively material. The woman who saw her brother's heart roasted and eaten was witnessing a prime symbol of love and emotion turned into mere food. Thus the survivors of the Donner Party faced a gruesome dilemma on the issue of social order. They could die, clearly violating the social order. On the other hand, they could stay alive by eating human flesh — an act that invariably defiled the social order by reducing human beings to nothing more than a source of protein.

## Dramaturgic Sociology

Laura and Hal had just arrived home from work. "How'd it go today, dear?" Hal asked.

"Well, I'm beginning to think that if I'm going to keep this job, I'd better get a plastic surgeon to carve a permanent smile on my face." With a weary sigh, she threw herself into a chair. "The problem is that I never get to really be myself."

As this exchange suggests, social interaction involves people acting out parts. **Dramaturgic sociology** is a theoretical approach that analyzes social interaction as if the participants were actors in a play. Erving Goffman (1959), the creator of this approach, suggested that actors perform their parts, follow the script most of the time, and im-

*The courtroom provides an interesting example of social interaction, which involves people acting out parts (and often improvising) on a fairly formal stage.*

provise whenever the script is unclear. People's daily performances are generally given in distinct settings. Rooms, furniture, food and drink, and so forth constitute props, the physical context of social interaction. Furthermore, as in an actual play, the setting tends to be immobile, and often the interaction cannot begin until the actors reach the setting. Even if all the people scheduled to participate in a meeting happened to gather by chance on the street a few minutes before the meeting was due to begin, they would probably not conduct their business right there. Customary procedures as well as efficiency would likely dictate that they head for the conference room.

Many performances are straightforward. Garage mechanics fix cars and dentists take care of teeth. Salespeople in clothing stores sell dresses, suits, shirts, socks, and underwear. But sometimes, Goffman emphasized, people's performances are deceptive, involving a form of activity that remains concealed from the public because of its incompatibility with a respectable, honest image. For instance, there is the cigar store or barber shop owner who secretly runs a bookie joint, or workers who routinely rob their employers by stealing tools, reselling food and other supplies, or traveling on company time. Another type of deceptive performance involves the concealment of errors and mistakes, a practice that provides the impression of infallibility so important in many performances. There is a well-known saying that doctors bury their mistakes. One of the discomforting features of a malpractice suit is its implication that doctors are not infallible.

### Frontstage versus Backstage

Like a theater performance, social interaction may be thought to have a frontstage and a backstage. The **frontstage** is the physical area or region where people present a performance. On the frontstage people are expected to maintain certain behavioral standards toward those with whom they interact: their audience. These standards fall roughly into two categories. One category involves the treatment of the audience; Goffman designated these standards "matters of politeness." Waiters or waitresses are supposed to be pleasant, respectful, and attentive when they wait on customers. The second category concerns performers' behavior when they are within visual or hearing range of the audience but not necessarily in direct communication; Goffman used the term "decorum" here. Often people within a given social context fail to appreciate the significance of standards of decorum until someone violates them. Most of us would readily accept the necessity of being quiet during a funeral service. The fact that this quiet signifies respect for the deceased and his or her family would strike us forcefully only if someone entered the service speaking in a loud, boisterous manner.

Unlike the frontstage, the backstage lies outside the audience's view. The **backstage** is the region where people construct the illusions and impressions they will use in a performance. Frequently the frontstage and backstage lie close to each other. This arrangement permits the performer to receive assistance from backstage if necessary and also allows him or her to spend brief periods of rest and relaxation in the back region, where members of the audience are unlikely to intrude. A waiter, for instance, passes through a swinging door into the kitchen, picks up "props"—the food and drink for customers—and then returns to the dining hall, which is the frontstage. In many restaurants, including the fanciest, it is essential that the audience—the customers—be kept out of the backstage, where they would probably discover conditions and practices that could destroy their appetites. George Orwell, who worked in the kitchens of many French restaurants, observed that most kitchens were insufferably dirty. The cook, he conceded,

> . . . is an artist, but his art is not cleanliness. To a certain extent he is even dirty because he is an artist, for food, to look smart, needs dirty treatment. When a steak, for instance, is brought up for the head cook's inspection, he does not handle it with a fork. He picks it up in his fingers and slaps it down, runs his thumb around the dish and licks it to taste the gravy, runs it round and licks again, then steps back and contemplates the piece of meat like an artist, judging a picture, then presses it lovingly into place with his fat, pink fingers, every one of which he has licked a hundred times that morning.
>
> *(Orwell, 1959: 59)*

Orwell believed that the less expensive the restaurant, the less thorough the cook's care and thus the more hygienic the preparation of food.

As people move from backstage to frontstage, they engage in **impression management:** the attempt to control others' evaluations by presenting themselves in the most favorable light. In some instances impression management is relatively easy, especially when we can anticipate others' reactions and can visualize a way to behave that will be mutually acceptable to everyone involved. However, in other situations the appropriate style of presentation is not readily apparent or is difficult to execute. Sometimes performers must be simultaneously concerned with impression management and with the effective maintenance of valued relationships. For instance, chief surgeons are likely to make joking comments if subordinates commit minor mistakes during operations. Such observations reflect well on the surgeons—clearly they retain a definite yet relaxed control over their team—and at the same time they ease the tension among team members anticipating punishment for their mistakes (Goffman, 1961: 122).

## Commentary

We have examined three perspectives on social interaction. The symbolic-interactionist approach emphasizes the significance of symbolic communi-

**Table 5.1**
**Three Theories of Social Interaction**

| THEORY | VIEW OF HUMAN BEHAVIOR | EXAMPLE |
|---|---|---|
| Symbolic interaction | Communication process supplies meaning, and people's actions reflect their interpretation of that meaning. | The highly impersonal communication process telephone operators engage in encourages limited emotional involvement in their work. |
| Ethnomethololology | An often unrecognized social order underlies everyday social activity. | Through informal research Garfinkel's students discovered some shared understandings that existed in their families. |
| Dramaturgic sociology | The participants in social interaction behave like actors in a play. | When interviewed for a job, an effective candidate will engage in impression management. |

cation in social situations. Ethnomethodology focuses on the part played by the underlying social order. Finally dramaturgic sociology analyzes social interaction as if the participants are actors in a play. None of these three theories can claim to be inherently superior to the others. Sometimes one perspective might seem more effective for examin-

ing a given social interaction. Often a sociologist chooses a particular approach because he or she simply favors it, feeling that the issues it emphasizes are more interesting and thought provoking than those raised by the other perspectives. (See Table 5.1.)

## Structuring of Social Interaction

The theoretical perspectives discussed in the previous section indicate that social interaction uses symbolic communication, that it contains an underlying social order, and that social interaction can be analyzed like the action of a play. In each case the theory reveals certain patterns that occur in social interaction. If we examine such concepts as status and role, leadership, conformity, and decision-making, other patterns will become apparent, and our understanding of social interaction will increase.

**Figure 5.2**
**Statuses and Roles**

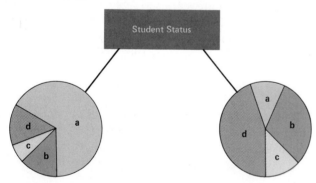

Jan's Proportion of Time in Different Student Roles

Jill's Proportion of Time in Different Student Roles

"a" represents time doing schoolwork (studying, attending classes, speaking to professors, etc.).
"b" is time at work to pay for schooling and basic expenses.
"c" stands for extra-curricular activities (school clubs, athletic teams, etc.).
"d" represents social activities.

*These two students differ profoundly in their interpretation of their student status. Knowledge of their respective priorities permits some predictions about role strains. Jill, for instance, would be much more likely to interrupt studying to socialize with her friends. The resolutions to role conflicts would be difficult to predict without more knowledge of the women. For instance, how would a conscientious student like Jan respond to the pressing needs of a sick relative at exam time?*

### Status and Role

Imagine that two twenty-year-old women—Jan and Jill—meet at a bus station. Both are on the way home from college for the spring break, and soon they are talking about their school experience. Jan has been studying over fifty hours a week ever since her freshman year. "It's the only way I can keep a high average," she explains. Jill, in contrast, is relaxed about her grades and spends a lot of time socializing, drinking, and going to parties, "We're certainly having a very different time at college," Jan says.

These two women occupy a common status: that of college student. A **status** is a position that indicates where a person fits into a group or society and how he or she should relate to others in the structure. Any particular status stands in a definite relationship to other statuses because of the rights and obligations associated with it. As college students, both Jan and Jill have the right to take courses for credit, and they are expected to pay for their schooling and to complete their assignments.

Whereas both Jan and Jill occupy the status of student, they perform the role of student differently. A **role** is a set of expected behaviors associated with a particular status. Several roles may be "attached" to one status. An individual occupying the status of student may emphasize academic performance; extracurricular activities such as student government, clubs, and athletics; or social life, particularly parties and friendships. As Figure 5.2 indicates, Jan and Jill visualize the student status differently. Jan concentrates on the academic role while Jill's chief concern is the partying role.

In modern societies people play many roles, and often two roles played by an individual will clash. **Role strain** is an incompatibility between two or more roles associated with the same status. For example, students experience role strain when they must decide whether to study for a test or go to a party.

**Role conflict** refers to incompatibility between two or more roles associated with different statuses. For instance, a man may have the statuses of husband and businessman. In the role of husband, he recognizes that he should be concerned about his wife's happiness—he knows that she is attached to the town they live in—and thus, as a husband, the man wants to remain in town. In the role of businessman, however, he receives an offer for a better-paying, more prestigious job with a company in another state, and so as a businessman he wants to leave town. Therefore this man's two role expectations are in direct conflict, and the decision on what to do will mean that either as a husband or as a businessman he will fail to meet the expectation.

In recent years there has been a large body of research developing on one topic involving role conflicts. What is the topic? Keep in mind that a rapid growth in social research tends to reflect events within the society. Have you got the answer? . . . The subject is the role conflicts faced by modern adults, who must meet the often conflicting demands on their time and energy made by family members and work obligations. The majority of studies focus on role conflicts of working women with children (for instance, Barnett and Baruch, 1985; Burden, 1986; Elman and Gilbert, 1984; Houseknect, Vaughan, and Macke, 1984), but some investigations examine the role conflicts both women and men face in reconciling the demands of family and job (for example, Kelly and Voydanoff, 1985; Regan and Roland, 1985).

Besides the problems produced by role strain and role conflict, people can end up in situations where they are compelled to fill roles they do not want to perform. As the following Contemporary Issue indicates, such a circumstance can encourage disruptive behavior.

## CONTEMPORARY ISSUE

## *The Evacuation of 400 Mental Patients*

We have just discussed statuses and roles. We have considered the fact that often individuals in the same status will perform a role differently. In addition, it should be noted that changing circumstances sometimes encourage or even compel people to alter the way they perform their roles. In this box we will see how these two conclusions about roles apply to a situation where patients were evacuated from one mental hospital to another and then later returned to the original hospital.

During the autumn of 1968, I accompanied a group of mental-health personnel and 400 mental patients from a state-run mental hospital near New York City to a facility 400 miles away, directly south of Buffalo. The pa-

tients were moved in anticipation of a strike of nonprofessional staff workers. Two weeks later, when it was clear there would be no strike, the patients were returned to the original hospital. In both cases the stage was the same—a train—but the attendants and the mood of many of the patients differed on the two trips. As a result the role performances were distinctly different.

On the trip westward, the attendants had been flown in from Holzlein Hospital, the receiving facility. Most of these people came from the town of Holzlein. There was a waiting list of people who wanted to become attendants at the hospital. The workers with whom I spoke valued their jobs, especially those working in units for the reha-

bilitation of long-term patients. The flight to New York City and the chance to take a tour of the city were a boost to the morale of the Holzlein attendants. Many had never been so far from home before. The train trip to Holzlein took about nine hours, and the attendants were kept busy, feeding the patients, providing medication, and helping the less agile to the bathroom. Yet even though they worked hard, most kept a positive frame of mind. The older attendants seemed pleased to see the younger, less experienced members of their units working efficiently.

On the trip to Holzlein Hospital, I was able to spend several hours walking through the cars and talking with the attendants and patients. None of the patients seemed negative about being moved, and some were definitely positive. The following comment from a young male patient was almost joyful: "This is great! I've been in Benedict for five years, and I've never been more than about thirty miles from the city. I'm really enjoying myself!"

Two weeks later the trip back to Benedict was an entirely different matter. This time the attendants came from Benedict, and they were quite unlike their counterparts on the trip out. The Benedict staff members were residents of the New York City area. In contrast to the Holzlein attendants, they seemed to take little pride in their jobs; the position of nonprofessional mental-health worker offered relatively low pay and prestige in a major metropolitan context. During an orientation meeting shortly before the return trip, there were indications that difficulties would develop. Several times a speaker had to rap on the table to quiet the attendants. One individual, in particular, had been drinking heavily and made loud, hostile comments throughout the meeting.

Once the train had departed, it became clear that the Benedict attendants would not perform their roles in the same pleasant, disciplined manner as their Holzlein counterparts. The

Benedict attendants frequently visited friends in other cars, leaving their patients unsupervised. They also slept and drank while on duty. The care they provided patients was minimal and often hostile. Some attendants played manipulative games with the patients. At one point, for instance, the attendants were distributing soup. As each patient's name was called, he rose from his seat and came forward. One man, anticipating that he would be called next, started to stand up. An attendant shouted: "Hey you son-of-a-bitch, get your fat ass down 'til I call you!" Then about five seconds later: "Now come up!"

In addition to the Benedict attendants' behavior, the patients' role performances helped make the return trip substantially different. Many of the patients enjoyed their two weeks at the Holzlein Hospital. The atmosphere there was relatively relaxed and pleasant. Some of the Benedict patients had formed new and meaningful ties with local patients, and they did not want to leave. A number of patients who had been optimistic and hopeful on the trip out were sullen or depressed on the way back. With their attendants frequently asleep, drunk, or absent, many of the patients were free to roam as they chose. And many did, sometimes moving from one car to the next. To make matters

worse, the train had to detour around a derailment, and the return trip took nearly fifteen hours compared to nine on the way out.

Both trips were under the leadership of the same nurse, who had been dispatched from the Department of Mental Hygiene headquarters in Albany. On the trip out, he had proudly explained his system of "loose centralization"—he would remain in a central car from which he would issue orders to attendants who would direct operations in the individual cars. On the return trip, this man's confidence visibly faded. He spoke less, appeared tense, and kept looking at his watch. When one of his associates burst into the car shouting that two attendants three cars back were making love—and this was scarcely an exaggeration—the head nurse threw his arms in the air and sighed loudly. Obviously "loose centralization" was not working well on the return trip.

Years later I'm still struck with how very different the two trips were. The two principal reasons for the difference seems related to the topic of roles: The two sets of attendants had entirely dissimilar conceptions of their roles; in addition, because of their attendants' neglect and hostility as well as other depressing conditions about the return trip, many patients performed their roles quite differently on the way back.

Source: Christopher Bates Doob. "An Evacuation of 400 Mental Patients: Implications for Continuity and Change." *Journal of Health and Social Behavior.* Vol. 10. September 1969, pp. 218–224.

## Leadership

A man pridefully watches his son playing with a group of other children in his backyard. His wife walks over, and he puts his arm around her. "That kid of ours, Judy, is giving orders like a shop foreman. He's one heck of a leader. You know what I think? I think some day Pete's going to be president." Like many people, Pete's father apparently believes that leadership is simply the ability to issue commands. As we will see, research has indicated that leadership is more complicated than that.

**Leadership** is the exercise of influence or authority within a group by one or more members.

The study of leaders and their effectiveness has been part of an on-going sociological investigation of the problem-solving activities of groups (Frost, Fiedler, and Anderson, 1983; Smircich and Morgan, 1982). Since early in the twentieth century, researchers have recognized that activities seem to follow a systematic pattern or, at any rate, that problem solving might be simplified if they did. In spite of this early interest, a thorough effort to map out small-group activities did not begin until after World War II. In the late 1940s, Robert Bales and his associates (Bales, 1953; Bales and Strodtbeck, 1968) set out to analyze all the basic types of interpersonal relations that occur in small groups.

*As the group therapy session below indicates, some group settings encourage role performances that are emotional and spontaneous, while in others, such as this business meeting, members' role performances are more structured and controlled emotionally and most likely follow a formal agenda.*

Bales studied twenty-two small groups involved in a wide variety of tasks, and he identified twelve types of communication that occurred in these groups. Six of these types are **instrumental,** intended to promote the pursuit of group goals. The other six types of communication are **expressive,** concerned with emotional or social issues. Expressive communications frequently are meant to restore the harmony disrupted in the pursuit of group goals. If a group is to function effectively, the competent performance of both types of tasks is essential. Laboratory studies indicate, however, that a single person seldom provides both expressive and instrumental leadership in a group (Bales and Slater, 1955). The skills required of each type of leader are different, and furthermore the considerable time and energy that must be devoted to providing one type of leadership often precludes actively pursuing the other type of leadership.

Small-group researchers have also assessed the consequences of different styles of leadership. One investigator studied the behavior of groups of boys subjected to three different adult leadership styles. **Authoritarian leaders** controlled all aspects of group activity yet stayed somewhat aloof from the group. **Democratic leaders** permitted group members to determine many policies and took an active role in discussions. In contrast, **laissez-faire leaders** left group members free to reach their own individual or group decisions. The research showed that:

Authoritarian leadership tended to be ineffective because the group members became bogged down in internal conflicts.

Democratic leadership proved to be efficient. The quality of work in democratically led groups was better than that performed by groups with authoritarian leadership, and work motivation was stronger in a democratically led group than in an authoritarian setting. In addition, originality was more common, and greater group-mindedness and friendliness prevailed.

Under laissez-faire leadership, the group members did less work, and the quality of the work accomplished was poorer than was the case in democratic contexts. More time was spent playing.

In any particular situation, a number of factors are likely to influence the effectiveness of a particular style of leadership. Among the relevant factors are:

*The followers' opinion of the leader.* If group members like and trust the leader, then compliance is likely.

*The amount of power invested in the leadership position.* If a leader has indisputable power in a group situation, then followers are likely to obey that person, whether or not he or she is popular with followers.

*The task involved.* If the task is an activity that seems understandable and reasonable to the participants, then they will probably try to accomplish it (Fiedler, 1967).

If all three factors are positive, then leadership is likely to be effective. If a popular, respected army captain receives an order from the general calling for a practice maneuver that the company has performed many times, the captain is likely to obtain the whole-hearted support of the troops. On the other hand, if an untrustworthy business executive who is likely to be dismissed according to rumor undertakes a vague project that none of the associates can really understand, the executive probably will not receive much support from subordinates.

An interesting problem involves the challenge of supplying leadership to groups that are largely self-managed. A study of self-managed work groups within a production plant has indicated that there is a fine line between over direction and under direction. So-called "unleaders" tend to be most effective when they have well-developed social skills and act as counselors or communication facilators. Frequently such people refuse to provide answers themselves; instead they ask reflective questions, throwing the burden of decision-making back on the group itself (Manz and Sims, 1984).

The following Cross-Cultural Perspective demonstrates that personal circumstances in people's lives can significantly influence their behavior as leaders.

**CROSS-CULTURAL PERSPECTIVE**

*Malcolm X's Revelation concerning Whites*

The discussion of leadership has emphasized that leaders differ in their priorities and approaches. But we have not considered why leaders choose to behave as they do. As this box suggests, the behavior might be traced to specific influences in the person's background. And if a significant new influence enters the leader's life, then, in turn, that individual's behavior might change.

The subject is Malcolm X, a prominent civil-rights leader. During the first half of his life, Malcolm X's contacts and relationships with whites were overwhelmingly negative. When he was six years old, his father was killed by the members of a white mob. As an adolescent living in Boston and New York City and holding a variety of underworld jobs, he encountered whites who were hustlers, prostitutes, gangsters, hard-drug users, or so-called "respectable middle-class citizens" looking for prostitutes or some other form of vice. In his late teens, Malcolm formed a robbery ring with two white women and a black male friend. Eventually they were caught, and even though all four were equally involved in the crimes, the white women received more lenient sentences than the black men.

Finally, while in prison, Malcolm joined the Nation of Islam, often known as the "Black Muslims." This organization, which has maintained loose ties with the Islamic faith headquartered in Saudi Arabia, taught that all whites are inherently weak and evil and that blacks' best course of action is to physically separate themselves from whites and form a separate nation. When he was converted, Malcolm completely accepted the Nation of Islam's understanding of whites. Clearly he found such conclusions consistent with his own experience. Upon his release from prison, Malcolm dedicated his considerable energy and intelligence to the Muslim cause. As a minister he gave powerful, fiery sermons about the evils of whites. Large crowds came to hear the young speaker, and people joined the Nation of Islam in record numbers.

But then, in the course of his ministry, Malcolm took a trip to the holy city of Islam—Mecca. He was overwhelmed by what he saw and experienced there. His fellow pilgrims came from all over the world, and they were people of different colors. They all participated in the same rituals and displayed a unity of understanding and purpose that Malcolm's experiences in America had led him to believe whites and blacks could never share. To Malcolm X this was a revelation. A letter he wrote at the time records his sentiments:

> During the past eleven days here in the Muslim world, I have eaten from the same plate, drunk from the same glass, and slept in the same bed (or on the same rug)—while praying to the same God—with fellow Muslims, whose eyes were the bluest of blue, whose hair was the blondest of blond, and whose skin was the whitest of white. And in the words and in the actions and in the deeds of the "white" Muslims, I felt the same security that I felt among the black African Muslims of Nigeria, Sudan, and Ghana.
>
> *(Malcolm X, 1965: 345)*

Malcolm recognized that it was necessary to change some of his beliefs. Whites were not inherently evil. If they were willing to forsake racist attitudes and behavior, the possibility of unified action and even brotherhood among blacks and whites did exist.

Years later Malcolm recalled a time before his Mecca trip when a white woman had flown to New York City to see him. She approached him in a Harlem restaurant, and asked with deep concern what she could do to improve America's racial problems. Malcolm was struck by the force of her appeal, but at the time he believed that all whites were evil, and so he told her that there was nothing she could do. Recalling the incident, he regretted not having her name and address. He would have told her that sincere whites and blacks could work together but that the whites should not try to prove that they supported blacks by working directly with them. Blacks needed to develop their options independently. Whites should go back to their home communities and try to explain the evils of racism to their friends and neighbors.

In the final months of his life, Malcolm X tried to convey to both black and white audiences the need to work together and yet separately —an idea that almost immediately had a profound effect on the civil-rights movement.

Source: Malcolm X. *The Autobiography of Malcolm X.* New York: Grove Press. 1965.

## Conformity

**Conformity** is an individual's behavior in line with the relevant social norms. Society could not survive without considerable conformity, and yet excessive conformity suggests mindlessness, an inability to think and act on one's own. In Hans Christian Andersen's fairy tale "The Emperor's New Clothes," all the subjects watching the king were excessive conformists, acting in line with the official norm that their ruler was wearing beautiful new clothes even though he was actually naked. Finally a little girl commented loudly that the king was wearing nothing. As soon as the little girl had spoken, her father said, "Just hear what the innocent says." Quickly the word spread through the crowd of conformists that the king was indeed naked.

A wide range of research has been conducted on the topic of conformity. Recent studies have demonstrated that conformity prevails in Christmas gift giving in a midwestern city (Caplow, 1984), in informants' judgments about the fashionability of women's clothing (Davis, 1984), and in interpersonal relations among management personnel at a telephone company (Feldman, 1985). The Asch experiments are among the best known investigations of conformity.

### The Asch Experiments

Some years ago Solomon Asch (1963), a social psychologist, devised an experiment to explore how group pressure affects judgment. The original study featured a control group and an experimental group. In the control situation, people sat in a room without talking and examined two set of cards. As Figure 5.3 indicates, there was one line on the card on the left, and the card on the right held three lines, only one of which exactly matched the length of the line on the first card. Each person recorded the number of the line on the second card that seemed to be the same length as the line on the first card. Altogether there were twelve sets of cards, and in each case there was one obvious match between the single line on the first card and the three lines on the second. Virtually no mistakes were made, indicating that normally people had no difficulty accomplishing this task.

In the experimental group, there were eight men. Seven of them were "confederates," who had met previously with the experimenter, who had instructed them to respond at certain points with unanimous, incorrect judgments. The eighth person, the so-called "naive" subject, who confronted this unanimous majority, was the real focus. Asch wrote, "He faced, possibly for the first time in his life, a situation in which a group unanimously con-

**Figure 5.3**
**A Sample Comparison of Lines in the Asch Experiment**

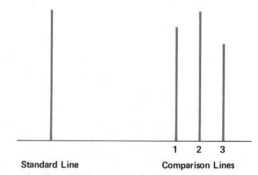

Standard Line          Comparison Lines

*Control subjects made correct matchings over 99 percent of the time. Experimental subjects conformed to incorrect matchings one-third of the time when faced with the unanimous incorrect matchings of seven confederates. (Source: Solomon E. Asch.* Social Psychology. *Englewood Cliffs, NJ: Prentice-Hall. 1952, p. 452.)*

tradicted the evidence of his senses" (Asch, 1963: 179).

The results from the experimental group were very different from those that emerged from the control group. In the experimental context, one-third of the total number of matchings made were factually incorrect but conformed to the prearranged stated judgment of the confederates.

Variations in the experimental setup produced different results. When there were two naive subjects, the incidence of conformity to the group opinion dropped sharply. If, however, this "true partner" suddenly stopped giving accurate answers and sided with the majority, then the incidence of conformity rose to 28.5 percent, nearly as high as in the original experiment. Asch also varied the group size of "confederates." When there was only one person who had been instructed to give incorrect answers, conforming responses by the naive subjects practically disappeared. With two confederates 12.8 percent of the naive subjects' responses were conforming. Conformity rose to the one-third level when there was a majority of three opposing the naive subject. Larger groups of confederates (four, eight, and sixteen) did not significantly increase the level of conformity.

Recent experiments have tried to refine Asch's results. For instance, in experiments similar to those conducted by Asch, Jennings and George (1984) sought to determine the extent to which the distortion of judgment produced by group influence was conscious or unconscious. They found that conscious distortion of judgment occurred four to five times more frequently than unconscious distortion. Since the research subjects were aware of their incorrect judgments, it can be assumed that they felt that it was more important to support the group judgment than to be correct.

### Commentary on Conformity

While some of us are probably disturbed by the mindlessness often accompanying conformity, conforming behavior generally does not arouse strong reactions until cases are revealed in which people felt compelled to obey orders to commit brutal acts. If a person is already inclined to commit such acts, then the support of authority figures simply makes such behavior easier, as the following illustration suggests. In January 1942 Adolph Eichmann, head of the Jewish Office in the German Secret Police (Gestapo), met with a group of top-level Nazi civil servants to coordinate efforts to the Final Solution, Hitler's plan to exterminate the Jews of Europe. Eichmann still had some doubts about "such a bloody solution through violence," but when he observed this group of elite civil servants competing with each other to take the initiative in the genocidal effort, he felt freed of guilt. As Eichmann told the court at his trial in Jerusalem, he not only obeyed orders but was also following the new law of the land (Berkowitz, 1980: 316–317). We well might wonder whether the members of modern societies can eventually eliminate the conditions producing Eichmanns.

## Decision-Making

There is an old saying that two heads are better than one. This proverb is certainly valid if the "two heads" are trying to make a decision that can be based on factual knowledge. For instance, a team of people will do better at a crossword puzzle than will a single individual. Similarly a clinic that employs a variety of medical specialists is likely to be better equipped than a single physician to diagnose and treat a wide range of illnesses.

In other situations it is less clear whether an individual or a group will make better decisions. One researcher first asked individual subjects to reach decisions on hypothetical problems and then combined the individuals into groups and instructed them to reach group decisions. The latter decisions often displayed a "risky shift," a move toward a more daring course of action (Stoner, 1961). One reason this occurred is that a group decision diffuses responsibility among the members, particularly if the decision turns out to be bad.

The vast literature on this topic includes recent studies on decision-making in the evaluation of medical technologies (Vinokur et al, 1985), grocery shopping (Murtaugh, 1984), and major life issues (Sloan, 1983). A number of factors affect group decision-making. Among them are:

*Members' personality characteristics.* More extroverted, dominant, and socially aggressive people are likely to control discussion and generally will have the lion's share of influence on the decisions reached.

*Prior commitments.* People who join a group with a particular solution in mind usually will argue forcibly in favor of their position and will firmly oppose alternative decisions.

*Group composition.* The more varied the available perspectives on a problem, the most likely that a high-quality solution will emerge. When group members encompass a diversity of personalities, leadership abilities, and points of view, their decisions are generally more creative and innovative than those that emerge from groups whose members have similar characteristics. However, different viewpoints can create strain, and when group members become openly antagonistic, they cannot fully capitalize on their diversity.

*Interpersonal relationships.* Positive feelings among group members increase people's sense of security, making them more willing to risk unusual solutions. In contrast, group members' loss of positive feelings about each other tends to block or distort their communication (Hoffman, 1979).

## Disruption of Patterns of Social Interaction

In the last two sections, we examined theories and concepts that demonstrate how the social-interaction process works. These analyses have emphasized the central role played by social interaction in human relations. Further support for that conclusion becomes apparent if we examine situations where there is a breakdown in the normal social-interaction patterns. The absence of such patterns will suggest their importance in maintaining people's sense of well-being.

Frequently people experience stress when isolated. Research indicates that there are several stages isolated people are likely to pass through (Schachter, 1959). In the beginning these people often experience full-blown anxiety attacks that increase with time and then decrease sharply in many cases. As the sense of isolation diminishes, there is apathy or even withdrawal and detachment. Finally the isolated individual may dream or even hallucinate about other people.

Many human beings are highly adaptive in a solitary condition. A small number of hearty individuals have sailed alone around the world, in small boats, apparently without suffering significant psychological damage. Admiral Richard Byrd, an experienced polar explorer, spent the entire winter of 1933 completely alone in his camp in Little America. Such people have been able to withstand their isolation because they have had activities to keep busy. Individuals in situations of forced isolation seem to do better when they invent tasks for themselves such as solving puzzles, reciting poetry, or performing exercises.

Patterns of social interaction are also disrupted when communities disintegrate because of such factors as disasters, widespread ill health, poverty, and rapid technological change. Various alternatives confront people: They can leave, rebuilding their lives elsewhere; they can stay, deciding that in spite of the disruptions, the possibility of rebuilding their community and reestablishing effective patterns of social interaction definitely exists; or they can stay because they no longer possess the will to take active steps on their own behalf.

Major disasters can produce the third reaction for many people. A number of years ago in a mining district in West Virginia, a large dam broke,

*As painfully suggested by this photo of flood victims outside their home, major disasters affect more than people's physical well-being.*

flooding a vast area and causing widespread death and destruction. When a sociologist interviewed survivors, he found that many were severely disoriented. One woman explained, "I feel that the disaster has affected almost everyone on Buffalo Creek emotionally. People have no sense of belonging anywhere. There are no existing community identities left, only desolation and indecision. People are not sure yet of what to do or where to turn" (Erikson, 1976: 214).

Totalitarian governments can also disrupt patterns of social interaction. During the Nazi period, nonparticipants and victims reacted in a number of ways to the events of the era.

Many average citizens were shocked by the persecution, mass torture, and murder of millions of Jews and other victims of the Third Reich. Both during and after World War II, many Germans found that the most expedient course of action was to avoid talking and, if possible, thinking about this dreaded subject. In some cases people's ability to avoid the topic was so well developed that they were simply unable to maintain their concentration whenever it arose in conversation (Hughes, 1968).

Under Hitler's rule life had become a nightmare for Jews. They were deprived of all civil rights, including the right to retain personal property, to be employed, to practice a profession, or to enter restaurants, cafés, bathing beaches, or public parks. They could expect to receive the foulest, most vicious insults or to suffer arrest. In Vienna many Jews spoke of committing suicide with no more emotion than discussing an hour's journey by train. Sometimes killing themselves seemed easier than living in a situation in which normal social interaction patterns had been shattered (Gedye, 1939).

Within Nazi concentration camps, inmates made significant adjustments in their outlook and behavior. Bruno Bettelheim, a psychologist and Nazi-concentration-camp survivor, noted that prisoners had made the ultimate surrender to camp life as soon as they accepted the Gestapo guards' values as their own and imitated their behavior. Many old prisoners would mistreat and even torture newcomers, appropriate any available patches of Gestapo uniforms and sew them on their own, and adopt guards' anti-Semitic sentiments, even if they were Jewish themselves (Bettelheim, 1958).

Yet even in concentration camps, some opportunities arose to elevate people's spirits, making them feel better about themselves and about the circumstances in which they lived. Viktor Frankl, a psychiatrist, was interned in a Nazi concentration camp during World War II. At a moment when the situation was particularly desperate and the prisoners' morale especially low, the lights in the compound went out. The block warden called on Frankl to provide some psychological counseling. Cold, hungry, irritable, and tired as he was, Frankl nonetheless realized that if he failed to say something helpful, many men were likely to commit suicide. Therefore he started by explaining that their situation was far from the most terrible imaginable. As long as they remained alive, health, family, happiness, professional standing, and social position could be restored. He told his companions that human life never ceases to have meaning and that it includes suffering, privation, and death. Frankl also spoke about sacrifice and its meaning. In the course of his speech, he established intense social interaction with his listeners that reminded them that love, hope, and other positive qualities had not disappaeared from the earth. Frankl wrote, "When the electric bulb flared up again, I saw the miserable figures of my friends limping toward me to thank me with tears in their eyes" (Frankl, 1959: 84).

# STUDY GUIDE

## Summary

1. Social interaction is the basic process through which two or more people use language and gestures to affect each other's thoughts, expectations, and behavior. Social interaction provides the foundation of people's development.

2. Theories of social interaction include symbolic interaction, ethnomethodology, and dramaturgic sociology. Symbolic interaction is a theory that emphasizes the importance of symbolic communication — gestures and, above all, language —

in the development of the individual, group, and society. To understand symbolic interaction, researchers must study unobservable as well as observable activity.

Ethnomethodology is the study of the sometimes recognized, often unrecognized social order. Harold Garfinkel's informal experiments have supplied the pioneer research in this theoretical area.

Dramaturgic sociology is a theoretical approach that analyzes social interaction as if the participants were actors in a play. The actors perform their parts, follow the script if possible, and improvise whenever the script is unclear or nonexistent. Dramaturgic sociology emphasizes that like a theater performance, social interaction involves a frontstage and a backstage. Performers also engage in impression management: an attempt to control other people's evaluations of them by presenting themselves in the most favorable manner.

3. Concepts that play a significant part in social interaction include status and role, leadership, conformity, and decision-making. A status is a position that indicates where a person fits into a group or society and how he or she should relate to others in the structure. A role is a set of expected behaviors associated with a particular status. Role strains and role conflicts also influence group activities.

Leadership is another important component of the social interaction process. Studies of leadership demonstrate that two broad sets of leadership tasks exist: the instrumental and the expressive; and that different kinds of leadership develop: the democratic, authoritarian, and laissez-faire varieties.

In examining social interaction, some researchers have studied conformity, an individual's behavior in line with the relevant social norms. The well-known Asch experiments have demonstrated how group pressure affects judgment.

Decision-making is another prominent social-interaction process. Factors affecting group decision-making include members' personality characteristics, their prior commitments, the group composition, and members' interpersonal relations.

4. Disruption of social-interaction patterns can profoundly affect people's lives. When people are experiencing the stress of being alone, of living in a destroyed community, or of surviving within a totalitarian setting, their behavior will demonstrate a number of different adjustments.

## Glossary

**authoritarian leader**　a leader who controls all aspects of group activity yet stays somewhat aloof from the group.

**backstage**　the region where people construct the illusions and impressions they will use in a performance.

**conformity**　an individual's behavior in line with the relevant social norms.

**democratic leader**　a leader who permits group members to determine many policies and takes an active role in discussion.

**dramaturgic sociology**　a theoretical approach that analyzes social interaction as if the participants were actors in a play.

**ethnomethodology**　the study of the sometimes recognized, often unrecognized social order, the set of underlying shared norms and expectations that promote harmony in most everyday social interaction.

**expressive**　concerned with emotional or social issues.

**frontstage**　the physical area or region where people present a performance.

**impression management**　the attempt to control others' evaluations by presenting oneself in the most favorable light.

**instrumental**　intended to promote the pursuit of group goals.

**laissez-faire leader**　a leader who does not take an active role in group discussions, leaving group members free to reach individual or group decisions.

**leadership**　the exercise of influence or authority within a group by one or more members.

**role**　a set of expected behaviors associated with a particular status.

**role conflict**　an incompatibility between two or more roles associated with different statuses.

**role strain**　an incompatibility between two or more roles associated with the same status.

**social interaction**　the basic process through which two or more people use language and gestures to affect each other's thoughts, expectations, and behavior.

**status**   a position that indicates where a person fits into a group or society and how that person should relate to others in the structure.

**symbolic interaction**   a theory that emphasizes the dominant part played by symbolic communication—gestures and, above all, language—in the development of the individual, group, and society.

## Learning Objectives

After studying this chapter, you should be able to:

1. Define social interaction and discuss its significance in people's lives.
2. Discuss symbolic interaction, ethnomethodology, and dramaturgic sociology, defining each theory and offering clear, detailed examples of all three.
3. Define status and role, distinguishing between the two concepts by using clear illustrations.
4. Discuss role strain and role conflict, clarifying their differences and providing an example of each.
5. Define leadership, examine the leadership styles of authoritarian, democratic, and laissez-faire leaders, and identify the factors determining leadership effectiveness.
6. Analyze conformity, defining the concept and summarizing the major findings of the Asch experiments.
7. Examine the factors that affect group decision-making.
8. Indicate how social-interaction patterns may become disrupted and how people may react or adapt to such disruption.

## Tests

### True-false test

_____ 1. Researchers using the symbolic-interactionist theory study both observable and unobservable activity.

_____ 2. Garfinkel's ethnomethodological study of his students' families showed that to most family members, the underlying social order was not an interesting subject.

_____ 3. According to the dramaturgic sociological perspective, frontstage and backstage areas often lie close together, allowing performers to receive assistance from backstage.

_____ 4. Several statuses may be "attached" to one role.

_____ 5. In a role-conflict situation, the fulfillment of one role expectation means that another role expectation will not be met.

_____ 6. In recent years there has been almost no research done on role conflicts.

_____ 7. Instrumental leaders are concerned with emotional or social issues.

_____ 8. Laissez-faire leaders discourage group members from making their own decisions.

_____ 9. In the Asch experiments that explored how group pressure affects judgment, the behavior in the experimental group was sometimes very different from the behavior in the control group.

_____ 10. Bettleheim reported that prisoners had made their final adjustment to Nazi concentration camps when they accepted Gestapo guards' values as their own and imitated the guards' behavior.

**Multiple-choice test**

_____ 1. A study of telephone operators:
   a. found that most of the informants were unhappy with their jobs.
   b. concluded that most operators are occupied by their work but remember little after talking to customers.
   c. made it clear that social setting has little impact on people's job performances.
   d. a and b

_____ 2. The Donner party described in the text faced a challenge to the social order when its members had to choose between death or survival by committing:
   a. war atrocities.
   b. cannibalism.
   c. violations against animals they worshipped.
   d. incest.

_____ 3. Using a dramaturgic sociological perspective, Goffman suggested that the performances people give are:
   a. independent of the social setting.
   b. only done in the backstage.
   c. always done without impression management.
   d. sometimes based on deception.

_____ 4. An incompatibility between two or more roles associated with the *same* status is a:
   a. role conflict.
   b. role strain.
   c. anticipatory status.
   d. conformity conflict.

_____ 5. Bales and Slater studied communication in task-oriented groups. They found that:
   a. instrumental and expressive leadership skills are similar.
   b. the typical leader has well-developed instrumental and expressive skills.
   c. only very nervous people have instrumental skills.
   d. effective performance of both instrumental and expressive tasks is necessary for a group to function effectively.

_____ 6. According to the text, all but one of the following conditions contributes to a leader's effectiveness. Which factor is NOT included?
   a. the leader's power
   b. followers' opinion of the leader
   c. the leader's attractiveness
   d. the task involved

_____ 7. Jennings and George's recent experiments, which sought to refine Asch's research on conformity, found that:
   a. surprisingly, Asch's results were incorrect.
   b. conscious distortion of judgment occurred four to five times more frequently than unconscious distortion.
   c. unconscious distortion of judgment occurred four to five times more frequently than conscious distortion.
   d. Americans are much less likely to conform than people in other countries.

_____ 8. According to the text, group decision-making is affected by:
   a. members' prior commitments.
   b. backstage activities.

   c. the influence of control groups.

   d. role strain.

_____ 9. Which of the following responses is NOT typical of people when they are isolated?
  a. aggressive behavior
  b. anxiety attacks
  c. apathy and withdrawal
  d. dreaming or hallucinating about other people

_____ 10. Victor Frankl, a psychiatrist, was interned in a Nazi concentration camp. He assisted prisoners by:
  a. helping them escape.
  b. helping them commit suicide.
  c. reminding them of positive qualities still existing on earth.
  d. obtaining permission to turn off lights and make horrors less visible.

## Essay test

1. List and discuss two theories of social interaction, providing definitions of each and your own examples (*not* those in the book) representing the major issues and concepts of each theory.
2. Define status and role, making a clear distinction between the two terms. Write about a social situation that demonstrates the meanings of the two concepts. Use this same situation to illustrate the meanings of role conflict and role strain.
3. Define leadership and also three different leadership styles. Discuss the leadership style in two groups in which you participate. Are the styles effective in both cases? Explain.
4. Define conformity and describe in detail the findings of the Asch experiments.
5. Discuss how people are likely to respond to the disruption of social-interaction patterns within their communities.

## Suggested Readings

Caughey, John L. 1984. *Imaginary Social Worlds: A Cultural Approach.* Lincoln: University of Nebraska Press. An innovative, interesting book discussing and analyzing the intimate relationship between imaginary social worlds (as represented, for instance, by television, in dreams, and in psychotic experiences) and the real social world.

Erikson, Kai. 1976. *Everything in Its Path: Destruction of Community in the Buffalo Creek Flood.* New York: Simon and Schuster. A nicely written, well-documented account of what happened to the social interaction patterns of a tightly knit mining community when it was ravaged by a flood.

Garfinkel, Harold. 1967. *Studies in Ethnomethodology.* Englewood Cliffs, NJ: Prentice-Hall. A set of eight challenging articles outlining Garfinkel's informal studies of the social order underlying all social interactions.

Goffman, Erving. 1959. *The Presentation of Self in Everyday Life.* Garden City, NY: Doubleday. An introduction to some of the intricacies and subtleties of social interaction. Goffman discussed the devices people use to influence others' perceptions of them. The illustrative material is colorful, wide ranging, and thought provoking.

Golding, William. 1954. *Lord of the Flies.* New York: Coward-McCann. A classic novel describing how a group of boys gradually deteriorates into savagery following an airplane crash. Group decision-making, leadership, and the influence of groups on individuals are important themes throughout the account.

Hare, A. Paul. 1982. *Creativity in Small Groups.* Beverly Hills: Sage. A clearly written, well-organized presentation of important processes, concepts, and theories involving the social interaction of small groups.

**114**

Janis, Irving L. 1972. *Victims of Groupthink.* Boston: Houghton Mifflin. Use of case studies of the Bay of Pigs invasion, the escalation of the Vietnam War, the Cuban missile crisis, and other important international confrontations to illustrate the process by which top governmental leaders make both foolish and effective decisions.

Leiter, Kenneth. 1980. *A Primer on Ethnomethodology.* New York: Oxford University Press. An overview of theory and research in ethnomethodology.

Manis, Jerome G., and Bernard N. Meltzer (eds.). 1978. *Symbolic Interaction.* Boston: Allyn and Bacon. Third edition. Nearly fifty articles discussing different elements of the symbolic-interactionist perspective and divided into six sections. The editors also provide a brief, useful introduction to symbolic interaction.

Orwell, George. 1959. *Down and Out in Paris and London.* New York: Berkeley Medallion Books. Originally published in 1933. The youthful adventures of the well-known writer when he was cleaning pots in Paris restaurants and living as a tramp in England. The book reads like a gripping novel and is filled with insights about social-interaction patterns.

## Student Projects

1. Select a place to eat—a fast-food restaurant, a student cafeteria, or a fairly expensive restaurant. As you eat, make mental notes (to be recorded as soon as you leave) regarding the physical layout, behavior of patrons, interaction of patrons and waiters and waitresses, or other important features of the setting. When you are alone, try to visualize the activity as if you were going to write and produce a play. Would social interaction flow more smoothly if any of the actions, settings, or props were changed? Did you detect any failures in impression management? Did any actions occur in the frontstage that more appropriately should have occurred backstage? Compare your findings with those obtained by other students.

2. Among people you like and trust (such as family members, roommates), violate a fairly minor social norm. Note people's immediate reactions. After the violation behave as though you had done nothing wrong or unusual and observe others' reactions for the next few minutes. Do they seem to be encouraging you to maintain conforming behavioral patterns? Complete this informal experiment by explaining what you have done and what sociologists seek to learn from such research. How did you feel during the experiment? What reactions did your study produce? Did this experience give you insight about the Garfinkel and Asch studies presented in the text?

## Answers to Test Questions

**True-false test**

| | | | | |
|---|---|---|---|---|
| 1. t | 3. t | 5. t | 7. f | 9. t |
| 2. t | 4. f | 6. f | 8. f | 10. t |

**Multiple-choice test**

| | | | | |
|---|---|---|---|---|
| 1. b | 3. d | 5. d | 7. b | 9. a |
| 2. b | 4. b | 6. c | 8. a | 10. c |

# 6
# SOCIALIZATION

The account began on a low note. Dibs was a five-year-old problem child attending a private school in New York City. Some of the teachers thought he was retarded. Certainly his behavior was unusual. Most of the time, he crawled around the edge of the room, sucking his thumb or chewing on his hand and lying rigid on the floor when anyone tried to involve him in school activity. After two years the teachers decided that something had to be done about Dibs. Parents were complaining about him, particularly on occasions when he scratched or bit children who came too close to him. Virginia Axline (1968), a clinical psychologist who specialized in working with children, was called in at this point. Dr. Axline was asked to meet with Dibs and his mother and then to offer suggestions. Interviewing Dibs's mother, Dr. Axline soon learned that she had been putting tremendous pressure to achieve on her son since early infancy. His response had been to withdraw.

The first time Dibs went to visit Dr. Axline he spent a long time just standing in the middle of the play-therapy room. Finally he walked slowly across the room and then moved along the walls. He passed from one toy to another, tentatively touching them. Then he began calling the toys by name—dog, cat, rabbit. He turned to the dolls and the doll house. He looked at the house and said over and over, "No lock doors. No lock doors. No lock doors." There was desperation in Dibs's voice. He kept playing with the doll house, eventually finding that the walls could be removed. "No like walls. Dibs no like walls." And in the playroom Dibs started taking down the emotional walls that had been built around him.

Every Thursday at 3 P.M., Dibs and Dr. Axline met for an hour. At each session Dibs's awareness that he was free to do as he wished increased. Never before had he been so free, and from one meeting to the next Dibs became more talkative and active. Dr. Axline's part was important. She was there to respond to Dibs in the free and open atmosphere of the play-therapy room, to let him know by her unspoken approval that what he was doing, and thus he himself, was acceptable to her.

With Dr. Axline's help, Dibs was undergoing **socialization,** the process by which a person becomes a member of a group or society, learning the necessary cultural content and modes of behavior. Socialization is most apparent in childhood when the basic elements of culture are learned, but the process continues throughout people's lifetimes as they change their group affiliations and thus must learn new ways of thinking and acting.

You are in many ways a product of socialization. For one thing you have been significantly influenced by your parents. Perhaps you do not even recognize the extent to which you have adopted their beliefs, values, and behavioral patterns as your own, but if you analyze your family life, you will recognize that many things you were taught and the patterns you observed in your family influenced the development of your standards and behavior. For this reason you are probably different from your friends or classmates. You get angry faster or perhaps slower, you drink more or perhaps less, or you study many more hours or perhaps fewer. You can recognize that others have also contributed to your socialization: friends, neighbors, and teachers. Furthermore socialization continues throughout the entire life span. Perhaps you have older parents, grandparents, or other elderly acquaintances, and you can observe the extent to which modern values and life-style and perhaps retirement have affected them. In our society people often pride themselves on being independent and self-reliant, but we are social animals and we require socialization in order to function competently in society.

The following section assesses the factors that determine human development. Next we consider the effects of deprived childhood socialization, followed by a summary of four important theories of socialization. Our fourth topic concerns sources of socialization, and the chapter closes with a look at certain common socialization experiences people find difficult.

# The Origin of Human Development

In the 1983 film *Trading Places*, two wealthy brothers have a bet. One wagers that if they use their influence to manipulate a number of circumstances, a certain successful businessman would become a criminal and a particular poor, uneducated con man would become a successful businessman. The other brother disagrees, believing that no matter what the circumstances, "breeding" will prevent the two men from trading places. The first brother wins the bet. His perspective on human development has been more prominent in our society, where achievement receives more emphasis than "breeding" (heredity). However, for over a century, controversy has raged on the issue of nature versus nurture: Are human beings the product of their **nature** (their inborn biological characteristics or heredity), their **nurture** (their socialization), or some combination of both?

The "nature" position dominated the thinking of most scholars in the nineteenth century. For example, the renowned biologist Charles Darwin emphasized "natural selection": the view that in the struggle for space, food, and shelter, the most adaptable members of a species will live and the less adaptable will perish. In sociologist Herbert Spencer's words, this is the principle of "the survival of the fittest." This principle proved useful to many elitist nineteenth-century political and economic leaders. They could justify their positions of dominance by arguing that the fact that they held such exalted posts was an indication of their natural superiority. Such people would say there was nothing wrong with exploiting the poor in the United States and elsewhere in the world. After all, individuals' poverty and deprivation were clear indications of innate inferiority, and like beasts of burden, inferior human beings should be exploited.

Some social scientists who shared the heredity-oriented approach began to focus their analysis on **instincts:** unalterable behavioral complexes that parents transmit genetically to their children. In the late nineteenth century, psychologists started to compile lists of what they believed to be human instincts and went on to attribute many behavioral patterns to them. Thus warfare was supposedly the result of an "aggressive" instinct, capitalism of an "acquisitive" instinct, and society of a "herding" instinct. These simplistic analyses overlooked the evidence suggesting that such types of behavior are principally learned. If these behaviors were instinctual, then they would occur in all societies, and they do not. Societies exist where most people are nonaggressive and nonacquisitive, and under certain circumstances people will voluntarily isolate themselves.

By the early twentieth century, the "nature" perspective had begun to lose support. Ivan Pavlov, a Russian physiologist, proved that he could train or "condition" dogs to exhibit an involuntary response such as salivation when they heard the ringing of a bell. The writings of John B. Watson, an American psychologist, emphasized the same general conclusion: that nurture is the most important factor in human development. According to Watson (1924), children can be turned into anything: doctors, lawyers, artists, beggars, or thieves, depending on how they are raised. The well-known contemporary psychologist B. F. Skinner (1972) has made a similar point, claiming that such environmental influences as parental approval and social custom lead us to want to do certain things.

In recent years a new school of thought emphasizing the importance of heredity has emerged. Proponents of **sociobiology** argue that through the evolutionary process, human beings have acquired tendencies that determine much of their behavior. Edward Wilson (1978), a zoologist, has claimed that among humans, behaviors such as aggression, selfishness, territoriality, and the tendency to form dominance hierarchies are both innate and universal. According to Wilson and other sociobiologists, government officials planning public policy should take into account certain alleged inflexible tendencies in human nature.

Many sociologists have sharply criticized socio-

**118**

biology, arguing that little supportive evidence has been presented in defense of this perspective and that unlike sociologists, sociobiologists pay almost no attention to the effects of social, political, and economic factors on the societies about which they generalize. In recent years, however, there has been a growing support for including a modified sociobiological position in sociological analysis. Thus it is argued that an understanding of human behavior will be enhanced if both genetic and cultural factors are examined (Parker, 1984; Wozniak, 1984).

Some social research, such as studies on intelligence, show the interplay of nature and nurture. Investigations demonstrate that pairs of identical twins, whose heredity is identical, obtain scores on intelligence tests closer together than those obtained by other pairs of siblings, even if the identical twins have been raised apart. Thus, heredity seems to be a significant factor in the determination of intelligence. On the other hand, any given genetically related pair, including not only identical twins but also fraternal twins or any other types of siblings, will usually show a closer match in intelligence test scores if the pair is raised together than if the pair is raised apart (Scarr and Weinberg, 1977; Skeels, 1966). On such topics as criminal behavior (Gabrielli et al., 1984; Mednick et al., 1984), communication development (Hardy-Brown and Plomin, 1985), and cultural transmission (Shand and Kosawa, 1985), carefully executed, contemporary studies have tended to emphasize the significance of socialization but have not ruled out the possible influence of biological factors.

## The Results of Deprived Socialization

Both nature and nurture affect human development, but the sociological perspective decidedly emphasizes nurture. The present section implicitly supports the nurture position, which suggests that from early infancy an intimate relationship between child and caretaker establishes a child's sense of well-being and permits the child to develop the social and intellectual skills necessary for effective participation in society. When children are deprived of such relationships, their development is seriously affected.

Several decades ago Harry Harlow and his associates at the University of Wisconsin conducted research on the effects of extreme isolation of young rhesus monkeys (Harlow and Harlow, 1962; Harlow and Zimmerman, 1959). Harlow found that the monkeys isolated in his labs showed behavior similar to that of human psychotics: They were afraid of and hostile toward other monkeys, and, in general, they acted sluggish and reclusive. In one experiment Harlow built two artificial "mothers." One was composed of wire mesh and dispensed milk while the other, which was similar in size and shape, was made from a terrycloth bath towel and offered the comfort of soft contact but not milk. During the 165-day period that the infant monkeys spent with both "mothers," they showed a marked preference for the cloth substitute, spending an average of sixteen hours per day clutching the cloth figure compared to one and a half hours on the wire "mother." Apparently the need for contact with a soft object proved more compelling than the need to reduce hunger.

Of course, researchers cannot devise experiments where children are purposely deprived of nurture. One investigator, however, discovered a situation where caretakers for children were scarce. René Spitz (1945) conducted a study that compared infants raised by their own mothers with infants of the same age raised in an orphanage. The first group of infants had extensive social involvement with their mothers while the orphans were kept isolated in small cubicles, with no human contact beyond feeding, clothing changes, and doctoring. After eighteen months the two groups showed dramatic differences. One third of the orphans were dead, and the remainder were physically, intellectually, and emotionally retarded while the children reared by their mothers were physically and mentally healthy.

Kingsley Davis's (1948) case studies of two isolated girls provide further evidence for the harmful effects of depriving children of conventional socialization. The first little girl, an illegitimate, unwanted child named Anna, was kept isolated in an upstairs room for nearly six years. When Anna totally isolated during the first six years of life. At her death Anna's social and cognitive development was equivalent to that of a normal two- or three-year-old. The possibility that Anna was retarded might have prevented more progress.

Davis's other case study involved a girl named Isabelle, found at about the age of six. Her mother was a deaf-mute, and the two of them spent most of their time together in a dark room. They communicated by gestures, not by speech. Because of lack of sunshine and poor diet, Isabelle was in poor health. At first she seemed incapable of forming relationships, and it was not clear whether or not she was deaf. When it was established that she could hear, specialists started working with her. People first believed she was feebleminded, but under a program of skillful guidance, she began to show signs of a rapidly expanding intelligence. A little more than two months after speaking her first words, Isabelle started making sentences. Nine months later she could read and write quite well, add to ten, and retell a story after hearing it. Seven months later she had a vocabulary of between 1500 and 2000 words and was asking complicated questions. By the age of eight-and-a-half, she had reached a normal level of knowledge, covering in two years the development that usually requires six. The case of Isabelle suggests that, with conscientious and skillful effort, specialists can overcome the deficiencies produced by deprived socialization.

The Spitz research and the Davis case studies show the devastating effect of isolation on children. These are extreme situations, and yet one might wonder whether some negative impact is apparent in less extreme situations.

Without doubt the answer is affirmative. A recent study of abused toddlers concluded that some impact of the abuse they had received was revealed when other children cried. Toddlers from non-abusing homes responded with interest, empathy, or sadness when agemates were distressed. In contrast, toddlers from abusing homes reacted to age-mates' crying with physical attacks on the distressed child, fear, or anger. For instance, Thomas, an abused one-year-old, was playing when he heard a child crying in the distance. The researchers wrote:

Suddenly, Thomas becomes a statue: His smile fades and his face takes on a look of distress also. He sits very

The Wild Child, *a movie based on an historical account first published in 1800, describes an extreme case of social deprivation. The wild boy had no attachments to other humans (he didn't even seem interested in the company of those who captured him), and displayed the behavior of the animals with whom he had shared the forest for years — getting food, sleeping, and running from predators. Like other such stories, this one raises questions about the degree to which our social environment molds us and essentially "creates" our humanity as well as the degree to which we, unlike other animals, inherit the capacity to respond to socialization.*

was discovered, her clothing and bedding were filthy, and she had received no instruction or friendly attention whatsoever. She could not walk, talk, feed herself, or do anything that showed intelligence. She was emaciated, with skeletonlike arms and legs and a bloated stomach. Anna made considerable progress after she was discovered. She learned to follow directions, to string beads, to identify a few colors, and to build with blocks. Eventually she also learned to talk (though in phrases and not full sentences), to wash her hands, and to brush her teeth. Anna died before she was eleven, but the progress she made demonstrates that it is possible to teach many things to a child

**120**

still, his hand frozen in the air. His back is straight, and he becomes more and more tense as the crying continues. The fingers on his hand slowly extend a bit. . . . The (distant) crying diminishes. Suddenly, Thomas is back to normal, calm, mumbling and playing in the sand.

*(Main and George, 1985: 410)*

Children's socialization affects their behavior in a variety of ways, and those who have been abused are more likely to respond stressfully to other children's pain and stress. One of the more frightening aspects of such a situation is the legacy it can produce: It is possible that an adult who was abused as a child will be more harsh and abusive than most people in stressful situations.

We have seen the effects that deprived socialization can have on individual children. But what happens if all the children within a society experience deprived socialization? The following Cross-Cultural Perspective considers such a situation.

## CROSS-CULTURAL PERSPECTIVE

### *Socialization among a People Driven Mad: The Case of the Ik*

Colin Turnbull (1979), an anthropologist, studied the Ik (pronounced "eek"), who live in a mountainous region of the central African nation of Uganda. The details of the Ik case make it clear that the deprived socialization experienced by Ik children was one result of living in what has become a seriously deprived society.

Before World War II, the Ik were nomadic hunters and gatherers. Traditionally Ik children regarded all adults living in the same village as parents and all other children as brothers and sisters. During prosperous times such a social arrangement meant that a village was in effect one large family. But then disaster struck. Following World War II, much of the Ik's traditional land was turned into a national park, and the Ik were forbidden to hunt and gather there. The tribespeople were forced to settle on barren and arid land. In the United States, victims of disasters generally receive relief from the government and from the local community. In

addition, family members usually pull together in such circumstances, helping each other as much as possible. In contrast, the Ik receive no outside help, nor do they possess family or other group structures to provide support.

In this situation the socialization process has deteriorated rapidly. At the age of three, children are normally thrown out of the home by their parents. These children survive by forming "age bands," with each child seeking others close to his or her own age for protection against older children. However, these alliances are temporary. Each child eventually turns on the ones with whom he or she has become closest, and the fragile bond they called friendship is ended. Three or four such friendships will be formed and then broken. At that point the child is twelve or thirteen and has learned the wisdom of acting on his or her own while acknowledging it is occasionally profitable to associate temporarily with others.

Only the strongest and craftiest children survive. Turnbull wrote that a young girl named Adupa, unable to accept her parents' rejection, kept going back for food and shelter, but they laughed and drove her away each time. Adupa kept returning to them, and finally they did let her stay, leaving the hut themselves and shuttering the door so tightly that the half-starved little girl could not open it. Turnbull learned later that that was how Adupa died.

Grown children treat their parents in the same spirit. When Turnbull departed, he left a sack of ground cornmeal with the police for an old man. The cornmeal was enough to last the old man for months, and Turnbull promised to send money for more when the sack was finished. However, the anthropologist had underestimated the old man's son. Within two days the son had persuaded the police that it would save them a lot of bother if he looked after the cornmeal for his father. Later Turnbull heard that the old man had died of starvation within two weeks.

Novelists and filmmakers often try to shock their audiences, devising horrifying scenes that show human beings' capacities to hurt or to destroy each other. But what could be more horrifying than the case of the Ik, which demonstrates that under certain social conditions parents will completely reject their children, leaving them to die?

Source: Colin M. Turnbull. "The Mountain People." In Phillip Whitten (ed.), *Readings in Sociology: Contemporary Perspectives.* New York: Harper & Row. Second edition. 1979, pp. 19–26.

# Theories of Socialization

The **self** is one's perception of his or her own person, which forms as a result of other people's response in the course of socialization. In the last section, we noted that children who grow up as isolated as Anna and Isabelle seem to have an undeveloped sense of self.

The present discussion examines four theories that analyze the growth of the self. Two of the theories are sociological and two are psychological.

## Sociological Theories of Socialization

Cooley's and Mead's theories have clear differences, but on one point they agree: The self is the product of a learning process that occurs in interaction with others.

### Cooley and the Looking-Glass Self

A child of scarcely eighteen months toddles toward her parents, smiles, and then dives to the floor. The parents clap their hands and roar with laughter. The little girl perceives that her parents see her as cute and funny and that they heartily approve of her action. She feels happy and proud and begins to think of herself as a funny person and will repeat her performance or some version of it in the future.

This situation illustrates a concept Charles Horton Cooley (1864–1929) called the **looking-glass self:** Our understanding of what sort of person we are is based on how we think we appear to others. Cooley wrote: "We always imagine, and in imagining share, the judgments of the other mind" (Cooley, 1964: 185).

According to Cooley, there are three steps in the development of the looking-glass self:

1. Our perception of how we appear to another person.
2. Our estimate of the judgment the other person makes about us.
3. Some emotional feeling about this judgment, such as pride or shame. Looking back you can see that the little girl in the previous example experienced these three steps.

Of course, one person does not have direct contact with another's thoughts or feelings; an individual only makes guesses from other people's responses. Faulty communication or confusion sometimes happens: A disapproving expression might be mistaken for an approving smile; or a person may receive mixed messages from different people. The diving child's mother might applaud while her father registers stony disapproval. The child is not certain whether or not she should do funny things in the future. If such mixed messages continue, she is not likely to develop a clear sense of whether or not she is a funny person. Children who grow up with a constant supply of mixed messages are likely to become adults who are confused and unsure of themselves.

### Mead's Conception of the Development of Self

George Herbert Mead (1863–1931) accepted the idea of the looking-glass-self theory. However, he believed that the development of the self-concept is the product of more than people's perceptions of others' reactions to them (Mead, 1930). According to Mead, the socialized individual has learned to read complicated social situations before taking whatever actions are judged the most appropriate. Mead visualized the development of the self as a three-stage process:

1. The preparatory stage occurs in early childhood. In the course of their second and third years, children imitate others' behavior. They copy the way their parents or older siblings hold a spoon, do a dance step, or make an obscene gesture. Children do learn some useful skills through imitation but discover little about how roles work.

2. Children enter the play stage at the age of four or five. **Play** is the process of taking the role of specific individuals and thereby starting to learn the rights and obligations that particular roles entail. Mead wrote, "A child plays at being a mother, at being a teacher, at being a policeman; that is, it is taking different roles . . ." (Mead, 1934: 150). At this stage children's role performances begin to give them an understanding of their significance. But these performances are definitely "play" in the sense that children are not committed to these roles and are able to make up the rules as they proceed.

3. The final stage is the game stage. According to Mead, a **game** is a group activity in which each participant's role requires interaction with two or more individuals. In order to take part in games, a person must have a **generalized other:** an image of the role expectations for all the game participants with whom a person must interact. Mead noted, "The fundamental difference between play and the game is that in the latter the child must have the attitude of all the others involved in that game" (Mead, 1934: 153–154). Unlike the play stage, the game stage is serious business. Children are expected to commit themselves to the roles they perform, and to perform effectively they must learn the rules governing all participants' behavior. Not following the rules can lead to a sense of personal failure.

An actual game provides an illustration. In baseball, for instance, the infielders must be aware of not only their own role expectations but also those of their fellow infielders. The first baseman must realize that without a runner on base, he must take the throw on a ground ball to the shortstop. With a runner on first base, the first baseman knows that the shortstop's throw will go to the second baseman, who then will throw to first.

The concept of game also applies to social situations. Let us imagine, for example, that Jackie is having problems with her boyfriend. She wants to discuss the situation with her friend Angela, and so she gives her a call. They agree to meet an hour later at the college cafeteria. Angela arrives, however, with her younger sister Peggy. "Mom had to go shopping," Angela says apologetically, "and she asked me to bring Peggy along." Peggy is ten years old, always curious, and is likely to pass on any information she hears to her mother, who in turn will tell Jackie's mother. In this situation the Meadian game includes the following facts: Both Jackie and Angela are aware of how Peggy is likely to act in this situation, and each knows that the other is aware. Thus the two young women engage in a careful conversation, avoiding references to certain issues: that Jackie frequently spends the night with her boyfriend, that all their friends drink liquor and smoke marijuana, and that Jackie has seriously considered dropping out of school. They also convey some information with facial expressions and gestures when Peggy is not looking. As they are leaving, Jackie whispers to Angela, "Ma's pretty understanding about my personal life. She really tries not to ask too many questions. She knows she'll just get upset and that I'll end up doing what I want anyway."

The two young women understand how the generalized other applies here. They know what behavior to expect from Peggy, their mothers, and each other. With this knowledge they perform their roles smoothly in this Meadian game. The skills demonstrated by Jackie and Angela in the conversation just described involve a level of social sophistication that far exceeds what is necessary to develop a looking-glass self.

## Freudian Theory of Socialization

Like Cooley and Mead, Sigmund Freud analyzed the development of the self in the course of socialization.

Sigmund Freud (1856–1939), certainly one of the most prominent theorists in psychology, described the different impulses to which we are subjected. All of us experience desires pulling us in different directions: Our wish to have another piece of pie conflicts with concern for our waistline; the wish to sleep through an early morning class clashes with concern that the material covered in the lecture will be featured on the next test.

Freud (1952) contended that socialization is a process that requires people to sacrifice personal impulses and desires for the common good. Without such a sacrifice, society would disintegrate as people pursued their most selfish goals. According to Freud, the energy inherent in these impulses and desires is redirected along socially acceptable paths by the socialization process.

Freud identified three distinct parts of the personality that exist as concepts, not in a physical form. One part is the **id,** which is unconscious, primitive, and constantly pleasure seeking. The second part is the **superego,** which has internalized standards of right and wrong, a conscience. Parental influence is strong in the development of the superego, but other authority figures such as teachers or the police also affect its development. Struggle between the superego and id is not inevitable, but Freud suggested that in modern life almost continuous warfare will occur between them. In short, there is an on-going conflict between basic impulses produced by the id and standards of society supplied by the superego. Generally the superego tries to force the id to modify or renounce its urges or at least to postpone them. The final part of the personality is the ego. The **ego** is Freud's conception of the self. It must cope with pressures from three often contradictory forces: the outside world, the id, and the superego.

In everyday life one can easily visualize the struggle among the three parts of the personality Freud described. Suppose that a student has an important test scheduled the next day. That evening a party will take place at a friend's apartment. The party promises to be a lot of fun — plenty to drink and eat — and many of the student's friends will be there. The id urges, "There's only one way to handle a party like this one — go early and stay late!" The superego takes the opposite tack. It argues, "This test could make or break your grade. You must study all evening and then turn in early. Parties are for weekends, after all." The ego is forced to evaluate both arguments. What decision will be reached? The party? Studying? Perhaps the ego will compromise: Study most of the evening, then spend two hours at the party, and have only one or two drinks. From a Freudian point of view, the decision reached will reflect the relative abilities of the id and the superego to "convince" the ego.

## Piaget's Theory of Cognitive Development

Jean Piaget (1896–1980) was a Swiss psychologist and a leading expert on children's thought processes. Piaget's work has complemented George Herbert Mead's analysis, with the latter focusing on the child's growing understanding of social relations and Piaget emphasizing **cognitive ability:** the capacity to use perception, thought, memory, and other mental processes to acquire knowledge. Piaget (1970) contended that a child's cognitive ability develops through four principal stages. These stages are age related because the brain must develop physically over time in order to allow certain types of cognitive processes to occur and because passage into a given stage requires a successful experience in the preceding one. Indeed, people are generally aware that cognitive abilities are age related. We would be shocked to hear a six-month-old infant speaking in full sentences or an eight-year-old discussing the theory of relativity or symbolic interaction. The four stages cover the time period from birth to the age of fifteen.

1. *The sensorimotor stage.* This phase involves the first two years of life. During these years infants learn to coordinate sensory experiences (such as seeing objects) with motor activities (such as touching objects). Infants discover that if they reach for bright-colored objects like mobiles or rattles, they can touch, grasp, or even jiggle them. They are starting to distinguish themselves from the surrounding environment, an ability an infant does not possess for the first three or four months of life. Eventually infants develop **object permanence,** the childhood recognition that specific objects still exist after they are removed from one's line of vision. A child of four months might play with a toy but will not seem to notice when it is taken away. However, a child of nine months will start looking for the same toy if removed. The older child

has developed object permanence, recognizing that the toy has an existence independent of his or her own perception.

2. *The preoperational stage.* This phase is named from the fact that a child of two to seven does not yet fully understand certain basic concepts one must grasp in order to function effectively in the everyday world. These concepts include weight, volume, speed, and cause and effect. Children's apparent abilities at this stage can be deceptive, sometimes dangerously so. For instance, a baby-sitter is with Jamie, a four-year-old, in his family's yard. "I'm thirsty," Jamie says. "I'd like a glass of milk." The sitter stands up, and as she heads for the kitchen door she says, "Now you stay right here, Jamie. I don't want you going into the street." Just to check, she might add, "Now tell me what you're supposed to do, Jamie," The little boy will apparently be able to explain—he seems to understand danger—but in reality he does not yet truly comprehend the speed of cars nor does he grasp the process of cause and effect (that is, that if hit he will be injured or killed). Thus even though he has understood his baby-sitter's words, he is too young to grasp their significance, namely the personal danger that speeding cars represent.

3. *The concrete operational stage.* This phase involves children approximately seven to eleven, and in the course of it, they master the cognitive skills necessary for everyday life. They come to understand measurement, speed, weight, time, and cause and effect. Unlike younger children they are able to appreciate other people's outlooks and, as Mead suggested, to coordinate other people's viewpoints and actions with their own. Children at the concrete operational stage, however, lack the ability to think abstractly.

4. *The formal operational stage.* Children's responses to the following set of sentences display the difference between the concrete operational and the formal operational stages:

    (1) All children like spinach.
    (2) Boys are children.
    (3) Therefore boys like spinach.

Younger children, especially if they do not like spinach, will focus on the content of the syllogism, while adolescents are much more likely to examine the argument because they are impressed by its logical form (Phillips, 1969). This stage occurs from ages eleven to fifteen. Children develop the ability to think abstractly, to manipulate concepts not linked to experience in the immediate environment. In the formal operational stage, children are beginning to explore the vast capacities of the mind, and education is a prominent vehicle for these explorations.

Piaget's theory has some interesting implications for education. Because expanded cognitive abilities are the result of both the physical maturation of the brain and intellectual experiences, it would be difficult and counterproductive to force children to think abstractly before they are intellectually ready. On the other hand, once they have developed their full intellectual capacities, there is no reason to move slowly. A child of fourteen has completed the formal operational phase, suggesting that most high-school students are fully capable of the same sort of abstract thinking college students must perform.

## Commentary

The four theories of socialization we have discussed all recognize the changing nature of the self. Three of the theories contend that social interaction determines the development of the self, while Piaget's theory claims that brain maturation is the source. Furthermore each theory has its own particular focus. Cooley's approach concludes that a person's perceptions of how other people evaluate his or her behavior determines the content of the self. Mead's analysis accepts Cooley's central point but emphasizes that the development of the self requires an understanding of how roles work. Unlike the two sociological theories, the Freudian perspective suggests that there is a conflict-laden relationship between the individual and society in the on-going struggle between the id and superego. Finally Piaget's theoretical contribution involves an entirely different aspect of socialization, focusing on children's development of cognitive abilities and not on their increasing understanding of social relations. (See Table 6.1.) A complete theory of socialization must include all the major points these four theories raise.

**Table 6.1**
**Four Prominent Theories of Socialization**

| THEORIST | PRINCIPAL CONCEPT(S) | CENTRAL IDEA(S) | INDIVIDUAL'S RELATIONSHIP TO SOCIETY |
|---|---|---|---|
| Charles Cooley | Looking-glass self | That people's sense of self is based on how they imagine they appear to others | Continuous effort to adjust one's behavior to one's perception of others' desires and expectations |
| George Mead | Play, generalized other, and game | That the development of the self is a three-stage process, where each stage represents a more sophisticated understanding of the world | The necessity to understand the generalized other for each game in which one participates |
| Sigmund Freud | Id, ego, and superego | That there is an on-going conflict between a person's primitive impulses and societal controls, with the ego (self) serving as negotiator | Requirement that the ego places heavy restraints on the id in line with the demands of the superego |
| Jean Piaget | Cognitive abilities | That the acquisition of knowledge is a four-stage process occurring in childhood and featuring a particular set of mental operations at each stage | Expectation that at each stage a child meets socially approved cognitive demands, such as in school performance |

# Sources of Socialization

The focus now shifts from an examination of theories, which attempt to designate the central influences and steps in the process of socialization, to an analysis of fundamental influences in the process—key sources of socialization. In fact, one of these sources, the family, received some attention in the previous section.

## The Family

Children are born into families, and it is within the family context that they obtain their first exposure to the values, norms, beliefs, and knowledge characteristic of their society. Recent research has shown that parents significantly affect their children's outlook on such wide-ranging issues as drinking behavior (Barnes, 1986), gender-role identity (Costos, 1986), religion (Hoge, Petrillo, and Smith, 1982), and marijuana use (Yamaguchi

and Kandel, 1985). Furthermore the socialization experience within the family continues for many years. Most American children live with their parents until they are in their late teens, and many continue living with them much longer. As the Cooley and Mead theories emphasize, parents and other family members have a tremendous impact on children. Sometimes family influences involving distinctive patterns of facial and bodily expression or behavioral patterns are readily apparent. In other cases these traits are not obvious, and yet the parental influence remains equally pervasive.

Americans usually think of childhood as a distinct period of time in people's lives, but such a conception has not always been maintained.

### The Changing Conception of Childhood

During the Middle Ages, children were treated as little adults. Parents had no perception of themselves as people involved in child-rearing, and the family was generally thought of as an institution for the transmission of a name and inheritance. Between the thirteenth and the seventeenth centuries, this outlook gradually changed. Religious groups began to take an increasingly important part in the education of children, and the members of these groups started to emphasize that parents were the guardians of their children's souls. From the seventeenth through the nineteenth centuries, the growing involvement of parents showed itself in increasingly stricter codes of discipline. This trend became particularly apparent in the early nineteenth century when the Industrial Revolution encouraged a sharp role distinction between men and women, forcing many wives to remain in the home where they were expected to concentrate much of their energy on rearing their children. By the end of the nineteenth century, the combined forces of the family and the school had firmly established the conception of childhood (Ariès, 1962).

With the existence of childhood confirmed, people have disagreed about what child-rearing patterns are appropriate. Before the 1920s a restrictive approach to parenting generally prevailed. There was a widespread belief that it was critical to maximize children's obedience to the social norms. Most parents felt that the use of punishments and rewards was the best means of securing this obedience. During the 1920s the increasing acceptance of the ideas of Sigmund Freud, educator John Dewey, and others led to an almost complete reversal of the earlier approach. Now parents became aware that children have their own individual perceptions and needs and that bad experiences suffered in childhood can produce psychological damage that will carry into adulthood. Different opinions regarding discipline have also been apparent in recent years. Some critics of the student protest of the 1960s, for example, suggested that a major cause of the unrest was the supposedly overly permissive child-rearing typical of the post-World-War-II era.

People often believe that a particular approach to rearing children is best. However, many social scientists argue that there is no single "right approach." Americans are inclined to believe that infants are inherently helpless and must establish strong emotional bonds with their caretakers. The ethnocentrism within many Americans will arise when they learn that traditional Japanese mothers believed that their young children were uncivilized creatures whose emotions needed to be soothed and tamed—quite the opposite of the American approach. It will further strain Americans' capacity for cultural relativism to discover that many Indian mothers in the highlands of Guatemala believe that their children's day of birth will determine their dispositions and therefore make no effort to shape their personalities. However, in all three of these societies, most children grow up to be relatively well-adjusted, productive adults; research indicates that children do not need exposure to a particular set of socialization patterns to develop properly. Beyond basic care and feeding, there appear to be no universal needs among children. One psychologist has concluded, "To ask what a child needs is to pose half a question. We must always specify the demands the community will make upon the adolescent and young adult" (Kagan, 1983: 411). Thus the child-rearing of American children will prepare them for American society, not for traditional Japanese or Guatemalan societies.

## Mass Media

The **mass media** are the instruments of communication that reach a large audience without any personal contact between the senders and receivers. Books, records, newspapers, magazines, television, radio, and movies are the most prominent mass media. Figure 6.1, based on national survey data, indicates how extensively Americans employ various types of media information during the typical day.

As Figure 6.1 implies, of any of the mass media, television probably has the most extensive impact on Americans; four of the categories in this figure involve television. One study indicates that by the age of eighteen, the average American child will have spent more time watching television than performing any other waking activity (Liebert and Poulos, 1972). Since 1950 the amount of time Americans have spent watching television has steadily increased. In 1983 American households with televisions averaged seven hours, two minutes of television time a day, an increase of fourteen minutes from the previous year (*U.S. News and World Report,* 1984).

Television and other commercial media are profit oriented. Television networks and local channels, radio stations, newspapers, and magazines sell time or space to advertisers, whose investment proves worthwhile only if a large audience pays attention to the medium. A team of experts noted: "The purchase of a 30-second spot on CBS or a page in *Time* is a meaningless act—and a poor business decision—unless there are audiences involved. In reality, advertisers buy the audience, which is a byproduct in the mass communication process" (Hiebert, Ungurait, and Bohn, 1974: 39). Television programming involves vast sums of money, and thus competition for the audience is intense. The producers of most major network shows attempt to develop programs that will "hook" the viewers, reel them in like fish. So the central concern is audience appeal; any consideration of artistic merit is secondary.

One of the most effective ways to hook an audience is with violent activity. It has been estimated that an average American child will see over 13,000 television killings by age fifteen. There is twice as much violence in American television as there is in British programming. Yet it is difficult to assess the effects of television violence. A rigorous study of the relationship between violent programming and violent behavior has determined that previous research claiming a relationship is inconclusive (Baron and Reiss, 1985). Still certain developments appear possible: that audiences that have had extensive contact with violence in the mass media are relatively likely to perform violent acts in situations where they expect to be rewarded for such behavior or when they encounter a situation similar to the one where media violence was presented (National Commission on the Causes and Prevention of Violence, 1969).

**Figure 6.1**
**Media Use in the Last Twenty-Four Hours**

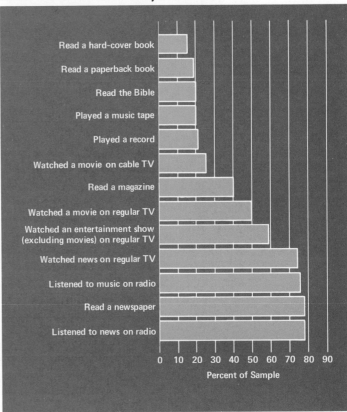

*Americans make extensive use of the mass media. With the exception of reading the newspaper, they are more likely to watch TV or listen to the radio than they are to read. (Source: Roper Organization.* Roper Reports. *April 1982.)*

The following Contemporary Issue considers one of the perplexing current issues of the mass media—the freedom of the press.

---

## CONTEMPORARY ISSUE

### *What about Freedom of the Press?*

As we have noted, the mass media are the instruments of communication that reach a large audience without any personal contact between the senders and receivers. The lack of personal contact, however, does not prevent people from having strong feelings about the press—newspapers, magazines, television, and radio—and their personnel. In our society viewpoints about the freedom of the press are diversified. Many Americans believe that media personnel have too much freedom. Nationwide surveys conducted by the National Opinion Research Center in the middle 1970s and again in the middle 1980s indicated that the percentage of Americans with a great deal of confidence in the press dropped during that decade from 29 to 14. Furthermore a majority of Americans would favor repealing the First-Amendment clause guaranteeing freedom of the press. Commenting on this information, Joseph Kopec, a public-relations specialist, suggested that the American public perceives the press as arrogant, unnecessarily intrusive, and as distant from the everyday struggles of average citizens as big business or big government. Kopec proposed ways for press officials to reform this situation: policing themselves; using whatever means necessary to correct errors and establish credibility with the public; and reestablishing contact with the people by holding meetings where reporters and editors can candidly communicate with local citizens.

But other observers of the press would suggest that Kopec's reforms are insufficient. The problem, some critics observe, is that the mass media are a prime portion of the corporate world. Michael Parenti noted that just ten major companies control fifty-nine major magazines (including *Time* and *Newsweek*), fifty-eight important newspapers (including the *New York Times* and the *Washington Post*), the three major television and radio networks, thirty-four television stations, 201 cable systems, and twenty record companies. The owners of the major media have diversified business involvements, and they emphatically do not see it as in their interest to examine big-business activities in depth, especially when those businesses have significant problems. Thus an investigation of the media coverage of the major oil spill at Santa Barbara in 1969 showed that the local news media, which were not owned by large corporations, were about equally likely to provide coverage to environmental groups and oil companies. In sharp contrast the nonlocal press, which was considerably more likely to be controlled by large corporations, generally excluded the environmental groups, giving six times as much coverage to the oil companies.

Is the central issue in freedom of the press simply a question of power and influence? Do powerful corporations control mass media in line with their interests? While some apparently believe this is the basic concern, others don't. Leo Szilard, a Hungarian-born scientist and writer who lived in the United States, contended that Americans are subtly socialized to censure themselves. In a short story, he described the process by which a brilliant dolphin was taught the workings of modern societies. What he learned about American society was often complicated and perplexing.

Thus, on one occasion, Pi Omega Ro [the dolphin] asked whether it would be correct to assume that Americans were free to say what they think, because they did not think what they were not free to say. On another occasion, he asked whether it would be correct to say that in America honest politicians were men who were unable to fool others without first fooling themselves.

*(Szilard, 1961: 42–43)*

Herbert Marcuse, a philosopher, agreed with Szilard's dolphin, indicating that even members of the press will monitor and control themselves. Why do members of the press respond this way? The reason, Marcuse claimed, is because they are all playing the same game: They want to become rich and successful and revel in the good life, glorifying in material wealth. The press is no different from any other sector of American society in this respect. Thus mass media are not a particularly significant factor shaping Americans' perceptions and views. "The preconditioning does not start with the mass production of radio and television and with the centralization of their control. The people enter this stage as preconditioned receptacles of long standing . . ." (Marcuse, 1964: 8).

What do you think? Do we have freedom of the press? And if your answer is wholly or partially negative, what do you believe is the source of the limitation?

Sources: Joseph A. Kopec. "The Big Chill." *Vital Speeches.* Vol. 50. June 1, 1984, pp. 528–530; Herbert Marcuse. *The One-Dimensional Man.* Boston: Beacon. 1964; Harvey Molotch and Marilyn Lester. "Accidental News: The Great Oil Spill as Local Occurrence and National Event." *American Journal of Sociology.* September 1975, pp. 235–260; Michael Parenti. "The Moneyed Media." *Economic Notes.* Vol. 51. October 1983, pp. 7–12; Leo Szilard. *The Voice of the Dolphins and Other Stories.* New York: Simon and Schuster. 1961.

## Peers

In a scene from the 1982 film *Diner,* one young man was complaining that since he was getting married, all the good times would be over. His male companion, whom everyone regarded as knowledgeable about sexuality, suddenly looked strangely at the other young man. Then he smiled confidently and said, "You're a virgin." The other, acutely embarrassed, admitted that his friend was "technically" correct.

Research indicates that American males are likely to face strong peer pressure to become sexually experienced and that virgins are sometimes made to believe that they are not demonstrating proper masculinity and that something must be wrong with them (Kirkendall, 1968).

Sex is hardly the only activity over which peers exert influence. Recently published articles have shown that peers influence such activities as risk-taking behavior (Lewis and Lewis, 1984), psychiatric treatment (Odom and Strain, 1984), and cigarette smoking (Westman et al., 1985). The fact that young people of school age spend an average of twice as much time with their peers as they do with parents, and that they like that arrangement, underlines the significance of teenage peer groups (Bronfenbrenner, 1970).

We might wonder why peer groups have become so important to young people. One line of sociological analysis points out that in a highly complex industrial society, the family turns over many of its primary functions, such as moral training, to the schools. Within the school, however, a close, emotional relationship is unlikely to develop between adolescent students and their teachers. Thus students must look to their own age group (their peers) for much of their emotional support and guidance (Coleman, 1961).

## Schools and Day-Care Centers

The first day of school is an important moment sociologically. When they enter school, children encounter for the first time a significant source of socialization outside the bounds of the family. In school children obtain formal knowledge from teachers and from books and also much more. In some of their courses, they are likely to receive a stronger emphasis on patriotism than is normally provided at home. In addition, children in school will find out how to behave in group settings. They learn to sit quietly and to obey teachers providing instructions, whether the instructions make sense or not. Children are encouraged to compete, to attempt to produce higher quality work than do their classmates. A body of criticism has developed concerning the regimentation that occurs in the early school years. One writer, for instance, suggested that kindergarten is "an academic boot camp," where the system of routines and orders prepares young children for blind obedience over the next dozen years of schooling and also within the large-scale occupational bureaucracies of current society (Gracey, 1977).

Parents, educators, politicians, and others are well aware that schools are a critical means of socialization in modern society. This awareness sometimes leads to debate and conflict about the proper means of handling certain controversial issues in the schools. A national survey conducted in February 1982 gave evidence of the American public's divided opinion about three such controversial issues. At that time 69 percent favored prayer in public schools while 24 percent opposed it. Fifty-five percent supported the requirement that public schools teach the creation theory if they also taught Darwin's theory of evolution, and 30 percent opposed this parity. Finally 29 percent backed the banning of school and library books some people consider objectionable while 64 percent were against such a censorship (Roper Organization, *Roper Reports,* April 1982).

The controversy concerning day-care centers surrounds the question of whether or not to have them. Proponents of day-care emphasize that programs work well if the children come from stable families and if a satisfactory ratio of children to caretakers is maintained. For infants the ratio to caretakers should be about 3 to 1; for toddlers (two and over) no higher than 6 to 1 (Belsky and Steinberg, 1978). Opponents argue that no outsider will maintain a parent's sensitivity and interest. In the course of reviewing the issue of day-care, sociologists Brigitte and Peter Berger made the following careful statement: "From the point of view of the individual child, the shift [to day-care] has meant ever earlier and ever longer separation from intimate family contacts. We are not persuaded of the harmlessness of this" (Berger and Berger, 1984: 155).

## Additional Agents of Socialization

Parents, the media, teachers, and peers are important agents of socialization. But are there others as well? Several types come to mind.

*Institutional "caretakers".* Staff members provide significant socialization for orphans, juvenile delinquents, and mentally and physically handicapped children. However, the fact that these staff members are frequently overworked generally means that the quality of socialization they can provide would be considered inadequate by most people.

*Social workers.* Individuals of various ages often receive help from such organizations as child-abuse centers; programs for the elderly; drug-, alcohol-, or gambling-treatment centers; and social-welfare departments. In some cases a kindly, insightful staff person (or the opposite —a cold, uncaring individual) can have an impact that seems out of proportion to the time and energy spent with the person needing help.

Sometimes people will encounter individuals whose guidance or example may lead them to decisions about their best future course of action. For example, a charming, articulate pro-fessor or physician may inspire a young man or woman to prepare for the same profession. Or, in a different vein, a pleasant, kindly representative of the Unification Church ("Moonies") may offer what seems to be a message of hope to a confused, unhappy young man or woman who relinquishes control over his or her destiny in exchange for the promise of happiness and fulfillment.

Figure 6.2 represents the possible impact of different agents of socialization on two individuals.

## Total Institutions

Unlike the other socialization agents discussed in this section, total institutions are concerned with resocialization. A **total institution** is a place of residence where inhabitants experience nearly complete restriction of their physical freedom in order to be effectively resocialized into a radically new identity and behavioral pattern. Frequently such barriers as locked doors, high walls, water, cliffs, or barbed wire are used to prevent unrestricted contacts with outsiders. Psychiatric hospitals, prisons, monasteries, boarding schools, and some army camps are examples.

Inhabitants' resocialization in closed institu-

**Figure 6.2**
**Agents of Socialization**

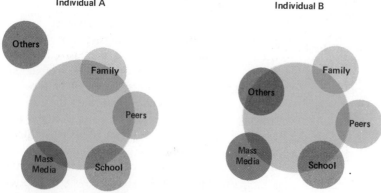

*In the course of socialization, different agents exert varying degrees of influence. For Individual A the family and peers were especially significant. In contrast, Individual B received much less influence from these two agents. In this case the school, particularly two teachers, and others—a couple that owned a local small business— were the most influential.*

*In prison, inmates frequently spend a great many hours alone and inactive, highlighting the fact that prisons generally fail to resocialize inmates to function effectively in society.*

ting, issuing institutional clothing, instructing as to rules, and assigning to quarters.

*(Goffman, 1961: 16)*

Obviously the mortification process in a psychiatric hospital will be different from the one in a boarding school. In both cases, however, significant portions of inmates' former identities are stripped away by admissions procedures and other new, often deeply disturbing situations they must experience. As the mortification process continues, inmates are gradually exposed to the **privilege system:** a framework for inmates' resocialization. The three parts of the privilege system are the "house rules," which are norms that indicate the main requirements of inmate conduct; punishments for breaking the rules; and rewards or privileges provided in exchange for obedience to staff. Goffman noted:

The building of a world around these minor privileges is perhaps the most important feature of inmate culture, and yet is something that cannot easily be appreciated by an outsider, even one who has previously lived through the experience himself. This concern with privileges sometimes leads to generous sharing; it almost always leads to a willingness to beg for such things as cigarettes, candy, and newspapers.

*(Goffman, 1961: 50)*

Does the resocialization that occurs within closed institutions prepare people to function effectively in the greater society? While the question is so general that neither "yes" nor "no" would be an adequate answer, a negative response often seems more appropriate. The American prison system, in particular, has been largely ineffective in this respect. In fact, two experts in criminal justice recently acknowledged this conclusion when they suggested that in the future prisons might be reserved for only dangerous individuals. Others might be treated at community-based correctional centers and reintegrated, as rapidly as possible, into society as useful citizens (Montgomery and MacDougall, 1986).

tions is a two-step procedure: The old identity must be stripped away and replaced with a new one. This begins with a **mortification process,** a series of degradations and humiliations of inhabitants that are systematically carried out by staff members of total institutions. The mortification process begins the moment an individual enters the total institution. Erving Goffman wrote:

We very generally find staff employing what are called admission procedures, such as taking a life history, photographing, weighing, fingerprinting, assigning numbers, searching, listing personal possessions for storage, undressing, bathing, disinfecting, haircut-

# Tough Times: Major Transitions in the Socialization Process

In the last two sections, we have learned something about how socialization works. Most of the time the process runs smoothly. However, when people

make major transitions in their lives, they must undergo socialization, and at these times they can have difficulties learning or accepting the new cultural standards or modes of behavior. Adolescence, job loss, divorce, and the death of a spouse are significant "tough times."

## Adolescence

Several years ago in Hartford, Connecticut, a fifteen-year-old girl named Kathy stood on the steps of a church and slashed her arms with a knife. Later, when asked why she tried to kill herself, Kathy explained that it was because she realized how confused and unhappy her family life was. An investigation revealed that her life had been unstable, involving shifts from one foster home to another as well as occasional stays in institutionalized settings (Papirno, 1976). This girl's socialization had been inadequate, and it is easy to understand why she possessed an unclear, undeveloped sense of self.

Far less disruptive upbringings than Kathy's can lead to confusion and hopelessness for adolescents. While the majority of adolescents do not end up slashing themselves, many, perhaps most, find the transition difficult.

Numerous investigations document the fact that adolescence is a confusing time. For instance, Offer (1969) studied fourteen- to eighteen-year-olds, and his subjects and their parents generally agreed that the greatest turmoil occurred between ages twelve to fourteen. Research conducted by Simmons, Rosenberg, and Rosenberg (1973) of nearly two thousand urban school children in grades three through twelve found that the most disturbed sense of self developed among early adolescents. Compared to the other children, these early adolescents tended to be more self-conscious, less stable in their self-image, less positive in their self-esteem, and less confident about the evaluations of them maintained by parents, teachers, and peers of the same sex. The researchers suggested that the move from the relatively protected, personalized atmosphere of the junior-high school to the more impersonal environment of the high school contributed significantly to their informants' disturbed sense of self.

Elements in middle-class socialization sometimes compound adolescents' confusion and uncertainty. Middle-class adolescents commonly grow up in households where their fathers are so dedicated to occupational success that they spend little time with their families, thereby producing limited interaction with their children. As a result middle-class adolescents often become skeptical about the pursuit of material success and uncertain about their occupational future. Yet, because of parental emphasis on success, they are likely to have "vague yearnings for recognition and fame" (Flacks, 1979: 30). Middle-class boys are especially likely to identify with their mothers because of their fathers' frequent absence. They tend to be less inclined to be dominant, less physically tough and aggressive, and more emotionally expressive than the traditional standard for American male behavior. Middle-class girls' educational opportunities and career aspirations have made them less submissive, more assertive, and more self-confident than expected in the past. For both sexes these personality traits are at least somewhat inconsistent with many parents' role expectations. If the inconsistency is sharp, then adolescents are likely to experience confusion and a sense of inadequacy (Flacks, 1979).

Another source of adolescent confusion in modern cultures is the failure to provide youths with a clear indication of their status. In preindustrial cultures a rite of passage is normally provided: a formal ceremony initiating both boys and girls into adulthood. Such ceremonies contribute to young people's socialization, giving them strong assurance that their status has truly changed and that in the future people will regard them differently. No such assurance is provided to teenagers in modern societies. In the United States, boys and girls gradually emerge from childhood into adolescence, putting away childish things and taking up adult activities — drinking, drugs, sex, and more mature types of entertainment forms — but not yet assuming full adult responsibilities. When does one actually become an adult? We have no generally accepted way of marking the transition. Adolescence in America can be considered a "big waiting room" (Davison and Davison, 1979).

Thus adolescence can be a difficult, confusing period of time. Sometimes young people feel overwhelmed by their problems; yet they often lack the motivation and skills to discuss them. Can anything be done to encourage disclosures? Recent research indicated that adolescents were more encouraged to discuss their problems if the conversation started off with such easily approached topics as music or hobbies than if it began with an analysis of such emotionally demanding subjects as unhappy or happy moments in their lives. Furthermore disclosure of personal problems was more extensive in group than in individual interviews. In the former context, adolescents used each other as models; once one individual disclosed his or her problems, others were encouraged to do so as well (Mills, 1983).

## Job Loss

Most people value their jobs, and this is revealed when they lose them. Recent studies have concluded that loss of job produces such reactions as diminished self-esteem, a sense of uselessness, and feelings of life being out of control (Baum et al., 1986; Davies, 1985; Kinicki, 1985).

Powell and Driscoll (1979) studied seventy-five scientists and engineers who lost their jobs. The informants averaged forty-one years of age, had a mean of sixteen years of education, and had experienced 9.5 months of unemployment. As they were gradually socialized to the unemployed status, these men passed through four stages that involved the learning of new values and norms:

*People who lose their jobs suffer the loss of both the tangible and intangible rewards of work. This photo shows unemployed steelworkers waiting in line at a food bank.*

*Stage 1: Period of relaxation and relief.* In most cases the men were aware of the layoffs in advance, and they were relieved when they finally took place. There was a sense of being "between jobs," and while most of the men made a definite effort to look for work, they tended to treat this period like a vacation at home, spending time with their families, sleeping late, and reading or tinkering in their workshops.

*Stage II: Period of concerted effort.* After about twenty-five days, the men usually felt rested and sometimes also bored. At this point they initiated a systematic effort to find new work, using such well-established strategies as calling friends, sending out resumés in response to ads, and going to job-placement centers. This phase averaged about three months, but the length varied considerably depending on such factors as the individual's ability to sustain his morale in the face of repeated rejection letters from potential employers, the amount of savings or other financial resources available to tide over the family, and the extent to which the wife provided moral support and handled the secretarial chores that accompany job seeking. During this

stage the men often avoided others who were unemployed. "I'm not like them," one engineer said. "They are out of a job. I am waiting for an offer from Corning Glass."

*Stage III: Period of uncertainty and doubt.* At this point the men had been unemployed longer than they had ever been before. After repeated unsuccessful encounters with the job market, their optimism began to erode. During this stage many men lost a clear sense of their occupational competence, often starting to feel that they were losing to younger men in the job competition or that their own knowledge and skills had become obsolete. Depression and rage often set in, with the rage frequently directed inward because there was no suitable external object on which to vent it. Toward the end of this period, a decline in job-hunting activity took place. The men made comments like the following: "I've stopped using certain approaches like sending out resumés. I push a little harder only when an opportunity comes up."

*Stage IV: Period of cynicism.* The transition to this stage was fairly smooth. The intervals between efforts to secure a job became longer and longer. The researchers concluded that a man was socialized to the status of unemployed person when he went two months without personally contacting a potential employer or job counselor. At this time many of the men in the study started to lose the conviction that they were in control of their occupational lives. The following statement was typical. "No matter what I do, it just doesn't make any difference. It's just a throw of the dice, whether I'll get the job or not." A strong sense of powerlessness and pessimism appeared. "Why go in for an interview?" a physicist asked. "I'll never get past the secretary anyway." This cynicism seemed to be a way of avoiding a confrontation with the reality that a return to work would require a major change in life-style—in particular, that any jobs the men would be able to obtain would pay much less than the ones they had previously. Once in this stage, men were likely to spend more time at home and to associate less with friends. While financial limitations played a part in this change, the major reason seemed to be a deliberate avoidance of people whose life-style now differed sharply from their own. With their husbands out of work, wives frequently sought full-time employment, and husbands assumed a more active role on the domestic front. Further developments would depend on changes in the job market and on the willingness of the man to accept a more modest position than the one he previously held.

## Divorce

Do you think that divorce tends to be a difficult experience? A study of stressful life events ranked the relative impact of forty-three issues. The death of one's spouse was placed first, and divorce was second. But a pair of researchers recently asserted that these findings have actually minimized the effect of divorce. They concluded that the impact of divorce is ". . . often much more disruptive, both immediately and in the long term, than losing one's spouse" (Counts and Sacks, 1985: 151).

Paul Bohannon (1970) suggested that divorce is especially difficult because it encompasses six different dimensions simultaneously and because our society does not yet possess effective means of helping people cope with these experiences. What

Bohannon has called the "six stations of divorce" include:

1. *The emotional divorce.* The spouses withhold emotion from each other—they grow apart—because their trust in and attraction for each other has ended.
2. *The economic divorce.* When the household is broken up, an economic settlement is necessary, separating the shared assets into two portions.
3. *The legal divorce.* In the courts the formal termination of the marriage takes place, along with the right to remarry.
4. *The coparental divorce.* Decisions are made about the custody of the children, visitation rights, each parent's financial and child-rearing responsibilities, and so forth.
5. *The community divorce.* Changes occur in the way friends and acquaintances react to the former marital partners when they learn about the divorce. Like property, friends too are often divided, becoming "her friends" or "his friends."
6. *The psychic divorce.* When marriage partners break up, an uncoupling occurs, and the sense of self alters. Each spouse must realize that he or she is no longer part of a couple. Once again the person is single, and for many, this is a shock.

Divorces are normally unsettling; remarriages can be also, especially when children are involved. In such cases the socialization of the stepparent includes learning how to build a relationship with his or her spouse's children. At present our society lacks clear standards on how stepparents should treat their spouses' children. Even the terms to use are unclear. What do children call their parents' new spouses—"Dad," "Mom," or do they refer to them by their first names? One obvious problem is that the missing biological parent is likely to resent the new spouse being called "Dad" or "Mom": It symbolizes a seizure of the parental role (Cherlin, 1983). Additional questions arise: For instance, does the new spouse have a parent's full rights and obligations—the right to use discipline on the children or the obligation to become a full partner in the long list of tasks that accompany parenthood?

# Death of Spouse

Recent research has indicated that elderly citizens who had lost a spouse in the past two months were more likely to report a newly developed or worsened illness, extensive use of medication, and poor health than a comparison group of elderly citizens who had not suffered such a loss (Thompson et al., 1984).

People inevitably undergo a period of adjustment after the death of a spouse. This socialization experience is often referred to as **grief work:** the process by which people attempt to establish a new identity after the death of a loved one. Grief work involves several stages. First, numbness and disbelief dominate. In the beginning surviving spouses often cannot accept the fact that their husbands or wives have actually died. This stage frequently continues for several weeks after the funeral. Second, longing for the lost spouse becomes obsessive. Constant crying, psychosomatic symptoms such as headaches and insomnia, feelings of guilt about failing to prevent the spouse's death, hostility toward doctors, and other strong emotional reactions occur at this time. Third, depression is likely;

sadness and loneliness become incapacitating. The surviving spouse no longer follows his or her normal routine and often expresses no motivation to keep living. Finally recovery occurs. The surviving husband or wife recognizes that, with adjustments, life can continue. When people reach this point, they have completed the grief work (Hiltz, 1980; Hultsch and Deutsch, 1981).

Because American women average about seven more years of life than do American men and also tend to be younger than their husbands, wives generally survive longer. At any given point in time, in fact, there are about five times more American widows than widowers (Hiltz, 1980). Studies on women suggest that several factors determine how difficult they will find the acceptance of the new role. One consideration involves the circumstances of the husband's death. If there is a long illness, the wife has some opportunity to prepare for her new role. On the other hand, if the death is unexpected, she finds herself thrust into the role of widow despite being unprepared to meet the psychological, economic, and social problems before her. Another important factor is the character of the relationship between the husband and wife.

**Table 6.2**
**Some Facts and Figures about "Tough Times"**

| ISSUE | PERTINENT STATISTICS | | |
|---|---|---|---|
| Adolescence | *The Age Group* | *The % of Total Arrests in 1983* | *The Age Group's % of American Population* |
| | 13 to 15 | 6.7% | 4.7% |
| | 16 to 18 | 13.3 | 4.9 |
| | 19 to 21 | 15.5 | 5.4 |
| | Unemployment rate of civilian labor force, February 1986 | | |
| | 16- to 19-year-olds | | 19.0% |
| | Overall | | 7.3 |
| Job loss | In February 1986, 4.2 million Americans, representing 3.6% of the civilian labor force and 48.7% of the unemployed, had lost their jobs. | | |
| Divorce | Divorced Americans, 1983: 11.6 million or 6.5% of the adult population 15 years old and over | | |
| Death of spouse | Widowed Americans, 1983: 12.8 million or 7.2% of the adult population 15 years old and over; 10.9 million widows or 11.7% of the female population 15 years old and over; 1.9 million widowers or 2.3% of the male population 15 years old and over | | |

Sources: U.S. Bureau of the Census. *Current Population Reports,* Series P-20, No. 389, *Marital Status and Living Arrangements: March 1983.* Table 1; U.S. Department of Justice. *Sourcebook of Criminal Justice Statistics, 1984.* Figure 4.4; U.S. Department of Labor. *Employment and Earnings.* Volume 33 (March 1986). Tables A-38, A-40.

A wife who was dependent upon her husband to make decisions and to handle practical matters is in a more difficult situation than is a wife who was more active in family affairs. A third issue concerns the age at which a woman becomes a widow. If it happens when she is still young, she is probably the first widow in her circle of friends. If she becomes a widow at a later age, she is likely to have friends to help her learn how to play the role of widow. These women can serve as role models and perhaps make her adjustment to the new role easier. A final factor involves the woman's marital-role orientation. Research indicates that women who have given their highest priority to the wife role have more difficulty accepting the death of their husbands and assuming the widow role than do those who have emphasized the mother role as their strongest priority (Loether, 1975).

Table 6.2 provides some statistical information about "tough times."

# STUDY GUIDE

## Summary

1. Socialization is the process by which a person becomes a member of a group or society, learning the necessary cultural content and modes of behavior. The most fundamental socialization occurs in childhood, but the process continues throughout people's lifetimes.

2. Sociologists address the question of whether human beings are the product of their nature (their innate biological characteristics or heredity) or their nurture (their socialization). While recognizing the significance of the nature issue, sociologists emphasize the importance of nurture or socialization.

3. When children grow up in isolated circumstances or are the victims of deprived socialization, their sense of self is likely to be underdeveloped, confused, or unusual in some other respect. Studies of isolated infant monkeys, isolated children, and abused children have demonstrated these patterns of development.

4. Several well-known theories analyze development of the self. Cooley's looking-glass self and George Herbert Mead's discussion of "play" and "game" indicate how the self develops as a result of interaction with others. Freudian theory divides the self into three parts, with one of the parts — the ego — acting as a mediator between the conflicting demands of the other two. Jean Piaget's theory of cognitive abilities involves four age-graded stages, where progressive knowledge builds from the experience obtained in the previous stage or stages. The four theories of socialization we have examined all recognize the changing nature of the self.

5. Sources of socialization include the family, mass media, the school and day-care, and peers. Families have a prominent socialization impact on children because they receive their first exposure to values, norms, beliefs, and knowledge in the family context. The conception of childhood and appropriate child-rearing practice vary in different eras and social settings. The mass media, especially television, are also a modern agent of socialization for people. The influence of television in the area of violent programming is a source of widespread concern. The school is another prominent socialization force. The content of children's schooling often arouses controversy. Day-care for small children is also a controversial issue. With so many mothers working, however, the continuance of day-care in the future seems inevitable. Peers are another agent of socialization. In industrialized societies peer groups appear to have assumed some of the socialization functions performed by the family in the past. Besides the previous agents of socialization, a variety of others can be important influences on individuals. Inhabitants in total institutions experience resocialization, with the mortification process and the privilege system contributing to that outcome.

6. In the course of their lives, people encounter certain "tough times," transitional periods when new standards and new activities affect them. Some of these periods are elicited by adolescence, job loss, divorce, and the death of a spouse. Adolescence is a difficult, confusing time period because it involves a shift from childhood to adult roles. Job loss can be a disturbing experience. Peo-

ple who suffer it can pass through four stages that involve a gradual socialization to their unemployed status. Divorce also involves a significant readjustment. Bohannon described six levels on which divorce occurs. The loss of one's spouse also produces new socialization experiences. Learning to live without one's spouse can be described as a four-step process.

## Glossary

**cognitive ability**   the capacity to use perception, thought, memory, and other mental processes to acquire knowledge.

**ego**   Freud's conception of the self that must cope with pressures from three often contradictory forces.

**game**   according to Mead, a group activity in which each participant's role requires interaction with two or more individuals.

**generalized other**   an image of the role expectations for all the game participants with whom a person must interact.

**grief work**   the process by which people attempt to establish a new identity after the death of a loved one.

**id**   according to Sigmund Freud, the part of the personality that is unconscious, primitive, and constantly pleasure seeking.

**instincts**   unalterable behavioral complexes that parents transmit genetically to their children.

**looking-glass self**   according to Charles Cooley, our understanding of what sort of person we are is based on how we imagine we appear to other people.

**mass media**   the instruments of communication that reach a large audience without any personal contact between the senders and the receivers.

**mortification process**   a series of degradations and humiliations of inhabitants systematically carried out by staff members of total institutions.

**nature**   inborn biological characteristics or heredity.

**nurture**   socialization.

**object permanence**   according to Jean Piaget, the childhood recognition that specific objects still exist after they are removed from one's line of vision.

**play**   according to George Herbert Mead, the process of taking the role of specific individuals and thereby starting to learn the rights and obligations that particular roles entail.

**privilege system**   a framework for inmates' resocialization.

**self**   one's perception of his or her own person, formed as a result of other people's response in the course of socialization.

**socialization**   the process by which a person becomes a member of a group or society, learning the necessary cultural content and modes of behavior.

**sociobiology**   a field in which the proponents contend that through the evolutionary process, human beings have acquired tendencies that determine much of their behavior.

**superego**   according to Freud, the part of the personality that has internalized standards of right and wrong, a conscience.

**total institution**   a place of residence where inhabitants experience nearly complete restriction of their physical freedom in order to be effectively resocialized into a radically new identity and behavioral pattern.

## Learning Objectives

After studying this chapter, you should be able to:

1. Define socialization and discuss its importance for human life.
2. Discuss the interplay of nature and nurture in human development.
3. Describe the effects on human development of deprived socialization in childhood.

4. Discuss in detail Cooley's, Mead's, Freud's, and Piaget's theories of socialization.
5. Examine the socialization impact of the family, analyzing how conceptions of childhood have changed over time.
6. Discuss mass media, peers, and schools and day-care centers as sources of socialization.
7. Define total institution and describe the two-step process of inmate resocialization.
8. Examine the following "tough times," major transitions in the socialization process: adolescence, job loss, divorce, and death of spouse.

# Tests

## True – false test

_____ 1. Socialization continues throughout the entire life span.

_____ 2. Sociobiologists argue that the tendency to form dominance hierarchies among humans is neither innate nor universal.

_____ 3. Cooley and Mead both believed that the self is the product of a learning process that occurs in interaction with others.

_____ 4. Piaget's theory is concerned with children's increasing understanding of social relations.

_____ 5. During the Middle Ages, children were treated as little adults.

_____ 6. A rigorous study of the relationship between violent television programming and violent behavior has determined that violent programming is the main reason many people engage in violence.

_____ 7. Resocialization in closed institutions always prepares people to function smoothly in the greater society.

_____ 8. A consequence of job loss and nonsuccess in job seeking is that eventually one becomes socialized to the status of unemployed person.

_____ 9. Grief work is a type of socialization.

_____ 10. In a given year, there are about equal numbers of widows and widowers in the United States.

## Multiple-choice test

_____ 1. Darwin's idea of "natural selection" is consistent with the idea of:
   a. nurture.
   b. the id.
   c. instinct.
   d. survival of the fittest.

_____ 2. Cooley's concept of the looking-glass self:
   a. was rejected by George Herbert Mead.
   b. involves an image of the role expectations for all the game participants with whom a person must interact.
   c. suggests that our understanding of what sort of person we are is based on how we imagine we appear to other people.
   d. is closely related to Freud's concept of the superego.

_____ 3. All but one of the following are stages in the development of the self as described by Mead. Which is NOT a stage?
  a. play
  b. game
  c. generalized
  d. preparatory

_____ 4. In Freud's theory of the self, the internalized standards of right and wrong (conscience) exist in the:
  a. superego.
  b. id.
  c. ego.
  d. instinct.

_____ 5. In Piaget's theory of cognitive development, the ability to think abstractly occurs in which stage?
  a. concrete operational
  b. formal operational
  c. sensorimotor
  d. preoperational

_____ 6. On the topic of child-rearing, it now seems apparent that:
  a. children in all societies should be reared the same way.
  b. beyond basic care and feeding, there are no universal needs among children.
  c. Americans have developed the best approach to child-rearing for all societies.
  d. non-Westerners rear their children more effectively than Westerners do.

_____ 7. A recent study has concluded that adolescents were more encouraged to discuss personal problems if:
  a. conversations began with such easily approached topics as music or hobbies.
  b. they remained anonymous during interviews.
  c. conversations were conducted over the phone and not face-to-face.
  d. interviewers were teachers known to the adolescents.

_____ 8. Powell and Driscoll studied scientists and engineers who had lost their jobs. Depression and rage occurred during which stage of response to job loss?
  a. period of relaxation and relief
  b. period of concerted effort
  c. period of uncertainty and doubt
  d. period of cynicism

_____ 9. Which of the following is a common problem of remarriage?
  a. lack of clear standards for stepparent's treatment of spouse's children
  b. less value attached by society to second marriages
  c. lack of strong parental support for second marriages
  d. absence of formal rituals to legitimate second marriages

_____ 10. Which of these statements about widowhood in America is true?
  a. There is a formal mourning period.
  b. Role models (other widows) seldom make adjustment to the new role easier.
  c. Women who give the highest priority to the wife role have less difficulty accepting the death of their husbands than do those who most strongly emphasize the mother role.
  d. Wives whose husbands die suddenly adjust to widowhood more slowly than wives whose husbands die after a long illness.

**Essay test**

1. Define socialization. Why is this process important?
2. Distinguish nature and nurture and discuss the development of the "nature" position, including sociologists' reaction to it.
3. How does deprived socialization affect young children? Discuss the different issues raised in the section on this topic.
4. What is the self? Describe Cooley's, Mead's, Freud's, and Piaget's analyses of the self. Indicate significant similarities and differences between and among the theories.
5. Discuss the impact of three important sources of socialization on American college students.
6. Describe three difficult transitions that can occur in the socialization process, making references to relevant concepts and studies.

## Suggested Readings

Axline, Virginia. 1968. *Dibs: In Search of Self.* New York: Ballantine. A vivid account of a withdrawn child's effort to clarify his sense of self with the aid of a highly skilled therapist.

Erikson, Erik. 1964. *Childhood and Society.* New York: Norton. Revised edition. A theoretical analysis of socialization and the development of the self. The book contains an eight-stage developmental process through which modern people pass.

Goodman, Paul. 1960. *Growing Up Absurd.* New York: Vintage. A sociologist's uncompromisingly critical account of the frustrations and confusion that all children face growing up in American society where, according to Goodman, useless, destructive, and above all absurd standards and activities are dominant.

Intintoli, Michael James. 1984. *Taking Soaps Seriously: The World of "Guiding Light".* New York: Praeger. A study of the process by which a soap is put together. The author emphasizes that the soap's morality and domesticity themes are dictated by Proctor and Gamble, the show's owner and chief sponsor.

Kagan, Jerome. 1984. *The Nature of the Child.* New York: Basic. A noted psychologist's highly readable summary of what is known about children. A wealth of cross-cultural references are included. Traditional theory and research are challenged.

Roth, Henry. 1932. *Call It Sleep.* New York: Cooper Square. A novel that sensitively describes fear, confusion, and loneliness encountered by a young Jewish immigrant boy living in early twentieth-century New York City.

Spock, Benjamin, and Michael B. Rothenberg. 1985. *Dr. Spock's Baby and Child Care.* New York: Pocket Books. Sixth edition. This forty-year-old book continues to be the country's leading guide for parents seeking practical knowledge about how to care for their children.

Zelizer, Viviana A. 1985. *Pricing the Priceless Child: The Changing Social Value of Children.* New York: Basic. An interesting book showing how the conception of children has shifted from perceiving them in economic terms to perceiving them within a moral framework.

## Student Projects

1. In the course of an ordinary school/work day, observe the behavior of someone (without being noticed), noting how often and under what circumstances this person seems to alter his/her behavior in order to fit in with others' expectations. Alternatively you might make mental notes on your own behavior, recording your own behavioral changes when you are with other people. Discuss your findings with other class members. How do your observations fit with Cooley's and Mead's theories? How do your findings fit with Goffman's theory (dramaturgic sociology) discussed in Chapter 5?

2. Make a list of the different agents of socializa-

tion with whom you have been in close contact today. Then ask yourself which of these agents of socialization you would consult regarding the following issues: problems with school, difficulties in interpersonal relations (such as your love life), career choices, self-improvement goals, and the need to release strong emotions (such as love, hate, or fear). What does this exercise suggest about the varied influences of different agents of socialization? Would you have made the same consultations five years ago?

## Answers to Test Questions

### True–false test

| | | | | |
|---|---|---|---|---|
| 1. t | 3. t | 5. t | 7. f | 9. t |
| 2. f | 4. f | 6. f | 8. t | 10. f |

### Multiple-choice test

| | | | | |
|---|---|---|---|---|
| 1. d | 3. c | 5. b | 7. a | 9. a |
| 2. c | 4. a | 6. b | 8. c | 10. d |

# 7
# Gender Roles and Sexuality

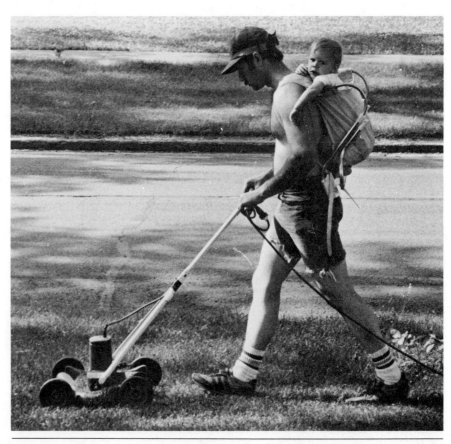

He is the kind of man she had hoped to meet: intelligent, confident, amusing. But the party ends, and there is no dinner invitation. However, that is no problem. She is a young, successful, liberated woman, and the next day she gives him a call and asks him for a date.

Is this what happens? Many young female professionals support the idea of such a course of action, but they remain reluctant to pursue it.

> "Theoretically, it should be perfectly fine if a woman asks a man for a date, but I'm not comfortable with it," said . . . [a woman] who is with the Department of Commerce in Washington. "I'm embarrassed to admit I feel that way," she added, "because it seems to me I should feel comfortable doing it, but I don't."
>
> *(Nemy, 1982: 1)*

A twenty-seven-year-old vice-president of a major investment banking firm admitted that she would be reluctant to ask a man out but that she would "certainly let a man know I was interested." She added, "I have to be aggressive all day in my business, and I don't like to be the aggressor in personal relations. I like to assume the female role" (Nemy, 1982: 1).

Nancy Reagan's deputy press secretary explained that her mother had taught her never to call a man "and I don't." This woman, who is in her early thirties, seldom writes off a man who interests her but does not call. She does what thousands of other women do: She creates a situation where she will see him again. "What I might do is have a dinner party and ask him," she said. "I wouldn't ask him to dinner alone" (Nemy, 1982: 16). Other women will call a man for a date when they are sufficiently motivated. "Dating is not like the bomb, it's not serious," said . . . a law librarian in Washington. "When you take it in that spirit, it's no big deal. It's absolutely antiquated that someone should sit home waiting for their phone to ring" (Nemy, 1982: 16). This woman feels that men are usually so flattered by her unexpected calls that they cannot wait to go out with her.

A sociological analysis of the preceding discussion requires the use of three concepts — sex, gender, and gender role. All women share the same **sex**. A variety of animal forms, including human beings, are divided into the biological categories of male and female.

Distinctions of gender, however, are not as fixed. **Gender** consists of the general behavioral standards that distinguish males and females in a given culture. In the United States, men and women traditionally have been expected to dress and behave differently. Gender is a status, specifying for both women and men their culturally supported rights and obligations. In the 1980s the definition of female gender is being reevaluated as the traditional expectation that women should be subordinate to men in all social activities has come under strong attack.

For many women some **gender roles** — sets of specific behavioral patterns associated with either the male or female gender — are more straightforward than others. For instance, most women are more comfortable interacting with men as equals in student and worker roles than in the more personal role of single women seeking dates. For men too the redefinition of gender roles is often easier to accept in impersonal than in personal areas.

It is noteworthy that until recent years the concept "sex role" was used instead of the term "gender role." The switch has been occurring as people have increasingly recognized that the ability of women and men to perform roles effectively is usually determined by sociocultural factors, including socialization, not by the fact that one has been born a male or female (Berger and Berger, 1984: 54–59).

As you read this chapter, you might consider how issues involving gender roles apply to you. You might evaluate the different ways parents, peers, and others have shaped your conception of

*The addition of a person of the opposite sex to an all-female or all-male group can have a more noticeable effect on conversation and behavior than the addition of a person of the same sex.*

yourself as a male or female as well as the various gender roles you have played. It might be interesting to analyze the extent to which you have accepted traditional female or male roles.

You undoubtedly realize the prominent part that gender and gender roles play in everyday life. For example, the addition of a person of the opposite sex to an all-female or all-male group will often have a more marked effect on the conversation than will the addition of an individual of the same sex. In a sense an intruder has appeared. To some extent, one might argue, men and women form separate subcultures. Furthermore it is likely that you are aware that your gender-role behavior differs from what was conventional in your par-

ents' generation. What would you emphasize? Freer, more relaxed sex? Greater leeway in the realm of gender-role definitions? Better communication between the sexes? Or is some or all of this nothing but hogwash?

The following section considers the biological and cultural bases for differentiating people into female and male gender roles. Then the discussion shifts to the leading theoretical perspectives on gender roles. The next topic is sexuality in premarital, marital, and extramarital situations. Fourth, we consider homosexuality, a subject on which ignorance, tension, and antipathy are widespread in U.S. society. Finally we look briefly at the future of American gender roles.

## Gender-Role Development

What factors account for gender-role development? Biological? Cultural? A combination of both? Let us consider.

### Biological Differences between the Sexes

Sigmund Freud believed that "anatomy determines destiny." Critics correctly note that this stance has been used to justify keeping women

subordinate to men in the workplace and at home. But what are the facts? How much does the physical reality of being male or female influence a person's attitudes and behavior? In order to address this question, we must start by examining the importance of chromosomes and hormones in shaping human activity.

*The Differentiation between Male and Female*

The differentiation—the development of (in this case biological) differences—between males and females is fundamental, depending on whether or not a Y chromosome was present at the zygote (single-cell) stage of development. About half of all human sperm cells contain a Y chromosome, and the other half an X chromosome. The human egg always includes one X chromosome. If a Y-bearing sperm unites with the egg, an XY sex-chromosome pattern is produced and a male results. An X-bearing sperm uniting with the egg creates an XX pattern and a female. The single-celled zygote divides, then divides again and again, and at adulthood a person has at least 100 trillion cells, each of which contains either an XX or an XY sex-chromosome pattern. From a biological perspective, therefore, sex is fundamental.

About six weeks after conception, the fetal sex chromosomes direct the formation of either testicles (from the XY pattern) or ovaries (from the XX pattern). In turn, the embryonic testicles or ovaries start producing male or female sex hormones (androgen and estrogen), which mold the originally undifferentiated reproductive tissues into either male or female genitals and internal reproductive systems. The hormones also influence the brain centers, controlling such adult reproductive functions as ovulation, menstruation, and erection. The second most obvious effect of sex hormones occurs at puberty, with a sharp increase in hormone production creating sexual maturation.

### Evidence of Biological Factors in Sexual Differentiation

Men and women experience different physiological processes related to reproduction—such as the menstrual cycle in women and the erection of the penis in men—and so the controlling brain centers must also be different. But current research is finding further evidence of differences in men's and women's brains. Research on epileptics, who had portions of their brains removed to control seizures, has led to some interesting findings. Men lose verbal skills after surgery on the left half of their brains and spatial abilities after damage to the right half. Women, on the other hand, lose both verbal and spatial skills, no matter which half of their brains has been damaged. This suggests that women's verbal and spatial abilities are duplicated on both sides of the brain while men

seem to have the speech center located on the left and the center for spatial skills on the right side of the brain. The implications of the research are noteworthy. Because the halves of women's brains are less specialized, it might be simpler for them to perform tasks combining the two skills—for instance, reading or learning to understand someone's behavior on the basis of both facial expression and words. On the other hand, the structure of men's brains may make it easier for them to do a verbal task and a spatial task at the same time, such as simultaneously reading a map and talking (Goleman, 1978).

## Cultural Differences between the Genders

It seems indisputable that biological factors play a significant part in the development of gender roles. However, the sociological perspective compels one to recognize also the significant contribution of culture. Even before a child is born, people's expectations about what is appropriate male or female behavior begin to appear. Late in pregnancy a parent might say, "The baby's kicking a lot. It must be a boy." Mothers tend to look at and talk to female infants more than to males and to respond to girls more quickly when they cry. As toddlers, girls are encouraged to spend more time touching their mothers and staying close to them than are boys.

Different treatment for boys and girls intensifies at about the age of two when parents are able to use children's rapidly expanding language ability to mold their behavior. There are "boy" toys (trucks, airplanes, and rubber balls) and "girl" toys (dolls and dollhouses). Many two-year-old boys who would prefer dolls are steered away from them and warned not to become "sissies." By the age of five or six, children's preferences are relatively stabilized. Young children's appearance and dress also conform to our cultural norms of masculinity and femininity. For example, a girl's hair is expected to be carefully combed and decorated. She will be clothed in dresses, encouraged to play with her mother's jewelry and makeup, and warned to stay clean, to keep her underpants always covered, and to be restrained, cute, and coy. Boys, on the other hand, are permitted and even encouraged to participate in physically active

*Gradually gender roles are becoming less sex-typed, with some men taking a more active role in the performance of domestic tasks.*

games and sports, to get as dirty as they wish in the process, and to be generally noisy, aggressive, and even combative (Kagan, 1964).

As we noted in Chapter 6 ("Socialization"), children internalize their parents' conceptions of appropriate behavior. When asked how boys and girls differ, children explain that boys are noisy, dirty, and active while girls are quiet, clean, gentle, and inclined to cry. Men, they indicate, become protectors, adventurers, laborers, and decision-makers while women engage in cooking, sewing, and child-rearing (Gagnon and Greenblat, 1978).

A study of hermaphrodites (people with genitals part male and part female) supports the cultural basis for sex differentiation. Matched pairs were employed, with each pair involving two people similar in chromosome pattern (both had either an XX or XY pattern) and in personal characteristics (such as age, income, and education). One, however, had been raised a female and the other a male. In each case the hermaphrodite who was a

chromosomal male but had been raised a female was typically "feminine" behaviorally while the hermaphrodite who was a chromosomal female but was reared as a male acted typically "masculine" (Money and Ehrhardt, 1972).

### Cross-Cultural Evidence

A look at gender roles in different societies suggests that certain sex-linked tasks seem to be partly rooted in the biological differences between males and females. On the other hand, the fact that gender-role standards can vary from one culture to another demonstrates that cultural factors are also important.

#### ANTHROPOLOGICAL RESEARCH

Joel Arnoff and William Crano (1975; Crano and Arnoff, 1978) studied data drawn from cultures carefully picked to represent six broad geographical areas encompassing the planet. Their findings suggest that generalizations about typical male or female behavior must be carefully made. They note that food production (hunting, gathering, fishing, animal husbandry, and agriculture) has frequently been considered a male-dominated, instrumental task, but their evidence indicates that, in reality, women often participate. Furthermore in spite of widespread belief to the contrary, women do not dominate child-rearing in all cases. In the 186 societies they studied, the investigators found that women invariably were responsible for most of the child-rearing during infancy (the first nine months). As Figure 7.1 indicates, mothers were the principal or almost exclusive caretakers of infants in over 90 percent of the societies. However, in early childhood (aged nine months to four or five years), no societies confined most care responsibilities to the mother. In 32 percent of the cultures studied, most or practically all of the young child's time was spent apart from the mother. Fathers were excluded or nearly excluded from child-rearing in only 16 percent of the societies, and in 55 percent, fathers maintained a frequent or regular relationship with their children.

The following Cross-Cultural Perspective demonstrates that, in spite of some biologically influenced gender-role tendencies, societies can develop highly varied gender-role patterns.

*Evidence from Modern Societies*

Jeanne Block (1973) studied gender-role stereotypes in six countries—Norway, Sweden, Denmark, Finland, England, and the United States. She found that male and female college students shared similar images of ideal male and female behavior in these six Western, technologically advanced societies. Adjectives that described the ideal man included the following: practical, assertive, dominating, competitive, self-controlled, and rational. For females the list contained such adjectives as affectionate, impulsive, generous, sympathetic, perceptive, sensitive, and shy. American men placed the most emphasis on males being "macho" while American women described their ideal female as being more "masculine" than did women from the other societies. Furthermore in several respects American child-rearing values differed sharply from those of the other five countries studied. Americans placed especially strong emphasis on early and clear differentiation of male

**Figure 7.1**
**Cross-Cultural Comparison of Mothers' and Fathers' Contribution to Child-Rearing[1]**

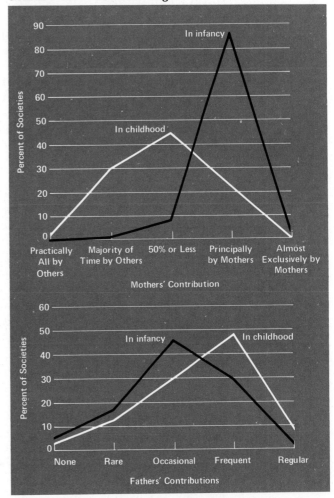

[1] A total of 186 societies were included in the study, with data on 141 societies in the infancy phase and 122 in the childhood phase.

*While across societies mothers make a distinctly more substantial contribution to child-rearing than fathers, men nonetheless do provide significant assistance in many societies. (Source: Adapted from Joel Arnoff and William D. Crano. "A Cross-Cultural Study of Expressive and Instrumental Role Complementarity in the Family." American Sociological Review. Vol. 43. 1978, pp. 466–467.)*

and female gender roles and also stressed competitive achievement while putting relatively little emphasis on the control of male aggression.

In such socialist nations as the Soviet Union and the People's Republic of China, both sexes are expected to participate actively in the labor force.

**148**    CROSS-CULTURAL PERSPECTIVE

*Gender Roles among the Arapesh and the Tchambuli*

Margaret Mead (1963), an anthropologist, studied three preindustrial societies located within a hundred miles of one another on islands in the South Pacific. Her analysis of socialization practices characteristic of two cultures provides some indication of why the Arapesh of both sexes were gentle and strongly concerned with each other's emotional needs and why the Tchambuli women tended to fill their culture's principal breadwinner roles while Tchambuli men customarily spent the entire day insulting each other and laboring over their appearance. The larger implication of Mead's research is that gender roles are highly flexible, primarily developing from prevailing socialization patterns.

Among the Arapesh both mothers and fathers participated equally in child-rearing. Fathers tended to show as little embarrassment as mothers in disposing of infants' feces and as much patience teaching young children to eat from spoons too large for their small mouths. Throughout Arapesh society it was recognized that men played a prominent role in child-rearing. If an observer were to comment that a middle-aged man was good-looking, people would reply, "Good-looking? Ye-e-s. But you should have seen him before he bore all those children" (Mead, 1963: 39).

According to the Arapesh standards, a young child's crying was "a tragedy to be avoided at any cost." The most trying period of time in child-rearing occurred at about the age of three when children were too old to be comforted by breast-feeding and yet too young to explain why they were weeping. The best way to ensure that infants maintained their sense of well-being, the Arapesh believed, was to provide the continuous comfort of human voices and skin contact. Thus when a mother was working in the garden, she would bring along a young child to hold her infant instead of laying it on the ground.

Arapesh children were not pressured to grow up quickly. Their socialization was informal and easy, and attentive adults and older children were always around to help.

Among the Tchambuli Mead found that boys were raised by hard-working mothers who nursed them "generously but nonchalantly" while busily weaving reeds into baskets. There were always women present, willing to attend to a boy's needs while they worked. Mead wrote, "If his father's other wife failed to feed him as generously as his mother, his mother needed only to make the light reproach: Are children so plentiful that you should neglect them?" (Mead, 1963: 248). Like the

Arapesh children, Tchambuli boys were raised indulgently. Their childhood days were spent tumbling around the floors of the great dwelling houses where the mothers worked. After being weaned, they were fed delicacies, such as sugar cane, whenever they cried.

However, a significant change happened somewhere between the ages of eight and twelve when boys were subjected to the ritual of scarification required of all males approaching manhood. The boy was held squirming and howling on a rock while a maternal uncle and an expert scarifier cut patterns on his back. Then he was painted with oil and tumeric (a spice) and kept in seclusion for as long as three months until his father decided that the best moment for the ceremonial washing of the child's body had arrived; the boy's immense discomfort was never considered. When the ritual washing was completed, the child's seclusion ended. He was given an elaborately woven belt, shell ornaments, and other decorative items to carry around with him.

Tchambuli men did not trust each other. As a boy grew into manhood, his father and elder brothers watched him jealously to be certain that he made no advances toward their wives.

Mead wrote little about the socialization of Tchambuli

girls. Apparently they were raised to identify with their mothers, to become the workers and breadwinners. Among women there was always an emphasis on "comradeship, efficient, happy work enlivened by continuous brisk banter and chatter" (Mead, 1963: 252). While the women worked and chatted, the men labored over their appearance, their flute playing, and dancing and were always prepared to reply to caustic comments and insults from jealous rivals.

Margaret Mead's research has received a fair amount of criticism. Most recently, in 1983, Derek Freeman has claimed that Mead's well-known book *Coming of Age in Samoa* was a distorted analysis of the lives of Samoan adolescent girls. It is also possible that her studies of the Arapesh and Tchambuli contain some exaggerated conclusions. Nonetheless it is proba-ble that the gender roles of people in both societies differ sharply from those that Americans typically associate with men and women.

Certainly Mead's data emphasize an important theme in this chapter: In spite of biologically influenced gender-role tendencies for both men and women, societies can produce highly diversified gender-role patterns.

Source: Margaret Mead. *Sex and Temperament in Three Primitive Societies.* New York: William Morrow. 1963.

Compared to women in the United States and other Western countries, Soviet women seem to have more educational and occupational opportunities. This appearance, however, is somewhat deceiving. While it is true that the majority of physicians in the Soviet Union are women, medicine as a profession provides much lower prestige and pay in the Soviet Union than in the United States. In medicine and in other job areas as well, women are generally excluded from high-level positions (Smith, 1976). Before the advent of socialism, Chinese women were clearly subordinate to men. Some were forced to bind their feet, crippling them and making it impossible for them to walk. Women were also beaten, physically abused, and treated as servants. Since the Chinese Revolution, women have received increased educational and occupational opportunities. However, few women attain higher levels of education, and few hold managerial positions or prestigious government posts (Stacey, 1975).

## The Biosocial Position

As we have seen, some uncertainty currently exists on the issue of whether sex-linked abilities and psychological attributes are principally biologically or culturally determined. In Chapter 6 we noted that the field of sociobiology has developed as a response to the nature-nurture debate on whether human beings are the product of their inborn biological characteristics, their socialization, or both. The **biosocial position** is a recently developed perspective that acknowledges the sig-nificance of both biology and social experience in the development of gender roles and that emphasizes their interplay, contending that the independent significance of each factor is impossible to assess since they never exist in isolation from one another. This position suggests that biological factors determine a few limits and lead to a number of predispositions but that culture generally has the "final say" about development.

Consider several examples. Advocates of the biosocial position will observe that in female rats the release of the hormone prolactin will stimulate the production of milk and encourage them to display mothering behavior toward their offspring (Terkel and Rosenblatt, 1972). In human females the production of prolactin will also produce milk, but mothering tendencies require cultural support before they can occur. Consider another example. Among such nonhuman primates as baboons and gorillas, for which defense is frequently a life-and-death struggle, males tend to be much larger and stronger than females and to exert considerable dominance over them (Gough, 1983). Human males also tend to be larger and stronger than their female counterparts, but the extent to which males exert dominance will vary considerably from one culture to another.

In her presidential address to the American Sociological Association several years ago, Alice Rossi suggested that in order to most effectively understand gender-role issues ". . . it is my firm conviction, and conclusion, that the goals we seek are best approached through an integrated biosocial science" (Rossi, 1984: 15).

# Theories

There is no doubt that biological factors affect the development of gender roles. However, the three theories discussed in this section—the structural-functional, the conflict, and the symbolic-interactionist theories of gender roles—focus on social influences.

## The Structural-Functional Theory of Gender Roles

Parsons and Bales's (1955) analysis supports the traditional outlook on gender roles, suggesting that men and women exhibit distinct, task-related gender roles. Such a sharp distinction between women's and men's roles no longer exists in our society, but this theory remains important, because the different socialization patterns for males and females described by Parsons and Bales still occur to some extent.

A central concept in the structural-functional theory of gender roles is **identification,** a process by which an individual incorporates another person's values, standards, and expectations into his or her own behavior and sense of self. Parsons and Bales contended that, as infants, children of both sexes identify with their mothers. As they become older, girls continue that identification, but boys are encouraged to start finding male role models. Therefore boys turn toward their fathers as a model for identification. The fact that girls identify with their mothers is apparent from their patterns of play. According to Parsons and Bales, little girls tend to play with dolls and to play "house." They become directed toward domestic chores like those done by their mothers. Little boys, on the other hand, are more inclined to play with trains, cars, and airplanes and to act out masculine roles such as fireman or soldier (Parsons and Bales, 1955: 100).

Parsons and Bales suggested that the basic gender-role patterns formed in childhood extend into adulthood. As girls grow up, they concentrate on domestic roles, and marriage becomes their primary concern. A woman establishes her basic social status by competently performing the roles of wife and mother. For a man, Parsons and Bales wrote, the carryover of the breadwinner role from childhood to adulthood "is so clear as to need relatively little comment." Boys are brought up with an emphasis on attaining knowledge, and as they progress through school, growing importance is placed on preparing for an occupation (Parsons and Bales, 1955: 127–128).

Parsons and Bales (1955) claimed that the nuclear family, composed of husband, wife, and children, obtains positive functions from these distinctive male and female gender roles. Role complementarity develops. The wife stays at home and cooks, cleans, raises the children, and seeks to maintain the family's emotional health and stability. The husband, in turn, is the breadwinner. In short, ". . . he is in the first instance "giver-of-care" or pleasure, and secondarily the giver of love, whereas the wife is primarily the giver of love and secondarily the giver of care or pleasure" (Parsons and Bales, 1955: 151). Parsons and Bales recognized that any social structure, such as the nuclear family, can vary in its form and function in different societies. However, they believed that the nuclear family will operate efficiently only if there is a sex-linked division of labor within it, with men chiefly performing the breadwinner and women the domestic roles.

## The Conflict Theory of Gender Roles

The development of the modern women's movement has helped produce a growing sense that women should have a right of equal access to edu-

*As perspectives on traditional roles change, occupational opportunities for women appear to be broadening. This in turn may result in new role models and further changes. Shown here is Sandra Day O'Connor, the first woman to be sworn in as a Justice of the United States Supreme Court. (Her husband is standing in the center.)*

cational and occupational opportunities and a corresponding distaste or even repugnance for traditionally defined men's and women's roles. At present, therefore, it is understandable that many modern Americans feel that Parsons and Bales's analysis represents little more than a defense of the status quo and that a different approach, a conflict perspective, is necessary.

In her book *Sexual Politics,* Kate Millett (1970) has emphasized that men traditionally have dominated women in all institutions and activities. The conflict perspective on gender roles makes the same point. Randall Collins (1971; 1974) concluded that gender inequality, like any other inequality, involves a conflict for scarce resources between a dominant group (males) and a subordinate group (females). In order for men to have superior political, social, and economic status, women must have inferior status in all respects.

According to conflict theorists, economic inequality is the underlying source of sexual inequal-ity. Cross-cultural evidence provides support for this argument. For instance, in hunting-and-gathering societies, where men and women make a fairly equal contribution to food production, little sexual inequality exists. In more technologically advanced societies, the economic contributions of men have overshadowed those of women, with a corresponding growth in sexual inequality.

The link between economic and sexual inequality is clearly borne out by events during the industrial era. Until women had the option of work outside the home, they were entirely dependent on the care and protection of their husbands, who, if they chose to (and apparently many often did), could beat or sexually abuse their wives without any fear of legal action. The first factory jobs for women offered pathetically low pay (one-third of men's) and gruesome working conditions, but women were earning money for themselves and, from this point on, their role in family decision-making began to increase gradually.

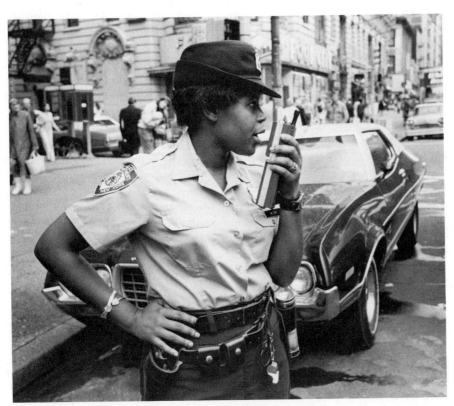

*Police work, which until recent years was overwhelmingly a male profession, now contains a steadily increasing percentage of women. As women move into what were once exclusively male professions, they serve as possible role models for girls, who are learning what constitutes the range of acceptable modern female behavior.*

**152**

While structural-functional and conflict theorists are sharply opposed to each other, some points of agreement do exist. Many structural-functional theorists recognize that extreme gender inequalities are no longer functional in the modern world —such inequalities lead to discontent, conflict, and the loss of female talent for an array of occupations. An up-to-date structural-functional perspective will allow for women's greater involvement in occupations and men's increased participation in domestic tasks. On the other hand, conflict theorists, though critical of traditional gender roles, will recognize that these roles were functional in the past. Furthermore both schools agree that gender roles are based primarily on cultural, not biological factors.

## The Symbolic-Interactionist Theory of Gender Roles

Theories, such as that of Parsons and Bales, which emphasize children's imitation of their parents and parents' reinforcement of their children's appropriate behavior, tend to highlight children's passivity and downplay their active participation.

According to George Herbert Mead (1934), young children learn to act out the roles of significant people in their lives—in particular, parents. As the children do so, they begin to understand what these roles really involve. Their developing conceptions of the roles of mommy, daddy, or other significant individuals will differ depending on whether or not the model plays his or her gender role in a traditional or a nontraditional manner.

As children grow older, Mead observed, they gradually begin to understand that the roles they have learned to play are not necessarily and exclusively bound to specific individuals. Children begin to recognize that expectations are associated with the roles themselves and also that roles are interconnected. When children understand this, they have started to realize that norms guide the behavior of all participants in social situations. At this point children grasp the fact that not only must they know what behavior to perform in a particular interaction, but they also must be aware of whether or not their actions are roughly in line with the attitudes and expectations of others. A little boy who plays with dolls at home will probably stop playing with them at a day-care center if caretakers

and male peers verbally or nonverbally suggest to him that his behavior is inappropriate. A little girl accustomed to playing with fire engines, trucks, and other traditionally male toys will be likely to do the same if she encounters decisive disapproval.

Kohlberg (1966) has concluded that children's conceptions of the appropriate behavior in male and female gender roles derive from what they have seen, heard, and been told. These observations are a distortion of reality because they consider only features children observe, such as hairstyles, clothing, and facial expressions. Frequently children's judgments are oversimplified. A case in point would be the four-year-old girl who insists that girls can become nurses but not doctors, even though her mother is a doctor.

According to Kohlberg, children face two problems in learning and adopting appropriate gender-role behavior. First, they must be able to distinguish between behavior appropriate for boys and that appropriate for girls. Second, they must have a clear sense of their own sexual identity in order to know which kind of behavior they ought to display. Neither children's understanding of what constitutes "masculine" or "feminine" behavior nor their perception of their own sexual identity is always clear. A boy of four, for instance, may be able to distinguish boys from girls, but he may lump all men and women into the category "adult." Until he can separate men from women and identify with the former, he will be unable to develop a full understanding of what constitutes appropriate masculine behavior based on observing the kinds of things done by men as opposed to those done by women.

Modern research suggests that the development of people's gender-role perceptions is a complicated, subtle process. For instance, a recent study of college students concluded that while informants frequently made use of simplified gender-role generalizations (stereotypes) for males and females, these stereotypes tended to be discarded as more information about the individuals in question was provided (Deaux and Lewis, 1984).

## Commentary

In summary, the structural-functional theory of gender roles assumes a traditional stance, emphasizing distinct, task-related gender roles for males and females. Conflict theory opposes that tradi-

**Table 7.1**
**Theoretical Perspectives on Gender Roles**

| | STRUCTURAL-FUNCTIONAL THEORY | CONFLICT THEORY | SYMBOLIC-INTERACTIONIST THEORY |
|---|---|---|---|
| Prominent features of gender roles | Expressive roles for women; instrumental roles for men | Distinct cross-cultural tendency for men's roles to provide higher political, social, and economic status than those of women | Children's gradual understanding of gender-role expectations, with behavior modeled after the expectations |
| Major source of gender-role development | Identification with parent of the same sex | Economic inequality between women and men | Children's conception of appropriate gender-role behavior based on their interaction with parents and other influential individuals |
| Support for changing gender roles | Not a consideration | Emphasis on its necessity | Acknowledgment of the possibility |

tional arrangement, contending that women have generally suffered inferior political, social, and economic status. The symbolic-interactionist theory does not support the position expressed by either of the other two theories but focuses on the process by which children develop their conceptions of gender roles. A recent study about the relationship between gender and power concluded that theories of gender role tend to be oversimplified analyses, and that the most effective approach is to combine their respective strengths in a single, integrated theory (Molm, 1986). (See Table 7.1.)

# Sexual Behavior

As the conflict perspective on gender roles emphasizes, women have traditionally been treated differently and been given fewer opportunities than men. Since sexual activity is one aspect of gender roles, it is not surprising that unequal standards for the sexes have developed.

## Premarital Sex

In recent years two patterns involving premarital sexual behavior have become apparent: First, females continue to be more likely than males to perceive sex in a context of love and marriage — to be less inclined to accept sex for sex's sake — and, second, considerable change is occurring in the sexual realm, with females' attitudes and behavior gradually changing toward those of males.

## Male–Female Differences in Outlook on Sexuality

A recent cross-cultural study of adolescent sexual behavior concluded that in 186 societies boys tend to have more sexual freedom than girls (Barry and Schlegel, 1984). In our society boys and girls typically hold different attitudes toward sexuality. With the implicit, if not explicit, approval of parents, teachers, and other adults, boys are frequently encouraged to experiment with sex, talk about it, and joke about it. Girls, on the other hand, are taught to avoid such easy familiarity with sexuality. Females learn that sexual activity is not supposed to be an act in its own right, that it is supposed to occur for the sake of love and the creation of children.

Given this, it is not surprising that male and fe-

**154** male sex-related behavior is often different. Male adolescents, for instance, often treat sexual contacts with females as a means of building social status in their peer groups. They talk about "scoring," "how far one can get," or "hitting a home run." The emphasis is on sexual access—a highly goal-oriented approach that sometimes resembles the negotiation of a business deal more than an expression of love. Young women, in contrast, are more likely to focus on the emotional element, emphasizing the affection they feel and demonstrations of fondness or love on the male's part (Gagnon and Simon, 1973).

Since men's approach to sexuality is more opportunistic than that of women, it is reasonable to expect that males will lose their virginity at an earlier age than will females. A national sample of nearly 1200 undergraduates from twelve American colleges and universities found a higher percentage of nonvirginal men than women in each college year. Among freshmen 36 percent of the males were nonvirgins compared with 19 percent of the females. Among seniors the respective percentages were 68 and 44. Women are more likely than men to develop a strong emotional tie with their first sexual partner. In the study just cited, the researchers found that 59 percent of the women planned to marry their first sexual partner following their first sexual experience while a much lower 14 percent of men had the same intention (Simon, Berger, and Gagnon, 1972). Recent research on college students has produced supportive findings. In assessing the significance of the relationship as a factor in reaching a decision about whether or not to engage in sexual intercourse, female virgins were more inclined to consider the relationship as a factor than male virgins (Christopher and Cate, 1985).

### Changing Patterns of Sexuality

While to some extent, men and women still hold somewhat different sexual attitudes and behavior, changes are occurring. Ira Reiss (1960) suggested that patterns of premarital sexual behavior may be divided into four categories: abstinence, the double standard, permissiveness with affection, and permissiveness without affection. **Abstinence** means total restraint from sex. The **double standard** asserts that men may engage in premarital sex but women may not. The two standards have tradi-

**Table 7.2**
**Americans' Attitudes Toward Premarital Sex**

| YES, IS WRONG | NO, IS NOT WRONG | NO OPINION |
| --- | --- | --- |
| 38% | 52% | 10% |

Source: George H. Gallup. *Gallup Poll.* April 12, 1985.

*People who are younger, better educated, Catholic, and from the West (as opposed to those from other regions of the United States) are more inclined than other individuals to feel that premarital sex is not wrong.*

tionally coexisted, with abstinence the official norm while the double standard was widely practiced. In recent years, however, young people have come to accept two different standards. The **permissiveness with affection** position argues that men and women who love each other and have a stable relationship have the right to express their feelings sexually. Those who endorse **permissiveness without affection** contend that men and women should feel free to have sexual relations whether or not there is commitment or affection between them. Emphasis here is on sexual pleasure. While all four standards of sexual behavior were found in a sampling of couples from four colleges in the Boston area (Peplau, Rubin, and Hill, 1977), a recent investigation has emphasized that college students' behavior has become increasingly consistent with an equal standard for sexual conduct—in short, the restriction or even elimination of the double standard (Keller, Elliot, and Gunberg, 1982).

Table 7.2 indicates that in 1985 more than a majority—52 percent of a representative sample of adult Americans—felt that premarital sex is not wrong. Americans' changing attitudes on the subject are revealed by comparative responses in earlier years: In 1973, 43 percent indicated premarital sex was not wrong, and in 1969, just as sexual standards were becoming more flexible, the figure was only 21 percent (George Gallup, *Gallup Poll,* April 1985).

## Marital Sex

Modern married couples tend to engage in sex frequently, and wives play a significant part in the initiation of sexual activity. A study revealed that in

**Table 7.3**
**Married Couples' Sexual Frequency**

| | YEARS TOGETHER | | |
|---|---|---|---|
| | 0–2 | 2–10 | 10+ |
| Sex once a month or less | 6% | 6% | 15% |
| Sex between once a month and once a week | 11 | 21 | 22 |
| Sex between one and three times a week | 38 | 46 | 45 |
| Sex three times a week or more | 45 | 27 | 18 |

Source: Adapted from Philip Blumstein and Pepper Schwartz. *American Couples.* New York: William Morrow. 1983, p. 196.

*The results of this study, which involved over 3600 married couples, indicated that the longer couples are together, the less frequently they have sex. However, this table also suggests that the majority of married couples, no matter how long they have been together, tend to have sex frequently.*

the 1970s husbands and wives in five different age categories estimated higher rates of sexual frequency than did their counterparts in the 1940s (Hunt, 1983). Table 7.3 points out that modern married couples' frequency of sex tends to be high. A recent investigation indicated that 51 percent of husbands and only 12 percent of wives said they were more likely than their spouses to initiate sexual activity. However, 33 percent of husbands and 40 percent of wives suggested that the initiation of sex was equally likely to come from either partner (Blumstein and Schwartz, 1983: 207).

Some research suggests that people with certain social characteristics are more likely to experience uninhibited, mutually pleasurable sexual activity than those without them. For women, age and social class seem to be two significant considerations. When women are younger and come from middle-class or upper-middle-class backgrounds, they are likely to have been socialized to believe that sex should be a pleasurable experience for women as well as for men. Social class is also a factor for the couple as a unit. Because of their more extensive educational background, middle-class spouses are likely to communicate their needs to each other more effectively than their working-class counterparts, and effective communication often en-

hances sexual relations (Bell and Lobsenz, 1977; Rainwater, 1972; Rubin, 1983).

A number of agents of socialization currently influence marital couples' sexual attitudes and behavior. Peers, the mass media, and sex-therapy clinics have been particularly influential. The following quotation shows how the first two socialization agents combined to affect the sexual activity of a twenty-six-year-old mechanic and his wife. He explained:

> My wife works, and at lunchtime she and all the girls talk about things, and she comes home one time and tells me she hears there's nothing like pornography for a turn-on. So I go along with it; I go out and buy an armful of stuff—mostly picture magazines—and bring it home. First, it embarrasses her, but then she gets to see it differently, and to like some of the things she sees. Same way with a stag film I borrowed and brought home to show her. Personally, I think it's good and wholesome; it stimulates and opens the mind.
>
> *(Hunt, 1983: 226)*

The widespread availability of contraceptive devices has been another important influence on marital sexuality. In particular, the pill, the IUD (intrauterine device), and the vasectomy have freed couples from the fear of unwanted pregnancy and permitted new spontaneity and joy to enter marital sex.

Finally the woman's liberation movement has affected married couples' sex lives. The effect has been twofold. First, the movement has encouraged women to forsake passivity and to take a more active part in all aspects of living, including sex. Second, many women have openly struggled to gain more power in their marriages, and the struggle has often extended to the bedroom. Many husbands who strongly support a tradition of male sexual dominance are unable to cope with wives' sexual assertiveness. It appears that one symptom of this failure has been an increase in the incidence of impotence (Hunt, 1983).

## Extramarital Sex

What factors encourage people to engage in extramarital sex? One determinant seems to be residential location. Recent research has concluded that large communities are more permissive toward extramarital sex than small ones. It appears that increases in population are accompanied by a diversity of subcultures, supporting and encouraging tolerance toward a variety of life-styles (Weis and Jurich, 1985). Another study discovered several factors that seem to be associated with permissive attitudes toward extramarital sex. These include the individual's perceived sense of freedom to associate with members of the opposite sex and the person's level of marital satisfaction. Most significantly related to permissive attitudes, however, was an informant's diffuseness of intimacy: the willingness to share one's most personal and private feelings with someone besides the spouse (Saunders and Edwards, 1984). It is an interesting, thought-provoking conclusion—a point that seems to imply the great importance of effective communication in marriage if one wishes the marriage to avoid this threat to its existence.

Let us move from attitudes to behavior. An investigation of upper-middle-class business and professional men concluded that those who were alienated (had lost their youthful idealism and felt powerless and isolated) were more inclined to initiate extramarital involvements than those who were not alienated (Whitehurst, 1972). Sometimes the affairs involved "office wives"—executive secretaries or other female office personnel with whom the man worked closely. The following quotation suggests the special closeness that can develop on the job. A forty-year-old scientist's assistant said:

> We do have an advantage over the wives at home. If I help him draft a proposal that comes through with flying colors, I can really feel overjoyed at our mutual success, can feel that I have been a real part of it. But if the proposal falls through, I'm the one closest to his disappointment and I find deep comfort myself in my efforts to comfort him . . .

> *(Cuber and Harroff, 1972: 117)*

In this section we have seen that Americans' sexual outlook and behavior have been changing. The amount of premarital and marital sexual activity is increasing, and there are indications that many Americans are trying to improve the quality of sexual intercourse, making it a more pleasurable and meaningful aspect of their relationships. There is, in short, a trend to develop a more relaxed, open-minded approach toward sexual relations between men and women. Does this trend include attitudes toward homosexuality?

## Homosexuality

During the 1970s and 1980s, many gay Americans have decided that their interests will be best served if they seek to change the political, economic, and social injustices they have suffered. Gay people's public actions to produce these changes have received extensive media coverage. Yet homosexuality remains a mysterious, confusing subject for most Americans. In fact, even social workers and other clinicians doing therapy with gay people generally lack a clear definition of homosexuality (Berger, 1983).

Myths about the subject abound. One is that homosexuals come from conflict-ridden families. Evidence from a study of over 320 gay men and women disputed such a conclusion, indicating that two-thirds perceived their relationships with their fathers as either satisfactory or extremely satisfactory and three-quarters felt that they maintained either a satisfactory or extremely satisfactory relationship with their mothers (Robinson et al.,

1982). It is also widely believed that homosexuality is an indication of serious psychological disturbance. The results of psychological tests done on gays offer no support for such a conclusion (Gonsiorek, 1982).

In addition, many people believe that homosexuality is particularly communicable to children in contact with adult gays. A preliminary study disputes this claim, suggesting that children with gay parents almost invariably prefer the toys, games, clothing, and activities typical of their own sex and as they become older report sexual fantasies or activities that are heterosexually oriented (Green, 1978). Finally it is often felt that homosexuals, whether male or female, assume either an "active" or "passive" role in sexual relations. The evidence indicates, however, that gays of both sexes commonly alternate between active and passive roles (Saghir and Robins, 1971).

## Types of Homosexuality

"Straight" people's outlook on gays is often influenced by the fact that their observations of homosexuals are largely confined to the more obvious. The majority of gays lead unremarkable lives except for their sexual orientation, which often remains a well-kept secret from most people. In colleges, for example, large numbers of gay students never reveal their sexual preference to campus friends and even roommates, although a "coming-out" trend has become more popular in recent years.

The following five types of life-styles were identified in the course of a major study on gay men and women (Bell and Weinberg, 1980).

*Close-Coupleds.* The partners in this kind of relationship were closely bound and tended to turn to each other rather than to outsiders for sexual and interpersonal satisfactions. Compared to other respondents in the research, the close-coupled individuals were less paranoid and tense and more exuberant. An interviewer offered a typical portrait of a close-coupled pair: "The apartment which he shares with his lover is very clearly 'their' home. A lot of love went into fixing it up. Interestingly, when I ask him questions about his own siblings, he called in his roommate to help him out with the answers!"

*Open-Coupleds.* Like their close-coupled counterparts, the men and women in this category were living with a special sexual partner. The difference was that one or both members of the couple found the exclusive relationship insufficient and sought additional sexual satisfaction outside the partnership. As a result, both males and females spent a fair amount of time "cruising"—looking for new sexual partners in bars and elsewhere. The open-coupleds often worried about the possibility of being arrested and publicly exposed while cruising. One of the prime reasons they worried was that they did not want their partners to find out about these activities.

*Functionals.* Of all five types, the functionals were the least likely to regret being homosexual, cruised frequently, displayed the greatest interest in sex, and generally showed an extensive, even exuberant involvement in the gay world. They were also the ones most likely to have been

arrested, booked, or convicted for an offense involving homosexuality. Investigators provided comments like, "She was friendly and completely comfortable during the interview. She had a very pleasant, lively personality."

*Dysfunctionals.* Of all the types of homosexuals, the dysfunctionals were the least well adjusted. They reported the most regret about their homosexuality and, in spite of fairly frequent sexual activity with a variety of partners, listed the most sexual problems. Dysfunctionals were most likely to complain about not having enough sex and were the most inclined to indicate that they and their partners could not agree on what kind of sexual activity should take place.

*Asexuals.* The most distinct characteristic of the asexuals was their lack of involvement with other people. They had the least sexual activity of all the categories, rated their sex appeal very low, and tended to have a fair number of sexual problems. Among the different types, asexuals were the least likely to consider themselves exclusively homosexual and among the men were the least likely to be overt about their homosexuality. Generally they described themselves as lonely and (among the men) unhappy.

## Homosexuality and Modern Society

What are the conditions that produce homosexuality? To respond to this question, we might begin by setting aside certain factors. No firm evidence suggests that either imbalances in sex hormones (Rose, 1975) or genetic factors (Brodie et al., 1974) play a significant role. In addition, research findings do not show any clear differences between the family backgrounds of homosexuals and heterosexuals (Siegelman, 1974).

There are, however, some indications that experiencing homosexuality as a normal, pleasurable activity encourages its acceptance. A study of seventy-six preindustrial societies concluded that forty-nine of them (64 percent) accepted some form of homosexual activity as normal behavior. Among the Siwans of Africa, for instance, men who did not engage in homosexuality were considered peculiar. The Keraki of New Guinea believed that boys would not grow up healthy and well adjusted unless adult men practiced anal intercourse on them. Among the Mbundu and Nama of Africa,

**158** women were expected to perform mutual masturbation, using an artificial penis (Ford and Beach, 1951).

In U.S. society, experience also seems to be a determining factor. One researcher who studied lesbians (female homosexuals) concluded that in an examination of the sources of lesbianism ". . . one factor stands out as having more . . . weight than others. This is the importance of the first sexual experience and whether it is pleasurable and positive with a woman or discomforting and negative with a man" (Rosen, 1974: 70). If, indeed, this finding is maintained by further research, it will be a powerful indication of how single episodes can significantly affect people's gender-role socialization.

While pleasurable experience seems to encourage people to become gay, homosexuals' lives are often difficult because of the severe economic and social sanctions they experience. Recognizing gays' adjustment problems, many expert observers have urged the decriminalization of homosexual acts between consenting adults in private. In 1961 Illinois was the first state to repeal its statutes against homosexual acts between consenting adults in private, and seven other states took similar action during the 1970s. In recent years a number of towns and cities have experienced bitter struggles over gay civil rights, including debates over whether or not gays should be allowed to teach in the public schools. Sometimes the debates have sunk to an absurd level, as indicated by the charge that male homosexuals are cannibals because they swallow sperm. Such charges document the intense emotion and fear generated in many people by the increased visibility of contemporary homosexuality.

At present the greatest threat to gays comes from a nonhuman source—AIDS (Acquired Immune Deficiency Syndrome). This disease, which

**Table 7.4**
**Americans' Outlook on Gays**

| LEGALIZATION OF HOMOSEXUALITY | | | |
|---|---|---|---|
| | *Yes* | *No* | *No Opinion* |
| 1985 | 44% | 47% | 9% |
| 1982 | 45 | 39 | 16 |
| 1977 | 43 | 43 | 14 |

| HOW AIDS HAS AFFECTED ATTITUDES TOWARD HOMOSEXUALITY | | | |
|---|---|---|---|
| | *Better* | *Worse* | *No Difference* | *No Opinion* |
| 1985 | 2% | 37% | 59% | 2% |

Source: George H. Gallup. *Gallup Poll.* November 11, 1985

*People who are younger, better educated, and more affluent are more inclined than other individuals to favor legalization of homosexuality and to feel that AIDS has not affected their attitudes toward gays.*

can be transmitted by sexual contact or blood transfusion, destroys the body's immune systems, leaving victims vulnerable to a variety of bacteria and viruses, including forms of cancer. According to the Centers for Disease Control in 1985, about 72 percent of AIDS victims in the United States are male homosexuals (Feldman, 1985: 344). Even though the vast majority of male homosexuals do not have AIDS, many Americans' attitudes toward homosexuals have been adversely affected by the link between gay males and AIDS. Table 7.4, which addresses two issues on Americans' attitudes toward gays, includes this topic.

Chapter 15 ("Science and Medicine") contains a Contemporary Issue, which examines Americans' knowledge about AIDS and also dispels some myths about the disease. The following Contemporary Issue considers a topic that, like AIDS, is a subject where public knowledge is limited and often confused. It is hoped that this material will provide some clarification.

**CONTEMPORARY ISSUE**

*Why Are Some Homosexual Men So Promiscuous?*

 Evidence suggests that some homosexual men are very promiscuous. Many psychoanalysts argue that this extensive sexual activity indicates that these men are mentally ill. However, another position is steadily gaining support among researchers— that given some special social conditions encountered by gay males, promiscuity is appropriate male gender-role behavior.

Let us start with some facts. Frequently the American public hears or reads that male homosexuals have extensive sexual activity. A 1982 study of fifty AIDS victims, for example, found that the median number of lifetime sexual partners for these men was 1,100; for a matched sample of 120 men without the disease, the median was about half that figure—550.

Many psychoanalysts, as well as other therapists, use such figures as evidence to support their belief that being homosexual is a disease. For instance, Charles W. Socarides, a longtime advocate of the disease model, believes that male homosexuals are strongly identified with their mothers. Socarides has suggested that as a result of this identification, these men visualize themselves as symbolically having lost their penises. In order to preserve themselves, the argument continues, they must bring into themselves the penis of another man. The more fragile the sense of self, the greater the need to perform homosexual acts to allay one's anxiety.

Here is an opposing line of argument. In several respects one can contend that many gay and straight men's pursuits are similar. Among both categories of men, there are many who covet young bodies and seek quick, anonymous sex. Perhaps the big difference between the straights and the gays on this point is that the former are more likely to find it difficult to satisfy their wishes; often they are forced to pay for sex.

Many straight men are pro-

miscuous, but if they choose to establish a stable relationship with a woman, they receive most people's blessing. Gays do not. After his homosexual relationship with a congressional page was revealed, Congressman Gerry Studds explained:

> To grow up and to enter adulthood as a gay person in this country is to be in a situation where all the messages one receives with respect to the deepest feelings inside oneself tell one that those feelings are not legitimate at best, and that they are sinful and evil at worst.

*(Meredith, 1984: 59–60)*

One might suspect that the development of a gay-rights movement and the growth of gay communities would help support and legitimate gay-couple relationships. However, probably in part because of the lack of general societal support, this has not been the case. In *American Couples* Blumstein and Schwartz wrote, "The problem with gay male culture is that much of it is organized around singlehood or maintaining one's sexual marketability. Meeting places like bars and baths promote casual sex rather than couple activities" (Blumstein and Schwartz, 1983: 322).

For gay men society provides few supports—few social anchors. They cannot form couples and move to the suburbs as heterosexual couples do, because they will not fit in. Like everyone else, they want intimacy and love, but

the lack of social supports often convinces them that a sustained relationship is impossible. Frequently such men feel isolated and alone. They want to validate their sense of self-worth, but believing that a sustained relationship is impossible, they are inclined to engage in what Paul Walker, a gay clinical psychologist, has called "compulsive promiscuity." He distinguishes this behavior from recreational promiscuity; there is no joy involved, only a continuous restless effort to validate one's worth.

Walker has suggested that the appearance of AIDS has had a profound effect on the lives of many gay men. It is as if a panel of experts declared that monogamy, not sexual freedom, had to be the standard for gay behavior. While some gay men continue to have a variety of sexual relations, the previously uninhibited atmosphere surrounding many gay groups and their activities has been severely restricted.

In summary, the material here seeks to analyze some gay men's sexual promiscuity. Like many psychoanalysts, one can label homosexuals' promiscuity as a disease. However, I contend that such an analysis fails to note gay and straight men's similar outlook on sexual activity. A big difference is that gay men receive little or no societal support for stable relationships. Thus the pressure driving them toward promiscuity is generally stronger.

Sources: Philip Blumstein and Pepper Schwartz. *American Couples.* New York: William Morrow. 1983; Nikki Meredith. "The Gay Dilemma." *Psychology Today.* Vol. 18. January 1984, pp. 56+.

# American Gender Roles in the Years Ahead

If we look back over the major topics of this chapter, we see that in each case behavioral standards have altered, providing more rights and opportunities for certain groups. Traditionally gender roles were sharply divided, with men working and women caring for the family and home. Sexual behavior, especially for women, was supposed to be restricted to marriage. Finally homosexuality was considered misguided, perhaps even evil, and homosexuals were to be avoided by the general public. Now a steadily increasing proportion of women are rejecting traditional limitations and seeking the educational and occupational opportunities once largely restricted to men. Sexual standards and behavior have altered, with the rejection of the double standard receiving widespread support. In addition, the pursuit of a gay life-style is considered legitimate by many Americans. Even with the negative impact produced by the relatively high incidence of AIDS among male homosexuals, a recent survey indicated that nearly half the public would be willing to legalize homosexuality.

Nonetheless, a liberalized attitude on these issues does not mean that participants' struggles are eliminated. Consider modern women's role.

The survey data presented in Table 7.5 indicate that in 1985 about 72 percent of married women wanted to be married and have children and that over half of those women (38 percent) also wanted a full-time job. Is this possible? According to Betty Freidan (1981), the most effective way to accomplish both work and domestic goals involves cooperation. In recent years, Friedan reported, many equality-minded women are consciously and effectively implementing two ideologies once believed contradictory. One is the woman-as-individual ideology, often involving careers pursued part time or on different shifts from their husbands; the other is the woman-serving-her-family ideology, ideally supported by husbands willing to assume much more extensive domestic roles than they did in the past.

Both men and women might benefit from such an approach. Research suggests that the **androgynous** person, who possesses a definite blend of both traditionally masculine and traditionally feminine traits, is usually healthier emotionally and better adjusted than someone strongly masculine or feminine (Bem, 1975).

Such people can make special contributions in many situations. If an androgynous person were the chairperson of a college committee or a business meeting, he or she would be concerned about the effective accomplishment of the goals at hand —such as the evaluation of colleagues for promotion or the planning of a marketing campaign— and would also be tuned into the participants' emotional needs, taking the time and trouble to ensure that they were met as adequately as possible.

It is not easy for most Americans to combine these two skills. The majority of Americans have been raised with a distinct emphasis on one capacity or the other. Yet research has shown that under supportive circumstances androgynous women and men can and do effectively share leadership (Porter et al., 1985). Perhaps the most socially significant conclusion about gender roles that has emerged from the social change of the last two decades is the realization that all of us can develop both traditionally masculine and traditionally feminine skills that we can use to benefit others and ourselves.

**Table 7.5**
**Women's Views of the Ideal Life-Style**

| | 1975 | 1980 | 1985 |
|---|---|---|---|
| Married with children | 76% | 74% | 72% |
| With full-time job | 32 | 33 | 38 |
| With no full-time job | 44 | 41 | 34 |
| Married with no children | 9 | 10 | 9 |
| With full-time job | 6 | 6 | 6 |
| With no full-time job | 3 | 4 | 3 |
| Unmarried with full-time job | 9 | 8 | 9 |
| Not sure | 6 | 8 | 10 |
| (Total) | 100% | 100% | 100% |

Source: George H. Gallup. *Gallup Poll.* May 1, 1985.

*Over a ten-year period, women's view of the ideal life-style has remained fairly stable. The most noteworthy change, perhaps, is the increased proportion that want to be married with both children and a full-time job—a jump from 32 percent in 1975 to 38 percent in 1985.*

# STUDY GUIDE

## Summary

1. Sex is the division of a variety of animal forms, including human beings, into the biological categories of male and female. Gender consists of the general behavioral standards that distinguish males from females in a given culture. A gender role is a set of specific behavioral patterns associated with either the male or female gender.

2. Sex differentiation is determined by both biological and cultural factors. Whether a fertilized egg develops into a male or female depends on whether or not a Y chromosome was contained in the human sperm cell. Besides chromosomes, the sex hormones—androgen and estrogen—seem to influence sex differentiation, producing somewhat different male and female brain structures and behavioral patterns.

Culture is also an important factor determining sex differentiation. From birth our cultural standards of treatment for girl and boy babies are different, and these cultural standards are sufficiently powerful to insure that hermaphroditic children will effectively adopt the gender role in which they are raised. Cross-cultural evidence further endorses the impact of culture on gender-role development. Most likely biology and culture both influence sex differentiation, and therefore a biosocial position seems to be a sensible outlook.

3. One theory on gender roles is the structural-functional theory. Parsons and Bales took a traditional view, arguing that men and women have distinct task-oriented gender roles—men at work and women in the home. The conflict theory emphasizes the inequalities in the traditional arrangement, contending that the underlying source of

sexual inequality is in the economic realm. The symbolic-interactionist theory of gender roles focuses on the development of gender roles. Kohlberg contended that sex-typed behavior is a set of ever-changing rules children compile from what they see, hear, and are told.

4. The discussion of sexual behavior divides the topic into three parts: premarital sex, marital sex, and extramarital sex. In the premarital area, men approach premarital sex with more emotional detachment than women do. However, studies indicate that women's approach to premarital sexual activity is becoming more like that of men.

A number of factors currently support more uninhibited and pleasurable sex for married couples. Age, social-class background, socialization agents, effective contraception, and the women's liberation movement are significant influences.

Extramarital relations are encouraged by various conditions, including residential location and the diffuseness of intimacy.

5. Gay people do not fit any neat, standardized image. One study designated five life-style types: the close-coupleds, the open-coupleds, the functionals, the dysfunctionals, and the asexuals. Like gender-role activity generally, homosexuality is the product of a combination of biological and social factors, with the latter more influential than the former.

6. The future of American gender roles is difficult to predict. It seems likely, however, that in the years ahead people will be judged more by their competencies and less by the assumption that males have greater skills.

## Glossary

**abstinence**   total restraint from sex.

**androgynous**   possessing a definite blend of both traditionally masculine and traditionally feminine traits.

**biosocial position**   a recently developed perspective that acknowledges the significance of both biology and social experience in the development of gender roles and that emphasizes

their interplay, contending that the independent significance of each factor is impossible to assess since they never exist in isolation from one another.

**double standard**   a position asserting that men may engage in premarital sex but women may not.

**gender**   the general behavioral standards that

distinguish males from females in a given culture.

**gender role**    a set of specific behavioral patterns associated with either the male or female gender.

**identification**    a process by which an individual incorporates another person's values, standards, and expectations into his or her own behavior and sense of self.

**permissiveness with affection**    a standard arguing that men and women who love each other and have a stable relationship have the right to express their feelings sexually.

**permissiveness without affection**    a position contending that men and women should feel free to have sexual relations whether or not there is commitment or affection between them.

**sex**    the division of a variety of animal forms, including human beings, into the biological categories of male and female.

## Learning Objectives

After studying this chapter, you should be able to:

1. Define sex, gender, and gender roles.
2. Discuss the influence of biological, cultural (including cross-cultural) factors on gender-role development.
3. Summarize the biosocial position.
4. Examine the structural-functional, conflict, and symbolic-interactionist theories of gender roles.
5. Describe the traditional patterns of premarital sexuality and indicate how and why these patterns are changing.
6. Discuss marital couples' sexual attitudes and behavior and identify the factors influencing marital sexuality.
7. Summarize trends in extramarital sex.
8. Analyze homosexuality, discussing myths about the subject, life-style types, and conditions producing it.
9. Examine the changes that seem to be occurring in Americans' gender-role outlooks.

## Tests

### True – false test

_____ 1. In recent years the term "sex roles" has started to replace the term "gender roles."

_____ 2. Women's and men's brains have identical locations for both speech and spatial centers.

_____ 3. Arnoff and Crano's cross-cultural study of gender roles concluded that men do not always dominate food production or women child-rearing.

_____ 4. Jeanne Block indicated that Americans more strongly emphasize gender-role differentiation and competitive achievement than the respondents from five other technologically advanced nations.

_____ 5. Collins's conflict perspective on gender roles focuses on a struggle for scarce resources between a dominant group (males) and a subordinate group (females).

_____ 6. Structural-functionalists believe that gender roles are determined by cultural factors while conflict theorists contend that they are produced by biological factors.

_____ 7. The symbolic-interactionist theory of gender roles has concluded that children's conceptions of appropriate gender roles are a distortion of reality because they consider only what they have seen, heard, and been told.

_____ 8. Females' sexual attitudes and behavior are becoming less like males'.

_____ 9. Recent research found that diffuseness of intimacy is strongly associated with a permissive attitude toward extramarital sex.

_____ 10. Studies have concluded that an androgynous person is usually healthier emotionally and better adjusted than is someone who is strongly masculine or feminine.

## Multiple-choice test

_____ 1. General behavioral standards that distinguish males from females in a given culture are referred to as:
  a. biosocial role.
  b. sex role.
  c. gender role.
  d. gender.

_____ 2. Crano and Arnoff examined data from cultures in six broad geographical areas and found:
  a. most traditional generalizations about female and male behavior are true.
  b. men dominate food production in all societies.
  c. women often participate extensively in food production.
  d. fathers are excluded from child care in most societies.

_____ 3. The biosocial position:
  a. concludes that anatomy determines destiny.
  b. presumes that biology produces some limits and predispositions but that culture has the "final say."
  c. has been officially rejected by the American Sociological Association.
  d. rejects all cross-cultural research.

_____ 4. According to conflict theorists, the source of sexual inequality is:
  a. identification.
  b. genetic factors.
  c. economic inequality.
  d. cross-cultural causes.

_____ 5. Kohlberg identified problems in learning and adopting appropriate gender-role behavior. Which of the following did he include?
  a. distinguishing which behavior is appropriate for boys and which is appropriate for girls
  b. separating adult from child behavior
  c. awareness of social context of behavior
  d. understanding peers' gender roles

_____ 6. Emphasis on sexual pleasure for both partners is found in which of the following patterns of premarital sexual behavior?
  a. permissiveness with affection
  b. permissiveness without affection
  c. double standard
  d. abstinence

_____ 7. Compared to those who oppose extramarital sex, those who are more permissive toward it are:
  a. more likely to be from rural than urban areas.
  b. more likely to be satisfied with their marriages.

       c. less likely to discuss intimate issues with someone besides their spouse.
       d. more likely to be from urban than rural areas.

——  8. Studies of homosexuality have provided evidence that:
       a. gays come from conflict-ridden homes.
       b. homosexuality is not particularly communicable to children in contact with adult gays.
       c. homosexuals typically adopt either an active or a passive sexual role.
       d. a and b

——  9. In the study of homosexual life-styles, the individuals expressing the least regret about being homosexual were the:
       a. dysfunctionals.
       b. close-coupleds.
       c. open-coupleds.
       d. functionals.

—— 10. Androgynous women and men:
       a. can and do share leadership under supportive circumstances.
       b. tend to focus their time and energy on bisexuality.
       c. tend to be weak in task performance.
       d. have unusual chromosome patterns.

## Essay test

1. Define sex, gender, and gender role. What do you believe is the most significant gender-role issue today in our society?
2. If females and males received identical treatment in American society, would their outlooks and behavior be the same? Discuss, drawing from material in the section on gender-role development.
3. Summarize the structural-functional, conflict, and symbolic-interactionist theories of gender roles. What point(s) would you extract from each theory in constructing a general theory of gender roles?
4. Has Americans' sexual behavior changed in the past twenty years? Discuss, drawing from material in the section on sexual behavior.
5. Summarize three myths about homosexuality. What are the five types of homosexual life-styles that emerged from the Bell and Weinberg research?
6. Discuss possible changes in gender-role activity in the years ahead.

## Suggested Readings

Bell, Alan, and Martin Weinberg. 1978. *Homosexualities: A Study of Diversity among Men and Women.* New York: Simon and Schuster. A study of almost 1000 male and female homosexuals and nearly 500 heterosexuals in the San Francisco area, contrasting gay and straight attitudes, behavior, and problems.

Bergman, Ingmar. 1974. *Scenes from a Marriage.* New York: Pantheon Books. Translated from Swedish by A. Blair. A sensitive account of a Swedish professional man and woman who appear to be ideally suited for each other but then separate and divorce, eventually realizing that their marriage failed because of their efforts to meet culturally defined gender-role expectations.

Block, Jeanne H. 1984. *Sex Role Identity and Ego Development.* San Francisco: Jossey-Bass. A book containing Block's major articles and papers. Collectively they provide a great deal of information and insight about female and male development.

Blumstein, Philip, and Pepper Schwartz. 1983. *American Couples.* New York: William Morrow. A sociological study based on over 12,000 surveys and 300 interviews with married, heterosexual cohabitational, and gay couples. The book focuses on the issues of money, work, and sex.

Maccoby, Eleanor Emmons, and Carol Nagy Jacklin. 1974. *The Psychology of Sex Differences.* Palo Alto, CA: Stanford University Press. A painstaking review of hundreds of studies of the psychological similarities and differences between males and females.

Masters, William, and Virginia Johnson. 1975. *The Pleasure Bond: A New Look at Sexuality and Commitment.* Boston: Little, Brown. An easy-to-read, nontechnical discussion of human sexuality, based on a massive experimental research program conducted by these two prominent investigators.

Nass, Gilbert D., Roger W. Libby, and Mary Pat Fisher. 1981. *Sexual Choices: An Introduction to Human Sexuality.* Monterey, CA: Wadsworth. A stimulating text that provides an overview of human sexuality. The presentation is aided by an effective conceptual framework.

Twain, Mark. 1962. *Adventures of Huckleberry Finn.* Boston: Houghton Mifflin. A marvelously funny novel describing the off-beat gender-role socialization of a nineteenth-century boy who seemed to thrive on getting himself and his friends into trouble.

## Student Projects

1. Take one of the following topics—androgyny, extramarital sex, homosexuality, or premarital sex—and develop an explanation of why it occurs, using these three theories of gender roles: structural-functionalism, conflict theory, and symbolic interaction. Use printed media, films, radio and television programming, and information in the text to provide support for each of the theoretical analyses of the topic. Is any theory clearly superior or inferior in its explanation?

2. Watch an hour of rock videos, if available, or select television shows that are likely to contain more than one setting where gender roles are displayed. Keep a tally on the frequencies with which males and females present themselves as either sex or love objects and also the frequencies with which females and males present members of the opposite sex as either sex or love objects. If the information is available, analyze gay males and lesbians in a similar manner. Do any patterns in media portrayals of gender-role relationships emerge? Discuss the significance of these portrayals.

## Answers to Test Questions

### True–false test

| | | | | |
|---|---|---|---|---|
| 1. f | 3. t | 5. t | 7. t | 9. t |
| 2. f | 4. t | 6. f | 8. f | 10. t |

### Multiple-choice test

| | | | | |
|---|---|---|---|---|
| 1. d | 3. b | 5. a | 7. d | 9. d |
| 2. c | 4. c | 6. b | 8. b | 10. a |

# Research on Sexuality and Its Acceptance: Reflections of Changing Values

For the past half-century, research on sexuality has been surrounded with controversy. What is notable is that the substance of that controversy has changed as dominant values have changed. In the 1930s and 1940s, the focus of people's opposition was the existence of research on sexuality. Nowadays the opposition revolves around different issues.

## Confronting Resistance to Research on Sexuality

Before 1938 there were nineteen published studies of human sexuality. Most of them used only (written) questionnaires—not nearly as satisfactory a method as interviews to encourage people to expose the intimate details of their sexual lives. Furthermore none of the investigations were extensive enough to obtain a detailed sexual life history. Alfred Kinsey's research was a departure in both respects. Kinsey and his associates conducted detailed interviews of both American males and females. Each interview contained a minimum of 350 questions and as many as 521. In the 1980s it probably seems commonplace to undertake a detailed study of human sexuality. In the 1930s and 1940s, however, such a study was unprecedented. Kinsey was widely criticized for undertaking his investigation, and yet most of his research subjects cooperated when interviewed. Why?

One reason was the highly organized nature of the interview. In the beginning the researcher (Kinsey himself or one of his carefully trained assistants) would painstakingly explain the value of the individual's contribution and emphasize the fact that everything said in the interview would remain completely confidential. Then the actual interview would begin. The early questions were nonthreatening: about the person's age, place of birth, religion, education, and other such matters. For fifteen or twenty minutes, the informant answered questions that had nothing to do with sex. In fact, even when the interviewer switched to sex, the questions were easy and nonthreatening: about early knowledge of the subject. By the time the questions on adult sexual feelings and activities were reached, many people were relaxed. However, others were not; in fact, some people stayed tense throughout. Interviewers did what they could to alleviate this condition. If an individual seemed especially nervous, the interviewer might switch momentarily to another subject and then back to the first topic, hoping that this time the individual would be more relaxed.

Overall Kinsey and his assistants were successful in obtaining cooperation. However, Kinsey did not feel that it was wise to use a random-sampling technique, because he believed that even a modest refusal rate would invalidate any claims that the sample accurately reflected the adult American population. Instead Kinsey chose to interview a variety of different groups—the teachers in a certain school, the employees of a factory, or whatever. As the research progressed, Kinsey became increasingly determined to obtain 100 percent of each chosen group. So while he could not claim to have a random sample, at least he was able to state that once a group was picked to be included in the study, all or nearly all its members had been interviewed.

The following situation illustrates the value Kinsey placed on this approach. A magazine sent a questionnaire to its college-student readers and sought information about their sex lives. Only 20 percent of those contacted filled out the questionnaire and returned it. Kinsey was asked to comment on the limited response. He wrote:

If you are getting something like 20 per cent response, you are left completely in the dark as to the 80 per cent of the persons who fail to answer the questionnaire. This is very different from our 100 per cent sampling, where we get the histories of everybody in a group . . .

(Pomeroy, 1982: 225)

Kinsey's two massive volumes on the sex lives of American males and females were well received. In fact, it was the favorable response to Kinsey's second book—on the sex lives of American females—that encouraged William Masters, a gynecologist, to launch his own studies of sexuality. Masters's plan was to do an exhaustive physiological study of human sexual activity. In order to perform this research, Masters and his associates needed to observe and take physiological measures of research subjects engaged in masturbation and sexual intercourse. Masters originally became interested in this research in the late 1930s. At the time a well-known authority on the biology of sex supported the research in principle but urged Masters to follow three rules to insure that both experts and the public would take his work seriously: wait until he was forty before starting; earn a scientific reputation in a medical specialty; and obtain the sponsorship of a major medical school or university. Masters conscientiously followed his mentor's suggestions. He became a gynecologist, affiliating himself with Washington University School of Medicine and publishing twenty-five papers in his specialty. Furthermore he did not start his study of sexuality until the age of thirty-eight, thus waiting nearly as long as his advisor suggested.

## Current Controversy in Research on Sexuality

As Americans' sexual attitudes and behavior have been liberalizing in the past two decades, there has been little opposition to the idea of conducting research on sexuality. Disagreements and debates have erupted around more specific issues. As we noted at several points in Chapter 2 ("Doing Research in Sociology"), social researchers have a variety of motives for conducting studies. Controversy can develop when the researchers' motives conflict with others who have a stake in the investigation.

In the middle 1970s, difficult economic times encouraged government officials to look for ways of saving money. In the spirit of those times, Senator William Proxmire of Wisconsin began to issue his tongue-in-cheek "golden

fleece awards"—a monthly acknowledgment of what he considered a particularly effective means of wasting taxpayers' money. One month the award went to a study of romantic love. The senator wrote, "I believe that 200 million Americans want to leave some things in life a mystery, and right at the top of the things we don't want to know is why a man falls in love with a woman and vice versa" (Rubin, 1980: 284). Perhaps one can understand Proxmire's conclusion. Nonetheless it is not the position taken by researchers interested in love and sexuality. They believe that their task is to obtain information about their subjects and that often this information will be interesting, revealing, and even prove useful in helping improve people's lives.

When sociologist Morton Hunt undertook a major study of American sexuality in the 1970s, his outlook was entirely different from Proxmire's. He wanted to discard mystery and ignorance and reveal dominant trends in sexuality. He believed that a revelation of modern trends could supply important, practical information about couple relationships. Hunt stated:

> Lacking a major census of American sexual behavior, we have had no good way to judge whether that behavior has changed radically or merely come out in the open; whether such changes as have taken place are affecting only a highly visible minority or the largely unseen majority; whether the increase in freedom, whatever its scope, has strengthened love relationships and marriage among the sexually liberated or weakened them; whether sexual liberation is bringing the liberated greater satisfaction or only a frenetic quest for stronger sensations and new kicks; and whether America is becoming a dissolute and degenerate nation or a sensuous and healthy one.
>
> *(Hunt, 1974: 15)*

Feminists have raised a different set of criticisms of research on sexuality. A number of feminists have contended that like all or most elements in American society, this body of research has been male-dominated and male-oriented. For instance, Carole Vance attended an important conference on human sexuality given at a major center for research on sexuality and concluded that while prominent researchers spoke in favor of openness and general tolerance, the conference was structured to maintain male dominance, heterosexuality, the preeminence of a highly traditional nuclear family, and little or no tolerance for alternative perceptions and life-styles.

Martha Vicinus made a related point. She argued that the conceptualization of sexuality continues to be viewed in male terms—what she has called "the energy-control (or hydraulic) model."

> Sex is always something to be released or controlled; . . . . Sexual modernists, such as Alfred Kinsey and more recently Masters and Johnson, have continued to describe sex as a force seeking release. The male bias of the energy-control model reflects both the gender of the major theoreticians

and the unchanging assumption of a male-dominated society.

*(Vicinus, 1982: 136–137)*

Vicinus goes on to explain that a number of analysts of sexuality have been starting to examine the subject using other models, where they reject sexuality as an autonomous force and examine it as a product of social and historical conditions.

These feminist criticisms represent a thought-provoking commentary about recent research on human sexuality. In the years ahead, it will be interesting to observe whether studies are able to successfully incorporate the new insights and make a significant contribution to this body of research.

Sources: Philip Blumstein and Pepper Schwartz: *American Couples.* New York: William Morrow. 1983; Edward M. Brecher. *The Sex Researchers.* Boston: Little, Brown. 1969; Morton Hunt. *Sexual Behavior in the 1970s.* Chicago: Playboy Press. 1974; Wardell B. Pomeroy. *Dr. Kinsey and the Institute for Sex Research.* New Haven: Yale University Press. 1982. Revised edition; Zick Rubin. "The Love Research." In Arlene Skolnick and Jerome H. Skolnick (eds.), *Family in Transition.* Boston: Little, Brown. 1980. Third edition, pp. 279–285; Carole S. Vance. "Gender Systems, Ideology, and Sex Research." In Ann Snitow, et al., *Powers of Desire: The Politics of Sexuality.* New York: Monthly Review Press. 1983, pp. 371–384; Martha Vicinus. "Sexuality and Power: A Review of Current Work in the History of Sexuality." *Feminist Studies.* Vol. 8. Spring 1982, pp. 133–156.

# 8
# Deviance

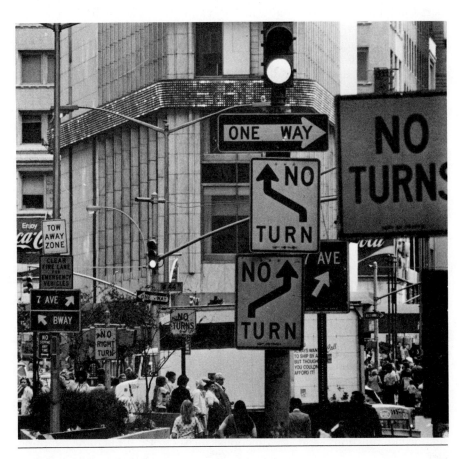

At a news conference, Representative Daniel Crane spoke with tears in his eyes. "I've broken the law of God, and I can only ask for God's forgiveness, my wife's forgiveness and my friends'" (Alter, 1983: 16).

Crane and fellow House member Gerry Studds had just been censured in the House of Representatives for having sexual relations with House pages, Crane with a seventeen-year-old female in 1980 and Studds with a seventeen-year-old male in 1973. The punishment of censure required the two congressmen to stand before their colleagues while the Speaker of the House read a brief censure resolution. The House ethics committee had recommended that the two congressmen be given the mildest possible punishment—a reprimand, which would not have required public criticism. But the majority of the House voted against the milder punishment. "The idea of a reprimand was not strong enough for the American people," said Representative Bill Alexander, Democrat of Arkansas. "After all, these guys molested minors. I was out in my district over the weekend and I was overwhelmed. The reaction was brutal" (Roberts, 1983: B22).

The reaction of people in Representative Studds's district was mixed but primarily sympathetic. Representative Crane, on the other hand, had campaigned against moral laxity, presenting himself as a staunch supporter of traditional values, and this scandal hardly endorsed that image.

Clearly both congressmen had engaged in deviant behavior. What is deviance? Sociologist Albert Cohen has suggested that it includes "knavery, skulduggery, cheating, unfairness, crime, sneakiness, malingering, cutting corners, immorality, dishonesty, betrayal, graft, corruption, wickedness, and sin . . ." (Cohen, 1966: 1). But simply listing types of deviant activities, colorful though they may be, does not indicate precisely what qualifies them as deviant. I offer the following definition. **Deviance** is any condition or behavior that the more powerful members of a social group consider a reasonably serious violation of their more important values or rules. The word "deviance" conveys the strong feeling that the people who engage in this behavior—the "deviants"—are different or even inferior and generally set apart from the rest of us.

Since social groups determine whether a thought or action qualifies as deviant, it should be apparent that what is considered deviant behavior will vary across space and time. Perhaps one of the reasons Representative Daniel Crane's affair with a House page created such a negative reaction in his district was that many of the citizens were traditional, believing that extramarital sex is wicked behavior that will destroy the precious family unit. Representative Studds, on the other hand, came from a socially and politically more liberal district, where the voters were inclined to focus on his work record and to ignore his personal life.

But three hundred years ago, Studds's district was part of the newly established Commonwealth of Massachusetts, where Puritan settlers had just founded a colony of fervently religious people who wanted to free themselves from the decadence and corruption they believed were sweeping across Europe. Those caught engaging in sexual activity outside marriage would have been imprisoned, exiled, branded, or even put to death. Today extramarital sex is commonplace.

Deviance is a broad and interesting topic. In the following section, we examine the functions and dysfunctions of deviance. Then we consider some of the most useful sociological theories of deviance, followed by a discussion of crime. The chapter closes with an examination of the social control of deviance.

## The Social Consequences of Deviance

This section considers how deviance provides significant functions and dysfunctions in society.

### Functions of Deviance

It might be tempting to assume that deviant behavior is inevitably destructive for groups and societies. However, deviant behavior can have a number of positive consequences.

## Unifying the Group

According to Émile Durkheim (1964), deviant behavior can act like a war, flood, or other disaster to unite people in the face of danger. Shared values and interests that otherwise might appear unclear are brought into focus. In a study of deviant behavior among the founders of the Massachusetts Bay Colony, Kai Erikson illustrated Durkheim's argument, contending that the Puritans' emphasis on harsh punishment for offenders reinforced their sense of shared community. Magistrates and ministers sought zealously to obtain statements of repentance from convicted felons, sometimes as they stood at the gallows a mere moment before their deaths. These confessions emphasized to all the fact that the moral standards broken by the deviants were, in fact, just and appropriate. Erikson argued that the Puritans' focus on a clear relationship between punishment and community unity has had a prominent influence on the development of the American prison system with its frequent emphasis on group discipline. Erikson pointed out that in Europe, where the Puritan influence has been weaker, the dominant prison system has emphasized that criminals are best rehabilitated through solitude and personal reflection (Erikson, 1966: 194–205).

## Endorsing Conformity

When the deviant behavior of an individual or of a number of individuals is singled out and censured, it is implied that the others, the nondeviants, are behaving in a desirable manner (Cohen, 1966: 10). Charles Dickens's (1859) *A Tale of Two Cities* is a novel set during the French Revolution. There were a series of public executions toward the end of the narrative. A guillotine was used, and each time a head was lopped off, a cluster of women seated in chairs and busily knitting counted out in unison the numbers of the victims beheaded that day. The victims were all aristocrats or friends and associates of aristocrats. The people watching and counting were the common people, the nonaristocrats who had overthrown the elite. For those watching and counting, each falling head symbolized the justice of their cause. In short, the guillotine not only chopped off heads, but also it cleaved a division between deviants and nondeviants.

## Supplying a Warning Signal

A rapid increase in the occurrence of deviance may indicate that there are serious defects in an organization or more generally in the structure of society. Such an increase suggests the necessity of making changes that can improve efficiency and heighten morale (Cohen, 1966:10). Analyzing Arab terrorists, Robin Wright (1985) concluded that these individuals believe that the only way they can compel the United States and other Western nations to take their political and economic grievances seriously is to use terrorists acts as warning signals. If the Western powers continue not to address their grievances and, in fact, use force against the terrorists or their countries, an escalation of terrorism will continue indefinitely.

## Providing a "Safety Valve"

Sometimes the fact that individuals engage in relatively mild forms of deviant behavior prevents them from pursuing more serious deviant activity. Since the 1960s there has been occasional criticism

*For the Puritans the world was an arena of struggle between God and Satan. Appropriate behavior was rigidly defined and anything else was deemed a threat to society. The Salem witch trials resulted in the execution of twenty people regarded as deviants.*

**172** of certain government policies contending that they have covertly encouraged the spread of hard drugs among blacks, other minority groups, and young people in order to siphon off energies that might otherwise explode into militant protest. The "safety-valve" function applies to other situations as well. Several decades ago the dean of students at a well-known college commented that "boys will be boys," especially in the springtime. He was therefore willing to overlook such pranks and infractions as panty raids and drinking bouts in the dormitories so long as these transgressions did not become more serious. In other words an implicit bargain had been struck between the dean and the students. Overall there were few serious disciplinary problems as a result.

## Dysfunctions of Deviance

The negative consequences of deviance are perhaps more obvious than its functions. Three will be discussed.

### Making Life Unpredictable and Tense

When deviance from significant norms happens, life becomes less predictable, encouraging tension and conflict between the conforming and deviant groups or individuals. The wives of alcoholic men, for instance, have often found that their husbands' erratic, even brutal behavior creates so much tension and conflict that living with them becomes intolerable. When wives reach the point where they realize they cannot control their husbands' drinking, they are likely to begin to worry about maintaining their own sanity (Jackson, 1978).

### Diverting Precious Resources into Social Control

Occasionally we read that a municipal police chief is planning to launch a large-scale attack against a particular type of crime. The chief will explain that a hand-picked elite force will go undercover in order to capture, arrest, and ultimately immobilize these particular criminals. If a local police force actually implements such a plan, then some of its best personnel must be removed from other much-needed duties. A somewhat similar situation can develop in schools. Teachers sometimes find themselves spending their valuable time on hallway duty, checking the restrooms for illicit drug use, and breaking up fights. Such misuse of time and energy might even convince some teachers to seek other employment.

### Undermining the Enthusiasm or Support Provided by Members of an Organization or Society

A number of studies have indicated that the Watergate revelations and related scandals have undermined the respect of a generation of young children for politicians and political activity. Evidence has suggested that adults' outlooks on the political system are largely based on their childhood perceptions of presidential authority (Greenstein, 1960; Hess and Easton, 1960). After studying over 12,000 children during the 1960s, David Easton and Jack Dennis (1969: 177) were unable to find a single child not expressing the highest esteem for the president. In the following years, however, the situation changed decisively. F. Christopher Arterton (1974) compared questionnaire results obtained from third, fourth, and fifth graders in 1962 with the answers given by children in the same grades in 1973 during the Watergate disclosures. In 1973 politicians generally were considered ". . . more selfish, less intelligent, more dishonest, and less likely to keep their promises" (Arterton, 1974:278).

# Sociological Theories of Deviance

Our discussion about the social consequences of deviance used a functional approach. In this section the theoretical emphasis continues with a discussion of four prominent and useful theories of deviance.

## The Anomie Theory

**Anomie** is the confusing situation produced when norms are either absent or conflicting. Societies that experience widespread anomie risk disintegration because their members no longer possess guidelines for achieving common purposes. The individual members often feel isolated and disoriented.

Robert Merton (1968) used the concept "anomie" more specifically, suggesting that it is a discrepancy between a socially approved goal and the availability of means to achieve that goal. Merton indicated that the attainment of wealth has been a strongly emphasized goal all Americans have been encouraged to seek. However, he also noted that many strivers for wealth and success, especially members of minority groups, have found the channels to achievement relatively closed. Either these individuals have lacked easy access to the culturally acceptable means to attain wealth or, primarily because of their socialization experience, they have not possessed the appropriate personality qualities that would have allowed them to become achievers.

Merton described five courses of action or adaptations to being in such a condition of blocked opportunity. Only in the case of conformity does the individual continue to accept both the pursuit of culturally prescribed goals and to feel favorable toward using solely legitimate means. The other four adaptations are regarded as deviant. They involve the nonacceptance of legitimate means, goals, or both. (See Figure 8.1.)

1. **Conformity.** This is a nondeviant adaptation. Individuals pursue legitimate goals and the culturally accepted means to achieve them, even though it is likely they will not attain those goals. In the 1920s a young black person who went to college with the hope of eventually becoming a wealthy professional was pursuing a culturally legitimate means to a legitimate goal. However, with the widespread discrimination that existed, it was unlikely the goal would have been achieved.

2. **Innovation.** This common deviant adaptation develops when a person seeks legitimate goals but is blocked from effectively using culturally accepted means to achieve them. If the drive to become wealthy cannot be satisfied through legitimate means, then some people turn elsewhere. For instance, some poor but ambitious members of economically deprived ethnic groups have turned to organized crime. There has been a definite pattern of ethnic succession

**Figure 8.1**
**The Five Modes of Adaptation in Merton's Anomie Theory**

— Accepts a means or goal
— Rejects a means or goal
---- Creates new means or goals

*People limited in their access to wealth and other socially approved goals will pursue one of the five modes of adaptation. (Source: Adapted from Robert K. Merton.* Social Theory and Social Structure. *New York: Free Press. 1968. Third edition, p. 194.)*

in this activity. In the nineteenth century, organized crime was initially dominated by the Irish, followed by Jews and then Italians. Blacks and Puerto Ricans are the latest in line. As each ethnic group has found conventional channels of success becoming increasingly available to them, they move gradually out of the underworld (Bell, 1962: 148).

Organized criminals are not the only success-oriented people who display innovative behavior. Merton observed that most great American fortunes were accumulated at least in part by techniques generally considered culturally illegitimate and even illegal. The respect most Americans show toward those who have accumulated such wealth indicates that the goal itself—the achievement of wealth—generally is considered more important than the legitimacy of the means by which it is achieved (Merton, 1968: 195–203).

**174**

3. **Ritualism.** This pattern occurs when culturally prescribed success goals are no longer actively sought, but the legitimate means for achieving those goals are conscientiously pursued. The ritualist avoids the dangers and possible frustrations of open competition and simply follows safe and easy routines of living and working. Ritualism is marginally deviant. Perhaps, therefore, it is more appropriate to label it eccentric. Merton mentioned a number of well-known clichés that apply to the ritualist—"I'm not sticking my neck out," "I'm playing safe," and "Don't aim high and you won't be disappointed." As a prime example of ritualism, Merton cited the "zealously conformist bureaucrat" (Merton, 1968: 203–205). Such a person accepts the organization's goals or rules as personal goals or rules and is characterized by an unquestioning allegiance to the organization.

4. **Retreatism.** A person is a retreatist if he or she pursues neither the culturally prescribed goal of success nor the means for achieving this goal because of limited opportunities or a sense of personal inadequacy. Among the types of deviants who may be regarded as retreatists are "psychotics, . . . outcasts, vagrants, vagabonds, tramps, chronic drunkards, and drug addicts" (Merton, 1968: 207). In short, retreatists are dropouts, and they are frequently condemned by many people because of their inability or unwillingness to lead normal, productive lives.

5. **Rebellion.** This deviant adaptation happens when an individual decides that the existing society imposes barriers preventing the achievement of success goals. Therefore that individual strikes out against the society, seeking to change its goals and also the existing means for achieving goals. According to Merton (1968: 210), people who engage in rebellion withdraw their allegiance from the existing society and develop "a new myth." This myth or set of beliefs claims that the source of frustration lies in the organizational and cultural patterns of the present society. Thus the myth proposes new cultural arrangements that do not display the problems emphasized by the people involved in the rebellion. In the past fifteen years, women, blacks, students, welfare recipients, antiwar activists, antinuclear protestors, work groups, and environmentalists have been prominent groups initiating social movements that support rebellious activity.

*Commentary*

A major contribution of the anomie theory is that it allows us to interpret a wide variety of deviant behavior by means of a single theory. As one writer noted, the scheme includes such diverse deviant personality types "as Cubists, alcoholics, lone-wolf inventors, religious martyrs, executives, and beggars" (Hunt, 1961: 59). Furthermore this theory contributes significantly to an understanding of deviance by indicating that social forces play an important role in encouraging people to behave in a deviant manner and by opposing the widely held belief that all responsibility for deviant acts should be placed on the individuals in question.

On the other hand, Merton's analysis has been criticized. Some individuals have claimed that the scheme provides no more than a general idea of how anomie can contribute to deviance; the precise process by which people learn deviance still needs to be mapped out much more thoroughly and systematically (Agnew, 1985; Cohen, 1966: 77). Merton (1976: 32) himself admitted that his theory addresses only selected issues as it analyzes sources of deviance and contributes nothing about how people learn to be deviant. That task is left to other theories, in particular the differential-association perspective.

## Differential-Association Theory

What is the process by which criminal behavior is learned? Edwin Sutherland's theory of differential association addresses this issue. Essentially this perspective emphasizes that people's behavior is largely determined by the company they keep. The following four steps summarize the differential-association process.

1. Criminal behavior, like behavior generally, is learned in interaction with others, mostly in intimate groups.
2. Learning criminal behavior consists of acquiring both criminal techniques and the motives, drives, and attitudes appropriate for criminal behavior.
3. A person becomes a criminal "because of an excess of definitions favorable to violation of

law over definitions unfavorable to violation of law." Therefore someone is likely to become a criminal if that person's values and the values of the individuals who have the greatest influence on him or her more strongly support criminal than support noncriminal activity.

4. A person's criminal associations can vary in certain respects. In particular, the frequency, length, and intensity of these contacts will help determine the impact of these associations on the individual (Sutherland and Cressey, 1978: 80–83).

The differential-association theory can be applied to diverse forms of criminal and delinquent behavior. For example, some evidence suggests that a number of inner-city youths may turn to hard drugs in order to display the much prized attributes of "toughness, daring, and adventure." Using heroin apparently makes a young man "somebody" in the eyes of peers (Feldman, 1968). Thus the individual encounters an excess of definitions favorable to the use of hard drugs over those unfavorable to their use.

During the first half of this century, juvenile gangs were often the context where young men could learn the values, skills, and motivation necessary for a criminal career in association with others (Shaw and McKay, 1942; Thrasher, 1926). The minority and ghetto gangs of the 1970s seem to have been less clearly linked to criminal life. If these gangs have had one distinguishing factor, it has been that they provide an excess of definitions favoring violence as a means of self-glorification and status achievement in a situation where the gang members are usually characterized by limited social ability and training, excessive aggression, and a desire to retaliate against others and against the society in general. As one gang member graphically stated, "A knife or a gun makes you feel ten feet tall" (Haskell and Yablonsky, 1974: 525).

*Commentary*

Critics of the differential-association perspective have charged that some of the terminology of the theory is vague, making verification through research difficult. For example, it is not entirely clear how the phrase "excess of definitions favorable to violation of law over definitions unfavorable to violation of law" can be tested (Sutherland and Cressey, 1978: 83–92).

On the other hand, differential-association theory has made a significant contribution: It emphasizes the fact that the development of criminal behavior can be understood only by examining the particular needs and values that specific criminal groups provide to their members.

## Conflict Theory of Deviance

Like conflict theory in general, the conflict theory of deviance focuses on the consequences of the concentration of wealth and power in the hands of a few people. The main thrust of this approach is that powerful groups of people with shared economic and political interests—power elites—use their power to develop and enforce legal standards that protect their interests.

Proponents of conflict theory offer somewhat different explanations of why the situation they describe has arisen in modern societies. Chambliss and Seidman (1971) contended that such a condition will occur in any complex society that has a multilevel class system. On the other hand, Richard Quinney (1974) argued that Western capitalism is the prime source of these inequities.

Quinney's (1975: 37–41) version of the conflict theory of deviance has focused on "the social reality of crime." He described four conditions that help explain high U.S. crime rates and also the prevailing system of criminal justice. First, the power elite defines as criminal those behaviors that threaten its existence. Second, the elite uses these definitions of criminal behavior to protect its own interests. Third, because of the limited life chances available to them, members of the subordinate classes are virtually compelled to engage in the sorts of behaviors defined as criminal. Finally the power elite develops an ideology that explains criminal behavior and that, in effect, downgrades the subordinate classes or groups, which are said to contain a disproportionate number of dangerous people.

*Commentary*

Conflict theory suggests that those defined as criminals are generally members of subordinate classes; this is an oversimplification. Consider the crimes of the prominent politicians, businessmen, and labor leaders who have been indicted in the post-Watergate years.

*Gang membership may provide a supportive context for attributes such as toughness and daring as well as an "excess of definitions" favoring violence as a means of achieving status within the gang, if not in the larger world.*

Conflict theory has also been criticized for its failure to describe the causes of deviant behavior. However, the theory makes no claim to do so; it pursues a specific task. The theory attempts to explain why certain standards for criminal behavior are established and not others. For instance, why are homosexuality, excessive drinking, the habitual use of powerful prescription drugs, and uncontrolled gambling frequently considered deviant but not classified as criminal? According to the conflict perspective, the reason is that it is not in the interests of the power elite to establish a criminal definition for these activities.

## Labeling Theory

Labeling theory is a form of symbolic interaction, and because it falls within this theoretical tradition, the perspective is centrally concerned with interaction between deviants and conformists. In addition, since the interaction is symbolic, labeling theory is concerned with the meanings the participants derive from each other's actions and reactions. Labeling theory emphasizes that behavior itself does not distinguish deviants from nondeviants. Instead the distinction is provided by the actions of the conforming members of society. These members interpret certain behavior as deviant and then apply the deviant label to individuals. Like conflict theory, the labeling perspective does not seek the causes of deviance but raises such questions as who applies the deviant label to whom and what are the consequences for the people labeled.

Labeling theory emphasizes that labels are applied by people powerful enough to impose their standards on society—for instance police, judges, prison guards, and psychiatrists. Those labeled include criminals, juvenile delinquents, drug addicts, alcoholics, prostitutes, homosexuals, mental patients, and retardates (Thio, 1978: 56–58). Recent studies have examined the rationalizations heroin addicts use to minimize the self-rejection of being labeled an addict (Covington, 1984), police and mental-health officials' impact on the development of juveniles' deviant self-images (Palamara, 1986), and the process by which self-labeling leads to seeking help for mental illness (Thoits, 1985).

If labeling theory were concerned only with the issue of who imposes labels on whom, then it would be closely related to conflict theory. However, labeling theory also examines another important issue: the consequences of being labeled deviant.

## Consequences of Labeling

The labeling process can be divided into two stages, primary deviance and secondary deviance (Lemert, 1951: 75–76). With **primary deviance** individuals violate a social rule but are not labeled and so do not see themselves as deviant. **Secondary deviance** occurs when authorities label individuals deviant and those individuals accept the status of deviant. The label seems to fit. "Yes," the person admits, "I am an alcoholic," or "I did commit a crime by embezzling the company funds."

Why does primary deviance tend to become secondary deviance? Edwin Lemert (1951: 77) has suggested that there is a process of interaction between the person and various forces of social control. Primary deviance is followed by the imposition of social penalties. Additional primary deviance happens, followed by stronger penalties and rejections. Further hostilities and resentment occur, perhaps with a hostile focus on those penalizing. The community now takes formal action, labeling the individual as a deviant. Eventually the person accepts the deviant role and incorporates an awareness of being deviant into his/her life pattern. At this point secondary deviance has taken place.

In a study of two groups of white male high-school students, William Chambliss (1973) demonstrated the selective nature of the labeling process. Both groups were frequently involved in delinquent acts—truancy, drinking, petty theft, vandalism, and (for one group) wild driving. The members of one group, however, were never arrested, while the members of the other were in constant difficulty with the police. The boys who were never in trouble—in the study they were called the "Saints"—came from respectable families. They had established good, sometimes excellent reputations in school; tended to have good grades; and were careful "to cover their tracks" so that they would not be caught following their misdeeds. If confronted by the police, the Saints were polite and apologetic, and if necessary their parents would intervene on their behalf. These boys engaged in primary deviance but carefully avoided run-ins with the authorities. In other words they escaped the labeling process that would have led them to see themselves as deviants.

The other group, whose members were called the "Roughnecks" in the study, came from much lower-status families. The Roughnecks had poor reputations and grades in school; they were less likely to have cars than the Saints, and so if they got into trouble they were less easily able to escape the situation. Being without cars also encouraged the Roughnecks to stay in the center of town, where everyone, including teachers and the police, could see them. Unlike the Saints, the Roughnecks appeared hostile and disdainful if confronted by the police. Furthermore the parents of the Roughnecks, feeling powerless, were unlikely to intervene with the police on behalf of their children. In short, various social forces in the community propelled the Roughnecks toward secondary deviance.

It proved difficult to make an accurate comparison of the relative severity of the deviance engaged in by members of the two groups. The Saints took part in a greater number of deviant acts and may have caused greater damage with their drunken driving. The Roughnecks were much more inclined toward physical violence. From the point of view of the community, however, the comparison was easy. Selective perception operated. As the products of upper-middle-class families, the Saints were perceived to be "good;" the lower-class Roughnecks were seen as "bad." The police frequently took action against the Roughnecks and never against the Saints, setting the secondary deviance process in motion for the Roughnecks.

## Commentary

There are several limitations to the labeling perspective. First, this theory applies only to a relatively small range of deviant behavior. The majority of the people who take part in deviance are never caught or labeled. This generalization applies to types of deviance as diverse as stealing, homosexuality, extra-marital sexuality, marijuana use, drunken driving, and crimes committed by businessmen or politicians. Second, sociologists who employ the labeling perspective tend to focus primarily on lower-class people who are easily labeled and to ignore middle- and upper-class individuals who have considerable ability to resist labeling. This situation seems unavoidable. After all,

**Table 8.1**
**Four Sociological Theories of Deviance**

| THE THEORY | ITS BASIC QUESTION | THE ANSWER |
|---|---|---|
| 1. Anomie theory | 1. What are the social conditions that produce deviance? | 1. Limited access to culturally approved goals and/or the means to achieve them |
| 2. Differential-association theory | 2. How do people learn deviant norms, values, and behavior? | 2. By the influence of the company they keep |
| 3. Conflict theory | 3. What is the primary motivation behind a society's definitions of deviance and crime? | 3. That the definitions protect wealthy and powerful people's needs and interests |
| 4. Labeling theory | 4. What happens to a person who is labeled deviant? | 4. A two-part process that is likely to produce a deviant career |

the labeling process is initiated by middle- and upper-class people in positions of authority, and these people are not likely to permit themselves or their children to be labeled deviants (Thio, 1978), as the Chambliss study on high-school boys illustrates.

Despite such limitations, labeling theory does contribute substantially to our understanding of many kinds of deviant activity. In particular, the theory emphasizes that a force other than the deviant act itself—namely, the reactions of others—frequently contributes to the development of deviance (Clinard, 1974: 25–27). (See Table 8.1 for a summary of all four theories of deviance.)

The following Contemporary Issue shows a different perspective on labeling: An individual's behavior can be affected by the absence of labeling.

## CONTEMPORARY ISSUE

## *Confessions of a Closet Addict*

It's probably best to begin very straightforwardly. I'm speaking about myself—as a television watcher. There! I feel a bit better already.

Actually I've never felt that this particular problem puts me in quite the same league as a ravaged alcoholic or drug user. The addiction has never been so compelling that I've had to stop whatever I've been doing to take a TV "jolt" or "fix." To no one do I give the appearance of destroying myself. Certainly TV watching has never led to the label of deviant being attached to me. In fact, many, perhaps most of my friends and acquaintances often watch many of the same programs . . . And we even discuss them, especially the sporting events in the cafeteria over a cup of coffee.

So what's the problem? I'm not breaking any laws; I'm not doing anything generally considered morally wrong. My friends watch TV too, and most of the American public is immersed in it. As far as I know, there's been no public call for a Television Watchers Anonymous.

Truthfully this last set of points leaves me somewhat uneasy. All but the last argument could be used with alcohol. Adults can drink booze legally. Often they do their drinking in public, and the American culture is swimming in it. Yet there are millions of alcoholics—deviants.

The comparison with alcohol seems to yield further insight. Both TV and booze can be used as escapes—to block out one's problems and concerns. In the past when I watched more TV than now, I often found it difficult to remember the program I'd just seen. Is this similar to the alcoholic who loses count of the number of drinks? The loss of memory—that's what I remember most vividly about those situations. I was just filling in time, and at the end when I either fell asleep or became so bored and disgusted that I finally did something else, I felt as though I were bloated with spiritual junk food. It's not a pretty memory, but perhaps its impact was necessary before I could come to grips with this problem.

I've also been helped in this effort by what I've seen TV do to other people. Most notable perhaps was the twelve-year-old boy I knew while I was doing my dissertation research. He was a pale, thin, intense child, who tended to spend most of his free time in his parents' apartment. He had good drawing skills, and when I encouraged him to do drawings for me, he sketched TV characters. He drew them impressively well, clearly. That was fine. But then he'd talk about them, and they seemed just as real and clear to him as the drawings — much clearer and more admirable to him than the people in his neighborhood. He seldom wanted to talk to them, especially the children. Often they laughed at him, calling him a sissy. Although he didn't say it, my impression was that he felt he was accepted by the TV characters; they weren't only his heroes but also his friends. I worried about how he'd ever adjust to a real, often demanding world in the years ahead. This boy might have been an extreme case, but it seems that many of us experience some of the same process.

So I've been struggling with my addiction. Lately I've been comforting myself with the fact that I've cut back on television and that my tastes have changed; I'm much more inclined to watch public than commercial TV. But what does that really mean? Maybe it's no different than the heavy drinker who no longer swigs a cheap muscatel but instead sips martinis. Some alcohol-treatment programs emphasize that the only way to eliminate alcoholism is to give up alcohol entirely. Is it the same with TV?

I'm not sure what's ahead. Perhaps some day I will give up TV entirely. Not tonight, though. It's the fifth game of the NBA (professional basketball) finals.

# Crime

In the last two sections, we have encountered a number of references to crime. The majority of crimes are, in fact, regarded as deviant activities — for instance, murder, rape, assault, robbery, burglary, embezzlement, and a host of others. On the other hand, some people who talk to themselves in public or who do not bathe would qualify as deviant but not criminal in U.S. society. In addition, some technically illegal behaviors are often not regarded as deviant. There is widespread violation of some outdated laws, such as restrictions against premarital sexual relations or Sunday sports. Criminal laws reflect the prevailing standards of deviant behavior, and when those standards change, the laws are likely to be altered or disregarded.

**Crime** is an act that violates criminal law. Punishment for crime is provided by the criminal-justice system of a society. Behavior is likely to be defined as criminal when it is too disruptive to be permitted and cannot be controlled by informal means.

In this section we examine the limitations of criminal statistics, the different types of crime, and criminals' characteristics.

## Limitations of Criminal Statistics

Official crime statistics drawn throughout the United States are reported in the FBI's annual *Uniform Crime Report*. We should emphasize that serious biases exist in these data, and we examine three sources of these biases.

### From Complaints to Official Statistics

One of law enforcement officials' chief tasks is to respond to people's complaints. The officer must decide whether or not to file a formal report of the complaint, thereby making it a crime known to police. Research (Black, 1971) has suggested that the following factors are among those that determine whether such a report will be made. There is a greater likelihood that official reporting will take place if the crime in question is a felony, for which the perpetrator may be sentenced to death or to a long prison sentence, than if it is a misdemeanor, for which a fine or a short sentence would normally be imposed. Second, the less closely associated the person complaining and the offender are, the more likely it is that a report will be issued. When friends and family are involved, injured parties are much less inclined to press charges. In addition, some evidence indicates that socioeconomic status is related to the likelihood of an official report, with police being more inclined to officially report acts brought to their attention by upper-middle-class injured parties—but only in felony cases. Finally the more courtesy or respect the person complaining shows the police, the better the chances that the crime will be reported.

A recent study emphasized fewer factors, concluding that the major variable affecting the reporting and recording of a crime is its perceived seriousness—more important is the victim's perception and less significant is the officer's view—and that offenders' and victims' personal characteristics seem to have a minor impact on reporting and recording crimes (Gove et al., 1985).

### Issues Involving the Victim's Willingness to Cooperate

Other factors also strongly affect the official crime statistics. The victim's willingness to cooperate is often significant. It is unlikely that rape will be made known to the police and that an arrest will be made unless the victim reports the crime and cooperates with the investigation. Between 1967 and 1984, the number of rapes known to the police increased by 205 percent (U.S. Bureau of the Census, *Statistical Abstract of the United States: 1980.* No. 302; U.S. Bureau of the Census, *Statistical Abstract of the United States: 1986.* No. 279). While it is likely that the actual amount of rape increased during that time period, there undoubtedly was also an increase in the victims' willingness to cooperate with an investigation. A couple of factors have supported this trend. Some women's groups have argued that a war against rapists should be declared—"We shall win back the night"—and many police departments have supported this campaign. In some cases they have taken steps to encourage the report of rape, such as using female officers to process victims' reports.

### Administrative Distortions

Sometimes crime rates appear to increase because a police force has become more professionalized. For example, in 1950, under pressure from the FBI, the New York City Police Department changed its system of reporting crime, and in one year the city's robbery rate "increased" 400 percent and the burglary rate "rose" 1300 percent.

Furthermore some law-enforcement officials or politicians—in an effort to serve their own purposes—deliberately alter statistics in order to "prove" that there has been an increase or decrease in crime. For instance, the FBI reported that of the people arrested and then released by the courts in 1963, 92 percent were rearrested within six years. Careful investigation revealed, however, that the FBI did not include all persons released in 1963 in this study. Seventy-six percent of the records involving people in that category were conveniently lost, and apparently most of these people were not rearrested. J. Edgar Hoover, then the director of the FBI, wanted to show that the courts were too lenient with offenders. He therefore distorted FBI crime statistics in order to support that conclusion (Zeisel, cited in Reid, 1982: 50–51).

## Types of Crime

The people who commit different types of crime are likely to vary in their background characteristics, life-styles, and subcultures. However, all are probably affected by some of the social forces referred to in the theories we have examined. Many are, in Merton's terminology, innovators: seeking wealth through crime because legitimate access to its pursuit has been blocked. Furthermore as differential-association theory indicates, most lawbreakers are exposed to criminal reference groups, providing an excess of definitions favorable to violation of the law. And in line with conflict theory, most criminals are engaged in behavior that influential citizens have—to their advantage—designated as criminal. Finally many lawbreakers experience the process of being labeled as criminals and, especially if sent to prison, enter the phase of secondary deviance.

## Crime against Persons and Property

The crime statistics reported in the FBI's *Uniform Crime Reports* are divided into two categories, Part I offenses and Part II offenses. Part II offenses are less serious crimes, such as drunkenness, fraud, prostitution and commercialized vice, and disorderly conduct. Part I offenses are further divided into two subcategories: (1) violent crimes, namely murder, negligent manslaughter, forcible rape, robbery, and aggravated assault; and (2) property crimes, specifically burglary, larceny (theft), motor vehicle theft, and arson. The *Uniform Crime Reports* focus on these particular offenses because they have uniform definitions throughout the states and because they occur frequently enough to be statistically significant.

### VIOLENT CRIME

In recent years at least one member of about 6 percent of all households has been raped, robbed, or assaulted each year. In 1984 a violent crime known to the police took place every twenty-five seconds on the average. A murder occurred every twenty-eight minutes, a forcible rape every six minutes, one robbery every fifty-five seconds, and one aggravated assault every seventy-eight seconds. In 1984 there were over 1.3 million violent crimes out of the nearly 11.9 million total Part I crimes known to the police, with violent crime representing 10.7 percent of that total. However, law enforcement officials place special emphasis on violent crime, arresting suspects in 30 percent of the known violent crimes compared to 13.7 percent of the suspects in property crimes (U.S. Bureau of the Census, *Statistical Abstract of the United States: 1986.* No. 279 and No. 297).

Many Americans today fear being murdered. Americans often think of murderers as deranged people like the Son of Sam, Charles Manson, the Zodiac Killer, the Boston Strangler, or Jack the Ripper, who strike quickly and unexpectedly, murdering and perhaps raping victims they have never met. Of course, such murders do happen, and they are often well publicized. However, these murders make up only a small proportion of the total. Most murders occur after social interaction between the murderer and the victim. In a substantial number of cases, the victim precipitated the violence, perhaps by striking the first blow or by attempting to use a deadly weapon. Furthermore most people who kill lack apparent psychotic tendencies.

Murders, in fact, tend to occur in the course of ordinary behavior. A recently developed theory—the "routine activities" approach—suggests that most murders are committed in the midst of people's everyday routines, which tend to vary according to such personal characteristics as age, sex, race, marital status, and employment status. For example, since the very young and the very old are more likely to have their routine activities centered in the home than are other people, these two age categories are more likely to be murdered at home than are others (Messner and Tardiff, 1985).

Studies suggest that men kill and are killed four to five times more frequently than women; that there is usually an increase in homicides during the summer; that most murders take place on weekends, particularly on Saturday night between 8 P.M. and 2 A.M.; and that in nearly two-thirds of all murders, either the victim or the offender (or both) has been drinking (Wolfgang, 1967). As Figure 8.2 indicates, the homicide rate is higher in the United States than in other Western nations.

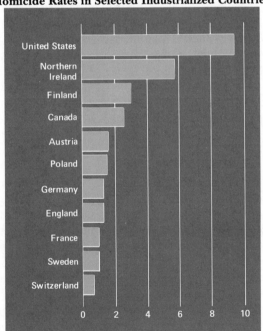

**Figure 8.2**
**Homicide Rates in Selected Industrialized Countries[1]**

[1] *Homicide rates per 100,000 populations of all ages in 1978. Homocide rates are slightly higher than murder rates because the former also include such seemingly justified acts as a policeman's killing of a felon.*

*The homicide rate in the United States is much higher than it is in other Western nations. (Source: U.S. Bureau of the Census.* Statistical Abstract of the United States: 1982–83. *No. 297.)*

Unfortunately rape is widespread in the United States. At some colleges, security has been increased, and members of fraternities and other men's groups volunteer to escort unaccompanied women home at night.

Violent sex offenders generally do not consider themselves criminals, although they recognize themselves as "different." Except in the sexual realm, their behavior is usually conventional, and they rarely have previous criminal records. Repressed sexuality frequently appears in case studies, but its source is unclear (Gibbons, 1977: 389–391). When asked why they engaged in rape, a group of 114 convicted rapists referred to revenge or punishment (with another woman substituting for the actual object of the rapist's anger), a means of access to unwilling or inaccessible women, or a bonus in a burglary or robbery (Scully and Marolla, 1985).

In recent years some women's groups have strongly protested the general availability of pornographic magazines, films, and album covers, claiming that these materials blatantly encourage men to see women as objects for exploitation. Efforts to legislate against pornography are now underway. In major cities around the country, supporters of such legislation have worn buttons that make statements like: "Women against Pornography: It's About Time" (McCarthy, 1981). As the research section at the end of the chapter indicates, the modern women's movement has also helped produce a steadily growing body of research on rape.

### CRIME AGAINST PROPERTY

People who know little about correctional institutions might assume they are filled to overflowing with murderers and rapists. Actually of the nearly 1.5 million individuals under some form of correctional supervision, by far the greatest number are held for offenses against property. In short, the prisoners have stolen or damaged something that belongs to someone else. Property crimes are much more common than violent crimes. In fact, a property crime known to the police occurs in the United States every 2.9 seconds, more frequently than most of us blink. About one in twenty Americans is the victim of a property crime each year (U.S. Bureau of the Census, *Statistical Abstract of the United States: 1986*. No. 279).

Between 1967 and 1984, the amount of crime known to the police increased by 101 percent (U.S.

Bureau of the Census, *Statistical Abstract of the United States: 1980*. No. 182; U.S. Bureau of the Census, *Statistical Abstract of the United States: 1986*. No. 279). Part of the increase resulted not from an actual increase in crime but rather from improved procedures for collecting and reporting crime statistics. Furthermore during this period, the population of young people was increasing substantially, and the members of this group are especially likely to commit property crimes. In 1984 people under twenty-five accounted for 62.2 percent of larcenies, 72 percent of motor-vehicle thefts, and 74.3 percent of burglaries (U.S. Bureau of the Census, *Statistical Abstract of the United States: 1986*. No. 297). In addition, some current social conditions seem to promote increasing rates of property crime. Americans are living in a "ripoff society," one critic asserted. He suggested that impersonal urban conditions, the cost of adequate security in businesses and homes, the ability of the mass media — especially television — to stimulate an intense desire for worldly goods, and the lessening impact of organized religion have all encouraged an increase in property crime (Bacon, 1979).

In addition, use of computers has permitted a new type of property crime — "computer crime." Anyone with a small computer and a modem (a device costing approximately $100 that converts a computer's digital pulses into electromagnetic waves that can be transmitted over a phone line) can employ a relatively easy trial-and-error procedure to hook into thousands of business and military computers. Some experts estimate that computer criminals use such methods to steal as much as $300 million per year. One prominent computer scientist suggested that the low level of security at many computer centers is ". . . like leaving the keys in the ignition of an unlocked car" (Broad, 1983: 1). It is now widely acknowledged that the most sophisticated computer systems cannot be protected from penetrators who have high-level skill, knowledge, and resources.

### Victimless Crime

A **victimless crime** is defined as the willing (hence "victimless") exchange among adults of strongly desired but illegal goods or services. As the term suggests, those who engage in victimless crimes are generally not preying on others. The list of victimless crimes includes gambling, illicit drug use, prostitution, loansharking, vagrancy, and public drunkenness.

Prostitutes, vagrants, and drunks are public eyesores who often draw police complaints. Arrests are frequent. In 1984, 9.9 percent of all arrests were for public drunkenness, with about 900,000 people arrested. There were also 562,000 arrests for drug abuse, 88,000 for prostitution, 67,000 for juvenile curfew violations and loitering, 27,000 for gambling, and 23,000 for vagrancy (U.S. Bureau of the Census, *Statistical Abstract of the United States: 1986.* No. 297).

Defining the types of behavior just discussed as crimes has a couple of dysfunctional consequences. First, when highly desired goods and services are made illegal, black-market activities will develop to supply users. If these operations are profitable enough, organized crime is likely to step in. It is hard to deny that in the 1920s the Volstead Act, which made the sale of alcoholic beverages illegal, helped organized crime to flourish and that the continuing illegal status of drugs, prostitution, and to some extent gambling have also strongly benefited organized crime. Second, the illegal status of these goods and services keeps prices high and quality questionable. For example, street-bought heroin varies markedly in its strength, and occasionally users take lethal or near-lethal overdoses because the strength of the drugs they have purchased exceeds expectations. With prescription drugs, in contrast, the strength and purity of the drugs are always guaranteed.

## Organized Crime

*The Godfather* has been one of the most financially successful films of all time. At one point Marlon Brando as the Godfather—a major organized-crime leader—turns to an associate and says in his gravelly voice, "I'm going to make you an offer you can't refuse." This phrase summarizes the powerful mystique of the Godfather, whose wealth and influence control a vast underworld network. With a snap of his fingers, he can make fortunes or end lives. From the perspective of Merton's anomie theory, organized-crime leaders are highly successful innovators, achieving great wealth and power through illegitimate channels.

Organized-crime activities fall roughly into three categories:

1. Illegal activities, such as gambling, prostitution, and narcotics. Public opinion varies widely on the morality of these different activities.

2. Legitimate businesses. Organized crime has infiltrated many ordinary businesses, which provide significant income and some measure of respectability to the participants.
3. Racketeering, which is the systematic extortion of funds over a period of time. For instance, if owners pay for "protection," their businesses will not be destroyed by the mob (Clinard and Quinney, 1967: 390).

Organized crime maintains a mystique and also provides certain goods and services not otherwise available. However, the consequences of some of its activities have been devastating. For instance, organized crime has the cash to finance the heroin trade, which frequently employs expensive and elaborate equipment such as computers, processing laboratories powered by electric generators, and radar-equipped private planes.

What are the effects of organized crime's control of the heroin trade? For one thing this situation has created an army of muggers, who are estimated to initiate over half the violent crime in major cities. Courts and prisons are overloaded with addicts. Many billions of tax dollars are spent on efforts to combat and treat addiction. Furthermore government officials estimate that drug-related murders and overdoses account for some 15,000 deaths a year. Finally, in order to keep law-enforcement officials from interfering in the heroin trade, organized crime has corrupted the police departments of many large cities (Newfield and Dubrul, 1979).

We should emphasize that American drug laws, which make the use of heroin and other hard drugs a felony, have permitted organized crime to control the drug trade. Some, perhaps most, of that control could be taken from organized crime if drug addiction were reclassified as an illness and the government made a major effort to establish effective treatment programs. These programs quite possibly would include controlled distribution of heroin to some users during the early stages of treatment.

With the formation of the Organized Crime Drug Enforcement Task Forces in 1982, the federal government has used a different approach to attempt to destroy organized crime's control of the drug trade. Noting that $70 billion of illicit drugs are imported and distributed each year, one proponent of the new program observed that ". . . the major trafficking organizations can be

*Although organized crime still thrives in the U.S., its leaders are now somewhat more vulnerable to arrest than in the past.*

dismantled by using task forces as organized as the drug traffickers themselves" (Giuliani, 1985).

### White-Collar Crime

A number of different studies support the conclusion that serious criminal behavior is widespread among middle- and upper-middle-class people (Shapiro, 1980; Wheeler, Weisburd, and Bode, 1982). Unlike the poor, affluent individuals often have excellent opportunities to engage in **white-collar crime**—crime committed by members of higher socioeconomic classes in the course of their business activities. The list of white-collar crimes includes bribery; sale of dangerously defective cars, military equipment, and pharmaceuticals; criminal price-fixing; serious consumer fraud; Medicare theft; deliberate shipping of defective products to unsuspecting foreign markets; and systematic violation of safety and pollution-control standards. Consumer advocate Ralph Nader recently wrote, "By almost any measure, crime in the suites takes far more money and produces far more casualties and diseases than crime in the streets—bad as that situation is" (Nader,

1985: 3). According to Nader, corporations, like fish, rot from the head down. To attack white-collar crime in corporations, law-enforcement officials need to start at the top.

Some prosecution for white-collar crime has occurred, and those prosecuted experience various impacts on their careers. Professionals (lawyers, in particular), government workers, and people in licensed occupations (for instance, accountants) tend to suffer a negative response from their occupational groups and frequently are barred from continued activity in their fields. On the other hand, business people or employees of private business generally encounter few such negative responses (Benson, 1984).

## Who Commits Crime?

A number of years ago, I was speaking with a man who had spent fully half his life in prison. "You know, Chris," he said, "you and your friends grew up aware that you'd be going to college. For me and my friends, the college we saw ahead was the slammer." Several of the theories we have discussed, most obviously the anomie and differential-association perspectives, support the conclusion that certain types of people are especially susceptible to becoming involved in crime. The person just referred to was black, male, of urban origin, as well as young when he started in crime. All these are factors associated with a high likelihood of being arrested. By no means, however, is it being suggested that the mere presence of these factors predestines a life of crime and arrest. We are simply addressing statistical probabilities here. Moreover, there may be biases involved not only in how crime statistics are compiled but also in arrest patterns.

### Age

According to official statistics, people under twenty-five accounted for about 62.5 percent of all arrests for Part I crimes in 1984. People in this age range were responsible for 50.5 percent of all arrests in 1984 (U.S. Bureau of the Census, *Statistical Abstract of the United States: 1986.* No. 297). (See Table 8.2.) A number of factors contribute to this high rate of arrests among young people. For one thing the police are more inclined to arrest those under twenty-five than they are to arrest older persons. In addition the rate of serious crime commit-

**Table 8.2**
**Serious Crimes[1] Committed by Different Age Groups (percent)**

| | AGE GROUP | | | | | | |
|---|---|---|---|---|---|---|---|
| | UNDER 15 | UNDER 18 | 18–24 | 25–44 | 45–54 | 55–64 | 65 AND OVER |
| Total arrests | 5.9 | 17.2 | 33.3 | 40.5 | 5.4 | 2.7 | .9 |
| Serious crimes | 13 | 31.1 | 31.4 | 31.4 | 3.4 | 1.8 | .9 |
| Murder and nonnegligent manslaughter | 1.0 | 7.3 | 34 | 47.9 | 6.4 | 2.9 | 1.5 |
| Forcible rape | 5.2 | 15.5 | 31.3 | 46.1 | 4.6 | 1.8 | .7 |
| Robbery | 6.6 | 25.6 | 41.3 | 31.2 | 1.4 | .4 | .1 |
| Aggravated assault | 4.3 | 13.4 | 31.3 | 46.4 | 5.6 | 2.4 | .9 |
| Burglary | 14.9 | 38.2 | 36.1 | 23.8 | 1.3 | .5 | .2 |
| Larceny–theft | 15.5 | 33.6 | 28.6 | 30.4 | 3.9 | 2.3 | 1.3 |
| Motor vehicle theft | 9.1 | 36.3 | 35.7 | 25.3 | 1.8 | .6 | .2 |
| Arson | 27.9 | 42.5 | 21.4 | 29.1 | 4.5 | 1.8 | .6 |

[1] Part I crimes.
Source: U.S. Bureau of the Census. *Statistical Abstract of the United States: 1986.* No. 297.

ted by those under twenty-five has apparently risen more sharply than has the rate for older persons (Cohen and Short, 1976: 59–60). Finally, until recent years, the number of young people had been increasing. This had meant an increase in the number of crimes committed by youths, whether or not their crime rate rose. Since the youthful group has begun to decline in size, it seems likely that the number of crimes committed by youths will start to decrease.

## Sex

Men are considerably more likely to be arrested than are women. In 1984, 83.3 percent of the people charged were male, meaning that about five times as many men as women were arrested. The only categories of crime in which men are arrested less frequently than women are prostitution and running away from home. However, the general trend over time has been for the female arrest rate to rise more rapidly than the male rate. In recent years the ratio of males to females appearing before juvenile courts has dropped to 4 to 1, probably the lowest of any Western society. At the turn of the century, ratios of 50 to 60 to 1 prevailed. In recent decades arrests of females for property crime have increased more rapidly than arrests of males for property crime, but a similar trend has not occurred for violent crime. One fact that might help explain these findings is that women are socialized to restrain their emotions and especially their violent tendencies much more effectively than are men. Furthermore women's inclination toward property crimes may be partially related to expectations associated with the contemporary female role, especially in difficult economic times — the female shopper becomes a shoplifter or the female casher of good checks turns into a passer of bad checks. It seems apparent that there are no simple, broad patterns of female criminality and that the variety of existing patterns will be most effectively revealed by detailed studies of the lives of women engaged in different criminal behaviors (Box and Hale, 1984; Simon, 1975; U.S. Bureau of the Census, *Statistical Abstract of the United States: 1986.* No. 297).

## Ethnicity and Race

High ethnic crime rates can be explained in part by the recency of a group's immigration — for example, Puerto Ricans and other newly arrived Latin American groups currently display high crime rates; or by the amount of cultural conflict and deprivation each group has encountered — blacks and Native Americans are the most obvious cases. Some ethnic groups, such as the Jews and the Irish, were once very active in crime, but as they have gained some access to the legitimate channels that may be used to obtain economic success, they have tended to move out of crime. On the other hand, certain Oriental groups, once relatively crime free, have become more actively involved because of lessening economic opportunities and partial community disintegration.

## Place of Residence

**186**

The extent to which an area is urbanized is definitely related to its arrest rate. Specifically the larger the population of a community, the higher its arrest rate is likely to be. For instance, in 1984, cities of 250,000 or more had an arrest rate for violent crime that was nearly two-and-one-half times as high as that of cities with populations of 50,000 to 100,000. With regard to property crime, the rate was 37 percent higher in cities of 250,000 or more than in those with between 50,000 and 100,000 residents (U.S. Bureau of the Census, *Statistical Abstract of the United States: 1986.* No. 283). Arrest rates are higher in more urbanized areas because larger cities are more likely to house high percentages of low-income people and to be characterized by physical deterioration and high population density. It is also possible that large cities, which tend to have professionalized police forces, place more emphasis on a high arrest rate than the police in small cities.

In order to combat crime and other forms of deviance, societies have various ways of maintaining social control.

# The Social Control of Deviance

A young child disobeys a parental command and is sent to his or her room. An adult breaks a law and must pay a fine or go to prison. Both individuals are punished by means of **social control** — the application of systematic behavioral restraints intended to motivate people to obey social expectations. Most people usually obey the rules because they have **internalized** cultural standards. This means that through socialization, social expectations have become part of the personality structure. People therefore feel guilty when they deviate. For some people in certain situations, however, these internalized standards are not sufficient to ensure conformity. In such situations informal or formal social control is necessary.

## Informal Social Control

Most of the time people obey the norms, but sometimes the rules are violated, and informal social control is unleashed. **Informal social control** consists of unofficial pressure intended to convince potential deviants to conform to social norms. Consider a student who has recently transferred to a new college. He wants to be accepted by the other students in the dormitory, but he is too pushy. He jumps into conversations and then monopolizes them. When two close friends go out for a beer, he forces his company on them. Informal social control is soon applied. The new arrival gets the "cold shoulder." Everyone says, "I'll see you later" whenever he appears. Perhaps the newcomer will eventually realize his behavior is unacceptable, and he will tone down his efforts to gain acceptance. Perhaps he will fail to come to this realization and will continue to be shut out by the others.

### Use of Informal Social Control

Most people are very responsive to informal social control. Few of us pick our noses publicly, make frequent obscene gestures, or speak loudly at weddings and funerals. We fear others' disapproval.

Informal social control is also commonly exercised in occupational settings. Numerous studies suggest that a certain kind of person is especially likely to be in business — the "organization man" (Whyte, 1956). Such people realize that the best way to get ahead and to escape the disapproval of their superiors is to be first and foremost a conformist. They subscribe to the organizational leadership's prevailing values and interests, displaying total loyalty to the organization and avoiding, at all costs, creative suggestions or pursuits. But it is not just people's superiors who impose informal social control. One investigation concluded that informal social control initiated by one's coworkers can be a powerful deterrent to committing deviant acts on the job (Hollinger and Clark, 1982).

### Effects of Ignoring Informal Social Control

Sometimes people risk a great deal when they ignore others' wishes. Loss of support from one's family and severed friendships are possible. Even bodily harm can result. A case in point is the "maverick," the person who in many situations stubbornly refuses to conform. Americans often have mixed feelings toward mavericks. Such people tend to be highly individualistic, a trait Americans widely admire. Yet their individualism, if uncontrolled, frequently triggers the disapproval of others and restricts their access to such highly valued items as wealth and power. Mavericks generally risk disapproval or even stronger reactions because they are unusually moral. They follow the dictates of their own internalized sense of right and wrong and not the external directives that bring material success. "Whistle-blowers" are a case in point—people who expose the existence of defective merchandise, cost overruns, and safety and health violations in the companies or government agencies for which they work (Parmerlee, Near, and Jensen, 1982; Spiegel and Katz, 1973). Common reactions to whistle-blowing include colleagues' and superiors' anger and hostil-ity, dismissal, and even lawsuits. A study has recently suggested that whistle-blowers are more likely to suffer retaliation if they lack the support of supervisors and managers, if the situation suggests serious wrongdoing, and if they use channels outside the organization to blow the whistle (Near and Miceli, 1986). Not all whistle-blowers, however, suffer adverse effects. U.S. society offers fame and even fortune to the few mavericks whose accomplishments have made them nearly invulnerable to the effects of criticism and disapproval. Consumer advocate Ralph Nader and columnist Jack Anderson have become household names as a result of their efforts to expose and eliminate government and business secrecy and corruption.

The preceding discussion has suggested that there are many different ways to provide social control. The following Cross-Cultural Perspective describes a rather unusual example.

## CROSS-CULTURAL PERSPECTIVE

### *Art Rides Shotgun on the Paris Subway*

We have noted that social control is the application of systematic behavioral restraints intended to motivate people to obey social expectations. Social control, in short, means the imposition of limits. The following situation demonstrates an innovative way that social control has been imposed and, at the same time, has created a situation providing some interesting new entertainment and experiences.

In the fall of 1982, the Paris Opéra Ballet presented a benefit performance. That fact alone was hardly unusual. What was unusual was the setting—hundreds of feet below ground in the white-tiled corridors of the Opéra subway stop. The Opéra's performance of the ballet, "Massacre on Mac-Dougal Street," was the latest in a series of artistic activities sponsored by the Paris Transport Authority as part of a plan to use art to help fight crime. The program has included performances by thirteen theater troupes, 200 musicians, and a two-ton hippopotamus brought into the subway by elevator because it could not make it down the stairs.

Crime in the Paris subways is infrequent by American standards, but the number of muggings and thefts has more than tripled in a decade, reaching 1100 in 1981. In addition, acts of vandalism have been increasing by about 25 percent a year. Parisians were particularly shocked by two brutal murders, in which an elderly woman was stabbed to death and a man was thrown in front of a moving train.

One of the reasons for this increase in crime is that machines have replaced the sharp-sighted women who punched subway tickets, increasing efficiency but leaving miles of corridors deserted and unprotected. Events such as the ballet are intended to support social control—to fight crime by restoring the human presence that was removed due to the introduction of modern technology. Claude Quin, the president of the Transport Authority, explained: "Criminals are bound to have a harder time if you have large numbers of people standing around listening to concerts and watching plays . . ." Although the crime rate has not dropped since the advent of the programs, Quin contended that it would have increased much faster without them. He said: "We estimate that 10,000 people are directly affected by every week-long program . . . There's no doubt that the activities are a deterrent."

Some of the more successful programs have attracted up to 3000 people. Several events, such as the ballet, have been held in the huge main hall of the Auber stop. Others, such as the Festival of French Song, were performed in twenty or thirty stations in order to reach more people. Not all of the activities involve theater, music, or dance. For one program, which was entitled "Vive le Cirque," trapezes were rigged at a major subway stop, and clowns and jugglers rode the trains, performing at different stations. During "Hobby Week" passengers learned how to paint porcelain, do Japanese flower arrangements, and make croissants in a baker's oven lowered into the subway for the occasion.

The most popular events are the Friday afternoon classical concerts held from July to September at the Auber stop. In the future Quin plans to expand the subway's offerings to include public-service activities such as explanations of the intricacies of the social-service system and advice to the unemployed.

It will be interesting to learn whether the Paris subway program really does serve as a mechanism of social control. If, in fact, the program can demonstrate substantial success, perhaps other large cities will adopt similar strategies.

Source: *New York Times.* "Culture Rides Shotgun on the Paris Metro." November 30, 1982, p. C13.

## Formal Social Control: The Criminal-Justice System

The American image of justice shows a woman blindfolded to insure equal treatment for all people who appear before her. However, many feel that the blindfold must have holes in it because in practice the American criminal-justice system is clearly biased. From arrest to sentencing, the likelihood of being ignored, released, or lightly treated improves as one's affluence increases. This relationship will be apparent as we examine the different steps in the process: arrest, pretrial and trial, and sentencing. Prisons will also be discussed.

### Arrest

For any particular crime, the poor are more likely than the affluent to be arrested. A study of 3475 delinquent boys in Philadelphia compared middle- and lower-class boys with similar arrest records detained for equally serious offenses. It concluded that the police were considerably more likely to refer lower-class youth to juvenile court (Thornberry, 1973).

How can we explain these findings? A number of factors seem to be relevant. For one thing poor people have less privacy. More affluent people can engage in certain illegal activities—gambling or drug use, for example—in the seclusion of their homes. The poor, however, are more likely to be forced into the public arena, where they can be directly observed by the police or where the complaints of others are likely to draw the attention of law enforcement officers. Second, in some cases the police are less likely to arrest affluent than poor youth because they believe that it is probable that middle-class parents will take a more active, effective role in disciplining their children. In addition, many researchers feel that police training and experience tend to make officers especially inclined to attribute criminality to certain groups—in particular, lower-class youth, blacks, Puerto Ricans, Mexicans, and Native Americans. Finally some evidence indicates that law-enforcement officers often are most willing to arrest those least able to bring political pressure to bear in their own behalf—in short, the poorest members of society (Reiman, 1979: 104).

### Pretrial and Trial

Poor people usually have little hope of raising bail. Being in jail during the pretrial period means that defendants are unable to work actively for their own defense. Furthermore defendants out on bail are able to walk into court off the street, like anyone else. In contrast, defendants not released on bail are likely to be led into court from a nearby detention center and thus give the appearance of being guilty, probably influencing juries and judges. Research indicates that among defendants accused of the same offenses, those who receive bail are more likely to be acquitted than those who do not (Foote, 1954).

Besides bail another issue that can influence the outcome of a defendant's case is the quality of the legal assistance. Since the *Gideon* v. *Wainwright* decision in 1963, all defendants must be provided with a lawyer. But the effectiveness of legal assistance varies considerably. The poor often receive "assembly-line" legal aid from a public defender or a private attorney assigned by the court. In both instances the lawyer's payment is likely to be modest, and public defenders' case loads are usually much larger than those of private criminal lawyers. Because of these facts, poor people's lawyers tend to be strongly motivated to bring cases to a quick conclusion. They may work out a deal with the prosecutor, whereby the defendant pleads guilty to a somewhat reduced charge.

In business, time is money, and defendants without funds are normally unable to command more than a minimum of a lawyer's time. In contrast, wealthy, white-collar defendants are able to hire a battery of skilled lawyers with sufficient resources to make it in the prosecutor's interest to settle quickly and leniently out of court. When white-collar criminals appear before judges, they frequently find themselves in friendly surroundings. The judge often sees the defendant as someone whose style of dress and general behavior are much like his own — a prominent, wealthy man who may well belong to the same country club as he does and who is the kind of person whom the judge represented when he was in private practice. One corporation lawyer explained that ". . . it is best to find the judge's friend or [former] law partner to defend an antitrust client — which we have done" (Green, Moore, and Wasserstein, 1979: 543).

*Sentencing*

The poor experience a double bias when they appear before a judge for sentencing. First, the crimes committed by poor people receive harsher penalties than do the "crimes in the suites" of the more affluent. For instance, a *New York Times* story on the fate of twenty-one business executives found guilty of making illegal campaign donations during the Watergate scandal indicated that most of these men, including New York Yankees owner George Steinbrenner, are still presiding over their companies. Only two went to prison, serving no more than a few months each. Upper-class criminals, in short, were punished leniently for their attempts to undermine the independence of the electoral process and to endanger the basic vitality of our democratic form of government (Jensen, 1975).

Furthermore the poor are likely to be the objects of discrimination. They more frequently receive long prison terms than do more affluent people convicted of the same crimes. Recent research has suggested that even when equitable standards of sentencing are established and stressed, subtle ways to affect the lengths of sentences can be found. For instance, blacks are more readily charged than whites with the use of a weapon in the course of committing a crime. Bearing in mind that, on the average, blacks and other nonwhites are poorer than whites, it is not surprising that the average sentence for a nonwhite inmate in federal prison is 144 months, compared to about 102 months for white inmates (Miethe and Moore, 1985; Reiman, 1979: 117; U.S. Bureau of the Census, *Statistical Abstract of the United States: 1982 – 83*. No. 331). (See Table 8.3.)

*Prisons*

What functions are served by prisons? Retribution is certainly one of them. Prisons are supposed to punish people who have made the lives of other

**Table 8.3
A Comparison of the Average Sentences for Whites and Nonwhites in Federal Prisons in 1981**

| SELECTED CRIMES | WHITES' AVERAGE SENTENCE (IN MONTHS) | NONWHITES' AVERAGE SENTENCE (IN MONTHS) |
| --- | --- | --- |
| Drug violations | 75 | 105 |
| Robbery | 178 | 178 |
| Larceny (theft) | 61 | 49 |
| Forgery | 55 | 49 |
| Kidnapping | 374 | 400 |
| Burglary | 95 | 113 |
| Juvenile Delinquency | 15 | 68 |

Source: U.S. Bureau of the Census. *Statistical Abstract of the United States: 1982 – 83*. No. 331.

**190**

people unpleasant. The Old Testament doctrine of "an eye for an eye and a tooth for a tooth" has often been the justification for putting people in prison.

Second, prison life is expected to act as a deterrent, encouraging individuals not to return to crime once they are released. But some research suggests that the kinds of criminals generally put in jail, such as drug addicts and sex offenders, are less likely to be deterred by prison sentences than are such criminal types as shoplifting housewives and white-collar criminals, who normally manage to avoid prison (Chambliss, 1969; Pittman and Gordon, 1968). There has also been the widespread belief that punishment can deter the noncriminal public from engaging in crime. This might be an accurate claim, but there is limited research evidence to support it (Reid, 1985: 88).

Third, prisons are supposed to isolate criminals, thus protecting the law-abiding public. Incarceration does produce this effect for the period of time that the individual is imprisoned. An important question, however, is whether or not the person still pursues crime after being released. If so, the protection provided is only temporary.

The final function of prisons is rehabilitation, the effort to reform inmates so that they will become productive citizens and no longer commit crimes. In recent years vocational education and psychotherapy have been used sporadically in attempts to rehabilitate inmates. Prisons have successfully punished and isolated inmates, but they have been much less effective at deterrence and rehabilitation.

The prison population has grown rapidly. The number of people held in federal and state prisons increased from 196,000 in 1970 to 445,000 in 1984, a rise of 127 percent in fourteen years (U.S. Bureau of the Census, *Statistical Abstract of the United States: 1986.* No. 321; U.S. Department of Justice, 1983).

A number of steps would probably help prisons function more effectively. These include removing those convicted of minor crimes from prisons and putting them in alternative programs; separating violent and property criminals; developing alternatives to incarceration such as restitution of destroyed property or public service (Stephens and Tafoya, 1985); and providing more prison space. The accepted minimum in the American penal system is 60 square feet per person. However, 65 percent of all state and federal inmates and 68 percent of local prisoners are confined in cells and dormitories that provide less space than the accepted minimum (U.S. Department of Justice, 1981: 49). A study conducted for the National Institute of Justice learned that long-term inmates of overcrowded prisons die, are killed, or commit suicide more frequently than do prisoners confined in cells of at least 60 square feet per person (Wilson, 1981).

In the preceding pages, I have offered evidence that people who are less affluent are likely to receive harsher treatment at different steps in the criminal-justice system. Not surprisingly a recent summary of survey research found that people who are poor or black are more likely to perceive injustices in the criminal-justice system (similar to those we have discussed) than people who are not poor or are white (Hagan and Albonetti, 1982).

# STUDY GUIDE

## Summary

1. Deviance is any condition or behavior that the more powerful members of a social group consider a reasonably serious violation of their more important values or rules.

2. Deviant behavior has both functional and dysfunctional consequences. The functions of deviance include unifying the group, endorsing conformity, supplying a warning signal, and providing a "safety valve." Dysfunctions are making life unpredictable and tense, diverting precious resources into social control, and undermining the enthusiasm or support provided by members of an organization or society.

3. Sociology provides a number of theories of deviance. Merton's anomie perspective indicates that U.S. culture strongly emphasizes monetary

success for all, without placing an equally strong emphasis on the legitimate means to achieve that success. The theory describes five individual adaptations, four of which are deviant.

The differential-association perspective claims that someone is likely to become a criminal if that person's values and the values of the influencing individuals show greater support for criminal activity than for noncriminal activity.

According to the conflict theory of deviance, a power elite uses its strategic location to develop and maintain the legal standards the group desires, to the advantage of middle- and upper-class and the disadvantage of lower-class people.

Labeling theory contends that certain people are labeled as deviant by those powerful enough to impose their standards on society. The labeling process can be divided into two stages, which are designated as primary and secondary deviance.

4. Crime is an act that violates criminal law.

Limitations to criminal statistics occur because many complaints are never reported, some victims refuse to cooperate, and administrative distortions happen. Among the different types of crime are crime against persons and property, victimless crime, organized crime, and white-collar crime. People with certain social characteristics — the young, males, minority-group members, and city dwellers — are more likely to be arrested.

5. The social control of deviance is the application of systematic behavioral restraints intended to motivate people to obey social expectations. Both informal and formal means of social control exist. More affluent people fare better with the criminal-justice process at all stages — arrest, pretrial and trial activity, and sentencing. Prisons are supposed to serve the functions of retribution, deterrence, isolation, and rehabilitation. Prisons are seriously overcrowded, and the penal system in general needs major reform.

## Glossary

**anomie** the confusing situation produced when norms are either absent or conflicting.

**conformity** a nondeviant adaptation, where individuals pursue legitimate goals and the culturally accepted means to achieve them, even though it is likely they will not attain those goals.

**crime** an act that violates criminal law.

**deviance** any condition or behavior that the more powerful members of a social group consider a reasonably serious violation of their more important values or rules.

**informal social control** unofficial pressure intended to convince potential deviants to conform to social norms.

**innovation** a deviant adaptation that develops when a person seeks legitimate goals but is blocked from effectively using culturally accepted means to achieve them.

**internalized** through socialization, social expectations have become part of the personality structure.

**primary deviance** violation of a social rule but the individuals in question are not labeled and so do not see themselves as deviant.

**rebellion** a deviant adaptation displayed when a person decides that the existing society imposes barriers preventing the achievement of success goals. Therefore that individual strikes out against the society, seeking to change its goals and also the existing means for achieving goals.

**retreatism** a deviant adaptation in which an individual pursues neither the culturally prescribed goal of success nor the means for achieving this goal because of limited opportunities or a sense of personal inadequacy.

**ritualism** a behavioral pattern that occurs when culturally prescribed success goals are no longer actively sought, but the legitimate means for achieving those goals are conscientiously pursued.

**secondary deviance** authorities label individuals deviants and the individuals accept the status of deviant.

**social control** the application of systematic behavioral restraints intended to motivate people to obey social expectations.

**victimless crime** the willing (hence "victimless") exchange among adults of strongly desired but illegal goods or services.

**white-collar crime** crime committed by members of higher socioeconomic classes in the course of their business activities.

# Learning Objectives

After studying this chapter, you should be able to:

1. Define deviance and discuss changing definitions of deviance across time and space.
2. Identify and examine functions and dysfunctions of deviance.
3. Define, discuss, and evaluate the anomie, differential-association, conflict, and labeling theories of deviance.
4. List and describe the limitations of criminal statistics.
5. Examine the following prominent types of crime: violent crime, property crime, victimless crime, organized crime, and white-collar crime.
6. Determine who is likely to commit crimes and why by analyzing the following factors: age, sex, ethnicity and race, and place of residence.
7. Define informal social control, indicate how it is achieved, and describe the effects of ignoring it.
8. Identify and discuss the four steps of the criminal-justice process, examining the discriminations suffered by poor people at each stage.

# Tests

## True–false test

_____ 1. Deviant behavior is inevitably destructive for groups and societies.

_____ 2. Robert Merton uses the concept of anomie to designate a discrepancy between a socially approved goal and the availability of means to achieve the goal.

_____ 3. Sociologists' studies of gangs, in which members were provided with an excess of definitions favorable to violence over definitions unfavorable toward violence, contain findings consistent with differential-association theory.

_____ 4. Labeling theory analyzes primary but not secondary deviance.

_____ 5. It is possible to engage in behavior that is considered deviant but not criminal.

_____ 6. A recent study concluded that the major factor determining the reporting and recording of crimes is offenders' personal characteristics.

_____ 7. The "routine-activities" theory suggests that most murders occur in the midst of people's everyday routines, which tend to vary according to such personal characteristics as age, sex, race, marital status, and employment status.

_____ 8. The majority of people under correctional supervision are held for violent crimes.

_____ 9. Some, perhaps most of the control exercised by organized crime over the drug trade might be removed if drug use were reclassified as an illness and the government made a major effort to establish treatment programs.

_____ 10. In the past decade, the construction of many new prisons has sharply reduced problems of overcrowding in correctional facilities.

## Multiple-choice test

_____ 1. A dysfunction of deviance is:
   a. unifying the group.
   b. making life unpredictable and tense.

    c. supplying a warning signal.

    d. encouraging retreatism.

_____ 2. According to anomie theory, the only nondeviant adaptation one can make to a condition of blocked opportunity is:

    a. innovation.

    b. ritualism.

    c. retreatism.

    d. conformity.

_____ 3. Quinney's "social reality of crime" version of the conflict theory of deviance focuses on:

    a. definitions of criminal activity by the power elite.

    b. socialism as a cause of crime.

    c. secondary deviance.

    d. learning criminal skills from peer associations.

_____ 4. Labeling theory:

    a. is a form of symbolic interaction.

    b. analyzes causes of deviance.

    c. does not explain consequences of being labeled deviant.

    d. demonstrates how behavior distinguishes deviants from nondeviants.

_____ 5. Biases exist in official crime statistics because:

    a. official reporting of misdemeanors is more likely than is official reporting of felonies.

    b. of administrative distortions in reporting crimes.

    c. officers are more likely to report complaints made by low-income groups.

    d. of the widespread reporting of crimes when actually no crimes occurred.

_____ 6. Which statement is true of murder?

    a. It is a Part II offense.

    b. It is a crime more common in Europe than in the United States.

    c. It is likely to occur after social interaction between the murderer and the victim.

    d. Arrest for murder is less likely than arrest for property crimes.

_____ 7. Organized crime:

    a. is confined to illegitimate business activities.

    b. has not been attacked by the federal government.

    c. is no longer in the prostitution business.

    d. is involved in such illegal activities as gambling and narcotics, legitimate businesses, and racketeering.

_____ 8. Arrest patterns indicate a greater likelihood of arrest for those who are:

    a. over twenty-five years of age.

    b. male.

    c. from small towns.

    d. white.

_____ 9. Which of the following statements is true of the arrest process?

    a. The poor are more likely than the affluent to be arrested.

    b. Since middle-class people have less privacy than do the poor, their crimes are more readily observed.

    c. There is no evidence suggesting that police officers are more likely to arrest those least capable of exerting political pressures on their own behalf.

    d. Police are strongly inclined to arrest middle-class adolescents because they believe that their permissive upbringing has encouraged delinquent behavior.

———— 10. Prisons have successfully performed which function?
    a. inmates' punishment
    b. prisoners' deterrence from further crimes
    c. inmates' rehabilitation
    d. prisoners' improved health

## Essay test

1. What is deviance? Discuss the variations of standards of deviance across time and space.
2. List and discuss two functions and two dysfunctions of deviance. Provide examples of each, using those supplied in the book and also some of your own.
3. Define, discuss, and evaluate two theories of deviance.
4. Is there bias in the reporting of criminal statistics? What factors seem to contribute most substantially to this bias?
5. What categories of people are more likely to be arrested for crimes? Discuss.
6. Define informal social control and assess the effects of ignoring it.
7. By examining the four steps in the criminal-justice process, indicate whether or not this system truly provides justice.
8. What changes should be made to improve jails and state and federal prisons? Discuss.

## Suggested Readings

Cockerham, William C. 1981. *Sociology of Mental Disorder.* Englewood Cliffs, NJ: Prentice-Hall. A sociological text examining the concepts, sources, social context, and treatment of mental illness.

Douglas, Jack D., and Frances C. Waksler. 1982. *The Sociology of Deviance.* Boston: Little, Brown. A text that effectively analyzes the principal topics in the sociology of deviance. The four chapters that review different theories of deviance are particularly well done.

Erikson, Kai T. 1966. *Wayward Puritans.* New York: Wiley. A study of deviance among Massachusetts Puritans. Erikson explains how the activities of the Puritan era contributed to the development of American standards of deviance and crime.

Green, Hannah. 1964. *I Never Promised You a Rose Garden.* New York: Signet. A beautifully written, fictionalized autobiography describing the thought patterns of a mentally ill girl as well as the frustrations and torments of life in a mental institution.

Kennedy, William. 1983. *Legs.* New York: Penguin Books. A powerfully written fictional account of the last years in the life of "Legs" Diamond, the famous gangster. The novel is particularly effective in conveying a sense of why many people have admired, even glorified major crime figures.

Reid, Sue Titus. 1985. *Crime and Criminology.* New York: Holt, Rinehart and Winston. Fourth edition. A comprehensive introduction to criminology, offering both detailed legal and sociological perspectives on crime.

Shoemaker, Donald J. 1984. *Theories of Delinquency: An Examination of Explanations of Delinquent Behavior.* New York: Oxford University Press. A text that effectively describes the principal bodies of theory seeking to interpret delinquent behavior. This is a useful, up-to-date book for students interested in this subject.

Spiegel, Don, and Patricia Keith-Spiegel (eds.). 1973. *Outsiders USA.* San Francisco: Rinehart Press. Twenty-four well written, effectively documented analyses of different types of deviance.

# Student Projects

1.  The following list contains a combination of noncriminal deviant forms and criminal behaviors:
    a.  alcoholism
    b.  assault
    c.  behavior demonstrating mental illness
    d.  dependence on legally available drugs
    e.  embezzlement
    f.  murder
    g.  nonviolent student protesting
    h.  organized crime
    i.  rape
    j.  theft

Ask five people (not in your sociology class) to rank these activities from 1 to 7, with 1 being the most serious. Compare and discuss your results with other students in the class. Is there strong consensus about the seriousness of the different activities? In particular, are the crimes always considered more serious violations than the noncriminal deviant activities?

2.  Select an interesting prominent person, such as a celebrity, political figure, or religious leader. Prepare a short biography that outlines this person's well-known deviant and nondeviant activities. On the whole, can you conclude that this person's prominence occurred because of deviant or nondeviant behavior? Ask other students to name something famous this person did. Which did students name more frequently—deviant or nondeviant activities?

# Answers to Test Questions

## True–false test

| | | | | |
|---|---|---|---|---|
| 1. f | 3. t | 5. t | 7. t | 9. t |
| 2. t | 4. f | 6. f | 8. f | 10. f |

## Multiple-choice test

| | | | | |
|---|---|---|---|---|
| 1. b | 3. a | 5. b | 7. d | 9. a |
| 2. d | 4. a | 6. c | 8. b | 10. a |

# RESEARCH IN SOCIOLOGY: SECTION III

## Research on Rape: A Progressive Struggle

In the early and middle 1970s, social scientists' papers about rape were often strongly worded statements demanding greater societal concern with the issue. During the intervening years, as the modern women's movement has received stronger support, the issue of rape has become defined as a significant social problem worthy of scientific investigation. As a result the quality of research has steadily improved. However, research on rape is still in its infancy, and investigators face some special problems when they do studies on this topic.

To begin, let us consider the meaning of the statement that research on rape is in its infancy. For the most part, investigators have not yet approached the subject matter systematically. For instance, as we noted in Chapter 1 ("Introduction"), the relationship between research and sociological theory is an intimate one, with sociologists developing theory to guide research, and investigators, in turn, refining theory based on their conclusions. For research on rape, it appears that an individual theory, such as feminist theory or conflict theory, explains rape under some conditions but not under others. However, the range of different theories' explanatory power has not yet been effectively mapped out.

Besides the fact that researchers studying rape are charting new territory, they find themselves facing some special problems — in particular, biased sampling of victims and difficulties with studies of offenders.

### Biased Sampling of Victims

A significant problem with research on rape is that the victims studied represent a biased sample. In the United States, it is estimated that somewhere between 25 and 50 percent of actual and attempted rapes are reported. Thus a serious sampling problem exists. How do women who report rapes differ from those who do not? The troubling fact is that we really do not know. And since we do not know, any generalizations made about rape victims based on those who report are biased in unknown ways.

Researchers on rape have been concerned about the sampling bias among victims and have tried to figure out the characteristics of those who have reported and those who have not. Studies have suggested that the victim's age, race, marital status, and relationship to the rapist are the factors that most strongly influence the eventual decision not to report the crime. However, until recently, studies have produced inconsistent, seemingly unrelated conclusions about the impact of different factors.

After a number of studies of rape victims had been published, sociologist Linda Williams did a systematic investigation of bias in reporting, highlighting several steps in the research process discussed in Chapter 2 ("Doing Research in Sociology"). First, in the course of her literature review, she read the various studies on reporting of rape and noted their different, often inconsistent conclusions. Then, based on the information obtained from those studies, she formulated a hypothesis, which seemed to resolve the major inconsistencies: A woman was more likely to report a rape if it approximated a classic rape than if it did not. What she meant by a classic rape was a situation where a woman was raped in public by a stranger who threatened or used a high degree of force and frequently produced injury. After developing the hypothesis, Williams tested it. The results of systematic research paid off, generally supporting the hypothesis. In an article on the subject, Williams emphasized that the most significant factor related to reporting the crime was whether or not the victim had known the rapist. If she had known him, Williams concluded, then the woman found herself in a difficult, self-blaming situation. Many women have been socialized to believe that they should control all female–male interaction. If such women are raped, then they are likely to conclude that it is largely or wholly because they failed to control the situation. Feeling responsible, they are not inclined to report the crime. Williams wrote, "This study . . . shows that those circumstances in a classic rape which discourage the woman from blaming herself also increase the probability that she will report the crime to the police" (Williams, 1984: 265).

Another body of rape-victim research involves follow-up studies. Here too the conclusions that are drawn are affected by biased sampling; in this case the bias results not only from limited reporting but also because some informants cannot be tracked down at a later date. For instance, Carol Nadelson and her associates initially interviewed 130 women in a general hospital emergency room after they had been raped. One to two-and-a-half years later, the investigators were able to track down only forty-one of those women—just 32 percent. Once more one does not know to what extent those interviewed in the follow-up were typical or not typical of the original set of informants.

## Difficulties with Research on Offenders

The limited reporting of rapes is a prominent reason why the samples of offenders in rape studies are biased. If only 25 to 50 percent of rapes or attempted rapes are reported, then based on that factor alone, 50 to 75 percent of attempted or actual rapists are never caught. Furthermore, even when a rape is reported, a sizable percentage of offenders are not apprehended.

But wait! The sampling bias problem can be even greater than so far acknowledged. Consider, for instance, Diana Scully and Joseph Marolla's study of convicted rapists. In this study the researchers' informants were drawn from the approximately 25 percent of rapists incarcerated in seven maximum or medium security prisons in Virginia who volunteered to be included in the investigation. Were the 25 percent who volunteered significantly different from the 75 percent who did not? Again, we do not know.

The Scully and Marolla research also raises another research problem in rape-offender studies—a question about validity. In Chapter 2 we briefly discussed validity—the condition where a research item accurately measures what it claims to measure. In this case did the researchers receive valid answers to their questions? The authors did not examine this question, but they conceded that since the offenders talked more about their feelings and emotions when the interviewer was female, the interviewer's sex may have affected the information received. It is possible, for instance, that some of the harsh, brutal statements these men made about women could have been aroused by a woman's presence. On the other hand, one might argue that when the interviewer was a male, the offender might have been inclined to feel competitive with him and that he (the offender) might have asserted this competitiveness by demonstrating what he considered his mastery of women. While the researchers did not discuss the issue of the relationship between interviewer's sex and validity, they did acknowledge a general concern with validity, indicating that since prison inmates are known for "conning" outsiders, they had taken the normal precaution of comparing the data from their interviews with presentence reports on file at the prisons. For the most part, no significant discrepancies were found with rapists' earlier explanations of their crimes.

## Conclusion

Several decades ago research on rape represented a small set of studies, but in recent years that situation has changed. As competent studies on this topic increase, some investigatory problems are likely to decline. For example, as research on rape helps publicize the issue, a higher proportion of women are likely to report the crime and decrease the sampling biases that currently exist. Eventually, based on modern research, a sophisticated body of theory will develop. It is hoped that from this theory there will emerge powerful insights for taking legal and social steps to curtail, and some day eliminate, this dreadful form of behavior.

Sources: Mary Beard Deming and Ali Eppy. "The Sociology of Rape." *Sociology and Social Research.* Vol. 65. July 1981, pp. 357–380; Carol C. Nadelson, et al. "A Follow-Up Study of Rape Victims." *American Journal of Psychiatry.* Vol. 139. October 1982, pp. 1266–1270; Diana Sully and Joseph Marolla. "Convicted Rapists' Vocabulary of Motive: Excuses and Justifications." *Social Problems.* Vol. 31. June 1984, pp. 530–544; Diana Scully and Joseph Marolla. " 'Riding the Bull at Gilley's': Convicted Rapists Describe the Rewards of Rape." *Social Problems.* Vol. 32. February 1985, pp. 241–263. Linda S. Williams. "The Classic Rape: When Do Victims Report?" *Social Problems.* Vol. 31. April 1984, pp. 459–467.

# PART THREE
## Inequities in Modern Society

# 9
# SOCIAL STRATIFICATION

In early 1983 a few hopeful signs appeared in the American economy. U.S. Steel rehired 2 percent of its labor force, but that still left only 42 percent of its workers on the job. In Detroit auto executives were predicting that 1983 sales would be 10 percent higher than 1982, which had been the worst year since 1961. "Ten percent better than terrible is still terrible," the Chairman of General Motors said (Issacson, 1983: 17).

A slight resurgence appeared in a few industries, but overall the economic picture was bleak for many Americans. The unemployment rate had steadily risen, reaching 10 percent overall and attaining at least twice that figure in many communities. Such federal programs as food stamps, school lunches, student loans, mass-transit aid, and subsidies for alternative energy systems were cut or eliminated. A proposed jobs program planned to hire about 125,000 people to repair bridges, highways, and mass-transit systems. Putting 125,000 people back to work, however, represented a small step in the effort to eliminate unemployment.

The poor and the near poor have generally been the hardest hit economically, with the greatest losses in income striking those with incomes just above the poverty level. Unemployment for such people means status loss on more than one dimension, as the following commentary suggests:

> Unemployment does not merely add to the quantity of poverty. It changes its quality. Put simply, it robs poverty of its dignity. Working men and women, regardless of how little they earn, have their self-esteem. They have their pride in their sweat to make up for the position. They are not victims, but actors. They can face their families. All this the unemployed are missing. Their weakness, for which most of them are emphatically not to blame, is made to feel dishonorable.
>
> *(New Republic, 1982: 6)*

During the early 1980s, a substantial number of citizens slipped down the rungs of the American stratification system. In the course of this chapter, we consider how social stratification affects the lives of these people as well as other members of U.S. society.

**Social stratification** is the structured inequality of access to rewards, resources, and privileges that are scarce and desirable within a society. "Structured inequality" means that because of their roles and group memberships, some people have a better opportunity than others to obtain rewards, resources, and privileges. The poor, for instance, are often without jobs, and thus they frequently lack both income and respect.

You undoubtedly realize that because of family income, parental connections, and other factors some people have better opportunities to obtain these rewards and resources than others. At the same time, you probably are also aware that for most of us little of value simply drops into our laps. If you are going to obtain the benefits of the American stratification system, then you must plan your life and, in particular, your career. It is likely that you have decided that a college education will help you in this effort.

This chapter analyzes a number of important issues involving social stratification. The next section examines three theories of social stratification. Then we will look at the prominent dimensions of social stratification—wealth, power, and prestige. The fourth subject is the American social-class system, and in this discussion we see how stratification enters the everyday activities of Americans. The chapter closes with an examination of social mobility in American society.

## Theories of Social Stratification

The structural-functional and conflict theories always offer different perspectives on a particular issue. In this instance structural-functional theory indicates that people's talent and drive determine their occupational positions, and conflict theory disputes this conclusion, contending that job placement has little to do with talent and drive. We examine this difference of opinion and then briefly consider Gerhard Lenski's effort to combine the structural-functional and conflict theories.

## Structural-Functional Theory of Social Stratification

In 1945 Kingsley Davis and Wilbert Moore (1945) produced a structural-functional theory of stratification that attempts to explain the unequal distribution of rewards, resources, and privileges. Davis and Moore contended that all societies must face the problem of getting people to fill different positions and, once in those positions, to perform the duties associated with them. Some positions, however, are more critical to fill than others. The most critical jobs are those functionally important for the survival of society and those that require highly qualified personnel.

Davis and Moore suggested that functional importance alone will not assure job holders that they are well rewarded. Some positions make a major contribution, but their ranks are so easy to fill that high salaries are not necessary. Police, fire fighters, and sanitation workers are examples.

Other positions are both functionally important and require highly qualified personnel. The promise of rewards will increase the likelihood that a fairly large number of people will endure the long, costly training that will qualify them for these positions. The potential to be a physician, for example, probably falls within the mental capacity of many people, but the training is so expensive and difficult that it is unlikely that many individuals would seek to enter the profession without the promise of a high income.

Davis and Moore concluded that differences between one system of social stratification and another exist because of conditions affecting the two determinants of differential reward—namely, functional importance and scarcity of personnel. Doctors, for instance, would not receive a high income in a society where the members do not believe that modern medical techniques will work or where the training for medical personnel is fairly brief and inexpensive.

### *Criticism of the Structural-Functional Theory*

Critics of Davis and Moore's theory have claimed that this perspective does not establish a convincing link between the rewards provided by the stratification system and the contributions people make. According to Davis and Moore, the people who fill all high-paid positions are making an important, even necessary contribution to the society. But it seems impossible to argue that such individuals as underworld crime leaders, baseball superstars, and corrupt but wealthy business people are performing essential, even important services. Furthermore many affluent individuals have neither special talents nor special training. Children of wealthy parents or people who marry the wealthy are cases in point.

Conflict theorists have raised criticisms like the ones just mentioned. Unlike the structural-functionalists, who focus on how stratification systems meet the needs of the overall society, conflict theorists consider how stratification affects individuals and groups. Karl Marx made an early and important contribution in this theoretical area.

## Marxist Conflict Theory of Stratification

Karl Marx believed that the struggle between social and economic classes was a central feature in the development of societies. In his famous *Communist Manifesto,* he wrote, "The history of all hitherto existing society is the history of class struggles."

Marx was convinced that classes arise out of the productive system within a society. In an agricultural society, the principal positions are landowner and serf or tenant. In an industrial society, the principal positions are the **bourgeoisie**—the class of modern capitalists who own the means of economic production and employ wage labor—and the **proletariat**—the class of modern wage laborers who possess no means of production and thus must sell their own labor in order to survive.

According to Marx, the interests of the bourgeoisie and the proletariat are inevitably opposed. Those who own the means of economic production—the factories and the farms—are primarily interested in maximizing their profit, and the workers, in turn, invariably want to increase their wages and benefits. Because of their economic prominence, the capitalists are able to exert politi-

*Marx believed that the interests of wage laborers, such as these factory workers, are in fundamental conflict with the interests of those who own the means of production.*

cal influence to prevent any organized expression of workers' discontent.

Marx contended that even though the members of the proletariat are disorganized and often unaware that they constitute a social class, they nonetheless share class membership in two respects. First, they are all victims of the capitalist production process since they perform essential physical labor but receive minimal pay for their efforts. Second, workers are powerless to confront the political strength of the state, which prevents them from expressing their discontent.

According to Marx, the proletariat gradually begins to develop **class consciousness:** recognition by the members of a class of the role they play in the production process. The workers' class consciousness involves an awareness of their relation to the bourgeoisie, especially a recognition of the owners' determination to prevent them from receiving a fair share of company profits. Marx believed that industrial conditions invariably encourage the development of class consciousness. He wrote:

> But with the development of industry the proletariat not only increases in number; it becomes concentrated in greater masses, its strength grows, and it feels that strength more. The various interests and conditions of life within the ranks of the proletariat

are more and more equalized, in proportion as machinery obliterates all distinctions of labor and nearly everywhere reduces wages to the same low level . . . Thereupon the workers begin to form combinations (trade unions) against the bourgeois; they club [join] together in order to keep up the rate of wages . . .

> *(Marx and Engels, 1959: 16)*

Marx believed that in the final stage of class consciousness, the members of the proletariat recognize that the only way they will receive payment commensurate with their work efforts is to organize themselves into an army, overthrow the capitalists, and eliminate private ownership of the means of production.

## Criticism of the Marxist Conflict Theory

One point of contention involves Marx's claim that once a class of individuals recognizes its common interests and is willing to act on them in the public arena, it will always try to overthrow the existing system. This conclusion fails to appreciate that most politically disenfranchised people usually want to become part of the system rather than to overthrow it. Prominent American cases in point have been the labor movement, a variety of racial and ethnic movements, and the women's movement. In the specific case of industrial workers, Marx underestimated the improving opportunities many of them have historically gained —in particular, good pay, pensions, social security, tenure and seniority, trade unionism, and the chance for some individuals, especially potential leaders, to move from lower- to higher-status positions. Thus, as one writer noted, were Marx to return to earth a century after his death, he would discover ". . . that, in the most advanced capitalist countries, the proletariat had gained in many ways, despite the continuing exploitation against it, and that new middle classes had arisen, contrary to his expectation of class polarity" (Gurley, 1984: 112).

In addition, the Marxist scheme takes a highly oversimplified view of the human personality. For Marx people seemed to be little more than the products of a uniform class experience, shifted around in large numbers in response to general social conditions. In short, Marx minimized the extent to which individuals are capable of making their own decisions (Beeghley, 1978: 22–24; Rossides, 1976: 423–427).

## Lenski's Theory of Social Stratification

Gerhard Lenski (1966) was convinced that neither structural-functional nor conflict theory offers a complete and effective analysis of social stratification. He borrowed from both approaches in developing his own theory.

Lenski noted that the structural-functionalists believe that people are generally self-serving—that when individuals must choose between their own or their group's interests and the interests of others, they almost always choose the former. In contrast, the conflict theorists are much more likely to conclude that many people, especially members of the proletariat, are "good," putting the interests of their entire class above their own and their family's interests. On this point Lenski agreed with the structural-functionalists.

On the other hand, Lenski supported conflict theorists' observation that societies contain individuals and groups that constantly struggle to obtain precious, scarce goods. Lenski was critical of Davis and Moore's conclusion that "perfect" systems of social stratification develop in order to meet the precise needs of the societies in which they are located. He asserted that since

> . . . there is no such thing as a perfect social system, we should stop spinning theories which postulate their existence and direct our energies toward the building of theories which explicitly assume that all human organizations are imperfect systems. Second, social theorists (and researchers too) should stop trying to find social utility in all the varied behavior patterns of men; they should recognize that many established patterns of action are thoroughly antisocial and contribute nothing to the general good.
>
> *(Lenski, 1966: 34)*

Lenski has suggested that on some issues the accuracy of the structural-functional or the conflict perspective varies with the type of society. For instance, structural-functionalists have contended that consensus (shared agreement) maintains social stratification systems, and conflict theorists have concluded that coercion plays the dominant part. Lenski's analysis of societies led him to the conclusion that consensus is considerably more important in societies with little or no economic surplus, while coercion is more significant in societies that possess a substantial economic surplus. Unlike the simpler societal forms, the latter kinds of societies have inevitably developed a small governing class that controls the political process and requires the people outside the elite to turn over most of their economic surplus; the use of force or the threat of its use has been the only way to insure such compliance.

Structural-functionalists are generally positive about modern industrial stratification systems, and Lenski's analysis offers some evidence favoring such an outlook. He noted that until the advanced industrial age, major technological innovations tended to increase social inequality within societies. In recent decades, however, this trend has reversed. The United States and other major industrialized nations show somewhat more equitable distribution of power, privilege, and prestige than was apparent in less advanced industrial societies. On the other hand, Lenski's analysis has provided evidence in support of the conflict theorists' criticism of modern industrial stratification systems. In particular, he noted that the gap between the wealthy and the poor nations has been growing since the beginning of industrialization. One expert has estimated that between 1860 and 1960 the wealthiest quarter of nations increased their share of the world's income from 58 to 72 percent, and during the same time period the income of the poorest quarter dropped from 12.5 to 3.2 percent (Lenski and Lenski, 1982; Zimmerman, 1965: 38).

The chief difference between Lenski's theory and the other two is that Lenski's analysis does not take a firm ideological position into which facts are fitted. Instead basic theoretical conclusions are determined by available evidence. The Lenski theory, in short, is a more effective scientific endeavor than its predecessors.

## Dimensions of Social Stratification

The focus now shifts from theories to the major dimensions of stratification systems. As you read this section, you might consider whether the facts you encounter are more consistent with structural-functional or with conflict theory.

Max Weber (Gerth and Mills, 1946: 180–195)

emphasized that there are three dimensions of social stratification, which will be referred to as wealth, power, and prestige. The relationship among these dimensions is not self-evident. Sometimes they are highly interdependent. For instance, a person with great wealth might be able to exert considerable power in the political process by making substantial contributions to legislators' campaign funds. In other situations no apparent relationship exists. The members of the long-time wealthy families in the locale just mentioned might feel that the wealthy person is low in prestige, lacking the education and social contacts that would make that person an acceptable member of their set of friends.

## Wealth and Income

The United States has about a half-million millionaires, or—in 1985—about one in every 475 citizens. The largest number reside in big business centers—in New York, California, and Illinois—while Idaho, Maine, and North Dakota have the highest per capita ratio of millionaires. Historically the majority of millionaires have had inherited wealth, but in recent years that proportion has diminished, with entrepreneurs in such high-tech businesses as computer software, skilled professionals in fields like neurosurgery and the law, and corporate executives being among the most prominent new entries.

**Wealth** is people's economic assets—their cars, homes, stocks, bonds, and real estate—and individuals can convert these assets into cash. A disproportionate share of economic assets belongs to the wealthy. In 1984, 1.9 percent of American households (those with assets of $500,000 or more) possessed 63.3 percent of all economic assets, including 73.8 percent of stocks and mutual funds, 71.1 percent of business and professional ownership, and 60.5 of rental property (U.S. Bureau of the Census, *Household Wealth and Asset Ownership: 1984.* Tables 1 and 3).

Data on **income,** which is people's earnings obtained through wages, salaries, business profits, stock dividends, and other means, are more accessible and easily measured than data on wealth. For this reason researchers study income more frequently than wealth. However, a study of income fails to acknowledge various sources that are not reported or are indirect, such as professors' research grants and business executives' use of company cars and recreational facilities.

*Absolute versus Relative Wealth and Income*

Analysts often make a distinction between two types of wealth—absolute and relative. **Absolute wealth** is the cash value of an individual's economic assets. **Relative wealth** is the value of an individual's economic assets compared to the assets possessed by other citizens in that society.

Through most of American history, rising industrial productivity, the tax structure, and various supplemental income programs have produced an absolute increase in wealth for all classes. However, over time the relative inequality of class income has remained stable. One sociologist suggested that modern stratification systems are like ". . . a fleet of ships in a harbor: an incoming tide—rising productivity and a rising standard of living—does not diminish the difference between rowboats, cabin cruisers, cargo vessels, and giant ocean liners" (Rossides, 1976: 112).

These two assessments of income distribution focus on different issues. For instance, absolute income figures suggest that until the mid-1970s people at all income levels were able to purchase increasing quantities of goods and services, thereby steadily improving their standard of living. Since the mid-1970s, however, the trend has reversed, and a growing proportion of Americans now find that their standard of living is declining. Absolute figures also make it clear that a significant number of Americans—about 33.7 million or 14.4 percent of the national population—have insufficient income to provide a nutritionally adequate diet (U.S. Bureau of the Census, *Statistical Abstract of the United States: 1986.* No. 767).

Relative income figures highlight the fact that over time the distribution of income has changed little. Thus in 1947 the lowest fifth of the American population received 5 percent of all income, the highest fifth 43 percent, and the top 5 percent 17.5 percent. In 1983 the respective figures were 4.7 percent, 42.7 percent, and 15.8 percent (U.S. Bureau of the Census, *Current Population Reports,* Series P–60, *Money Income of Households, Families, and Persons in the United States: 1983,* 1984. Table 17). (See Table 9.1.)

**Table 9.1**
**Relative Family Income[1] over Time**

| | Lowest Fifth | Second Fifth | Middle Fifth | Fourth Fifth | Highest Fifth | Top 5 Percent | Mean Income |
|---|---|---|---|---|---|---|---|
| | PERCENTAGE DISTRIBUTION OF INCOME | | | | | | |
| 1983 | 4.7% | 11.1% | 17.1% | 24.4% | 42.7% | 15.8% | $28,638 |
| 1977 | 5.2 | 11.6 | 17.5 | 24.2 | 41.5 | 15.7 | 18,264 |
| 1967 | 5.5 | 12.4 | 17.9 | 23.9 | 40.4 | 15.2 | 8,801 |
| 1957 | 5.1 | 12.7 | 18.1 | 23.8 | 40.4 | 15.6 | 5,443 |
| 1947 | 5 | 11.9 | 17 | 23.1 | 43 | 17.5 | 3,546 |

[1] Unrelated individuals living in the household were included until 1978 and since then have been excluded.
Source: U.S. Bureau of the Census. *Current Population Reports,* Series P–60, *Money Income of Households, Families, and Persons in the United States: 1983.* Table 17.

*The figures in this table demonstrate that relative family income has remained remarkably stable over a thirty-six-year period.*

## Effect of Taxes

The tax structure is a prominent means by which unequal economic distribution is kept fairly stable. Certain taxes—those on property, sales, and on behalf of social security—are regressive, meaning that all people pay the same percentage of a product's value, regardless of their income. Therefore, if the state sales tax is 7 percent, any person making a purchase must pay an additional 7 percent beyond the cost of the item.

On the other hand, income taxes are supposedly progressive, apparently taking a greater percentage of people's income as it increases. If income taxes truly were progressive, then economic inequality might be significantly reduced. However, the tax system is progressive only for low- and middle-income people. For those with high and very high income, a range of available tax loopholes permits them to keep significant portions of their income untaxed or taxed at sharply reduced rates. For example, people financially involved in the search for such exhaustible resources as oil or natural gas receive tax breaks because they are investing in the procurement of scarce but essential resources. In addition, people in various businesses and professions are able to "write off" a wide range of activities as business expenses. Sometimes these meals, travel costs, and rented cars, hotel rooms, and villas will represent legitimate business costs, and sometimes they will not.

Thus, on the surface, the U.S. tax structure is progressive, but the more significant fact is that the number and size of tax loopholes increase as people's income increases. In 1972 a person with an income under $3000 a year averaged a $15.00 yearly benefit from tax loopholes, but at high income levels (over $500,000 per year) the savings provided by loopholes rose sharply, reaching an average of $726,198.00 for people with incomes over $1 million per year (Surrey, 1973: 71).

The instillation of tax loopholes is an example of the close relationship between wealth and power. As we will see in Chapter 14 ("The Political and Economic Institutions"), interest groups attempt to influence politicians to pass favorable legislation, and wealthy interest groups tend to be more successful than their less affluent counterparts. In recent decades there has been a rising citizen dissatisfaction about the tax breaks available to the wealthy. One result was that in 1969 a seemingly major tax reform passed Congress. However, in spite of the apparently sweeping changes this law enacted, wealthy people have continued to find multiple tax loopholes. Furthermore in 1971, after the furor over tax reform had died down, Congress passed a law restoring some of the loopholes plugged in 1969. Therefore wealthy people influence Congress through their interest groups, which act in a carefully planned series of maneuvers. "Rarely is a frontal assault undertaken, lest the self-interest of the wealthy be exposed. Rather, the progressivity of the tax structure is eroded by a persistent series of skirmishes" (Turner and Starnes, 1976: 113).

Efforts to reform the income-tax system continue. In September 1986 Congress passed a tax reform bill, which enacted some important

**208** changes. About 6 million low-income people were removed from the tax rolls, and about 60 percent of taxpayers faced reduced payments. Many corporations taxed at or close to the maximum received a tax cut, while others, especially those benefiting from special tax subsidies that were repealed, were compelled to pay more. Overall it has been estimated that business tax payments will increase by about $120 billion over six years to counterbalance an equivalent amount of tax cuts received by individuals (Egan, 1986; Koepp, 1986). Will corporations actually assume a larger share of the tax burden, or will a new set of "skirmishes" erode such a change? We must wait and see.

The following American Controversy is meant to encourage readers to analyze an important issue related to wealth and income—inheritance.

---

## AMERICAN CONTROVERSY

# *What Should Be Done about Inheritance?*

Let me tell you about the very rich. They are different from you and me. They possess and enjoy early, and it does something to them, makes them soft where we are hard, and cynical where we are trustful, in a way that, unless you were born rich, it is difficult to understand. They think, deep in their hearts, that they are better than we are because we had to discover the compensations and refuges of life for ourselves. Even when they enter deep into our world or sink below us, they still think that they are better than we are. They are different.

— *F. Scott Fitzgerald*

In this chapter we will encounter some information backing Fitzgerald's position: that the wealthy not only have more valued material resources than the rest of us but they think of themselves as different, in significant ways superior. Should our society permit conditions encouraging people to maintain such a sense of superiority? A critical issue underlying this question is the subject of inheritance. After all, it is the opportunity to inherit that allows wealth to be passed from one generation to another. Let us consider different positions on inheritance.

A position in favor of inheritance: We live in a capitalist society, which rewards an individual's intelligence and perseverance. One of the most satisfying rewards that can be bestowed upon successful business people is the knowledge that their families will be able to inherit the wealth that they have accumulated. The existence of inherited wealth serves as an incentive to others to produce similar achievements. Were inheritance eliminated or severely restricted, it is possible that many potentially excellent business ventures would not be pursued. Not only would individual families suffer, but the society would not obtain the benefits provided by these enterprises.

A position against inheritance: We live in a society that emphasizes equality. One of the most effective ways to achieve equality is to place a priority on economic equality, and the elimination of inheritance would be a significant step toward such an achievement. The government could use the enormous wealth that it obtained from taking over all inheritance to eliminate poverty, hunger, and disease and to reorganize and revamp a vast range of public structures and facilities, including the education system, health care, antiquated public buildings, highways, and other public works. It is unlikely that the elimination of inheritance will significantly discourage business people from pursuing commercial ventures: Immediate economic success and glory are considerably more important to those who engage in such activities than a consideration of their children's inheritance. Finally one might argue that for the wealthy, inheritance weakens or even kills the work ethic, a highly prized value in our society. Most of us work because we have no alternative means to purchase goods and services. Those born wealthy, however, have no such incentive.

What do you think? Do you

strongly support one of the positions presented here, or do you find yourself somewhere in between? Discuss the issues in class or outside of class with several others in the course. In particular, try to assess the impact different policies would have on various groups as well as on the society overall.

## Power

**Power** is the ability of an individual or group to implement wishes or policies, with or without the cooperation of others. A young girl who forces a smaller child to give her a cookie is exercising power. So is a college teacher who assigns two tests, three quizzes, and two short papers at scheduled intervals through the semester. However it is in the realm of politics that sociologists most frequently study power, and we focus on the topic in Chapter 14 ("The Political and Economic Institutions"). At this time we briefly consider two sharply opposed theories on the operation of power in the American political process: the pluralist perspective and the power-elite approach.

The two theories differ in their assessment of whether or not political power is concentrated. The pluralist perspective emphasizes that power is not concentrated, that it is dispersed to different centers that must represent their constituents' needs and interests or lose their access to political power (Dahl, 1967). The pluralists contend that the only way elected officials can effectively represent their constitutents' interests on different issues is to form a separate alliance on each issue. Thus a state legislator might be aligned with one set of politicians on a tax reform bill and be working with an entirely different set on an antipollution measure. In both cases the legislator is seeking to promote constituents' interests.

The power-elite perspective popularized by C. Wright Mills (1956) opposes the pluralist approach. This theory claims that there is a group of high-status men who are well educated, often wealthy, socially prominent, and located in occupational positions where they can exert considerable power. Members of the elite control basic government policy in the political, economic, and military realms. Mills visualized three levels of society. At the top is the power elite. Then there is a middle class of politically unorganized white-collar employees dominated by the corporations and government agencies for which they work. At the bottom are the masses, whose access to channels of power and influence is entirely cut off.

Overall neither the power-elite view nor the pluralist perspective provides a fully accurate picture of the role of power in American society. The power-elite thesis probably exaggerates the extent to which upper-class people operate as a group with strongly shared interests. Competition sometimes exists among the rich and powerful for limited resources like government contracts or political offices. On the other hand, the pluralist thesis fails to recognize that exploitation, privilege, corruption, and powerlessness are deeply rooted in American politics. Both theories seem to provide a part of the truth.

## Prestige

**Prestige** is the possession of attributes that elicit recognition, respect, and some degree of deference. Overall Americans tend to be fairly consistent in their assessments of prestige. A recent study found that two groups of informants—one from the working class and the other from the middle class—were similar in their prestige rankings for eighty-four Long Island communities (Logan and Collver, 1983). A similar consistency occurs with occupations, which are frequently linked with prestige. (See Figure 9.1.) In 1947 the National Opinion Research Center (NORC) at the University of Chicago used a national sample of 2920 informants to rank ninety occupations in relation to each other, and across the nation there was remarkable consistency obtained from the informants. The NORC study was repeated in 1963, and with minor variations the occupational rankings were strikingly similar (Hodge, Siegel, and Rossi, 1966). Research in other industrialized as well as nonindustrialized countries reveals a similar pattern (Treiman, 1977).

The fact that Americans are highly consistent in the occupational rankings they provide suggests that for high-status jobs there is a nationally shared

**Figure 9.1**
**Prestige of Selected White-Collar Occupations**

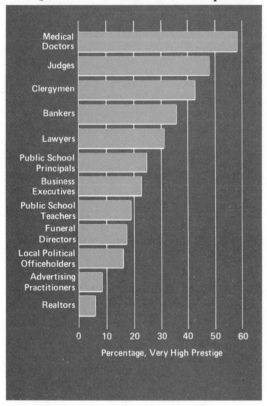

*As this assessment of twelve occupations illustrates, Americans consider some white-collar positions much more prestigious than others. (Source: George Gallup.* Gallup Poll. *October 7, 1981.)*

respect, which legitimates the performance of people in these positions. On the other hand, those ranked low are consistently valued in a negative way, an evaluation that tends to legitimate their economic failure and justify their placement at the bottom of the occupational prestige structure. Evidence suggests that the American public is particularly inclined to maintain generalized negative images of low-status occupational groups, refusing to recognize that such categories as farm workers contain people with diversified personal characteristics and life-styles (Whitener, 1985).

People in low-status positions obviously feel the brunt of their prestige rankings. Taxi drivers, for example, do not possess an unusual or specialized skill. Sometimes drivers will try to convince their fares that they do indeed have a special talent and "will resort to darting nimbly in and out of traffic, making neatly executed U-turns and leaping smartly ahead of other cars when the traffic light changes" (Davis, 1969: 160). Tenants generally believe that custodial work is low in prestige. Custodians usually recognize the tenants' estimations of their work and will sometimes attempt to enhance their image by representing themselves as similar to professionals, especially doctors. Some custodians will tell their tenants to call only during daylight hours except for emergencies, or like some doctors they will charge their tenants on a sliding scale for any extra jobs that their tenants might request (Gold, 1952).

In the first section, we looked at theories that consider why social stratification exists in societies. We continued an analysis of the macro-order in the next section, examining the distribution of wealth, power, and prestige throughout the society. Now the focus narrows, and we analyze the micro-order in the everyday life of people belonging to various social classes.

## Social Class in America

A **social class** is a large category of people who are similar in income level, educational attainment, and occupational prestige ranking. The members of a social class share a set of values and also similar opportunities to obtain desired goals and experiences.

Sometimes people speak about "the social-class structure" as if a single, distinct way of determining an individual's social-class placement exists. In reality a number of approaches have been used.

The **subjective definition of social class** is a measuring technique that requires people to indicate the social class to which they belong. In some cases the investigators provide a range of choices, and in other cases they do not. One problem with this approach is that research suggests that some people are not sure to which class they belong. One sociologist has reported that a substantial number of Americans have been unable to decide whether they are middle or working class (Kahl, 1957).

**Table 9.2**
**Three Ways to Measure Social Class**

| THE APPROACH | WHO DETERMINES THE RESPONDENTS' SOCIAL CLASS? | A PROBLEM WITH THE APPROACH |
|---|---|---|
| Subjective definition | The respondents themselves | Some people's uncertainty about their own class membership |
| Reputational definition | Local "judges" | Modern, urbanized living making it impossible for any citizens to have sufficient knowledge of all fellow residents to serve as judges |
| Objective definition | Researchers using certain quantifiable factors, such as occupational evaluations, income, or education level | Limited agreement about what factors to use or the weight to provide each given factor |

The **reputational definition of social class** is a measuring technique where researchers use resident experts from the community—"judges"—to assess their neighbors' social-class position. This approach will work well in residential areas that have a population that is sufficiently small and stable to permit the researchers to find judges who know all the local citizens well enough to place them in social classes. In the majority of modern American communities, however, the population is too large and physically mobile to make the use of this technique possible.

Finally the **objective definition of social class** is a measuring technique that uses certain quantifiable factors—income, occupational prestige level, or level of education, for example—as the basis for determining an individual's social-class position. Investigators sometimes employ a single factor, and in other cases they use a combination of several. Among sociologists the objective approach is the most popular one, but what factors to use and how much weight each should receive is not an issue on which unanimity exists. Table 9.2 summarizes the three approaches.

As we study social class, we should keep in mind that there is not unanimous agreement about how the American class system is structured. Most sociologists, however, would accept some approximation of the following scheme:

1. A capitalist class, with considerable wealth, whose members, if working, maintain executive positions, have been educated at prestigious universities, possess a family income of about $450,000 a year, and represent about 1 percent of the population. (All the income figures presented in this discussion were calculated for the United States in 1985.)

2. The upper-middle class, containing people who are managers and professionals, have an income of about $45,000 or more, have attended college and perhaps done postgraduate study, and constitute about 14 percent of the population.

3. The lower-middle class, with members who work as lower-level managers, semiprofessionals, salespeople, craft workers, and foremen, earn about $28,000 a year, have at least a high-school education, and comprise about 33 percent of the population.

4. The working class, who are operatives, clerical and sales workers, or low-paid craftspeople, receive about $20,000 a year, have graduated from high school, and represent about 32 percent of the population.

5. The working poor, employed as service workers, laborers, and low-paid operatives, have some high-school education, make below $13,500, and are about 11 percent of the population.

6. The underclass, who are unemployed or underemployed and sometimes are maintained by welfare, tend to have a primary-school education, receive $10,000 a year or less, and comprise about 9 percent of the population (Gilbert and Kahl, 1982: 348).

People within a particular social class share a common sense of outlook and experience. Those in various social classes, for instance, have different opportunities and life-styles (Tumin, 1967).

## Opportunity and Social Class

Social classes offer different opportunities. The higher people's social class, the longer their life expectancy, the less likely they will suffer mental illness, the more effective their capacity to communicate, and the higher their self-esteem.

### Life Expectancy

People can pay to lengthen their lives in a number of ways. In particular, the higher classes benefit from longer life expectancy in situations where death is preventable since, because of income and other advantages, they have greater access than lower-class people to effective means of prevention. For example, when the *Titanic* was rammed by an iceberg and sunk, sufficient lifeboats for everyone were not available. Only 4 of 150 women and children in first class (3 percent) went down with the ship, compared to 13 of 117 in second class (11 percent) and 141 of 244 in third class (58 percent). It appears that third-class passengers suffered two distinct disadvantages; they were much more likely to be denied entrance to the lifeboats and their residential areas were much farther from the boat deck (Hall, 1986).

A variety of more general conditions promote longer life expectancy for people in higher social classes. For example:

Front-line troops have tended to come from the lower social classes. A researcher who studied combat soldiers in Vietnam found that about two-thirds of the soldiers in the units with which he stayed were from working-class backgrounds and the remainder had lower-middle-class origins. Nearly two-thirds had graduated from high school, and most of the others were high school dropouts. Several had attended college, but none were college graduates (Moskos, 1969).

A study of four societies—Belize, Kenya, Nepal, and American Samoa—found that individuals given a high social-class ranking locally were two to four times more likely to be healthy than those given a low social-class ranking (Munroe and Munroe, 1984).

### Mental Illness

Robert Faris and Warren Dunham (1939) examined over 30,000 people admitted to hospitals in Chicago for the treatment of mental illness. They found an inverse relationship between social-class position and the rate of mental illness: the higher the social-class position, the lower the rate of mental illness. Another study, which assessed the psychiatric condition of a random sample of 1600 New Yorkers, reached a similar conclusion (Srole et al., 1962). Later research has produced consistent results, concluding that people in higher social classes have lower rates of schizophrenia, depression, unhappiness, and anxiety (Syme and Berkman, 1981).

We might wonder why. On the one hand, people in higher social classes generally have greater educational and occupational opportunities, which can promote a positive sense of self and decrease the likelihood of mental illness. On the other hand, less affluent people's general life condition, where most items that are highly prized are in short supply, is likely to encourage a negative, even fatalistic, outlook on reality. Such an outlook will make it difficult to deal resourcefully with stress in the course of everyday life (Kessler and Cleary, 1980; Kohn, 1976).

### Communication Effectiveness

The higher the social class of the family, the earlier and the more effectively speech will develop (Berelson and Steiner, 1964: 69). Leonard Schatzman and Anselm Strauss (1972) conducted 340 interviews with witnesses of tornados. They found that the social class (especially the amount of education) of the individuals involved in these disasters significantly influenced the effectiveness of the accounts they gave. In particular:

The working-class participants could see the events only through their "own eyes." In contrast, the middle-class witnesses could also offer explanations from the point of view of another person or a group of other people.

The working-class respondents were often unable to realize what the listener who had not been present during the disaster did or did not know about it. The result was that the accounts from working-class people were often hard to follow beyond the description of their personal reactions. On the other hand, the middle-class person stood "between his own images and the hearer and . . . [implicitly said], 'Let me introduce you to what I saw and know.'"

The working class informants could describe individuals, but they were not able to discuss effectively the activities of categories of people (the rich or the poor, the hurt or the unhurt) or organizations. Seemingly without effort middle-class people tended to analyze their perceptions in relation to these different categories and to convey information about them in an effective, coherent manner (Schatzman and Strauss, 1972).

## Self-Esteem

The wealthy can afford to purchase particularly expensive goods and services, thereby setting themselves apart from the rest of humanity. After World War I, employees of William Randolph Hearst toured Europe, Asia, and Africa collecting tapestries, paintings, statues, furniture, and even buildings and creating a priceless homestead of mammoth proportion, where Hearst gave fabled parties for the rich, famous, and glamorous in the years between the two world wars. During the same era, William Vanderbilt sailed his yacht around the world, collecting specimens for his private museum.

However, the economic elite do not need to go to such lengths to separate themselves from other people. In his study of Philadelphia gentlemen, for example, E. Digby Baltzell observed that the typical male member of that class has tended to imitate his English counterpart in clothing, sporting activities, and club memberships. For many years one of the Philadelphia gentlemen sent his shirts to London to be laundered (Baltzell, 1971: 57).

In contrast, a major problem often accompanying working-class life is the "hidden injury" of class, the fact that working-class people are denied a sense of worth in the eyes of others and of themselves. This lack of esteem, Sennett and Cobb (1973) suggested, has two sources: first, the idea that class placement is the result of ability, and second, the often futile pursuit of efforts to improve one's class position. Sennett and Cobb undertook a study in Boston, conducting 150 in-depth interviews of working-class men and women ranging in age from their late teens to their sixties. The study offered many illustrations of working-class people's low self-esteem.

For example, an informant told the researchers about his sense of inferiority in the presence of middle-class people.

> [W]henever I'm with educated people, you know, or people who aren't my own kind . . . um . . . I feel like I'm making a fool of myself if I just act natural, you know? See, it's not so much how people treat you, it's feeling like you don't know what to do.
>
> *(Sennett and Cobb, 1973: 110)*

The man went on to describe a time when he had appeared at a meeting of middle-class people and felt out of place and isolated.

It seems that children's sense of relationship between their social class position and self-esteem develops gradually. A recent study concluded that among children ranging from fifth to eighth graders, the perceived relationship between social class and self-esteem rose with age. Apparently, as children become older, they pay more attention to social class, increasingly allowing their own position within the system to determine their self-image (Demo and Savin-Williams, 1983).

## Life-Style and Social Class

People demonstrate differences in life-style, as the following discussion of fertility, child-rearing patterns, sexual behavior, and clubs and friendships indicates.

## Fertility

In a chart that attempts to represent humorously the relationship between family life and social class, Simon and Gagnon (1972: 86–87) suggested that upper-class couples tend to have one child each by previous marriages or as many as God provides; upper-middle-class couples produce 2.4 children; lower-middle-class couples usually have three children; and lower-class couples have as many as God provides.

In fact, this summary is somewhat accurate. An inverse relationship—in this case the higher the social class, the fewer the number of children—often exists between social class and family size. Blacks generally have more children than whites, and this pattern is apparently class linked. When researchers compare black and white families of the same social class, the difference in family size disappears.

Several factors explain the statistical relationship between social class and family size. The higher the social class, the greater the tendency for women to be career oriented and thus to want to control family size. Furthermore people in the middle or upper-middle class are more likely than lower-class individuals to plan their lives in accord with the dominant value patterns of the day as represented in the media, and having a modest number of children is such a prevailing value pattern (Bronfenbrenner, 1966; Duberman, 1976: 244–255; Wrong, 1966).

### Approaches to Child-Rearing

A major review of studies on child-rearing concluded that middle-class parents tend to use an approach to socialization that is "acceptant and equalitarian," while parents in the working class are "oriented toward maintaining order and obedience" (Bronfenbrenner, 1966). Philip Slater (1976) discussed the distinction between "love-centered" and "fear-centered" child-rearing. In the middle-class setting, Slater contended, children are pressured to internalize their parents' standards, to make them their own. If the children do not internalize their parents' standards and abide by them, then they will be punished by the withdrawal of their parents' love and approval. According to Slater, for the working-class child, the situation is somewhat less subtle. In this setting children obey their parents, or they are punished, often physically.

During the Vietnam War, different class attitudes toward rearing children became a political issue. Vice-President Spiro Agnew, a man of working-class origins, made a number of speeches in which he sharply criticized the behavior of upper-middle-class antiwar activists. Agnew suggested that these young people were products of "permissive" child-rearing practices, practices that allowed or even encouraged the activists not to respect their parents and their political leaders.

It appears that the difference between working-class and middle-class families has sometimes been exaggerated. In an analysis of ten surveys on punishment practices, Erlanger (1974) concluded that the difference between social classes is not great and that, in fact, it has never been. It is true that working-class fathers have frequently resorted to the use of physical punishment, but what generally receives much less attention is the fact that working-class mothers have widely favored reasoning and emotionally supportive instruction, both of which are standard middle-class approaches (Hurvitz, 1964).

### Sexuality

Wardell Pomeroy (1972: 469) has suggested that by comparing adolescent boys' sexual histories one can conclude which individuals will be more likely to attend college. For instance, one boy has intercourse with a number of girls, does not remove his clothes for sexual relations, disapproves of oral sex, masturbates less at eighteen than in his early teens, and has few "wet dreams." The sexual history of a second boy shows that he has little or no sexual intercourse, engages in a great deal of petting and may try oral sex, and considers sexual activity more enjoyable in the nude. The first boy, according to Pomeroy, displays sexual behavior typical of a lower-class background, and coming from this background he is unlikely to attend college. On the other hand, the sexual behavior of the second boy is typically middle class, and middle-class adolescents are likely to attend college.

Lower-class people tend to begin their sexual lives somewhat earlier, but their sexual activity tends to be less frequent and less fulfilling, especially for wives (Howell, 1973). A study of low-status marriages in four places—the United States, Puerto Rico, Mexico, and England—suggests that the belief frequently exists that "sex is a man's pleasure and a woman's duty." This particular attitude seems to be a product of segregated gender roles, which permit a very limited sharing of interests and activities between women and men (Rainwater, 1964). On the other hand, middle- or upper-class spouses are likely to share common interests and a sense of closeness, openly discussing their sexual relations and remaining sensitive to their partners' needs (Reiss, 1980: 275–285).

The modern era of sexual permissiveness can be particularly confusing for working-class women. Like many modern men, most working-class husbands recognize the value placed on women's orgasm. Many of them now believe that unless their wives achieve orgasm, they have failed as lovers. The wives, on the other hand, have often been raised by mothers who stress "a grin-and-bear-it" approach to sex, and they are unlikely to enjoy sex and achieve orgasm (Rubin, 1983).

## Friendships and Clubs

An upper-middle-class man spoke to a researcher about the prospect of having working-class friends. He said, "I am not a snob, but it is a fact of life that in most of those occupations we would have nothing in common" (Laumann, 1966: 28).

Many people would agree with this man. When classes are defined on the basis of occupation, people are more likely to choose friends from among their own or adjacent classes. In one study the pattern was most distinct at the extremes, with unskilled and semiskilled workers finding more than three-quarters of their friends close to their own class level and with the professional and business classes doing the same (Laumann, 1966: 65). Another study offered additional information about the process of choosing friends: While most people tend to choose their closest friends from members of the same social class, the principal reason is the social context in which they reside, not the tendency to seek friendships among one's own class. Individuals who live in a neighborhood dominated by people whose social class is different from their own are more likely to have close friends from that social class than from their own (Huckfeldt, 1983).

The members of different social classes tend to join certain kinds of organizations, and the prestige of the organizations depends on the prestige of the members. There are upper- and upper-middle-class social clubs: athletic clubs, men's clubs, women's gardening clubs, and charitable organizations. These same classes support professionally oriented clubs: chambers of commerce, business and professional associations, and service clubs. These organizations can serve a variety of purposes for their members. Typically men's professional organizations provide the opportunity to make valuable contacts, to obtain useful information, and to engage in interesting, stimulating discussion. In contrast to men's clubs, women's orga-

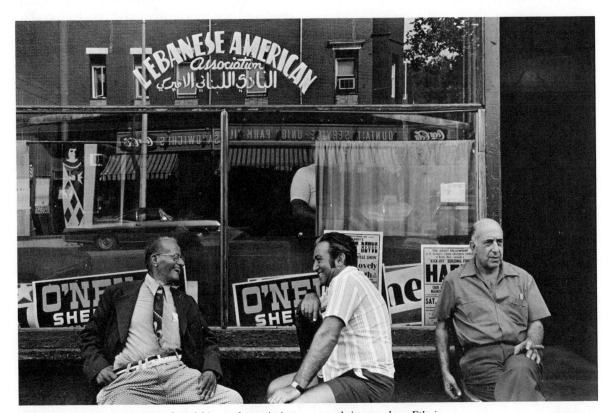

*People are more likely to choose friendships and associations among their own class. Ethnic and racial similarities may also affect the choice of organizations and clubs people join.*

nizations are more likely to be local than national, and upper-middle-class wives usually belong to more clubs than their husbands and to place greater emphasis on clubs as a source of status advancement (Hodges, 1964; Lerner, 1982).

Clubs and friendships can be effectively used to help people "get ahead." In the following section, we discuss Americans' efforts to improve their social-class position.

# Social Mobility in American Society

At the end of the nineteenth century, Horatio Alger's novels about poor boys who rose from rags to riches through hard work sold more than thirty million copies. These novels underlined the American belief that the United States is an open society where enormous opportunity for personal success exists and that people will receive rewards of wealth, power, and prestige in correspondence with the effort they make. Actually, how open is the social-class system? To address this issue, we must first examine the concept of social mobility.

**Social mobility** is the movement of a person from one social class or status level to another, either upward or downward with accompanying gains or losses in wealth, power, and prestige. In the past couple of decades, there have been many studies of mobility processes (Kerckhoff, 1984; Smith, 1981) and also debates about how this complex topic should be conceptualized (Slomczynski and Krauze, 1984; Sobel, 1984).

Sociologists generally study two kinds of social mobility. **Intergenerational mobility** is a comparison of a parent and a child's social-class position. This comparison will indicate whether the child's social-class position is higher or lower than the parent's or has remained the same. Most prominent studies of intergenerational mobility have compared fathers' and sons' social-class position, using occupational status as its measure. An increasing number of intergenerational mobility studies on women seems inevitable as they enter the work world in rapidly increasing numbers. Recent research in sixteen countries concluded that in spite of some differences among the nations, their patterns of intergenerational mobility are basically similar (Grusky and Hauser, 1984).

**Intragenerational mobility** is an analysis of an individuals's occupational changes in the course of

a lifetime. Thus a researcher might observe that a particular woman started as a bank teller, advanced to management status, and eventually retired as the bank president. One recent study of intragenerational mobility in three countries—Austria, France, and the United States—found that because of different conditions governing the move from lower-status to higher-status jobs, the three cultures differed significantly in their intragenerational mobility patterns (Haller et al., 1985).

We consider current evidence of social mobility, the causes of social mobility, some of the effects produced by it, and prospects for upward mobility.

## Evidence on the Social-Mobility Issue

Perhaps you have participated in a conversation like the following. A group of friends are having lunch together. Jane says, "Last night I spoke with my grandfather, and all he talks about these days is how much things have changed. Yesterday he kept harping on the fact that you can't work your way up from the bottom anymore. The big corporations run the whole show, and they keep people pretty much locked in. If your family has got money and power it's one thing, but for the rest of us . . ." She shakes her head unhappily.

Ron smiles. "I don't agree. It seems to me that if you have a good idea and can market it, you can still make a pile and gain all the power and prestige that go with it. My mom and dad went to high school with Frank Trudeau. In his early twenties, he had a simple idea for a household device, and he turned it into a multimillion-dollar business."

Many Americans have bits and pieces of opinion and knowledge that suggest that U.S. society is either more or less open than it was in the past. We need to look beyond bits and pieces and see if we can detect a broad pattern. In the first place, we must be aware that it is difficult to make meaningful comparisons of social-mobility rates over long periods of time. It is misleading, perhaps impossible, to compare people in an agrarian society with those in an industrial one. If the grandson of a blacksmith who earned $500 a year becomes an automobile worker making $10,000 per year, he is likely to be downwardly mobile in a relative sense, in spite of a sizable increase in income. In this case "relative sense" means that the automobile worker will be proportionately lower in the modern stratification system. When agrarian societies become industrial most people become ". . . wealthier, healthier, more skilled, better educated, and the like than their forebears, but modern populations are just as unequal, relative to their own societies, as people were in the past" (Rossides, 1976: 99).

Comparisons over short periods of time involving a society with a fairly stable economic system are easier to understand. In 1962 sociologists Peter Blau and Otis Duncan (1967) conducted a study that David Featherman and Robert Hauser (1978) repeated a decade later. In both cases the investigators arranged with the Bureau of the Census to add two pages containing questions on career history and parental background to the regular monthly survey of employment and unemployment. Blau and Duncan received data on 20,000 fathers and sons, and Featherman and Hauser obtained information on 33,000 fathers and sons.

The researchers focused on their respondents' occupations. They divided the men into five categories based on their type of job—white-collar, lower white-collar, upper manual, lower manual, and farm. In the 1973 study, Featherman and Hauser found that 49 percent of sons moved up, 32 percent stayed in the same general category, and 29 percent went down. The Blau and Duncan findings from eleven years earlier were just slightly different. The percentage of upward mobility was the same, but 2 percent more stayed the same, and thus 2 percent fewer went down.

Blau and Duncan examined findings from some older studies that allowed them to make comparisons back to 1947. They found that between 1947 and 1962 an increasing percentage of men moved from manual origins into white-collar jobs and that

no corresponding downward move occurred. Furthermore, in that fifteen-year span, an increasing proportion stayed at the same occupational level as their fathers (Blau and Duncan, 1967: 103).

Thus the American occupational structure has shown a trend toward upward mobility. However, some distinct limitations to that pattern occur.

### Cases of Limited Access

In the first place, it is difficult for lower-class people to move up. Many sociologists contend that millions of poor people are trapped in a **vicious cycle of poverty,** a pattern where the parents' minimal income significantly limits the educational and occupational pursuits of the children, therefore keeping them locked into the same low economic status. Does such a cycle of poverty actually occur? Bradley Shiller (1970) studied 1017 males who grew up in families receiving Aid to Families with Dependent Children. Sixty-three percent of the informants were in some kind of unskilled jobs, and only 8 percent achieved a white-collar position. Therefore a few men did succeed in breaking the vicious cycle of poverty, but nearly two out of three remained in marginal job slots, leaving them likely candidates to carry the cycle into the next generation.

For decades governmental programs have tried to combat the cycle of poverty, but they have generally been unsuccessful. How could such programs be improved? An expert on the subject has suggested that all welfare programs seeking to eliminate the cycle of poverty have had a common deficiency: the failure to recognize the inadequacies of the head of household. These programs have not ". . . sought to break the cycle of dependency and poverty by trying to improve the care and upbringing of young children on welfare. This task was left exclusively to the mother, often a teen-ager, completely disregarding her obvious limitations" (Bernstein, 1986: A35). Effective governmental intervention in the welfare family would insure good nutrition and health for infants, early-childhood education, and the development of values that would encourage children to remain in school and to avoid activities that promote the cycle of poverty.

The following Contemporary Issue demonstrates how the cycle of poverty can develop.

**CONTEMPORARY ISSUE**

*The Vicious Cycle of Poverty: A Case Study*

The vicious cycle of poverty consists of the transmission of limited opportunity from one generation to the next. But how does the process actually occur? One concrete answer comes from looking at case studies of individuals, such as the life account of José Alvarez, who grew up in East Harlem, a Puerto Rican district of New York City. For José and other people caught in the cycle of poverty, the opportunity to obtain affluence, good jobs, and prestige has been remote.

At the time of the research, José was eighteen years old, a dropout from high school. He had a host of interests and talents including photography, electrical gadgetry, and sports. His photographs were widely acclaimed by local residents and outsiders who saw them. After studying a stack of José's photos, one expert declared that the young man had a rare knack of "catching that special moment." José was also mechanically inclined; he could put together a television from spare parts or repair serious automotive problems without even a manual.

In spite of José's talents, a number of factors made his future bleak, beginning with his family. When José was young, his mother died and his father remarried. The new wife was not enthusiastic about raising her husband's son, and soon he was shipped to his grandmother. This

small, white-haired woman, always dressed in black, had come to New York City before José was born. She survived on public assistance, living an almost reclusive existence, and she forced the same life-style on her grandson. José explained, "I never got to go downstairs and play outside like the kids now. So on the way home from school I'd sometimes stop at the library and pick up a book. All I ever did was read."

Although he read constantly, José generally did not take school seriously. As a boy he failed to grasp its relation to occupational success. Neither his grandmother nor his counselors ever encouraged him to do anything but "just get by." He went to a vocational high school, but several of his friends explained to him that the best he could hope for in the future with a vocational degree was a job as a factory worker. As a result of this advice, he transferred to an academic high school, but then another hurdle appeared in front of him. He became involved with Maria Pagan.

Maria was divorced with two children, and soon after she and José started going together, she was pregnant again. José explained, "I quit school and got myself a job. Like the people say, when the woman gets pregnant you've got to forget about school and go to work!"

Several years later José re-

turned to school, but his attendance was irregular, and he seldom did his homework. I met José at this time, and he would speak enthusiastically about school, about the teachers who stimulated him, and about friends applying to college. The way he spoke made it clear that he felt that college and the good jobs that would come from higher education were fascinating but not attainable.

I told José that if he wanted to go on to college, he could. José pointed out to me that it was easy for me to say that. My life, after all, had been simple. I admitted that he had a point, but still I persisted. If José really wanted to go to college, he would be able to in spite of the difficulties involved. José laughed bitterly and gave me a paper he had written. One paragraph read in part:

POVERTY: WHO KNOWS WHAT IT REALLY IS?
You have to know from experience what it is like to be poor. You have to learn about a life where you can't afford to pay $1.25 for a hair cut. You have to get to know the smell of second-hand mattresses after too many babies have lain on them.

When I returned the paper to José, he told me that this was true, that you couldn't learn about poverty from books, only from experience. I agreed but added that José could still go to college. He stared blankly and said nothing.

Fifteen years have passed, and José has had a long list of menial jobs, a lengthy involvement with hard drugs, a short jail sentence, two broken marriages, and five children. Not surprisingly he never went to college. Certainly there were economic and practical problems, but for José the cycle of poverty seems to have set its most vicious trap at the interpersonal level. As Cooley's looking-glass-self concept suggests, we see ourselves as others see us. It appears that no one ever visualized José as a college student, or for that matter as any kind of consistent success. So he never visualized himself in any successful roles either, and his talents have simply gone to waste.

Source: Christopher Bates Doob. *The Development of Peer Group Relationships among Puerto Rican Boys in East Harlem.* Unpublished Ph.D. dissertation. Cornell University. 1967.

Blacks are another category of people who encounter special difficulties when they try to advance themselves in social-class position. On the average, blacks have certain distinct disadvantages compared to whites—poorer parents, fewer years of education, less sympathetic and thorough supervision early in their careers, and extensive discrimination. Yet in spite of these disadvantages, the black community is no longer lower class occupationally. Employed black males divide roughly into thirds, with one-third in the underclass or among the working poor, another third in working-class jobs, and the final third in some level of middle-class positions.

Let us consider some advancement problems blacks face. The black underclass continues to experience high unemployment rates, high welfare rates, and a decrease in movement out of poverty —in short, the vicious cycle of poverty (Gilbert and Kahl, 1982: 202–203; Wilson, 1980). An editorial in *Economist,* a British journal, recently offered a distinctly non-American viewpoint on the plight of the black underclass in the "land of opportunity," where upward mobility tends to be a dominant national concern. It was suggested that unlike Europeans, who are obsessed with the idea of people ending up relatively equal in wealth and income, Americans only want to ensure that people start out equal. Now, however, "with the emergence of a huge . . . largely black, underclass, that belief is now impossible to sustain"(*Economist,* March 15, 1986: 29). To many Americans black middle-class people appear successful, but evidence suggests that they are concentrated in areas serving black consumers and communities and that in the 1980s the Reagan administration has altered policies that have assisted middle-class blacks to rise (Collins, 1983).

Women also face special problems attaining upward mobility. One difficulty is the sex-typing of occupations. Traditionally people in occupations classified as "male" have considered women who tried to enter them as deviants and have placed obstacles in their paths. In recent years women have managed to join many previously exclusive male professions, but in certain high-status positions they are still nearly absent: for instance, architecture, surgery, engineering, commercial piloting, and top business management.

Another difficulty is the informal, sex-linked, "old-boy" network that prevails in most professions. Like females, males often interact as members of a subculture. They talk about sports, about women, and about other "masculine" topics at lunch or over drinks in situations that implicitly or explicitly exclude women. This exclusion can be a serious problem for women since career advancement often emerges out of these informal contexts. For the few women who possess the social skills to function in these male-oriented situations, this informal colleague system can prove to be an asset for career advancement.

Another problem women encounter is an outgrowth of the last issue. In many situations men's occupational advancement results from the sponsorship of an established professional. The younger man serves an apprenticeship, in which he "learns the ropes." Established professionals are less likely to develop such a relationship with women because they are often incapable of or are unwilling to visualize women as their successors. Furthermore an apprentice relationship with a woman is likely to be awkward—to raise questions in people's minds about the possibility of a personal relationship between the two of them. Thus women frequently do not have the opportunity to participate effectively in male-dominated professional structures (Duberman, 1976; Epstein, 1970).

## Causes of Social Mobility

A number of factors, which have been present in American society, encourage upward mobility.

First, there is circulation mobility. Some people are downwardly mobile, opening up positions for others moving up.

Second, reproductive mobility can occur. As we noted earlier in the chapter, a relationship between social class and number of children exists — the higher the social class, the fewer the children. Before World War II, estimates indicated that professional men were not producing a sufficient number of sons to replace themselves: 870 sons to every 1000 professional fathers. Farmers, however, were averaging nearly double that number — 1520 sons to every 1000 farmers. Estimates suggest that if fathers of all status levels, including professionals, had produced families of equal size, then the upward mobility of blue-collar sons would have decreased by 7 percent.

Third, immigration mobility can encourage upward mobility. If immigrants fill a large number of the unskilled labor jobs, then opportunities increase for native-born citizens to move up the status ladder. For example, at the turn of the century, a strong demand existed for workers in the mines and factories. During those years the arriving immigrants provided a major source of unskilled and semiskilled labor, allowing native-born citizens, including the sons of foreign-born parents, to move into skilled manual and white-collar positions.

Finally a significant factor affecting upward mobility is occupational or structural mobility, which occurs because technological innovation or organizational change creates more new jobs at the middle or upper levels of the occupational structure than at the lower levels. For instance, from 1940 to 1970, professional and technical jobs for men increased 192 percent, while jobs for farm laborers dropped by 75 percent (Gilbert and Kahl, 1982: 170–174).

## The Effects of Social Mobility

Fifty million fans watch as the television coverage shifts to the locker room. The announcer moves through the crowd of players, coaches, and media personnel until he reaches the game's hero, whose hair and face are glistening with a combination of champagne and perspiration.

"How does it feel?" the announcer asks.

"I . . ." The player shakes his head. "I don't have the words to explain it. I've waited so long for this moment . . ."

Some semblance of this scene has occurred many times in American professional sport. The television camera catches the sporting hero at the moment of glory. Professional sport stars have been upwardly mobile — they have achieved wealth and prestige — and yet many have drug, alcohol, or other serious personal problems. Other upwardly mobile people do too.

Melvin Tumin (1957) has suggested that upward mobility can produce "diffusion of insecurity." The upwardly mobile have departed from their original social-class position and thus feel lost, no longer firmly grounded in a social-class tradition with its associated family, friends, and life-style. Other sociologists make a similar assessment (Ellis and Lane, 1967; Sorokin, 1927).

One study indicated that upwardly mobile people are more likely to show high levels of anxiety and psychosomatic illness than the socially stable, whereas downwardly mobile individuals exceed the average on serious forms of psychotic illness (Kessin, 1971). The last conclusion receives support from another investigation, where the major finding was that higher suicide rates occur among downwardly mobile men (Breed, 1963). Some social conditions can offset such tendencies. An investigation of upwardly mobile black families has concluded that the family (generally with the woman serving as a full-time homemaker) has played a significant role in blunting the impact of stress in members' lives (McAdoo, 1982).

In spite of the difficulties involved, a strong incentive exists for many Americans to improve their social-class position. Let us consider the current prospects for continuing upward mobility.

## Prospects for Upward Mobility

Many Americans apparently believe that opportunities still exist to enter the higher social classes. Studies conducted in Boston and Kansas City indicated that Americans feel that getting ahead depends on four things: parental encouragement, an effective education, ambition to get ahead, and plenty of hard work. In particular, when the informants in these studies talked about upward mobility ". . . the phrases they most freely applied in explaining how it happened were 'pure effort,' 'perseverance,' 'just plain hard work,' 'sheer work,' 'work, work, and more work,' and 'he wasn't ever afraid of working' (Coleman and Rainwater, 1978: 240). In addition, recent research has revealed a specific attribute that seems to contribute to upward mobility: the ability to keep one's emotions under control in situations which could easily provoke anger or irritation. This quality makes people easier to work with and more socially acceptable than individuals without it (Snarey and Vaillant, 1985).

Today if people are planning to move into the middle or upper-middle class, they must be aware of the choices they are making. They must realize that in a slumping economy, certain occupations offer prospects for affluence and others do not. People who have jobs where salary advances have been running behind inflation include middle management, secretaries and other office personnel, salespeople, retail clerks, college professors, public employees, construction laborers, and factory workers. Those who have stayed ahead include top management, doctors, dentists, lawyers, and computer programmers. Figure 9.2 lists a number of occupations that kept pace with inflation between 1970 and 1980 and others that did not.

During the 1970s and 1980s, many people have not only found themselves entering occupations with receding incomes, but many others also discovered no work available. In the last decade, a third of male college graduates and two-thirds of female college graduates had to accept work outside their chosen field, often in jobs not requiring any college training.

Certain life-style choices are also likely to promote a middle-class affluence or to prevent it. The employment of wives can substantially increase family income. The decision to have one or two children instead of three or more children will mean significant savings, particularly in an era when the cost of food, clothing, higher education, and many other goods and services paid for by parents has been skyrocketing. Finally the avoidance of divorce can be a decisive factor affecting family affluence. The capacity to support or partially support two families is clearly beyond the

*Politics involves many upwardly mobile people, who often find themselves working hard while others are relaxing.*

**Figure 9.2**
**Occupational Battles against Inflation, 1970–1980**

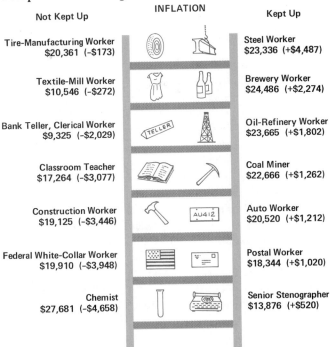

| Not Kept Up | INFLATION | Kept Up |
|---|---|---|
| Tire-Manufacturing Worker $20,361 (−$173) | | Steel Worker $23,336 (+$4,487) |
| Textile-Mill Worker $10,546 (−$272) | | Brewery Worker $24,486 (+$2,274) |
| Bank Teller, Clerical Worker $9,325 (−$2,029) | | Oil-Refinery Worker $23,665 (+$1,802) |
| Classroom Teacher $17,264 (−$3,077) | | Coal Miner $22,666 (+$1,262) |
| Construction Worker $19,125 (−$3,446) | | Auto Worker $20,520 (+$1,212) |
| Federal White-Collar Worker $19,910 (−$3,948) | | Postal Worker $18,344 (+$1,020) |
| Chemist $27,681 (−$4,658) | | Senior Stenographer $13,876 (+$520) |

*In 1980 some occupations had kept up with inflation and others had not. For instance, the purchasing power of a steel worker's average annual salary was $4,487 greater (in 1980 dollars) than a steel worker's average salary in 1970. For tire-manufacturing workers, the average annual 1980 salary represented a decline of $173 from a decade earlier. (Source: Adapted from Lawrence Maloney. "America's New Middle Class." U.S. News and World Report. March 30, 1981, p. 40.)*

economic scope of most modern citizens (Maloney, 1981).

Some Americans, including many college students, are in a situation that permits them to move from the working class into the middle class. For many Americans, however, upward mobility simply involves an escape from poverty or near poverty. For the 46 million families with incomes below $15,000, significant advances in their social position would probably not occur without some changes in federal policies.

Such changes would include a reallocation of federal spending to meet the basic needs of the poor and near poor. Student loans or subsidies would seem particularly useful since educational opportunity could help people obtain jobs that would permit them to escape poverty.

The elimination of tax inequities would be a sig-

nificant policy change. Evidence suggests that tax incentives to corporations in order to stimulate economic growth do not produce any more growth than when the incentives are absent.

Another change that would offer considerable assistance to less affluent Americans involves a much broader issue: a reorientation in economic planning. Americans, and especially their elected officials, need to realize that many activities that would greatly benefit large numbers of citizens would not be short-term, profit-making enterprises. The formation of an effective national mass-transit system and a program of full employment are good examples. Neither would prove to be profit making immediately, but both would undoubtedly promote economic growth in the long run (Bluestone and Harrison, 1982).

# STUDY GUIDE

## Summary

1. Social stratification is structured inequality of access to rewards, resources, and privileges that are scarce and desirable within a society.

2. The structural-functional and Marxist conflict theories take very different approaches. The structural-functional theory of stratification indicates that people who perform the most important and difficult-to-fill positions in a society will receive the largest rewards. The Marxist conflict theory of social stratification emphasizes the inequity of the rewards, contending that their distribution has little to do with drive, talent, and the functional significance of the positions filled. Both theories have received extensive criticism, and Gerhard Lenski's theory is an effort to use their respective strengths and avoid their weaknesses.

3. Three prominent dimensions of social stratification are wealth, power, and prestige. Wealth is people's economic assets that can be converted into money. Over time Americans have experienced an increase in absolute wealth, but relative wealth has remained fairly stable. The current tax system contributes to the sharp economic inequalities that persist in U.S. society.

Power is the ability of an individual or group to implement wishes or policies, with or without the

cooperation of others. Sociologists have tended to use two approaches to examine power: the pluralist and the power-elite perspectives.

Finally prestige is the possession of attributes that elicit recognition, respect, and some degree of satisfaction. Survey research indicates that Americans show some consistency on ranking the prestige of a range of occupations.

4. A social class is a large number of people who are similar in income level, educational attainment, and occupational-prestige ranking. Sociologists have used a number of different approaches to measure social class. The members of different social classes vary in their life expectancy, mental illness, communication effectiveness, and self-esteem.

People from various social classes also differ in life-style. Fertility, approaches to child-rearing, sexuality, and friendships and clubs are life-style activities that vary among the social classes.

The topic of social mobility, which is the movement of a person from one social class or social status to another, addresses the issue of the openness of the American social-class system. A comparison of large studies conducted in 1962 and 1973 suggests that the amount of social mobility varied little at those two times. Certain people—the poor, blacks, and women—have below-average opportunities for upward mobility.

Upward mobility occurs because of circulation mobility, reproductive mobility, immigration mobility, and occupational or structural mobility. The effects of social mobility include the "diffusion of insecurity," anxiety, psychosomatic illness, and high rates of suicide.

In the 1980s upward mobility into the higher social classes is still possible, with the choice of profession and life-style serving as significant determinants. Changed governmental policies could help more people escape the poor or near-poor categories.

## Glossary

**absolute wealth**   the cash value of an individual's economic assets.

**bourgeoisie**   the class of modern capitalists who own the means of economic production and employ wage labor.

**class consciousness**   recognition by the members of a class of the role they play in the production process.

**income**   people's earnings obtained through wages, salaries, business profits, stock dividends, and other means.

**intergenerational mobility**   a comparison of a parent and a child's social-class position.

**intragenerational mobility**   an analysis of an individual's occupational changes in the course of a lifetime.

**objective definition of social class**   a measuring technique that uses certain quantifiable factors—income, occupational prestige rank, or level of education, for example—as the basis for determining an individual's social-class position.

**power**   the ability of an individual or group to implement wishes or policies, with or without the cooperation of others.

**prestige**   possession of attributes that elicit recognition, respect, and some degree of deference.

**proletariat**   the class of modern wage laborers who possess no means of production and thus must sell their own labor in order to survive.

**relative wealth**   the value of an individual's economic assets compared to the assets possessed by other citizens in that society.

**reputational definition of social class**   a measuring technique where researchers use batteries of resident experts from the community to assess their neighbors' social-class position.

**social class**   a large category of people who are similar in income level, educational attainment, and occupational prestige ranking.

**social mobility**   the movement of a person from one social class or status level to another.

**social stratification**   structured inequality of access to rewards, resources, and privileges that are scarce and desirable within a society.

**subjective definition of social class**   a measuring technique that requires people to indicate the social class to which they belong.

**vicious cycle of poverty**   a pattern where the parents' minimal income significantly limits the educational and occupational pursuits of the children, thereby keeping them locked into the same economic status.

**wealth**   people's economic assets—their cars, homes, stocks, bonds, and real estate—and individuals can convert these assets into cash.

## Learning Objectives

After studying this chapter, you should be able to:

1. Define social stratification and consider its significance in modern life.
2. Discuss and evaluate the three theories of social stratification examined in the text—structural-functional, Marxist conflict, and Lenski's.

3. Identify and analyze the three dimensions of social stratification.
4. Define social class, identify and define the three principal ways of measuring social class, and list and briefly discuss the American social-class structure.
5. Describe the impact of social class on people's opportunities and life-styles.
6. Define social mobility, distinguish between intergenerational and intragenerational mobility, and summarize current evidence on the social-mobility issue, including cases of limited access.
7. Identify and discuss the causes of social mobility, examine its effects, and describe the life-style and social policy changes that can promote upward mobility.

## Tests

### True–false test

_____ 1. Evidence that many affluent people have neither special talents nor special training supports the structural-functional theory of social stratification.

_____ 2. Marx believed that in the final stage of class consciousness, members of the proletariat would be able to use negotiations to resolve their differences with capitalists.

_____ 3. Lenski's theory of social stratification accepts some ideas from both the structural-functional and the Marxist conflict theories.

_____ 4. Relative income figures highlight the fact that over time the distribution of American income has changed little.

_____ 5. The U.S. tax system is progressive only for high-income people.

_____ 6. The members of a social class share a set of values and also similar opportunities to obtain desired goals and experiences.

_____ 7. A recent study concluded that as children become older, their social-class position has less impact in determining their self-esteem.

_____ 8. The "hidden injury" of class is that working-class people are denied a sense of worth in the eyes of others and of themselves.

_____ 9. When individuals live in a neighborhood dominated by people whose social class is different from their own, they are more likely to have close friends from that social class than from their own.

_____ 10. A recent study of sixteen countries has concluded that the patterns of intergenerational mobility are strikingly different.

### Multiple-choice test

_____ 1. The theory of social stratification that emphasizes the need to fill jobs critical for the survival of society with highly qualified personnel was developed by:
a. Marx.
b. Davis and Moore.
c. Tumin.
d. Lenski.

_____ 2. Marx suggested that the members of the proletariat share social-class membership because of which common characteristic?
   a. They are disorganized.
   b. They are unaware of their social-class position.
   c. They are victims of the capitalist production process.
   d. They are profit-oriented.

_____ 3. Lenski's theory of social stratification is different from the structural-functional and conflict theories in which respect?
   a. It is more scientific.
   b. It is less scientific.
   c. It emphasizes social mobility to a greater extent.
   d. It demonstrates less commitment to the existing stratification system.

_____ 4. People's earnings obtained through wages, salaries, business profits, stock dividends, and other means are called:
   a. wealth.
   b. income.
   c. relative income.
   d. relative wealth.

_____ 5. In Mills's power-elite theory, the politically unorganized white-collar employees of corporations and government agencies belong to which social class?
   a. the power elite
   b. the pluralist class
   c. the proletariat
   d. the middle class

_____ 6. When researchers use community judges to assess their neighbors' social-class position, the approach is called:
   a. the reputational definition of social class.
   b. the subjective definition of social class.
   c. the power definition of social class.
   d. the objective definition of social class.

_____ 7. The higher one's social class, the better his or her chances are for:
   a. mental illness.
   b. communication problems.
   c. long life.
   d. low self-esteem.

_____ 8. Which statement about the relationship between social class and sexuality is true?
   a. The claim that "sex is a man's pleasure and a woman's duty" has become increasingly applicable to upper-middle-class marriage in the last decade.
   b. Working-class wives tend to enjoy sex and easily achieve orgasm.
   c. Working-class boys tend to begin their sexual lives earlier than middle-class boys.
   d. a and b

_____ 9. For middle-class blacks:
   a. upward mobility has been an unqualified success.
   b. employment is concentrated in areas serving black consumers and communities.
   c. the vicious cycle of poverty is often a reality.
   d. a and c

_____ 10. The situation in which some people are downwardly mobile, encouraging upward mobility for others, is called:

    a. occupational or structural mobility.
    b. immigration mobility.
    c. reproductive mobility.
    d. circulation mobility.

## Essay test

1. Define social stratification and discuss the general significance of social stratification in American society.
2. Summarize and evaluate the three theories of social stratification discussed in this chapter.
3. What are three major dimensions of social stratification? List and discuss them, focusing on recent evidence about each dimension.
4. Define social class and discuss two issues citing social-class differences in opportunity and two issues indicating social-class differences in life-style, using studies and examples presented in the chapter.
5. What is social mobility? Discuss the causes and effects of social mobility as well as prospects for upward mobility in the years ahead.

# Suggested Readings

Berreman, Gerald D. (ed.). 1981. *Social Inequality: Comparative and Developmental Approaches.* New York: Academic. Anthropological studies examining the structured inequalities that exist in societies ranging from the primitive hunting-and-gathering type to the modern socialist variety. The papers share a conflict theoretical perspective.

Burris, Beverly H. 1983. *No Room at the Top: Underdevelopment and Alienation in the Corporation.* New York: Praeger. An interesting study of how underemployed clerical workers in a service corporation react to their jobs and why they react as they do.

Dreiser, Theodore. 1953. *An American Tragedy.* New York: Random House. Originally published in 1925. The gripping novel of a young man with aspirations to marry into the upper class. The sharp contrast between lower-middle- and upper-class life-styles appears throughout the book.

Gilbert, Dennis, and Joseph A. Kahl. 1982. *The American Class Structure.* Homewood, IL: Dorsey Press. Revised edition. A revised edition of Kahl's leading sociological text on American social class published over thirty years ago. The current edition is comprehensive and easy to read.

Heller, Celia S. (ed.). 1969. *Structured Social Inequality.* New York: Macmillan. A book of readings containing more than forty articles and covering a variety of issues on social stratification, including theoretical contributions from Marx, Weber, and Davis and Moore.

Rubin, Lillian Breslow. 1976. *World of Pain: Life in the Working-Class Family.* New York: Basic Books. A study based on intensive interviews with fifty blue-collar couples and a comparison group of twenty-five upper-middle-class couples. Rubin concluded that norms that originated in the upper-middle class are filtering to working-class people and are producing huge strains in their marriages.

Sennett, Richard, and Jonathan Cobb. 1973. *Hidden Injuries of Class.* New York: Vintage. An account of the pain, disappointment, and lack of confidence associated with American working-class life. This book is based on competent sociological research, and yet its poignant, well-written material makes readers feel they are caught up in a novel.

Warner, W. Lloyd, J. O. Low, Paul S. Lunt, and Leo Srole. 1963. *Yankee City.* New Haven: Yale University Press. A single, slim volume presenting the principal conclusions of the historic, five-volume Yankee City study, the earliest analysis of the American class structure.

Williams, Terry, and William Kornblum. 1985. *Growing Up Poor*. Lexington, MA: Lexington Books. Based on interviews conducted in four American cities, this study shows poor adolescents' everyday struggles with poverty.

---

## Student Projects

1. Interview a dozen people with varied social characteristics—age, sex, race, and occupation. Ask them the following questions:

a. Is there a difference in the contribution to the welfare of society made by people in high- or low-status jobs?

b. What substantial differences, if any, exist between people who are successful economically and socially and those who are not?

c. Does class consciousness exist in the United States? Should it?

d. Is America the "land of opportunity"? Explain.

From the answers to these questions and perhaps others you might wish to add, try to construct a simple theory or perhaps several theories of social stratification. What are the similarities to and differences from theories examined in this chapter?

2. Select advertisements or photos from various magazines, choosing models, clothing, and activities that you believe to be representative of upper-, middle-, and working-class groups. Ask at least five people to guess the social class being represented in each picture. How much agreement did you find? Did you uncover cases of widespread agreement, suggesting that some items or situations definitely represent certain social classes?

---

## Answers to Test Questions

**True–false test**

| | | | | |
|---|---|---|---|---|
| 1. f | 3. t | 5. f | 7. f | 9. t |
| 2. f | 4. t | 6. t | 8. t | 10. f |

**Multiple-choice test**

| | | | | |
|---|---|---|---|---|
| 1. b | 3. a | 5. d | 7. c | 9. b |
| 2. c | 4. b | 6. a | 8. c | 10. d |

# 10
# RACIAL AND ETHNIC GROUPS

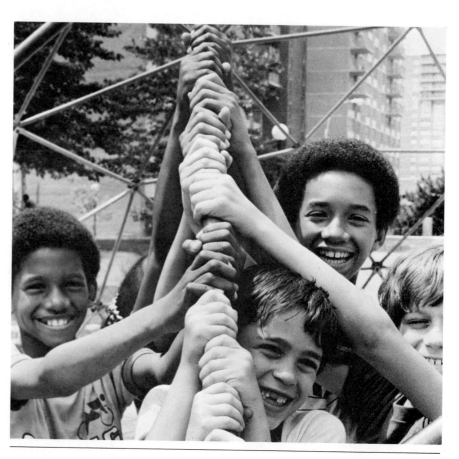

After some time in the American corner of heaven, Captain Stormfield turned to his guide Sandy and asked a question: "Sandy, I notice that I hardly ever see a white angel; where I run across one white angel, I strike as many as a hundred million copper-colored ones—people that can't speak English. How is that?"

Sandy explained that this situation was the normal way of things. After all, America had been occupied for centuries by Indians before the arrival of whites, and so it was reasonable that the Indians in heaven would vastly outnumber the whites. The Indians so outnumbered the whites, in fact, that Sandy on occasion had traveled a whole week at a time through the American part of heaven and had never seen a white face or heard a word of English.

The fact that whites were vastly outnumbered in the American corner of heaven was a disappointing discovery for Captain Stormfield. But Sandy had even more disturbing information to pass on. From time to time, Sandy indicated, the learned men from other planets and other solar systems came to the American part of heaven, and then they returned to their own part where they would write books about their travels. Sandy continued:

> And what do they say about us? They say this wilderness is populated with a scattering few hundred thousand billions of red angels, with now and then a curiously complected diseased one. You see, they think we whites . . . are Injuns that have been bleached out . . . for some peculiarly rascally sin, mind you. It is a mighty sour pill for us all, my friend—even the modestest of us, let alone the other kind, that think they are going to be received like a long-lost government bond, and hug Abraham into the bargain.

*(Twain, 1973: 93–94)*

In his special way, Mark Twain attempted to demonstrate to white Americans how ridiculous their sense of racial superiority has been. Yet this kind of lesson often fails to take hold. In spite of the fact that all human beings are members of the same species, many people pay more attention to their few differences with members of other groups than to their numerous shared qualities.

Undoubtedly you are aware that in U.S. society racial and ethnic issues often have a decisive, sober side. If you are the member of a racial or ethnic group that has been badly treated, then you have directly experienced the anger and frustration produced by discrimination in a country that ostensibly treats all its citizens equally. On the other hand, if you belong to the so-called dominant group, you also suffer the effects of American racial and ethnic problems. You are likely to feel confusion and fear—fear to talk seriously and honestly with members of certain groups, fear to walk or even drive through their neighborhoods.

Anger, frustration, and fear are certainly emotions that traditionally have been part of the American racial and ethnic picture. However, people of different heritages can also have positive relations, and colleges and universities are places for such contacts. In these settings students of different backgrounds can meet on esssentially neutral ground, where the fears and prejudices they might have grown up with are likely to be muted. On campuses and elsewhere in many American communities, different ethnic and racial groups sometimes sponsor festivals, fairs, plays, dances, and other activities that can help make the American public aware of their particular cultural experiences. Quite possibly more of those kinds of activities occur in your locale than you realize. Local mass media, both on campus and in the surrounding towns and cities, will reveal the events that different groups sponsor.

In the course of this chapter, we consider a number of important issues involving racial and ethnic groups. The next two sections concern basic concepts—first, the classification of race, ethnicity, and minority group, and then in the following part, the important processes of prejudice and discrimination are examined. In the next section, the various behavior patterns that can emerge when different racial and ethnic groups encounter each other are discussed. The following subject is American ethnic and racial groups. The chapter finishes with a look at racial and ethnic relations in the decades ahead.

# Race, Ethnicity, and Minority Group

In Chapter 3 ("Culture"), we examined the linguistic-relativity hypothesis, which emphasizes that language influences people's perceptions and behavior. As far as the present topics are concerned, language allows people to place themselves and others in distinct categories that focus on differences considered significant.

## Race

The call reaches the patrol car from police headquarters. "Liquor store robbed at the corner of Hudson and Grove. The suspect is a . . ." Usually the next word is a reference to the person's race. Americans and the citizens of many other Western nations often use a person's race as a basic means of identification. Race and sex are the two most prominently used status characteristics for identification, but while people fall into either the male or female category, race does not divide as neatly.

Superficially a basis for classification of races seems to exist. Westerners designate three broad racial categories: Caucasian, Mongol, and Negro. The Causasians, who originally lived in western Europe, northern Africa, and western Asia, have light skin pigmentation, frequent male balding, prominent chins, and fairly long trunks. The Mongols, who first inhabited northern and eastern Asia, have brown to yellow skin, black hair, broad cheekbones, low nose bridges, and eye folds, which produce the sense of slanting eyes. Negroes, the first residents of Africa, have dark pigmentation, low-bridged noses, and kinky or curly hair.

This three-part classification scheme is well known, but many groups, including some large groups, do not fit easily into the categories. Specialists have developed nearly 200 categories to account for discrepancies like the following. The Australian aborigines have Negroid skin and Caucasoid hair and are sometimes classified as a fourth race. Among Native Americans, who are a subrace of Mongoloid people, there are great differences in height and head shape. The tallest people in the world, the Watusi, and the shortest, the Pygmy, are both in the Negroid category and live within a few miles of each other.

Racial classifications are imprecise, and their functional significance seems modest. Admittedly certain biological adaptations have probably been functional. The original inhabitants of areas with high solar radiation appear to have received protection from their dark skin, and Negroes apparently have developed a much greater resistance to malaria forms than the Caucasians and Mongols arriving later in Africa. But no evidence suggests that one racial group is more intelligent, more creative, more athletic, more ferocious, in fact "more anything" involving brain power, personality, or capability than other groups. Sometimes the behavior of different racial groups suggests otherwise, but that is because one group receives better opportunities than another. Human beings are a single species, with all members possessing the same skeletal structure, the same complex nervous system, and the same intricate sensory organs.

If the classification of races has limited functional use, one must wonder why racial distinctions are so important. In a sentence the answer is that race is significant because people consider it thus. No matter what its biological meaning, therefore, race has sociological significance. Sociologically speaking, **race** refers to distinct physical characteristics, such as skin color and certain facial features, used to divide people into broad categories. Racial classification often creates a **self-fulfilling prophecy:** an incorrect definition of a situation that comes to pass because people accept the incorrect definition and act on it to make it become true. In such instances when the dominant group within a society declares a racial group inferior, they limit the opportunities of those group members, and so those individuals will demonstrate more limited capabilities than the members of the dominant group. Ethnic groups can also suffer the effects of the self-fulfilling prophecy.

## Ethnicity

**Ethnicity** is a set of cultural or national qualities that distinguishes a particular category of people from other categories. Ethnic groups differ on such issues as values, ideas, food habits, family patterns, sexual behavior, beauty standards, political outlook, work orientation, and recreational behavior, and the culture of an ethnic group creates a sense of identity among the members. Outsiders recognize ethnic group membership, and hostilities between different ethnic groups have been a major source of conflict in human history.

In U.S. society ethnicity is often synonymous with national group membership: So there are Chinese-Americans, Irish-Americans, Italian-Americans, Cuban-Americans, Polish-Americans, or whatever. Then there are linguistic groups that maintain their own cultural identity, such as the English-speaking and the French-speaking Canadians. Sometimes religious groups develop as ethnic groups: for instance, the Amish and Hutterite religious communities in the United States.

In many situations ethnic and racial groups have minority-group status.

## Minority Group

A **minority group** is any category of people with recognizable racial, religious, or ethnic traits that place it in a position of low esteem and that serve as the basis for unequal treatment. The members of a minority group are inevitably aware of the unequal treatment they all share, and this awareness helps create a sense of belonging to the group. It is important to understand that minority status has no intrinsic relationship to group size. Sometimes a minority group is hundreds of times larger than the dominant group in the society. Such a situation existed when the European countries established colonies in Africa, Asia, and the Americas. In other cases — blacks in the United States, for instance — the minority group is smaller in numbers than the dominant group. Minority status is the result of a subordinate position in society, not the size of its membership.

All the racial and ethnic categories discussed in this chapter are minority groups. What are the processes that create minority status? The following section answers this question.

# Prejudice and Discrimination: Producing Inequality

"All people are created equal." As infants, all human beings generally behave in accord with this principle. Yet in the course of socialization, many Americans accept the belief that some groups are superior to others. They accept both prejudice and discrimination.

**Prejudice** is a highly negative judgment toward a group, focusing on one or more negative characteristics that are supposedly uniformly shared by all group members. If a person rigidly believes that all members of a racial or ethnic group are innately lazy, stupid, stubborn, and violent, then that person is prejudiced toward the group in question. Racial, ethnic, and religious prejudice are the most prominently discussed types; in general, prejudice is not easily reversible. The fact that prejudice is not easily reversible distinguishes it from a "misconception," where someone supports an incorrect conclusion about a group but is willing, when confronted with facts, to change his or her opinion. The companion concept to prejudice is discrimination, which is the behavioral manifestation of prejudice. **Discrimination** is the behavior by which one group prevents or restricts another group's access to scarce resources.

Prejudice and discrimination are often a one-two punch: The behavior directly follows the judgment. The two situations do not always appear together, however. Discrimination sometimes takes place without prejudice. In the 1950s in Little Rock, Arkansas, many white ministers were not prejudiced toward black people (they wanted integrated congregations), but they continued to support discrimination against blacks. The ministers realized that a movement to integrate would have meant the disaffection of many affluent, white members who provided the major economic support for the churches (Campbell and Pettigrew, 1959). In other situations prejudice fails to evoke discrimination. From 1930 to 1932, a white social scientist traveled throughout the United States with a Chinese couple. They received courteous treatment at hotels, motels, and restaurants, and yet 90 percent of questionnaire responses sent to the establishments visited made it clear that Chinese would be unwelcome (LaPierce, 1934). The

**232** study does contain some problems—for instance, there is no assurance that the person answering the survey was the one who had served the researcher and the Chinese couple—and yet similar findings appear in later research (Kutner, Wilkins, and Yarrow, 1952). Thus, in some situations, prejudice and discrimination do not automatically occur in tandem.

It is possible to analyze prejudice as an ideology. An **ideology** is a system of beliefs and principles that presents an organized explanation of the justification for a group's outlooks and behavior. **Racism** is the ideology contending that actual or alleged differences between different racial groups assert the superiority of one racial group. Racism is a rationalization for political, economic, and social discrimination.

There are a number of explanations for prejudice, discrimination, and racism.

## Sources of Prejudice and Discrimination

The old man nodded and smiled as she walked by, pushing the baby carriage. Her impulse was to hurry past the bench—he was unshaven, his clothes were threadbare, and the near-empty bottle leaning against his knee was no testimony to his sobriety—but she slowed down as he looked at the baby. And when he said, "Could I see her, ma'am?" she immediately pulled back the blanket. The old man's face relaxed and softened. "She's a beauty, ma'am, just a plain beauty! Look at her, laying there, peaceful and innocent. And she don't hate nobody. Black, white—it's all the same to her."

Like the old man, we will make the assumption that prejudice and discrimination are learned forms of behavior. Psychological, social, and economic explanations all contribute to an understanding of the development of prejudice and discrimination.

### Psychological Explanations

A number of psychological perspectives exist. One approach suggests that the acquisition of prejudice and discrimination is a three-stage process that occurs to children in the course of socialization. A girl of six runs home to her mother and says, "Mother, what is the name of the children I am supposed to hate?" This child is at the "first stage" in learning prejudice. She has not yet associated prejudicial attributes with the culturally supported target group. In fact, a recent study concluded that until children reach the age of eight, they do not have a clear, stable sense of people's ethnicity. The "second stage" in learning prejudice occurs when children connect prejudice with the culturally supported target group. In a social context where racial or ethnic prejudice exists, children in the first and second grade often intermingle, but by the fifth grade they are usually more exclusive, choosing to stay with members of their own group. The "third stage" involves the ability to practice prejudice and discrimination subtly. In high school young people are able to express polite acceptance and tolerance toward members of other ethnic groups, while often rejecting those ethnically different. This approach stands in sharp contrast to the behavior of eight-year-olds who have learned the prejudicial categories and speak as if they completely reject people in different ethnic groups, but their behavior is often nondiscriminatory (Aboud, 1984; Allport, 1954: 307–311).

Another psychological explanation contends that a major source of prejudice and discrimination is a certain personality type—the authoritarian personality. According to a five-year research project (Adorno et al., 1950), the **authoritarian personality** is a personality pattern where the individual rigidly supports conventional middle-class values, uncritically admires and obeys strong, controlling people, bullies the weak, and exhibits extensive superstition about and fear of the unknown. The backers of the theory suggest that such a person has a powerful tendency to demonstrate prejudice and discrimination toward members of other ethnic groups. The appropriate conditions of socialization can encourage the development of the authoritarian personality. This personality type generally results from a harsh, disciplined upbringing, where children must unquestioningly obey their parents and are punished for showing insufficient respect for them.

Social scientists have been receptive to authoritarian-personality theory as demonstrated by the fact that studies on the topic have continued to be published in recent years (Heaven, 1985; Ray, 1984; Zaenglein-Senger and Stewart, 1985). Yet, historically, studies of the authoritarian personality have been criticized for poor sampling tech-

*Since prejudice and discrimination must be learned, children of different races are not disposed to hate and fear each other. Such emotions, however, are often acquired in the course of socialization, and the modern resurgence of the Ku Klux Klan, an organization with a violent, anti-black tradition, offers ample evidence of this tendency.*

nique and other methodological inadequacies. Furthermore some social scientists have opposed the perspective of the authoritarian-personality theory—that prejudice and discrimination are conditions produced only by poorly reared individuals and not "normal" people. In fact, plenty of evidence indicates that other factors besides au-

thoritarian socialization encourage these tendencies (Bahr, Chadwick, and Stauss, 1979).

An alternative psychological approach is the **scapegoat theory.** This explanation emphasizes that people blocked from achieving a goal will sometimes be unable or unwilling to take out their frustration on its source, and so they direct their aggression against an accessible individual or group. The displacement of the hostility from the real source of frustration to the scapegoat permits a release of tension, called catharsis.

Three conditions make it likely that a racial or ethnic group will become a scapegoat. First, the group must be easy to identify, whether it be a skin color, a tattoo, or some insignia such as the Star of David the Nazis forced Jews to wear. Second, the ethnic group selected must be weak enough so that it is unlikely to retaliate. Finally, in order to qualify as a scapegoat, a group must be accessible (Simpson and Yinger, 1972: 66–69).

In a pre-World-War-II experiment that tested the scapegoat theory, all three conditions existed. The subjects were white boys attending a summer camp. The first step was to give them a pretest assessing their prejudice toward Japanese and Mexican-Americans. Then the boys received a tedious paper-and-pencil test that lasted long enough to make them miss the weekly opportunity to go to town and see a movie. Finally the subjects were given a post-test measure of prejudice toward the two minority groups. This time the rate of prejudice increased significantly (Dollard et al, 1939: 43–44). The results support the scapegoat hypothesis, which contends that people — in this case white boys — are inclined to direct their hostility toward visible, vulnerable, and accessible minority groups (here Japanese and Mexican-Americans) when the true source of their frustration (in this situation the adults administering the test) is too powerful to attack.

## Cultural Explanations

Language is a significant component of culture. Without the words "black," "white," "yellow," and "red," Americans would be unable to distinguish skin-color differences. Furthermore the words associated with "black" and "white" are often highly tinged with emotion. *Roget's Thesaurus* has about 120 synonyms for "blackness," most of which are negative — for instance, blot, blight, smut, evil, wickedness, and malignance. The 134 synonyms for whiteness have primarily favorable connotations. The list includes brightness, innocence, honor, purity, fairness, and trust. Without language we would also not be able to produce such unflattering racial and ethnic designations as "frog," "honky," "kike," "kraut," "nigger," "slope," and "spic" or phrases like "lazy as a

nigger" or "jew him down." Words also permit the development of stereotypes.

A **stereotype** is an exaggerated image, maintained by prejudiced people, of the characteristics of the group members against whom they are prejudiced. For instance, in U.S. society blacks have been traditionally stereotyped as superstitious, lazy, happy-go-lucky, ignorant, stupid, and pleasure loving and Jews as shrewd, mercenary, grasping, intelligent, ambitious, and aggressive. Countless jokes about blacks, Jews, and other minority groups elaborate these stereotypes. "What harm can a little joke be?" an observer might ask. "They're just meant to be funny, not to hurt anyone." The problem is that jokes directed at minority groups do emphasize the negative, distorted image represented by the stereotype. As a result people hearing the joke will perhaps more readily accept that members of the target group are "that way." Furthermore, while members of the dominant culture might see such humor as harmless, minority-group members are likely to be infuriated and offended.

The use of stereotypes demonstrates the existence of **social distance:** the feeling of separation between individuals or groups. In the 1920s Emory Bogardus developed a scale to measure social distance. The scale has become so widely known that social scientists simply call it "the Bogardus scale." The scale asks people to indicate their willingness to interact with various racial and ethnic groups in certain social situations, which represent seven degrees of social distance. The seven items involve an increasing social distance as one moves down the list. Informants must indicate whether they will accept members of the particular group:

To close kinship by marriage.

As a regular friend.

To the street as a neighbor.

To employment in one's occupation.

To citizenship in one's country.

As visitor only to one's country.

Would exclude from one's country.

Over a forty-year period (from 1926 to 1966), research in the United States showed that white Americans and northern Europeans scored in the top third of the hierarchy, eastern and southern Europeans in the middle, and Asian minorities in the bottom third. The rankings stayed consistent over the forty-year period, and not just for whites. When Jewish-, Asian-, and black Americans took the test, their results were similar to white Americans, with one exception—in each case their own group was placed at the top (Bogardus, 1968).

Social distance can be situational, operating more strongly in some contexts than in others. One recent study conducted in three British cities concluded that Asian residents' choice of whether to go to Asian- or white-run shops was strongly affected by the amount of contact required between customer and shop keeper. When they patronized clothing stores and restaurants where fairly extensive contact between shop keeper and customers was required (and thus social distance tended to be emphasized), Asians were more likely to go to Asian-run shops. When the shops sold newspapers, tobacco, and candy, and little contact between shop keeper and patron was necesssary, Asians were more willing to go to white-run shops (Aldrich et al., 1985).

One final point about social distance. To some extent social distance is self-fulfilling. A person says, "I can't stand that group. I don't even want them in my country." It is fairly certain that this person will avoid contacts with members of that group. It is unlikely, therefore, that the unfavorable stereotype will break down. The simplifications and exaggerations of stereotypes thrive on extensive social distance. In fact, it is likely that stereotypes cannot survive with frequent, relatively pleasant contacts among racial and ethnic groups. (See Figure 10.1.)

## Economic Explanations

"Big bucks" in prejudice and discrimination? The immediate reaction might be to laugh at that idea, but a short reflection should produce a different response. In the United States and in other countries, slavery developed because it was the cheapest form of labor. A study of American history shows that a strong economic incentive for the practice existed. The northern states received little or no economic benefit from slavery, and they outlawed it soon after the Revolutionary War. Even in the South, slavery lost its popularity in the late 1700s, and many people saw it as a "necessary evil." By 1835, however, cotton had become the

**Figure 10.1**
**Americans' Perception of Different Ethnic Groups**

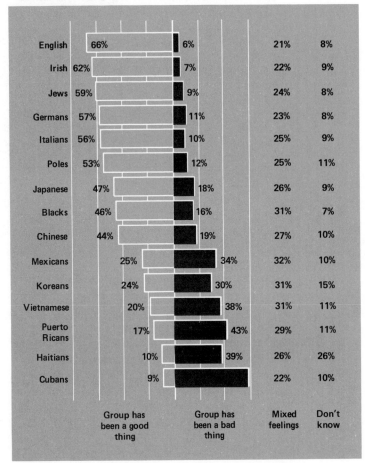

*This figure suggests that the more recently an ethnic group has arrived in this country, the less favorable Americans' attitude toward that group tends to be. (Source: The Roper Organization.* Roper Reports. *May 1982.)*

primary commodity of American foreign trade. At this point most white southerners did not consider slavery a necessary evil but as a positive good that served as the foundation of a stable society and a prosperous economy (Lacy, 1972).

In some cases the economic factor is present but not readily apparent. In 1942, during World War II, the American government ordered the removal of Japanese-Americans from the West Coast on the pretext that they were potential collaborators with the Japanese. A major impetus behind the relocation was an organized effort by newspaper leaders, congressmen, and wealthy farmers to convince President Roosevelt of the necessity to un-

**Table 10.1
Explanations of Prejudice and Discrimination**

| APPROACH | CENTRAL IDEA | ILLUSTRATIONS |
|---|---|---|
| Psychological explanations | That prejudice and discrimination derive from individuals' socialization or frustrations felt toward a strong, inaccessible group | Authoritarian-personality approach or scapegoat theory |
| Cultural explanations | That different components of culture—language, values, and beliefs—contribute to the development of prejudice and discrimination | The concepts "stereotype" and "social distance" |
| Economic explanations | That the existence of prejudice and discrimination are economically beneficial for the dominant group | The American slavery system or the relocation of Japanese-Americans during World War II |

dertake the endeavor. For the wealthy farmers, this was an unprecedented opportunity to divert less affluent white farmers' attention from their own unpopular domination of agriculture and to redirect the small white farmers' hostilities toward the Japanese. Other economic advantages were less subtle. At the time of the relocation, Japanese had to sell homes, farms, businesses, and personal possessions at a fraction of their real value. The official government estimate is that Japanese-Americans lost over $400 million (in 1940, preinflated dollars). The American government reimbursed scarcely 10 percent of that sum (Berry and Tischler, 1978: 370–371).

The economic factor encourages prejudice and discrimination, but the factor does not act alone. A person must have personal inclinations supporting these tendencies and must also receive cultural backing. Table 10.1 summarizes explanations of prejudice and discrimination.

## Effects of Prejudice and Discrimination

A man named Eldridge Cleaver was in prison, and like many other prisoners he decided to put a pinup girl—from the center of *Esquire* magazine—on the wall of his cell. But one evening when Cleaver returned to his cell, he was shocked and enraged to find his pinup torn into little pieces and floating in the toilet. Cleaver said that ". . . it was like seeing a dead body floating in a lake."

The next day he asked the guard why he had done it. There were rules against pinups, the guard said. Cleaver would not accept that reply. The rule was never enforced, he pointed out. The guard

smiled, immediately making Cleaver wary. He would compromise, the guard said. If Cleaver would get himself a black pinup, he would let it stay.

Cleaver was embarrassed. He called the guard two or three dirty names and walked away. But he was disturbed by what the guard had revealed. Without realizing it, he, a black man, had chosen a picture of a white woman over the available pictures of black women. Was it true? Did he really prefer white to black women? The conclusion was inescapable. He did (Cleaver, 1970: 20–21).

Putting aside for the moment the serious sexism in the above anecdote, Cleaver's reaction links to a widespread belief: that the members of minority groups tend to denigrate themselves and to value majority-group status more highly. Is it true that minority-group members have low self-esteem?

Let us consider a large study that tested the issue of self-esteem with a random sample of 2625 Baltimore school children. Rosenberg and Simmons (1971) concluded that black children do not have lower self-esteem than white children. In fact, 46 percent of the black children interviewed had high self-esteem compared to 33 percent of the whites.

The researchers uncovered certain factors that affected black children's self-esteem. Blacks who did well in school and who came from higher social-class backgrounds tended to have high self-esteem. Black children who attended integrated schools were more likely to have low self-esteem. It seemed that these black children had many opportunities to compare themselves with high-achieving white children. Apparently integrated schools can improve black students' academic achievement and provide interracial friendships, but they

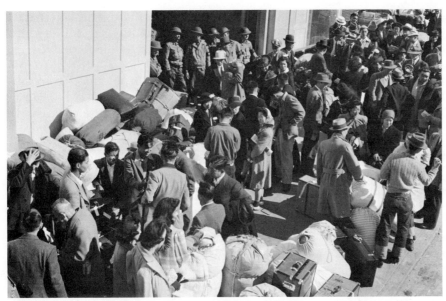

*This photo taken in 1942 shows the first 660 Japanese-Americans evacuated from San Francisco under army orders. Guarded by military police, they are shown awaiting trains that would take them to a detention camp.*

do not raise their self-esteem.

Backed by other recent research, the Baltimore study makes it clear that black children do not usually hate themselves, idolize whites, and maintain low self-esteem. Further research on this topic, not only with blacks but also with other racial and ethnic groups, needs to consider the cautions previously mentioned—in particular, the likelihood that such factors as social class, school performance, and the racial, ethnic, and class statuses of classmates have a significant effect on children's self-esteem, perhaps a more significant effect than their own race or ethnicity.

At the same time, it would be misleading to conclude that prejudice and discrimination do not produce negative effects upon people. Writing on the subject of racism, a psychiatrist stressed that experiencing racism can be devastating to an individual's self-esteem and that effective therapy can help patients explore their coping mechanisms and develop more productive ways of dealing with the anxiety triggered by racism (Brantley, 1983).

### Functions of Prejudice

It might be distasteful to consider, but prejudice can be functional for the people who practice it. First, prejudice can help protect an individual's self-esteem. An applicant fails to gain admittance to a college, and instead of conceding that his credentials are inadequate, he blames it on the fact that "the place is run by Jews, and they just look out for their own." Second, as we have seen, prejudice can produce economic, social, or political gain. An employer might get away with paying minority members less than other people; in the past poor Southern whites, though at the bottom of the white stratification ladder, could still claim a higher prestige ranking than even affluent blacks. Third, prejudice serves as a kind of "cognitive economy." In a complex world where people meet hundreds of individuals, the prejudiced person can take shortcuts, making judgments and taking actions based on stereotypes. "She's Irish, and those people all love to drink. I'd better lock the liquor cabinet when she comes to clean the house."

## Majority and Minority Behavior Patterns

Some evidence suggests that over time Americans have become less inclined to support prejudice and discrimination. Consider the following two situations. In 1906 Mark Twain attended a banquet

**238**

where a speaker received thunderous applause when he fervently told his audience of lawyers, bankers, and other middle-class professionals, "We are of the Anglo-Saxon race, and when the Anglo-Saxon wants a thing *he just takes it*" (Twain, 1973: 3). These respectable American citizens showed no inclination to support the rights of anyone besides their fellow Anglo-Saxons. Yet less than sixty years later in the fall of 1963, several hundred thousand black and white Americans marched in Washington, D.C., on behalf of full civil rights for all Americans. Neither of these events was out of character with its time. Both were consistent with the dominant-group racial policies during the respective eras.

As we examine six dominant-group policies involving racial and ethnic relations, it should be kept in mind that each policy is also the product of its era. The same point emphatically applies to the various responses to minority-group status, which we also discuss.

## Dominant-Group Policies

The first three patterns tend to maintain or increase social distance, while the last three tend to decrease it (Simpson and Yinger, 1972).

1. *Extermination.* The most extreme pattern is the elimination of the minority group. In the nineteenth century, the British decimated the Tasmanians and Dutch South Africans exterminated the Hottentots. In the effort to establish a "master race," the Nazis murdered six million Jews and thousands of Romany people, known as Gypsies. Americans wiped out most of the native people of Hawaii and the continental United States.

2. *Continued subjugation.* Short of destroying a people, members of the dominant group can hold them under complete control. In the United States, slavery was the outstanding example of this policy. The European colonial powers in Africa and Asia successfully maintained such an intergroup pattern in some countries until after World War II. As the following Cross-Cultural Perspective indicates, white South Africans currently maintain a policy of subjugation.

3. *Population transfer.* Sometimes the leaders of the dominant group decide that the most desirable solution is the movement of an ethnic group from one locale to another. In some cases leaders force the minority members to leave the country. Idi Amin, the former president of Uganda, compelled all Indians to mi-

---

## CROSS-CULTURAL PERSPECTIVE

### *South Africa and Its Apartheid Policy*

 Since it achieved independence in 1948, South Africa has maintained a pattern of subjugation for all nonwhite people. This policy poses a serious threat to the future stability of the country.

The Republic of South Africa is a multiracial state with four racial groups. In 1980 the population was 27.7 million people, with black Africans representing 71.5 percent, whites 16.2 percent, coloreds (mixed black and white) 9.4 percent, and Asians 2.9 percent.

In 1795 the British acquired South Africa and controlled it until 1948. The British introduced Indians as sugar-plantation workers and freed blacks, who had been the slaves of Dutch farmers, known as Boers. The blacks also received most political and civil rights. The Boers were unhappy with these developments, and throughout the nineteenth century there were violent confrontations with the increasing number of British colonists. The culmination was the Boer War,

which the British won with the help of the blacks. Once in power, however, the British felt that the blacks' greater numbers posed a significant threat, and so the white leadership imposed limitations—for instance, property qualifications for voting were established and blacks' geographical movement was restricted.

In 1948 South Africa received its independence, and the Nationalist Party assumed governmental control. Afrikaners, the Boers' descendants, have dominated the Nationalist Party, and under their leadership white supremacy, which existed during the colonial period, has become more and more formalized by law. Most significantly the whites have established the *apartheid* policy to insure their domination. In Afrikaans, the Afrikaners' language, *apartheid* means "separation" or "apartness" —a policy of compulsory segregation. Most blacks are forced to live in rural homelands. These homelands are too long a commute for blacks and other nonwhites who work in the cities, and so these people obtain residences in townships outside the cities. While in the cities, nonwhites must use separate facilities: restaurants, taxis, restrooms, staircases, and so forth.

In South Africa the blacks suffer second-class citizenship under *apartheid*. So far the government's strong military backing, along with steadily increasing economic benefits for black workers, have helped prevent open civil war. However, other conditions encourage such an outbreak: In particular, in urban areas, blacks' income is one-fifth that of whites, and in rural areas the ratio is worse; the blacks have no political rights and no prospects of receiving any; and neighboring black-run nations might offer extensive support. In fact, some support is

already apparent. Thousands of young black South Africans are supposedly training outside the country, mainly in Angola. They can return home without weapons, because large caches of weapons are available, as those periodically discovered by the police demonstrate. Since the late 1970s, some black South Africans have launched increasingly skilled guerrilla attacks on police stations, banks, and industries. White leaders realize that the threat of extensive industrial sabotage can seriously damage the climate for much-needed foreign business investment.

In recent years relations between blacks and whites have gotten worse. In spite of increasing economic and political pressures from many Western industrialized nations, the government of President P. W. Botha has continued to take a hard line. In June 1986, following twenty months of violence in which 1600 people, most of whom were black, were killed, the Botha government imposed a national-emergency decree. This order permits the police and army to arrest without making charges and to search without warrants. In other words, terrorism by the state has been legalized.

It is unclear whether a negotiated settlement between blacks and whites is still possible. Clearly any negotiations must recognize certain non-

negotiable positions. For blacks a solution must provide a genuine share in political power, and whites must receive assurance that because of their greater numbers blacks will not establish complete control. The hostility between blacks and whites impedes the determination of compromises. A black South African union leader explained:

> People talk about black and white consciousness. But it's not black consciousness, it's hatred. It's not white consciousness, it's hatred. Someone has said "To hell with the other person." What we need are ways and means of living together. We must recognize ourselves as humans because of our two feet, two hands, one head, and we must recognize that we are equal.
>
> *(Study Commission on U.S. Policy toward Southern Africa, 1981: 381)*

Other industrialized nations have eradicated their most visible forms of racism, and many nations consider the *apartheid* policy a visible insult. Since 1947 motions to censure South Africa have been introduced each year in the United Nations. For over twenty years, regardless of ideological differences, most African states have voted as a bloc to isolate South Africa politically and economically. It seems inevitable that the *apartheid* policy will change. What is unclear is when and by what means.

Sources: Alan Cowell. "South Africa Tightens the Vise on Black Dissent." *New York Times.* June 15, 1986. Section 4, page 1; Richard T. Schaefer. *Racial and Ethnic Groups.* Boston: Little, Brown. 1979; Study Commission on U.S. Policy toward Southern Africa. *South Africa: Time Running Out.* Berkeley and Los Angeles: University of California Press. 1981.

grate, even though most of them were natives of the country. American authorities have also resorted to population transfers, forcing Indian tribes to move to reservations. In the 1830s government officials ordered the Cherokee tribe to travel the thousand-mile "Trail of Tears" from the deep South to Oklahoma. Disease, starvation, and winter cold killed thousands along the way.

4. *Legal protection of minorities.* In some instances government officials recognize that to insure the rights of minorities they must pass special legislation. The Civil Rights Act of 1964 has been the most significant American legislative effort to eliminate discrimination. The act covers employment practices of all businesses with more than twenty-five employees, access to all public accommodations such as hotels, motels, and restaurants, and the use of such federally supported organizations as colleges and hospitals. The Civil Rights Act of 1964 also includes voting, but other legislation focuses on this issue. The Voting Rights Act of 1965 has suspended the various qualifying tests for voter registration that many southern states used, and this act has also authorized federal examiners to enter these states and register black voters. As a result of these actions, the opportunity for the registration of black voters has greatly increased.

5. *Cultural pluralism.* This policy emphasizes the existence of ethnic groups living peacefully but separately from each other. Switzerland, for example, has four separate ethnic areas, each with its own language — French, German, Italian, and Romansh. In U.S. society many Americans have retained a strong sense of ethnic identity, and successful politicians often find it necessary to acknowledge and support ethnic interests. Since the 1960s blacks and other minority groups have frequently focused on their racial or ethnic affiliation in the pursuit of political or economic goals that will benefit their particular group.

6. *Assimilation.* This approach assumes that the most productive course of action is to eliminate separate ethnic interests and develop a common identity. Assimilation can occur at a cultural level, a racial level, or both. Brazil is a country where both types of assimilation are widely practiced and approved, with intermar-

riage between blacks and whites causing little or no interest and concern. In the United States, assimilation among people of northern European ancestry has been extensive. In general, though, Americans marry within the same broad religious and racial categories. The early twentieth-century concept of the melting pot, where ethnic identities would disappear through complete assimilation, has not come to pass, not even to the originally proposed extent of eliminating all ethnicities of European origin.

Thus majority groups have established a number of different policies toward minority groups. Extermination, continued subjugation, and population transfer tend to maintain or increase social distance, while the legal protection of minorities, cultural pluralism, and assimilation tend to decrease it. The policies established by majority groups will determine or influence the responses of minorities.

## Minority Responses

Beginning with the southern civil rights activities in the late 1950s, blacks and eventually other ethnic groups started engaging in various protest activities in order to combat the discrimination and limited opportunities faced by their respective groups. Some Americans were frightened and surprised by this particular response to prejudice and discrimination. They were familiar with avoidance, acceptance, and assimilation, the other three responses, but now there was also aggression (Vander Zanden, 1972).

### Avoidance

For many people avoidance is impossible. People have skin color or other physical characteristics that make their ethnic or racial status undeniable. In other cases an accent in speech or extensive involvement in the local community would make avoidance difficult. But many others have the opportunity. A study shows that during the 1920s, in Washington, D.C., many light-skinned blacks chose to "pass." Former associates took pains not to betray the people who slipped into white society, and if those who remained were envious, they did not reveal it. In those years so many people attempted to pass that the National Theatre hired a black doorman to locate and bounce passers whom whites could not detect (Green, 1967: 207–208).

Little research on passing exists, but some issues that studies could address come to mind. Does guilt often accompany the act? Certainly the possibility exists. People who deny their ethnic or racial status are cutting themselves off from family, friends, and heritage. And what about the fear of discovery—the nagging thought that a former associate would inadvertently or perhaps even purposefully reveal one's identity?

For people who accept their ethnic status these problems do not develop.

## Acceptance

The majority of people in an ethnic or racial category generally accept their minority status. The acceptance, however, does not mean that their self-esteem must suffer. Acceptors can take a number of productive steps to boost their self-esteem and pride. First, they can base their self-evaluations on comparisons with members of their own group, instead of the more advantageously situated majority-group members. Second, they can use traditional structures—family, neighborhood, and friends—to provide mutual support and self-enhancement. Finally, those who accept their racial or ethnic status can establish special organizations, such as ethnic professional groups, study programs, or city-sponsored awareness projects, to nurture ethnic and racial pride through the use of available mass media (Bahr, Chadwick, and Stauss, 1979: 329–336).

Several decades ago American cultural standards strongly supported "second-class citizenship" for many minority groups. Writing in the 1930s, a researcher described a black man who had lived his entire life in the South, where blacks faced a highly restrictive life-style. Once the man and his wife took a trip to the North. The experience was unsettling. The man was surprised to see only one entrance to the railroad station instead of two, and he was almost dumbfounded to sit with a white family at the dinner table, to sleep in their guest room, and to drive around and meet their friends. The black man said "that it felt like 'being treated as a man'" (Dollard, 1937: 266).

After a lifetime of accepting a highly restricted minority status, this man found it difficult to adjust to a social situation where assimilation was possible.

## Assimilation

Minority-group members are pursuing assimilation when they attempt to eliminate their minority status and become socially and culturally unified with the dominant group.

Dominant-group policies play a significant part in determining the extent to which assimilation can occur. In American society European immigrants have been able to pursue this course of action successfully. Nonwhite groups, most notably blacks, have encountered severe difficulties.

Black executives serve as an illustration. Like all executives they experience pressures, but in addition many feel they must face a special kind of stress—the effects of American racism. One writer offered the following commentary on black executives:

> Their climb to the top, they assert, is made more difficult by the historical and psychological burden of American racism. They have coped, they say, with segregated schools and neighborhoods; some have lived with Ku Klux Klan violence and others have memories of whites-only drinking fountains. But many say the strains of working in a white-dominated structure and the evidence of corporate racism, cloaked by a subtly worded memo or a promotion that never comes, are new and strangely disturbing. In a recent survey by *Black Enterprise* magazine on work, nearly 75 percent of those earning more than $35,000 a year reported discrimination on their jobs. The perception of many blacks is that whites-only signs still hang on the higher rungs of the corporate ladder.
>
> *(Campbell, 1982: 37):*

Historically situations that have made blacks and other minority groups feel that assimilation was impossible have sometimes encouraged aggressive responses.

## Aggression

What constitutes minority-group aggression varies sharply across time and space, often determined only by the distorted perception of the majority group. In the 1930s some Southerners felt that it was aggressive behavior for blacks to hold a prestigious job, own a tract of land, or have a special talent. In some towns it was even considered an aggressive act for blacks to appear in public dressed up during the week. The whites apparently wanted to see blacks in only one place: the fields (Dollard, 1937).

In the 1960s a new, much more aggressive approach became popular. Some blacks, along with some other minority-group members, became strong advocates of equal opportunity and justice for members of their respective groups. Most of this activity was nonviolent, but the threat of violence was often present, particularly as a response to whites who wanted to use violence to keep blacks in positions of inferiority.

In the middle 1980s, blacks' aggression tended to be less frequent and more restrained but not uncommon. For instance, noting that minorities were underrepresented on the faculty and staff,

the president of the Black Student Union at an eastern state university told a reporter for his school newspaper that ". . . it was a 'never ending story.' He also said that the BSU 'will take drastic actions' to force changes. . . ." The president of the BSU noted that "he will 'always stand up for what is right and never step down from a fight.' He wants to 'stir things up' at Southern. . . " (Muraskin, 1986).

At a given point in history, members of a minority group often pursue more than one response. All these four responses appear in a discussion of American minority groups.

# American Minority Groups

An account of American minority groups is actually many accounts, one for each group. Space limitations make an extensive discussion impossible. In this section we examine the largest and most prominent of the American minority groups. Figure 10.2 indicates the size of each group and its percentage of the overall population.

**Figure 10.2**
**Prominent American Racial and Ethnic Groups**[1]
Total Population: 226.5 million

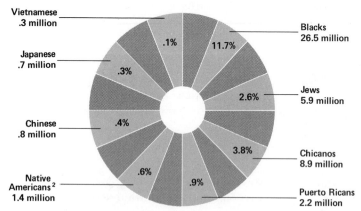

Vietnamese .3 million — .1%
Japanese .7 million — .3%
Chinese .8 million — .4%
Native Americans[2] 1.4 million — .6%
Blacks 26.5 million — 11.7%
Jews 5.9 million — 2.6%
Chicanos 8.9 million — 3.8%
Puerto Ricans 2.2 million — .9%

[1] Within the present figure, the representation of each group is the same size, not adjusted to its proportion of the total population.
[2] Includes Eskimos and Aleuts.

*This figure indicates the size of most prominent minority groups in America and the percentage each represents in the overall population. (Sources: Adapted from U.S. Bureau of the Census.* Statistical Abstract of the United States: 1982– 83. *No. 36;* American Jewish Year Book, 1982. *"Jewish Population in the United States, 1981.")*

## Black Americans

Black slave labor existed in Virginia as early as 1619, but black slaves were more expensive than white servants in the short run, and their foreignness in appearance, language, and general behavior offended the ethnocentric English. Almost all these early colonists preferred white laborers. In 1640 there were only 150 blacks reported in Virginia. The figure rose to 300 in 1650, 3000 in 1680, and 10,000 by 1704. During the latter third of the seventeenth century, the plantation economy was developing, and an acute need for cheap labor arose. A new type of labor known as "chattel slavery" gradually took shape. The laws on which the system was based came from English property law. Thus blacks became property that could be bought and sold. They would serve their masters for life, and children automatically became the property of their masters. The only limits upon owners' treatment of slaves was their personal discretion.

Slavery ended in 1865, but the oppression of blacks did not cease. In the South there were the "Jim Crow" laws that legalized discrimination against blacks in all institutional areas. There were also lynchings, and in many southern towns the Ku Klux Klan conducted terrorist raids. From 1880 to 1930, blacks often lived under very poor conditions. Rural southern blacks frequently had substandard diets inferior to those received under slavery, and infectious diseases spread more rapidly because of poor diet. Gonorrhea and syphilis became prevalent among blacks during this period, with many pregnancies ending in stillbirths.

In the 1920s federal legislation restricted immigration, and as a result factories lost their chief source of cheap labor. Recruiters sought southern blacks, and a migration of blacks from the South began. This migration stopped during the depression of the 1930s, but it resumed when industrialization revitalized with American involvement in World War II. The black migration to the North has continued, and by 1970 the states outside the South had about half the black population. Blacks migrating to the North usually experienced extensive discrimination in educational and occupational opportunities, in the availability of housing, and in the use of public facilities (bars, restaurants, grocery stores, buses, and trains, for example).

In the late 1950s and early 1960s, nonviolent demonstrations in the South protested discrimination against blacks. There were marches, pickets, and "sit-ins" at restaurants, on buses, and in other public facilities. During these years well-organized campaigns to register black voters occurred in southern states so that blacks would be able to use the political machinery to improve their living conditions.

Gradually, imperceptibly at first, the tone of the protest efforts changed. Whites, who had taken a prominent role in much of the early protest activities, were told to devote themselves to eliminating racism in their own communities. In the black protest groups, a sense of black culture and consciousness began to appear: Afros became fashionable, dashikis (African-style shirts) were worn, and black literature was widely read. A sense of black pride developed. "Black is beautiful" became a frequent slogan. The rhetoric and style of the black protest movement lost its nonviolent character. The young black leaders of the 1960s began advocating and predicting massive violence of blacks against whites if discrimination against blacks continued. On several occasions black protesters appeared carrying guns in public. For example, a group of armed Black Panthers marched through one of the state buildings in Sacramento, California, to announce their demands, and protesters emerged from a building occupation at Cornell University carrying rifles. No documented evidence has indicated, however, that blacks initiated violence during major protests.

On the other hand, blacks were often the victims of violence. The two most prominent black protest leaders of the 1960s—Malcolm X and Martin Luther King, Jr.—were assassinated. Other prominent blacks were killed, including a number of the most active, outspoken leaders of the militant Black Panther Party. Large segments of the white public were terrified of blacks revolting, and so many whites were willing to accept if not condone the killings of black leaders. The only killing of a black leader that created widespread public sympathy among whites was the assassination of Martin Luther King, Jr., and King always advocated nonviolence in protest activity.

## Situation of Blacks Today

An assessment of the situation of blacks in different institutional areas shows progress has occurred, and some of this progress took place during the protest years. In the case of *Plessy* v. *Ferguson* (1896), the Supreme Court affirmed state court rulings that separate facilities for blacks and whites could exist as long as the facilities were equal. This segregationist standard survived largely unchallenged for nearly sixty years until *Brown* v. *the Topeka, Kansas, Board of Education* (1954). At that time the Supreme Court declared that the segregation of public schools is illegal and that separate educational facilities are "inherently unequal." The same philosophy supported the Civil Rights Act of 1964, which legislated against discrimination in employment and the use of public facilities and threatened to withdraw federal funding from organizations practicing racial discrimination. In addition, during the mid-1960s, strong federal legislation assured equal rights for blacks and other minorities in voting and housing. Enforcement of the legislation, however, has been difficult because a limited number of government personnel have been available for the task, and their powers are often sharply restricted.

Blacks have tended to live in segregated, crowded, low-quality housing. The fact that blacks are usually poorer than whites is one reason housing for blacks is relatively inferior. Other reasons also exist. Federal government housing policy supported segregation until the 1960s, and it has taken a limited role in opposing segregated housing since then. Real-estate agents have often cooperated with neighborhood associations and banks to keep blacks and other minorities out of all-white residential areas. Sometimes zoning restrictions exist, such as a minimum lot size, and in many cases

**244** local politicians will rigidly impose restrictions on blacks but relax them for whites. In addition, many blacks are reluctant to leave inner-city areas, not wanting to destroy their community ties and feeling wary about possible hostile reactions from whites in a new neighborhood.

In spite of these problems, blacks sometimes do seek housing in all-white areas. A black woman with whom I spoke offered this reason: "Some whites believe I want to come into an all-white neighborhood as a status move. Nothing could be farther from the truth. The fact is that a white neighborhood is the only place I can hope to find a decent place to live."

As far as jobs, income, and education are concerned, improvements for blacks have occurred, but these must be kept in perspective. A gradual increase in the percentage of blacks in white-collar jobs and in skilled blue-collar jobs has taken place, but blacks still dominate in the low-skilled, low-paid jobs. The fact that black income has remained about 60 percent of white income since 1966 serves as a reminder of that fact. It is noteworthy that the percentage gap was actually narrower before the 1954 Supreme Court decision against school desegregation, a decision supposed to be a major step in eliminating discrimination against blacks. The amount of education people receive influences their occupational and income opportunities. Thus it is significant that on the average, there is a gap of more than two years of schooling between blacks and whites. In addition, predominantly black schools are inferior to predominantly white schools in multiple respects—for example, in peer stimulation offered, in the age and condition of school buildings, and in the range and quality of facilities and supplies (such as science and language laboratories, textbooks, and libraries) (Bailyn et al., 1977; Blackwell, 1975; Farley, 1977; Killian, 1975).

With financial austerity in the 1970s and 1980s, there has been a strong effort to cut back on programs that have benefited poor citizens, many of whom are black. One social scientist has suggested that the 1980s features what he has called "respectable racism." Code words such as "tax revolt," "competency-based education," "merit," and "tuition tax credits" are polite yet effective means of discriminating against many black citizens, without ever bringing up the issue of race (Piliawsky, 1984).

## Hispanic-Americans

Americans of Spanish descent number over 14.7 million and are classified separately from whites in the census records. About 8.9 million are Chicanos (Mexican-Americans), 2.2 million are Puerto Ricans, and the remaining 3.6 million come primarily from Central America, South America, or Cuba. Although Chicanos and Puerto Ricans both speak Spanish, there are marked differences in historical experience and cultural tradition.

### Chicanos

The first serious colonization by the Spanish occurred north of Sante Fe, New Mexico, in 1598, more than twenty years before the Plymouth settlement in Massachusetts. Large-scale Mexican immigration to the United States, however, did not start until the social upheaval accompanying the Mexican Revolution of 1909. During the next two decades, migration was steady, and by the early 1930s, there were nearly 1.5 million Chicanos. Migration declined during the war years when Mexican farming was prosperous, but since the 1950s a steady flow of Mexicans has occurred. In the middle 1980s, worsening economic conditions in Mexico and Central America produced an increase in illegal immigration. The number of illegal immigrants captured was 40 percent higher in 1986 than in the previous year. According to immigration officials, 1500 people a day were arriving by train at Mexicali, Mexico, and most were continuing by bus to Tijuana on the border. The combined impact of rapid immigration and a high fertility rate have made Mexican-Americans the fastest growing of all ethnic or racial groups in the United States.

Mexican-Americans are frequently poor and badly educated. The Chicano population aged fourteen or more averages about two-and-a-half years less schooling than whites and about $7500 less income per family in a given year. Most Mexican-Americans are blue-collar workers, primarily in service jobs. Only about 7 percent of men and about 3 percent of women do farm work, an occupation that many Americans closely associate with Chicanos.

One of the reasons many Americans associate Chicanos with farm work is the well-publicized and remarkably successful effort of Cesar Chavez and his associates to organize migrant Mexican-American workers into the National Farm Workers' Association, which has sought to obtain livable wages and benefits for union members. Among Chicano youth extensive political organizing has occurred in recent years. A Chicano political party exists— *La Raza Unida*. The sense of ethnic identity and pride that has developed in the course of these political activities is called "Chicanismo."

Chicano political militancy combined with extensions of the Voting Rights Act of 1965 and growing mainstream political activity have helped win an increase in elected political positions. Between 1950 and 1979, the number of Chicanos in five southwestern state legislatures increased from twenty to eighty-two. Mexican-Americans have not done as well in Congress. In 1983 they had only six congressmen and no senators. Nonetheless, Mexican-American political activity is extensive at the federal level. A number of well-organized interest groups present the Chicano or Hispanic cause, and since the "Viva Kennedy" campaign in 1960, both political parties have made efforts to gain the Mexican-American vote (Moore and Pachon, 1976; Pachon and Moore, 1981; Shenon, 1986).

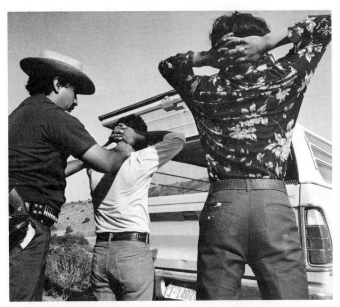

*Although some individuals illegally entering the U.S. from Mexico are arrested and deported, illegal immigration from Mexico and its equally impoverished neighboring countries continues at a rapid rate.*

## Puerto Ricans

In October 1898 Puerto Rico became an American possession, permitting people to move back and forth without restriction between the island and the mainland. By 1910 about 1500 Puerto Ricans had come to New York City, and their number rose to about 70,000 in 1940. Many of the early migrants were merchants who had lost their businesses when sugar became the dominant island crop. On the mainland, jobs were available because of the restrictions in European immigration.

The major migration of Puerto Ricans started after World War II. Most of the new arrivals came in search of better-paying jobs. The majority of Puerto Ricans moving to the mainland still settle in New York City, but urban concentrations are developing in Chicago, Philadelphia, Jersey City, Newark, Los Angeles, Miami, and a number of other cities.

Occupationally and economically, Puerto Ricans have a difficult time in the United States. They have generally suffered high unemployment, with their rates running about double those of non-Hispanics. Family income averages scarcely half that of American families overall, and two out

of five Puerto Rican families fall below the official poverty level. The professional contingent is small, with under 4 percent of the group having graduated from college.

Because of nonrestrictive travel and the closeness of the island to the mainland, Puerto Ricans, unlike other migrants, often return to their ethnic homeland. Trips to the island are made in order to visit relatives, or sometimes, if living on the mainland proves unsatisfactory, to resettle permanently. For many members of this ethnic group, adjustment to life in New York City and other cities has been difficult. Often language barriers increase the problem of finding a job. Then, too, there is a more pronounced color discrimination than exists in Puerto Rico.

On the other hand, Puerto Ricans choosing to return to the island encounter some definite difficulties. In Puerto Rico the unemployment rate approaches 40 percent with about 56 percent of the islanders receiving food stamps. Wage levels are lower than in the United States. The alcoholism rate, the suicide rate, and the automobile-accident rate are much higher than in the United States. With such poor conditions on the island, it is not surprising that a recent study concluded that stu-

*As with other racial and ethnic groups, many members of the Puerto Rican community who accept their minority status have done so with great pride and self-respect, resisting pressures to assimilate themselves completely into the dominant culture.*

dents who returned to Puerto Rico to live permanently had a less positive image of their teachers, schools, and themselves than a matched group of students who moved back and forth between Puerto Rico and the mainland (Fitzpatrick, 1975; Fitzpatrick and Parker, 1981; Prewitt-Diaz, 1984).

Puerto Ricans and other Hispanic-Americans fall below American averages educationally and economically. Table 10.2 offers some comparisons involving blacks, whites, and Hispanic-Americans.

## American Jews

It is not simple to determine the criteria that make a person a Jew. Certainly Jews are not a race. Among Jews one will find a wide variety of head and nose shapes, skin types, body builds, and hair colors. Jews also do not form a religious group. They include agnostics, atheists, and also converts to many different religions. Nor are Jews a nation. They come from many countries. It seems that the critical factor is "the consciousness of being a Jew." In short, Jews are people who think of themselves as Jews and are considered by others to be Jewish. Even in Israel, the reestablished homeland of Jews, uncertainty exists on this topic. Onetime Prime Minister Ben-Gurion suggested that ". . . being a Jew is so difficult that anyone professing to be one should be believed" (Berry and Tischler, 1978: 29–30).

The largest number of Jews reached the United States in the late nineteenth and early twentieth century from eastern Europe, where they had been poor, living in segregated villages or city ghettos. About 5.9 million Jews now live in the United States, forming about 2.6 percent of the American population. About three-quarters of American

**Table 10.2**
**Some Important Statistical Facts in the Lives of Whites, Blacks, and Hispanic-Americans**

| ISSUE | TOTAL POPULATION | WHITE | BLACK | HISPANIC |
|---|---|---|---|---|
| Median family income | $24,580 | $25,757 | $14,506 | $16,956 |
| Percent of persons below poverty line | 11.6% | 9.1% | 30.9% | 25.2% |
| Education[1] | | | | |
|   Four years of high school or more | 73.3% | 75% | 58.5% | 47.1% |
|   Four years of college or more | 19.1% | 19.8% | 10.4% | 8.2% |
| Lifetime births expected from a woman 18 to 34 | 2.079 | 2.064 | 2.16 | 2.405 |
| | | Male Female | Male | Female |
| Life expectancy (in years)[2] | 74.7 | 71.8  78.8 | 67.3 | 75.2 |

[1] All education figures are for people 25 years and older.
[2] The life expectancy figures compare whites to nonwhites.
Sources: Adapted from U.S. Bureau of the Census. *Current Population Reports, Population Characteristics: 1984*, Series P–20, No. 386. Table 2; U.S. Bureau of the Census. *Statistical Abstract of the United States: 1986*. Tables 106, 216, 753, and 770.

*Whites fare better than blacks and Hispanic-Americans on all these measures. Hispanic-Americans average higher income than blacks while blacks tend to be better educated.*

Jews live in large cities or their suburbs. Nearly half reside in the greater New York City area.

Jews often have been the target of hostile stereotypes and prejudices. **Anti-Semitism** is the complex of prejudicial attitudes toward Jews. The roots of this behavior lie in historical and economic conditions that go back many centuries in Asia and Europe. Anti-Semitism has also occurred in America. By the 1880s Jews appeared in newspaper and magazine cartoons that pictured them as "long-nosed, garishly dressed merchants speaking in broken English" or as revolutionaries trying to take over the American government. Industrialist Henry Ford contributed to anti-Semitism, financing a crusade against Jews in the 1920s. In recent years a gradual improvement in feelings toward Jews has occurred. In a national survey conducted in 1981, 40 percent of the sample had a highly favorable opinion of Jews, up from 33 percent in 1975 (Gallup Organization, *Gallup Poll.* April 16, 1981).

In spite of discrimination against them, American Jews have tended to be unusually successful in their occupational pursuits and income attainment. Success, however, often developed under trying circumstances. In the 1930s, for example, Jews were heavily represented in clothing, textiles, films, and other industries on the edge of the mainstream economy and vulnerable to unusually high risk. In Carey McWilliams's phrase, Jews were "the ragpickers of American industry." In the 1950s American Jews showed a much higher proportion of men in white-collar employment than the national average. Yet from 1900 to 1950, Jews obtained few top-management positions, a fact suggesting that in this area Jews have also been the victims of discrimination.

For American Jews two significant trends have been occurring in the past twenty years. As Jews have divested themselves of their languages and customs and moved into higher-status jobs, an increasing amount of intermarriage has taken place. At the same time, there has been a renewed interest in the survival of Jews as a distinct ethnic and religious group. Signs of this shift have been a revitalization of Jewish religious traditions, a greater focus of Jewish philanthropies exclusively on the needs of Jews, and a renewed emphasis on the importance of commemorating the Holocaust with courses, memorials, and museums (Cohen and Fein, 1985; Quigley and Glock, 1979; Sklare, 1971; Waxman, 1981).

# Asian-Americans

There are about 2.5 million Asian-Americans in the United States. About 800,000 are of Chinese, 700,000 are of Japanese, and 260,000 of Vietnamese descent. Although Asian-Americans reside in communities throughout the country, the West Coast, especially California, is where most live. In Hawaii, Asian-Americans probably maintain greater economic and political prominence than in any other state.

## Chinese-Americans

After 1850 Chinese arrived in the United States in substantial numbers and sought employment as laborers for mines and railroads. Within several decades the Chinese had become a source of fear to whites, who felt that they were a "yellow peril" that hated American institutions and only maintained loyalty to the homeland and their emperor. Motivated by fear, Congress passed the Chinese Exclusion Act of 1882, and the rate of immigration declined sharply.

Many Chinese-Americans have remained in ghettos (Chinatowns) and have suffered from the problems that usually accompany depressed urban living. The Chinatowns of America are located in the most deteriorated parts of cities. In New York City's Chinatown, more than a third of the tenements have rats and three-quarters have roaches. In San Francisco two-thirds of Chinatown housing is substandard compared to one-fifth substandard for the rest of the city. The Chinatowns across the country have become seriously overcrowded because of recent immigration.

Overall, however, the Chinese have done well in basic achievement areas. Twenty-five percent of group members have received a college degree; the national average is scarcely half that figure. Twenty-nine percent of Chinese-Americans are professionals, and once again the national average is little more than half that number. Furthermore the median family income for Chinese-Americans is slightly higher than the overall amount.

One reason for the success of the Chinese seems to have been their willingness to adjust to the standards of American life. For instance, immigrant parents generally do not try to restrict their children's career or marital choices. In spite of their own flexibility, the Chinese have often found evidence that they have not been accepted as full-fledged members of American society. As a college professor who was a third-generation American, a Korean War G.I., and a Stanford doctorate noted, it is infuriating to be frequently asked such questions as "How long have you been in the United States?" and "Where did you learn to speak English so well?" (Ikels, 1985; Kitano, 1981; Lyman, 1977; Ten Broeck, Barnhart, and Matson, 1968).

### Japanese-Americans

Japanese began arriving in the United States in the 1880s, at the time when restriction on Chinese immigration was occurring. About 28,000 Japanese settled in the United States between 1880 and 1900 and then over 213,000 in the next twenty years as demands for low-wage agricultural workers grew on the West Coast. By the first decade of the twentieth century, the hostile, fearful images that had developed toward the Chinese started focusing on the Japanese: "Now the Jap is a wily an' a crafty individual—more so than the Chink," warned one writer in the *Sacramento Bee* (Okimoto, 1971: 15).

In spite of discrimination, the West-Coast Japanese were successful as farmers, gardeners, and business people. In March of 1942, the *Los Angeles Times* revealed that Japanese agricultural products brought $40 million in sales annually. Japanese-Americans were growing 40 percent of the crops produced in California, on over 200,000 acres of land. As we have noted, this economic success did not protect Japanese-Americans during World War II. The American government ordered the forcible evacuation of 110,000 people of Japanese ancestry from the West Coast on the pretext that they might aid the Japanese war effort against the United States. In 1983 a group of former camp inmates initiated a suit seeking billions of dollars from the government on behalf of inmates and their descendants. Three years later the suit was still tied up in court.

The forced migration was devastating to Japanese-American families. The average loss per family was about $10,000 in goods, property, income, and expenses (in 1940, preinflated dollars). Yet after World War II, Japanese-Americans were able to reestablish themselves in the American economy. Like the Chinese, the Japanese have used education as a means of self-advancement. In recent years Japanese-Americans have had the highest college completion rate of any group in U.S. society, including majority groups. Furthermore

the annual income has averaged above the national average.

Japanese-Americans have been having an increasing amount of contact with other groups, and by 1985 over half of all new Japanese-American marriages have involved a non-Japanese spouse. Reasons for the increase include the lessening of segregation and isolation, economic mobility, and the declining control imposed by the Japanese family (Connor, 1977; Fugita and O'Brien, 1985; Kitano, 1981; Leighton, 1964; Taylor, 1986).

### Vietnamese-Americans

The arrival of the Vietnamese in the United States has produced publicity out of proportion to their numbers. Some of the approximately 260,000 refugees arriving in the United States were "boat people," who left Vietnam, Laos, and Cambodia in small, often ill-equipped craft. Some died en route, but many others were picked up at sea, brought to temporary compounds, and then distributed to various countries. Other Vietnamese reaching the United States were war orphans adopted by American families, and a few children were American servicemen's offspring who joined their fathers. Understandably many newly arrived Vietnamese felt confused and alienated. In part, such a reaction occurred because of the disruptive conditions under which they departed, but it also took place because of the significance of what was left behind: a family network in which rights and duties were clearly specified, and a sense of interdependence, support, and belonging were strongly emphasized.

Compounding these immigrants' problems has been the fact that they have arrived in the United States during a difficult economic era. Frequently they have found themselves pitted against American citizens in the struggle to make a living. In Texas some fishermen working in the Gulf of Mexico have charged that since the arrival of the Vietnamese, certain areas have been fished out. To protest the increased competition, a local chapter of the Ku Klux Klan sponsored a fish fry during which the participants burned a fishing dinghy labeled the "U.S.S. Viet Cong." In Denver, workers in a meat-packing plant were furious when they were dismissed and Vietnamese were hired at half the wage they had received (*New York Times,* February 26, 1981; Schmidt, 1981; Timberlake and Cook, 1984).

*Many Vietnamese-Americans are rapidly integrating themselves into mainstream American society, despite the difficulties of relocating and gaining acceptance among established communities.*

Since the newly arrived Vietnamese are often willing to work hard for low wages, they are likely to find themselves in the midst of similar disputes in the future. This general willingness to work hard also makes it likely that the Vietnamese, like earlier American ethnic groups, will become progressively integrated into the educational, economic, and social mainstream.

## Native Americans

The number of Native Americans or Indians is about 1.4 million at present. When Columbus arrived in America (San Salvador) in 1492, the figure was only slightly less, probably between 700,000 and a million. Experts believe that the number declined to under 250,000 at the end of the nine-

teenth century, and the Indian population has increased steadily since then.

Native Americans treated early European settlers well. For example, most of the English people who landed at Plymouth in 1620 probably would have starved without gifts of corn and information about how to fish and grow corn. As more settlers arrived, they sought increasing amounts of land. The American government signed many treaties with Indian tribes, but when new arrivals needed more land, the government agreed that they could break the treaties. If the Native Americans resisted the invasion of their lands, then the military imposed compliance.

Eventually the Indians had to leave their lands and enter reservations. This policy weakened or destroyed their traditional economies (such as the buffalo-hunting life-style of Plains Indians), political systems, and religious systems. In addition, the requirement that children enter white schools undermined the family structure. Control of the reservations was strict, and yet some rebellions did occur.

Perhaps the best known rebellion was nonviolent. It was called the Ghost Dance, and in 1890 the practice of this dance spread quickly from tribe to tribe. The belief behind the dance was that some day all Indians, both the living and the dead, would unite on a new earth containing great herds of buffalo and wild horses and protected from death, disease, and misery. Those who performed the Ghost Dance would supposedly rise into the air and remain suspended until the new earth moved into place beneath them. Then they would come down onto this new earth, that was without white people but did contain all their ancestors.

Government and military personnel watched warily as the Ghost Dance developed. They acknowledged that it was nonviolent, but they were apprehensive about the enthusiasm for traditional customs and activities it generated. Then, when it seemed that the renowned Sioux warrior Sitting Bull was joining the movement, government officials became increasingly nervous. Officials ordered the arrest of Sitting Bull, and when he resisted, he was shot and killed. Two weeks after Sitting Bull's death, a Sioux chief named Big Foot was leading his people toward Pine Rock reservation, hoping to find protection from the army. At Wounded Knee, South Dakota, the cavalry stopped the march to check the men for weapons. Fighting broke out, and about 150 men, women, and children were killed. Many were wearing the fabled ghost shirts, which were supposed to protect the wearers from any harm, including bullets. With the Wounded Knee Massacre, the belief that Indians would be elevated to a better existence ceased to exist.

In modern times Native Americans retain less than 3 percent of the land area in the United States. Officials of the Bureau of Indian Affairs estimate that Indian land ranges between critically and slightly eroded. None of it is prime land for supporting crops or animals. Native Americans are the poorest ethnic group in the United States. Per capita income is less than 60 percent of the American average. The male unemployment rate is three times the national average. The same trend holds for education, with the Indian dropout rate from high school twice the national figure. In addition, crime and delinquency rates have been high, and the adolescent suicide rate in the 1960s was 100 times the rate for the general population. During that decade death from tuberculosis was 400 times the national average.

Indians approach the future in different ways. Some believe that like all bad experiences, domination by white Americans will pass. Others have launched a legal battle to protect their rights and reclaim their lands. One significant activity has been the renewal of tribal traditions. Many tribes now emphasize teaching the younger generation tribal languages, craft skills, tribal histories, and religious ritual and ceremonies. Will these revitalized cultural traditions continue to develop, or will they be submerged by the continuing efforts to Americanize Native Americans in schools and jobs? Many modern Indians are fearful that the latter course of action will dominate (Brown, 1972; Deloria, 1981; Hodge, 1981; Robbins, 1984; Utley, 1963).

In the last few pages, we have been reading about the history of various racial and ethnic groups. As the following Contemporary Issue indicates, modern novelists' works also examine many of the topics we have discussed.

---

**CONTEMPORARY ISSUE**

*Prejudice and Discrimination in Modern Literature*

Prejudice is a highly negative judgment toward a group, and discrimination is the behavior by which one group prevents or restricts another group's access to scarce resources. In recent years many novelists have been writing about the impact of prejudice and discrimination. A well-written novel can be particularly effective in representing the negative emotions surrounding these issues. Between 1982 and 1985, three prominent novelists published books about the prejudice and discrimination suffered by their respective ethnic groups. The three groups, all of which are discussed in this chapter, are blacks, Mexicans, and Native Americans.

In *The Color Purple,* Alice Walker wrote about rural life in the American South in the 1930s. As we have already noted, in that time and place, whites were often free to terrorize blacks. One day Sofia, a strong-willed black woman, was in town with her children. The mayor's wife complimented her on how clean her children were and asked Sofia if she'd like to work as her maid. "Hell no!" she said. The mayor came forward and asked her to repeat the words. "Hell no!" she said again. He slapped her. She slapped him back, and then she knocked him down. The police came, and they beat her. A friend described Sofia after the beating.

> When I see Sofia I don't know why she still alive. They crack her skull, they crack her ribs. They tear her nose loose on one side. They blind her in one eye. She swole from head to foot. Her tongue the size of my arm, it stick out tween her teef like a piece of rubber. She can't talk. And she just about the color of eggplant.
>
> *(Walker, 1982: 87)*

When Sofia recovered, she was sent to prison. Then when she was released from prison, she was required to work as a maid for the mayor's family.

In *The Old Gringo,* Mexican novelist Carlos Fuentes wrote about a different kind of oppression. People from the United States, the author emphasized, were determined to compel Mexicans to embrace their own cultural standards. The Mexicans, they believed, needed to be scrubbed, educated, modernized, and democratized, while according to one of the novel's Mexican characters, the Yankees for their part surely ". . . did not enjoy good food . . . or beautiful churches, and broke with all tradition just for the sake of it, as if there were good things only in the future and in novelty. . ." (Fuentes, 1985: 128).

By the end of the account, the principal woman in the story—a school teacher from Washington, D.C.— began to understand that it was not important to save Mexico for progress and democracy but ". . . that what mattered was to live with Mexico in spite of progress and democracy" (Fuentes, 1985: 187). However, her understanding and her words had no impact on her fellow citizens, who were convinced that the United States had to lead Mexico into the modern world. Fuentes's novel takes place in Mexico early in this century, and yet what he said about the failure of people in the two cultures to understand each other certainly has implications for current relations between Chicanos and members of the dominant American culture.

In *Love Medicine,* Louise Erdrich also examined the impact of prejudice and discrimination upon an ethnic group—Native Americans. At one point a young man went to mass with his grandfather. The old man yelled his prayers, and the grandson was embarrassed. The young man explained:

> So afterwards I out and asked him. "How come? How come you yelled?"
> "God don't hear me otherwise," said Grandpa Kashpaw.
> I sweat. I broke right into a little cold sweat at my hairline because I knew this was perfectly right and for years not one damn other person had noticed it.
>
> *(Erdrich, 1984: 194)*

The young man went on to review the misfortunes that had occurred to friends and family members. Then he mentioned old-time Indians who had been purposefully infected with diseases or butchered by whites. Yes, he concluded, his grandfather was correct: God certainly could not hear the Indians very well.

These are just three examples of how modern novelists have examined prejudice and discrimination against their own ethnic groups. In the years ahead, there undoubtedly will be many new works that also effectively illustrate these processes.

Sources: Louise Erdrich. *Love Medicine.* New York: Holt, Rinehart and Winston. 1984; Carlos Fuentes. *The Old Gringo.* New York: Farrar, Straus, and Giroux. Translated by Margaret Sayers Peden and Carlos Fuentes. 1985; Alice Walker. *The Color Purple.* New York: Pocket Books. 1982.

## White Ethnics

White ethnics are primarily of Irish, Italian, Polish, Slavonic, and Greek origin. They generally come from southern and eastern Europe and often have a Catholic heritage. They are usually blue-collar workers with incomes slightly below the national average. Part of the enormous popularity of the television program "All in the Family" was that Archie Bunker expressed the furies and frustrations often attributed to white ethnics. Archie was an unabashed, devout conservative, suspicious of and hostile toward blacks, Puerto Ricans, and other nonwhite ethnics, contemptuous of people on welfare, and unyieldingly, unquestioningly patriotic. Others in public life have expressed the same fears and frustrations. During Nixon's first term, Vice-President Spiro Agnew gained great popularity speaking out for what he called the "Silent Majority" of hard-working, nonprotesting, patriotic Americans, many of whom were white ethnics.

Some evidence, however, disputes a conservative stereotype for white ethnics. A study suggested that white Catholics were more likely than white Protestants to have opposed the Vietnam War and to have supported such liberal causes as a guaranteed annual wage, governmental assistance for the poor, medicare, and the racial integration of public facilities (Greeley, 1977: Chapter 5).

Among the most traditional white ethnics are farmers who lead isolated lives and as a result tend to maintain cultural patterns from other countries for many generations. For other white ethnics, particularly those who move to suburban areas, the sense of ethnicity rapidly fades. Factors contributing to this loss of identity are an increased rate of intermarriage, physical breakup of the extended family, decreasing influence of religious organizations, and integration into the local educational, occupational, and recreational structures (Alba, 1981; Fallows, 1979; Novak, 1972; Salamon, 1985).

The present discussion of racial and ethnic groups provides a background for a consideration of some future trends.

## Moving toward the Twenty-First Century

One theme that has been carried through this chapter is the idea that ethnic consciousness frequently emerges within American racial and ethnic groups. On the question of whether a revival of ethnic consciousness is good for America, the two broadest positions would indicate:

*No.* Increasing ethnic consciousness means the projection of individual conformity or "groupism." As more ethnic groups enter a society, the keener the struggle becomes for the scarce resources of power and wealth and the greater the pressure for each group to develop a unified set of ethnic interests. Americans should disavow the "ethnic crutch," breaking away from their individual group affiliations and seeking self-betterment and success on their own (Patterson, 1982).

*Yes.* In truth, no ethnic revival is necessary. Ethnic pluralism has been an ongoing condition since the beginning of the United States. Those who oppose continuing ethnic diversity often seek a neat, homogenized society dominated by "Americanized" standards that downgrade the cultural influence of any people whose ancestors were not from northern Europe. The maintenance of ethnic consciousness permits the members of a racial or ethnic group to come to grips with their own "roots," thereby allowing them to become more thoroughly developed, vital people (Greeley, 1982).

In the 1980s these two positions—the Americanization and pluralist perspectives—are likely to clash over such issues as the following:

*No special recognition or differential treatment.* Those supporting Americanization emphasize that government should provide no formal recognition to categories of people based on race or ethnicity, leaving people free to work out things for themselves. On the other hand, pluralists indicate that racial and ethnic groups should receive separate recognition, with a formula insuring increased opportunities for the less advanced groups to make up "lost ground." In the United States, government-mandated affirmative action programs in employment and education and also busing of schoolchildren are current illustrations of this second approach.

*Contact or separation.* The Americanization position stresses that ideals of freedom and equality develop most effectively if all citizens readily establish friendships and marriages across all racial and ethnic boundaries. In contrast, the supporters of ethnic pluralism emphasize that ethnic-group membership plays an important role in educational access, occupational placement, and income. Thus pressure exists to stay within one group for marital partners, personal friendships, and work contacts.

*Area openness or exclusivism.* The proponents of Americanization recall the racial segregation of public facilities and residential areas and vow that such practices must disappear from U.S. society. The pluralist supporters are not necessarily staunch advocates of separation, but they reserve the right to establish ethnic neighborhoods, schools, and other structures if their development will foster an effective ethnic consciousness and pride.

*One language versus many.* The supporters of Americanization and the backers of pluralism sharply divide here. The first group believes that institutionally one language should prevail in this country. In schools English should be the only language, and the central issue for children of a non-English-speaking background is the need to catch up with the other children. The pluralists strongly disagree, feeling that no reason exists why English should be the only official language. Children should be helped to retain their ancestral language, and perhaps all Americans should be encouraged, even compelled to become bilingual or multilingual. When asked whether state and local governments should conduct business in languages other than English in parts of the country where many people speak another language, 60 percent of the informants in a nationally conducted survey supported the Americanization position, saying to use only English, and 36 percent adopted the pluralist perspective, choosing to use other languages too. (*New York Times/CBS News Poll,* October 26, 1986).

People will discuss and debate such issues in the years ahead. Outcomes are difficult, even impossible to anticipate. Will the fear, anger, and hate that currently exist in American ethnic and racial relations have decreased at the beginning of the twenty-first century? What do you think?

# STUDY GUIDE

## Summary

1. Although all human beings are members of the same species, they are often more inclined to emphasize their racial and ethnic differences than their shared similarities.

2. Certain concepts divide the human species into different categories. Race involves such physical characteristics as skin color and curl of hair, and ethnicity concerns distinctive cultural or national qualities. A minority group is a racial or ethnic category that suffers low esteem and unequal treatment.

3. Prejudice and discrimination are the processes producing minority groups. Prejudice is a highly negative judgment toward a group, focusing on one or more negative characteristics that are supposedly uniformly shared by all group members. Discrimination is the behavior by which one group prevents or restricts another group's access to scarce resources. Prejudice and discrimination do not always occur in tandem, but they often do. Different explanations of prejudice and discrimination exist. Psychological perspectives include a three-stage analysis of the development of prejudice, the authoritarian-personality approach, and the scapegoat theory. Cultural explanations emphasize the contributions of language to prejudice and discrimination and also the part played by the social-distance factor. Economic

**254** issues also encourage the development of prejudice and discrimination.

Studies have examined the effects of prejudice and discrimination. One prominent study found the self-esteem of black children higher than that of white children. It seems likely that such factors as social class and school performance have a more significant effect on children's self-esteem than their race or ethnicity. Besides the harm that it does, prejudice also has functional effects for the majority groups involved.

4. Dominant-group policies toward racial and ethnic groups include extermination, continued subjugation, population transfer, legal protection of minorities, cultural pluralism, and assimilation. Minority responses involve avoidance, acceptance, assimilation, and aggression.

5. The members of American racial and ethnic groups have distinctive histories. Blacks are the largest group, with 26.5 million people representing 11.7 percent of the population. The original American blacks were slaves, and persecution of blacks has persisted since the freeing of the slaves. In the past several decades, some improvements in the economic, political, and social conditions of blacks' lives have occurred. However, in spite of these improvements, current living conditions for blacks still tend to be substantially inferior to the living conditions maintained by whites.

Over 14.7 million people of Spanish descent live in the United States. About 8.9 million are Chicanos, 2.2 million are Puerto Ricans, and about 3.6 million come from Central America, South America, or Cuba. They are frequently poor and badly educated, and the majority work in blue-collar jobs.

The United States has about 5.9 million Jews. They come from many countries and are diversified in religion and biological characteristics. In spite of having been the target of vicious stereotypes and discrimination, Jews have traditionally done well in businesses that were on the edge of the mainstream economy. In recent years Jews have attained income and educational levels that are well above the national averages.

About 2.5 million Asian-Americans live in the United States. About 800,000 are of Chinese, 700,000 of Japanese, and 260,000 of Vietnamese descent. Chinese-Americans began arriving about 1850 and found jobs as laborers for mines and railroads. Many have remained in ghettos and have suffered the problems of depressed living, but overall their educational and income attainments exceed the national average. Japanese-Americans started to reach this country in the 1880s, and in spite of discrimination, they have become the most successful nonwhite ethnic group, both economically and educationally. The Vietnamese have primarily arrived in the past decade. Like earlier ethnic groups, their willingness to work hard for low pay pits them against Americans in a variety of occupations.

At present U.S. society contains about 1.4 million Native Americans, slightly more than when Columbus reached San Salvador in 1492. The history of the relationship of white Americans with Native Americans includes a long string of broken treaties and wars that have forced Indians to inhabit increasingly smaller amounts of inferior land. Today Native Americans are the poorest ethnic group in the United States, and in the 1960s the adolescent suicide rate was 100 times the national average.

White ethnics are primarily of Irish, Italian, Polish, Slavonic, and Greek origin. They generally come from southern and eastern Europe and often have a Catholic heritage. White ethnics are sometimes stereotyped as very conservative, and yet some evidence disputes such a claim. White ethnics and blacks often share common interests, interests that will most effectively prosper with unified action.

6. The resolution to the issue of whether or not ethnic consciousness is good for America will affect the future of ethnic and racial relations in U.S. society. In the years ahead, debate will involve a struggle over choices on such issues as no special recognition or differential treatment, contact or separation, area openness or exclusivism, and one language versus many.

## Glossary

**anti-Semitism**  the complex of prejudicial attitudes toward Jews.

**authoritarian personality**  a personality pattern where the individual rigidly supports conventional middle-class values, uncritically admires and obeys strong, controlling people, bullies the weak, and exhibits extensive superstitions about and fear of the unknown.

**discrimination**  the behavior by which one group prevents or restricts another group's access to scarce resources.

**ethnicity**  a set of cultural or national qualities that distinguishes a particular category of people from other categories.

**ideology**  a system of beliefs and principles that presents an organized explanation of and the justification for a group's outlooks and behavior.

**minority group**  any category of people with recognizable racial, religious, or ethnic traits that place it in a position of low esteem and that serve as the basis for unequal treatment.

**prejudice**  a highly negative judgment toward a group, focusing on one or more negative characteristics that are supposedly uniformly shared by all group members.

**race**  distinct physical characteristics, such as skin color and certain facial features, used to divide people into broad categories.

**racism**  the ideology contending that actual or alleged differences between different racial groups assert the superiority of one racial group. Racism is a rationalization for political, economic, and social discrimination.

**scapegoat theory**  an explanation emphasizing that people blocked from achieving a goal will sometimes be unable or unwilling to take out their frustration on its source, and so they direct their aggression against an accessible individual or group.

**self-fulfilling prophecy**  an incorrect definition of a situation that comes to pass because people accept the incorrect definition and act on it to make it become true.

**social distance**  the feeling of separation between individuals or groups.

**stereotype**  an exaggerated image, maintained by prejudiced people, of the characteristics of the group members against whom they are prejudiced.

## Learning Objectives

After having studied this chapter, you should be able to:

1. Define and discuss race, ethnicity, and minority group.
2. Define prejudice, discrimination, ideology, and racism and distinguish between prejudice and discrimination, providing examples.
3. Identify and analyze the psychological, cultural, and economic explanations of prejudice and discrimination.
4. Discuss the effects of prejudice and discrimination.
5. List and describe the six dominant-group policies.
6. Examine the four minority responses to minority-group status.
7. Discuss the following large, prominent American minority groups: blacks, Hispanic-Americans, Jews, Asian-Americans, Native Americans, and white ethnics.
8. Compare the Americanization and pluralist perspectives on ethnic consciousness.

## Tests

### True–false test

_____ 1. Racial classification often creates a self-fulfilling prophecy.

_____ 2. Prejudice and discrimination have exactly the same meaning.

_____ 3. The authoritarian personality is a personality pattern that no longer exists in modern times.

_____ 4. A recent study of social distance conducted in three British cities concluded that when a particular kind of service required extensive contact between customers and shop keepers, Asians were more likely to patronize white-owned shops.

_____ 5. The economic factor played a significant role in the relocation of Japanese-Americans during World War II.

_____ 6. As a minority response, avoidance means staying away from dominant-group members.

_____ 7. In the 1980s "respectable racism" has involved discrimination using such phrases as "tax revolts," "competency-based education," and "tuition tax credits."

_____ 8. In the middle 1980s, the number of illegal immigrants from Mexico has decreased.

_____ 9. Vietnamese immigrants have encountered hostility in the United States because they have been willing to work hard for low wages, thus competing with other workers for jobs.

_____ 10. Native Americans are the poorest ethnic group in the United States.

## Multiple-choice test

_____ 1. Which of the following statements about race is true?
a. Its classifications are imprecise.
b. There are six categories of race.
c. Members of different races vary considerably in intelligence, creativity, and athletic ability.
d. It never creates a self-fulfilling prophecy.

_____ 2. Which of the following is a psychological explanation for the development of prejudice and discrimination?
a. authoritarian personality
b. stereotype
c. social distance
d. economic incentives

_____ 3. If a racial or ethnic group is easy to identify and weak, it may become the victim of aggression when groups are unable to direct hostility toward the real source of their frustration. This is the basic idea of:
a. the authoritarian personality.
b. the scapegoat theory.
c. social distance.
d. the stereotype.

_____ 4. A dominant-group policy that tends to decrease social distance is called:
a. continued subjugation.
b. legal protection of minorities.
c. population transfer.
d. extermination.

_____ 5. The decision of a light-skinned black person to "pass" into white society is an example of:
a. acceptance.
b. aggression.
c. assimilation.
d. avoidance.

_____ 6. The Supreme Court decision in the case of *Brown* v. *the Topeka, Kansas, Board of Education* (1954):
a. affirmed the doctrine of separate but equal facilities for blacks and whites.
b. declared separate educational facilities to be inherently unequal.

    c. indicated that segregated restrooms are unconstitutional.
    d. stated that interracial dating would be unlawful.

_____ 7. Rapid immigration and a high fertility rate have made which group the fastest growing of all racial or ethnic groups in the United States?
    a. Vietnamese-Americans
    b. Puerto Ricans
    c. Chicanos
    d. Jews

_____ 8. Signs of a renewed interest in the survival of Jews as a distinct ethnic group include:
    a. a revitalization of Jewish religious traditions.
    b. a rapidly rising fertility rate.
    c. a sharp increase in the number of American Jews emigrating to Israel.
    d. a and c

_____ 9. Which statement best describes white ethnics?
    a. They are likely to be Protestant.
    b. They tend to be white-collar workers.
    c. They live only in urban areas.
    d. They have been stereotyped as patriotic and conservative.

_____ 10. Advocates of the ethnic pluralist perspective, contending that a revival of ethnic consciousness is good for America, would support:
    a. no special recognition for people because of race or ethnicity.
    b. intermarriage.
    c. bilingual or multilingual ability.
    d. integration of all residential areas.

## Essay test

1. Define race and ethnicity and consider their sociological significance.
2. Define prejudice and discrimination and discuss in detail situations where both prejudice and discrimination exist as well as a situation where each exists without the other.
3. Summarize two explanations of prejudice and discrimination and analyze an event that illustrates each explanation.
4. What are the principal majority-group policies and minority-group responses? Discuss the relationship between the two sets of behavior, providing several examples. In other words, how will a certain course of action taken by either a majority or minority group affect the other group(s) in question?
5. Summarize the history and current situation experienced by three minority groups examined in Chapter 10.
6. If you were in a position to significantly shape the development of American ethnic and racial relations, would you support an Americanization or an ethnic pluralist perspective? In your discussion refer to three of the issues examined in the last section of the chapter.

## Suggested Readings

*American Jewish Year Book*. Philadelphia: Jewish Publication Society. The leading reference book on American Jews. This yearbook, which has been published annually since 1899, contains new articles in each edition as well as updated biographies, bibliographies, and statistics.

Blalock, Hubert M., Jr. 1982. *Race and Ethnic Relations*. Englewood Cliffs, NJ: Prentice-Hall. A brief, readable introduction to race and ethnic relations, covering a range of important concepts, theories, and processes.

**258**    Brown, Dee. 1972. *Bury My Heart at Wounded Knee.* New York: Bantam. An eloquent, easily read history of the devastations suffered by Native Americans during their first 400 years of contact with whites.

Dworkin, Anthony Gary, and Rosalind J. Dworkin. 1982. *The Minority Report.* New York: Holt, Rinehart and Winston. Second edition. A combination text/reader on ethnic, racial, and gender relations. An introductory section on theoretical perspectives is followed by updated articles on the largest American racial and ethnic groups and on women.

Erdrich, Louise. 1984. *Love Medicine.* New York: Holt, Rinehart and Winston. A vivid, sometimes humorous series of first-person accounts representing modern Native Americans' hardships and tragedies as well as their spiritual resilience.

Grier, William H., and Price M. Cobbs. 1968. *Black Rage.* New York: Basic Books. Two black psychiatrists' analysis of the psychological effects of the oppression American blacks have suffered. The book contains considerable disturbing but thought-provoking case-study material.

Helmreich, William B. 1982. *The Things They Say Behind Your Back: Stereotypes and the Myths Behind Them.* Garden City, NY: Doubleday. An informative, nicely written discussion about American ethnic and racial stereotypes.

Mowat, Farley. 1965. *Never Cry Wolf.* New York: Dell. While observing a family of wolves, a biologist develops a clearer and deeper understanding of them. Although the terms never appear, prejudice and discrimination are central issues of this nicely written, sometimes humorous, and always compelling account.

Myrdal, Gunnar. 1944. *An American Dilemma.* New York: Harper & Row. A massive, influential study of a value clash many white Americans experience between their belief in the equality of all people and their prejudice and discrimination toward blacks.

Ortega, Phillip D. (ed.). 1973. *We Are Chicanos.* New York: Pocket Books. An anthology of creative and political Chicano writing.

Walker, Alice. 1982. *The Color Purple.* New York: Pocket Books. A powerful, often moving account of life for southern blacks in the years before World War II.

Wu, Cheng-Tsu. 1972. *Chink: A Documentary History of Anti-Chinese History in America.* New York: Meridian Books. Important legislation and ordinances against the Chinese appear here, along with an effective introduction and editorial commentary.

X, Malcolm. 1965. *The Autobiography of Malcolm X.* New York: Grove Press. The life story of the man who rose from a career of crime and drug addiction to become a leading spokesman of black rights. Besides Malcolm X's own history, this book gives a vivid picture of the places and times in which he lived.

## Student Projects

1. Read television programming for one week. Tally the number of programs based on or including people belonging to an identifiable racial or ethnic group. What can you conclude, if anything, about the way television represents minority-group members as featured characters? Are minority-group members who are secondary characters represented differently from those who are principal characters?

2. Have minority-group attitudes and behavior changed over time? One, somewhat unusual way to answer this question is to read novels that represent the lives of people from various ethnic groups at different times. Form groups of six to eight students. Each group should choose one ethnic or racial group and every member should read a novel about a different era. After reading his or her novel, each member of the group should be able to summarize the following issues:

a. The life-style of the minority-group members described in the novel.

b. Minority-group members' relationship with majority groups.

c. How members' minority status affects their self-images.
d. How, if at all, members of the minority group plan to change/improve their position in society.

This information should provide basic material for a group report about how minority groups' attitudes and behavior have changed over time.

## Answers to Test Questions

**True–false test**

| | | | | |
|---|---|---|---|---|
| 1. t | 3. f | 5. t | 7. t | 9. t |
| 2. f | 4. f | 6. f | 8. f | 10. t |

**Multiple-choice test**

| | | | | |
|---|---|---|---|---|
| 1. a | 3. b | 5. d | 7. c | 9. d |
| 2. a | 4. b | 6. b | 8. a | 10. c |

# 11
# EMERGING MINORITIES

It was 1885, and Charlotte Perkins Stetson had recently given birth to a daughter, Katherine. She loved the child and referred to her as "a heavenly baby." Yet she was unhappy all the time, and when she nursed the child the tears ran down onto her breasts.

The doctor explained that she had "nervous prostration." To her ". . . a sort of gray fog [had] drifted across my mind, a cloud that grew and darkened" (Ehrenreich and English, 1980: 217). The fog never entirely left Charlotte Perkins Stetson (later Gilman). Years afterwards, in the midst of an active career as a feminist writer and lecturer, she would suddenly feel overwhelmed by the same sense of despair, unable to make even the smallest decision.

Charlotte Perkins Stetson was only twenty-five when depression struck her. Jane Addams, the social reformer, was about the same age, scarcely twenty-one. Addams was affluent, well educated, and anxious to study medicine. Then in 1881 she fell into a "nervous depression" that immobilized her for seven years and continued to disturb her long after she had begun her work as a social reformer.

> She was gripped by "a sense of futility, of misdirected energy" and was conscious of her estrangement from "the active, emotional life" within the family, which had automatically embraced earlier generations of women. "It was doubtless true," she later wrote of her depression "that I was 'Weary of myself and sick of asking what I am and what I ought to be.'"
>
> *(Ehrenreich and English, 1980: 217–218)*

For women like Gilman and Addams, it was not clear what they ought to be. While they might have felt drawn to the "men's world" of business, politics, and science, that world was not ready to accept them. The domestic life, which their mothers and aunts had readily joined, was certainly available to them, but choosing that option meant turning their backs on the progress and opportunities late nineteenth-century society promised. These women felt they had no place to go. They were trapped, isolated, and, in their own perceptions, useless.

In this chapter we discuss three emerging minorities—women, the elderly, and the disabled. Each of these three minorities is "emerging" by starting to overcome the prejudice and discrimination imposed in the past.

About half of the readers of this text are women. One issue that women students might consider is whether or not you have faced discrimination because you are a woman. Perhaps your parents have shown less concern for your education and job plans than they have for your brothers' efforts. Sometimes you might feel that your boyfriend or husband treats you as little more than a sex object. For some of you, discriminatory treatment represents a greater insult than it does for others.

On the other hand, about half of the readers of this text are men. You might examine your approach to women. You might assess whether you value their advice and opinions as highly as you do men's. You might analyze your attitudes and behavior toward the different women with whom you come in contact in the course of a day.

In contrast to women, relatively few of you belong to or have frequent contact with the other two emerging minorities we examine: the elderly and the disabled. Therefore the problems these two groups must face as minorities might seem less familiar to you, but we shall see that in many respects the prejudice and discrimination processes are similar for all three groups.

A chapter on emerging minorities could include some other minority groups: homosexuals, for instance. There was a discussion of this minority group in Chapter 7 ("Gender Roles and Sexuality"). In addition, if the space were available, we might examine people with more than one emerging minority status: for instance, elderly women or the disabled elderly.

## **262** The Emergence of Women

Betty Friedan (1963) has called it "The problem that has no name." It was a "problem that lay buried, unspoken for many years in the minds of American women." It was a sense of dissatisfaction women suffered, and women struggled alone with it. Friedan suggested that as they made beds, bought groceries, or lay beside their husbands at night, housewives had a sense of yearning and a fear that emerged as a silent question: "Is this all?" Each woman was alone, confronting a sense of dissatisfaction for which no label existed. In Chapter 7 ("Gender Roles and Sexuality"), we examined the development of male and female gender roles. In the present discussion, the focus will be on women's minority-group status. We analyze the ideology of sexism, with a consideration of its costs included. Then the focus shifts to the women's movement, the effort to curtail and eventually eliminate women's minority-group status. Finally we briefly discuss the future for women.

### Sexism

Any "ism" is an ideology, a system of beliefs and principles that presents an organized explanation of and justification for a group's outlooks and behavior. **Sexism** is the ideology emphasizing that actual or alleged differences between males and females establish the superiority of males. While sexism can be practiced by both sexes, it usually serves as a rationalization by men for political, economic, and social discrimination against women. Let us consider how the ideology of sexism has traditionally developed in American society.

First, unless observers can distinguish one group from another, then sexism or any other discriminatory practice is impossible. Thus women's visibility makes sexism possible. Their secondary sex characteristics and distinctive manner of dress make them easily distinguishable from men. Even modern "unisex" styles seldom make the designation of a person's sex difficult.

Second, women have been ascribed certain attributes of inferiority. The sexist ideology has emphasized that women are less intelligent than men. At the emotional level, sexism claims that women are more likely to be irresponsible, inconsistent,

and unstable. Frequently descriptions refer to them as "the weaker sex," the reference generally extending well beyond the physical realm.

Third, sexism involves rationalizations about women's status summed up by the following sentence: "Women's place is in the home." The "feminine mystique" in the title of Betty Friedan's well-known book refers to the claim that the "occupation of housewife" will provide a glamorous, fulfilling role for modern women.

Fourth, sexism appears in the behavior patterns women have traditionally learned. These patterns are accommodations to the ascribed attributes and rationalizations of status just described. Traditionally, in the presence of men, women have learned to hide their intelligence or to restrict its demonstration. Women have been expected to be ever smiling, laughing, and helpless in appearance, thereby solidifying the conclusion that they are content with their situation as long as men supply direction and control.

Finally discrimination is an aspect of sexism. In American society women have traditionally encountered more limitations on education than men. In the occupational area, women have suffered confinement to less prestigious jobs, with little access to supervisory positions. In politics women have historically had almost no important roles. Women have also encountered extensive discrimination in everyday life, with men usually given greater leeway in their sexual activity and general public behavior (Hacker, 1951).

Not surprisingly sexism has produced various costs for women.

### *Costs of Sexism*

Three prominent costs involve psychological, career, and physical issues.

#### PSYCHOLOGICAL COST

Americans believe that both men and women possess positive qualities, but those attributed to women have emphatically not been those for which society offers its highest rewards. The positive traits attributed to males include their tendency to be aggressive, independent, unemotional, competitive, skilled in business, self-centered, and capable of leadership. For women the list includes the capacity to be talkative, tactful, gentle, aware of the feelings of others, interested in their own appearance, and quiet (Cox, 1981; Freeman, 1975).

Historically the media have presented a narrow, stereotyped image of women. In 1974 an analysis of ten of the most popular children's television programs found dramatic differences between the treatment of male and female characters. Four of the programs had no regular female characters, and even with these four excluded, the male characters outnumbered the female two to one. Males appeared aggressive, constructive, and helpful, while females normally seemed passive and sometimes were punished if they were too aggressive (Sternglanz and Serbin, 1974). Similar gender-role stereotypes appear in adult programming. In one study it was observed that prime-time television presented about two male characters for every one female, and three-quarters of the leading characters were men. Most of the females did not have jobs, and the successful ones often had special or "magic" powers. For instance, Wonder Woman and the Bionic Woman helped popularize female television characters, but it is noteworthy that when the heroics subsided, Wonder Woman worked as a secretary and the Bionic Woman taught elementary school (Schaffer, 1981: 115).

Although in recent years women have obtained an increasing proportion of significant roles on television, sexist images of women persist in the mass media. A study concluded that network television commercials emphasizing physical attractiveness tend to use female performers and male voice-overs, providing the commentary. Apparently this pattern supports viewers' tendency to link attractiveness to women; men's voices are felt to be authoritative, forging the link between women and attractiveness (Downs and Harrison, 1985). Another recent investigation found that in comic strips men were represented as principal characters far out of proportion to their numbers in the population. Furthermore both women and men tend to be presented in stereotyped roles—women mainly as housewives and mothers and men primarily as breadwinners (Chavez, 1985).

Therefore the psychological cost of sexism is that women have traditionally received negative or restricted images of themselves that tend to lock them into narrow roles offering little opportunity to achieve a high level of income, recognition, or personal satisfaction.

## CAREER COST

If a woman feels fulfilled doing housework, then she suffers no sense of career cost. However, many women do not feel fulfilled when limited to this work role. A study of British women, whose household tasks are basically similar to those of their American counterparts, indicated that 70 percent of the women expressed an overall dissatisfaction in their assessment of housework. The monotony of the work and its loneliness were other frequent complaints. This housewife's statement sums up the most typical criticisms: "It's ridiculous to pretend that anyone actually likes cleaning floors and washing dishes—how can they? Housework is awful work. It's lonely and boring. There's nothing to show for it—it's all got to be done the next day. You don't get paid for it, either" (Oakley, 1974: 186).

Today many women extend themselves beyond the housewife role. Women comprise over half the population and more than 40 percent of the labor force. Yet they are much less successful than men in the occupational realm.

Socialization is one contributing factor. As we saw in Chapter 7 ("Gender Roles and Sexuality"), traditional socialization has emphasized domestic tasks for women and breadwinning tasks for men. No wonder, then, that women seeking careers have often been confused and ambivalent. Perhaps no study makes this condition more apparent than Matina Horner's (1969) research, which involved a sample of ninety female and eighty-eight male students at the University of Michigan. When asked to finish a story about Anne who was at the top of her class after a term in medical school, 65 percent of the women were concerned that Anne would lose her friends, feared that she would tarnish her womanly image, or denied the possibility of a woman finishing so high. Only 9 percent of the men who found John at the top of the class wrote such negative stories about his success. Horner concluded that while many legal and educational barriers to female achievement have been removed, a psychological barrier persists: "The motive to avoid success has an all-too-important influence on the intellectual and professional lives of women in our society" (Horner, 1969: 62). Social scientists have criticized the Horner study in a number of ways, and yet this basic finding remains noteworthy.

Women with successful careers have often received a socialization that has made them feel particularly secure and certain about being successful. Margaret Hennig and Anne Jardim (1977) studied female presidents and vice-presidents of nationally recognized medium-to-large business firms and compared them with a group similar in age, education, and family background whose members had never risen beyond middle management. The basis for the achievement differences apparently lay in the family dynamics. Each high-achieving executive was either an only child or the first born of an all-girl family containing no more than three siblings. Both the mother and father simultaneously valued their daughter's femaleness and achievement and saw no contradiction to the enhancement of both. The parents wanted the girl to learn early to set her own goals and standards of excellence and to gain satisfaction from effectively performing any task she approached. One other distinctive quality about the families of top women executives was that both parents had strong relationships with their daughter. As one informant said:

> From my earliest recollections my parents and I were friends. . . . I always wanted to be just like my mother and just like my father, something which I am sure gave those hearing me say it no end of amusement! Yet in spite of this I think my parents really encouraged me to think through things very carefully and to venture my own opinion, even when I was very very young. I think they really trusted me and I them.
>
> *(Hennig and Jardim, 1977: 84)*

It appears that more than socialization accounts for most women's relatively limited career chances. For instance, the factor of socialization does not seem to account for the fact that between 1956 and 1980, women's earnings declined in relation to men's—from $.63 to $.59 on the dollar. This increased earning gap seems to have several causes.

In the first place, when education, training, and work experience obtained by men and women are held constant, pay differences do occur. Thus to some extent, women are the victims of "unequal pay for equal work." However a more significant factor helps explain sex differences in pay. By and large women and men work in different occupations, and the distribution usually favors higher pay for men. In particular, men have a greater representation in management and administra-

tion, crafts, and transport-equipment operation, and women show a higher percentage in clerical work and service activities (Rotella, 1980). And why do the different distributions occur? Many factors undoubtedly contribute: psychological, educational, and career limits on women most of all.

In spite of the discriminations they have encountered in the work world, women generally dismiss the idea of preferential treatment for jobs and places in college and instead favor ability. When asked whether women and minority groups should receive such preferential treatment, 82 percent of women said no and 11 percent yes. For the overall sample, the figures were almost the same: 83 and 10 percent respectively (Gallup Organization, *Gallup Poll,* May 1981).

Table 11.1 offers some statistics that compare women and men on job types, income, and several other important issues.

**Table 11.1**
**Some Bread-and-Butter Issues: Men versus Women**

|  | FEMALE | MALE |
|---|---|---|
| Education for people 25 and over: 1984 | | |
| Four years of high school or more | 73.1% | 73.6% |
| One year of college or more | 31.3 | 39.0 |
| Four years of college or more | 15.7 | 22.9 |
| Occupation of people 16 and over: 1981 | | |
| White-collar positions | 69.4 | 44.9 |
| Managerial/professional | 23.7 | 25.1 |
| Technical/sales/clerical | 45.7 | 19.8 |
| Blue-collar positions | 30.6 | 55.1 |
| Median income of full-time workers 14 and over: 1983 | $14,479 | $22,508 |

Source: Adapted from U.S. Bureau of the Census. *Statistical Abstract of the United States: 1986.* No. 218, No. 764; U.S. Department of Labor. *Employment and Earnings.* May 1986. Table A–23.

*On bread-and-butter issues, women generally do not fare as well as men—for example, the 1983 woman's median salary was 64.3% a man's median salary. Sometimes gender differences are deceptive at first glance. Thus women have a greater percentage of their workers in white-collar positions than do men, but as the present table indicates, about two-thirds of women's white-collar jobs are in technical/sales/clerical positions, which generally do not pay well.*

PHYSICAL COST

A study suggests that, roughly speaking, women agree on ranking of the hurtfulness of different kinds of violence against women (Leidig, 1981). At the least hurtful end of the continuum is "street hassling," which includes male verbal harassment, rude stares, and noises directed at women as they walk along the street. A more aggressive form of "hassling" is touching or grabbing a woman without her permission, including seemingly accidental physical contact with a woman's body in subways, elevators, or other crowded areas.

A stronger form of harassment would be sexual harassment on the job or sexual abuse by male psychotherapists and other professionals; these acts can extend from patting a woman on her knee or bottom to more extensive sexual overtures. Pornography and prostitution also fall in this intermediate area of the continuum. Both activities designate women as an object for male exploitation, with violence often intruding in fantasy or reality.

The continuum of violence reaches the extreme with outright, unadulterated violence: rape and/or physical abuse. Three prominent types of rape can occur: "date" rape, marital rape, and stranger-to-stranger rape. Police often receive reports of the third type but not of the other two. Nonetheless, it is likely that marital rape occurs more often than stranger-to-stranger rape. Many overt acts of violence against women, such as wife abuse, often contain both a sexual and physical component. An act of violence most people regard as extremely serious is girl-child incest. A trusted family member, usually a father or stepfather, forces a girl to have sexual intercourse with him over a protracted period of time.

Certain trends appear among the violent acts against women. In the first place, nonreporting is a pattern whether the issue is indecent exposure, battering, girl-child abuse, or rape. Reasons for nonreporting include the expectation that nothing will be done, the belief that claims will receive ridicule, and the victims' fear of repercussions if they complain. Another trend has been that violence against women was not considered a serious problem until the advent of the women's movement in the late 1960s. Historically women have listened to jokes about wife battering and rape and heard incest described as "the game the whole family can play." A third trend that appears in the acts of violence against women is the tendency to blame

*Throughout the U.S. women's shelters have been started to assist women and children who are the victims of family violence.*

them for the acts perpetuated against them. When a man is robbed or assaulted, police seldom ask if he provoked the crime, encouraged it, or dreamed about it. However, when a woman is physically or sexually assaulted, she traditionally has had to endure such questions from the police, therapists, physicians, and clergy. (In recent years many police departments have begun to demonstrate increased sensitivity in interviewing rape victims; the use of female officers for this task has been particularly effective.) Closely linked to this blaming-the-victim trend has been a broad belief in "female masochism." A widespread and extremely harmful contention is that women not only do not mind pain and humiliation but that they also often like it — thus the common male claim that rape victims frequently "lie back and enjoy it" (Frieze, 1983; Leidig, 1981; Russell and Howell, 1983).

Because of the toll sexism takes, women have mobilized to combat the inequalities and brutalities imposed on them.

## 266    The Women's Movement

Through the centuries women have become increasingly aware of their position in society. Some prehistoric cave paintings appear to be women's first representation of their social organization. Ancient Sumerian and African mothers wrote poems about being women, and speeches attributed to medieval women condemned as witches have survived to the present. Inevitably women's recognition of their subordinate position has expanded during periods that stressed the importance of new ideas and influences, particularly the significance of individual rights. In the course of the eighteenth-century era called the Enlightenment, the importance of rational thought and the value of the individual man received an increasing recognition. In 1792 Mary Wollstonecraft was extending the Enlightenment tradition when she published *The Vindication of the Rights of Woman.* In this book she stated:

> My own sex, I hope, will excuse me, if I treat them like rational creatures, instead of flattering their fascinating graces, and viewing them as if they were in a state of perpetual childhood, unable to stand alone. . . . I wish to persuade women to endeavor to acquire strength, both of mind and body, and to convince them that the soft phrases, susceptibility of heart, delicacy of sentiment, and refinement of taste, are almost synonymous with epithets of weakness . . .
>
> *(Wollstonecraft, 1980: 459)*

In the early twentieth century, a new wave of enlightenment swept across western Europe and the United States: New ideas and new ways of doing things were supported by the spread of industrialism; World War I and the rise of Marxism occurred; and the behavioral and social sciences developed rapidly. The most concrete accomplishment of the new enlightenment was the 1920 passage of the Nineteenth Amendment, which provided women the right to vote. After the passage of the Nineteenth Amendment, women's activities became less explicitly organized and involved less public fanfare. In the 1920s, however, various important women's organizations were formed: the League of Women Voters, the National Council of Women, and the International League for Peace and Freedom. After World War I, women increasingly entered the public workplace, taking an active role in the trade-union movement and also producing such professional organizations as Business and Professional Women (BPW).

*The first women's movement focused heavily on the right to vote. The modern movement, which evolved in the 1960s and continues today, has sought both broader and more profound changes and has drawn in women from a variety of racial and ethnic backgrounds. Over the past two decades, rallies on behalf of women's rights have become commonplace in the U.S.*

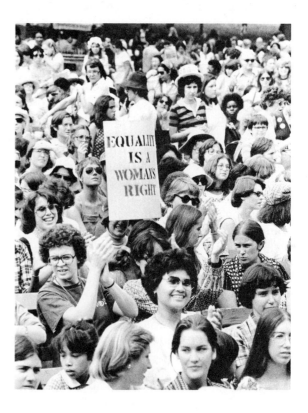

Like earlier women's consciousness efforts, the modern women's movement has been a product of its time. This movement has contained two separate sections. The first, which has been more traditional, received its impetus from the President's Commission on the Status of Women established by President Kennedy in 1961, the challenge to the status quo encouraged by Betty Friedan's bestselling book, and the influence of a "sex" provision in the Civil Rights Act of 1964. In 1966 the National Organization for Women (NOW) was formed. Its members were primarily from the professions, labor, government, and communications and ranged in age from about twenty-five to forty-five. Its self-assigned task was to obtain equality and justice under the law, and its initial target was the executive branch, with the intention of bringing federal power to bear on behalf of women. In the intervening years, NOW's major activities have been in the economic and political spheres, most notably the narrowly defeated effort to seek passage of the Equal Rights Amendment.

The second section of the modern women's movement emerged from the 1960s civil rights and antiwar movements, where general human rights received extensive emphasis but women's rights commanded little attention. The idea of women's "liberation" first appeared at a meeting of Students for a Democratic Society (SDS) in 1965, but the suggestion "was laughed off the floor by the male radicals." Two years later SDS women finally succeeded in passing a resolution calling for the full participation of women in SDS. Such early efforts brought no explicit resolution, but they did help create a "radical community" where women became increasingly aware of shared grievances and intentions. In such a context, five women's groups formed independently in 1967 and 1968 in five different cities: Chicago, Toronto, Seattle, Detroit, and Gainesville, Florida. The initial efforts to publicize a women's movement received an indifferent or hostile reaction from men (Freeman, 1980).

Throughout the 1970s, however, the women's movement has expanded, affecting every aspect of human existence. Its growing influence becomes apparent upon examining the results of a national sample of Americans who were asked whether they favor or oppose most of the efforts to strengthen or change women's status in society today. The percentage favoring an improvement of status has increased from a mere 42 percent in 1970 to 67 percent in 1981 (Louis Harris and Associates, *Harris Survey*, August 1981).

But what about the future of women's rights in America?

## The Future of Women's Rights

Let us focus on the woman interested in the pursuit of full, equal rights. Such a woman believes and supports the pursuit of such rights because without them she feels trapped in a life deprived of meaning and power. But how is it possible for such a woman to establish intimate relations with men? One option emphasized in some women's groups has been to associate as little as possible with men: to avoid having them as lovers or spouses. To most women, however, such a course of action presents another type of deficiency: the denial of their deep-seated belief that heterosexual coupling is a highly desirable part of human existence. Women who maintain this belief and are simultaneously committed to women's rights often find themselves in a difficult position. What does such a woman do if she falls in love with a man who falls far short of her feminist ideals? Does she try to increase his awareness of her own values and needs? Does she grin and bear it? Does she pull out?

The result will vary depending on the people and the circumstances involved. In recent years Betty Friedan (1981) has suggested that women and men would do well to cooperate more fully. Often compromise is possible, in the realm of couples' career and domestic responsibility, for example. According to preliminary research, Friedan reported, many equality-minded women are consciously and effectively implementing two ideologies that most people once considered contradictory. One ideology is the woman-as-individual, often enhanced through a career that women pursue part time or on different shifts from their husbands. The other ideology is woman-serving-her-family, and wives receive support in this area when husbands become more involved in domestic activities than they traditionally have been. Working out such problems seldom makes headlines, and yet the significance of this process for many modern women is enormous.

Compounding many women's difficulties has been the fact that American mothers have received

**268**

relatively little federal help in the area of child-care. In Sweden and Italy, women earn about 80 percent of the male wage, and in France, Germany, and Great Britain, the figure is about 70 percent. In contrast, women in the United States earn about 64 percent of what men do. The major reason for women's greater earning power in European countries has been the various types of governmental economic assistance provided when they have children. In the 1970s and 1980s, American women have pushed effectively for improved rights in the occupational, educational, and credit areas, but their European sisters have fought more effectively for assistance to working mothers (Hewlett, 1986).

The majority of the elderly are women, but whether they are women or men, the elderly frequently encounter patterns of prejudice and discrimination similar to those discussed in the section on women.

---

## Emergence of the Elderly

No one doubted that Alexander Freiheit was a first-rate college teacher. In lecture his breadth of vision gracefully combined with a vast store of anecdotal information about historical figures and events. Throughout the hour Professor Freiheit would pace quickly around the room, seemingly generated by the excitement of the ideas he was

**Figure 11.1**
**Percentage of Population 65 and More in the United States, West Germany, and Japan over Time.**

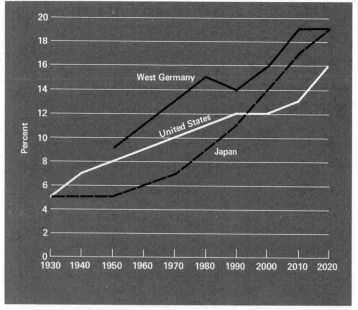

*This graph illustrates that these three advanced industrial nations have a steadily increasing percentage of people in the elderly bracket. (Source: U.S. Bureau of the Census.* Historical Statistics of the United States: Colonial Times to 1970. *Series A 119–134; U.S. Bureau of the Census.* Current Population Reports: Population Estimates and Projection, *No. 74. Tables 4 and 8.)*

expressing. But what about possible signs of senility? When asked, most faculty members readily admitted that Professor Freiheit was considerably more intelligent, alert, and witty than many colleagues half his age. The problem he confronted was bureaucratic. As a publicly funded organization, the university was under the jurisdiction of state law, which required mandatory retirement at age seventy unless the employer—in this case the university president—strongly supported continuing employment. The vice-president, speaking for his superior, refused such support, indicating that the planned "configuration" for the next two decades emphasized the decline of the history department and an increase in other subject areas where student demand was greater. "But the man is irreplaceable," one of Professor Freiheit's supporters argued. "I'm afraid that ultimately everyone is replaceable," the vice-president replied.

A group of students and faculty formed an organization to keep Professor Freiheit employed at the university. They sought and received publicity from the school paper, a faculty newsletter, and the local newspaper as well as support from several local politicians. Finally they initiated a lawsuit, but the judge ruled against the teacher. Professor Freiheit was angry and discouraged. "The president of the United States is two years older than I am, and I could have gone to school with most of the Supreme Court justices. It looks like you need to be prominent and powerful to avoid being put out to pasture."

Obviously Professor Freiheit was feeling that the laws involving retirement were meaningless and that he was powerless to do anything about them. The elderly frequently must face such situations — not an insignificant issue when we consider their numbers. As Figure 11.1 indicates, the American elderly—people aged sixty-five and older—are now about 25 million in number, representing 11 percent of the population, and will increase in both numbers and percentage in the United States and other industrialized nations too. The elderly is the one minority group most of us can eventually expect to join.

In this section we discuss ageism and its costs, the reactions to ageism, and the future of the elderly as a minority group.

## Ageism

**Ageism** is an ideology asserting the superiority of the young over the old. While ageism can be practiced by people of all ages, it usually serves as a rationalization by the nonelderly for economic, political, and social discrimination against the elderly. Like sexism, ageism is a process that is readily apparent in daily life.

First, like sexism, ageism could not occur without high social visibility. The elderly do possess such visibility. Their skin is wrinkled, and some of them walk slowly or stooped over. In addition, the elderly tend to dress more blandly than more youthful people. On this point they can face a dilemma. Colorless elderly fashions mark people off as old, and yet if they wear bright, fashionable clothes, they are accused of "failing to act their age."

Second, the elderly have various negative qualities attributed to them. The prevailing stereotype of old people includes images of physical deterioration, passivity, dependency, rigidity, senility, inefficiency, and the loss of alertness and intelligence (Nuessel, 1982; Williamson, Munley, and Evans, 1980). When adolescent, middle-aged, and elderly people were asked to evaluate adults in these three age groups, the elderly received the lowest overall evaluation (Luszcz and Fitzgerald, 1986).

Third, there is a rationalization of old people's status—the image of the "happy disengager," the picture of smiling, fulfilled elderly people reveling in their extensive free time and nearly endless opportunities to play with grandchildren. But it is not that simple. Research shows that adjustment to retirement depends on such factors as the availability of money, friends, and the capacity to make decisions for oneself (Atchley, 1976).

Like other minority groups, the elderly make some accommodation to their status. This accommodation can appear as a graceful acceptance of retirement, in spite of personal reluctance, or a decision to give short, even truncated responses to an interviewer in order to avoid the slightest hint of being a rambling, senile old person.

Inevitably the elderly face discrimination, with retirement laws having been one of the most obvious illustrations. Thus it was a legislative landmark when Congress, in October 1986, passed a law eliminating mandatory retirement for nearly all employed Americans. Claude Pepper, an eighty-six-year-old Congressman, who was the chief sponsor of the bill, declared, "Abolishing age discrimination will offer new hope to older workers who are desperate to maintain their independence and dignity . . ." (Noble, 1986: E6). The elimination of mandatory retirement has removed the most celebrated example of ageism. The elderly's minority status, however, continues to produce other costs.

*In 1986 Claude Pepper, the oldest member of Congress, was the chief sponsor of the bill which virtually eliminated forced retirement in the U.S.*

## 270   *Costs of Ageism*

In a study of 502 people aged forty-six to seventy-one, the respondents indicated that health was the principal factor contributing to life satisfaction, followed by participation in organizational or group activity, and sense of control over one's destiny (Palmore and Luikart, 1974). Let us consider some ways ageism asserts itself as a cost in each of these areas.

### HEALTH AND MEDICAL-CARE COST

Ageism appears to be a factor that influences health by affecting the quality of medical care. Several studies suggest that generally an inverse relationship exists between a person's age and the speed of emergency treatment—therefore, the older the patient, the more slowly he or she receives treatment (Simpson, 1976; Sudnow, 1967). Certain characteristics of aging people can make

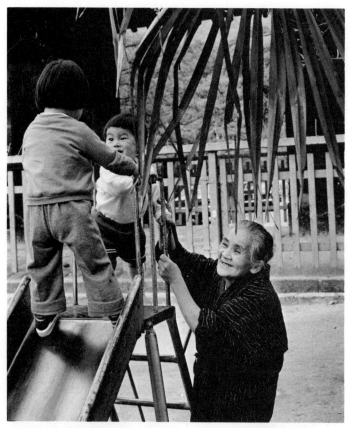

*In Japan, as in some other cultures, older people are regarded as vital contributors to society, both in their role as family members and, for many, as part of the work force.*

them undesirable from a treatment point of view. Old people's illnesses are often chronic, tedious, uninteresting, and difficult to treat. Doctors frequently subscribe to the common sentiment that medical treatment should be immediately successful, not spoiled by situations that defy the doctor's ability to supply an instant cure. Furthermore, like the general public, physicians can be frightened by aging and death (Butler, 1975) and frustrated by family members, colleagues, and hospital administrators who want to prolong life in the inevitably vain hope that somehow a miracle will occur (Duff and Hollingshead., 1968).

The elderly seem to vary considerably in their ability to confront health problems. A recent study found that when urban elderly were involved in social networks composed of neighbors, friends, or kin, they tended to be healthier than old people without such networks (Cohen et al., 1985). Research on medical problems of black and white female elderly concluded that these two categories had some similar coping mechanisms but also some differences. In particular, the black elderly had stronger support from friends, made more extensive use of prayer, and were more inclined to use nonprescription drugs (Conway, 1985).

### GROUP-INVOLVEMENT COST

Often the elderly feel lonely, cut off from frequent, positive interaction with others. One reason some of them commit minor crimes, most notably shoplifting, is to draw attention to themselves. Arrest can lead to sessions with a counselor who can provide a reality-based relationship, or it might produce renewed contact with a distant son or daughter who had ignored many plaintive invitations to visit. "The arrest becomes a reproach: See what you let happen to your father? And to get an extra bit of attention . . . many are arrested on their birthdays" (Gustaitis, 1980: 14). Recent research found that the elderly who are married, healthy (according to their own perception), fairly affluent, socially active, and socially fulfilled tend to be less lonely. In this study the measurement of social fulfillment was compiled from three items — a person's sense of having or not having enough friends, sufficient activities to keep busy, and a sense of being needed—and was the factor which best predicted loneliness (Creecy, 1985).

With the introduction of the concept "disengagement," researchers on aging have addressed the issue of the desirability of elderly people's group involvements. **Disengagement** is a process of mutual withdrawal involving decreasing interaction between an elderly person and others in the social system to which he or she belongs (Cumming and Henry, 1961). Elaine Cumming and William Henry, who developed the concept, originally contended that disengagement was functional for society, providing a process by which power can transfer from older to younger members, and also functional for individuals, initiating a less active and therefore more satisfying life-style. The early usage of the disengagement concept has received widespread criticism. At the very least, the original analysis was an oversimplification. A later study suggested that disengagement only becomes a satisfying outcome if the person voluntarily reduces role commitment and maintains high self-esteem in the process (Neugarten, Havighurst, and Tobin, 1968). Some recent research has emphasized the dysfunctions of disengagement, indicating that the process is likely to be destructive for elderly spouses when they withdraw emotional support, respect, and health-related assistance from each other (Depner and Ingersoll-Dayton, 1985).

The following Cross-Cultural Perspective describes activity that stands in bold contrast to most elderly Americans' experience.

## CROSS-CULTURAL PERSPECTIVE

### The Elderly in Abkhasia

Do the same conditions that encourage long life also discourage disengagement? That is a difficult question to answer. It is clear, however, that in Abkhasia the living situation experienced by the elderly does promote both results.

In the Soviet Republic of Abkhasia, an anthropologist raised a glass of wine to toast a man who looked no more than seventy. "May you live as long as Moses (120 years)," she said. The man was not pleased. He was 119.

No exact figures exist for the total number of aged people in Abkhasia. However, in the village of Dzhgerda, where this researcher did her study, 15 percent of the population was eighty-one and over. In 1954, the last year for which figures are available, 2.58 percent of the Abkhasians were over ninety. For the Soviet Union overall and the United States, the comparable figures were 0.1 and 0.4 percent respectively.

Why the difference? We will see that the elderly Abkhasians experience a number of conditions very different from those encountered by their American counterparts.

First, the life of the Abkhasian elderly has a broad base of uniformity and certainty. Sexual behavior, for instance, occurs without any sense of guilt. It is a pleasurable activity to be regulated for the sake of one's health, like a good wine. The same outlook exists with work. From the beginning of life until the end, Abkhasians do the amount of work they feel capable of doing. Work, they believe, is vital to life, and the concept of retirement is unknown to them. As they become older, they gradually cut back. Observations on twenty-one men and seven women over the age of 100 showed that they averaged a four-hour workday. The men weeded and helped with the corn crop, and the women strung tobacco leaves. They worked at their own pace, moving evenly and without waste motion, taking breaks on occasion. Both the Soviet medical doctors and the Abkhasian elderly feel that work habits have a lot to do with their long lives. The doctors suggest that the work patterns allow the vital organs to function more efficiently. The Abkhasians say, "Without rest, a man cannot work; without work, the rest does not give you any benefit."

Like other elements in Abkhasian life, the diet is stable. Investigators have found that people who are 100 years and older have eaten the same foods throughout their lives. At each of their three meals, the Abkhasians have *abista,* a corn-meal mash cooked in water without salt. Other prominent foods include cheese, buttermilk, fresh fruits, especially grapes, and fresh vegetables, particularly green onions, tomatoes, cucumbers, and cabbage. Although they are the main suppliers of tobacco for the Soviet Union, few Abkhasians smoke. They drink neither coffee nor tea but do consume a local red wine of low alcohol content. At meals the food is cut into little pieces, and the people take small bites, chewing their food very slowly. As a result effective digestion usually occurs.

One more special quality about Abkhasian culture is the highly integrated nature of life coupled with the respected role of the elderly. Abkhasians bear a close, interdependent relationship with a variety of kin, and these relationships tend to enhance the strong sense of security that underlies their existence. For the elderly that sense of security is further entrenched by the deep respect they receive. The elders preside at important ceremonies, mediate dis-

putes, and offer their experience and knowledge about farming. Quite the opposite of burdens, they serve as valued resources. As one ninety-nine-year-old Abkhasian told his doctor, "It isn't time to die yet. I am needed by my children and grandchildren, and it isn't bad in this world — except that I can't turn the earth over and it has become difficult to climb trees."

Source: Sula Benet. "Why They Live to Be 100 or Even Older, in Abkhasia." *New York Times Magazine*. December 26, 1971, p. 3+.

### COST OF LOSING CONTROL OVER ONE'S DESTINY

One of the problems elderly people face is that they encounter many social norms that place highly limiting expectations upon them—in the sexual realm, for instance. As one elderly commentator pointed out, people do not "chide young people for being horny . . ."; there is no such expression as a "dirty young man." The idea of "the dirty old man" is an accusation. The writer noted, "At the nonyouth time of life one has no business . . . being sexual. It is unwarranted, bizarre, if not obscene" (Neubeck, 1981: 314).

Relocation is another issue that can threaten old people's sense of control over their destiny. Choice and predictability are important elements in this process. Older people who relocate voluntarily are likely to adapt better than those who relocate involuntarily. In addition, new environments that are comfortable because of their similarity to the old environment are generally easier to adapt to than those that are less similar (Bourestom and Pastalan, 1981; Schultz and Brenner, 1977).

Adaptation to nursing homes can be particularly difficult. A guiding principle of these organizations is that patients' social and psychological needs are less significant than the efficient performance of patient care. The rigid scheduling of meals and activities as well as movement en masse to entertainment, religious services, or therapy can be efficient practices, but they are highly disruptive activities for people who have lived a largely independent existence (Gubrium, 1975).

Recent research has emphasized the importance of the quality of care provided in nursing homes. Does the nursing staff maintain a rigid, highly controlled setting, where communication between staff and patients and among patients is minimized, or do nurses establish a therapeutic environment, where patients participate in decision-making and meaningful social contacts are maximized? The quality of care is likely to have a significant influence on patients' quality of life in a nursing home (Bagshaw and Adams, 1986).

The elderly encounter ageism and other problems. What measures can they take to improve their situation?

## The Elderly's Fight to Feel Useful and Satisfied

Maggie Kuhn, the founder of the Gray Panthers, an activist organization on behalf of the elderly, has said that three things please her about being old: She can speak her mind, she has succeeded in outliving most of her opposition, and she can reach out to others (Shapiro, 1982: 11). Maggie Kuhn has a useful, satisfying old age. Let us consider the strategies people employ to produce such results at the individual level, at the community level, or at the national level.

Some people focus at the individual level, finding that continuing to work produces positive results. In a study of 4000 retired people who had held a variety of jobs, 73 percent of those who reported that work was a major source of satisfac-

*While many elderly Americans choose to retire, others, like this 70-year-old man, prefer to keep working.*

tion returned to work after retirement (Streib and Schneider, 1971). Others found satisfaction at the individual level in entirely different ways—foster grandparenting, for instance. Before entering such a program, one woman reported that she ". . . felt like I was dead but alive. I wasn't doing much." Her husband had died years earlier, and her children had long since left home. She heard on the radio that a local hospital wanted foster grandparents for retarded children. The prospect frightened her, but she went anyway. She was brought to see a little boy. "They called him a mongoloid, but I couldn't tell. The first thing he did was hug me. He squeezed my legs so tight, I thought I'd fall over. . . . We didn't talk much that day. We just sat and hugged. I felt warm all over" (Hultsch and Deutsch, 1981: 330). This woman eventually became the foster grandparent for five children, and she convinced one of her friends to enter the program.

At the individual level, old people can find different ways to feel useful and satisfied. But can they form a subculture at the community level to accomplish mutually sought goals? The answer, unequivocally, is yes. The inflationary pressures of recent years have provided a major impetus for the elderly to speak out and to act collectively on their own behalf. Like other minority groups, they have started to realize that they will be much more successful if they visualize what they had once considered individual problems as group problems. Thousands of organizations composed of elderly citizens now lobby local government officials on behalf of old people's needs. Housing, medical care, tax relief, and the construction of senior centers are some of the issues dealt with. Many elderly citizens have become highly politicized, recognizing that their power as a voting bloc is sufficiently strong to produce a sympathetic ear from many elected politicians. On the other hand, those who try to organize the elderly often find themselves frustrated. Maggie Kuhn has suggested that many old people "want to keep their lives as bland and as pleasant and as uncontroversial as possible. You don't talk about anything disagreeable" (Shapiro, 1982: 7). Certainly it is a common belief that old age should ideally be a happy time, free of significant worries, when a person can enjoy the well-earned fruits of toil during the earlier years. Organized efforts by the elderly to protest their common grievances hardly support such an image.

What is the possibility for a national subculture of the elderly—a shared sense of age consciousness? One recent summary of research concluded that some evidence supporting such a trend exists.

While the elderly generally do not like to think of themselves as old, there is

> . . . a fellow feeling, a sense of kinship with other elderly. They generally believe that the status of the old should be improved. But there is not a consensus about specific proposals for bringing about change. In general, a picture of age consciousness emerges which is neither clear-cut nor consistent.
>
> *(Foner, 1986: 89)*

What conditions might produce more solidarity among the elderly? One condition might be worsening economic conditions, with growing recognition by the elderly that such important issues as the availability of part-time work (Howard, 1983) and effective health care (Neugarten, 1983) could be determined by their ability to influence legislators. Organizations like the Gray Panthers could be sources for launching a human-rights campaign that could accomplish the same kind of rights for the elderly that the labor, civil-rights, and women's movements have accomplished for their members.

As we move on to the disabled minorities and their problems, we see many parallels with the elderly.

# The Emergence of Disabled Minorities

There are at least 36 million disabled Americans. This category includes people with deformities and noncrippling injuries that cause them the emotional pain of being labeled physical deviants. Disability is one minority status that shows no regard for age, race, sex, or class privilege. As one observer noted, "Anyone can become disabled. A skiing accident, a highway collision, a mistaken dose of medicine—it may take seconds or it may take years" (Bowe, 1978: viii).

In this section we examine the process of prejudice and discrimination encountered by the physically, mentally, and emotionally disabled. Then we look at the costs of this treatment and prospects for the future.

## Process of Prejudice and Discrimination Encountered by the Disabled

The same steps that occur in the sexism and ageism processes occur for the disabled. In the first place, the disabled frequently have high social visibility. For physically disabled people, the visibility can be dramatic. When a psychologist showed over a hundred students pictures of human faces lacking in noses or ears or partly caved in, they all expressed horror and disgust (Smith, 1973). In other cases social visibility is just as obvious but less startling—the physically disabled in wheelchairs, for instance.

Second, the disabled encounter a range of ascribed characteristics that will vary with their disability. Like other minorities the disabled are generally considered both different and inferior. The stereotypes formed about the disabled frequently lack substantiating evidence. For instance, one woman who had been in a wheelchair ever since she had been hit by a car pointed out that often people falsely assume she cannot have sex (Bowe, 1978). This same assumption exists for other handicapped Americans. A frequent misperception about the disabled is that their central disability must link with others. Thus blind people often find that those addressing them will speak loudly, believing that they must also have a hearing problem. Many people readily classify physically handicapped people as retarded. In some situations a basis exists for such conclusions. Cerebral palsy and mental retardation are frequently present in the same person, and yet one does not cause the other—some cerebral palsied people are intellectually gifted and many retarded people have no physical handicaps. It seems clear that accurate judgments about handicapped people require an evaluation of their individual characteristics and capabilites.

Third, a variety of rationalizations support prejudice and discrimination against the disabled. A number of studies indicate that people generally believe that they live in a "just universe." Given this condition, then why are some individuals suffering from serious handicaps? A number of people assume that one reason is that the disabled have done something wrong or that they are going to do something wrong. In short, the assumption goes, the disability represents a punishment for wrong-doing (Shaw and Skolnick, 1971). Another rationalization is that disabled people's problems are always inherited and of sufficient magnitude that little or nothing can be done to help them. Toward the end of the nineteenth and the beginning of the twentieth century, it was widely believed that mental retardation was an inherited condition that was largely responsible for crime, delinquency, vagrancy, poverty, and immorality. The so-called experts felt that it would be a waste of resources to allocate funds for training schools for the retarded to improve their mental and physical functioning. Instead the retarded were placed in institutions, where they received no more than custodial care (Katz, 1973).

Fourth, like other minorities, the disabled often accommodate to the expectations or desires of the majority. The blind, for instance, frequently recognize that they are likely to receive greater acceptance if they consider the visual dimension when dealing with sighted people. Thus they learn to face others when talking to them instead of just turning an ear to the sound of their voice. Or they will teach themselves automatic use of such phrases as "I see" or "It looks like . . ." (Bowe, 1978:51). One study of individuals with rheumatoid arthritis indicated that there was frequent "covering up," hiding the disability from others, and also "keeping up," pushing themselves to perform as if they were not suffering from the pain and swelling that interferes with normal activity (Wiener, 1975).

Finally the disabled encounter a range of discriminations: attitudinal, architectural, educational, housing, occupational, and transportational. Perhaps U.S. society is less aware of and has taken fewer steps to confront discrimination toward the disabled than those toward other major minority groups.

The prejudice and discrimination process endured by the disabled involves the same five steps as sexism and ageism. Table 11.2 summarizes the three processes.

## Costs of Prejudice and Discrimination against the Disabled

The prejudice and discrimination suffered by the disabled inevitably carry some heavy costs. We consider three types of costs — the psychological, the physical, and the occupational.

### PSYCHOLOGICAL COST

A labeling process often occurs with disabilities. For instance, a child not doing well in school receives a battery of diagnostic tests that educators themselves are likely to consider inadequate. If a disability is "discovered," then the officials involved can sigh with relief as they conclude, "No wonder Susie wasn't learning. She is learning disabled." With the label placed, the school is now off the hook for the child's inability to learn. For the child, however, the problems are just starting. Once applied, labels are difficult to remove, even when observers demonstrate they are inappropriate. There are several reasons why. First, labels are concise designations that justify an organization or activity. "He wouldn't be in this mental hospital, would he, unless he were crazy as a loon?" Another reason labels remain is that they are self-fulfilling. A child is labeled "mildly retarded" and then receives less instruction to insure that she or he is not unduly burdened. When this child learns less than others who have been pushed harder, she or he "confirms" the original diagnosis (Bowe, 1978: 139).

Perhaps the most devastating psychological effect of disability for many people is the expectation of powerlessness they encounter. Those working on behalf of the rights of the disabled stress that many, perhaps most, Americans believe that handicapped people are generally powerless to do anything significant for themselves. Sometimes the explicit efforts to help the handicapped receive such criticism. For instance, an organizer working to improve the civil rights of the disabled made the following comment about the annual cerebral palsy telethon: "It's absolutely degrading. Watching those telethons one might think that all palsied adults are mentally retarded, pathetically trusting, asexual children" (Gliedman, 1979: 60).

Powerlessness is one debilitating condition the disabled have thrust upon them. They also frequently encounter another negative situation — isolation and aloneness. Many disabled people live an existence that sharply contrasts with that of other minorities. Ethnic groups, women, and the elderly can usually find others who share their experiences and problems, but people with major deformities, injuries, or other disabilities often

**Table 11.2**
**Prejudice and Discrimination against Emerging Minorities**

| COMPONENTS | SEXISM | AGEISM | PREJUDICE AND DISCRIMINATION AGAINST THE DISABLED |
|---|---|---|---|
| High social visibility | Secondary sex characteristics and distinctive clothing | Aging appearance—wrinkled skin, white hair, or stooped walk—and also bland clothing | Detectable physical disabilities or deformities |
| Ascribed attributes of inferiority | Less intelligent than men; irresponsible, inconsistent, and unstable | Images of passivity, dependency, rigidity, senility, and inefficiency | Unsubstantiated convictions about people with various disabilities, such as the widespread suspicion that blind people will also have hearing problems |
| Rationalization of status | "Women's place is in the home." | Claims that the elderly are "happy disengagers" | Belief that a multiplicity of handicaps are a punishment for wrongdoing or are so incapacitating that little or nothing can be done to help |
| Accommodating behavior patterns | Hiding intelligence or acting helpless | Graceful acceptance of retirement in spite of deep-seated reluctance | Blind people's facing sighted speakers during conversations and using visually oriented phrases |
| Discriminations | In education, occupation, and political activity | In forced retirement policies and laws | In attitudes, architecture, education, housing, occupation, and transportation |

Adapted in part from Helen Mayer Hacker. "Women as a Minority Group." *Social Forces.* Vol. 30. October 1951, pp. 60–69.

know nobody experiencing their same fate. In fact, the disabled often seek to avoid such a sense of community. Most of them view their minority status as more abnormal and undesirable than other groups view their respective minority statuses. A study of people with skin disease found that many reported shame and embarrassment and made largely unsuccessful efforts to hide evidence of their disease (Jowett and Ryan, 1985). And a little person said, "Didn't all of us, at the beginning, avoid little people because we didn't want to be identified with them? I didn't want to admit that I was little, too" (Smith, 1973: 125).

Often handicapped individuals with serious psy-chological problems find it difficult to get help. Those with severe physical disabilities, for example, face several barriers to mental-health service, including a decline in federal funding, lack of professionals trained to assist people with severe physical disabilities, and limited transportation facilities for those whose mobility is seriously impaired (Pelletier, 1985).

When we consider the loneliness and isolation of many disabled people, it is not surprising that they treasure moments that help them escape those conditions. The following Contemporary Issue describes several episodes that produced such positive effects for one person.

## CONTEMPORARY ISSUE

*Humor and Honesty Help a Disabled Woman Survive*

How does a lively, spirited person who has led a life dominated by the crippling ugliness of arthritis cope with her existence? The answer, in a phrase, is not easily. But Gloria Maxson learned that when people offered her support generously sprinkled with humor, she was often "snatched from the abyss." It was clear humor helped Gloria visualize herself and her situation more positively, thereby curtailing the sense of desolation that tended to flood through her life.

For instance, there was her fourth-grade teacher. When Gloria was lamenting about how homely she was, the teacher said, "Well, stop talking about it and your insides will never know; then you will grow up just gorgeous!" They laughed, and the young girl felt better.

Her Aunt Grace was also a big help. Once Gloria was crying about the fact that she had a blind eye, and her aunt explained that she needed only one eye to see the outside world. The bad eye was a special one to see inside herself, and it was crooked to see better into the corners. Another time she was outside in her wheelchair, and a snake ran over her foot. She screamed to her aunt that if she could not leave her chair, then she had no way to escape a snake. Aunt Grace smiled mischievously and replied, "Well, if you can't run from a snake, you'll have to sit and charm it." Gloria was so delighted with the idea that she spent a long time thinking about the possibility. Eventually she imagined charming a large python until it not only danced gracefully but also sang "Mephisto's Serenade" from *Faust*.

Gloria was also grateful to the friends and family who realized that put-down words like "gimp" were pleasant to hear, that they represented "the full extension of friendship and acceptance" when uttered by a friend. What Gloria found hard to accept were "the modern euphemisms" for various handicaps: "hearing-impaired," "language-impaired," "motion-impaired," and "vision-impaired." Such terms sounded squeamish to her. "They are Mother-Hubbard words clapped around our nakedness with missionary zeal to make us 'respectable' and cover our 'shame'. So I much prefer the tough Old Testament words like deaf, dumb, blind and crippled that tell the plain truth and set us free."

Source: Gloria A. Maxson. "Talking to My Self." *Christian Century*. Vol. 98. July 15, 1981, pp. 749–750.

### PHYSICAL COST

Seriously disabled people, those in wheelchairs for example, frequently encounter both architectural and transportation barriers. Most buildings can be entered only after people climb steps or pass through narrow doorways. These buildings are inaccessible to people in wheelchairs.

Even though an increasing number of buildings are now constructed with accessibility in mind, no effective national policy controls either architectural or transportation barriers (Poister, 1982). This deficiency makes physical movement arduous for the disabled. They often find it difficult or impossible to enter buildings, and barriers can be a major problem when planning trips. Are there any steps at the airline terminal? And what about the hotel? The management has assured the disabled person that she will be able to reach her fourth-floor room, but she knows that the building is old. So there are inevitable questions about the width of doors and accessibility to the elevator, not to mention that other ever-present problem: steps.

Some cities are becoming more receptive to the physical needs of the disabled. Atlanta is one, and Berkeley, California, is another. Two-thirds of the Berkeley intersections have either wheelchair ramps or curb cuts. In addition, the Bay Area Rapid Transit System, a modern bus and subway complex that connects Berkeley and San Fran-

*The capuchin monkey in the photo is shown providing a life-giving service to her owner: literally feeding her. A behavioral psychologist who trains monkeys to help the handicapped has claimed that capuchins—which grow to a maximum of only 5 pounds—might become as useful for certain disabled persons as seeing eye dogs are for the blind.*

cisco, is fully accessible to people in wheelchairs. In addition, all buildings constructed in the last ten years are accessible, and even the automated tellers at local banks are built at wheelchair height. One disabled resident explained, "It's easy to forget you're in a wheelchair here . . . But in most small towns where the disabled aren't as prevalent, it's not the same story" (Langway, 1982: 84).

### OCCUPATIONAL COST

A variety of barriers combine to produce an adverse effect on the work lives of many disabled people. Segregated and inferior schooling deprive millions of disabled people of the preparation they need to compete for well-paying jobs. Architectural barriers at job sites may deny entrance to the disabled. Transportation limitations may make it impossible to commute to and from work each day without paying exorbitant taxi fees. Employers' or prospective employers' attitudes can also be a problem. Many will resist hiring the disabled, mistakenly believing that they will be absent more

often and generally prove less reliable. A recent experiment concluded that physically disabled people received a lower evaluation than nondisabled individuals for comparable task performances (Russell et al., 1985).

For the disabled the chance to work can provide an opportunity to attain considerable personal satisfaction, daily stimulation and challenge, ongoing contacts with a variety of people, and a sense of supporting oneself. In contrast, enforced idleness means the absence of all these opportunities, and it is a condition that readily stimulates self-hate and disgust (Bowe, 1978; Langway, 1982).

The present situation in which the disabled of America find themselves is not a particularly positive one. What are the prospects for the future?

## The Future for Disabled Americans: Regression or Progression?

During the 1970s major legislation seemed to bring many of the 36 million disabled American citizens closer to the mainstream of American life. The Rehabilitation Act of 1973 served as a bill of rights for the disabled. It prevented any recipient of federal aid from engaging in architectural and economic discrimination against the disabled. To enforce the law, the government founded the Federal Architectural and Transportation Barriers Compliance Board. Then in 1975 a special-education bill required schools to "mainstream" disabled students into regular classrooms whenever possible.

But while some laws are progressive on paper, they have received limited funding and casual enforcement. In 1981, for instance, the federal government was supposed to pay 30 percent of New York City's mainstreaming costs, and yet it paid only 12 percent. Then in the early 1980s, the Social Security Administration reviewed cases of those supposedly too crippled, too ill, or mentally disturbed to hold a job, and 500,000 individuals were cut from public support. Soon it was apparent that the cuts had been excessively harsh, as indicated by the fact that within a short period of time 200,000 people won back their benefits (*Economist*, December 21, 1985: 18).

Whether seeking to change a government policy or some other goal, the disabled, like other minorities, have learned that they can accomplish much more collectively than individually. In the early 1970s, disabled students at the University of California campus at Berkeley founded the Center for Independent Living. The center rapidly became headquarters for a civil-rights movement for the disabled, referring people to jobs and apartments and dispensing legal advice. Lobbying groups composed of disabled people exist in other states too, and these groups seek opportunities to work for equal rights. A blind woman who has served as an aide to the speaker of the Illinois House of Representatives explained that the disabled are no longer the mere pawns of politicians: "It used to be that if you took ten people with white canes to the legislature, you could get them to do anything you wanted. . . . Now it's more complex; legislators have begun to accept what we've been saying, that we are people like everyone else" (Langway, 1982: 84).

Disabled people will undoubtedly obtain a broader base of support if they establish more effective relations with nondisabled individuals. Research is demonstrating that the way to improve these relations is to increase contact in situations where the nondisabled can learn about their disabled contemporaries: begin to appreciate the fact that beyond their particular disabilities, disabled citizens have interests, outlooks, and capabilities that are similar to those of everyone else (Gething, 1985; Langer et al., 1985).

# STUDY GUIDE

## Summary

1. Women, the elderly, and the disabled are three prominent emerging minorities. A similar process of prejudice and discrimination affects all three groups.

2. Sexism is the ideology emphasizing that actual or alleged differences between males and females establish the superiority of males. In American society sexism has received a number of supports. The sexist ideology has also produced a variety of costs. Psychological costs include the widespread belief that women possess a smaller quantity than men of the qualities considered desirable for a person. In addition, the media have traditionally presented a narrow, stereotyped image of women. Women have also suffered career costs. It has been widely believed that women can be fulfilled in the housewife role, and yet it is clear that this often is not the case. Women in the work force have been less successful than men. Research shows that socialization patterns are one source of women's disadvantage. Pay differences result from outright discrimination and the differing distribution of men and women into occupations. Women also encounter a variety of physical costs. Physical violence experienced by women ranges from "street hassling" to rape and/or physical abuse. Trends that appear among the violent acts against women include nonreporting, the failure to take the reports of violence seriously, and the tendency to blame the victim herself for the occurrence of the act.

In response to sexism, a modern women's movement has developed. Like earlier efforts by women to develop consciousness or to start a women's movement, the modern movement seems to be an outgrowth of the era in which it developed. The National Organization for Women (NOW) represents one source from which the modern women's movement originated. Another has been local women's groups that emerged from the 1960s civil-rights and antiwar movements.

How will women maximize their rights as individuals and at the same time associate with men? We discussed this question as we considered the future of women's rights.

3. Like women, the elderly are frequently victims of modern society. Ageism is an ideology emphasizing the superiority of the young over the old. Like sexism, ageism is a process that receives a number of supports in daily life. One cost of ageism is health, which is adversely affected by the medical care some elderly people receive. Another cost for some aging Americans involves the limited organizational activity they experience. In addition, many aging people feel a limited control over their destiny. This sense of powerlessness appears frequently when old Americans face relocation and especially relocation to a nursing home.

**280** We can speculate about the future of the elderly in America. One significant question to ponder is whether or not a strong political movement of the elderly will develop. At present mixed indications exist.

4. The 36 million disabled Americans often face prejudice and discrimination similar to that encountered by women and the elderly. In fact, the same steps that occur in sexism and ageism also occur for the disabled. Not surprisingly the costs of prejudice and discrimination are also similar. Psychological costs include the destructive effect of labeling. Unlike women and the elderly, disabled people who would like to share experiences with others suffering the same minority status often find it more difficult to locate such people or receive less cultural support for seeking out those with a shared experience. The physical costs of being disabled include limited access to buildings and to transportation. No systematic national policies exist in either area, making it difficult for wheelchair-bound people to be physically mobile. The occupational costs encountered by disabled Americans are the result of a variety of barriers—educational, architectural, transportational, and attitudinal.

The future for disabled Americans seems unclear. It is possible that the landmark legislation of the 1970s will not survive the 1980s. However, some indications suggest that a movement of disabled people could develop, and such a movement could exert considerable political force, thereby reducing the sense of powerlessness that often accompanies being disabled.

## Glossary

**ageism** an ideology asserting the superiority of the young over the old.
**disengagement** a process of mutual withdrawal involving decreasing interaction between an elderly person and others in the social system to which he or she belongs.

**sexism** the ideology emphasizing that actual or alleged differences between males and females establish the superiority of males.

## Learning Objectives

After studying this chapter, you should be able to:

1. Define sexism and summarize the five steps in the process.
2. Discuss the psychological, career, and physical costs of sexism.
3. Examine the modern women's movement and the future of women's rights.
4. Define ageism and summarize the five steps in the process.
5. Analyze the following effects of ageism—health and medical-care cost, group-involvement cost, and the cost of losing control over one's destiny.
6. Describe the strategies elderly people pursue to feel useful and satisfied.
7. Summarize the five steps in the process of prejudice and discrimination encountered by the disabled.
8. Examine the psychological, physical, and occupational costs of prejudice and discrimination suffered by the disabled.
9. Indicate how the disabled act collectively to overcome their powerlessness.

## Tests

**True–false test**

_____ 1. In the 1980s sexism is no longer an ideology.

_____ 2. About half of the principal characters in modern comic strips are female.

_____ 3. Horner's study of women's motive to avoid success found that modern women do not possess such a motive.

_____ 4. In recent years American women have pushed effectively for improved rights in the occupational, educational, and credit areas, but their European sisters have fought more effectively for assistance to working mothers.

_____ 5. Like sexism, ageism could not occur without high social visibility.

_____ 6. Recent research has revealed that when urban elderly are involved in social networks composed of neighbors, friends, or kin, they tend to be less healthy than old people without such networks.

_____ 7. There are at least 36 million disabled Americans.

_____ 8. One reason that labels on the disabled are hard to remove is that they are self-fulfilling.

_____ 9. A recent experiment concluded that physically disabled and nondisabled individuals receive similar evaluations for comparable task performances.

_____ 10. Lobbying groups composed of disabled people are illegal in thirty-two states.


## Multiple-choice test

_____ 1. Which statement about sexism is true?
   a. Women's ability to perform, not their intelligence, has been questioned.
   b. In American society women have traditionally encountered more limitations on education than men.
   c. There are no rationalizations about women's traditional status.
   d. Women are the only minority group without social visibility.

_____ 2. Recent research shows that stereotyped images of women persist in:
   a. comic strips.
   b. television commercials.
   c. television.
   d. a, b, and c

_____ 3. Hennig and Jardim studied female presidents and vice-presidents of business firms and found that their achievement differences seemed to be produced by:
   a. family dynamics.
   b. work experience.
   c. training.
   d. social visibility.

_____ 4. NOW:
   a. was organized by the more traditional, older segment of the modern women's movement.
   b. was developed by the younger, more radical section of the modern women's movement.
   c. still maintains close relations with communist groups.
   d. members are primarily concerned with developing the ideology of woman-serving-her-family.

_____ 5. Which statement is true of the elderly?
   a. They have low social visibility.
   b. They have negative qualities attributed to them.
   c. Extensive disengagement is rare.
   d. Most Americans will face mandatory retirement for the next couple of decades.

——

6. Compared to black female elderly, white female elderly are more inclined to:
   a. use prayer.
   b. use nonprescription drugs.
   c. have weak support from friends.
   d. a and b

—— 7. Which of the following is a situation that is likely to threaten the elderly's sense of controlling their destiny?
   a. loss of the ability to vote
   b. religious conversion
   c. relocation
   d. too much control imposed by friends

—— 8. Prejudice and discrimination against the disabled are supported by the rationalization that:
   a. their disabilities represent punishment for wrongdoing.
   b. there are not enough jobs for everyone.
   c. we cannot afford the cost of all the environmental modifications they need.
   d. they are being cared for effectively enough by our welfare system.

—— 9. Which of the following factors is a psychological cost of being disabled?
   a. casual enforcement of laws to aid the disabled
   b. powerlessness
   c. transportation limitations
   d. architectural barriers

—— 10. A city that has made impressive physical adjustments to meet the needs of the physically disabled is:
   a. Rome (Italy).
   b. New York.
   c. New Delhi (India).
   d. Berkeley (California).

## Essay test

1. Define sexism and discuss the steps in the process, offering illustrations at each stage.
2. Discuss in detail three costs of sexism.
3. On what issue(s) is women's struggle for rights likely to focus in the future?
4. What is ageism? Discuss and illustrate stages in the process of ageism.
5. Discuss several significant costs of ageism.
6. Examine and illustrate the steps in the process of prejudice and discrimination against the disabled.
7. Describe the principal costs encountered by disabled Americans.
8. Discuss different ways that the disabled can confront and overcome their powerlessness.

## Suggested Readings

Blekher, Feiga. 1979. *The Soviet Woman in the Family and in Society: A Sociological Study.* New York: Wiley. An overview of research on modern Soviet women. The author considers a number of current problems, such as the effects of the high divorce rate, the impact of widespread negative attitudes toward marriage, and the effects of increasing friction between husbands and wives.

Bowe, Frank. 1978. *Handicapping America.* New York: Harper & Row. A book for a general audience describing the state of affairs for disabled people in modern America. The author, who is deaf, is a leading authority on and advocate for disabled people.

Cicirelli, Victor G. 1981. *Helping Elderly Parents: The Role of Adult Children*. Boston: Auburn House. An interesting, useful study of the conditions encouraging adult children to assist their aging parents. The author contends that the quantity and variety of services that adult children provide will vary with the parent–child relationship and with the elderly parent's dependency characteristics.

Cruzic, Kathleen. 1982. *Disabled? Yes. Defeated? No*. Englewood Cliffs, NJ: Prentice-Hall. A nurse's detailed account of the various resources available for the disabled, their families, friends, and therapists. The book contains sixteen chapters offering detailed information on such issues as shortcuts in the kitchen, pursuit of new careers, tips for traveling, and aids for recreation.

Cumming, Elaine, and William Henry. 1961. *Growing Old: The Process of Disengagement*. New York: Basic Books. The study from which the disengagement theory originated. This work provides an in-depth look at the development of this well-known, highly controversial theory.

de Beauvoir, Simone. 1957. *The Second Sex*. New York: Alfred A. Knopf. Translated and edited by H.M. Parshley. A scholarly yet passionate study of the subjugation of women. This prominent pioneer in the international modern women's movement reviewed the biological, historical, literary, developmental, and social structural sources that have traditionally compelled women to be "the second sex."

Foner, Anne. 1986. *Aging and Old Age*. Englewood Cliffs, NJ: Prentice-Hall. A concise, informative, wide-ranging, and up-to-date discussion of old age in modern society.

Friedan, Betty. 1963. *The Feminine Mystique*. New York: Norton. The widely read treatise that helped initiate the modern women's movement in U.S. society. As you read this book, it might be valuable to pretend that you are a woman of more than two decades ago suddenly discovering that someone has articulated the sense of confusion, uneasiness, and anger you experience as a housewife and mother.

Friedan, Betty. 1981. *The Second Stage*. New York: Summit Books. Friedan's thoughtful commentary on contemporary women's plight — seeking to fill both career and wife and mother roles.

Kahn-Hut, Rachel, Arlene Kaplan Daniels, and Richard Colvard (eds.). 1982. *Women and Work*. New York: Oxford University Press. A set of readings examining the effects produced at home and outside of it by growing numbers of women entering the work force.

Kesey, Ken. 1962. *One Flew over the Cuckoo's Nest*. New York: Signet. A chilling look at the alienated life of men living in the ward of a mental hospital. Kesey's novel makes it painfully clear how the process of controlling people's thoughts and actions is successfully conducted in this setting.

Stone, Deborah A. 1984. *The Disabled State*. Philadelphia: Temple University Press. An original, provocative analysis of the development of western nations' political definitions of disability.

Walker, Lenore E. 1984. *The Battered-Woman Syndrome*. New York: Springer. A detailed study of 435 battered women, examining their personalities and their inability to control the violence against them.

Williamson, John B. 1982. *Humanizing Institutions for the Aged*. Lexington: MA: Lexington Books. A study seeking to discover ways to make nursing homes for the elderly better places to live.

## Student Projects

1. Find ten people, preferably five females and five males. Ask them to rank the following occupations from 1 (most prestigious) to 12 (least prestigious). How much agreement did you find regarding the prestige of each occupation? Did men and women rank them differently? Compare findings with other class members and relate the trends you discover to information in your text chapter, indicating, in particular, how much the sex typing of occupations appeared to affect rankings.

The occupations

1. Flight attendant
2. Housewife
3. Truck driver
4. Waiter
5. Fashion model
6. Steward
7. Househusband
8. Photographer
9. Doctor
10. Waitress
11. Nurse
12. School bus driver

(Note occupations 2 and 10 are considered female occupations; occupations 4, 6, and 7 are considered male occupations. All other positions could have either male or female job holders, but we culturally identify females with occupations 1, 5, and 11 and males with 3, 8, and 9.)

2. Imagine yourself having a significant disability—being legally blind, confined to a wheelchair, or hearing-impaired. Over a two-day period, keep a record of what you discover regarding the physical facilities you use on campus, such as stairs and doors. What conclusions can you draw about your ability as a disabled person to participate in campus activities? How could your school make improvements to assist disabled students?

## Answers to Test Questions

**True–false test**

| | | | | |
|---|---|---|---|---|
| 1. f | 3. f | 5. t | 7. t | 9. f |
| 2. f | 4. t | 6. f | 8. t | 10. f |

**Multiple-choice test**

| | | | | |
|---|---|---|---|---|
| 1. b | 3. a | 5. b | 7. c | 9. b |
| 2. d | 4. a | 6. c | 8. a | 10. d |

# PART FOUR

## The Institutions of American Society

# 12
# FAMILY: ALTERNATIVE LIFE-STYLES

Anne Taylor Fleming was married in 1972, not in a church but on her father's terrace. Nobody gave her away, and nobody asked her whether she would honor and obey the man she was marrying. Like most of her friends, Ms. Fleming further defied tradition by not wearing a fancy gown, by writing her own ceremony, and by keeping her own last name. The modern women's movement was just getting launched. It seemed that the times were changing.

By the middle 1980s, however, old standards had reasserted themselves. Fancy weddings were back, and defiance of tradition was no longer popular. In fact, bookracks were filled with best sellers ". . . on how to please, get, hold, and handle a man" (Fleming, 1986: 31). Not surprisingly modern times have been difficult for American wives. Many struggle with the multiple demands imposed by their husbands, children, and jobs. Many receive limited psychological support or help around the home from their husbands. Often the wives are unclear about what they want. Fleming summarized the kinds of difficulties many modern American wives must face:

> Right now, at a time when there is no discernable women's movement left, so many of them seem caught between the parts of themselves they can't reconcile — the part that wants a hero for a husband and the part that wants to be the perfect career woman. They're caught and they're uneasy, wondering just how much backsliding is going to go on and just how much of it comes from the irreconcilable differences within their own psyches.

*(Fleming, 1986: 39)*

Modern social conditions have had a profound effect on American wives. In the pages ahead, we will see that besides their impact on American wives, social conditions have been affecting American families generally.

A **family** is traditionally defined as a social unit composed of two or more people who live together and are related by blood, marriage, or adoption. In the United States, the **nuclear family** has been the dominant form. This is a two-generation family that includes a father, a mother, and their children living separately from other relatives. In many other societies, however, the **extended family,** involving two or more generations of people related by blood and living together or close to each other, plays a more important role. The extended family has prevailed in rural settings. As societies have become increasingly industrialized and urbanized, the nuclear family has assumed a steadily more significant part.

The first section of this chapter discusses the functions of the family and also kinship terms. Next we analyze the development of the modern American nuclear family. The chapter then considers changing patterns of love, courtship, and marriage and closes with a look at divorce and contemporary alternatives to marriage.

## Selected Features of the Family

In this section we examine functions of the family and also kinship terms. It will become apparent that families share these features, even though the features often differ historically and cross-culturally.

### Some Functions of the Family

Throughout human history families have provided basic food and shelter and emotional comfort for their members. They have also supplied status placement; Americans' sense of their location in the social-class system is provided by their family membership. In addition, families are the groups that are supposed to engage in reproduction, thereby supplying new citizens for the society. Families also perform the three functions we will examine cross-culturally in this section: sexual regulation, economic activity, and socialization.

## Sexual Regulation

People are likely to become nervous when contemplating the prospect of extreme sexual promiscuity. Most of us could not cope effectively with a society where everyone was permitted to have sexual intercourse with everyone else. The universality of incest taboos demonstrates the importance that all cultures place on keeping sexual activity carefully controlled and limited.

### THE INCEST TABOO

An **incest taboo** is a rule outlawing sexual relations between certain kin-group members believed to be too closely related as defined by the cultural standards of a given society. In all known societies, the incest taboo normally restricts sexual relations within the nuclear family to the husband and wife. The incest taboo serves several important functions. First, the rule eliminates the conflicts and jealousy that would result if there were sexual rivalry among members of the nuclear family. The taboo, in short, helps maximize cooperation within the family unit. Second, the incest taboo forces people to marry outside their own nuclear families, thus reducing isolation and encouraging families to cooperate with each other. These marital alliances increase the possibility that families will share inventions and discoveries, work together in the procurement or production of food and other valued commodities, and engage in mutual protection against enemies. Third, the taboo helps keep the roles of family members clearly defined. Without the incest taboo, a single individual could be simultaneously a wife and a daughter, or a brother and a husband, and so on. If this occurred, authority within the family would become confused, and the continued existence of the nuclear family as a functioning social unit would be seriously threatened (Murdock, 1949: 295–297). Given the fundamental importance of the family within societies and the critical part that the incest taboo plays in maintaining the family, it is not surprising that the taboo exists universally.

## Economic Activity

How often do we hear the phrase "That's women's work" or "That's a man's job"? These clichés reflect traditional gender-role definitions currently under heavy attack by many modern women and men. If we consider societies other

*Extended families, like this one from the Aboure tribe on the Ivory Coast, remain the norm in many societies.*

than that of the United States, we will see that there are no tasks consistently categorized as "male" or "female" across cultures. For example, societies have existed where women were the warriors and others where men prepared the food. Societies have even existed where men have "recovered" from childbirth while their wives went back to work. Although men's and women's family tasks often differ widely from one society to another, they all have gender-linked tasks. They also have age-linked tasks. Because of the complexity or danger associated with some important tasks, children must reach a certain level of growth before being allowed to undertake them. Hunting, warfare, and the manufacture of many intricate or important objects provide good examples.

In modern societies families generally no longer produce food, clothes, housing, and other basic subsistence items. Instead men and women work for organizations and buy with the money they earn the essential items formerly produced by the united activity of the family unit. As people become increasingly integrated into a modern industrial setting, they tend to break away from extended families, where the function of economic production is often important, and to reside in nuclear-family units (Handwerker, 1973). As we will see, the nuclear family is especially compatible with a modern, industrial setting.

*Socialization*

Social norms compel parents to provide socialization for their children, whether or not they wish to do so. However, within a given culture, socialization patterns often vary considerably (Leighton, 1984).

There are many different patterns of socialization cross-culturally. For example, anthropologist Margaret Mead (1963: 40–41) noted that women in Bali hold their children in a looser and more relaxed manner than do American parents. Mead suspected that because of this manner of being held, Balinese children retain much greater physical flexibility than do American children.

Research has also suggested that personality differences can be attributed in part to variations in socialization practices. Beatrice and John Whiting and their associates (1975: 172–185) studied the typical socialization patterns in six cultures; five were non-American and agricultural and one American, specifically a New England town. The children in two of the traditional societies tended to have unsociable, aggressive, and authoritarian (rigid, conformity-oriented, and excessively obedient to authority) personalities, while the children of the New England town were relatively sociable and less aggressive. The children with aggressive, authoritarian personalities came from societies with extended families in which an adult male was the most powerful individual. With many relatives living together, often amid numerous conflicting interests, family interaction tended to be controlled by clear, sharp commands from the dominant male. In contrast, a much more casual, intimate setup is possible in the nuclear family characteristic of American towns, and this pattern is similarly reflected in the American children's personalities. The Whitings concluded that by the age of six, children have assimilated the respective values of their cultures, and their personality structures are basically established.

Socialization is usually a major function of all families, but it has been partially usurped from this institution by governments in some modern societies. In the Soviet Union and the People's Republic of China, children generally spend most of the day in a collective setting. Similarly the increase in the number of working mothers within U.S. society has meant that day-care facilities for infants and young children have been rapidly expanding. In the kibbutzim (collective settlements) scattered throughout Israel, communal living is emphasized; socialization is a communal enterprise with children of the same age living together entirely apart from their parents. Although the members of one kibbutz told a researcher that they were deliberately attempting to undermine the nuclear family structure, ties between parents and children remained strong. Families came together two hours a day and also on Saturdays and holidays. An observer wrote, "The eagerness of parents to see their children is equalled only by the eagerness of the children to see their parents" (Spiro, 1970: 125).

## Kinship Terms

A **kinship system** is a number of people related by common descent, marriage, or adoption. Cross-culturally kinship systems have several types of marriage, customs for marriage eligibility, residential rules for newly married couples, and patterns of power within the family.

*Types of Marriage*

**Polygamy** is a marriage practice where one spouse has two or more spouses of the other sex. **Polygyny** is the form of polygamy in which a husband has two or more wives; **polyandry** is the form of polygamy in which a wife has two or more husbands. **Monogamy** is a marriage practice in which there is one husband and one wife. In the United States, polygamy is illegal. About 90 percent of societies permit some form of polygamy, but it is not widely practiced because of the cost of maintaining two or more households. Polygyny is a much more common form of polygamy than polyandry. Since there is a higher death rate among male infants and men's life expectancy is shorter, there are fewer men in most societies than women. When polyandry does occur, it is because some practice creates an artificial scarcity of women; for example, the Todas of India used to drown some of their newborn infant girls.

*Customs for Marriage Eligibility*

**Endogamy** is a custom requiring a person to marry within a specific social unit, such as a kinship group, religious organization, or social class. **Exogamy** is a custom compelling someone to marry outside a specific social unit. In the United States, most marriages involve individuals similar in social-class background, religion, and race. All states have laws prohibiting marriage between members of the immediate family as well as between first cousins; some states will not permit second cousins to marry. Other societies also impose endogamous and exogamous standards. In some traditional societies, endogamy helps to strengthen a kinship group or community; thus people who refuse to obey this standard and marry within a particular unit are likely to suffer strong penalties.

### Residential Rules for Newly Married People

**Matrilocal** residence involves settling with or near the wife's parents. **Patrilocal** residence requires settling with or near the husband's parents. **Neolocal** residence occurs when married people establish an independent place to live. The respective roles that men and women play in the society largely determine the residential patterns. Therefore, if men within a particular society have an especially important role in obtaining food, then a patrilocal residential pattern is likely to exist. This is even more likely if men own property that can be accumulated and if males are the heads of elaborate political systems. On the other hand, if women have the dominant role in the procurement of food and if the political organization is relatively simple, then matrilocal residence is likely to take place. Neolocal residence generally occurs in societies where the nuclear family is economically independent. In the United States, where many people must be free to move where they can find jobs, neolocal residence predominates.

### Patterns of Power within the Family

A **patriarchal** family is a family in which the husband–father is the formal head and the absolute

*Members of the Mormon community in the United States commonly used to practice polygyny. Shown here is a photo taken in the 1870s of a Mormon husband, his two wives, and nine children.*

or nearly absolute source of power. A **matriarchal** family is a family in which the wife–mother is the formal head and the absolute or nearly absolute source of power. An **egalitarian** family is a family in which the wife–mother and husband–father share power and also permit their children to participate in the family decisions. In most societies the husband–father usually had the final say in most important matters. No societies qualify as true matriarchies. American families have traditionally been patriarchal, but a gradual movement toward the egalitarian form has been encouraged by women's steadily improving educational and occupational status in the society at large.

## The Modern American Nuclear Family

The American family is somewhat egalitarian, with neolocal residence and a monogamous marriage pattern. The dominant form is nuclear. In this section we consider how industrialization has encouraged the development of the nuclear-family type and also examine the declining functions of the American nuclear family.

### Industrialization and the Nuclear Family

William Goode (1963) has suggested that the industrial era has encouraged people to discard the extended family and live exclusively in the nuclear family. What specific features of industrialization have prompted such a shift?

The increased need for physical movement from one specific location to another is one factor. In an industrial setting, it is impractical to move an entire extended family in order to allow one person to take a desirable new job.

In addition, social mobility, prevalent in industrial societies, plays an important role. An emphasis on upward social mobility has supported the increased prominence of the nuclear family, which is relatively small and flexible and allows people to conform their life-styles, dress, and speech to the standards of the successful mainstream without encountering extensive criticism from kin. Such changes frequently help people get jobs (or better jobs) in an industrial context, thereby contributing to their advancement.

Third, a member of an extended family normally has time-consuming domestic obligations toward a variety of kin. For an individual to perform effectively in an industrial setting, these obligations need to be severely limited, and the nuclear family radically reduces kinship obligations.

Finally industrial society requires a family that, like the nuclear family, can afford to support children during a lengthy period of education or training provided by such social organizations as schools, corporations, and the military. In the extended family, children were expected to begin making an economic contribution to the family's upkeep soon after they started walking; for the most part, children in these families received no formal education at all.

Thus, Goode declared, industrialization has increased the prominence of the nuclear family. He has also noted that the relationship between the two structures has not always been smooth and harmonious (Goode, 1982: 181). Sociologist Richard Sennett (1974) has developed the last point, suggesting that the nuclear-family type may be less supportive of its members' emotional and occupational growth than the extended family. He found that males living in nuclear families when they immigrated to Chicago in the late nineteenth century tended to be less occupationally successful than men who had recently moved to the city but were still living in extended families. Sennett suspected that the first group of men viewed their nuclear families as protection against the new and alien urban social life. These men were, in fact, isolated. There were no adult males with whom they could readily discuss their fears and aspirations. Such

men tended to view their work defensively; they generally accepted modest positions and held on to them. Furthermore they passed the same introverted, self-protective attitudes on to their sons.

On the other hand, when male members of extended families arrived in Chicago, they tended to react to the city much less defensively because their family was more active and supportive. Work was frequently discussed with other men in the household, and sometimes friendly competition for jobs and occupational advancement would develop among them. The sons in extended families not only had a more optimistic, less-tension-laden outlook on work but also tended to be more successful than their counterparts in nuclear families.

Modern people often recognize some assets of extended families. A recent study conducted in a small city found that more than half the adults in a randomly selected sample indicated that among their relatives there was someone who could be considered a "kinkeeper" — usually a woman — who used telephoning, writing letters, visiting, and organizing or holding family gatherings to keep extended-family members in contact with each other (Rosenthal, 1985).

## Declining Functions of the Nuclear Family

The American nuclear family has lost a number of functions since the colonial era. Because of the Industrial Revolution, the economic-productive function has been transferred from the home and family to factories and businesses, where one or more family members often work in order to meet the family's economic needs. Therefore the family is no longer both producer and consumer, just the latter. This might seem entirely natural to Americans, but it would not seem so to most people of the past. In fact, many preindustrial people — the Greeks and Romans, for instance — visualized production and consumption as so thoroughly fused into a single life-giving function that they even lacked a separate word for consumer.

Other functions have also been largely separated from the family. Recreation was once centered in the home or the church, but it has become increasingly specialized along age lines and is now located outside the home. Little-league sports, ice- and roller-skating rinks, motion-picture theaters, and video arcades provide a few illustrations. In addition, the protective function is no longer handled by the family but rather is now the responsibility of the police, the fire department, and other community agencies. Health care too has moved out of the home, with the dominant role played by doctors and nurses, drug stores, hospitals, and health-care agencies. Religious training, once rooted in the home, is now restricted to certain times and places outside it. Finally dramatic institutional expansion and specialization have occurred in education. Today the law makes it impossible to do what most parents routinely did 200 years ago: educate their children in the home. From the age of four or five onward, children are now removed from home for thirty to forty hours a week (Adams, 1980: 87–88).

### Consequences of the Loss of Functions

As we have noted, Richard Sennett believed that extended families were healthier places for the development of nineteenth-century American men than were nuclear families. The French historian Phillipe Ariès (1962) has extended this argument to include women and children. Ariès contended that before the industrial era, women and children often encountered far fewer restrictions than they do today. The expectations that family members should constantly display mutual affection and that parents were obliged to ensure their children's maximum social and intellectual development simply did not exist. Once their household duties were completed, women and children were relatively free to do what they wanted. In contrast, Ariès has described the modern nuclear family as a "prison of love."

Arlene Skolnick (1971) has made a similar point. She has suggested that the nuclear family is characterized by "built-in strains." Men are freed from most obligations to the extended kinship unit, but they are compelled to support their wives and children in "the style to which they aspire to become accustomed." Skolnick has contended that women's plight is sometimes "obscured by the myth that women are the main beneficiaries of marriage." While women today have been released from their role obligations in extended-family units, they now find themselves living in isolated households, often with extensive domestic duties. Skolnick pointed out that while labor-saving devices can facilitate the completion of specific tasks, they do not necessarily reduce the total number of work hours. It is possible that these devices simply raise the standards for meal preparations, house cleaning, and child care. Furthermore women now comprise over 44 percent of the labor force, and working wives and mothers tend to bear the burden of domestic responsibilities, even when the husband–father is vocally supportive of his wife's career and expresses a willingness to make a substantial contribution to the domestic chores.

## Changing Patterns of Love, Courtship, and Marriage

The modern American family is the product of an industrialized, urbanized age. That same social context has produced some new developments in other types of cohabitation. In this section we examine living together, choice of partners, and changing marital patterns.

### Living Together

> I always say we never got married, because we bought our own toaster.
>
> *Danny DeVito, who played the dispatcher on "Taxi"*

When he made this statement, Mr. DeVito had been living with the same woman for over ten years; this fact suggests that this particular couple belonged to a distinct numerical minority. Ira Reiss (1980: 106) has identified two types of cohabitation: courtship cohabitation, where no desire for a lifelong union exists, and nonlegal marital cohabitation, DeVito's type, where a desire for a lifelong union and possibly children has developed. The majority of people living together, Reiss contended, fall into the first category. Saxton (1980: 300) designated five types of cohabitation arrangements:

1. Temporary, casual cohabitation, with a man and a woman sharing the same living quarters chiefly out of short-term convenience.
2. Affectionate cohabitation, which continues only so long as both partners remain pleased by it.

**294**

3. Trial marriage, whereby a couple deliberately examines and tests their relationship before making a formal commitment.
4. Cohabitation as a temporary alternative to marriage, with each partner committed to a permanent relationship but waiting, because of financial, legal, or other reasons, until that condition becomes more feasible.
5. Cohabitation as a permanent alternative to marriage, a situation in which a long-term commitment exists.

Most cohabitation arrangements meet the participants' needs at a particular point in time. Until recent years most of these relationships did not serve as trial marriages. A recent study, however, has observed that in the modern era where premarital sex has become widely acceptable, a new stage in the courtship process might be emerging, with many couples using premarital cohabitation as an intermediate step between dating and marriage (Gwartney-Gibbs, 1986).

Table 12.1 shows that the American public is divided about the practice of cohabitation.

## Who Engages in Cohabitation?

Cohabitation has sharply increased in the past two decades. Among students the relaxation of college rules and increased opportunities to live off campus have encouraged this trend. Further-

more changing sexual attitudes—a general increase in sexual permissiveness and openness—have occurred among young people. Living together has also been encouraged by some people's disenchantment with marriage and by the belief that cohabitation can help to develop interpersonal skills that will be useful when people marry at a later date (Gagnon and Greenblat, 1978: 174–179). In 1960 about 439,000 couples were living together outside legal marriage. By 1981 the figure had risen to about 1.8 million couples, a total that was more than four times greater than the earlier figure and represented about 4 percent of all couples (Reiss, 1980: 103; Spanier, 1983).

Overall the similarities between cohabitants and the general public appear to be more striking than their differences. In fact, among students, opportunity may be the single most significant factor differentiating between those who do and those who do not cohabit, although the participants must also possess sufficient interpersonal skills and personal attractiveness to be able to initiate a relationship.

Some research indicates that cohabiting women are more likely to consider themselves aggressive, competitive, independent, and managerial than are noncohabiting women. On the other hand, cohabiting men are more likely to regard themselves as warmer, less managerial, less competitive, and more emotionally supportive than are their non-

**Table 12.1**
**Feelings about the Practice of Cohabitation**

|  | Overall | AGE | | | |
|---|---|---|---|---|---|
|  |  | *18–24* | *30–44* | *45–59* | *60+* |
| Agree | 48% | 70% | 54% | 34% | 26% |
| Disagree | 42 | 24 | 35 | 55 | 63 |
| Mixed feeling or do not know | 10 | 6 | 11 | 11 | 11 |

|  | POLITICAL PHILOSOPHY[1] | | |
|---|---|---|---|
|  | *Conservative* | *Moderate* | *Liberal* |
| Agree | 35% | 56% | 69% |
| Disagree | 55 | 34 | 23 |
| Mixed feelings or do not know | 10 | 10 | 8 |

[1] Based on respondents' self-assessment.
Source: Adapted from the Roper Organization. *Roper Reports.* March 1981.

*Certain categories of people are especially likely to support the practice of cohabitation and other categories are noticeably inclined to oppose it. Young people and liberals strongly support the practice, while the elderly and conservatives generally oppose it.*

cohabiting counterparts. Both male and female co-habitants are more politically liberal, perceive themselves to be more androgynous (possessing a blend of both traditionally masculine and feminine traits), and more liberated in terms of traditional gender-role expectations. Cohabitants also seem more inclined to major in the arts and in social sciences than in engineering or physical sciences (Macklin, 1983).

Why do these correlations develop? It seems likely that while living together is becoming increasingly acceptable, its practice still divides people: Those who do it are more liberal, more inclined to engage in marginally acceptable behavior if they feel that it is socially progressive and meaningful. People with such viewpoints are probably more likely to reject traditional gender-role standards and also to major in the arts and social sciences.

### Consequences of Living Together

People who have cohabited do value the experience, arguing that it added to their personal growth and maturity, and usually feeling that they would not marry without having lived with that person first (Macklin, 1983).

In the legal realm, there are some decisive consequences of cohabitation. A child born to a co-habiting couple is considered illegitimate and is subject to a variety of legal and social difficulties. Cohabiting people deny themselves some of the protections provided by the law to married couples. In some states merchants and landlords may legally refuse to sell or rent to a cohabiting couple. In addition, living together can be grounds for eviction in those states where cohabitation is illegal. Finally a cohabitant has traditionally lacked a spouse's legally protected status, at least until recently. In the celebrated *Marvin* v. *Marvin* case, Michelle Marvin sued for "palimony," contending that she and actor Lee Marvin had an oral contract entitling her to half the property he earned during their seven years of living together. In April 1979 Michelle Marvin was awarded $104,000.

## Choice of Partners

Americans prize freedom of choice. It is easy to imagine someone saying, "I'll marry anyone I choose. After all, people are created equal, and so marriage should simply be a question of whom I love." Despite such attitudes, most Americans practice **homogamy,** marriage with a person having social characteristics similar to one's own. Why is this? In the first place, many of us desire mates whose values are similar to ours. Those who share our racial, religious, ethnic, and social-class statuses are especially likely to also share our values. Furthermore opportunity plays a part in promoting homogamy. Our residential areas, schools, and workplaces are usually somewhat segregated on the basis of race, ethnicity, and class, and so in these areas we are often going to meet people whose social characteristics are similar to ours. Another important factor promoting homogamy is informal pressure from family and friends to marry one's "own kind." We sometimes do not clearly perceive that these forces have an impact upon our lives, but for most of us, they are definitely significant. The data on homogamy support this conclusion.

Recent research has revealed that when people marry, they tend to find partners who are similar in age, race, religion, ethnic background, income level, educational attainment, overall physical attractiveness, and various personality characteristics (Atkinson and Glass, 1985; Buss, 1986).

Even though Americans are highly diversified in their status characteristics, American marriage ceremonies possess a number of common features, as the following Cross-Cultural Perspective indicates.

---

**CROSS-CULTURAL PERSPECTIVE**

## *The American Ritual: Contributions from Other Cultures*

Human societies frequently borrow practices from other cultures. The traditional American marriage ceremony contains elements that originated in a number of other places. A discussion of the origin of these elements provides some sense of their earliest meanings as well as their meanings in contemporary American life.

The wedding ring is probably the oldest and most widespread symbol of marriage.

Some ancient people apparently broke a coin in half, and each partner took one of the halves. The use of rings appears to have evolved from this practice. Ancient Romans, Greeks, and Egyptians all used wedding rings; in those times rings represented the highest form of trust and power. In the Middle Ages, men in many European cultures still wore engagement rings, but this practice seems to have declined as rings gradually lost their earlier meaning and became symbols of bondage and obedience. In recent years, however, the number of double ring ceremonies has increased, reflecting the growing emphasis on sharing and mutuality in modern marriage.

Throughout history couples have generally tried to choose a lucky wedding day. The Romans believed that it was unlucky to marry during the time when religious ceremonies and holidays occurred. As a result marriages did not occur for about a third of the year. The English traditionally regarded Friday as a bad day to begin any enterprise, and so they normally considered it a poor choice for a wedding day. Most Americans seem to display few superstitions about the choice of when to marry.

Brides have worn veils in many cultures. Christian, Hindu, Jewish, and Moslem brides have used them, and tradition has emphasized that veils protect brides from malicious spirits—from the "evil eye."

Through the ages candles or torches have enhanced weddings. By the time the wedding procession in ancient Greece or Rome got under way, it was usually dark. Thus the torchbearers both provided light for those in the procession and also carried the flame that symbolized the enduring spirit of marriage. In early Christian marriages, the wedding was supposed to occur in the presence of God, who was represented by a single large candle.

Flowers too have been prominent in wedding ceremonies. Wreaths of flowers represented the bride's virtue. In medieval Europe women decorated both the bride's and the groom's house with olive and laurel leaves in order to symbolize abundance and virtue. This practice probably served as a forerunner of the later custom of decorating church alters with flowers and greenery.

Sources: Barbara Jo Chesser. "Analysis of Wedding Rituals: An Attempt to Make Weddings More Meaningful." *Marriage and Family 82/83.* Guilford, CT: Dushkin. 1982, pp. 57–61.

## Changing Marital Patterns

Several years ago a film called *The Turning Point* portrayed two women who had made decisive choices about their lives. One had opted to become a ballerina and was successful in her career but was also lonely, with nothing in her life except her career. The other woman had married, turning away from a promising career, and while satisfactorily married, was always painfully aware of the choice she had made. The film raised a difficult question: Do women have to make a choice between career and family?

Women's increasingly common pursuit of careers is one reason the birthrate has been declining in recent years. Improved methods of contraception, the relentlessly increasing cost of raising children, and a growing concern about population control are others. In the period 1920–1924, there were about 3.3 children per woman. The figure rose to 3.7 children per woman in 1955–1959 and then generally declined, reaching 2.1 children per woman in 1983 (U.S. Bureau of the Census, *Population Profile of United States: 1981.* Table 5.1; U.S. Bureau of the Census, *Fertility of American Women: June 1983.* Table 2).

### Voluntary Childlessness

While most couples still want children, some do not. About 5 percent of all couples choose childlessness, concluding that one's adult status can be produced by means other than parenthood, especially through a career. Voluntarily childless couples emphasize that children drain away time and energy that could otherwise be devoted to one's career and personal interests.

J. E. Veevers (1973) studied fifty-two voluntarily childless wives and found that many of the informants came from unhappy homes where the parents had supposedly stayed together for the sake of the children, thus passing on to their offspring a feeling that children generally can be a cause of strife in marriage. Some of the voluntarily childless wives were the oldest children in large families and had shouldered major responsibilities for the care of their younger brothers and sisters. These women grew up with a sharply focused awareness that motherhood can be a burdensome responsibility.

One investigation discovered that career success is often a priority for women who remain voluntarily childless (Silka and Kiesler, 1977). Another study concluded that childless couples have two features that set them apart from couples with children: a tendency to more highly value women's achievement and independence and an inclination to interact more extensively with each other in such positive ways as exchanging ideas, working together on projects, and having sexual relations (Feldman, 1981).

About two thirds of Veevers's informants remained childless because of a series of decisions to put off childbearing until a later date. The other third had agreed not to have children as a part of an informal marriage contract (Veevers, 1973). Recent research has produced data supporting the last point; compared to other couples who are deliberating about whether or not to have children, childless couples are more inclined to stay with their original decision (Oakley, 1985).

*Working Mothers*

Working mothers are a prominent segment of the work force. In 1984, 60.5 percent of working women had children under eighteen, a considerable increase from 1975 when the figure was 47.3 percent (U.S. Department of Labor, *The United Nations Decade for Women, 1976–1985: Employment in the United States.* Table 14).

Women enter the work force for various reasons. A study of married mothers of infants concluded that white mothers tended to work because they wanted to be employed while black mothers chose to work because of financial need (Avioli,

1985). An important factor affecting women's motivation to work is the economic component: As family income increases, women are more inclined to work for noneconomic reasons.

Families in which women work or want to work outside the home frequently experience conflict because such behavior clashes with traditional attitudes about women's proper role. An extreme example is provided by the husband who says, "I'm the provider. You're the homemaker. Case closed." Or perhaps the wife works, and this produces severe strains on the family. In dual-career marriages, neither parent is centered in the home, caring for the children and keeping the house in order. Sometimes career-oriented wives find themselves forced out of their work and back in the home. Alternative resolutions include divorce, "commuter" marriages, or both spouses' lowering their career aspirations (Regan and Roland, 1985).

Despite some husbands' negative attitudes, many wives now work, partly because they may simply desire to do so, partly because of the necessity for additional income. While many husbands are willing or even happy to accept this situation, the lion's share of the domestic responsibility still almost always falls on the woman's shoulders even though she may be working full time. Researchers now emphasize that women who work and rear children cannot be expected to meet traditional expectations that they bear the sole or principal responsibility for child-care. They must be able to use day-care or some other arrangement to lessen the physical and emotional burden placed on them by child-care (Kamerman and Kahn, 1981; Lein and Blehar, 1983).

Contention may also arise over the issue of whether or not children will be damaged if their mothers work. Until a few years ago, it was widely believed that this was inevitable or at least likely. However, if the mother likes her work and if effective child-care is available, most studies suggest that the children will not be harmed. In fact, the daughters of working mothers are much more likely to score high on tests of independence, achievement, and positive self-image than are the daughters of nonworking mothers (Hoffman and Nye, 1974). Research also suggests that working women are less likely to be highly possessive of and overly ambitious for their sons largely because they are actively seeking their own fulfillment, rather than living vicariously through the children

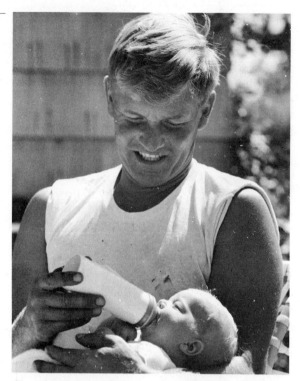

*Changing patterns of marriage have affected the division of labor within many families. An increasing number of husbands, for example, share the responsibility for rearing and caring for their children.*

(Holmstrom, 1972). Children's evaluation of their mothers' work will vary, depending on a number of circumstances. For example, one study found that children are more likely to have a positive outlook toward their mothers' work if they perceive that their mothers view it positively (Thimberger and MacLean, 1982). This finding suggests that if mothers can locate jobs that please them, their children might benefit.

The physical, mental, and emotional well-being of employed mothers is often better than that of their nonworking counterparts. Some concern and even guilt is frequently aroused by the effort to combine the roles of mother, wife, and worker, but this is frequently not a major problem. Working women usually feel useful, valued, and competent, giving them higher self-esteem than nonworking mothers. Working mothers generally display greater enjoyment of their activities and relationships with their children and have more realistic expectations for their children and for themselves as mothers (Green, 1978: 171–173). All in all, if the working wife–mother is able to balance her time and energy between her family and work, she usually constitutes a healthy influence on the domestic scene.

## Divorce and Alternatives to Marriage

The previous section makes it clear that the norms that influence people's patterns of love, courtship, and marriage have become considerably more flexible in recent years. The same tendency is apparent when we examine divorce and the alternatives to marriage.

### Marital Failure

While jogging on the beach in Guam, Chris Willie found a bottle containing a love note that was several years old. The writer said he was dropping the bottle into the Pacific halfway between Hawaii and Seattle. Mr. Willie followed directions in the bottle and mailed the note to the writer's wife in Seattle. The envelope was returned, however, marked "No longer at this address," and so Mr.

Willie sent it to the *Seattle Times*. The newspaper reached the woman by phone, and she asked that the note be read to her. It said:

> If, by the time this letter reaches you, I am old and gray, I know that our love will be as fresh as it is today. It may take a week, or it may take years for this note to find you. Whatever the case may be it shall have traveled by a strange and unpredictable route—the sea. If this should never reach you, it will still be written in my heart that I will go to extreme means to prove my love to you. Your husband, Bob.

The woman laughed and laughed, the newspaper reported. "We're divorced," she said and hung up the phone (Krebs and Thomas, 1981: 18).

Although surviving data are limited, recent research has concluded that in nineteenth-century America, there were fairly high rates of divorce, separation, and desertion (Schultz; 1984). Twen-

**Figure 12.1**
**Marriage and Divorce Rates: 1910 to 1980**

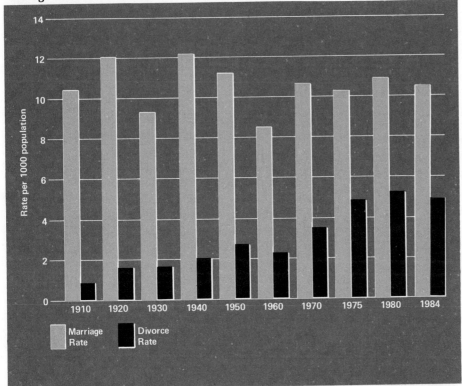

*While the marriage rate has varied little over time, the divorce rate has risen steadily. In 1910 the marriage rate of 10.3 per 1000 people was more than eleven times the divorce rate of .9 per 1000. By 1984 the marriage rate of 10.5 per 1000 people was scarcely twice the divorce rate of 4.9 per 1000. (Source: Adapted from U.S. Bureau of the Census.* Statistical Abstract of the United States: 1986. *No. 81.)*

tieth-century data are more thorough. As Figure 12.1 indicates, divorce has increased sharply in this century. In 1910 there were just 83,000 divorces, 385,000 in 1950, and about 1.2 million in 1984. The rate rose gradually, from .9 divorces per thousand people in 1910 to 4.9 per thousand in 1984. In 1940 there was one divorce for every six marriages. This figure rose to one divorce for every four marriages in 1950, and then rose to nearly one divorce for every two marriages in 1984 (U.S. Bureau of the Census, *Statistical Abstract of the United States: 1986.* No. 81). It is not surprising that with divorce so prevalent, the majority of Americans supports the prospect of divorce when a marriage has major problems. (See Table 12.2.)

**Table 12.2**
**Feelings about Divorce**

That when a marriage has serious difficulties, divorce is an acceptable solution even when children are involved

| | |
|---|---|
| Agree | 61% |
| Disagree | 25 |
| Mixed feelings | 14 |

Source: Adapted from the Roper Organization. *Roper Reports.* March 1981.

*People in different sex, age, income, education, religion, and occupation categories are about equally likely to support divorce under this condition. There is a somewhat greater tendency for self-styled political conservatives than self-styled political moderates or liberals to oppose divorce in this situation.*

*Some Factors Influencing the Divorce Rate*

### PLACE OF RESIDENCE

Since the nineteenth century, the divorce rate has consistently been higher in the western than in the eastern states. In fact, the rate is three or four times as high in the West as it is in the Northeast, with the South second to the West and the north central states next. It is likely that life is generally less stable in a rapidly growing state like California than it is in the more established East. Furthermore those who migrate westward may already have a disproportionate number of unstable marriages. Finally residents of western states tend to be younger, and younger people are generally more divorce prone (Leslie, 1979: 531; Reiss, 1980: 320).

### INDUSTRIALIZATION

Modern industrialized nations are characterized by relatively independent courtship patterns, which permit love to become a critical criterion in mate selection. Love-based marriages tend to be especially unstable, frequently ending in divorce if the parties come to feel that love no longer endures. Consequently increasing levels of industrialization tend to mean higher divorce rates. The United States achieved a high degree of industrial growth before 1930, and at that time its divorce rate was running well ahead of those typical of the European societies. Between 1930 and 1965, the American divorce rate grew slowly, while the rates in many European countries, which were experiencing rapid industrialization, rose sharply (Reiss, 1980: 321).

### AGE OF THE COUPLE

Age at the time of marriage is an important factor. Youthful marriages tend to be less likely to last for several reasons. First, the young are often more likely than older people to grow apart over time in their values and personal interests. Second, young people are the most inclined to turn to marriage as a means of escaping from an unhappy home environment, often failing in the process to realistically assess the chances of success. Third, young people are the most likely to decide to marry because of pregnancy, once again often without objectively assessing whether each partner is really ready to marry (Adams, 1980: 375–376).

A recent study has taken the analysis of the relationship between age and marital instability further, pointing out that besides very young people, those in their late twenties or older are less likely to maintain stable marriages. In both cases, the investigators concluded, inadequate role performances seems to be the major explanatory factor. In youthful marriages a major source of this inadequacy might be the peak interest in sexuality, especially among males, discouraging young married people from focusing on their marriages. For the older category, the researchers simply suggest that the traits that encouraged people to marry late might be the same ones producing marital instability (Booth and Edwards, 1985). Another investigation suggested that marital instability among older people might be produced by a "marriage squeeze"; thus a relatively limited number of potential partners often limits people to mates with characteristics different from their own, and this situation encourages marital instability (Bitter, 1986).

### CHANGING ROLE DEFINITIONS WITHIN MARRIAGE

None of the previous factors explain why the divorce rate shot up in the late 1960s. One significant influence was that role definitions within marriage began to change. The social protests of the 1960s, the increasing proportion of women in the work force, and then the development of the women's movement all encouraged women to seize the opportunity to be more independent and assertive than they had been in the past. Freed of traditional economic and psychological dependence on their husbands, an increasing number of wives decided that they did not need to grit their teeth and accept unhappy marriages.

### CHANGING DIVORCE LAWS

In 1970 California enacted the first no-fault divorce law in the United States, and forty-eight states have now adopted this standard in some form. No-fault legislation simplifies divorce proceedings. One spouse no longer needs to establish grounds for divorce, testifying to the other's adultery, cruelty, or desertion and bringing in witnesses to support his or her testimony. The wife and husband are no longer forced to be adversaries. With no-fault divorce, the legal focus becomes the partners' joint endeavor to end as quickly as possible a marriage that does not work (Weitzman and Dixon, 1983).

## Consequences of Divorce

If someone's parents are divorced, he or she is said to come from a "broken home." This phrase calls to mind the image of a home in shambles, with everything—relationships, personalities, and even furniture—in disarray or even destroyed. It seems obvious that the product of a "broken home" is likely to have psychological problems, perhaps serious ones. But is this true? What, in fact, happens to spouses and children after divorce?

### CONSEQUENCES FOR THE COUPLE

Paul Bohannon (1970: 33) has suggested that, in a sense, divorce reverses the courtship process. Instead of having been "selected" out of the whole world, the exspouse now feels "deselected." Not surprisingly recent research has concluded that following divorce people tend to become more depressed than they were before it occurred. The level of depression seems to be affected by the magnitude of one's economic problems, the availability of close, confiding relationships, and the extent to which one's former standard of living is maintained (Menaghan and Lieberman, 1986).

Economically women tend to suffer more from divorce than men do. In one study two-thirds of the women reported that their income following divorce was considerably lower than before, while only 19 percent of the males described such a situation. The researcher concluded that ". . . the divorce experiences of males and of females are not the same. Although some of these differences lessened the negative consequences of divorce for women, most of them clearly favored the male" (Albrecht, 1980: 67).

Nonetheless, there are indications that in many cases men have a more difficult time adjusting to divorce than women. While the suicide rate for divorced women has been three times that of married women, four times more divorced than married men have killed themselves (Moffett and Scherer, 1976). Furthermore evidence has indicated that men who have not remarried within six years after divorce have increased rates of car accidents, alcoholism, drug abuse, depression, and anxiety (Brody, 1983). Why do women seem to adjust more effectively to divorce? One factor seems to be that women have more skills for developing supportive social networks. For instance, one recent study found that following divorce women with children tended to receive strong support from social networks of kin and friends living relatively close to them (Leslie and Grady, 1985). Another factor operating here might be that men are more likely than women to lose custody of their children. Research concluded that some newly separated men's difficulties are compounded by

*Traditionally, when parents divorce, the wife has kept the children. In the immensely popular film* Kramer vs. Kramer, *however, the wife gave up her son and then a year later initiated a court battle to obtain the boy's custody.*

**302** their failure to accept the fact that the adaptation to their new existence will be greatly enhanced if they radically limit their interaction with their former spouse and also alter their relationship with their children (White and Bloom, 1981).

Age is another social characteristic that appears to affect people's adjustment to divorce. The Hunts (1980) found that most childless people who divorce at a young age soon rejoin the never-married group, rapidly putting both the marriage and former spouse out of their minds. In contrast, people with children who divorce after many years of marriage never really become single again. Such people form a group apart; the Hunts called them "the formerly married."

The unhappiness associated with most divorces does not mean that unhappily married people should stay married. A study indicated that individuals with unsatisfying marriages were more depressed, lonelier, and more socially isolated than were divorced people (Renne, 1974).

### CONSEQUENCES FOR THE CHILDREN

When divorce occurs, young children sometimes blame themselves. "I'll be good, Mommy and Daddy," a four-year-old pleads, "if we can all live together again." Certainly many children suffer because of divorce, but what is the overall picture? To begin, the number of children whose parents divorce has been increasing. Today about 60 percent of divorces involve minor children, and about one million children encounter divorce every year (Leslie, 1979: 553). It is estimated that by 1990 about one third of American children will experience their parents' divorce before they reach the age of eighteen (Kurdek, 1981). Following a divorce the relationship between children and the nonresident parent tends to change dramatically. One study concluded that in divorce situations, most children have little contact with their nonresident parent, usually the father, and what contact occurs is fairly superficial, with the nonresident parent often acting more like a pal than a parent (Furstenberg and Nord, 1985).

A number of status factors seem to affect children's adjustment to divorce. Younger children seem to find the experience more difficult than older children, with children under five suffering the strongest emotional reactions. Boys tend to have more difficulty adjusting to divorce than girls (Lowery and Settle, 1985). Probably both younger children and boys adjust more slowly because of more limited social skills. Another factor affecting children's adjustment is the custodial parent's reaction to the divorce. Goode (1956: 317–321) found that the more trauma mothers experienced from their divorces, the more likely that they would describe their children as hard to handle following the split. Eighty-one percent of the mothers studied admitted that they were concerned about the impact of the divorce on their children. However, 55 percent encountered no increase in problems with their children afterwards, and only 14 percent found that their children were more difficult to deal with in the months following the divorce.

One researcher has analyzed the impact of different time periods in the divorce process. In interviews with college students, Deborah Luepnitz (1979) learned that about half the students felt that the conflict between their parents was considerably more stressful than the divorce itself. Luepnitz suggested that much of the social-scientific literature on the "children of divorce" can be better thought of as concerned with "children of marital conflict"; in other words the symptoms long thought to be produced by divorce really result from years of being exposed to bitter parental fighting. It may well be much more harmful for children to grow up in conflict-ridden homes than in "broken" ones.

Divorce generally disrupts relationships between parents and children. When a divorced parent is also gay, there are likely to be additional

## CONTEMPORARY ISSUE

*Gay Parents*

 Research on homosexuals indicates that those who have children possess the same need to love and care for their children as other parents do. But gay parents' relationships with their children are often complicated by their sexual preference.

Brenda Maddox conducted forty-seven long interviews with male and female homosexuals and with the present and past spouses of most of them. She also received dozens of letters from other individuals who were too far away to be interviewed.

One conclusion from her research was that for some homosexuals the desire to have children was the principal reason that they married, and fear of being isolated from their children is the main barrier to being open about their homosexuality.

Many struggle with the issue of whether they should tell their children. The gay parents who choose secrecy are terrified that their children will reject them if they find out. On the whole women are more likely to tell their children than men are. When told, children generally accept their parents' homosexuality. Maddox wrote:

> There are many accounts in the gay press of . . . moments of revelation, which boil down to the child saying: "You're still my parent, aren't you?" The children are loving and understanding, and if they live in a liberated place like California, they dare to be proud. They take the news much better than wives, and why not? Children are not interested in their parents' sex life. Even as adults, they keep a

protective amnesia about what their parents probably had to do to bring them into the world.

*(Maddox, 1982: 66)*

While children are unlikely to reject gay parents, knowledge of parents' sexual preference can cause the children to question their own sexual identity. The overwhelming majority of these children eventually decide that they are heterosexual, but some, particularly boys, experience considerable stress before the decision has been made.

As more gay parents "come out," their homosexual lovers find themselves in the stepparent role, where they encounter the same difficulties divorced parents' heterosexual lovers must confront. Maddox noted:

> They are faced with many of the familiar problems, such as how much to discipline the child and how much to hide their resentment of the intruder. The child is a constant reminder of the partner's intercourse with someone else, and a constant drain on money and attention, someone who makes a lot of work and who often arrives just when the couple wants to

relax. The child can carry stories back to the other parent—who may be looking for tales of homosexual hanky-panky to take to court to plead for a cessation of visiting rights.

*(Maddox, 1982: 67)*

Gays and their children face some special problems, and yet the results of a number of studies suggest that the children of divorced homosexuals are no more confused, disturbed, or homosexual than the children of divorced heterosexuals. One psychiatric researcher has suggested that children take their cues for sexual identity from a variety of people, not just from their parents.

Evidence on the effects of gay parenthood on children is limited, however, and judges in most custody cases generally subscribe to the traditional view that it is best for children to grow up in a household headed by a heterosexual couple. Yet times are slowly changing. In 1970 lesbian mothers won custody of their children in about 1 percent of the contested custody cases in America. By 1982 they were winning 15 percent of the cases.

Source: Brenda Maddox. "Homosexual Parents." *Psychology Today.* Vol. 16. February 1982. p. 62+.

---

problems, as the following Contemporary Issue suggests.

## Remarriage

Several years ago the hostess at a party received a phone call, which occupied her for nearly three quarters of an hour. "Who was that?" she was asked when she returned.

"Poor woman!" the hostess replied. "She's desperate. Several months back her husband divorced

her, and tonight she feels trapped at home, alone on a Saturday night with no place to go and no one even to talk to. The funny thing is that I don't even know her very well and really don't like her much. She's very uptight. I invited her over but she turned me down. So I just talked to her."

William Goode (1956) contended that the norms governing the behavior of divorced people are often unclear. Should they continue to socialize with their old married friends? Should they stay in the same town or move elsewhere? How should they deal with acute, even desperate loneliness such as that felt by the woman just described? One common course of action is to remarry.

As we have already noted, people tend to marry homogamously. This generalization also applies to divorced people. While over 90 percent of single men and women marry another single person, over half of divorced men and women remarry another divorced person. Among those who remarry, over 15 percent will do so within a few months of the completion of divorce proceedings and another 50 percent within three years. It takes an average of seven years for those who divorce to leave their first marriage but only three years for those who remarry to enter a second marriage (Reiss, 1980: 340–342). In 1960 the remarriage rate was 197 women per thousand widowed and divorced women. The rate rose steadily reaching 510 per thousand in 1975 and then 610 per thousand in 1982 (U.S. Bureau of the Census, *Statistical Abstract of the United States: 1986*. No. 124).

How satisfactory are remarriages? Glenn and Weaver (1977) claimed that divorce and remarriage are fairly effective mechanisms for replacing bad marriages with good ones—that second marriages that do not end quickly in divorce seem to be almost as successful as intact first marriages. In another study Albrecht (1979) asked his informants to evaluate how happy their remarriages were compared with their first marriages and also how well each of their marriages compared with their acquaintances' marriages and with the level of happiness that they expected to find in marriage. The second marriages came out ahead on all these counts. When second marriages produce problems, therapists can work with clients to help them sort out unresolved issues, sometimes suggesting legal help to overcome the economic confusions and complexities remarried families often face (Bernstein and Collins, 1985).

The presence of children seems to be a factor strongly affecting the satisfaction level of remarriages. In one investigation informants who were remarried with stepchildren reported less satisfaction and were more inclined to seek divorce than remarried people without stepchildren (White and Booth, 1985).

## Alternatives to Conventional Marriage

In recent years a number of factors have made people feel freer to choose various alternatives to conventional monogamous marriages. These include a sharp decrease in social pressure to have children, vast improvements in the availability of effective methods of contraception for women, increased economic self-sufficiency among many single people, and rapid improvements in the communication of new ideas (Ramey, 1978: 3–5).

In the following pages we examine single-parent households, voluntary singlehood, gay relationships, and communes.

### Single-Parent Households

Between 1970 and 1984, the number of children under eighteen living in single-parent households rose from 8.2 million to 14 million, representing an increase from 12 to 26.9 percent of the total of American households containing children under eighteen (U.S. Bureau of the Census, *Marital Status and Living Arrangements: March 1982*. Table E; U.S. Bureau of the Census, *Statistical Abstract of the United States: 1986*. No. 66). (See Figure 12.2). Although the majority of single-parent families are headed by women, an increasing number of men are running families by themselves. Single-parent families tend to have modest incomes, with father–child families having incomes that are more than twice those of mother–child families. While about 24 percent of all children are living below the poverty level, the figure is 57 percent for one-parent families (Norton and Glick, 1986).

Single parents face some other significant problems. Probably the most frequently expressed complaint is the overload of role commitments. Single parents must be all things to their children, not only mother but father as well, the breadwinner, the cook, and the nurse. Work schedules often conflict with parental obligations. How can the parent drive a child to day-care, a little-league game, or a recital during working hours? Another difficulty is that single parents often have no one who can validate how they are treating their children. In a two-parent household, a mother or father can seek feedback for decisions from the other spouse. When single parents are challenged by their children, they often have no one who can effectively provide this feedback. As a result many begin to compromise their definition of reality, doing such things as giving in to a child whose personality development might be much more ef-

**Figure 12.2**
**Living Arrangements of Children under 18 Years Old: 1970 to 1984**

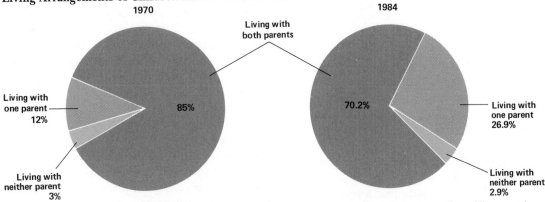

*The most noteworthy finding is the decline in percentage of children living with both parents—from 85 percent in 1970 to 70.2 percent in 1984. The figure suggests that children increasingly experience parental divorce while growing up. (Source: Adapted from U.S. Bureau of the Census.* Current Population Reports, *Series P–20,* Marital Status and Living Arrangements: *March 1982. Table E; U.S. Bureau of the Census.* Statistical Abstract of the United States: 1986. *No. 66.)*

fectively nurtured if firm guidelines were established (Glenwick and Mowrey, 1986; Sanik and Mauldin, 1986; Turner and Smith, 1983).

*Singlehood*

Being single was frowned upon during the colonial era. Women were considered old maids if they were not married by the age of twenty-five, and bachelors were scorned, ridiculed, and sometimes even forced to pay a special tax. The Bible declares that people should be fruitful and multiply, and single people were seen to be defying this command.

In modern times, however, a significant number of people have chosen to remain single. In 1960 about 32.8 percent of the adult population was unmarried. In 1982 about 36.9 million adults had never been married, while 13.2 million were widowed and 12.3 were divorced. This total of 62.4 million represented 36.8 percent, nearly two fifths of the adult population (U.S. Bureau of the Census, *Statistical Abstract of the United States: 1986.* No. 43). It appears that the percentage of unmarried people will continue to increase; one specialist has predicted that among young people in their mid-twenties to early thirties, 12 percent of women and 10 percent of men will never marry—three times as high a proportion as in their parents' generation (Glick, 1986). Singles include recent col-

lege graduates, who are on their own for the first time, as well as senior citizens, who reside together in order to make the most of two social-security checks. In between, one finds millions of single people pursuing a diversity of life-styles, including a host of single parents.

Currently many cities offer singles' apartment complexes as well as singles' bars, magazines, dating services, vacation packages, and resorts. However, the "swinging singles" side of singles life has received widespread criticism. Urban "body shops"—bars and clubs where sexual partners can be easily found—are felt by many to cater to men and degrade women.

The category of single people contains diverse outlooks toward marriage. For instance, never-married people are much more likely than divorced singles to define singlehood as a permanent life-style, and marriage rates are higher for divorced than never-married singles (Cockrum and White, 1985). People who are voluntarily single are probably most strongly committed to this status. Peter Stein (1980) studied singles and found a number of "pushes away" from marriage as well as "pulls toward" being single. "Pushes away" from married life included the possible suffocation of a one-to-one relationship, sexual frustration, and, interestingly, fear of isolation and loneliness. "Pulls toward" singlehood involved the

**306**  exciting life-style, self-sufficiency, and the availability of sexual variety.

### Gay "Marriages"

Donna Tanner (1978) found that homosexual (lesbian) relationships generally pass through three stages. First, there is the "trial phase," in which a regularized sexual association begins. Second, "insulation" occurs, with the couple living together covertly and attempting to develop a permanent commitment to each other. Finally "stabilization" takes place. At this point the couple lives together openly although in a relationship that lacks legal validation, something like a cohabitational arrangement between a man and woman. The third stage is important because it is at this point that social recognition is conferred upon the relationship by others; for instance, the lesbian couple may be invited out to parties as a social unit.

Many gay couples, however, want more than the informal recognition of friends. They would like a legally sanctioned marriage. In 1971, in the case of *Baker* v. *Nelson,* two men appealed to the Minnesota Supreme Court after a lower court ruled in favor of a county clerk who refused to grant them a marriage license. The couple contended that the state's statutes did not expressly forbid same-sex marriages. The court conceded that they were correct on this point but that marriage laws using such terms as "husband" and "wife" or "bride" and "groom" were meant to refer exclusively to a union between a man and a woman.

One reason many gays want a legally sanctioned relationship is for psychological support. If a relationship is clearly regarded as a marriage in the eyes of other people, then the participants themselves are likely to feel more comfortable and secure in it. There are also practical reasons. Gay couples face problems with insurance, tax laws, and inheritance. Even something as simple as a hospital visit can pose difficulties. A report in the London *Times* told of a dying lesbian who could be visited only by her family and was therefore denied deathbed visits from her partner of twenty years (Scanzoni and Scanzoni, 1981: 242–245).

### Communes

**Communes** are planned, intentional communities, bringing together biologically unrelated people in order to build a large, family-like group. Many, perhaps most, communes permit couples to maintain their social and sexual exclusiveness as a couple. About 250,000 people are estimated to live in communes in the United States.

Rosabeth Kanter (1968) studied thirty nineteenth-century American communes in order to determine what qualities increased or decreased the likelihood that a commune would survive. Nine of these communes were rated as successful, defined as lasting thirty-three years or more, and twenty-one were unsuccessful, enduring less than sixteen years and averaging a life span of just four years. The successful communes tended to build strong group commitments in a number of ways. They required significant personal sacrifices (ceasing sexual activity and alcohol and tobacco use, for instance) and also major investments of time, energy, money, and property. In addition, the more successful communes also created strong in-group feelings, often demanding that members give up all primary-group contacts with the outside world. Furthermore the participants' sense of individuality was largely eliminated; their identity was shaped and controlled by community standards.

The most comprehensive study of American communes is based on data derived from a sample of almost 700 men and women living in sixty urban communes in Los Angeles, Houston, Atlanta, Boston, New York, and Minneapolis. Some of the communes were intensely committed to certain religious positions or other values, while others were simply places where economic sharing occurred. Some were highly structured, and others were not. In a number of cases, children were present, but such groups were in the minority. Most of the participants were single, and all the communes included both men and women. In rank order the following were the primary reasons that members cited for joining the groups:

1. Financial advantages
2. Order and regularity
3. Friendship and support
4. A means of leaving home
5. A way to break from the past
6. A life-style that provided new and interesting experiences
7. A search for like-minded people
8. Companionship or community

The average participant stayed for two years, with some moving on to other communes, while others returned to more traditional life-styles. A significant proportion of the commune members in the sample led otherwise normal lives as students or as workers in conventional jobs (Zablocki, 1977).

Many Americans who are now living in communes do not fit 1960s stereotypes of long-haired hippies sitting around campfires in the evening singing folksongs. Often they lead ordinary middle-class lives, and instead of using the term "commune," they speak of "intentional communities." Such settlements have become one modern means of combatting food and heating bills, rising land prices, and high interest rates, while also serving as a way of restoring a sense of community frequently missing in modern life. In Florida, for instance, an intentional community of 100 families has permitted participants to live comfortably on less than $10,000 per year. The members have pooled their resources in order to build houses and buy land and tools. Typically houses have been built by a combination of do-it-yourself efforts, house-building parties, and outside contracting. The residents have used each other's expertise through voluntary labor exchange. Families have controlled their own land, but the community members' cooperative efforts have created a positive situation in which to live — as one observer has phrased it, "an atmosphere where things are possible" (*Futurist*, 1985).

## Conclusion

In 1980 a conference, which originally had been called the White House Conference on the Family, was renamed the White House Conference on Families. It might seem that changing one word in the title from the singular to the plural form was not significant, but it was. The change reflected the growing understanding in American society that there is not one form of the modern American family but many (Berger and Berger, 1984: 59).

Until recently most Americans expected to grow up in nuclear families and develop this type of family themselves. While the option remains popular, it is just that — an option. Nowadays Americans have a variety of life-style choices, but they also find themselves faced with the confusion and uncertainty of making choices. Was it better to grow up several decades ago when nearly everyone was expected to marry and start a family or is it better now? What do you think?

# STUDY GUIDE

## Summary

1. A family is traditionally defined as a social unit composed of two or more people who live together and are related by blood, marriage, or adoption. The family provides functions that are critical for its survival and also for the maintenance of society.

2. The functions of the family include sexual regulation, economic cooperation, and socialization. In other societies these functions are often performed in ways that differ sharply from those carried out by Americans. Prominent kinship terms involve the type of marriage, customs for marriage eligibility, residential rules for newly married people, and patterns of power within the family.

3. Like other institutional structures, the modern American nuclear family has been shaped by industrialization. In the course of the industrial era, the nuclear family has lost some of its preindustrial functions, with distinctly negative consequences for family members sometimes produced.

4. U.S. society has experienced changing patterns of love, courtship, and marriage. Living together has become a widely practiced activity, with a number of social conditions contributing to the increased incidence. People tend to practice homogamy, marrying people whose social characteristics are similar to their own. Among the changing marital patterns are an increase in childlessness and an increase in working mothers.

5. Divorce has increased sharply since the mid-1960s. Place of residence, industrialization, age of the couple, changing role definitions within marriage, and changing divorce laws are factors

affecting the divorce rate. There are significant, sometimes damaging effects of divorce for spouses and children. On the other hand, people's lives can become happier and more fulfilling once unhappy marriages are terminated. Frequently divorced people remarry, with second marriages often more satisfying than the first. Many Americans pursue alternatives to a conventional monogamous marriage. Among them are single-parent households, singlehood, gay "marriage," and communes.

## Glossary

**commune**   a planned, intentional community, bringing together biologically unrelated people in order to build a large, family-like group.

**egalitarian**   a type of family in which the wife–mother and husband–father share power and also permit their children to participate in the family decisions.

**endogamy**   a custom requiring a person to marry within a specific social unit, such as a kinship group, religious organization, or social class.

**exogamy**   a custom compelling someone to marry outside a specific social unit.

**extended family**   a family involving two or more generations of people related by blood and living together or close to each other.

**family**   traditionally defined as a social unit composed of two or more people who live together and are related by blood, marriage, or adoption.

**homogamy**   marriage with a person having social characteristics similar to one's own.

**incest taboo**   a rule outlawing sexual relations between certain kin-group members believed to be too closely related as defined by the cultural standards of a given society.

**kinship system**   a number of people related by common descent, marriage, or adoption.

**matriarchal**   a type of family in which the wife–mother is the formal head and the absolute or nearly absolute source of power.

**matrilocal**   a type of residence that involves settling with or near the wife's parents.

**monogamy**   a marriage practice in which there is one husband and one wife.

**neolocal**   a type of residence that occurs when married people establish an independent place to live.

**nuclear family**   a two-generation family that includes a father, a mother, and their children living separately from other relatives.

**patriarchal**   a type of family in which the husband–father is the formal head and the absolute or nearly absolute source of power.

**patrilocal**   a type of residence that requires settling with or near the husband's parents.

**polyandry**   the form of polygamy in which a wife has two or more husbands.

**polygamy**   a marriage practice where one spouse has two or more spouses of the other sex.

**polygyny**   the form of polygamy in which a husband has two or more wives.

## Learning Objectives

After studying this chapter, you should be able to:

1. Define family and indicate why it is socially important.
2. Discuss with illustrations the three basic functions of the family examined in the text.
3. Identify and define kinship terms for marriage types, marriage-eligibility customs, residential rules, and family-power patterns.
4. Describe the effects of industrialization on the family and explain the nature and consequences of the nuclear family's loss of functions.
5. Discuss contemporary patterns of cohabitation, including the consequences of living together.
6. Examine the topics of voluntary childlessness and working mothers.
7. Identify and discuss the factors that influence the divorce rate.

8. Describe the consequences of divorce for the couple and for children.
9. Examine prominent alternatives to conventional marriage.

## Tests

### True–false test

_____ 1. The incest taboo exists only in Western cultures.

_____ 2. The nuclear family is compatible with a modern, industrial setting.

_____ 3. Polygyny is a much more common form of polygamy than is polyandry.

_____ 4. A law that will not permit second cousins to marry is an example of endogamy.

_____ 5. Richard Sennett's study of nineteenth-century Chicago families concluded that the nuclear-family type may be less supportive of male members' emotional and occupational development than the extended family.

_____ 6. The French historian Philippe Ariès suggested that in the preindustrial era, women and children encountered fewer restrictions than today.

_____ 7. Recent research indicates that in the past decade, premarital cohabitation has become less acceptable.

_____ 8. Research concludes that children are more likely to have a positive outlook toward their mothers' work if they perceive that their mothers view the work positively.

_____ 9. In the middle 1980s, the divorce rate was roughly one divorce for every two marriages.

_____ 10. Gay marriages are now legal in twenty-two states.

### Multiple-choice test

_____ 1. Which of the following has NOT been recognized as a function of the incest taboo?
   a. elimination of conflicts and jealousies produced by sexual rivalry
   b. clear definitions of family roles
   c. encouragement of alliances between families
   d. accomplishment of age-linked tasks

_____ 2. Compared to noncohabiting women, cohabiting women are more likely to consider themselves:
   a. aggressive.
   b. emotionally supportive.
   c. politically conservative.
   d. noncompetitive.

_____ 3. Homogamy:
   a. only involves gay couples.
   b. involves both race and religion.
   c. is not influenced by family and friends.
   d. does not occur in modern times.

_____ 4. The birth rate has been declining in recent years because of:
   a. involuntary childlessness.
   b. women's increasing pursuit of careers.

    c. increased fertility problems produced by environmental damage.

    d. reduced male willingness to be breadwinners.

_____ 5. Veevers's study of voluntary childlessness showed which of the following statements to be true?

    a. Women in the study tended to be youngest children and thus felt inadequate to provide child-care because of inexperience.

    b. Many of the women were neurotically dependent on others.

    c. Many of the informants came from unhappy homes in which parents had communicated to them the feeling that children generally cause strife in marriage.

    d. Most of the informants had tradition-oriented husbands.

_____ 6. Which of the following statements describes a condition affecting the divorce rate?

    a. The divorce rate is consistently lower in eastern than in western states.

    b. Love-based marriages tend to be particularly stable.

    c. No-fault divorce legislation has discouraged the occurrence of divorce.

    d. Changing role definitions within marriage have made modern marriages more stable.

_____ 7. Following divorce, women are more likely than men:

    a. to commit suicide.

    b. to have increased rates of car accidents, alcoholism, drug abuse, depression, and anxiety.

    c. to participate in clubs and organizations.

    d. to have financial problems.

_____ 8. In remarriages:

    a. it is unlikely that both partners will have been previously married.

    b. the level of happiness tends to be lower than in first marriages.

    c. children's presence has little or no impact.

    d. the norms governing the behavior of divorced people are often unclear.

_____ 9. Single-parent families:

    a. tend to be less affluent than most families.

    b. declined in number between 1970 and 1984.

    c. declined in their proportion of all families between 1970 and 1984.

    d. b and c

_____ 10. Singlehood:

    a. can be encouraged by "pushes away" from marriage.

    b. is likely to increase in the years ahead.

    c. is more likely to be defined as a permanent life-style by never-married individuals than divorced people.

    d. a, b, and c

## Essay test

1. Define family. Discuss the relationship between industrialization and the nuclear family. Examine the declining functions of the nuclear family.

2. Analyze cohabitation, indicating who engages in this practice and also the consequences of living together.

3. Are young Americans of the 1980s entirely free to choose their spouses? Use the concept of homogamy in answering the question.

4. Examine three factors that significantly affect the divorce rate. Discuss in detail the consequences of divorce for both couples and children.

5. Describe two alternatives to conventional marriage, indicating why some people find these particular options either necessary or appealing in modern society.

# Suggested Readings

Atwater, Lynn. 1982. *The Extramarital Connection: Sex, Intimacy, and Identity*. New York: Irvington. A study that uses fifty in-depth interviews to uncover social and psychological patterns in women's extramarital affairs.

Berger, Brigette, and Peter L. Berger. 1984. *The War over the Family*. Garden City, NY: Anchor Books. A sociological analysis of both the American family and reactions to it, offering thought-provoking endorsement of the nuclear-family form.

Cherlin, Andrew J. 1981. *Marriage, Divorce, Remarriage*. Cambridge: Harvard University Press. A description and analysis of recent trends in these three areas in which norms and behavioral patterns have been rapidly changing.

Goode, William J. 1982. *The Family*. Englewood Cliffs, NJ: Prentice-Hall. Second edition. A short, clearly written text, effectively introducing students to the sociological study of the family.

Hood, Jane C. 1983. *Becoming a Two-Job Family*. New York: Praeger. A study that follows sixteen couples over six years and indicates in detail the impact of women's working on the family. Previous research and theory is effectively incorporated into the analysis throughout the book.

McGrady, Mike. 1975. *The Kitchen Sink Papers*. Garden City, NY: Doubleday. A journalist's often humorous, frequently revealing account of switching roles with his wife and becoming a househusband while his wife became the breadwinner.

Skolnick, Arlene S., and Jerome H. Skolnick (eds.). 1986. *Family in Transition*. Boston: Little, Brown. Fifth edition. Thirty-six articles divided into eleven chapters on a variety of topics involving marriage, the family, and related issues. The book includes a good general introduction and effective part openers.

Stein, Peter J. (ed.). 1981. *Single Life: Unmarried Adults in Social Context*. New York: St. Martin's. Articles that examine some of the diverse types of unmarried people as well as singles' activities and problems.

# Student Projects

1. Write a set of marriage vows that you believe acknowledges the important matters to be covered in a marriage relationship. If you are involved in a serious relationship, you might want to seek input from your partner. Compare the wording of your vows with the content of typical vows, containing such phrases as "to have and to hold," "to love and to cherish (or obey)," "in sickness and in health," and "until death do us part." Is the marriage your vows describe traditional or nontraditional? Compare your vows with classmates' efforts.

2. Using the text's list of alternatives to conventional marriage and also the option of cohabitation, ask at least ten people to rate the different choices on desirability—"1" would be a very low desirability and "10" would be the highest. For your informants seek a balance of males and females and also younger and older people. What explanations can you supply for your results? Discuss findings with other classmates.

# Answers to Test Questions

## True–false test

| | | | | |
|---|---|---|---|---|
| 1. f | 3. t | 5. t | 7. f | 9. t |
| 2. t | 4. f | 6. t | 8. t | 10. f |

## Multiple-choice test

| | | | | |
|---|---|---|---|---|
| 1. d | 3. b | 5. c | 7. d | 9. a |
| 2. a | 4. b | 6. a | 8. d | 10. d |

# 13
# Religion and Education

In December 1985 the U.S. Circuit Court of Appeals ruled by a vote of eight to seven that creationism (the biblical story of the creation of the world and its inhabitants) need not receive as much attention in the schools as the teaching of evolution. The Louisiana attorney general was not impressed by the vote. He vowed to take the case to the Supreme Court, declaring that the seven-vote dissent represented strong support for the creationist position (Lewin, 1986).

In California the creationism–evolution dispute appeared in another form. In September 1985 scientists successfully lobbied with the state board of education for a sophisticated, accurate treatment of evolution in school books. But when the changes were made, many scientists were disappointed, feeling that the publishers were trying not to offend the creationists. For instance, one book stated:

> "Many scientists think that dinosaurs were the ancestors of modern reptiles." Publishers have retreated to words such as "think" and "believe" in an attempt to be as vague as possible on the subject of evolution. At one hearing, . . . [a specialist] brandished a dinosaur bone to show how little the theory rests on belief and how much on substance.
>
> *(Marshall, 1986: 19)*

The disputes continue. On both sides the feelings have been strong, because something important is at stake: the development of children's beliefs and values.

Religion and education are both personal forms of socialization. The above discussion highlights the fact that in their socialization of individuals, participants in both institutions are concerned that the beliefs and values they support are passed onto children. When the risk develops that this will not occur, people become agitated. Throughout this chapter it should be apparent that all issues addressed involve personal socialization in some way. Now let us consider the meanings of religion and education.

In sociology an analysis of religion is likely to begin with the concept of "the sacred." The **sacred** is anything that is superior in power, is set apart from the ordinary and practical, and creates a sense of awe. Something sacred is so special that it cannot be questioned. Members of the group or society accept sacred items or activities as representations of the fundamental meaning of life. That acceptance creates a sense of unity and common purpose among those people and serves as the basis for the formation of their religion. Thus what makes an item or idea sacred in a sociological sense is the way people regard it and the unifying effect it produces, not any quality inherent within it. The same wafers and wine that Catholics consider to be sacred, representing the body and blood of Christ, would be regarded as ordinary food and drink by non-Catholics. In contrast to the sacred, those things that people consider ordinary and closely linked to practical demands are termed **profane.** Profane items do not create unity and a sense of common purpose the way sacred things do.

A **religion** may be defined as a unified system of beliefs and practices that focuses on sacred things and serves to create a community of worshippers (Durkheim, 1975: 123). Among other things religions may be analyzed as efforts to develop philosophical and spiritual insights that can be used in facing the stresses, confusions, and complexities of human existence. In this chapter we consider functions of religion and prominent trends in religion today.

Like religion, education is a type of personal socialization. **Education** is the transmission of knowledge, skills, and values by either formal or informal means. This transmission occurs primarily between the adult generation and the generation that follows it, and the process is critical for the survival of the culture. In modern societies the education process is in general highly formalized. We examine theories of education, education and equality, and reform in American education.

*Many parents, like those of the children pictured here, choose to send their children to private schools which emphasize formal religious training.*

## Functions of Religion

Just as children must undergo socialization in order to become members of society, people must be socialized before they become members of a religious organization. Once socialized, people find a number of functions their religious organizations perform. We will examine four functions of religion, three of which are associated with prominent sociological theories, and then discuss functional equivalents of religion.

### Providing Social Cohesion

Émile Durkheim (1961; 1964) emphasized that as people in traditional societies performed religious rituals, they were focused on what was special and awe-inspiring—the sacred. Durkheim claimed that collective concentration on selected sacred ideas and activities helped create a sense of common purpose and unity.

The sense of common purpose and unity that religion provided assured preindustrial people's commitment to it, in part because of the demands it made upon them. Durkheim indicated that religion places

. . . constraint upon the individual. It forces him into practices which subject him to small or large sac-

rifices which are painful to him. He must take from his goods the offerings that he is compelled to present to the divinity; he must take time from his work or play in which to observe rites; he must impose upon himself every sort of privation which is demanded of him, even to renounce life if the gods ordain.

*(Durkheim, 1964: 92)*

The deep commitment that preindustrial religion required of all worshippers strengthened their sense of involvement within the local community or society.

In preindustrial societies, then, religion generally served a cohesive function. But with the advent of industrialism, secularization occurred. **Secularization** is the process by which religion loses influence within groups and societies. Secularization involves the replacement of religious faith with belief in scientific principles, and, in addition, it leads to an increasing separation between the religious and nonreligious areas of life. Activities such as work, war, government, commerce, and learning and science become increasingly divorced from religion (Johnstone, 1975: 296; O'Dea, 1966: 81–86).

But the impact of secularization should not be overemphasized in modern societies. At public

*Religion and religious rituals are an intimate part of the fabric of daily life for many people. This photo shows an Hassidic Jewish father and his son participating in a Bar Mitzvah, a ceremony in which the boy formally becomes a man and assumes all the religious duties of an adult member of the community.*

## Supporting and Maintaining Social Control

Many congregations contain prominent, wealthy, and powerful members of the community, and the clergy of such churches are likely to feel that they must support dominant standards of social control, no matter how their personal feelings differ, in order to retain these members' economic and social support. For instance, in the 1950s, white ministers in Little Rock, Arkansas, in spite of their personal inclinations, often publicly opposed the integration of their congregations because they feared that integration would drive out the wealthy and powerful white members (Campbell and Pettigrew, 1959).

Mark Twain, a strong opponent of organized religion, emphasized that churches backed dominant practices of social control with a vengence. On the issue of slavery, Twain suggested, religious leaders originally focused on biblical texts that supported the practice. In time, however, public opposition to slavery became widespread. "There was no place in the land where the seeker could not find some small budding sign of pity for the slave. No place in the land but one — the pulpit." Finally, Twain continued, organized religion started opposing slavery. "It . . . did what it always does, joined the procession — at the tail end" (Twain, 1973: 109).

Karl Marx (1970: 131 – 132) also suggested that the primary function of religion is to support the status quo. Marx's analysis was centrally concerned with the class distinction between the exploited workers and the wealthy capitalists, who own the factories and farms where the workers labor. According to Marx, religion provides "illusory happiness" for workers, promising that the righteous will receive their just reward in heaven. In an often quoted Marxist phrase, religion is "the opium of the people." Thus Marx believed that religion has advanced the interests of the dominant capitalist class, providing a means by which capitalists could distract workers from their own immediate, pressing interests. Marx believed that in order for workers to correctly perceive the exploitation that they suffer, they must abandon religion. Once freed, they could start organizing to change their economic and political situation.

A recent review of Marx's writings suggested

events — presidential inaugurations, political conventions, or graduation ceremonies, for example — prayers and religious references emphasize the underlying unity and shared values of those present. In many rural communities, churches have traditionally served as the center of local activities, providing recreational programs and opportunities to make friends and generally catering to the specific needs of congregation members. If, for instance, members of the church are looking for jobs, the organization is likely to take an active role in helping them secure employment. Furthermore in recent years, the advancement of secularization has been somewhat offset by a widespread religious revival, seeking a more prominent role for religion in modern people's lives. One expert has noted that many religions "have gotten their acts together," making aggressive, passionate appeals for new recruits in the United States and many other countries (Marty, 1985).

that were Marx to return to earth more than a century after his death, he would find plenty of evidence supporting his conviction about the destructive effect of religion on workers (Gurley, 1984).

## Promoting Social Change

In the course of a major study of world religions, Max Weber concluded that religion has promoted social change by supporting the development of capitalism. Unlike Marx, who considered religion little more than a reflection of the economic system, Weber suggested that this institution has played an important role in the development of the economy. Weber conceded that capitalism has also influenced religion, but he primarily reversed Marx's cause-and-effect relationship. Religion became the cause, and the economic system (capitalism) became the effect.

Weber (1958) developed his argument in *The Protestant Ethic and the Spirit of Capitalism.* He suggested that Calvinism is the religion that has had the strongest influence on the development of capitalism. In this Protestant denomination, God was originally thought of as an aloof, inscrutable being maintaining total control over the universe. Human beings existed solely for the glorification of God and were expected never to question God's decisions; they were supposed to accept them on faith. One critical article of faith involved the doctrine of predestination. This doctrine suggested that before birth people were destined for either salvation or damnation. While nothing could be done to earn salvation, God did provide certain signs that indicated whether or not particular individuals were likely to be among the minority who would be saved. In particular, if people dedicated themselves to their occupations and achieved wealth, then it was likely that they were destined for salvation.

Devout Calvinists, Weber contended, were thus given "a positive incentive to asceticism." They were driven to work hard, to save, and to invest what they had saved in order to become wealthy. Wealth itself had no spiritual value, but accumulated wealth gave evidence that people were fulfilling their calling, glorifying God. Furthermore they were proving both to themselves and to others that they were bound for salvation. Weber argued that precapitalistic merchants were stimulated in their quest for material success by what we might term the joy of the hunt. In contrast, early Calvinist capitalists were under the influence of a religious standard for the conduct of life.

According to Weber, this drive to obtain wealth through thrift and hard work — in short the spirit of capitalism — has endured despite the decline of Calvinism. As a case in point, Weber quoted from Benjamin Franklin, who wrote in the eighteenth century: "Remember, that money is of the prolific, generating nature. Money can beget money, and its offspring can beget more, and so on. Five shillings turned is six, turned again it is seven and threepence, and so on, till it becomes a hundred pounds" (Weber, 1958: 49). Saving, investing, and building wealth might no longer be seen as providing proof of salvation in the next world, but Franklin's words suggest these activities can become the key to the achievement of success in the present life. Thus the spirit of capitalism remains strong in the industrial era, even though its link to Calvinism was severed long ago.

It has been difficult to test Weber's conclusions in the United States. Numerous studies seeking to determine whether or not Protestant religion has influenced the development of capitalism have often been sharply criticized. One significant drawback to such research has been that comparisons of occupational success between Protestants and Catholics are probably invalidated by the fact that Catholics have tended to experience more discrimination, giving them an occupational disadvantage compared to Protestants. Some researchers have sought to broaden Weber's thesis, determining if there is a general relationship between religious values and business success. For instance, a recent study concluded that Japanese immigrants' religious values have significantly contributed to their economic achievements in the United States (Woodrum, 1985).

## Making the World Comprehensible

The biblical explanation of human creation is straightforward, concise, and complete. Like Christianity, many other religions provide answers to such cosmic questions about how humanity originated and why people were created. Some religions, such as the Unitarian–Universalist Association, either deemphasize or deny belief in God and salvation, but they still contend that the pursuit of good works, such as continuing service to humanity, can make the world more comprehensible.

In 1985, 61 percent of the people interviewed in a national survey said that religion can provide answers for contemporary problems, while 22 percent said that religion is largely old fashioned and out of date. In 1957, 81 percent of the public expressed faith in religion's ability to provide answers to contemporary problems, and only 7 percent considered it old fashioned in this regard (George Gallup, *Gallup Poll,* May 30, 1985). The declining popular support for religion's function of making the world comprehensible is not surprising in a society that has been becoming increasingly secularized. It seems that Americans nowadays more frequently turn to a number of nonreligious specialists, including scientists, social scientists, and psychiatrists, to receive answers to contemporary problems.

Table 13.1 summarizes the four functions of religion discussed above.

## Functional Equivalents of Religion

A **functional equivalent** is an organization or activity that serves functions an individual or group more commonly receives from some other organization or activity. A number of organizations may be analyzed as functional equivalents of religion. For example, Transcendental Meditation (TM) is a group that teaches meditation techniques claimed to promote physical, social, and spiritual well-being. Erhard Seminars Training (est) is a commercial program providing group workshops for the pursuit of increased self-understanding. Socialism is a political philosophy that many national governments have endorsed, beginning with the Soviet Union in 1917. In each case the leaders and members of these groups and movements deny that they are involved in religious activity. In a formal sense, they are correct. Their concerns focus on the immediate, empirical world, not on the supernatural level of existence. Like religions, however, each of these functional equivalents has a founding prophet, follows certain sacred or quasi-sacred texts, provides a world view that precludes or at least subordinates most other world views, and seeks to convert outsiders.

Furthermore, as previously noted, functional equivalents can serve the same functions as religions. Soviet socialism has supported social change. A French visitor to the Soviet Union in the 1930s was impressed by the changes that the leaders promised. He wrote, "Like many other visitors, I saw model factories, clubs, pleasure grounds, at which I marveled. I asked for nothing better than to be carried away with admiration and to convert others as well" (Crossman, 1952: 160). Soviet socialism has also fostered strong social cohesion; people have been unified by the hope that they have been building a better, more just world. The same French traveler observed "a feeling of humanity, an immediate up-surge of brotherly love." Children were "well-fed, well-cared-for, cherished and happy. Their eyes were clear and full of confidence and hope" (Crossman, 1952: 159).

In the United States, functional equivalents of religion also exist. A prominent example is American civil religion. A **civil religion** is a shared, public faith in the nation, a faith linked to people's everyday life through a set of beliefs, symbols, and rituals that contain religious elements and overtones that are not formerly affiliated with any particular religion. Common beliefs include statements made by American presidents ranging across time from Washington and Jefferson to Kennedy and Reagan and contending that the

---

**Table 13.1**
**Some Functions of Religion**

| THE FUNCTION | ILLUSTRATION |
|---|---|
| 1. Providing social cohesion | 1. Durkheim's contention that religion can support a common sense of purpose |
| 2. Supporting and maintaining social control | 2. Marx's conviction that religion is "the opium of the people" |
| 3. Promoting social change | 3. Weber's conclusion that Calvinism has served as an incentive for capitalistic expansion |
| 4. Making the world comprehensible | 4. The belief, which is shared by the majority of Americans, that religion can provide answers to contemporary problems |

*The respective theoretical contributions of Durkheim, Marx, and Weber on religion can be visualized as illustrations of three separate functions of religion.*

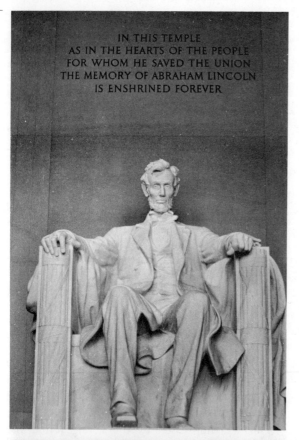

IN THIS TEMPLE
AS IN THE HEARTS OF THE PEOPLE
FOR WHOM HE SAVED THE UNION
THE MEMORY OF ABRAHAM LINCOLN
IS ENSHRINED FOREVER

*Prominent sacred symbols of the American civil religion include the Lincoln Memorial, the Liberty Bell, and the Capitol.*

United States is on a divinely supported mission to fulfill God's will for humanity. Sacred symbols of the American civil religion include the flag, a Judeo–Christian god, the Declaration of Independence, the Bill of Rights, the eagle, and a host of buildings and structures such as the Capitol, the White House, the Washington Monument, the Lincoln and Jefferson Memorials, and many more. Major rituals of the American civil religion include Memorial Day, Veterans Day, Thanksgiving, and the Fourth of July as well as the pledge of allegiance to the flag and the singing of the national anthem. A recent analysis has suggested that there has been too much emphasis on civil religion as a shared national experience and not sufficient recognition of the fact that civil-religious appeals are used by social movements and interest groups— for instance, by Ronald Reagan and associates in two successful campaigns for the presidency—to legitimate their own activities and goals (Demerath and Williams, 1985).

## Prominent Trends in Religion Today

Many Americans have been socialized to make attendance at religious services a consistent practice. In 1939, 41 percent of a national sample had attended services at a church or synagogue in the past seven days. The figure rose to 49 percent in 1955 and 1958 and then dropped back to 42 percent in 1985 (George Gallup, *Gallup Poll,* December 22, 1985).

In this section we examine religion from an organizational perspective. It is clear that membership is an important factor determining whether or not religious organizations survive. As we learn, modern religious groups have developed a number of ways of building membership, and no modern religious movement has been more successful in the area of membership growth than fundamentalism.

Figure 13.1 presents the percentages of the adult American population affiliated with major religious groups.

### The Declining Influence of Major Religions

Religion has sometimes been referred to as "a war for souls." If we think of religious activity in this way, then it seems as if the battleground has broadened in recent years. Many people display bumper stickers urging the unsaved to convert. Religious organizations purchase advertisements on radio and television. Various cults seek out young and confused people, offering them kindness and understanding and eventually imploring them to join their organizations.

Americans' feelings about the influence of religion have varied over time. In 1957, 69 percent of all Americans believed that the influence of religion was increasing, and only 14 percent felt that its power was decreasing. During the 1960s the percentage of the public that believed the influ-

**Figure 13.1**
**Americans' Religious Preferences**

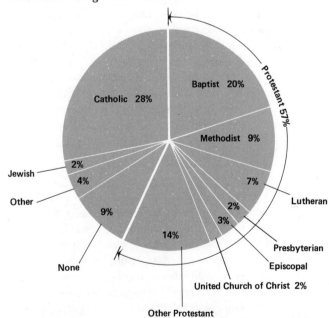

*The figure shows percentages of the adult American population affiliated with major religious groups. (Source: Adapted from George Gallup.* Gallup Poll. *1984.)*

**320**

ence of religion was increasing fell sharply, and then the figure gradually rose during the early 1970s until it reached 44 percent in 1976. After that it dropped again, registering 35 percent in 1980, but then it started rising once more, attaining 48 percent in 1985 (George Gallup, *Gallup Poll,* May 30, 1985).

In the mid-1950s popular ministers like Billy Graham and Norman Vincent Peale led a religious revival. The rapid increase in the size of the middle class and this group's widely held belief that attending church was "the thing to do" were also contributing factors to the growth of religion during this era. The 1960s were characterized by widespread disillusionment regarding social institutions, especially among young people. The present era has represented a mild religious revival.

### Fighting Back: Selling Organized Religion

The decline in interest in religion is a life-and-death matter for religious organizations. Consider some of the more dramatic shifts in membership. Since the mid-1960s the leading Christian fundamentalist denominations—Southern Baptists, the Assembly of God, and the Seventh-Day Adventists—have increased their membership by at least 30 percent, while the leading established "main-line" Christian denominations—the United Methodists, the Episcopalians, the Lutheran church in America, and Presbyterian church (U.S.A.)—have all lost membership (U.S. Bureau of the Census, *Statistical Abstract of the United States: 1966.* No. 45; U.S. Bureau of the Census, *Statistical Abstract of the United States: 1986.* No. 75). Many religious leaders have actively worked to reverse their organizations' declining influence. Three ways of attempting to revitalize established religion deserve special attention.

1. *Adjusting organizational practices to meet members' changing requirements.* Since Israel's Six Day War in 1967, many American Jews have been deeply concerned with Jewish survival. In response to this preoccupation, religious leaders have restored Hebrew to religious services and established many new religious schools (Cohen and Fein, 1985). Priest–sociologist Andrew Greeley has concluded that unless Catholic leaders become much more inclined to change traditional moral positions, such as the stance on birth control, there will be a profound alienation of lay Catholics and a continuing loss of members (McNamara, 1985).

2. *Using modern public-relations techniques.* A number of years ago, Catholic leaders in Michigan decided to conduct an intensive campaign to defeat a state referendum liberalizing abortion statutes. These leaders realized that one benefit of winning such a campaign would be a renewal of their followers' faith that the Catholic church remains a vigorous organization that can still defeat opponents' misguided efforts. The organizers hired an advertising and public-relations firm, and members of the church carefully coordinated the campaign, regularly providing up-to-date details to local personnel throughout the state. In addition, the church bought a great deal of television and radio time. Partly as a result, the antiabortion forces won on election day despite being considerably behind (according to independent polls) less than a month earlier (Hinsberg, 1974).

3. *Developing sales skills.* Some clergy have become proficient salespeople in order to gain converts. This is not a new development. In December 1734 Jonathan Edwards initiated the first American revival, a recruiting drive to counteract poor attendance at church services. This campaign was known as the "Great Awakening." With "terrible vividness and earnestness," Edwards urged his listeners to flee the wrath of God and seek refuge in religion (Sweet, 1950: 130). One of the most celebrated modern salesmen of religion is the Reverend Robert Schuller, the founder of the first (and still the wealthiest) drive-in church in the world, located in southern California. His "Hour of Power" television show is carried by eighty-eight stations, and he claims an audience of about thirty million people a week. According to Schuller, if a person continues to strive while putting his or her faith in God, success (material or otherwise) is inevitable. Schuller's supporters say that he provides hope and that he makes them feel good about their lives in a world where many people feel uprooted from traditional ties (Allman, 1976). His critics contend that he does not confront many important moral issues, but they concede "that he is bringing the unchurched within hearing distance" (Barr, 1977: 425).

## Fundamentalism

While the influence of many religious organizations has declined in this country, Christian fundamentalism has recently been very successful. In his well-known novel *Elmer Gantry,* Sinclair Lewis wrote about a fictional fundamentalist minister and how he achieved popularity. For the first sermon in the town of Zenith, Gantry chose the topic "Can Strangers Find Haunts of Vice in Zenith?" He was gratified to see four hundred people turn out when his predecessor had had to settle for a hundred. In his sermon Gantry told how he had gone to a local beach and found—What a shock! —"mixed bathing." The minister titillated the men in the audience by describing the ladies' legs. Then he mentioned the two women who had tried to pick him up, the waiter who had offered to sell him liquor despite Prohibition, the illegal, all-night poker game he had discovered, and more. As he spoke, Gantry became increasingly emotional, chastising his congregation for tolerating such rampant vice: "'We're lazy. We're not burning with a fever of righteousness. On your knees, you slothful, and pray God to forgive you and to aid you and me to form a brotherhood of helpful, joyous, fiercely righteous followers of every commandment of the Lord our God!'" (Lewis, 1970: 305). Gantry had let several newspaper reporters know that something special would be taking place in church that Sunday morning, and the papers reprinted almost the entire sermon. The next week 700 people turned out, and Gantry was solidly established as a local favorite.

It was during the period covered in *Elmer Gantry* —the post-World War I era—that the third of five Christian-fundamentalist revivals in the United States took place. The first revival occurred at the beginning of the nineteenth century; the fifth is taking place today. The five revivals have displayed six common themes:

1. *Individualism.* Fundamentalism focuses on personal woes and personal salvation, with supporters urged to examine their own private spirituality and to commit themselves to a personal relationship with Jesus Christ.
2. *Emotionalism.* Fundamentalism is a religion of the heart, not the head. Conversion is a highly emotional experience that remains almost unchanged since the early nineteenth-century revivals.
3. *Moralism.* Fundamentalism emphasizes living a Christian life. The path to salvation requires a recognition of one's own sinfulness and a determination to live righteously, resisting all temptations.
4. *Conservatism.* People who embrace fundamentalism are generally suspicious of most social change.
5. *Nondenominationalism.* Fundamentalists maintain that no one church has a monopoly on the attainment of salvation. While revivalists do not dismiss established religious organizations, their primary focus is on a moral crusade against evil, a crusade that rests on a nondenominational basis.
6. *Evangelism.* Revivalism depends on evangelistic ministers, who use oratory and personal magnetism to generate enthusiasm in revival campaigns. Evangelists are more likely to be prophets than messiahs, more interested in listeners than followers. Billy Graham, for instance, has characterized himself as "the Western Union Messenger of God" (Wilson, 1978: 67–68).

Modern fundamentalism represents a case where organized religion has been effectively sold. Graham is a prime example of a successful salesman. He was the first fundamentalist minister to use television as a means for religious salesmanship. Robert Schuller, Jimmy Swaggert, and many other fundamentalist ministers have followed his lead, building enormous followings from both their television and personal appearances. Fundamentalism seems to have become so popular in recent years because once individuals choose Christ as their personal savior, they are not only comforted but also spared the necessity of needing to personally struggle with interpretations of such complex modern issues as the possibility of nuclear war and the apparent end of economic growth (Hammond, 1985).

In the past decade, a fundamentalist group called the Moral Majority has become active politically. Reverend Jerry Falwell, the most prominent leader of the Moral Majority, has suggested that the Moral Majority has four basic aims:

1. The members are "prolife," believing that the legalization of abortion should be overturned.

2. The Moral Majority is "pro-traditional family," opposing any movement toward granting increased legitimacy to homosexuality.
3. Falwell and his associates are "promorality," opposing the legalization of marijuana and other currently illegal drugs and also opposing the spread of pornography.
4. Finally the Moral Majority is "pro-American," supporting a strong national defense (Falwell, 1981: 17).

Falwell has denied the frequent charge that the Moral Majority has distributed a "hit list" of prominent liberal politicians, who had to be defeated at any cost. However, in 1980 an organization affiliated with the Moral Majority launched a successful $1 million political campaign called "Target 80," during which television and radio spots and mailings of campaign literature strongly suggested that the primary intention was to give reasons why five prominent liberal Democratic senators should be defeated rather than why their opponents should be elected. The Moral Majority has worked with a large number of single-issue interest groups, such as those opposing abortion, gun control, the Equal Rights Amendment, and sex education in the schools, to achieve its political objectives (Ellerin and Kesten, 1981; Lienesch, 1982).

The following American Controversy addresses an issue raised in the discussion of fundamentalism — the role of religion in public life.

---

## AMERICAN CONTROVERSY

## *Religion in the Public Arena*

Should religious leaders be permitted to participate extensively in public life? We will consider positions favoring and opposing this possibility.

### The Position Favoring Religious Leaders' Involvement in Public Life

Initially it should be emphasized that the first amendment to the Constitution not only indicates that people have the freedoms of speech, press, and assembly, but they also have the freedom to establish and practice religion, without fear of intervention. Thus the Constitution supports religious leaders' right to involve themselves in public life.

But it is more than a question of legality. When religious spokespeople comment on public issues or even political candidates, Americans receive information and opinions from people who are unusually moral, people who are struggling to understand the meaning of life and the significance of our existence on earth. Who could possibly be a better choice to make a thoughtful, worthwhile commentary on such issues as prayer in the schools, creationism in the curriculum, and the moral character and godliness of different political candidates?

A final point. In modern times people who criticize the right of religious officials' involvement in public life are, in reality, simply liberals who oppose conservative religious leaders' political philosophy. Such people would be happy enough if conservative clergy — in particular, Jerry Falwell and Pat Robertson — were banned from political participation, but they favor liberals' activities — for instance, Catholic bishops' recent calls for a reduction in nuclear weaponry and for a much more extensive national commitment to eliminating poverty in the United States.

### The Position Restricting Religious Leaders' Involvement in Public Life

How much restriction should be imposed on religious leaders? Some, perhaps many, critics of clergy's involvement in politics would say that there is a difference between a Jerry Falwell, who attempts to assess the religious quality of specific candidates, and people and groups that issue general pronouncements about social and political issues. The first activity means direct involvement in a political contest, while the second is usually no more than a general declaration of political and social opinions provided in sermons.

But there is a topic of even greater concern. In its indisputable wisdom, this country has preserved a separation of church and state, maintaining no official American religion. Were there a national religion, we would run the danger of a few unscrupulous people using the enormous influence that religion can generate to create a mass allegiance. While the prospect of our country becoming like Iran, which is controlled by a religious dictator and his team of Islamic officials, might seem far fetched to us, the analogy is also thought-provoking. Consider the influence exercised by Reverend Moon of the Unification Church over thousands of young people or the power maintained by the deranged Jim Jones, who led a mass suicide of more than 900 Americans in 1978. No, it is safer and saner to have religious leaders removed from public issues.

## Conclusion

What do you think? Do you agree wholly with one position or the other? If you end up somewhere between the two positions, indicate precisely which points you support and oppose. Either discuss these issues informally in small groups or examine them in class.

---

The focus now shifts from religion to education. It has been clear that religion involves socialization, that people involved in it are concerned about the transmission of beliefs and values. As we have already noted, education also involves transmission—in this case knowledge, skills, and values by either formal or informal means.

Furthermore the relationship between religion and education has been apparent throughout American history. In fact, the earliest American schools were run by churches. For instance, the Society of Friends (Quakers) opened a school in Philadelphia in 1689, and for the next 125 years the only schools in Pennsylvania were run by churches (Binzen, 1970: 38). In 1636 Harvard College was created because the Puritans dreaded "to leave an illiterate ministry to the churches when our present ministers shall lie in the dust" (Bailyn et al., 1977: 159). In recent years there has been a revival of religious schools, increasing from several hundred in the 1960s to 13,000 in 1985. What is parents' primary motive for sending their children to such schools? Apparently they are seeking a Christian education for their children, an education that they feel has been denied in tax-supported schools since the Supreme Court's ban on school prayer in 1962. As one British observer noted, "They want the moral and religious instruction that publicly-financed schools cannot now provide without bumping up against the constitution" (*Economist*, 1985: 25). These parents, in short, want to control the kind of education their children receive. In both religion and education, control over the content of socialization is often a major concern for people involved.

---

# Theories of Education

Among sociologists there exist different perspectives about the impact that education produces upon people. Does it provide socialization that permits people to fit smoothly into modern society? The structural-functional theory would answer in the affirmative while conflict theory would respond negatively.

## The Structural-Functional Theory of Education

The structural-functional theory of education emphasizes that education contributes signifi-cantly to the stability and conflict-free existence of modern society. Even though structural-functional theorists are likely to suggest that individuals can use education to become socially mobile, they emphasize that the education system basically helps to maintain the existing distribution of wealth and power.

### Cultural Transmission

For a society to survive, culture must be handed from one generation to the next. Once children in modern societies reach four or five, the schools begin to assume the burden of this task. American children must study such academic subjects as English, mathematics, geography, and history and also learn about such nonacademic topics as patriotism, culturally acceptable behavior, and morality.

The United States has been more inclined to stress patriotism in its schools than has England, perhaps because of the necessity of integrating a continuous flow of immigrants. High-school civics textbooks, for instance, have traditionally avoided virtually all unpleasant and controversial aspects of American life. A study concluded that American schools do a more effective job of molding loyal and obedient citizens than do those in the Soviet Union (Banks, 1976).

### Social Control

"How'd you like school today, Joey?" a mother asks her young son when he gets home.

"Oh, it's all right, mommy, I guess." He pauses with a puzzled look on his face. "The thing is, though, that I feel much looser when I get home."

Although Joey would probably have trouble explaining it in detail, he seems to be aware of the **hidden curriculum:** a set of school rules that emphasize blind obedience and that are seldom made explicit but are recognized as important by students. Pupils have traditionally been expected to sit only in assigned seats, to answer questions when called on to do so, to take tests when told to take tests, and to keep quiet the rest of the time. Many American teachers emphasize "repetition, redundancy, and ritualistic action" above all else (Jackson, 1968: 6).

Exposure to the hidden curriculum begins in kindergarten. Children are expected to take part in a number of carefully supervised activities. Those who submit to the imposed discipline and eventually learn the habit of unthinking obedience tend to be evaluated by the school as good students. Those who accept the routines of the school but do not personally identify with them will probably find themselves placed in the category of adequate students. Finally children who refuse to accept the rules of the school will often receive the label of "problem children" or "bad students." In modern times schools frequently engage clinical psychologists or other therapists to help teachers deal with such children (Gracey, 1977).

### Transmission of Knowledge and Academic Skills

Schools pass on critical knowledge and skills that make it possible for people to participate in the central activities of their society. Without the ability to read, write, and compute, Americans find themselves highly limited in the job market and are also unable to participate in a host of other activities that occur in daily life; they cannot calculate their own income tax, understand a street map, or keep a check book accurately.

Beyond certain basic topics, educators often find it difficult to justify studying the liberal arts to students who insist that they are unwilling to devote attention to any topic that will not contribute directly to their future economic success. People who are concerned only about the practical advantages that education can provide them will not appreciate the broader benefits that students can obtain from studying literature, social science, a language, or mathematics.

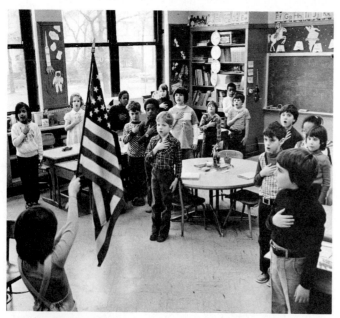

*From a functional perspective, education is viewed as a way of transmitting cultural values, such as patriotism, to successive generations.*

### Sorting

Another critical function that the schools perform is the sorting of people into different occupa-

---

tional roles. Research evidence strongly suggests that people's occupational placement is largely determined before they complete elementary school. Teachers and principals evaluate students' elementary-school records and then use this evaluation as the primary basis for recommending whether or not particular students should be placed in a high track, which will qualify them for a college-preparatory program, or a low track, which will direct them toward vocational courses or some other program that is not college bound. Sometimes the recommendation will change as a result of junior-high-school performance, but such changes are uncommon. Those who successfully complete college-preparatory programs then proceed to college, and ultimately its successful completion and perhaps further schooling lead to the more prestigious and higher-paying jobs. The occupational prospects of ten-year-olds, in short, are often determined (Parsons, 1968).

### Development of Social Skills

"Sally, I don't know how you did it!"

"It was easy, Hank. Really!"

"But you presented to the boss exactly the same proposal that I did. Nothing more and nothing less."

Sally smiles. "It's not what I said that was important, Hank. It's how I said it."

Sally is clearly aware of the importance of social skills. Tactfully (perhaps too tactfully for Hank to understand), she implies that his social skills could use some improvement. One of the functions of education is to help develop these abilities. Children who are evaluated as good students because they have learned to accept the rules that teachers emphasize also tend to develop the social skills that will help them behave appropriately in middle-class occupational spheres.

Research on successful management personnel has concluded that a high level of intelligence has been judged neither necessary nor desirable, and specialized or technical skills are of minor significance. The importance of managers' social skills is apparent when one realizes that corporate advancement often occurs when a manager becomes a member of a team or clique that provides assistance to a sponsoring higher executive. Failure in business can be largely explained by lack of social skills. A survey of seventy-six large corporations concluded that 90 percent of the managers fired from their jobs were believed to lack desirable personality traits (Collins, 1979: 32).

### Advancement of Knowledge

The role expectations for faculty in colleges and universities vary considerably. In the elite schools, the basic principle is "publish or perish." Either faculty members produce a substantial quantity of high-quality publications (books and/or articles), or they will be dismissed. Less elite colleges and universities favor publications and may require them for promotion or other forms of public recognition but do not consider them to be absolutely mandatory in order to keep one's job.

There is no doubt that contributions to the advancement of knowledge are highly prized throughout the academic world. One's colleagues may respect first-rate teaching, but the only way to receive really meaningful recognition, especially beyond the confines of one's own school, is to make a contribution to knowledge in one's field, normally in written form.

The process of advancing knowledge can bring new members into a discipline. When graduate students or undergraduate majors participate in a faculty-research project, they start to obtain the knowledge and skills that can make them productive members of that field and eventually contributors to its further advancement. Many academic departments provide courses that introduce students to the process of knowledge advancement in their field; the methods course in sociology is an example.

## The Conflict Theory of Education

While structural-functional theory emphasizes that education contributes to the stability and conflict-free existence of society, conflict theory makes the claim that education perpetuates existing inequalities among people. Conflict theorists will not accept the functionalists' claim that social control in schools simply promotes an orderly society. The advocates of conflict theory emphasize that the current education system tends to produce unquestioning obedience to authority: something like the frightening blind obedience Stanley Milgram created in the experiment reported in Chapter 2 ("Doing Research in Sociology").

**326**     *A Reexamination of Several Functions of Education*

Conflict theory considers the functions we have just examined in a different light. While structural-functional theory emphasizes that education provides students information that encourages them to intelligently interact in modern society, the conflict approach is less optimistic; it claims that schools are simply trying to prepare students to become dull, conforming members of modern society by developing unthinking patriotism, good work habits, and good manners. Since American public education started, the schools have tended to stress the transmission of conservative values. As early as the 1840s, textbooks and teachers propagandized for the positive qualities of the American way of life, especially the capitalist economic

system. In school, immigrant children were told that if they worked hard and lived virtuously, they would eventually become successful, honored, and even wealthy. Educators emphasized this theme constantly, even including it in the arithmetic lessons. The following example illustrates how one test simultaneously taught subtraction and sermonized about drunkenness: "There were 7 farmers, 3 of whom drank rum and whiskey and became miserable. The rest drank water and were healthy and happy. How many drank water?" (Quoted in Binzen, 1970: 43).

Like conflict theorists, West German educators have been deeply concerned about possible harmful effects of schools on children, as the following Cross-Cultural Perspective indicates.

---

**CROSS-CULTURAL PERSPECTIVE**

*Questioning Authority in German Schools*

As an important agent of socialization, schools are a major source of children's values. With this fact in mind, West German educators have been systematically teaching their pupils to question all authority. If children challenge and even refuse to obey authority figures, they argue, then no Nazi-style dictatorship will ever again receive public support.

In 1973 Gerda Lederer, an American mathematics teacher, first learned what West German educators were trying to do. She had come to Germany as part of a group of twenty-three American teachers whose chief purpose was to discover why German students, like students in a number of other countries, did better than their American counterparts on math achievement tests. But she found that the unlearning of

blind obedience was a much more interesting topic. The subject seemed to come up almost continuously. For instance, Lederer and a German colleague were at a train station preparing to take a class on a day trip. Lederer suggested that they line up the students and count them. "Oh no! We never line them up!" exclaimed the German teacher. "That would be too authoritarian. We don't treat children like that."

"I felt like Alice in Wonderland," Lederer explained. Everything was the opposite of what she expected. When she returned to the United States, almost nobody would believe what she had found happening in the German schools. The results were simply too distant from stereotypes of blindly obedient Germans. After Lederer entered a doctoral pro-

gram, she conducted a study comparing the values of German and American high-school students in the late 1970s with similar data from the two countries obtained in the 1940s.

Lederer found out the following:

1. When asked whether a soldier in wartime would be justified in refusing to obey an order to shoot an innocent prisoner, 44 percent of German adolescents and 29 percent of American adolescents said no in 1945. By 1979 the figure had dropped to 7 percent for German adolescents, while for their American counterparts it had also fallen but not as far—to 12 percent.

2. In 1945, 30 percent of German adolescents and 29 percent of their Ameri-

can age peers felt that a boy who disobeys his elders was worse than a boy who beats up small children. In 1979, 12 percent of the Germans and 16 percent of the Americans agreed with this view.

3. German adolescents were inclined to disagree with a statement that suggested that children should feel a deep sense of obligation to act in accord with their parents' wishes. American adolescents, on the other hand, tended to support this statement.

Lederer's findings generally indicated that German adolescents are less inclined to be obedient to authority figures than are their American counterparts. Yet some observers question how much the Germans have actually changed. Joseph Katz, a professor of human development at the State University of New York at Stony Brook, has suggested that: "It looks like an ideological compliance with 'the right kind of thing to say' and does not necessarily reflect underlying feelings . . ."

On the other hand, Gerda Lederer observed that the modern German effort to teach students not to obey authority figures does demonstrate the potential impact of education: "We, the teachers of the next generation, underestimate the influence that we have," said Lederer. "As a teacher it fascinates me—and terrifies me—to see what is in our hands."

Source: Maya Pines. "Unlearning Blind Obedience in German Schools." *Psychology Today.* Vol. 15. May 1981, pp. 59–60.

---

Structural-functional and conflict theory agree on only one point about the issue of sorting: that it does take place. The structural-functional perspective claims that students are placed in tracks according to their abilities. Conflict theory, on the other hand, focuses on the fact that there is a definite relationship between income and race and students' tracks. Specifically those who come from affluent families and are white are more likely to be in college-preparatory tracks than those who are not from affluent families and are nonwhite. Studies on tracking seem to agree that lower-status students are disproportionately represented in low tracks; however, there is disagreement on whether the placement in low tracks results because teachers and administrators steer students with a low-status background into them or because individuals with a low socioeconomic status are less likely to receive parental encouragement to do well in school, to develop high aspirations, and thus to achieve good academic skills (Davis and Haller, 1981; Oakes, 1982).

Structural-functional theory indicates that schooling will provide practical knowledge and skills that make it possible for people to participate in the central activities of the society. On the other hand, the conflict perspective, which focuses on the inequities existing in modern society, stresses that the knowledge that students obtain in school can make them aware of how and why injustices

have developed in U.S. society. While structural-functionalists find it difficult to demonstrate the practical significance of a liberal education, the

*While the law requires that free education be available to all children, those in less affluent areas generally have older, less effective facilities and equipment than their wealthier counterparts.*

**328**  advocates of a conflict approach emphasize that students who have received an effective liberal education will be able to think clearly and independently, thereby equipping themselves to resist any tyrannies the elite might contemplate (Lichtenstein, 1985; Oestereicher, 1982).

*Credentials and Social Skills*

It has been widely recognized that a steadily increasing proportion of Americans are overeducated for their particular jobs (Clogg and Shockey, 1984). Conflict theorists have sharply criticized this situation, claiming that beyond the development of mass literacy, education is generally irrelevant to on-the-job productivity and sometimes even has a negative impact on it. Concrete vocational skills seem to be learned much more commonly through work experience than in school. Furthermore the findings of a series of studies indicate that there is little or no relationship between school grades and success in the occupational world (Collins, 1979). If in reality the educational system provides few skills relevant to effective job performance, then why is there such a widespread emphasis on academic credentials among employers?

Conflict theorists offer an answer. They claim that most occupations in modern society require a loyal and obedient work force that will perform work tasks that entail limited responsibility and minimal independent decision-making. The advocates of the conflict approach contend that certificates of graduation from most high schools or colleges clearly indicate to employers that the young people in question have received training in school that has prepared them to serve effectively in the work world. Elite high schools and colleges might place more emphasis on responsibility and self-direction, but, according to conflict theorists, the differences are only superficial. The graduates of elite schools are socialized to be just as unquestioningly loyal and obedient on the job as individuals who receive their credentials from nonelite schools (Bowles and Gintis, 1976; Collins, 1979).

*Prospects for Change*

Conflict theorists contend that the current system of education will not change in any significant respects in the foreseeable future because the elite members of American society believe that their interests would suffer with any changes. According to the supporters of the conflict approach, the wealthy and powerful will usually tolerate and even encourage such innovations as open classrooms or newly developed teaching styles because they give the false impression that significant change is occurring, which might tone down some critics' protests. Conflict theorists argue that the educational reforms that the elite will find threatening are those that will develop less readily obedient workers or open up elite status to large numbers of people in the nonelite classes.

Supporters of both theories are likely to agree that significant measures of educational reform need to be initiated in our society.

## Educational Reform

From the time we are born, our socialization involves learning skills, and Americans are aware that this learning process applies to education. When the American public was asked in 1985 to evaluate fourteen possible educational goals, the ability to speak and write correctly received the highest score; 68 percent rated this ability a priority (George Gallup, *Gallup Poll,* January 15, 1985). This finding is one indication that when Americans judge the quality of education, they make the development of students' basic skills a major consideration. In recent years, however, there has been growing evidence that those skills are often not being effectively nurtured in school.

In April 1983 the National Commission on Excellence in Education issued its report on the state of American education. The commission indicated that unless significant educational reform occurred, the nation would be seriously endangered in the future. The report emphasized that throughout the world, other nations are overtaking the once unchallenged American lead in science, technology, commerce, and industry. If the American system of education continues to deteriorate, then American world prominence will also decline.

The commission report, entitled *A Nation at Risk,* paid tribute to "heroic" examples of educational excellence. Serious problems, however, were much more frequent. They include the following:

Some 23 million American adults are functionally illiterate.

About 13 percent of American adolescents (and 40 percent of minority teenagers) are functionally illiterate.

Between 1963 and 1980, there was a steady decline in average scores on the Scholastic Aptitude Test (SAT). Furthermore, during that time period, a significant decrease occurred in the number of students who achieved superior scores on the SAT.

The number of remedial mathematics courses offered in public four-year colleges increased 72 percent between 1975 and 1980 (Goldberg and Harvey, 1983).

Other recent research has suggested that the National Commission on Excellence in Education may have overstated its claims about the deterioration of American schools. Test scores and other data indicate that many students' actual performances have improved significantly in recent years. These improvements, however, have primarily taken place in lower grades and have involved "low-level" skills, such as the comprehension of a written passage and not the analysis of the author's purpose (Fiske, September 16, 1983).

Experts might disagree about the seriousness of the current decline in American education, but they all agree that widespread reforms are necessary. Most of them also believe that the curriculum is the place to start. The Carnegie Report, a study of American high schools supervised by a twenty-eight-member panel of prominent educators, recommended that the mastery of the English language, including writing, should be the "central curriculum objective" for all students. In addition, the Carnegie Report advocated the adoption of a "core curriculum" for all students, including those in vocational programs, and this set of courses would include detailed knowledge of a foreign language.

One social scientist has stressed that while American children's educational skills need improvement, it can be disasterous to emphasize only elevated standards. When this is done, teachers' control over students becomes the order of the day, and the hidden curriculum becomes a dominant presence. Procedures need to be developed so that both teachers and students can be innovative and autonomous — so that students can learn what the expected limits are and can also learn to experience and evaluate the effects of overstepping those limits (Deci, 1985). This conclusion seems to be supported by the results of a recent study that indicates that the more extensively students are permitted to use initiative and independent judgment in their schoolwork, the more effectively their intellectual skills will be developed (Miller et al., 1985).

Many educators emphasize that improvements in American education will be expensive. In particular, they point out that measures must be taken to encourage many of the ablest college graduates to enter teaching and to prevent effective educators from leaving the field. The Carnegie Report has suggested that there should be a gradual increase in teachers' salaries of 25 percent after making up for inflation and that the base pay of new teachers should be where this boost is first provided (Fiske, September 16, 1983).

Some states have taken decisive action to improve their educational programs. In 1983 the New York State Board of Regents adopted an "Action Plan" to increase the number of courses high-school students must take in math, science, social studies, the arts, and a language. The governor of New Jersey proposed a number of reforms, including an increase in teachers' starting salaries from $11,000 to $17,000.

Some people believe that the success of educational reforms will be strongly influenced by the role of the federal government. In the 1980s the administration has supported the idea of educational reform but has indicated that financing should be produced at the state and local level. Congress has been somewhat more cooperative. The associate executive director of the National School Boards Association indicated that the government role is crucial:

"The issue won't die out," he said, "and the Federal Government can't just tell the states to go ahead and do it [provide all the funding for education] because

**330**

there are rich and poor states as well as rich and poor districts. The Federal Government will have to pull a working oar."

*(Fiske, September 18, 1983: E20)*

In the next section, it is also apparent that the government plays an important role in significant efforts to equalize all citizens' educational opportunities.

# Education and Equality

Frederick Douglass (1968), a well-known, nineteenth-century black leader, published a book about his childhood experiences as a slave. He indicated that plantation owners were determined that their slaves should not learn how to read. The owners realized that literate slaves could obtain more extensive knowledge, and such knowledge could lead to discontentment with their situation and ultimately even encourage revolt. Douglass himself learned to read only by trading bread to poor white boys for "the more valuable bread of knowledge."

More recently black activists have consistently emphasized the importance of education. In the late 1930s and early 1940s, the National Association for the Advancement of Colored People (NAACP) and its allies began a concerted attack on segregated education, emphasizing that without equal educational opportunity, black people would forever be seriously handicapped in a highly competitive society. In the 1954 case of *Brown* v. *the Topeka, Kansas, Board of Education*, the United States Supreme Court ruled that segregated schools were inherently unequal. The years that followed saw widespread efforts to integrate America's public schools. The Coleman Report played a significant part in stimulating these efforts.

## The Coleman Report and Busing

As part of the Civil Rights Act of 1964, Congress ordered the federal Commissioner of Education to conduct a study of the availability of educational opportunities for Americans of different races, religions, and national origins. The project was massive. About 600,000 children in more than 4000 schools across the country were tested. Some 60,000 teachers, several thousand principals, and several hundred school superintendents were also interviewed.

More than halfway through the research, sociologist James Coleman, who had been named to direct the project, predicted that the study's findings on the differing quality of the education available to the average white child and to the typical black child were "going to be striking" (Hodgson, 1973: 37). They were not. To Coleman's surprise the results of the study indicated that the physical facilities and the formal curricula in segregated schools attended by blacks and whites were roughly similar and that the test scores of black and white students were only marginally affected by physical facilities, formal curricula, and other measurable characteristics of schools.

Nevertheless, about 85 percent of the black students scored below the white students' average on the standardized tests administered by the researchers. The reason for this seemed to involve a combination of nonschool factors operating among blacks: in particular, poverty, nonsupportive community attitudes toward education, and the low education level achieved by most black parents. Coleman and his associates found that black children and other poor, primarily nonwhite children generally possess less effective educational skills at the time when they enter school and that the schools have been largely unable to overcome this disadvantage (Coleman et al., 1966).

While the Coleman Report has received criticism, many educators and social scientists have accepted its basic findings. One particular finding has had an especially significant effect on social policy: that students from poverty areas were frequently able to substantially improve their academic performance when they attended schools with students living in affluent areas. This conclusion led directly to the practice of busing.

## Busing and Equality

Why is busing needed to promote school integration? To begin, recall that school districts normally serve only their immediate residential areas. Many of these areas are racially segregated, and in such situations the only way to bring affluent white children and poor black children into contact in the same schools is by physically moving them by means of busing. Busing in order to promote racial balance in the schools has provoked considerable controversy and even violence. Most white parents have not cited integrated classrooms as their reason for opposition. Instead they have claimed to be concerned about the possibility of endangering their children by busing them into high-crime areas, the lengthy school days that occasionally result from long-distance busing, and the erosion of the "neighborhood school principle" (Cassidy, 1972). In recent years a few educators and social scientists have also increasingly questioned the effectiveness of busing. Studying the effects of busing over time, researchers have either found that the positive educational impact of integration has been modest or nonexistent (Cohen, 1974) or that the costs outweigh the benefits (McClendon, 1985).

Sixteen years after the Coleman Report was published, James Coleman wrote about busing, acknowledging "the general unpopularity of this policy, greatest among whites, but also true for Hispanics and blacks. . ." (Coleman et al., 1982: 197). Coleman suggested that new ways of promoting equal opportunities in education need to be devised.

### Recent Developments

During the 1970s there was extensive emphasis on equalization of educational opportunity. Several court rulings addressed the concern that heavy reliance on property taxes as a means of financing public education tends to create sharp differences in the quality of education provided to children, with the richer districts characterized by better facilities and more highly qualified personnel. In the *Rodriguez* case, the U.S. Supreme Court urged the states to attempt to devise new ways of financing public education. During the 1970s about twenty-five states sought to equalize educational expenditures between rich and poor school districts. State legislatures, courts, and state educational agencies became involved in this process. Nevertheless, true equalization of school funding is still a long way off.

There was also significant legislation during the 1970s on behalf of the handicapped. By the middle of the decade, about twenty state legislatures had passed bills mandating equal educational opportunities for handicapped people. Educators struggled to comply, complaining of a lack of special teachers, instructional materials, and funds. In response Congress passed the Education for All Handicapped Children Act in 1975. This was a massive effort, designed to provide individualized schooling for five to seventeen million physically, mentally, and emotionally handicapped children (Brodinsky, 1979). Recently two educators suggested that the integration of severely handicapped children in public schools might benefit all students, making it possible for both the handicapped and the nonhandicapped to learn from each other (Hanline and Murray, 1984).

## Commentary

In this chapter we have examined two types of personal socialization. When people initiate religious activity, they are transmitting values and beliefs. Education too is a transmission — in this case of knowledge, skills, and values. In both institutional areas, many people feel strongly, and that is because they appreciate the processes that are unfolding: Members of society, especially children, can be strongly influenced by the content of either religion or education, and the nature of the content and its extent of influence obviously is determined by those in control.

## STUDY GUIDE

### Summary

1. A religion is a unified system of beliefs and practices that focuses on sacred things and serves to create a community of worshippers. The sacred is anything that is superior in power and dignity, set apart from the mundane and practical, and creates a sense of awe.

**332**　Education is the transmission of knowledge, skills, and values by either formal or informal means. Like religion, education is a type of personal socialization.

2. Religions serve a variety of functions, including providing social cohesion, supporting and maintaining social control, promoting social change, and making the world comprehensible. There are also functional equivalents of religion.

3. One trend in modern religion is the declining influence of major religions. In the past several decades, religious membership and attendance have been declining. Nonetheless, established religious organizations have fought back with a number of strategies for selling religion. Fundamentalism is a strong modern religious movement. Its basic themes are individualism, emotionalism, moralism, conservatism, nondenominationalism, and evangelism. The most renowned fundamentalist movement at present is the Moral Majority.

4. The structural-functional theory of education is a prominent theoretical perspective on that subject. Cultural transmission, social control, transmission of knowledge and academic skills, sorting, development of social skills, and advancement of knowledge are six important functions of education.

The conflict theory of education focuses on the part that education plays in the perpetuation of inequalities among people. This theory provides a reexamination of the functions analyzed by structural functional theory and offers its own conclusions about credentials and social skills as well as the prospects for change.

5. In the 1980s a number of national studies have concluded that the American education system has many serious problems and badly needs reform. Some states are already starting to make significant efforts to improve their schooling. Extensive federal participation would probably improve the likelihood that such reforms would be successful.

6. Attacks on inequality in American schools started in the 1930s. The Coleman Report concluded that the fact that black students on the average scored below whites on standardized tests was primarily because of nonschool factors. Findings in the Coleman Report supported the initiation of busing. During the 1970s extensive emphasis on equalization of education occurred.

## Glossary

**civil religion**　a shared, public faith in the nation, a faith linked to people's everyday life through a set of beliefs, symbols, and rituals that contains religious elements and overtones that are not formally affiliated with any particular religion.

**education**　the transmission of knowledge, skills, and values by either formal or informal means.

**functional equivalent**　an organization or activity that serves functions an individual or group more commonly receives from some other organization or activity.

**hidden curriculum**　a set of rules that emphasizes blind obedience and that is seldom made explicit but is recognized as important by students.

**profane**　anything that people consider ordinary and closely linked to practical demands.

**religion**　a unified system of beliefs and practices that focuses on sacred things and serves to create a community of worshippers.

**sacred**　anything that is superior in power, is set apart from the ordinary and practical, and creates a sense of awe.

**secularization**　the process by which religion loses influence within groups and societies.

## Learning Objectives

After studying this chapter, you should be able to:

1. Define religion and education and explain their significance in modern societies.
2. Identify and describe three major functions of religion.

3. Examine two prominent trends in religion today: the declining influence of major religious organizations and the prominence of fundamentalism.
4. Discuss the structural-functional and conflict theories of education.
5. Examine education and equality, describing the Coleman Report, busing, and recent activities in this area.
6. Analyze recent developments in educational reform.
7. Indicate why both religion and education are personal types of socialization.

# Tests

## True-false test

_____ 1. Profane items do not create unity and a sense of common purpose the way sacred things do.

_____ 2. Both Weber and Marx regarded religion as no more than an effect of the economic system.

_____ 3. In the United States, civil religion is supported by Protestants but not Catholics or Jews.

_____ 4. The text suggests that all major religious organizations have declined in membership in recent years.

_____ 5. Modern fundamentalist groups have sometimes become involved in politics.

_____ 6. The structural-functional theory of education suggests that the principal function of education is the pursuit of upward social mobility.

_____ 7. Research evidence has strongly suggested that people's occupational placement is largely determined before they complete elementary school.

_____ 8. Advocates of the conflict theory emphasize that the current educational system tends to encourage unquestioning obedience to authority.

_____ 9. It is now clear that the busing program has been an unqualified success.

_____ 10. According to the report issued by the National Commission on Excellence in Education, the United States still maintains an unchallenged lead over other nations in the quality of education provided to people preparing to work in the areas of science, technology, commerce, and industry.

## Multiple-choice test

_____ 1. According to Durkheim, secularization:
   a. is more prominent in preindustrial societies than in industrial societies.
   b. is more prominent in industrial societies than in preindustrial societies.
   c. declines as the influence of science increases.
   d. tends to promote cohesion in societies.

_____ 2. Marx's notion of "illusory happiness" relates to his view of religion as:
   a. the opium of the people.
   b. a support for slavery.
   c. a source of alienation for the wealthy and powerful.
   d. a Protestant ethic.

_____ 3. Weber believed that the reason Calvinism encouraged the development of capitalism was because it:
   a. created a common purpose and unity in communities.
   b. raised morale by indicating that everyone would eventually enter heaven.

    c. condemned the ruling class.
    d. encouraged people to work hard, to save, and to invest their savings.

———  4. Prominent functions of religion discussed in the text include:
    a. making the world comprehensible.
    b. limiting social control.
    c. lessening social cohesion.
    d. slowing down social change.

———  5. Which of the following is true of civil religion?
    a. It is represented by socialism in the Soviet Union.
    b. It has declined sharply in importance since the Civil War.
    c. It is simply another term for religious fundamentalism.
    d. It can be used by social movements and interest groups to promote their own interests.

———  6. Religion and education:
    a. are personal types of socialization.
    b. have not changed in any significant ways in recent years.
    c. are topics of rapidly declining interest to most Americans.
    d. a and c

———  7. The hidden curriculum in schools emphasizes students':
    a. sorting.
    b. blind obedience to rules.
    c. development of social skills.
    d. advancement of knowledge.

———  8. The structural-functional theory of education supports the idea that:
    a. cultural transmission should not occur in schools.
    b. schools pass on critical knowledge and skills that permit people to participate in the central activities of their society.
    c. knowledge helps students understand how and why social injustices have developed in U.S. society.
    d. education is irrelevant to on-the-job productivity.

———  9. Conflict theorists believe that:
    a. the wealthy oppose the open-classroom concept.
    b. loyalty and obedience should be central values in the classroom.
    c. the elite will support innovations that create a false impression of significant change in education.
    d. elite high schools and colleges encourage considerably more independent thought and action than nonelite schools.

———  10. Most experts believe that educational reform must begin with:
    a. the curriculum.
    b. a focus on SAT scores.
    c. state funding for education.
    d. improvement of higher education.

## Essay test

1. Define religion and distinguish between the sacred and the profane.
2. Discuss three functions of religion, giving illustrations of how they are performed in modern American society.

3. Define functional equivalent of religion and provide examples from two countries.
4. Why are major religions declining in the United States? What are three techniques for selling established religions? Which of these techniques do you think would be the most effective and why?
5. Define education. Indicate why it is important in American society.
6. Evaluate the contributions that both the structural-functional and conflict theories make to understanding the role of education in modern America.
7. Summarize the relationship between education and equality, evaluating the busing program in the course of the analysis.
8. Discuss major problems in the educational system and the steps that might be taken to initiate significant educational reform.

## Suggested Readings

Caplow, Theodore, et al. 1983. *All Faithful People: Change and Continuity in Middletown's Religion.* Minneapolis: University of Minnesota Press. A volume comparing the impact that religion has had on the residents of a modern-day community with the effect it had on its local citizens in the 1920s and 1930s.

Delamont, Sara. 1983. *Interaction in the Classroom.* New York: Methuen. A text for a course on the sociology of education, analyzing classroom research and activity. A book of readings has been developed to accompany the text.

Durkheim, Émile. 1961. *The Elementary Forms of the Religious Life.* New York: Collier Books. Translated by Joseph Ward Swain. A classic work in the sociology of religion, indicating how religion contributes to social cohesion in technologically simple societies.

Farber, Jerry. 1970. *The Student as Nigger.* New York: Pocket Books. A series of sharp, humorous essays demonstrating the repressive character of American higher education.

Fowler, James W. 1981. *Stages of Faith.* New York: Harper & Row. Analysis of faith as a process that moves through several stages. Fowler's conclusions are based on interviews with hundreds of people drawn from a variety of backgrounds.

Goodlad, John I. 1983. *A Place Called School: Prospects for the Future.* New York: McGraw-Hill. Research based on observations of more than 1000 classes in grades one through twelve as well as surveys from about 27,000 parents, students, and teachers. Building from his findings, the author discusses the reforms that might provide students a fuller, more meaningful educational experience.

Herndon, James. 1972. *How to Survive in Your Native Land.* New York: Bantam Books. A junior-high-school teacher's irreverent, humorous, and thoughtful account of his successes and failures with students.

*Journal of the Scientific Study of Religion.* The leading journal in the sociology of religion.

McGuire, Meredith B. 1981. *Religion: The Social Context.* Belmont, CA: Wadsworth. A highly readable textbook about the sociology of religion. Particularly appealing features are the effective integration of prominent sociologists' theoretical perspectives and the detailed analyses of contemporary religious movements and issues.

*Phi Delta Kappan.* A leading educational journal featuring essays, surveys, and studies. It is worth thumbing through if only to obtain a sense of the primary issues being analyzed and debated by American educators.

Ravitch, Diane. 1983. *The Troubled Crusade: American Education, 1945–1980.* New York: Basic. A history of developments in American education over a thirty-five-year period.

Roof, Wade Clark (ed.). 1985. "Religion in America Today." *Annals of the American Academy of Political and Social Science.* Vol. 480 (July). Thirteen recent articles offering detailed sociological commentary on contemporary American religion.

Sizer, Theodore R. 1984. *Horace's Compromise: The Dilemma of the American High School.* Boston: Houghton Mifflin. A detailed analysis of teaching that includes vivid descriptions of real classroom activity based on the observations of an educator who visited more than fifty classrooms in recent years.

**336** *Sociology of Education.* A contemporary sociological journal that specializes in sociological studies and essays addressing a range of educational topics.

Weber, Max. 1958. *The Protestant Ethic and the Spirit of Capitalism.* New York: Scribner's. Translated by Talcott Parsons. Original Parsons translation in 1930. Weber's best-known work in the sociology of religion. This challenging essay examines the relationship between the Calvinist ethic and the development of capitalism.

## Student Projects

1. In your school library, go to the periodicals file. Select two periodicals from different religious organizations. Look through at least five recent issues of each periodical. List the topics covered in each issue. Do the interests reflected in the two periodicals seem similar or different? What conclusions can you draw about the two organizations' efforts to "sell" their religion? What about their respective interests in social issues/problems?

2. Talk to at least five people about their memories of the teacher they liked most and the teacher they liked least. What characteristics seem to have been most significant in shaping their good/bad opinions of teachers? Has the information you received suggested support or criticism for either the structural-functional theory or conflict theory? What insights, if any, have your discussions provided about teacher training and educational reform?

## Answers to Test Questions

### True-false test

| | | | | |
|---|---|---|---|---|
| 1. t | 3. f | 5. t | 7. t | 9. f |
| 2. f | 4. f | 6. f | 8. t | 10. f |

### Multiple choice test

| | | | | |
|---|---|---|---|---|
| 1. b | 3. d | 5. d | 7. b | 9. c |
| 2. a | 4. a | 6. a | 8. b | 10. a |

# 14
# THE POLITICAL AND ECONOMIC INSTITUTIONS

Do you believe that the political and economic institutions are related? If you do, then your viewpoint is shared by many prominent business people. Consider Richard Dennis, a commodities trader, sitting in a noisy grill in Chicago and discussing politics with a reporter. At that moment, in 1986, he was a major contributor to the Democratic party, believing that the old-fashioned trading of votes for favors "means bargaining away the heart and soul of the political process." Dennis was using his contributions to influence the way in which party politics would be conducted.

Barton M. Briggs, the chairman of Morgan Stanley Asset Management, was also a political activist but for the Republicans. While his political views were different from Dennis's, they shared the belief that business people should become more involved in the political process. Briggs indicated that at one time he had not understood how the relationship between the political and economic institutions applied to him personally. He said, "There was a time . . . when we all sort of were traditionalists" (Lemann, 1986: 51). By 1986, however, that was no longer the case.

In the 1980s an increasing number of people saw that the intimate relationship between the economic and political institutions could be used to advantage. During the 1980 presidential election, business people started to become more active in national politics. In the Republican primaries, most big corporations backed John Connally and George Bush. When Ronald Reagan obtained the nomination, the southwesterners who provided most of his business support immediately became more prominent politically. In addition, Reagan's exuberant conservatism was appealing to big business people, and they tended to view his economic policies favorably.

After the 1980 election, the Democrats began to seek business people's support more aggressively than they had in many years. Like the Republicans, Democrats have developed a direct-mail operation that produces about half their funds and also three special committees for big donors. The largest of these committees, the Democratic Business Council, has about 200 members who give about $1.25 million per year.

As these examples demonstrate, both politicians and business people have a major stake in determining how society is run. Participants in both the political and economic institutions are concerned with power. **Power** is the ability of an individual or group to implement wishes or policies, with or without the cooperation of others. And why study power? Power, it seems, is an integral element of social relationships. All of us live with it, and, to some extent, exercise it. A child demonstrates power when he or she makes choices about what clothes to wear, breakfast food to eat, or film to attend. The president of the United States exhibits power when exerting influence on behalf of a federal tax cut or increased military expenditure. Extensive power is often "heady stuff," providing those who possess it the rare opportunity of having many others executing their wishes. Great power is sufficiently seductive that it often overshadows any associated distastefulness. Americans do not usually support organized crime, and yet display widespread interest, even fascination, in the Mafia leader who can literally order an enemy's death with the flick of his fingers.

Power and politics are closely related. The **political institution** is the system of norms and roles that concerns the use and distribution of power within a given society. Participants in the political process maintain social order and enact changes in the legal structure. The American political system is a democracy. A **democracy** is a government in which those in power are acting with the consent of the governed.

The **economic institution** is the system of norms and roles developed for the production, distribution, and consumption of goods and services. The economic institution meets the basic material needs and demands of the citizens within a society.

In the following section, we examine two prominent theories about the distribution of power, and the subsequent discussion deals with the three systems by which leaders obtain and exercise power.

Then the discussion shifts to American politics and its corruption. The next part examines modern economic systems, particularly the dominant role played by capitalism in our society, and the chapter ends with an analysis of work in modern times.

# Theories on the Concentration of Power

The following discussion demonstrates that social scientists have developed varied conceptions about the role of power in American society. The two theories discussed in this section provide such different perspectives that one might even begin to lose sight of the fact that their proponents are describing the same political system.

## Pluralism

**Pluralism** is a theory that emphasizes that a dispersion of power exists in American government. The supporters of this theory point out the existence of elected officials at the local, state, and national levels, all of whom are held accountable to constituents who in turn exercise power with their votes. Proponents of pluralism believe that if power is dispersed, then:

1. Power will be controlled and limited to decent purposes because different centers will counterbalance each other. The evil, coercive use of power will remain at a minimum.
2. Minorities, who will have the power to veto policies they strongly oppose, will be partners in the exercise of power and therefore be more cooperative in the long run.
3. Constant negotiations among different power centers will be necessary to reach resolutions on political issues. The process of negotiation will provide those engaged in politics with opportunities for learning how to reach peaceful decisions beneficial to all parties in contention (Dahl, 1967).

A large body of research has found evidence supporting the existence of pluralism in many societies. For instance, recent studies have documented pluralist tendencies in the politics of east central Europe (Arato, 1985), Latin America (Dealy, 1985), and France (Safran, 1985).

Some leading proponents of pluralism have acknowledged that American democracy has been plagued with serious problems—in particular, the abuse of power by political leaders during both the Vietnam War and the Watergate scandals as well as a failure to achieve the resolution to such social problems as the maldistribution of income and wealth, racial inequality, inadequate health care, and unemployment (Dahl, 1982; Lindblom, 1982). Although some leading pluralists have acknowledged various limitations to American democracy, they tend to be supporters of the political status quo. With this fact in mind, one critic has recently questioned whether pluralists are willing to advocate sufficient change in the political system to eliminate or even curtail the problems they now acknowledge (Manley, 1983).

## Power-Elite Perspective

This theory, popularized in the work of C. Wright Mills (1959), opposes the pluralist approach. The **power-elite perspective** is a theory emphasizing that in American society a group of high-status people—well educated, often wealthy, and placed in high occupational positions—control political power. The members of the power elite see themselves as an exalted group set apart from the other members of society. They ". . . accept one another, understand one another, marry one another, tend to work and to think if not together at least alike" (Mills, 1959: 11). According to Mills, the power elite controls basic political, economic, and military policy. Mills visualized three levels of society in America. At the top is the increasingly unified power elite. Then there is a middle class of white-collar employees. The members of this class are "in no political way united or coherent." They are dominated by the corporations and the government agencies for which they work. They have, in short, little or no control over their own lives. At the bottom there is a mass society of people whose lives lack purposeful direction and whose access to channels of power and influence is entirely cut off (Mills, 1959).

G. William Domhoff (1978; 1983) provided evidence supporting the power-elite theory in the United States. He studied the upper class composed of about .5 percent of the population and measured by membership in the Social Register (restricted to families that consider themselves an economic and social elite—"high society"), attendance at elite private schools, membership in exclusive clubs, and wealth. He found that members of this class have disproportional representation in high positions in business, politics, and the military. Extensive evidence also indicates that the American government has aggressively acted on behalf of powerful businesses, both nationally and internationally. Sometimes the government has even backed violent intervention in support of wealthy commercial interests. A number of years ago, a notable case in point was the participation of the Central Intelligence Agency

(CIA) and International Telephone and Telegraph (ITT) in the unsuccessful effort to prevent the election of Salvador Allende to the presidency of Chile and then later their involvement in the successful effort to overthrow his socialist regime (Wise, 1976; Wolfe, 1973). Domhoff concluded that the only possible way to adopt a pluralist perspective would be to ignore the privileged backgrounds, wealth, and diversified and interrelated activities and interests of people in the upper class.

Research documenting the power-elite theory has been conducted in many other countries as well. Recent studies have analyzed evidence of power elites in Thailand (Anderson and London, 1985), Syria (Aziz-al Ahsan, 1984), and black Africa (Bradshaw, 1985).

## A Combination of the Two Theoretical Perspectives

Domhoff dismissed the pluralist perspective. An alternative is to consider that the two theories emphasize different facts. We might examine, for instance, the escalation of the Vietnam War. Sup-

**Figure 14.1**
**Pluralist versus Power-Elite Perspectives on the Vietnam War Escalation**

**Pluralist Perspective**

1. Central decision-maker was a democratically elected president

2. Presidential advisers from diverse backgrounds

3. Majority of Americans eventually supporting the decision

**Vietnam War**

**Power-Elite Perspective**

1. Decision by a small group of men

2. Presidential advisers shared a socially elite or business-associated background

3. Lyndon Johnson's secrecy about the escalation of the war

*The facts people choose to emphasize in a given political situation often reflect the theoretical perspectives they support.*

porters of the pluralist thesis will stress that a democratically elected official — Lyndon Johnson — made the decision to escalate the war and that the president's key advisers came from diverse backgrounds and so clearly served the interests of different groups — specifically, business, academia, the military, and politicians. Besides, though the decision was initially unpopular, the majority of Americans eventually supported it.

In contrast, power-elite advocates will emphasize that a small number of people made the decision. These people shared a socially elite or business-associated background that may partially account for their willingness to have been more actively supportive of the escalation than the general public. In addition, in 1965, Johnson campaigned as a peace candidate opposed to escalation, but after his election he sought to keep the

process of growing involvement in the war secret — very different from the pluralists' ideal of the elected official implementing constituents' interests (Garson, 1977: 146–147). (See Figure 14.1.)

The pluralist and power-elite theories usually focus on different points. This condition suggests an important conclusion: Both theories can simultaneously apply. Or to put it another way, Americans live within a less-than-perfect democracy. Certainly Americans elect their representatives, but these representatives and their associates often boost their own interests and desires ahead of those maintained by the general public.

We have examined two opposing theories involving the dispersion of power. The upcoming section also focuses on power, offering a theoretical analysis of three authority patterns.

## Types of Authority

In this section the focus is on a special kind of power. **Authority** is power that people generally recognize as rightfully maintained by those who use it. If a person with a gun forces a driver over to the side of the road, then that person has demonstrated power. On the other hand, if a policeman flags down a motorist, he is employing his authority.

Max Weber, the German sociologist, described three systems of authority that exist in political systems throughout the world. These systems of authority are ideal types, and as we saw in the discussion of bureaucracies in Chapter 4 ("Groups"), ideal types are simplifications of reality made to improve understanding. Actual political systems usually contain elements of two or even all three of Weber's authority systems. In the course of its history, the American political structure has been affected by the three different types.

### Traditional System of Authority

A **traditional system of authority** is an authority system in which the standard of political leadership passes down from one generation to another. Weber said that within the traditional system, inherited authority is believed ''to have always existed.'' In this political context, the leaders' au-

thority ranges widely because followers must fulfill almost unlimited obligations (Weber, 1947: 341–342). Yet within such a system, people's loyalty focuses on the position and not the incumbent, as the following declaration indicates: ''The King is dead! Long live the King!''

Throughout American history citizens have demonstrated mixed reactions toward a traditional system of authority. During the first session of the Senate, Vice-President John Adams and others sought to make ''His Highness'' the title by which citizens would address the president. Adams and his associates lost out to the simpler title ''Mr. President.'' Some of the most prominent leaders, including George Washington, James Madison, Alexander Hamilton, and John Adams, saw themselves as a natural aristocracy, ''a gentlemanly elite to whom ordinary people, if they were only left alone, would naturally defer'' (Bailyn et al., 1977: 359). In his farewell address, Washington contended that political parties were a mistake. Parties would readily become factions and thus sources of conflict.

Thomas Jefferson shared Washington's dislike of political parties, but he believed that they were necessary. Jefferson was disturbed by the extent to which early government leaders had consolidated authority. He also believed that these leaders were

*Americans may admire and even romanticize traditional authority. Yet it is unlikely that most Americans would accept having a king and queen in their own country, even if they had no power to rule, which is the case with the British monarchy.*

detached from ordinary citizens' interests. Jefferson led the movement to form the Democratic Republican party (which later became the Democratic party) in order to defeat the aristocratic interests of Washington, Adams, and other prominent leaders.

Although the American government has had some traditional tendencies, it more resembles Weber's second authority type.

## Legal-Rational System of Authority

The **legal-rational system of authority** is an authority system based on laws enacted to produce rational behavior and the achievement of formally designated goals. The system depends on participants' competent performance. These people are "servants of the state" (nation), who work within government departments and agencies at the national, state, county, and local levels. Like bureaucrats generally, government officials must follow rationally determined rules and meet the formal qualifications of education and experience that will insure competent performance in their spe-

cific positions (Gerth and Mills, 1946: 79, 196–198).

Many Americans are generally critical of the legal-rational element in the government. People frequently claim that the federal government is too large and too encumbered with "red tape." For half-a-century politicians have spoken about curtailing the size of the federal government, with a particular emphasis on the elimination of overlapping functions performed by different agencies. In recent years presidents of both parties have stressed that the best way to restrict the size of the federal government is to transfer increasing responsibility in education, transportation, community development, and social services to the states.

On the other hand, the contributions of the legal-rational system of authority should be acknowledged. A recent analysis of the economic and political development of Western nations has argued that the legal-rational factor has been a significant agent in their rise to world prominence (Chirot, 1985).

Both the traditional and legal-rational systems tend to entrench themselves in societies, often persisting generation after generation no matter who are the individuals filling the leadership roles. As we will see, the charismatic system is different in this respect.

## Charismatic System of Authority

The **charismatic system of authority** is an authority system in which leadership develops because of the personal magnetism of an individual whose followers believe that he or she possesses superhuman qualities. In Weber's phrase the charismatic leader maintains authority "by proving his strength in life." If followers decide to reject a charismatic leader's sense of mission, then the leadership collapses. Few things are ordinary or regularized about a charismatic leader: no career pattern, no formal training, and the rejection of conventional institutions and behavioral standards.

Charismatic leaders often arise when deep-seated problems exist within a society, and their mission usually involves an effort to change society and eliminate social problems, thereby establishing a better life for their followers. Thus the behavior of charismatic leaders is disruptive, at least in the short term (Gerth and Mills, 1946: 245–250).

A number of prominent American politicians have been considered to possess charismatic qualities. One would be the late Senator Robert Kennedy. He was assassinated on the evening of his victory in the California presidential primary, when the road to the White House seemed unblockable. To Americans of wide-ranging political views, Robert Kennedy seemed to be the presidential candidate who could best move toward the resolution of the various social problems that helped create the dissensions and conflicts of the late 1960s. In this respect he was charismatic. In one Weberian respect, however, he did not qualify as a charismatic leader—he operated within the established political system.

Charismatic leaders are likely to appeal to the discontented, deprived members of society. By Weber's standard John Brown, Sitting Bull, Malcolm X, and Charles Manson qualify as charismatic. Outside the United States, Mao Tse-Tung, Fidel Castro, Adolph Hitler, Joan of Arc, and Napoleon would qualify. Manson and Hitler were charismatic individuals who clearly illustrate the fact that the possession of charisma is not an attribute restricted to people most of us would consider "humanitarian" or "good." For a leader to qualify as charismatic, he or she needs only to perform the function of the charismatic-leadership

*Mao Tse-Tung, one of the most influential charismatic leaders of the twentieth century, is so widely pictured and discussed in China that he seems to be a living presence.*

role. (This chapter concludes with a research section about charismatic leadership.)

The American political system has been influenced by elements of Weber's three authority types. (See Table 14.1.) Let us now move beyond theory and consider the actual workings of the political system.

**Table 14.1**
**Weber's Three Authority Systems**

| AUTHORITY SYSTEM | BASIS OF AUTHORITY | POSSESSORS OF AUTHORITY | CONTROVERSIAL APPEARANCE IN AMERICAN SOCIETY |
|---|---|---|---|
| Traditional | Standard of political leadership passed from one generation to another | Royalty or chieftains | Political orientation of the Federalists' "gentlemanly elite" |
| Legal-rational | Laws enacted to produce rational behavior and the achievement of formally designated goals | Government bureaucrats | Presidents' and other politicians' half-century effort to trim the size of the federal government |
| Charismatic | Followers' belief that a leader possesses special, even supernatural qualities | Individuals who appear at crisis times and promise to establish a better life for their followers | Political activities of leaders like Robert Kennedy and Malcolm X whose sense of mission primarily represented the dispossessed and conflicted with many Americans' economic and political priorities |

Source: Adapted from Hans Gerth and C. Wright Mills (eds.). *From Max Weber*. Oxford University Press. 1946.

# American Politics and Its Corruption

In the 1830s a young Frenchman named Alexis de Tocqueville (1966) visited American society and wrote about it. Some of his observations about the American political process remain accurate today. A pair of his insights summarize central themes of this section: the widespread desire of people to participate in the democratic process and the tendency of influential citizens to corrupt the process.

On the first point, de Tocqueville felt that a large amount of political activity occurred in America, with a wide range of groups mobilizing political action on behalf of their own interests. The Frenchman concluded that nothing was more important to Americans than discussion about their political involvement. According to de Tocqueville, Americans often became so involved in politics that they tended to speak as if addressing a meeting. In fact, Americans could become so excited with the subject that they would sometimes address an audience of one as "Gentlemen."

De Tocqueville claimed that many wealthy people appeared to support democracy. They tended to dress simply and to maintain a modest manner. If an affluent man met his shoemaker in the street, he would stop to talk with him, and most likely they would discuss politics. When they parted, they would inevitably shake hands as equals. If democracy would ever have been in peril, however, this same affluent man would have been happy to help bring about its demise if it would have been in his interest. Hence, while de Tocqueville saw power widely dispersed in American society, he recognized the dangerous potential for the concentration of power in the hands of a few. As we will see, both these issues have been apparent in the American political process.

## The Two-Party System

At the American Constitutional Convention of 1787, the delegates opposed "factions" because they feared that political parties would destroy the newly formed nation. Early advocates of political parties like Thomas Jefferson and James Madison believed that opposing, lasting differences of opinion, which political parties represent, are necessary in a free country, even if clashing party ambitions will sometimes endanger the existence of the country. Jefferson, Madison, and others felt that it would be impossible to support the basic freedoms of speech, press, and assembly and simultaneously oppose the development of political parties. The constitutional decision to hold periodic elections among the people also favored the development of political parties (Dahl, 1976: 275–277).

Political parties provide a number of functions. First, they make the transfer of power from one administration to another peaceful and smooth. When presidents, governors, or mayors leave office, the newly elected officials move in, bringing with them a slate of the party faithful who can fill government posts, judicial openings, or office-staff positions. Thus, for such transfers, parties can act as large personnel agencies. Second, parties are a major source of recruitment for government leaders. People who run for local, state, and federal offices have usually been active in party politics, where they display potential leadership qualities. Third, parties simplify voters' choices by providing party labels as a guideline. The majority of American citizens have limited knowledge about the wide array of candidates for whom they are entitled to vote, and without the party labels to assist them, they would often be completely lost. Fourth, American parties supply a series of platforms and policies. These directives may be somewhat vague and are not always clearly differentiated between the two major parties, but they do support the broad interests of various voter groups—more clearly with some issues than others (Grant, 1979: 196–197).

Certainly American political parties do not always meet their members' needs and interests. Yet two parties have been successful enough to have dominated most of U.S. political history. Two parties have prevailed for several reasons. In the first place, in the United States, a broad consensus on political issues exists. Americans generally express a commitment to democracy, the Constitution, the free-enterprise economic system, universal free public education, and religious and racial tolerance. In contrast, in some other democratic countries, sharp disagreement on specific issues can be the basis for lasting political factions—for instance, Catholic parties in Italy and the

Netherlands, farmers' parties in the Scandinavian countries, and working-class parties throughout Europe. Second, the electoral process also encourages a two-party system. In the United States, a winner-take-all situation prevails. For instance, in the congressional elections, each state is divided into districts, and within each district the person receiving the highest vote total obtains the seat. In a number of other democratic countries, on the other hand, there is a system of proportional representation, where each party receives the percentage of seats that corresponds with its total vote. Such a system encourages minority parties, which will receive little or no representation under the U.S. political system. Finally another factor supporting the two-party system is the force of habit and tradition. For over a century, the current two parties have dominated politics. Many Americans receive their party loyalties and political positions from their parents and in turn transmit similar loyalties and positions to their own children (Dahl, 1976: 287–291).

In the 1980s the two-party system worked more effectively for some Americans than for others. The Republican administration's tax and spending policies benefited most Republicans and also affluent Democrats. On the other hand, low-income Democrats either saw their tax burdens increase or received the proportionately smallest tax reductions (Edsall, 1986). In many other political systems, there would be one or more political parties to represent this group's specific interests.

For over two centuries, the United States has

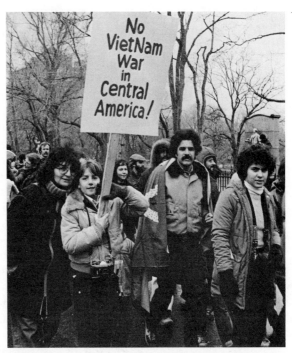

*Sometimes Americans, such as those opposing Reagan administration efforts to overthrow the socialist government in Nicaragua, conclude that the best way to express their opposition to a prevailing policy is to protest.*

maintained a stable political democracy. We are not directly aware of the problems a country must face as it moves from dictatorship to political democracy. Spain accomplished this shift in the late 1970s, as the following Cross-Cultural Perspective indicates.

## CROSS-CULTURAL PERSPECTIVE

### *From Dictatorship to Democracy: The Spanish Case*

The transition from dictatorship to democracy is a complex and ticklish process. Because of a combination of skillful national leadership and cooperative efforts from the major political parties involved, Spain successfully completed the transition in 1977.

On November 20, 1975, Francisco Franco, the dictator of Spain for thirty-six years, died. The new head of state was King Juan Carlos, who had been appointed by Franco as the individual most likely to perpetuate the standards and the structures of the Franco dictatorship. For a six-year period before Franco's death, Juan Carlos expressed public loyalty to the regime, but only his most intimate friends knew that he had strong sympathies for a

democratic form of government.

Nonetheless, Juan Carlos's first appointments were a disappointment to supporters of democratic rule. In particular, legal restrictions made it impossible to choose a democratically oriented prime minister, and he picked Arias Novarro, a strong backer of Francoist policies. Arias held office for about six months.

His refusal to support significant political and economic reform provoked strikes and major street demonstrations. Toward the end he even lost the support of his fellow Francoists, who were unwilling to make the most modest reforms to existing policies.

Arias resigned, and in his place King Juan Carlos appointed Adolfo Suárez. By all reasonable criteria, Suárez seemed to be the finest choice as prime minister for the difficult period of transition to democracy. He was experienced politically, having held diverse posts in the Franco regime. He saw clearly that the remaining Franco supporters lacked the backing to maintain their system but that no opposition parties had the public support or the organizational unity and strength to assume the leadership. Suárez realized it was up to him to lead his nation gradually but relentlessly toward democratic rule. Besides knowledge and perceptiveness, Suárez had the right personal qualities for the task. He was flexible, self-disciplined, emotionally controlled, energetic at public relations, and above all, forceful.

During the late 1970s, Suárez maneuvered skillfully around the obstacles that opposed a transition to democratic rule. He worked carefully with his closest allies: King Juan Carlos and a number of other influential, progressively oriented individuals. He also managed to maintain effective relations with the army, enlisting senior officers' support behind his reformist program. A prominent reason these individuals and groups were willing to back Suárez was his determination to act entirely within the guidelines of the legal processes set down in the Francoist Constitution.

While the Prime Minister was courting the support of established individuals and groups, he was also determined to obtain backing from the developing political parties. The moderate opposition to Francoism — the Liberals, Christian Democrats, and the Social Democrats — readily approved his program. Even the rapidly growing Spanish Socialist Workers' Party recognized that Suárez's program for restoring democracy was in the best interest of the nation — that, at times, as one leader said "it's most revolutionary to be moderate."

Finally the negotiations with the Communists were the only obstacle. Suárez was reluctant to cooperate with the Communists, whose support for his program seemed doubtful. Other moderates agreed that it would be better to keep the Communists out of the upcoming elections. The Communists were unhappy with this prospect, and one of their most prominent leaders appeared openly in Madrid — a public challenge to Suárez's government since his party was still illegal. To maintain his authority, Suárez had no choice but to arrest this Communist leader. That action, in turn, endangered Suárez's entire program. Most of the moderates had no use for the Communists, but the arrest of their leader undermined in their eyes the democratic credentials of Suárez and his administration. Suárez had no other option. He released the Communist leader and enlisted the help of King Juan Carlos and Vice-President Gutierrez Mellado to convince the military leaders, the staunchest opponents of Communism, that it was essential to permit the Communists to become a legal political party. Army leaders publicly expressed their dissatisfaction with this decision but said that out of patriotism they would cooperate. No military coup occurred. The Communist leaders, in turn, made a number of significant concessions.

In this context of cooperation and compromise, a national vote on the government's political reform was held on December 15, 1976. Of the electorate, 77.4 percent went to the polls, and 94.2 percent of those voters supported the government's political reform, which featured elections in June 1977.

The elections were a triumph for an expanding democratic program. The Suárez coalition received 34.3 percent of the popular vote, and the Spanish Socialist Workers Party was a highly respectable runner-up, with 28.5 percent. Both the remnants of Francoism and the Communists received modest support. In 1982 the Socialist Party won majority control in the national elections. Thus, within less than a decade, a modern European nation had used a democratic political process to move across the political spectrum: from a repressive, highly conservative dictatorship to an elected socialist government.

Sources: Raymond Carr and Juan Pablo Fusi Aizpurua. *Spain: Dictatorship to Democracy.* London: Allen and Unwin. 1981. Second edition, pp. 207–258; Meir Serfaty. "Spanish Democracy: The End of the Transition." *Current History.* Vol. 80. May 1981, pp. 213–217+.

## Interest Groups

Some efforts to influence politicians are illegal, but there is nothing inherently illegal about trying to influence such people. In fact, interest groups are widespread in American society. An **interest group** is a group whose members seek to influence elected politicians or government bureaucrats to initiate the legislation or policies they want. In the American political system, there are thousands of organizations ". . . representing or claiming to represent trade unionists, veterans, business people, industrialists, taxpayers, bankers, oil companies, copper importers, doctors, women's clubs, nature lovers, stream pollutionists, conservationists, foreign policy groups, old people" (Dahl, 1976: 482).

Some citizens' interest groups write letters to politicians, organize petition drives, or advertise in the media. Large, wealthy interest groups might advertise and write to politicians, but they are more likely than citizens' groups to engage extensively in lobbying activities. **Lobbying** is a face-to-face effort to persuade legislators and other government personnel to support the proposals of an interest group. Those proposals might involve the provision of tax loopholes that benefit various businesses, or lobbying might help produce legislation that protects the needs of organizations as diverse as the American Medical Association, the Associated Milk Producers, Inc., and United Aircraft. On the other hand, interest groups or their representatives might act to postpone legislation; the lobbying efforts of the National Rifle Association have prevented the passage of any effective gun-control legislation. Studies indicate that at the federal level, the amount of interest-group activity has increased in recent years. In particular, political-action committees (PACs) started by large corporations have been making major contributions to federal candidates (Berry, 1984; Masters and Keim, 1985). (See Table 14.2.)

**Table 14.2**
**PAC Contributions to Congressional Campaigns: 1983–1984[1]**

| | Corporations | Trade Associations[2] | Labor |
|---|---|---|---|
| **HOUSE OF REPRESENTATIVES** | | | |
| Democrats | 10.6 | 10.7 | 19.3 |
| Republicans | 13.4 | 10.0 | 1.1 |
| **SENATE** | Corporations | Trade Associations | Labor |
| Democrats | 3.8 | 3.0 | 5.1 |
| Republicans | 10.2 | 4.2 | .4 |

[1] In millions of dollars.
[2] A variety of occupationally affiliated organizations.
Source: U.S. Federal Election Commission. *Interim Report No. 9. U.S. Senate and House Campaigns.* May 1985.

*Political action committees or PACs raise money to support the candidates of their choice. This table shows that Republican congressional candidates receive a greater share of corporate contributions, while their Democratic opponents receive major support from labor.*

**348**

Why are interest groups so prevalent in U.S. society? A prominent reason is that the political system rests on the simple idea that government exists in order to protect people's rights. A well-known phrase states the condition widely believed by Americans to effectively protect these rights: The government governs best that governs least. John Locke expressed this political philosophy in his *Second Treatise on Civil Government,* and when Thomas Jefferson wrote the Declaration of Independence, he received much of his inspiration from Locke's book. In the more than 200 years since the signing of the Declaration, Americans have generally accepted this political philosophy. As a result there has been much less government regulation in the lives of the American citizenry than in many other societies. Wealthy and powerful interests have been prominent beneficiaries of this clear absence of regulation (Roelofs, 1967: chapter 6). When these groups have chosen to further their own interests at the expense of ordinary citizens, they have encountered few if any limits or penalties. Through the late 1970s and into the early 1980s, the rapid rise in oil prices accompanied by a large increase in company profits was a case in point.

While interest groups and lobbying are legal, payoffs to politicians obviously are not. The problem is where to draw the line. One could argue that even when lobbyists take politicians to dinner, they are actually offering them a low-level bribe: spending money on them in order to encourage action on behalf of their own interests. Evidence from the past fifteen years demonstrates that many prominent politicians have taken much more substantial bribes from lobbyists. On the list have been a president (Richard Nixon), a vice-president (Spiro Agnew), a Supreme Court justice who had been nominated for chief justice (Abe Fortas), and a long list of governors, congressmen, and mayors. In the 1980 Abscam scandal, a Senator and six congressmen accepted bribes from undercover FBI men pretending to act on behalf of Arab oil men seeking political favors. A team of historians claimed that these various scandals represent "the fall of the great men." Each new scandal "was more shocking than the last, and each set an historic precedent" (Bailyn et al., 1977: 1262).

Americans have become suspicious about the relations between the federal government and business. In 1958, 18 percent of a national sample

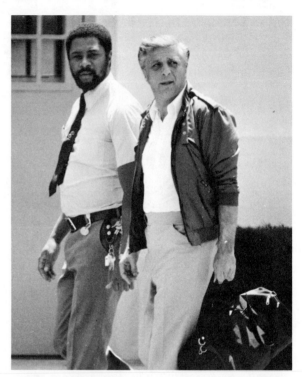

*Angelo Errichetti, a former mayor of Camden, New Jersey, was just one of many prominent people arrested and convicted for accepting bribes during the Abscam scandals.*

believed that government is run for a few big interests. That figure has risen steadily, reaching 76 percent in 1980 (Center for Political Studies of the Institute for Social Research, University of Michigan Elections Studies, April 1980).

## Corruption in American Politics

George Washington Plunkitt, a prominent, corrupt nineteenth-century politician, once said, "Men ain't in politics for nothin, they want something out of it" (Riordan, 1963: 21).

Candidates for political office would agree. If elected, they will reward those who worked for their election. The distribution of favors to political supporters is called **patronage.** Sometimes patronage means giving jobs, which can be done in a legal manner, but it can also involve illegal activities: provision of construction contracts, defense contracts, banking and insurance funds, and specialized treatment by government agencies (Tolchin and Tolchin, 1972: 6). Favors such as these will establish the loyalty of one's supporters and thus help secure a politician in power.

In the United States, civil-service systems require that applicants for many government jobs be chosen under a merit, not a patronage system (Ranney, 1966: 468). However, the most powerful nonelected government jobs remain appointments, which are subject to the patronage system. Evidence suggests, for example, that patronage is a prominent factor influencing presidents' selection of their cabinet members (Burstein, 1977).

Political machines also use a patronage system. A **political machine** is an organization established to control a city, county, or state government. At the head is a political boss, who seeks to dominate political activity within the machine's jurisdiction. In exchange for political control and often payoffs too, bosses and their associates provide certain advantages for different groups. These arrangements, though illegal, satisfy the following citizen needs:

1. The machine creates elaborate networks that offer food, jobs, legal advice, educational assistance, and many other forms of aid. The help supplied by political machines usually involves a style that is not demeaning to the recipient. Such a style of giving aid often stands in stark contrast to the approach of the official, culturally approved welfare agencies. Many recently arrived immigrants, among others, have been willing to pledge their voting loyalty to a political machine in exchange for much-needed assistance provided in a more respectful manner than the official welfare agencies offer.
2. Political bosses and their associates supply political privileges to large businesses. For example, transportation, utility, and communications companies seek permits, licenses, variances, and special ordinances from bosses;

a utility company will receive the only local permit to supply electricity, for instance. When businesses receive these privileges in exchange for payment or other favors, they are able to stabilize their operations and maximize their profits.
3. By affiliating themselves with political machines, many people are able to elevate their economic and social positions more quickly than otherwise would have been possible. The members of various newly arrived ethnic groups are prominent examples of this.
4. People involved in organized crime—drugs, gambling, and prostitution—often work closely with political bosses. In exchange for payments or other favors, the machine protects these illegal businesses from prosecution by law-enforcement officials (Merton, 1968).

The functions performed by political machines help ". . . explain why the periodic efforts at 'political reform,' 'turning the rascals out,' and 'cleaning political house' are typically . . . short-lived and ineffectual" (Merton, 1968:135).

From the earliest days of American history, a relationship between the political and economic institutions has existed. In 1629 John Winthrop, the first governor of Massachusetts, was a prosperous businessman. Throughout American history the two institutions have shared an ideology emphasizing people's right to pursue an unrestricted existence: There is the Jeffersonian ideal that the government governs best governs least, and Adam Smith's free-enterprise standard of the self-regulating market. Finally both politicians and business people are power brokers, affecting or controlling the destinies of thousands, even millions of people.

## The Corporate State

In his study of American society, Alexis de Tocqueville observed not only the American political process but successful American business enterprises as well. De Tocqueville claimed that the superiority of American businesses over their European counterparts was based on one factor: the ability to ship their goods more cheaply. But why? American ships cost as much as the European vessels, and the sailors received higher wages than their European counterparts. The reason, de Tocqueville concluded, was that the American sailors were willing to take more chances and to work harder. Admittedly they were shipwrecked more frequently, but no one else crossed the ocean so quickly, and this timesaving saved money. For example, a captain would leave Boston and go to

China to buy tea. He would arrive at Canton, stay a few days, and come back. In less than two years, he had gone around the world, and he had seen land only once. During an eight- to ten-month voyage, he had drunk brackish water and eaten only salted meat. The captain had fought the sea, disease, and boredom, but on his return he could sell tea a few pennies cheaper than his English competition. And that in a nutshell was what he was trying to do (de Tocqueville, 1966: 368–369).

In writing about what he called "the commercial greatness of the United States," de Tocqueville emphasized the daring and commitment of American sailors. But a number of other factors encouraged the explosive development of the economic system — in particular, a range of rich natural resources, a large adult labor force arriving from Europe and Africa, isolation from the disruptive European wars, and, in particular, Adam Smith's revolutionary ideas about economic development.

The rest of this chapter examines the economic institution — the system of norms and roles developed for the production, distribution, and consumption of goods and services. Throughout the material on the political institution, we have frequently seen its relationship with the economic institution — in particular, in discussions indicating that many business people attempt to influence politicians to establish policies or pass laws that they want. The relationship between the two institutions remains apparent in the upcoming sections, especially in the analysis of how corporations exert influence in the political sphere.

## Economic Ideologies: Capitalism versus Socialism

Perhaps we in the United States are more concerned than are the people of other nations with the threat of opposing values, beliefs, and activities. After all, we have a word for it: "un-American." The British or the French do not have a comparable word. Even our most powerful political rivals — the Soviets — do not classify any people's values, beliefs, and activities as "un-Soviet." We in this country are unique in this respect. In fact, at one time a congressional committee existed — the House Un-American Activities Committee — to investigate such matters. This kind of classification presents a problem: It tends to preclude thoughtful analysis. Consider, for instance,

the two economic systems we are about to examine. To many Americans capitalism is American/good, and socialism is un-American/bad. To some people there is no need to look further. We will.

To begin: Capitalism and socialism are economic systems, and therefore both concern themselves with the production and distribution of goods and services. The American system is capitalist. **Capital** is money, goods, or other forms of wealth invested to produce more wealth. **Capitalism** is an economic system where capital is controlled by private citizens who own the means of production and distribution of goods and services. **Socialism** is an economic system with collective ownership of the means of production and distribution of goods and services. Socialist measures range from limited steps advocating the public ownership of a few businesses to extensive control over economic planning and its implementation.

### The Development of Capitalism

To Americans 1776 is renowned as the year when the Declaration of Independence was written and signed and the nation officially began. To the rest of the Western world, however, 1776 has received more recognition as the year the Scottish philosopher Adam Smith (1723–1790) published *The Wealth of Nations,* in which he presented the first complete theory of economic behavior (Smith, 1930).

Smith began with the central idea that the great motivator of economic activity is all participants' powerful desire to better their own condition — in short, self-interest. Self-interest, Smith argued, produces the miracle of the capitalist system: the self-regulating market. If consumers are free to spend their money as they wish and if business people can compete equally for their patronage, then capital and labor certainly will be used where they are most needed. Thus if consumers want more shoes than are currently produced, they will pay high prices for shoes, and shoemakers will make a good profit. Those profits, in turn, will draw new investors into the shoe market. If more shoes are produced than consumers want, the price will fall, and investors will turn to other products — socks perhaps. In addition, competition wipes out the inefficient businesses, rewarding those who turn out the best products at the lowest prices and forcing even the successful people to invest in new products and procedures if they want to stay ahead of their competitors. Therefore, Smith explained, production keeps rising, pulling up wages at the same time. The overall result is that while business people are seeking only their own profit, they become part of a market process that promotes the common good.

In Adam Smith's view, however, business people are likely to attempt to undermine the common good by trying to fix prices and keep down wages, efforts Smith believed could succeed only if government actively helps business. For this reason Smith strongly advocated that the economic system be "laissez-faire" (literally, let do), meaning that it should be allowed to function without government intervention.

By the early nineteenth century, many people had read *The Wealth of Nations,* and most Western governments accepted Smith's basic ideas. Open competition in the marketplace became the standard of the day, and the power of Adam Smith's theory seemed indisputable to many. Businessmen accumulated and reinvested capital in awesomely large amounts compared to the amounts of pre-capitalist times. For instance, the world production of pig iron rose from 10 million tons in 1867 to 357 million tons a century later. As recently as 1850, human muscle and animal power produced 94 percent of the energy used in American industry, whereas today these sources supply less than 1 percent.

Although capitalism created industrial expansion, it was also a disruptive force. The Industrial Revolution wiped out the rural cottage industries and forced workers to enter the new factory towns, where living conditions were crowded and squalid. Wages were low, and to help support their families, children as young as eight would work up to fourteen hours a day in factories and mines. At the same time, Andrew Carnegie, John D. Rockefeller, and other capitalists accumulated vast fortunes. In addition, there were depressions, which caused economic analysts to question whether the market could be self-regulating.

The Great Depression of the 1930s inspired the economic theory of John Maynard Keynes. Keynes, a British economist, argued that a government can generate an economic upsurge by using tax cuts, extensive government spending, and the outright creation of more money. Since World War II, capitalist governments have adopted Keynesian measures, and none of them would ever consider leaving a depression to right itself. Consequently widespread agreement now exists that a modern capitalist system cannot be entirely self-regulating; at least some government intervention appears periodically necessary (Greenberg, 1974; Samuelson, 1980).

Adam Smith provided the theory on which capitalism was based. For socialism Karl Marx supplied the basic perspective.

## The Development of Socialism

In 1848, in *The Communist Manifesto,* Karl Marx described the conditions he believed would produce socialism from capitalism. Marx contended that within capitalism the interests of the capitalists and their workers are irreconcilably opposed. The capitalists' dominant interest is in increasing their profits. The workers' primary concern is increasing wages and improving job conditions. But since the owners are more powerful, their drive for profits will dominate. As a result certain developments will occur — in particular, the growing concentration of wealth in the hands of a few large businesses that absorb the small ones; the increasing use of machinery; the displacement of more and more workers, thereby creating widespread unemployment; and the recurrence of periodic, increasingly acute breakdowns in the economy.

At some point the workers will recognize that the economic system is the source of their problems and that these problems are shared by all workers. The workers will also see that since they represent the majority of the citizenry, they are potentially stronger than the owners. Eventually they will organize themselves into an army and will rise up and overthrow the owners. At this point the means of production and distribution will be in the hands of the people — in short, socialism (Marx, 1932).

### SOCIALIST PHILOSOPHY

Marx devoted his energy to the criticism of capitalism. He wrote little about the content of socialism and did not live to see the existence of a socialist nation.

A few elements characterize modern socialist philosphy. They include:

1. *Government ownership of productive resources.* Key industries such as railroads, coal, and steel are nationalized in the effort to downplay the role of private property.

2. *Planning.* Coordinated, centralized planning replaces the free play of the profit motive in a laissez-faire economy. There is an emphasis on "production for use rather than profit." Citizens are encouraged to develop craftsmanship and social services and to downplay the materialistic tendencies so strong in the Western "acquisitive societies."

3. *Redistribution of income.* Government taxing power sharply reduces inherited wealth. Social-security benefits and cradle-to-grave assistance programs will insure the well-being of previously poor people (Samuelson, 1980: 816–817).

The Soviet Union, the People's Republic of China, and Cuba practice socialism, and Sweden, Great Britain, Norway, Australia, and France have had governments with socialist platforms.

Americans have traditionally opposed socialism. In a 1942 survey, 25 percent of a national survey indicated that some form of socialism would be a good thing for the country, and 40 percent felt it would be a bad thing (Roper Organization, *Fortune Survey,* 1942). Thirty-four years later, only 10 percent of the respondents said they would support the introduction of socialism in the United States, whereas 62 percent opposed its introduction (*Cambridge Reports,* March 1976). These are not surprising findings when we consider the dominance of capitalist activities in U.S. society.

It should be emphasized that like all ideologies both capitalism and socialism seldom exist in absolutely pure form. Capitalist societies often contain some socialist elements: a range of governmental assistance programs in health care and income subsidy, for instance; and socialist nations sometimes permit limited capitalist ventures: for example, the sale of privately grown fruits and vegetables for personal profit in the Soviet Union.

## Capitalist Activity

Mark Twain once wrote that the leading capitalists live by the following gospel: "Get money. Get it quickly. Get it in abundance. Get it in prodigious abundance. Get it dishonestly if you can, honestly if you must" (Twain, 1973: 224). In Twain's day, especially at the end of the nineteenth century, the opponents of big business grew rapidly in number. Monopolies, which involve exclusive control by one or several corporations over the production of a commodity, were widely denounced as a conspiracy, evidence of greed, and a misallocation and underuse of resources (Bailyn et al., 1977: 843). But the critics had little effect upon the increasing concentration of corporate power and wealth.

### Corporate Power and Wealth

A **corporation** is a legally designated organization that has powers and responsibilities separate from its workers and owners. For instance, in an unincorporated business, the owner may be forced to sell his or her home and possessions to settle business debts. Investors in corporations, however, have limited liability. No investor is responsible for more than the initial investment, and this limited liability attracts backers and serves as a primary basis for extensive capital accumulation and massive growth in the size of some corporations.

In a given year, the 500 largest corporations account for over half—about 55 percent—of the Gross National Product, the sum total of the value of the goods and services produced in the United States in a year. The top 100 corporations have assets of over $1 billion each and yearly sales of more than $2.5 billion each.

The major corporations exert impressive political and social power through a number of sources. They include:

*Their wealth.* Because of their market domination, the business giants have enormous sums of money that their owners and managers can allocate the way they choose. They use these sums for continued market domination, especially for increased political and social power. For instance, vast expenditures on advertising support not only the sale of the particular products but also the company image and the legitimate use of the corporate system in general.

*Their accumulation of skilled and talented people.* No other modern organization has such a range of talented members, with the possible exception of the federal government. At a moment's notice, a giant corporation can mobilize scientists, social scientists, engineers, lawyers, accountants, management experts, and systems analysts to work together on a problem designated important by management, no matter what it may be—new product development, basic research, public relations, or overseas expansion.

*The linkage between citizen and corporate well-being.* Large corporations are massive organizations that employ hundreds of thousands of people, and each major corporation has numerous large companies to which it subcontracts its work. In the early 1970s, General Motors employed over 700,000 people, and in a single week in 1980 this largest American corporation laid off 155,000 workers, the population of a small city. In his campaign for a major government loan to stave off bankruptcy, Chrysler President Lee Iaccoca frequently emphasized that if his company went bankrupt, hundreds of thousands of citizens would be forced out of work and into the already long unemployment lines.

*Commitment of all public officials to the existing economic and social system.* Liberals and conservatives or Republicans and Democrats might have somewhat different outlooks on the economic and social order, but they agree on one fundamental point: The basic principles of the current economic system should not be challenged. With rare exceptions public officials do not make such radical proposals as massive income distribution, restraints on corporate autonomy, or the establishment of public control over the production process. In fact, the relationship between government personnel and corporate leadership is frequently intimate, especially in the realm of national defense and foreign policy. From 1940 to 1967, 77 percent of the individuals who directed the principal foreign-policy departments (secretaries and undersecretaries of state and defense, the military-service secretaries, the chairmen of the Atomic Energy Commission, and directors of the CIA) came from big business and high finance (Gilpin, 1975; Greenberg, 1974).

The power and influence of U.S. corporations extends well beyond the boundaries of our society. In the twenty-year period following World War II, the United States was dominant in productivity and in its ability to influence the world economy. In recent years its economic dominance has slackened as Japan and West Germany have surpassed the United States in the rate of economic development.

**Figure 14.2**
**Gross National Products Compared to Corporate Sales: Some Matchings[1]**

[1] The Gross National Product is the financial value of yearly goods and services in a national economy. In an economic sense, the GNP is comparable to corporate sales. Both represent the financial value of the products their respective units produce.
[2] The numbers in parentheses represent the U.S. corporate rank in sales for 1985.

*This figure clearly demonstrates the enormous wealth and associated power of some major American corporations by comparing their corporate sales in 1985 with the gross national products of foreign countries in 1985. (Sources: The 1985 (Fortune) Directory of U.S. Corporations; 1986 Information Please Almanac.)*

As American corporations helped establish their economic dominance by investing directly in the economies of other countries, multinationals have developed. A **multinational** is a large corporation with production plants and distribution centers in many countries. It draws its natural resources and labor supply and sells its products — as varied as autos, clothes, computers, and oil — around the world. About 200 American corporations are multinational. In the 1970s the ten largest multinationals were General Motors, Exxon, Ford, Royal Dutch/Shell, General Electric, IBM, Mobil Oil, Chrysler, Texaco, and Unilever, with all but Royal Dutch/Shell and Unilever centered in the United States. It is an understatement to say that multinationals are large. Of the 100 largest economic structures in the world, exactly half are multinationals. The total sales revenue for Exxon in 1982 was greater than the sum of the Gross National Products of Argentina, Portugal, and Cuba. (See Figure 14.2.)

Massive corporations invest their capital in a number of ways. Some investments bring raw products to the United States for use domestically: for example, shipment of oil for refinement and use. Other investments involve the sale of American goods abroad. In some cases, such as the automobile industry, a corporation will open a factory abroad to manufacture products for local sale. Frequently, though, the products manufactured abroad are sold in the United States.

What conditions have encouraged the development of multinationals? In the first place, in many countries tariffs restrict the importation and sale of American products. Any locally manufactured goods, including those produced by multinationals, escape that restriction. Second, foreign labor is likely to be considerably cheaper than in the United States. Third, the shift of operations abroad allows multinationals to avoid some payments of taxes; thus a corporate division in a country with high taxes can avoid these taxes by transferring products to a division in a country with low taxes. Fourth, a multinational strategy seems consistent with a basic capitalist belief — the conviction that continuous growth is a desirable condition — and foreign markets obviously represent a massive growth opportunity. Finally, since World War II, presidential administrations have encouraged large-scale foreign investment as a means of establishing American preeminence internationally (Gilpin, 1975; Greenberg, 1974; Salomon and Bernstein, 1982).

Material in this section has suggested that within our economic system, a small number of corporations have accumulated a lion's share of wealth and power and that their dominant concern is extension of their wealth and power. But what about workers' needs? This issue will be considered in the upcoming discussion.

# Work and the Worker

A staff member for a major management consultant firm posed a question to American white-collar workers. "Do you really need an office as such at all?" He went on to suggest that by the 1990s two-way communication will be sufficiently advanced to encourage widespread working at home. At present many office workers perform tasks — entering data, typing, retrieving, and totaling columns of figures — that require few, if any face-to-face communications. In addition, many of the tasks performed by engineers, draftsmen, and other white-collar employees could be done more readily or as readily at home as at the office with often nothing more required than a computer terminal. Such a change would provide greater work flexibility, an opportunity for more extensive family and community involvement, and a decisively lessened cost for transportation. Alvin Toffler has called this pattern of people increasingly working at home "the electronic cottage," a modern version of the preindustrial cottage industries, where workers performed their labors in their own homes (Toffler, 1981: chapter 16).

Whether or not Toffler is correct, the scheme he proposed is consistent with the historical trend by which significant social eras create major changes in people's work patterns. The industrial age brought people into central places — factories and offices. Perhaps, as Toffler suggested, the postindustrial age will allow many people to do their work, or most of their work, in their homes. In this section we examine changing outlooks on work over time and the modern perception of work.

## Changing Outlooks on Work over Time

People have attached as great a variety of meanings to work as they have to sex and to play. To the ancient Greeks, who had a slave-based economy, work was a curse. Homer claimed that the Gods hated humanity and therefore condemned people to work. Greek thinkers did consider the possibility that agriculture allowed independence and thus might be tolerable but were convinced that the mechanical arts were brutalizing to the mind. In general, the Greeks felt that work possessed two attributes: It was humiliating and necessary.

The Hebrews shared the Greek outlook on work, and they believed that people had to engage in it as a punishment for Adam and Eve's fall from divine grace. By working, people could regain some of their lost dignity. In fact, early Jewish scholars emphasized that working, no matter how lowly the labor one faced, was never as repugnant as idleness.

Like the Greeks and the Hebrews, the early Christians gave little respect to work, but they also despised idleness. The early Christians believed that the most honorable labor in which people could engage was the contemplation of heavenly existence and that any other work served as a diversion from this noble task. From the eleventh to the fourteenth century, the Catholic Church became more involved in community activities, and religious leaders started to give more consideration to work. St. Thomas Aquinas took a position that closely resembles the current Catholic view: Work is a natural right and duty providing the foundation for property and profit, but it is always just a means to a higher spiritual goal.

In the sixteenth and seventeenth centuries, a sharply different outlook on work developed: The only effective way to serve God was through good work. During this period scientific and technological innovations provided the basis for the development of capitalism, and Protestant theology supported the emphasis on work, as we noted in Chapter 13 ("Religion and Education"). The Protestant-ethic focus on the importance, even sanctity of work was consistent with a number of positions that both preceded and followed it. Examples are the early Christians' disgust for idleness as well as the outlook on work, thrift, and success maintained by such prominent American capitalists as Carnegie, Rockefeller, and Ford (Wilensky, 1966: 119–123).

The modern American conception of work has some distinct attributes as well.

## Modern Perception of Work

Americans' feelings about work seem to be linked to four cultural values:

1. *The good-provider conception.* Traditionally men have been the breadwinners, and a "real" man is one who can take care of his family.
2. *The ability to maintain independence.* A paying job is the way to establish freedom and independence. Most adult Americans are uncomfortable if they are financially dependent on others.
3. *The emphasis on material success.* The higher people's wages or salaries, the more capable they will be to purchase the expensive homes, cars, clothes, and other material items that they enjoy and that are indicators to others of their occupational achievement.
4. *The importance of performing a good job.* For Americans, work is a source of self-respect, and so the people who do their job well have higher self-esteem than those who do not (Yankelovich, 1974).

Unemployed people are unable to attain any of these cultural standards. Therefore it is not surprising that the effects of unemployment on individuals can be serious. One long-term study has indicated that when the rate of national unemployment rises 1 percentage point, suicide increases 4.1 percent, homicide 5.7 percent, and stress-related disorders such as heart disease 1.9 percent (Riegle, 1982). While other factors besides the increase in unemployment might contribute to the rise in these problems, that increase has probably played a dominant role. Table 14.3 indicates how large a problem unemployment represents in modern times.

### Job Satisfaction Today

In a journalistic study of Americans at work, Studs Terkel offered the following commentary about the significance of people's jobs.

**Table 14.3**
**American Unemployment Past and Present**

| UNEMPLOYMENT OVER TIME | | | RECENT FIGURES (APRIL 1986) | |
|---|---|---|---|---|
| | *Number (in millions)* | *Percent of Labor Force* | | *Percent of Labor Force* |
| 1950 | 3.3 | 5.2 | Total (all civilian workers) | 7.1 |
| 1955 | 2.9 | 4.3 | Men, 20 years and over | 6.0 |
| 1960 | 3.9 | 5.4 | Women, 20 years and over | 6.4 |
| 1965 | 3.4 | 4.4 | Both sexes, 16–19 | 19.6 |
| 1970 | 4.1 | 4.8 | White | 6.1 |
| 1975 | 7.9 | 8.3 | Black | 14.8 |
| 1980 | 7.6 | 7.0 | Hispanic | 10.4 |
| 1985 | 8.3 | 7.1 | Married men, spouse present | 4.2 |
| | | | Married women, spouse present | 5.3 |
| | | | Women who maintain families | 9.4 |

Sources: Adapted from U.S. Department of Labor. *Employment and Earnings.* February 1984. Table A–1; U.S. Department of Labor. *Employment and Earnings.* May 1986. Tables A–1 and A–39.

*This two-part table demonstrates two broad conclusions: first, that in general American unemployment has risen steadily since 1950; and second, that individuals with certain social characteristics are more likely to suffer unemployment. Such categories of people, by the way, are inclined to be in low-paying jobs that do not require extensive education or training.*

During my three years of prospecting, I may have, on more occasions than I imagined, struck gold. I was constantly astonished by the extraordinary dreams of ordinary people. No matter how bewildering the times, no matter how dissembling the official language, those we call ordinary are aware of a sense of personal worth—or more often a lack of it—in the work they do.

*(Terkel, 1974: xxiv)*

Sociological studies have uncovered the following causes of job satisfaction or dissatisfaction:

1. *Monetary compensation.* Satisfied workers believe that they are paid well for their efforts. Besides wages or salary, such fringe benefits as medical care, retirement, and paid vacation time are important considerations.
2. *Control.* People generally are happier in jobs that give them some chance for control, especially over their own schedules. Recent research, in fact, has suggested that for many people this is the factor most strongly affecting job satisfaction.
3. *Location issues.* Workers are more satisfied in a place that is pleasant in a physical sense—not too hot or cold, too dirty, or too noisy, for instance—and that is not dangerous.

4. *Organizational amenities.* Desirable facilities include cafeterias, lounges, and gyms and such features as training programs or promotion-from-within policies.
5. *Prevailing economic, political, and social conditions.* If prosperity exists within a society, then workers' outlook on their jobs will tend to be optimistic.
6. *Psychological satisfaction.* Employees are pleased when they have a chance to learn on the job, when the work relates to their particular abilities and preferences, and when it provides a sense of accomplishment (Boffey, 1985; Morton, 1977; Mottaz, 1981).

The Contemporary Issue on page 357 indicates that black executives face some particularly difficult psychological conditions.

#### WORK ALIENATION

Karl Marx noted that with the technological innovations of capitalism, the nature of work began to change. People's jobs were in factories, where the individual worker ". . . becomes an appendage of the machine, and it is only the most simple, most monotonous and most easily acquired knack that is required of him" (Marx, 1932: 328).

*In our society, the demands made by jobs vary considerably. Some, like construction work, require a strenuous physical effort while others, like selling ice cream, are much less taxing.*

## CONTEMPORARY ISSUE

*Black Executives and Corporate Stress*

All corporate executives experience stress, but for a number of reasons, black executives are likely to experience considerably more stress than their white counterparts.

Less than a century ago, the idea of blacks filling corporate-executive positions was inconceivable. The overwhelming majority of blacks worked in agriculture, forestry, fishing, or domestic service. Few had any hope for significant advancement in the job market. In fact, many want ads contained statements indicating that blacks need not apply.

It was not until the 1960s that the development of the civil-rights movement and also the growing fear of black violence encouraged some concessions to minority citizens, including companies hiring black professionals in more than token numbers. In recent years, however, the gains have been small. By 1982 only 4 percent of all corporate managers were black. Black executives face several types of stresses.

First, they experience the normal stresses of corporate life. Like whites, they must work hard and produce tangible results that lead to increased company profits. If they are unsuccessful, they will not advance, and perhaps they will lose their jobs. This issue alone is a source of considerable stress to many executives, both black and white.

Second, many black executives claim that they face racism on the job. Sometimes the racism is overt—such as a racist joke that a white supervisor will expect his black subordinate to appreciate—and in other instances the process is more subtle. Many black executives claim that their superiors withhold more strategic information from them than they do from their white counterparts. As a result, the blacks claim, they can be much less effective than their white colleagues.

Third, blacks often must confront the problem that

their backgrounds are different from those of whites. Frequently they feel ill-at-ease in a situation where they are unsure about the appropriate norms governing behavior. For instance, newly arrived black executives often do not know how to interact smoothly and comfortably with whites in social situations. Or, they will be unaware how to play company politics and still not compromise their own ethics. Dr. Ronald Brown, a psychologist who has counseled thousands of black and white managers in major corporations, offered this comment: "Back in the late 60's . . . it was obvious that black managers were having difficulty adjusting to the cues and norms of the corporate environment. Some of them are starting from ground zero."

Dr. Brown pointed out that a major contributor to problems of blacks in this area is that as a group they are new-

comers to the corporate world, and therefore they are less likely than whites to find members of their race to serve as mentors to help them learn the ropes. Thus blacks entering corporations suffer a double disadvantage. They are less prepared culturally for the white-dominated corporate world than whites, and once they arrive in that world, they generally receive less help.

For many black executives, the stresses they encounter manifest themselves in physical symptoms: migraine headaches, insomnia, and high blood pressure, in particular. Some alleviate the stress by joining black professional organizations where they can find the camaraderie and understanding lacking in their own white-dominated corporations.

Most successful black executives, however, usually work out their stresses alone. Frequently they pass through a

four-stage process. At entry they are likely to feel euphoria, thinking that fame and fortune are inevitable. The second stage features an adjustment where black employees detect racism and the workings of company politics. In the third phase, many black executives pursue their own programs of personal growth in which they gradually attempt to meet corporate demands. The last stage involves the effective pursuit of organizational goals accompanied by successful coping with stresses.

The black executives who reach this fourth stage are relatively free of stressful symptoms. One researcher of black managers noted, "Basically, what the successful black manager learns is how to manage the racism of others and to creatively funnel his anger into drive . . ."

Source: Bebe Moore Campbell. "Black Executives and Corporate Stress." *New York Times Magazine*. December 19, 1982, pp. 36–39+.

Since Karl Marx's era, many studies have focused on the absence of job satisfaction. An analysis of Marx's writings reveals two prominent sources of work alienation:

1. *Control over the product.* Workers are unhappy because they produce commodities whose sale falls under the direction of the company owner.
2. *Control over the process of one's labors.* As the quotation from Marx indicates, the nature of work itself can be dissatisfying to workers.

Melvin Kohn (1976) interviewed 3101 men in a wide range of civilian occupations, and he learned that these informants were much more concerned about the work process than about control over the product. In assessing the literature on work

alienation, Kohn concluded that three factors were intimately linked with satisfaction on the job: closeness of supervision, routinization, and substantive complexity. With Kohn's conclusions in mind, one might propose the following definition. **Work alienation** is loss of control over the process of one's labor, with the resulting dissatisfaction primarily caused by overly close supervision, highly routine tasks, and an overall simplicity to one's job.

In recent years a number of occupational groups have become increasingly alienated on the job. In particular:

1. During the protest years of the 1960s, blacks and other minorities started to reject dead-beat jobs and demanded more work respectability,

which training and higher education could produce.

2. Some teachers, government employees, social workers, and counselors have been demonstrating a growing discontent with their organizations' extensive bureaucratic regulations and limited job autonomy, conditions that often prevent advancement and the development of more refined job skills. Rapid unionization among these workers seems to have been one indication of their discontent.

3. A steadily increasing number of women have been rejecting the tradition that women's work is in the home, doing housework and caring for children. In 1950 about one in every five married women was in the labor force. Now about one out of every two married women is working.

4. Since the 1970s many factory workers have been openly responding in a negative way to their work. In 1972 at the General Motors plant in Lordstown, Ohio, factory workers went on strike, not for higher wages but in opposition to the alienating conditions of assembly-line work. The heart of the 1973 contract settlement between the Big 3 auto manufacturers and the

United Auto Workers involved a reduction in work demands. Central issues were a restriction on compulsory overtime and the establishment of a full retirement plan for those with thirty years seniority. In recent years difficult economic conditions have reestablished the priority of financial factors, but such a shift, of course, does not eliminate the underlying discontent.

5. The American Management Association has indicated that some managers have expressed dissatisfaction with their work, that they feel "robbed by computers" of decision-making duties. In the last couple of decades, professionals, managers, and executives in their forties and fifties have frequently changed their careers (Gartner and Riessman, 1974).

Thus work alienation cuts across occupational types and class lines. In *Working*, journalist Studs Terkel interviewed more than 130 people about a wide range of different jobs. An awareness of work alienation usually permeated the interviews. Many of the blue-collar workers made statements similar to this one expressed by a steelworker:

"After forty years of workin' at the steel mill, I am just a number. I think I've been a pretty good worker. That job was just right for me. I had a minimum amount of education and a job using a micrometer and just a steel tape and your eyes—that's a job that was just made for me . . . Bob [his son] worked in the mill a few months during a school vacation. He said, 'I don't know how you done it all these years. I could never do it.' I said, 'I been tellin' you all your life never get into that mill.' (Laughs.)"

*(Terkel, 1974: 557–558)*

White-collar employeess also made statements that demonstrated work alienation. For example, an audit-department head at a bank described his job in the following way:

"The job is boring. It's a real repetitious thing . . . It's always the same. Nothing exciting ever happens.

"It's just the constant supervision of people. It's more or less like you have a factory full of robots working the machinery. You're there checking and making sure the machinery is constantly working . . . If they break down, replace them. You're just like a man who sits and watches computers all day. Same thing . . .

"A man should be treated as a human, not as a million-dollar piece of machinery. People aren't

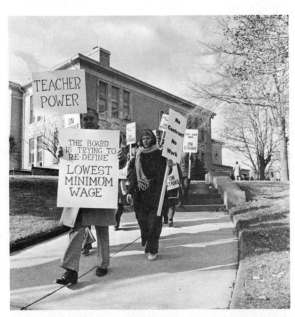

*In recent years an increasingly wide variety of occupational groups, including teachers, have concluded that demands for increased pay and other benefits are more likely to be granted if they militantly assert their demands by picketing or even going on strike.*

treated as good as an IBM machine is. Big corporations turn me off. I didn't know it until I became a supervisor and I realized the games you have to play."

(Terkel, 1974: 400)

What can be said about job satisfaction in the years ahead? One point seems obvious: As the structure of work changes, values will change, including people's sense of what is satisfying or dissatisfying work.

Computers have been becoming increasingly prominent in many jobs, and some observers believe that by the beginning of the twenty-first century, their prevalence in the work world will have a profound effect upon a variety of job holders. It has been suggested that working with computers supports an emphasis on personal freedom and self-expression on the job. One observer noted that the work force in the year 2000 might feature ". . . young workers wearing sunglasses and having their ears plugged in to their own private music. The personal freedom they choose is having

their inner consciousness free to roam" (Deutsch, 1985: 11).

Certainly this image will not represent the entire work force at the beginning of the next century. But if a significant component of Americans has computer-based jobs, several problems might develop. First, one might wonder whether there will be enough creative, computer-related work for all who are interested. If there is not — and certainly that seems to be a strong possibility — then those who have trained for it will be disappointed and easily become alienated if compelled to pursue what they perceive to be lower-quality jobs. Second, because of the autonomous, even solitary nature of many computer-based activities, it will be important and interesting to observe whether the holders of such jobs will be able to work smoothly with others in organizations. In the past people have been trained to function effectively in organizational settings, but perhaps the nature of computer-based work will undermine that capacity.

## Commentary

This chapter has examined both the political and economic institutions. The relationship between the two institutions has been apparent throughout. Both politicians and business people are prominent power brokers, whose decisions and activities can affect many people's lives. There are also numerous interrelationships between the two

institutions. For instance, politicians often find that business people are a major source of financial support. Business people, in turn, can use either legal or illegal means to influence politicians. In particular, the great wealth of modern corporations permits them to exert enormous power.

## STUDY GUIDE

## Summary

1. Power is the ability of an individual or group to implement wishes or policies, with or without the cooperation of others. The political institution is the system of norms and roles that concerns the use and distribution of power within a given society.

The economic institution is the system of norms and roles developed for the production, distribution, and consumption of goods and services.

2. The two leading theories on the concentra-

tion of power are the pluralist and the power-elite perspectives. Pluralism focuses on the dispersion of power in government, and the power-elite thesis claims that power concentrates in the hands of a privileged few. On a given issue, one finds that the two theories will focus on different facts, thus providing divergent insights into the political process.

3. Authority is power that people generally recognize as rightfully maintained by those who use it. Max Weber has designated three systems of

authority — the traditional, the legal-rational, and the charismatic — and elements of each system appear in the American political process.

4. One of the prominent features of the American political process is the two-party system. In U.S. society this system dominates for a number of reasons, including the existence of a broad consensus on political issues, the winner-take-all quality of the American electoral process, and the force of habit and tradition. Another feature of the American political process is the existence of interest groups. While these structures are legal, many of the wealthier interest groups lobby illegally. Traditionally corruption has been widespread in American politics, with political machines supplying a number of significant functions that the participants could not receive elsewhere.

5. In the United States, capitalism is the dominant economic system. It is an economic system where capital is controlled by private citizens who own the means of production and distribution of goods and services. In *The Wealth of Nations*, Adam Smith first described the theoretical workings of a capitalist system. He explained that self-interest would produce a self-regulating economy. In modern capitalist states, however, governments have found some regulation necessary. Socialism is an economic system in which collective ownership of the production and distribution of goods exists. Key elements in a socialist economy include government ownership of productive resources, coordinated, centralized planning, and a redistribution of income.

In the United States, the 500 largest corporations control about half of the Gross National Product in a given year. The major corporations exert political and social power through their wealth, their accumulation of skilled and talented people, the general support for business in the United States, citizens' link to corporate well-being, and the commitment of all public officials to the existing economic and social system. Multinationals, large corporations with production plants and distribution centers in many countries, are a major source of American corporate dominance.

6. Over time societal outlooks on work have been changing. The ancient Greeks and Hebrews shared a negative view of work, and whereas early Christians recognized that it might help insure the health of the body and soul, they too showed little respect for work. By the sixteenth and seventeenth centuries, a positive attitude toward work had developed: The only way to serve God effectively was through good work.

Americans' feelings about work appear to be linked to four cultural values: the good-provider conception, the ability to maintain independence, the emphasis on material success, and the importance of performing a good job. Satisfaction or dissatisfaction in one's occupation is the product of a number of causes. They include monetary compensation, control, location issues, organizational amenities, prevailing economic, political, and social conditions, and psychological satisfaction. Following the lead of Karl Marx, sociologists have studied work alienation — the loss of control over the process of one's labor. In recent years a number of conditions have encouraged work alienation. They include the protest tradition of the 1960s, white-collar workers' increased unhappiness with organizational bureaucracy and limited job autonomy, an increasing tendency for women to reject the traditional woman's role, factory workers' negative response to their work, and managers' dissatisfaction with their jobs.

## Glossary

**authority** power that people generally recognize as rightfully maintained by those who use it.

**capital** money, goods, or other forms of wealth invested to produce more wealth.

**capitalism** an economic system where capital is controlled by private citizens who own the means of production and distribution of goods and services.

**charismatic system of authority** according to Max Weber, an authority system in which leadership develops because of the personal magnetism of an individual, whose followers believe that he or she possesses supernatural qualities.

**corporation** a legally designated organization that has power and responsibilities separate from its workers and owners.

**362**

**democracy** a government in which those in power are acting with the consent of the governed.

**economic institution** the system of norms and roles developed for the production, distribution, and consumption of goods and services.

**interest group** a group whose members seek to influence elected politicians or government bureaucrats to initiate the legislation or policies they want.

**legal-rational system of authority** according to Weber, a system of authority based on laws enacted to produce rational behavior and the achievement of formally designated goals.

**lobbying** a face-to-face effort to persuade legislators and other government personnel to support the proposals of an interest group.

**multinational** a large corporation with production plants and distribution centers in many countries.

**patronage** distribution of favors to political supporters.

**pluralism** a theory that emphasizes that a dispersion of power exists in American government.

**political institution** the system of norms and roles that concerns the use and distribution of power within a given society.

**political machine** an organization established to control a city, county, or state government.

**power** the ability of an individual or group to implement wishes or policies, with or without the cooperation of others.

**power-elite perspective** a theory emphasizing that in American society a group of high-status people—well educated, often wealthy, and placed in high occupational positions—control political power.

**socialism** an economic system with collective ownership of the means of production and distribution of goods and services.

**traditional system of authority** according to Weber, an authority system in which the standard of political leadership passes down from one generation to another.

**work alienation** the loss of control over the process of one's labor, with the resulting dissatisfaction primarily caused by overly close supervision, highly routine tasks, and an overall simplicity to one's job.

---

## Learning Objectives

After studying this chapter, you should be able to:

1. Define power, political institution, and economic institution and indicate the general functions performed by the two institutions.
2. Compare and contrast the pluralist and power-elite theories of power.
3. Define authority and define and describe Weber's three types of authority—the traditional, legal-rational, and charismatic.
4. Discuss the American two-party political system and explain its dominance in the American political process.
5. Examine the influence of interest groups and lobbying in American politics.
6. Define patronage and political machine and examine the functions of American political machines.
7. Define capitalism and socialism and discuss their respective economic ideologies.
8. Analyze the political and social power of large American corporations and the conditions encouraging the development of multinationals.
9. Describe how outlooks on work have changed over time.
10. Identify and discuss the cultural values associated with Americans' feelings about work.
11. List and examine the factors associated with workers' satisfaction or dissatisfaction on the job.
12. Define work alienation and discuss groups that have become increasingly alienated on the job in recent years.
13. Examine the relationship between the political and economic institutions.

# Tests

## True – false test

_____ 1. As long as elections take place in a society, it can be considered a democracy.

_____ 2. A policeman who flags down a motorist is using power and not authority.

_____ 3. Charismatic leaders are likely to appeal to the discontented, deprived members of society.

_____ 4. A two-party system has dominated political activity in all Western nations.

_____ 5. Political machines often satisfy citizens' needs more satisfactorily than legal organizations do.

_____ 6. Adam Smith suggested that as business people pursue self-interest in a capitalist system, they are promoting the common good.

_____ 7. Keynesian economic measures support the maintenance of a laissez-faire economy.

_____ 8. A major source of political and social power in corporations is the accumulation of skilled and talented people these organizations can mobilize.

_____ 9. Work alienation occurs when people lose control over the process of their labor.

_____ 10. According to the text, the political and economic institutions are completely independent of each other.

## Multiple-choice test

_____ 1. Pluralism emphasizes that:
   a. the evil, coercive use of power will be frequent.
   b. elected officials tend not to be accountable to voters.
   c. minorities will be without power.
   d. constant negotiations among power centers will occur.

_____ 2. C. Wright Mills concluded that:
   a. a power elite no longer exists in the United States.
   b. white-collar employees are dominated by the corporations and government agencies for which they work.
   c. pluralism is a more accurate theory in the 1980s than in the 1960s.
   d. a and c

_____ 3. The text indicated that escalation of the Vietnam War can be explained by:
   a. pluralism.
   b. the power-elite theory.
   c. a combination of the pluralist and power-elite theories.
   d. symbolic interaction.

_____ 4. The system of authority that is least likely to persist for several generations is called:
   a. legal-rational.
   b. traditional.
   c. charismatic.
   d. democratic.

_____ 5. Factors encouraging a two-party system in the United States include:
   a. the force of habit and tradition.
   b. the electoral process.

c. a broad consensus on political issues.
d. a, b, and c

_____ 6. Lobbying is primarily done by:
   a. charismatic leaders.
   b. elected officials.
   c. interest groups.
   d. alienated workers.

_____ 7. Adam Smith's theory of economics emphasizes the importance of:
   a. group interest rather than self-interest.
   b. government intervention to prevent depressions.
   c. socialism.
   d. self-interest.

_____ 8. Which of the following statements is true of capitalism?
   a. It has created industrial expansion.
   b. It has encouraged the equalization of wealth in industrial societies.
   c. It is an ideology that opposes the development of multinationals.
   d. It is very compatible with socialism.

_____ 9. A source of corporate political and social power is:
   a. job enrichment.
   b. wealth.
   c. socialist philosophy.
   d. union labor.

_____ 10. Which of the following is a current indicator of work alienation?
   a. declining unionization among teachers, government employees, social workers, and coun-
      selors
   b. an increased proportion of women leaving the workplace to return to homemaking as a
      career
   c. blacks' rejection of executive training programs
   d. professionals, managers, and executives in their forties and fifties changing jobs

## Essay test

1. Define power, political institution, and democracy and give examples of each.
2. Summarize the pluralist and power-elite theories and apply them to the American political process.
3. Define Weber's three systems of authority. Describe an episode or event in American history illustrating each type.
4. Would American democracy be significantly different without a two-party system or would it be
   essentially the same? Consider the alternatives of a single party and a multiparty system.
5. What are interest groups? Evaluate their functions and dysfunctions in the American political process.
6. Why does corruption exist in the American political system? Discuss functions performed by political
   machines.
7. Define the economic institution. What are the similarities and differences between the capitalist and
   socialist economic systems?
8. How do major American corporations exert power and influence? Discuss various functions and
   dysfunctions of corporate activities.
9. What is a multinational? What conditions have encouraged their development?
10. Discuss the changing conceptions of work societies have maintained through different historical
    periods.

11. What are five prominent factors that determine people's satisfactions and dissatisfactions toward their jobs? Indicate five occupational groups that have become more alienated from their work in recent years. Why have they become more alienated?

## Suggested Readings

Breslin, Jimmy. 1976. *How the Good Guys Finally Won.* New York: Ballantine Books. A beautifully written, entertaining, sometimes humorous, always informative account of the congressional impeachment proceedings against Richard Nixon. In the course of the book, the reader learns a great deal about the workings of Washington politics.

Dahl, Robert. 1982. *Dilemmas of Pluralist Democracy.* New Haven: Yale University Press. A recent statement of pluralism written by the most influential proponent of the theory.

de Tocqueville, Alexis. 1966. *Democracy in America.* New York: Harper & Row. Translated by George Lawrence. Originally published in 1835. A young Frenchman's incisive study of American politics a century-and-a-half ago offers provocative, even startling insights into the modern political process.

Domhoff, G. William. 1983. *Who Rules America Now? A View for the Eighties.* Englewood Cliffs, NJ: Prentice-Hall. An updated version of Domhoff's analysis of modern American politics, providing a wealth of documented support for the power-elite theory.

Froman, Creel. 1984. *The Two American Political Systems: Society, Economics, and Politics.* Englewood Cliffs, NJ: Prentice-Hall. An analysis emphasizing the discrepancy between prevailing political ideology in the United States and the actual workings of the corporate political system.

Harvey, David. 1982. *The Limits to "Capital".* Chicago: University of Chicago Press. An effective, updated critique of Karl Marx's historically significant analysis of capitalism.

Kohn, Melvin L., and Carmi Schooler. 1983. *Work and Personality: An Inquiry into the Impact of Social Stratification.* Norwood, NJ: Ablex Publishing Corporation. A study that develops and tests an interesting theory about the interrelationship between social-class position, occupational placement and activity, and personality development.

Lerner, Max (ed.). 1948. *The Portable Veblen.* New York: Viking. The sharpest and most powerful writings of a well-known critic of American capitalism. Veblen lived and wrote at the end of the nineteenth and the early twentieth century, the era when the great corporate monopolies were establishing themselves.

Lipset, Seymour Martin. 1981. *Political Man: The Social Bases of Politics.* Baltimore: John Hopkins University Press. Revised edition. An updated version of a widely read book on political behavior originally published in 1960. Most notably the author analyzes major studies in a variety of countries to determine why certain class and occupational groups take their respective positions and actions.

*PS.* 1982. "The Equal Rights Amendment: Anatomy of a Failure." Vol. 15 (Fall), pp. 572–591. Four articles by political scientists carefully analyzing the reasons the ERA failed to obtain passage and how such a failure might be avoided in the future.

Schott, Kerry. 1984. *Power, Policy, and Order: The Persistence of Economic Problems in Capitalist States.* New Haven: Yale University Press. A thought-provoking effort to explain the performances of modern capitalist economies, integrating the ideas and data of a large body of modern literature on the political economy.

Terkel, Studs. 1974. *Working.* New York: Pantheon. A set of over 130 interviews showing how Americans in a wide range of occupations feel about their work. Terkel, a sensitive, perceptive writer, presents these detailed, insightful interviews as monologues—a form that increases the emotional power of people's commentary about their jobs.

Warren, Robert Penn. 1946. *All the King's Men.* New York: Harcourt, Brace and World. A fictionalized version of Huey Long's life, describing Governor Willie Stark's drive for power and privilege during the depression years.

Wilensky, Harold. 1966. "Work as a Social Problem," pp. 117–166 in Howard S. Becker (ed.), *Social Problems: A Modern Approach.* New York: Wiley. A sociologist's particularly effective analysis of work.

The essay includes a historical examination of work as well as a detailed, penetrating study of work alienation.

Zurcher, Louis A., Jr. (ed.). 1981. "Citizen Participation in Public Policy." *Journal of Applied Behavioral Science* 17 (Fall). Ten articles examining the role that citizens can play in affecting public policy on a variety of issues.

## Student Projects

1. Talk to at least six Americans who are old enough to have voted in two presidential elections. (If you can find three Democrats and three Republicans, that will be useful for sensitizing you to some party differences in perception.) Ask them the following questions:
   a. What were the main issues in the presidential election of _____ ? (Fill in year of most recent election.)
   b. What were the differences in Democratic and Republican presidential candidates' views on each of these issues?
   c. Who were the vice-presidential candidates for each party? What did they say about the issues?
   d. What factor(s) made you choose a particular candidate?
   e. How did the issues in the more recent presidential campaign differ from the campaign four years earlier?

On the basis of your findings, you can conclude that our two-party system does or does not encourage politicians' taking significantly different positions on issues? As you think about what your interviewees said, would you be optimistic or pessimistic about using the political process to produce changes you might advocate? Does the information you gathered stimulate any ideas about changing the American political process?

2. Without consulting the text, daydream for a few minutes about the occupation you are considering. Then make two lists—the positive and negative features you feel are associated with this occupation. Now consult the text material examining sources of job satisfaction/dissatisfaction. Are these factors consistent with your perception of what is satisfying or dissatisfying about the job you are considering? How does your occupational choice rate using these criteria?

## Answers to Test Questions

**True–false test**

| | | | | |
|---|---|---|---|---|
| 1. f | 3. t | 5. t | 7. f | 9. t |
| 2. f | 4. f | 6. t | 8. t | 10. f |

**Multiple-choice test**

| | | | | |
|---|---|---|---|---|
| 1. d | 3. c | 5. d | 7. d | 9. b |
| 2. b | 4. c | 6. c | 8. a | 10. d |

# The Case of Charisma: Research on an Elusive Concept

What is charisma? What is charismatic leadership? These words conjure up romantic notions, images of heroic, magnetic individuals arriving at crucial moments to lead their followers to victory or security. The charismatic individual makes the difference; it is the stuff of successful novels or films.

But even though awareness of charisma is widespread, there is not a vast body of research on the subject. Why not? For one thing charisma is a condition that is unusual, even rare in the real world. As we see in this research section, the rarity of true Weberian charisma has meant that individuals conducting studies of the concept have been compelled to follow one of two strategies: Either they revised Weber's definition or carefully chose research sites where something approximating Weber's definition could be claimed to exist. In the first instance, the definition had to be broadened to include modern leaders who did not actually meet the requirements of Weber's definition. In the second situation, investigators chose contexts that were either preindustrial or small, thus avoiding conventional modern political situations where Weber's conception of charismatic leadership could not legitimately be claimed to exist. After discussions about broadening the definition of charisma and researching charisma in contexts where Weber's definition was preserved, we will briefly consider the future of research on the concept.

The material in this section is about the definition of a research concept and related matters. To some observers this might seem at first to be an insignificant matter. It is not! As we saw in Chapter 2 ("Doing Research in Sociology"), good research builds on a series of separate stages. How could one effectively study charismatic leadership without having a clear sense of what charisma is? Actually it makes no more sense than sending a person out to buy bread or coffee when the person does not know what bread or coffee is.

## Broadening Weber's Definition of Charismatic Leadership

Politicians, sport celebrities, actors and actresses, and many others appear to possess charisma. Is charisma actually widespread in our society? No, not according to Max Weber's definition. Sociologists Joseph Bensman and Michael Givant have indicated that when Weber wrote of charisma, he was emphasizing three conditions: a personal relationship between leaders and followers, a radical or revolutionary situation, and irrationality (seeking followers not by an appeal to reason but by the magnetism of his or her personality).

Bensman and Givant have contended that most if not all modern uses of the term involve situations where these conditions are absent. In politics the very size and impersonality of modern mass societies have prevented the personal appeals of Weber's kind of charismatic leaders; furthermore politicians' communications are highly rational, often carefully planned by media experts to produce the most potent impact upon the public. Bensman and Givant have concluded that instead of using the term charisma, it makes more sense to speak of "pseudocharisma"—the use of the appearance and imagery of charismatic leadership as a rational device to obtain or maintain power.

Arthur Schweitzer's *The Age of Charisma* is an example of a study of charisma that, in reality, examines pseudocharisma. Unlike Weber, Schweitzer claimed that charismatic leaders are not truly radical or revolutionary but are adaptable, seeking to ally themselves with established political parties, ideologies, armies, and even state bureaucracies. The author examined fifty-five examples of twentieth-century charismatic leaders, including Churchill, DeGaulle, Hitler, John Kennedy, and Martin Luther King. Weber would not have considered any of these leaders charismatic, but then, as Bensman and Givant emphasized, Weber's definition of charismatic leadership is virtually nonapplicable to industrial societies.

## Preserving Weber's Definition of Charisma

Since charisma as Weber defined it is so difficult to find in industrial societies, those interested in using the concept for research can either broaden the definition as Schweitzer did, or they can keep Weber's definition and search out charisma in contexts where it conceivably can be found.

Richard Emerson, a sociologist, chose this second course of action, studying charismatic leadership in a preindustrial state. Emerson examined the formation of the state of Baltistan, a republic of Tibetan-speaking Islamic people in South Asia. His research included an analysis of the contribution of charismatic leadership, and his evidence came from somewhat unusual secondary sources. In Chapter 2 we learned that secondary sources are data banks produced by other individuals and organizations. Emerson's secondary sources were considerably more artistic than most—dances, songs, and other types of folklore. For instance, Emerson analyzed a long epic poem about King Kesar of the kingdom of Ling that has been passed on orally for over four centuries. King Kesar

. . . is a mythical charismatic warrior-king whose exploits and magical fighting powers are recounted in the saga at great length. But despite the supernatural powers of this warrior–ruler–deity, the vulnerability of his kingdom (Ling) is a major theme in the saga, symbolized by the frequent abduction of his wife, the queen Lomo Brugmo.

*(Emerson, 1983: 429)*

Emerson concluded that this and other examples from Baltistan folklore reveal an important point about charismatic leadership and vulnerability. He suggested that unless people consider themselves vulnerable, they will not follow a charismatic leader. For instance, no matter how appealing and magnetic the personality, the leader of a powerful army facing modest opposition will not inspire the fervent loyalty charismatic leaders normally receive; in this situation people do not feel vulnerable and thus the loyalty gladly given to a protecting leader is not inspired.

Emerson, in short, was suggesting that fol-lowers' perception of their own vulnerability will significantly affect whether or not they will perceive an individual as their charismatic savior. Is Emerson correct? Perhaps his conclusion is best viewed as a hypothesis that needs further testing.

Emerson's insights about charismatic leadership were based on information contained in ancient folklore. In contrast, Phyllis Day, a social researcher at Purdue University, obtained insights about charisma from investigating a contemporary home for troubled girls. An unusual feature of Day's project was the fact that it was a study of charisma at an organizational level. Like Emerson, Day was not studying charisma in a modern, political context. Therefore, again like Emerson, she could approximate the characteristics of charismatic leadership emphasized by Weber. Remember what those characteristics are: a personal relationship between leaders and followers, a radical or revolutionary situation, and an appeal based on the magnetism of the leaders' personality.

Roseland, the organization Day studied, possessed a leader with these three qualities. This woman, who was the director of an agency containing twenty-two residents and a staff of nine, had a powerful personal relationship with her followers and a magnetic impact on them. A staff member's statement suggests the existence of both conditions:

She's always with us, and she always has time for the kids, too, even if it's only five minutes. Her door is never closed. She tunes in with the kids. She's involved in everything and involves us—I'm learning as much here as in any grad school.

*(Day, 1980: 56)*

In addition, the leader's goal was widely considered controversial, even radical—namely the decision to shift the emphasis in the program from caring for pregnant girls to helping girls who were poor, emotionally disturbed, and frequently delinquent. After this shift in goal, Roseland was no longer a "nice" middle-class agency, and its support by the United Way and other established organizations was endangered.

## Commentary on Future Research of Charismatic Leadership

We have learned that researchers who have studied charismatic leadership have been compelled to follow one of two options. Either they have needed to broaden Weber's definition of charisma to acknowledge certain political conditions in industrial societies, or they have had to seek either preindustrial or organizational contexts that approximated the conditions described in Weber's definition of the context.

But what about the future? Let us consider two possibilities. One option is to suspend all research on charismatic leadership, recognizing, as Bensman and Givant wrote, that industrial society eliminates the conditions that promote charisma as defined by Weber. Another, seemingly more interesting approach would be to pursue studies seeking to determine whether or not industrial and postindustrial societies can produce leadership that, though not always charismatic in the literal Weberian sense, contains interesting, provocative elements found in his description of charisma.

I would argue that one of the interesting ideas in Weber's discussion of charisma is its suggestion that followers are willing to follow such leaders without question. The director at Roseland possessed such an appeal, and I did a year-long study of a federally funded agency in which the director possessed a similar control over staff members. It is an impressive, yet frightening, phenomenon to behold. In a recent paper on charisma, a psychiatrist indicated that in our society some charismatic, or perhaps we should say pseudocharismatic, people can be dangerous: "They offer *the* Answer, and promise purpose, meaning, and freedom from choice. It is the kind of intense charisma that especially needs to be explored" (Newman, 1983: 204).

What are your ideas about interesting directions for future research on charisma?

SOURCES: Joseph Bensman and Michael Givant. "Charisma and Modernity: The Use and Abuse of a Concept." *Social Research*. Vol. 42. Autumn 1975, pp. 570–614; Phyllis J. Day. "Charismatic Leadership in the Small Organization." *Human Organization*. Vol. 39. Spring 1980, pp. 50–58; Christopher Bates Doob. *How the War Was Lost*. Unpublished manuscript. 1970; Richard M. Emerson. "Charismatic Kingship: A Study of State-Formation and Authority in Baltistan." *Politics and Society*. Vol. 12. 1983, pp. 413–444; Hans Gerth and C. Wright Mills (eds.). *From Max Weber*. New York: Oxford University Press. 1946; Ruth G. Newman. "Thoughts on Superstars of Charisma: Pipers in Our Midst." *American Journal of Orthopsychiatry*. Vol. 53. April 1983, pp. 201–208; Arthur Schweitzer. *The Age of Charisma*. Chicago: Nelson-Hall. 1984.

# 15
# SCIENCE, MEDICINE, AND HEALTH CARE

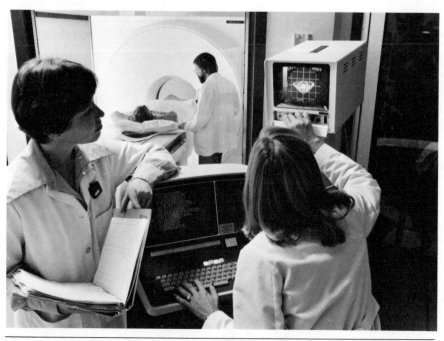

In January 1986 the U.S. space program had its greatest tragedy. As many millions of Americans watched on television, the space shuttle *Challenger* exploded soon after taking off. All of those aboard were killed.

Shortly after the disaster, a national poll was taken to reveal adults' and children's reactions. Americans of all ages were upset about the accident, but they also remained enthusiastic about the shuttle program. Eighty percent of adults and 84 percent of children said that the program should continue. Among the adults 68 percent said that an accident was bound to happen sooner or later.

Those interviewed were asked whether they would like to travel in space themselves. Forty-four percent of adults said that they would. Younger adults were more inclined to want to go than older people; 56 percent of those aged eighteen to twenty-nine indicated they would like to enter space. Children were even more enthusiastic about the prospect. For children aged nine to seventeen, 65 percent wanted to fly in space, and among twelve- to fourteen-year-olds, the figure was 77 percent (Clymer, 1986).

The results of this survey seem typical of Americans' reactions to scientific endeavors. It is widely realized that some are dangerous—that there will be accidents, even deaths—but that chances must be taken if progress is to be made. The same outlook generally prevails in the area of medicine, where scientific procedures are used. Americans generally appreciate that medical advances are made at a price—that if progress is going to be made, then lives must be risked, even sometimes lost. Transplant operations and various new techniques for treating different forms of cancer are cases where such a perspective is maintained. Thus as we will see in the pages ahead, Americans usually take a supportive, optimistic outlook on science and medicine. Let us define the major topics examined in this chapter.

**Science** is a systematic effort to develop general principles about a particular subject matter based on actual observations and stated in a form that can be tested by any competent person. The body of knowledge that comprises a science represents the consensus of a scientific community, not simply the results of individual experience. In modern times scientific investigation has become the most widely accepted activity for accumulating knowledge, and it has often taken over the role that religious specialists, astrologers, and philosophers had in preindustrial societies. We will discuss the development of science and also scientists and scientific work.

**Medicine** is the scientifically based practice concerned with the prevention and treatment of disease and the treatment of injury. Doctors and other medical personnel ideally use the most recent scientifically tested knowledge to treat illness and injury. The second half of this chapter is concerned with **medical sociology**—the study of the social settings in which health, sickness, and health care occur. This field, which has existed since the middle of the twentieth century, examines all subject matter involving health and health care but emphasizes disease and the medical professions. We discuss disease and death in the United States. After that we look briefly at American health care and the medical professions, and the chapter closes with an analysis of patient–doctor relations.

In both institutional areas, we will see that over time knowledge has increased and technical skill has improved. We will also learn that in spite of such advancements, problems and controversy often develop in both areas.

# The Development of Science

During most of human history, science and the scientist have had a negligible function in people's lives. Their potential to be important was always there, as science can be a major source of technological advances. For a number of reasons, however, science made modest contributions to societies until modern times. The reasons include:

*Limited range of practical tasks for science.* In the realm of astronomy, for instance, ancient societies made certain practical advances through crude scientific investigation—in particular, the formation of a calendar, the establishment of dates for seasonal festivals, and the prediction of eclipses. But after the early societies in Babylon, Egypt, Greece, India, and Mexico had mastered the technology necessary to complete these tasks, they visualized no practical reasons for further innovation. This was because innovation was motivated entirely by practical considerations and not by the modern scientific tradition emphasizing continuing research and development.

*Little incentive to incorporate scientific analysis in most areas where technological development was occurring.* In some preindustrial societies, technological advance was an ongoing process, but progress was possible without contributions from science. Architecture and construction engineering are good cases in point. Ancient architects and engineers learned from working directly with their materials. They transmitted little knowledge in writing, and any drawings they used were simple and free of abstraction. Early buildings, bridges, and other structures were much more precise than they would have been if their developers had relied on contemporary scientific formulations.

*Opposition to scientific inquiry.* In some cases the use of science opposed a traditional system of belief. For example, if an ancient priest or priestess used religious ritual to determine when to hold a seasonal festival, he or she probably would have opposed the adoption of a scientifically derived calendar that would have eliminated a ritual that he or she both enjoyed performing and believed represented a significant religious activity.

In one ancient society—Greece—science did play a significant part. For about 200 years (from the fourth to the second century B.C.), a flowering of pure science occurred in mathematics and physics, which both maintained a formal linkage with philosophy. However, the significance of these scientific disciplines declined when science and philosophy separated. With the separation many people turned to philosophy for answers to moral–religious and political problems. Science, widely considered little more than excess baggage, became the endeavor of a few learned men living an isolated existence in Alexandria. The most practical sciences—medicine and astronomy—continued to flourish until the second century A.D.

It was not until the seventeenth century in England that science received widespread acceptance. Two factors seem to have contributed to that development. In the first place, science gradually obtained a central part in the emerging conception of progress. Scientists and business people began to establish close relationships, with the production of better navigation techniques and instruments a particular concern. In England the mathematicians Robert Recorde and John Dee served as consultants to large trading companies. Henry Biggs, the first professor of mathematics at Gresham College in London, belonged to the London (later the Virginia) Company, which was the first commercial group to sail to the New World. Besides their common involvement in navigation, English scientists and business people showed mutual interest in machines, mining, lens grinding, and the construction of watches and other instruments.

A second factor that supported the rise of science to prominence in the seventeenth century was the contribution of Protestantism, which was much more inclined to permit individual believers to develop their own interpretations of the Bible than either Catholicism or Judaism. It was possible for Protestants to believe in good conscience that God's will and scientific progress were in harmony. Not all Protestants, to be sure, supported the development of science. In some small, self-contained Protestant communities in Switzerland, Scotland, and Germany, the citizens regarded science with less tolerance than the people of Catholic countries. But in England such religious

*The spectacular advances of modern science could not have occurred without the contributions made by scientists in the past.*

control was not imposed, and the rise of science received early acceptance. It was similarly supported in America, where the Puritan settlers emphasized a regularized, patterned quality to all activity and readily accepted the conclusion that scientific investigation could provide human beings with extensive knowledge about the universe.

## The Rise of Science in the United States

At the beginning of the twentieth century, the leaders of American industry began to recognize the potential contributions that a full-time professional scientific staff could make to the manufacture of new and more effective products. These industrial leaders encouraged the development of graduate programs where students could receive a

**Figure 15.1**
**Twentieth-Century Nobel Prize Laureates in the Sciences:[1] Selected Countries**

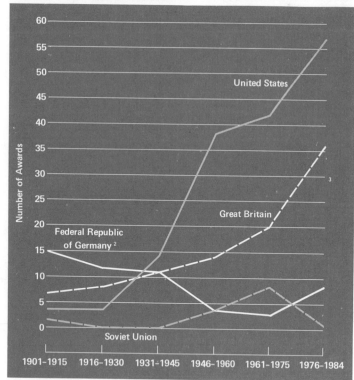

[1] Chemistry, physics, and physiology/medicine.
[2] Includes East Germany before 1946.
[3] The last span of time covers nine years compared to fifteen for all earlier spans. The number of American Nobel Laureates in science is actually proportionately higher in the nine-year period than in the previous fifteen-year span.

*Winning a Nobel prize in science is an individual achievement, but as this figure suggests, some countries provide better contexts for encouraging this kind of scientific achievement than others do. In the United States, the professionalization of science, which has received the combined support of industry, higher education, and government, has helped produce a record of unparalleled success in this area of scientific achievement. (Source: Adapted from U.S. Bureau of the Census.* Statistical Abstract of the United States: 1986. *No. 1003.)*

Ph.D. in a variety of scientific fields. Within the U.S. system of professional education, degree recipients were expected to keep abreast of scientific advances, to initiate research, and to contribute generally to the advancement of science. One of the outgrowths of this research emphasis has been the extensive development of professional–scientific associations, which often sponsor journals as well as regional and national conventions. In addition, the belief in the significance of the professional researcher has meant a stronger support for increasingly complex and sophisticated types of organized research than in Europe, where research has traditionally been less professional.

At present, large research units exist at universities and also in governmental and industrial settings. After World War II, a major impetus to government-sponsored research has been the interest of the federal government in nuclear weapons and atomic energy. Scientists have become advocates and consumers of federal expenditure for research and also advisers and decision-makers in important areas of public policy. Statistics indicate a steadily increasing federal governmental support for research. The federal expenditure for research and development activities rose (in current dollars) from $5.2 billion in 1953, to $26.1 billion in 1970, and to about $106.6 billion in 1985. Within universities, government, and private industry, more than one-half-million scientists and engineers are engaged in full-time research. Almost 100,000 scientific journals currently exist, and they publish more than 2 million scientific papers each year (Ben-David, 1971; Merton, 1973: 228–254; U.S. Bureau of the Census, *Statistical Abstract of the United States: 1984.* No. 1016; U.S. Bureau of the Census, *Statistical Abstract of the United States: 1986.* No. 994; Williams, 1970: 570–575; Wyngaarden, 1984). Figure 15.1 illustrates one result of the strong American scientific emphasis.

## Scientists and Scientific Work

Ninety-three percent of Americans favor scientific endeavors. In one national survey, 74 percent felt that it is very important—and 19 percent that it is fairly important—that the United States be a leader in scientific growth and development (Roper Organization, *Roper Reports,* May 1979).

The public support for scientific endeavors is undoubtedly one factor that has permitted scientists the freedom to conduct research without much concern for citizens' needs and interests. In this section the topics are the practice of scientific norms and two controversial areas of research.

Table 15.1 presents some significant characteristics of American scientists and engineers.

**Table 15.1**
**Characteristics of American Scientists and Engineers: 1983**

| | PERCENT |
|---|---|
| *Sex* | |
| Male | 87.3 |
| Female | 12.7 |
| *Highest Degree* | |
| Doctorate | 10.5 |
| Master's | 26.3 |
| Bachelor's | 52.7 |
| Other | 10.5 |
| *Type of Employer* | |
| Business/industry | 67.2 |
| Educational institutions | 12.0 |
| Nonprofit organizations | 3.4 |
| Federal government | 8.8 |
| Military | .5 |
| Another level of goverment | 5.4 |
| Other | 2.6 |
| *Scientific Specialty* | |
| Engineering | 55.9 |
| Life science | 10.7 |
| Computer science | 9.7 |
| Social science | 7.4 |
| Physical science | 6.9 |
| Psychology | 4.2 |
| Mathematics | 2.8 |
| Environmental science | 2.5 |

Source: Adapted from U.S. Bureau of the Census. *Statistical Abstract of the United States: 1986.* No. 1007 and No. 1008.

## The Practice of Scientific Norms

Are scientists morally superior beings who lead exemplary professional lives? Some evidence disputes such a claim, indicating that scientists have their fair share of such uninspiring traits as driving personal ambition (Lee, 1985) and indifference to scientific advancement in their fields (Moravcsik, 1985). Robert Merton (1973: 268–278), in contrast, described four scientific norms that he suggested promote a high moral standard of scientific behavior:

1. *Universalism.* **Universalism** is a norm stating that all scientific claims of truth need to be evaluated by impersonal criteria consistent with existing knowledge in that field. Scientists will disregard such considerations as class, race, and national membership when they assess colleagues' work.

2. *Communism.* As a basic scientific norm, **communism** signifies that the substantive findings of science represent a common heritage, not the exclusive property of individual discoverers and their heirs. Thus Newton's famous remark —"If I have seen farther it is by standing on the shoulders of giants"—both expresses indebtedness to the common heritage and acknowledges the expectation that all scientists will contribute to that heritage.

3. *Organized skepticism.* In scientific pursuits **organized skepticism** is the conclusion that no scientist's contribution to knowledge is acceptable without careful scrutiny. Sometimes this norm brings scientists into conflict with the members of other institutions—clergymen and politicians, for instance. A prominent controversy is the question of how humanity originated. Scientists' support for organized skepticism has made it impossible for them to accept the biblical story of creation when archaeological evidence suggests the occurrence of an evolutionary process.

4. *Disinterestedness.* The fourth norm of **disinterestedness** is a requirement that scientists avoid the pursuit of work that is self-serving and self-interested. It is possible that science draws people with higher ideals than other occupations, but no evidence supports this position. More likely the emphasis on disinterestedness is the result of the public nature of scientists' work, which tends to encounter more rigorous policing than the work in many other professions.

A study of forty-two scientists associated with the Apollo lunar missions offered some evidence opposing Merton's four scientific norms. One scientist spoke against the claim of organized skepticism, saying, "It takes commitment to be a scientist. One thing that spurs a scientist on is competition, warding off attacks against what you've published" (Mitroff, 1974: 588).

All the scientists rejected the idea of the objective, emotionally disinterested scientist as naive. One scientist noted, "The [emotionally] disinterested scientist is a myth. Even if there were such a being, he probably wouldn't be worth much as a scientist. I still think you can be objective in spite of

**Table 15.2**
**Scientific Norms and Counter-Norms**

| MERTON'S SCIENTIFIC NORMS | COUNTER-NORMS |
| --- | --- |
| Universalism: that scientists use impersonal criteria to evaluate all claims to truth | Particularism: that scientists accept or reject claims primarily on the basis of colleagues' personal characteristics |
| Communism: that the substantive findings of science represent a common heritage | Solitariness or "miserism": that scientists consider the disposition of their discoveries within the realm of property rights |
| Organized skepticism: that no scientists' contribution to knowledge is acceptable without careful scrutiny | Organized dogmatism: that scientists must have complete conviction about their own findings while doubting others' findings with all their worth |
| Disinterestedness: that scientists avoid the pursuit of work that is self-serving and self-interested | Interestedness: that scientists achieve self-satisfaction in work by serving special-interest communities such as their own research units |

Adapted from Ian I. Mitroff. "Norms and Counter-Norms in a Select Group of the Apollo Moon Scientists: A Case Study of the Ambivalence of Scientists." *American Sociological Review.* Vol. 39. August 1974, pp. 579–595.

having strong interests and biases" (Mitroff, 1974: 588).

A basic conclusion emerging from this research was that scientists were more likely to use the norms designated by Merton in situations where the problems were well defined and clearly structured. On the other hand, the less clear and less settled a problem, the more frequently the scientists were inclined to develop intensely personal hypotheses and interpretations. Under these circumstances they often rejected the norms described by Merton for a set of "counter-norms," which the previous quotations illustrate. (See Table 15.2.)

## In the Throes of Controversy: DNA and Nuclear-Weapons Research

Two richly funded areas of contemporary scientific research are the studies of DNA and of nuclear weapons. A discussion of these topics raises interesting and troubling questions about the conduct of scientific research. We turn now to a summary of the positions for and against each type of research and then consider the social conditions that permit these activities to continue unabated when they are so controversial.

### DNA RESEARCH

The basis for these investigations is the relatively recent discovery that the combination of genetic material from one organism with genetic material from another can produce a new organism with entirely new properties.

Some supporters of this new technology claim that it will revolutionize health care by introducing new means of curing various diseases created by genetic deficiencies. Other advocates contend that DNA studies will help solve world food problems by producing huge crops of corn and wheat capable of supplying their own nitrogen fertilizer or that new organisms can be invented to perform critical tasks like cleaning up oil spills, producing valuable hormones such as insulin, or possibly even curing cancer.

On the other hand, the opponents of DNA research point out that this modern technology contains unknown, perhaps devastating potential for human destruction and that the possible costs considerably outweigh the possible gains. One of the critics' greatest fears is that the *E. coli* bacteria used in most DNA experiments might accidentally escape a laboratory and produce disastrous results. For instance, a lab technician might breathe or swallow a few particles containing *E. coli*. These organisms might then combine with the *E. coli* that exists in the intestines of all human beings, and the result could be a particularly virulent virus that might eventually endanger or even destroy all humanity.

### NUCLEAR-WEAPONS RESEARCH

Two laboratories at the University of California are entirely responsible for the conception, design, and testing of every nuclear warhead the United States has ever developed—from the first bomb dropped on Hiroshima to the most recent nuclear weaponry. The University of California has operated the labs from their beginning—Los Alamos since 1943 and Livermore since 1952. The Department of Energy has provided about $3.8 million yearly to fund Los Alamos and Livermore.

The proponents of nuclear-weapons research contend that the only way to survive in the modern world is to maintain a superior military presence and that nuclear weaponry represents the most crucial component of that strength. Without a massive stockpile of nuclear weapons, the proponents state, the United States will be vulnerable to attack from the Soviet Union and perhaps lesser powers too. Nuclear weaponry, in short, represents a deterrent to World War III.

The opponents of nuclear-weapons research claim that the idea of nuclear-weapons superiority is a fantasy—that both sides would be destroyed in a nuclear war and that there would be only losers. Nuclear-weapons research, the opponents contend, should cease. Instead of enlarging their nuclear arsenals, the United States and the Soviet Union should curtail nuclear weaponry.

Both the scientific community and the American public are divided on these two research issues.

### The Conduct of Controversial Research

The following conditions help to sustain the research on DNA and nuclear weaponry in spite of their controversial nature:

1. *Scientists' strong support for the research goals.* Scientists need to believe sufficiently strongly in what they are doing so that they can block out, or at least significantly subordinate, the issues raised by opponents.

    It seems likely that most if not all scientists involved in controversial studies must personally support the value positions underlying their research. For nuclear-weapons research, a commitment to the proponents' position on nuclear weaponry seems necessary. A team of writers noted:

    Only by increasing the quantity and sophistication of our weapons, the proponents argue—improving their range, accuracy and maneuverability as

"*Something's gone terribly wrong. We cloned some duplicate Einsteins, and all they want to do is tap dance.*"

© *Sidney Harris*

well as total number of warheads—can we be sure they will not be used in warfare. Indeed, if this proposition is not true, in the context of today, there can be no point to weapons research: if it increases the chance of war, it is impossible to justify. As one Livermore Lab employee has stated, "In order to work here, you have to believe in nuclear deterrence."

(*University of California Nuclear Weapons Labs Conversion Project, 1980: 96*)

2. *Enthusiastic governmental sponsorship.* In order to conduct controversial research effectively, scientists need federal funding, government assistance in establishing favorable regulations, or both. In the case of DNA research, a number of the committee members who created the federal guidelines have had ties to the precise companies they have supposedly regulated. This situation has represented a blatant conflict of interest (Rifkin, 1980). In nuclear-weaponry research, the situation has been similar. For the Strategic Arms Limitation Talks (SALT) with the Soviet Union, a number of directors and former directors of both the Livermore and Los Alamos laboratories have served as technical experts and participants. It is difficult to believe that people committed to the development of increasingly potent nuclear weaponry would seriously commit themselves to nuclear-

arms limitation. Once again, a conflict of interest seems apparent.

3. *Policy of secrecy.* People conducting controversial research often conclude that an effective way to avoid controversy is to keep their research hidden, thereby preventing the public from learning about the dangers that might be developing. Several years ago an interviewer asked the Attorney General of New Jersey, who was in charge of investigating DNA research in his state, whether he knew of any firms planning to do P–4 (maximum-risk) DNA studies in New Jersey. The Attorney General replied that he did not. The interviewer then explained that the Hoffman-LaRoche Company was constructing a P–4 facility in Nutley, New Jersey (Rifkin, 1980: 151).

Secrecy also prevails in the nuclear-research area, as Senator Stuart Symington learned during an inspection trip. Symington, who was a member of the Joint Committee on Atomic Energy and a former Secretary of the Air Force, was relatively well informed on nuclear matters. Yet he explained:

> Not until I became a member of the Joint Committee and travelled to Europe with Sen. Pastore . . . in 1971, did I realize the military strength of the U.S. and become acquainted with the vast lethal power of our nuclear arsenal. I actually learned more about the true strength of the U.S. forces in Europe in those six days than I had in some 18 years on the Armed Services Committee. One cannot help but consider the implication to our defense and foreign policies if these facts were known by the appropriate committees of Congress, as well as . . . by the American people.

> *(University of California Nuclear Weapons Labs Conversion Project, 1980: 101–102)*

4. *An in-group for scientists.* Both kinds of controversial research are possible because of the primacy of the research goal, governmental support, and a context of secrecy. But another factor also seems to contribute. In the course of their work, individuals often need support and encouragement from others to perform effectively. Recall a concept from Chapter 4 ("Groups"): in-group. An "in-group" is any group whose membership maintains a strong sense of identification and loyalty and a feeling of exclusiveness toward nonmembers.

In both DNA and nuclear-weapons research, scientists and technicians encourage each other's efforts, emphasizing the tremendous importance of what they are doing and dismissing outsiders' criticisms of their work as the ignorant chatter of the lay public.

Thus controversial scientific research, like all social activity, is fostered by certain social conditions. Our analysis of four conditions related to two types of controversial research reveals that these activities are strongly supported by a number of groups and practices.

Controversy continues with the following American Controversy, examining the role of nuclear energy in modern society.

---

## AMERICAN CONTROVERSY

## *Do We Want Nuclear Energy?*

In April 1986 the worst nuclear accident in history occurred at Chernobyl nuclear plant in Pripyat, a Soviet town. This serious accident revitalized the debate about whether or not the use of nuclear power should be continued.

One might consider such an issue within a structural-functional framework: The opponents of nuclear energy emphasize its dysfunctions and the proponents its functions. Actually it is more specific than that: The opponents emphasize the *latent* dysfunctions of nuclear energy and the proponents its *manifest* functions. (If this distinction is unclear, check the meanings of these concepts in Chapter 1 "Introduction".)

Opponents of nuclear energy reading this chapter might be struck by the conclusions about controversial research discussed in the previous section. In particular, they might emphasize that those employed in producing a particular type of technology are unlikely to assess the risks carefully because their own livelihood is dependent on that technology.

Opponents will also stress

the problem of assessing the long-term impact of nuclear contamination. While nuclear proponents might say that the fallout from the Three Mile Island accident or the nuclear fire at Brown's Ferry, the routine emissions occurring at all plants, and leaks from stored nuclear wastes have not proved harmful, optimism is premature. The impact of strontium 90, which can cause leukemia, is not detectable for up to five years, and some tumor malignancies can take twenty or even thirty years to appear. A particularly serious problem is the magnified effect of nuclear fallout in the food chain; some fish concentrate the impact of radiation up to 100,000 times its occurrence in the environment. Furthermore our water-treatment systems are not equipped to remove radioactive particles, and health departments cannot monitor all our food.

No, we are better off har-nessing the wind, the sun, and the tides, the opponents conclude. We can burn municipal garbage, obtain methane from existing landfills, and mine coal safely and burn it cleanly as Australia does.

The proponents of nuclear power will say that opponents are exaggerating. They will point out that a large part of the cost of nuclear-power plants goes for insurance in the form of layer after layer of physical protection: fuel traps for radioactive gases, steel casings for uranium, and enormously strong concrete and steel containment buildings. Unfortunately the Soviets do not take the same precautions as we have; the differences are tragically apparent when one compares the minimal impact produced by the Three Mile Island accident with the much more extensive damage created in the Soviet situation.

Nuclear power now lights about one out of every six bulbs in the United States. In France, which uses plants based on our designs, it is about three out of every four bulbs. It seems important to continue to develop this cheap, safe form of power as a means of insuring our energy independence from foreign energy sources.

What do you think? Certainly a problem in debating this issue is that more specialized information is needed here than with most subjects analyzed in these American Controversies. For that reason perhaps it is tempting to let political leaders, with the advice of experts, resolve the issue. But can we trust them to make wise, balanced decisions that are truly in the American people's interest?

In discussing and debating the issue of nuclear energy, you might consider the reasons why people will take one side or the other on this issue. Evaluate not only experts but average citizens on this point.

Sources: Jeremy M. Hellman. "U.S. Plants Are Safe; Go Full Speed Ahead." *USA TODAY*. April 30, 1986, p. 12A; Jeanne Honicker. "To Save Ourselves, Stop Nuclear Pollution." *USA TODAY*. April 30, 1986, p. 12A.

We have just seen that science often involves itself with controversial subject matter; medical activity often stirs controversy as well. This tendency is hardly surprising because medicine, even more frequently than science generally, is concerned with life-and-death issues. The fundamental relationship between the two institutions is emphasized by the fact that our definition of medicine contains a reference to science: Medicine is the scientifically based practice concerned with the prevention and treatment of disease and the treatment of injury.

Over the past three-and-one-half centuries, scientific advances have been the source of medicine's rapid advancement. For instance, in 1628 William Harvey provided the first description of the circulation of blood; in 1673 Anton Leewenhoek invented the microscope; in 1797 Edward Jenner discovered smallpox vaccine; in 1846 William Morton perfected ether as an anesthetic; in 1866 Joseph Lister first used antiseptic methods in surgery; in the 1880s Robert Koch discovered the causes of anthrax, cholera, and tuberculosis; in 1954 Jonas Salk discovered polio vaccine; in 1970 John Charnley made the first hip-joint-socket replacement (Coe, 1978: 188). In modern times many people take these advances for granted. But what would life be like without them? Consider, for instance, a society periodically ravaged by smallpox, cholera, and tuberculosis, or having an operation without an anesthetic!

# **380** Disease and Death in the United States

Medicine is concerned with the treatment of disease. Most people are generally aware of what disease is, but they will be hard pressed to distinguish it from the related concepts of illness and sickness. **Disease** is a condition of biological nonhealth. Microorganisms, which are either bacteria or viruses, invade human beings and other organisms and produce specific diseases. **Illness** is an individual's sense that he or she has been affected by disease. Usually disease does produce illness, and it is widely believed that illness improves the likelihood of disease. Finally **sickness** is a social status in which an individual is treated as unhealthy. Sick people are usually suffering from a disease, but that is not always the case.

## Disease

The United States Public Health Service (USPHS) has long recognized that an effective attack on disease requires knowledge of how many people have contracted various diseases and the extent to which different categories of individuals are vulnerable to particular diseases.

In the late 1950s and early 1960s, USPHS started three monthly surveys that collected a wealth of data on health and health care throughout the country.

The results of these surveys make it clear that some definite trends in vulnerability to disease exist — in particular, in the likelihood that various groups will catch acute or chronic disorders. Acute diseases such as influenza, dysentery, and measles are likely to be intense, even incapacitating, but short term, whereas chronic diseases such as heart conditions and arthritis can usually be controlled but not cured.

One pattern is that the older people become, the more likely they are to develop chronic ailments and the less likely they are to catch acute diseases. From a biological point of view, one would expect to find a higher rate of chronic disease among older people because such ailments are primarily the result of the degeneration of bodily tissue and the increasing ineffectiveness of various organs. On the other hand, younger people are less likely

to have developed immunities through exposure to acute diseases than their elders have.

Women tend to have more acute and less chronic disease than do men. Once children pass the age of ten, females have a higher rate of acute disorders for the rest of their lives than males, and after the age of seventeen, males maintain a greater likelihood of developing chronic ailments than females. Several factors may account for men's greater susceptibility to chronic disease. It is possible that women are stronger physically than men — they do live longer — and therefore their bodies are more resistant to chronic disorders in old age. On the other hand, social conditions might play a significant part. Traditionally men have been more involved in the work world than women; perhaps work-related exposure to stress has made men more vulnerable to such chronic ailments as heart disease and ulcers. (See Table 15.3.)

There is also a relationship between income and disease. In general, the higher the income group, the lower the rate of disease. A number of factors are relevant. People in higher income groups generally live in cleaner and more sanitary situations; they also tend to have better nutrition, more effective medical services, and greater knowledge about disease and illness (Coe, 1978: 61–64; Twaddle and Hessler, 1977: 59–62).

## Death

Just as certain categories of people are more vulnerable to disease, some status groups are more susceptible to death.

Age is one important factor. During the first year of life, there is a high death rate; the likelihood of death then remains low until about the age of forty when physical deterioration and vulnerability to a number of serious chronic diseases cause the death rate to increase sharply.

At most ages males have a higher death rate than females. Working conditions, such as risk of injury and the likelihood of stress, are significant factors. As we have noted, it also seems possible that women are physically stronger than men, possess-

**Table 15.3**
**Americans' Disease Rates: 1982**

| | RATE PER 100 POPULATION | |
| --- | --- | --- |
| | SEX | |
| | *Male* | *Female* |
| *Acute Conditions*[1] | | |
| Infective and parasitic[2] | 16.3 | 21.0 |
| Upper respiratory[3] | 38.6 | 43.3 |
| Other respiratory[4] | 36.2 | 41.1 |
| Digestive system[5] | 6.2 | 6.8 |
| Injuries | 30.6 | 24.1 |
| *Chronic Conditions* | | |
| Heart conditions | 7.4 | 7.5 |
| Arthritis | 9.7 | 16.7 |
| Hypertension | 10.1 | 13.1 |
| Deformities or orthopedic (bone) impairments | 9.9 | 10.0 |

| | AGE | | | | |
| --- | --- | --- | --- | --- | --- |
| | *Under 6 years* | *6 – 16 years* | *17 – 44 years* | *45 – 64 years* | *65 years and over* |
| *Acute Conditions* | | | | | |
| Infective and parasitic | 45.0 | 32.4 | 15.4 | 9.0 | 7.3 |
| Upper respiratory | 93.7 | 62.3 | 35.9 | 23.9 | 16.2 |
| Other respiratory | 61.6 | 51.8 | 39.3 | 28.7 | 15.8 |
| Digestive system | 10.9 | 12.5 | 5.0 | 3.8 | 4.8 |
| Injuries | 28.1 | 35.5 | 28.5 | 20.6 | 20.6 |
| *Chronic Conditions* | *Under 45 years* | | *45 – 64 years* | | *65 years and over* |
| Heart conditions | 3.5 | | 13.7 | | 25.7 |
| Arthritis | 5.6 | | 27.6 | | 49.6 |
| Hypertension | 5.9 | | 24.6 | | 39.0 |
| Deformities or orthopedic | 13.9 | | 11.3 | | 4.6 |
| (bone) impairments | 10.7 | | 13.9 | | 16.9 |

[1] The acute conditions reported here required medical treatment or at least one day of restricted activity.
[2] E.g., tonsilitis.
[3] E.g., pneumonia.
[4] E.g., a cold.
[5] E.g., a bleeding ulcer.

Source: Adapted from U.S. Bureau of the Census. *Statistical Abstract of the United States: 1986.* No. 186 and No. 187.

*Like women in comparison to men, young people tend to have proportionately more acute and proportionately less chronic disease than older people. In this table, however, women's rates of chronic disease are higher than men's. This particular result probably has occurred because women tend to live longer than men and thus have a higher percentage of their number at ages where they are especially vulnerable to chronic disease.*

ing in particular the capacity to resist more effectively a variety of diseases.

Married people tend to live longer than people who are not. Widowed individuals have higher death rates than married people, and the rates are the highest among those who have never been married. Perhaps part of the explanation for the relationship between marriage and long life is that

**382**

married people are more likely to have an orderly existence and a range of relationships that will lessen the impact of stress.

Finally the higher an individual's social-class position, the lower the death rate. Some high-risk factors faced by individuals with low socioeconomic status include physically dangerous occupations, inadequate housing, poor nutrition, limited access to medical facilities, crowded living conditions, and exposure to a relatively high level of violence (Twaddle and Hessler, 1977: 78–84).

Table 15.4 lists the diseases that were the leading causes of death in 1982.

A disease that has captured public attention and produced a great deal of fear across the nation has been AIDS. The following Contemporary Issue provides some information about both the disease and people's reaction to it.

**Table 15.4**
**Death Rates for Different Diseases: 1982**

| | DEATHS PER 100,000 AMERICANS |
|---|---|
| Heart disease | 326.0 |
| Cancer | 187.2 |
|    Respiratory system | 50.2 |
|    Digestive system | 48.6 |
|    Breast | 16.3 |
| Cerebrovascular diseases[1] | 68.0 |
| Pneumonia and influenza | 21.1 |
| Chronic liver disease and cirrhosis | 11.9 |
| Diabetes | 14.9 |

[1] For instance, strokes.

Source: Adapted from U.S. Bureau of the Census. *Statistical Abstract of the United States: 1986.* No. 114.

## CONTEMPORARY ISSUE

## *AIDS and Americans' Fear of the Disease*

Throughout history people have been frightened by diseases. And why not? When a disease sweeps into one's locale, creating great suffering and death, and no one is aware of either the cause or cure, it is reasonable to be frightened. Gradually we have come to understand more about different diseases, and many have been subdued. Diphtheria, smallpox, tuberculosis, typhoid, typhus, yellow fever—all of these once devastating diseases are now under control. So is infantile paralysis, which many of us can remember at epidemic levels.

Some lethal diseases remain, however, and in recent years a new one has been added to the list—AIDS. Like the great killers of the past, AIDS and other prominent major diseases tend to produce considerable fear, including some concerns that are groundless.

When asked in a New York Times/CBS News Poll, what are the most serious medical problems facing the country today, 74 percent of a national sample mentioned cancer, 51 percent AIDS, and 41 percent heart disease. Concern about AIDS was found to be highest among blacks, residents of large cities, and younger adults.

The survey sought to determine the accuracy of public information about the transmission of AIDS. The Centers for Disease Control in Atlanta have obtained nearly conclusive evidence indicating that AIDS can be transmitted only through intimate sexual contact, use of a contaminated hypodermic needle, transfusion of blood containing the virus, and, in the case of newborn infants, infection while in the womb, during birth, or from milk of a mother suffering from the virus. Most informants knew about the proven modes of infection.

However, many of those interviewed thought that AIDS could be transmitted by less intimate means. Forty-seven percent thought that AIDS could be obtained by drinking from a glass just used by an AIDS victim. Thirty-two percent believed that the disease could be obtained through kissing, 28 percent felt that it could be transmitted from a toilet seat, and 12 percent indicated that AIDS could be contracted just by working in the same office with someone who is infected.

So it appears that many Americans have some inaccurate information about AIDS. It also seems probable that at least some people will continue to maintain false beliefs about the disease. One reason why this is likely to be the case is the complexity of reaching conclusions about disease transmission: It is impossible to prove that AIDS cannot be transmitted by casual contact. And if some people are skeptical about official commentaries on the disease, there is no way actually to prove them wrong.

Certainly one conclusion to be drawn from this survey data is that situations can arise where health-care personnel need to be concerned with much more than delivering medical treatment to the public. At times an important task will be educating citizens so that they can most effectively cope with a serious medical problem.

Source: Erik Eckholm. "Poll Finds Many AIDS Fears that the Experts Say are Groundless." *New York Times.* September 12, 1985, p. B11.

# Health Care in the United States

By seeking to avoid disease and death, people make these subjects significant issues in their lives. The significance is implied by the following statement: "Well, at least I've got my health." How many times have you heard someone make such a declaration? Fairly often, I suspect. Since people do not like to be unhealthy, they usually take measures to restore their health. **Health care** is the variety of public and private organizations that support an individual's effective physical, mental, and social adaptation to his or her environment. Modern American health care has some significant problems, which we will review.

## Sickness in the System

One prominent difficulty with modern health care is its cost. There has been a steady increase in the total expenditure, the per-capita expenditure, and the percent of the Gross National Product. For instance, between 1960 and 1984, the total expenditure rose from $26.9 billion to $387 billion, increasing from $146 to $1580 per capita and from 5.3 to 10.6 percent of the Gross National Product (U.S. Bureau of the Census, *Statistical Abstract of the United States: 1986*. No 146).

Physicians' increasing fees have contributed to the rising cost of health care. Before World War II, medical doctors averaged about two-and-one-half times the income of all full-time workers. Now they average more than five times the national average, making them the highest-paid occupational group in the country. The cost of specialization helps account for rising fees; six of seven practicing physicians are now specialists compared with about half in the early 1960s. Hospital costs, however, have made a more significant contribution to soaring health costs than doctors' fees. The increasing number of hospital workers as well as their rising wages or salaries have been contributing factors. A more significant influence on increasing costs has been the recent intensification of hospital care — the growing use of laboratory tests, x-rays, and such new and expensive advances as CAT scanners and heart-bypass surgery.

Admittedly most people do not pay for most of their health care. About 83 percent of health care is paid by "third parties": private health-insurance companies, company health plans, and government programs, especially Medicare and Medicaid. However, the rising cost of health care does come back to haunt the average consumer in such ways as relentlessly increasing expenditure for private health plans, the possibility that growing expenses in company plans will reflect on workers' wage packages, and the necessity to pay for public plans through federal taxation (Addiss, 1985; Conrad and Schneider, 1981).

Another major symptom of deficiency in American health care involves limited access to competent medical care. This difficulty is summed up by the sentence: "I can't find a doctor." The situation has two aspects. First, some people are unable to locate a physician qualified to treat their particular medical complaint. This is because throughout the country there are not enough doctors in certain medical areas — emergency care, home care, and care outside of regular working hours, in particu-

*It is likely that this little boy, who lives in a rural area, has less access to competent medical care than children living in cities.*

lar. Second, certain groups within the society face particular access problems. The poor, ethnic and racial minorities, and rural people are often deprived of effective medical care. The principal reason is that many members of these groups lack adequate income and insurance to pay for standard medical treatment. An additional factor operating here is that most physicians prefer to locate their offices in middle- or upper-income areas, and so poorer people's access problem is also geographical (Wolinsky, 1980: 416–419).

Sickness in the American health-care system is apparent when one compares Americans' life ex-

pectancy and infant mortality rates with rates in other major industrial nations. In spite of the fact that Americans pay more per capita for health care than people in other countries, American men's life expectancy is lower than that of men in such industrialized nations as Australia, Canada, Japan, and the Netherlands. On infant mortality (death in the first year), countries with a lower rate than the United States include Australia, France, the Federal Republic of Germany, Japan, the Netherlands, and Spain (U.S. Bureau of the Census, *Statistical Abstract of the United States: 1986*. No. 1468 and No. 1469).

How could American health care be improved? One way would be to introduce a different perspective on the subject. Since about 1900 American medicine has tended to focus on the analysis of specific diseases with the use of drugs as quick-fix cures. Medical personnel have generally failed to take a broad, environmental perspective, emphasizing that prevention of different diseases, most notably many types of cancer, could be obtained by controlling environmental factors in the home, in the work place, and throughout the country. For instance, if all Americans ceased smoking, in a given year about 80,000 people would survive who otherwise would have died (Feagin, 1986: 236–237). To initiate a successful program of disease prevention would require that program directors fight to clean up the environment. So far most health-care personnel are strongly inclined to avoid such controversial activities.

The focus now shifts from the health-care system to the central figures in that system: physicians and nurses.

## Medical Careers

When Americans think of professions, medicine will be at or near the top of the list. But what is it that separates a profession from other occupational groups? Within their specialty area, the members of a profession have the exclusive right to ". . . determine what the problem is, how the problem is to be dealt with, and what price is to be paid for dealing with it" (Freidson, 1970: 368–369).

The members of a profession, in short, have autonomy in their work, and they receive both cultural and legal backing in this regard. Physicians

are the only people permitted to diagnose and treat disease and injury, and they also set the fees for their work. No outsiders may interfere; the policing of any irregularities is done by members of the profession.

### Physicians and Their Professional Activities

What status characteristics do you associate with physicians? If "male" and "white" come to mind, then you are considering two prominent characteristics of most modern doctors. At present women and nonwhites are still underrepresented in medical schools. Women, who are 54 percent of the American population, comprise about one quarter of medical-school students, and nonwhites, who are more than 13 percent of the population, represent only about 8 percent of the medical-school population. In addition, medical students tend to come from professional backgrounds and from families with above-average incomes. We see, in short, that distinct characteristics prevail for students entering medical school (Wolinsky, 1980: 274–279).

## Socialization of Doctors

For the first two years, medical students' education is concentrated in the basic sciences associated with medicine: anatomy, biochemistry, biophysics, cellular biology, genetics, microbiology, pathology, pharmacology, and physiology. During those two years, students are expected to absorb a great deal of knowledge from these different specialties.

Medical students find themselves in an instructional environment that is generally much less structured than in college. At one medical school, a directive to beginning students reads in part:

> We do not use the comfortable method of spoon-feeding . . . Limits are not fixed. Each field will be opened up somewhat sketchily . . . You will begin to paint a picture on a vast canvas but only the center of the picture will be worked in any detail. The periphery will gradually blur into the hazy background. And the more you work out the peripheral pattern, the more you will realize the vastness of that which stretches an unknown distance beyond.
>
> *(Fox, 1978: 190)*

During their first two years, medical students begin to distinguish three kinds of "vastness" stretching in front of them. The first type involves their imperfect mastery of current knowledge. The second type concerns the limitation to current knowledge; physicians currently do not have answers to innumerable questions. A third type of "vastness" results from the inability to distinguish between the first two types. In the course of their schooling, medical students must be able to grasp the third uncertainty—to appreciate that grave consequences can result if they are unable to do so.

## Doctors' Relations with Colleagues

"Harry, I'm worried." Dr. Finchlow stares straight ahead, lost in thought. "I've called you in for this consultation because Mary Perkins doesn't seem to be responding to treatment. I wanted to talk to you because you're our top person in neurosurgery. I'll give you a detailed rundown on her condition and treatment to date, and then you tell me what you think." Such scenes appear frequently in soap operas, but they do not seem to be a prominent part of medical activity.

Elliot Freidson (1978) has pointed out that many people believe that the mere existence of group practice will encourage a higher level of medical performance than if each doctor works alone. However, for group practice to have such an effect, doctors must be able to exercise some social control over each other's behavior, and such control is possible only with systematic and extensive exchange of information about patients by their physicians. Studying the subject, Freidson found that this process did not generally occur.

Doctors would frequently make referrals to other doctors in their group practice, but the information contained in the referral was often brief and superficial, thus providing the physician receiving the referral little information about the colleague's competence. In addition, within the group practice, no effort existed to make information available to all others about each physician's performance. For instance, pediatricians and internists worked at parallel services, seldom if ever referring to each other and so having little opportunity to learn about the competence of each other's work.

An important issue involved mistakes. Doctors were willing to discuss their own and colleagues' mistakes if they were relatively minor, not reflecting on their basic competence. With a clear blunder, however, they tended to be self-protective or protective. Freidson interviewed a surgeon who had recently examined a young girl. The girl had a cancerous thyroid, that, according to her chart, had only "blossomed" in the last few weeks. The surgeon spoke with the physician who had made the referral. This man admitted that the family doctor who had been treating the case for years had made a mistake, and the referring physician told the surgeon, "Look, the less said about it the better. The man who sent her to me feels horrible about it. He realizes now he missed something and he said, 'Forget it. Don't say anything about it.' He really feels badly about it, you see." The surgeon agreed with his colleague's comments about the family doctor. The surgeon said, "All right, he knows. What more can you do? After a man knows and he realizes, you are not going to go in and twist a knife in his back" (Freidson, 1978: 237).

Freidson concluded that while group practice does provide a fine opportunity to collect and share information and to evaluate colleagues' performances, such tasks are generally not pursued. In fact, it has been his observation that the benefits of group practice are no more than negligible.

Other researchers, however, are somewhat more optimistic about the impact of group practice. For instance, a recent study of a large group practice concluded that the doctors involved varied considerably in the extent to which they consulted colleagues and made referrals to them. Those most inclined to engage in both activities were physicians who were older and more active in administrative and professional activities (Anderson and Jay, 1985). Presumably these individuals were both busier and more secure than most of their colleagues.

Looking beyond colleagues' examination of each other's work in group practice to the general issue of peer review, we see that this activity is complicated by a number of conditions. First, doctors strongly support the idea that they can only work effectively if they are allowed to exercise independent clinical judgment in the diagnosis and treatment of patients. Second, physicians emphasize that the evidence that can be obtained on colleagues' actual medical performance is limited unless one is present to observe. Third, there is the belief that during practice some mistakes are inevitable (Mechanic, 1978: 404). Finally physicians' high status often discourages damaging interpretations of acts that might violate the law (Pontell et al., 1982).

In spite of these difficulties, some physicians emphasize that modern medical practice should include the development of effective procedures for peer review. A recent president of the American Medical Association pointed out that there are a few physicians charging their patients outrageous fees and that this serious problem must be relieved by tough peer review: "We must seek the means to exercise increased professional discipline and serve as true patient advocates in correcting these physician excesses before they destroy us all" (*New York Times,* June 18, 1985).

For many physicians rivalry seems to be a dominant element in their relations with colleagues. In the United States, a "surgery surplus" now exists. With too few patients available for the number of surgeons, competition for new patients can develop. A salesman of orthopedic equipment reported that surgeons jealously watched to see how many artificial hips, knees, and other replacement parts their colleagues ordered from him. At the extreme, rivalry led to verbal assaults of one doctor by another. The salesman noted, "Doctors constantly asked me: 'How was that knee case with Dr. X? I hear it didn't go so well?'" Apparently they hoped the salesman would supply some information that could be used to undermine the colleague's reputation. This same observer explained that many surgeons wanted to be on the emergency-room roster, since a doctor on call in the emergency room would be in a good position to recruit new patients (MacKay, 1978: 102–103).

## Nurses and Their Professional Development

In the latter half of the nineteenth century, the women who provided nursing care were either patients themselves, residents of near-by prisons, or women hired off the street. Physical strength, particularly a strong back, and a pleasing disposition were the major job requirements. Hiring was often a casual process. In one case the matron of a Boston Hospital wanted a nurse, but none of the applicants met her qualifications. So she had a recuperating patient become the laundress, and the laundress was promoted to nurse (Reverby, 1981: 221).

Certainly nursing has changed a great deal in the past century. The first three accredited nursing schools in the United States were founded in 1873. Hospitals were willing to finance the early training of nurses in exchange for their services in the hospital. The first nursing schools were sufficiently successful to encourage the formation of a number of new schools during the late 1800s and early 1900s. At present three types of nursing education have emerged. In the hospital-diploma programs, the student receives three years of practical training, with a strong emphasis on the nurse's readiness to follow doctor's orders without questioning them. The second type of nursing education is the baccalaureate program. There are now more than 430 baccalaureate programs in the United States, producing over one-fifth of the new nurses each year. This training is less practical and more theoretical than the instruction received in the diploma program. The third type of nursing education—the associate-degree program—is a "fence straddler." The students receive a more theoretically oriented program than their colleagues at diploma schools—two years at a community college—but a less-extensive professional emphasis than the baccalaureate candidates.

No matter which type of program they complete, registered nurses (RNs) comprise 58 percent of all active health-care professionals. In fact, the current nurse per-capita rate is 246 percent higher than the physician per-capita rate. Traditionally nurses have been lower-middle-class or working-class women from small towns or rural areas. In recent years an increasing percentage have been coming from urban middle- to upper-middle-class families (Wolinsky, 1980: 315–340).

Nursing is taxing work. Nurses are not only expected to do their best to help patients get well, but they are also supposed to fill an emotional role, creating whenever possible a "therapeutic environment." Nurses interviewed in one study reported that they often felt badly equipped to do this, especially with critically ill patients (Gray-Toft and Anderson, 1981). A recent investigation of student nurses found that other major sources of stress include conflicts with other nurses and insecurity about professional skills (Parkes, 1985).

It is not surprising that student nurses feel this insecurity, because members of the profession face a number of status problems. First, there is resistance to this field receiving the social prestige, monetary rewards, and deference normally associated with major professions. The American public tends to view nursing with the limited respect accorded social work and elementary-school teaching. One reason is that many people believe that nurses are no more than assistants to physicians. In addition, as a "female" occupation, nursing receives the brunt of many people's antifeminist bias.

A second status problem encountered by nurses involves the multiple demands they must satisfy. In particular, hospital nurses must face the dual pressure of serving in administrative capacities and also performing nursing services for patients. Both are difficult tasks that together can make overwhelming demands on a nurse's time and energy.

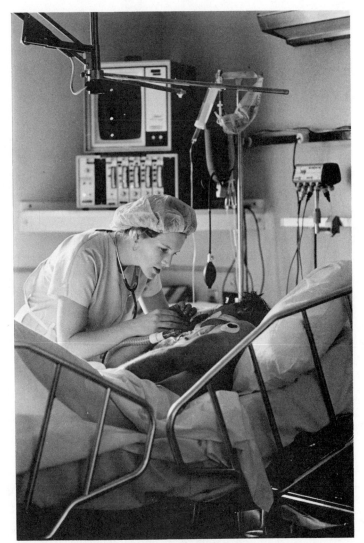

*Nurses, especially those working in intensive care units and other special areas, are highly trained and skilled professionals. But the relatively low status and limited advancement opportunities compel many to change careers.*

Finally a significant conflict often exists between the ideology of nursing and the realities of status advancement. Within the nursing profession, the conviction continues that the central activity should be the direct care of patients. However, in modern times, the greatest tangible rewards—increased salary and promotions—come from administrative work (Coe, 1978: 256–248).

# Patient–Doctor Relations

Portions of the two previous sections serve as effective background for the present one. Patient–doctor relations involve the problems of disease and death, and those relations are significantly affected by physicians' professional status.

## Conceptual Perspectives

Talcott Parsons (1951) analyzed the sick role. Like any other role, this one has a definite set of behaviors associated with it. First, if a person has a disease or injury, it is legitimate to consider oneself ill, to remain bedridden if necessary, and to be freed from normal obligations. Second, the sick person is expected to recognize that his or her disease or injury is undesirable and that it should be cured as quickly as possible. Third, sick people and the members of their families are aware that physicians supply the most effective treatment of disease and injury, and so they seek doctors when they become sick.

Parsons's conception of the sick role has been criticized. It has been pointed out, in particular, that this analysis fails to consider that the sick person plays a significant part in the treatment process (Honig-Parnass, 1981). In spite of limits to Parsons's perception of the sick role, however, the concept has been used widely by sociologists studying health, disease, and sickness in modern American society (Wolinsky and Wolinsky, 1981).

Unlike Parsons, Szasz and Hollender (1956) acknowledged that patients play a significant role in the treatment process. They produced a classification of the kinds of relationships likely to develop between doctors and patients. Szasz and Hollender suggested that the nature of a disease or injury will strongly influence or determine the relationship between doctor and patient. Three types of relationships are proposed:

1. *Activity–Passivity.* This type of relationship exists in medical emergencies when severe injury, delirium, coma, or blood loss makes the patient helpless. Treatment occurs whether or not the patient makes a contribution.
2. *Guidance–Cooperation.* Such a relationship develops in less dangerous circumstances than those just described. When patients have acute, especially infectious disorders, they are likely to be very ill, but they are able to follow physicians' orders, respecting their doctors as experts who know the best way to produce a cure.
3. *Mutual Participation.* This approach is often useful for the management of such chronic diseases as diabetes and hypertension, where the patient performs most of the treatment and only consults the physician occasionally. In this relationship doctors help patients to help themselves. The instructions that patients receive are often complex; thus, unlike the other two kinds of doctor–patient relationships, children and mentally retarded or profoundly immature individuals will often be unable to participate. One writer warned that unless the control exercised by physicians in traditional doctor–patient relationships is carefully analyzed and reformed, significant participation by patients will not occur (Barnard, 1985).

## Special Features of Patient–Doctor Relations

Hank Johnson calls up the garage. "Charlie, I can't get the Ford started again. Do you think you could send a man over before noon?" Hank Johnson has just purchased a service. When most of us encounter doctors, we too are purchasing a service, a service that, to be sure, has some noteworthy features. In the first place, those who perform the service—doctors—are held in high regard. As Table 15.5 indicates, 58 percent of a national sample assessed doctors as ranking very high or high in honesty and ethical standards. Only clergymen at 67 percent and druggists and pharmacists at 65 percent scored better (George Gallup, *Gallup Poll*, April 1985).

Another particular quality about medical service is that doctors will sometimes provide a less-than-complete summary of the patient's condition. One reason physicians withhold information is their belief that patients generally lack the expertise to assimilate the information they receive. Another reason is the nature of certain cases—cases of terminal illness, in particular. Doctors and nurses

## Table 15.5
## The Medical Profession in Comparative Perspective

|  | VERY HIGH OR HIGH STANDARDS OF HONESTY AND ETHICAL STANDARDS |
| --- | --- |
| Clergymen | 67% |
| Druggists/pharmacists | 65 |
| Medical doctors | 58 |
| Policemen | 47 |
| Lawyers | 27 |
| Senators | 23 |
| Congressmen | 20 |
| Realtors | 15 |
| Labor-union leaders | 13 |
| Insurance salesmen | 10 |
| Car salesmen | 5 |

Source: George Gallup. *Gallup Poll.* April 1985.

*The results of this survey demonstrate that doctors are well regarded compared to a variety of other occupational groups.*

are likely to find such cases emotionally trying, and so they may have as little as possible to do with such patients. In particular, contact with terminal patients reminds doctors that in these instances they are proving incapable of fulfilling their primary mission—to maintain life (Freidson, 1981: 189–190; Quint, 1978: 94). Several twentieth-century patterns—the growing professionalization of medicine, the increasing specialization within the field, and the expanding bureaucratization of health care—have tended to make patient–doctor communications appear less and less effective from many patients' point of view (Betz and O'Connell, 1983).

Another important aspect of medical service is the fact that physicians' examinations of illness involve a variety of risks and costs in situations that can literally determine life and death. For instance, in trying to decide whether or not to continue an exploration of an illness without a clear diagnosis, a physician must weigh the following factors: the time and financial cost, the possible risks of medical tests, and the psychological distress for patients of continued investigation (Mechanic, 1978: 422–423). In recent years there have been many claims

of unnecessary surgery. An analysis of the topic suggested that the best way to resolve questionable cases is close scrutiny by committees containing both medical and nonmedical personnel (Schacht and Pemberton, 1985).

A fourth noteworthy feature of medical services is that low-status people receive inferior medical care. One study, which involved research conducted in Michigan and Australia, found that doctors in both places had particularly negative stereotypes of certain categories of patients who possessed characteristics negatively valued in their societies and/or were especially difficult to treat—in particular, patients who were alcoholic, unhygienic, angry, addicted to drugs, obese, or mentally disturbed (Najman, Klein, and Munro, 1982).

The poor often receive inferior treatment. Compared with middle-class citizens, the poor usually have greater difficulty gaining hospital admittance, receive less effectively coordinated treatment, and are much more likely to obtain the burden of care from "beginners"—medical students, interns, and residents. In addition, poor patients receive much more public care than their middle-class counterparts. One observer commented on the public treatment of the poor person, "Several staff members will congregate to examine him, and talk about him, callously and contemptuously ignoring him, talking over him, not to him" (Ryan, 1976: 168).

Old people are another category of low-status people who often receive inferior medical treatment. Elizabeth Markson (1971) examined the records of 174 elderly people admitted to Fairview State Hospital, a publicly funded mental hospital in New York City. Markson found evidence backing the frequent claim that elderly people are often sent to low-status institutions, especially mental hospitals, to die. She learned that the patients admitted to this hospital had a multiplicity of serious physical illnesses, especially heart and circulatory diseases. In fact, a full quarter of the sample died within a month of admission, especially those arriving incapacitated. This sociologist concluded that little effort was made to separate people with symptoms indicating serious physical disorder from those suffering old-age mental disabilities. The staff doctors apparently supported the idea that the Fairview geriatrics patients should be provided little more than "a hiding place to die."

Commentary

We have now learned that medical practice is often controversial, and this trend was also apparent when we discussed science, another topic that involves life-and-death matters. We have also seen that the two institutional areas have changed rapidly over time, with progress a priority for each of them.

# STUDY GUIDE

## Summary

1. A science is a systematic effort to develop general principles about a particular subject matter based on actual observations and stated in a form that can be tested by any competent individual. Medicine is the scientifically based practice concerned with the prevention and treatment of disease and the treatment of injury.

2. Until modern times science made modest contributions to societies. Reasons included limited breadth of practical tasks for science, little incentive to incorporate scientific analysis into technological development, and opposition to scientific inquiry. In ancient Greece science did play a fairly significant role for about 200 years. Science began to receive widespread acceptance in seventeenth-century England. Factors contributing to this acceptance included the growing recognition of the part science played in the emerging conception of progress and the contribution of Protestantism, which permitted supporters to believe that God's will and scientific activity were harmonious. In twentieth-century America, science received a boost when graduate schools started to develop professionally qualified research workers. Since World War II, the American government has provided massive support for a wide range of scientific research.

3. In examining scientists and scientific work, we have considered the practice of scientific norms. Robert Merton has suggested that four norms dominate scientific practice: universalism, communism, organized skepticism, and disinterestedness. A study of forty-two scientists associated with the Apollo lunar missions provides some evidence opposing Merton's set of norms. A set of "counter-norms" seems to exist.

Certain conditions help to sustain such controversial research projects as studies on DNA and nuclear weaponry. These conditions include the scientists' strong support of the research goals, effective government sponsorship, a policy of secrecy, and an active in-group for scientists.

4. Disease is a condition of biological nonhealth. Illness is an individual's sense that he or she has been affected by disease. Sickness is a social status in which an individual is treated as unhealthy.

Some definite trends in vulnerability to disease exist. People's age, sex, and income are status characteristics that provide an indication of their likelihood of catching acute or chronic diseases. Just as certain categories of individuals are more vulnerable to disease, some status groups are more susceptible to death.

5. There is sickness in the American health-care system, including rapidly rising costs and, for many Americans, limited access to competent medical personnel. In some significant respects, health care in a number of other industrialized nations appears to be more effective.

6. There are certain particularly significant elements in doctors' careers. Inevitably doctors' training involves a standardized socialization—attendance at medical school and postgraduate studies. During their schooling they must learn to work effectively in a context where they face three different kinds of "vastness." Most modern doctors tend to exchange a fairly limited amount of information about their respective practices. In general, peer review is not an effective mechanism.

Nurses represent the largest category of health-care personnel. Three different kinds of nursing programs are available. Nurses encounter a number of severe status problems, including the difficulty of establishing nursing as a widely recognized profession, the necessity of satisfying multiple demands on the job, and the conflict between the ideology of nursing and the realities of advancement.

7. Parsons's analysis of the sick role focuses on three definite behavioral patterns. Szasz and Hollender produced a three-part classification of the kinds of relationships likely to develop between doctors and patients.

Four factors have a significant influence on doctors' relations with patients: the public's high regard for physicians, doctors' tendency to provide a less-than-complete summary of the patient's condition, life-and-death risks and costs involved in medical practice, and the provision of inferior medical treatment for low-status patients.

## Glossary

**communism** a requirement that the substantive findings of science represent a common heritage, not the exclusive property of individual discoverers and their heirs.

**disease** a condition of biological nonhealth.

**disinterestedness** a standard that scientists avoid the pursuit of work that is self-serving and self-interested.

**health care** the variety of public and private organizations that support an individual's effective physical, mental, and social adaptation to his or her environment.

**illness** an individual's sense that he or she has been affected by disease.

**medical sociology** the study of the social setting in which health, sickness, and health care occur.

**medicine** the scientifically based practice concerned with the prevention and treatment of disease and the treatment of injury.

**organized skepticism** the conclusion that no scientist's contribution to knowledge can be accepted without careful scrutiny.

**science** A systematic effort to develop general principles about a particular subject matter based on actual observations and stated in a form that can be tested by any competent person.

**sickness** a social status in which an individual is treated as unhealthy.

**universalism** a norm stating that all scientific claims of truth need to be evaluated by impersonal criteria consistent with existing knowledge in that field.

## Learning Objectives

After studying this chapter, you should be able to:

1. Define science and medicine and discuss their social importance.
2. Examine the development of science in ancient societies, seventeenth-century England, and the United States since the beginning of this century.
3. Identify and discuss the norms and counter-norms of scientific practice.
4. List and explain the factors that help sustain controversial scientific research.
5. Define disease, illness, and sickness and examine the trends on vulnerability to disease and death.
6. Examine sickness in the American health-care system.
7. Briefly discuss the socialization of doctors and their relations with colleagues.
8. Describe the development of nursing in the United States and examine nurses' status problems.
9. Summarize Parsons's analysis of the sick role and Szasz and Hollender's classification of doctor–patient relationships and indicate differences between the two approaches.
10. Discuss the factors influencing patient–doctor relations.
11. Describe the relationship between the two institutions examined in this chapter—science and medicine.

## True – false test

_____ 1. In some preindustrial societies, technological advance could occur without contributions from science.

_____ 2. Modern European research has typically been more professionalized than American research.

_____ 3. Figures indicate steadily increasing federal-governmental support for research.

_____ 4. Robert Merton's set of four scientific norms is based on information obtained from a study of scientists associated with the Apollo lunar missions.

_____ 5. According to the text, DNA research is no longer considered controversial.

_____ 6. The existence of their own in-groups encourages scientists to pursue controversial research.

_____ 7. Women tend to have more acute and less chronic disease than do men.

_____ 8. Research has determined that the mere existence of group practice will encourage a higher level of medical performance than if each doctor works alone.

_____ 9. At one time the practice of nursing was so casual that patients, prison inmates, and women hired off the street were allowed to serve as nurses.

_____ 10. Parsons's analysis of the sick role has focused on the contribution patients make to the treatment process.

## Multiple-choice test

_____ 1. Which of the following statements is true about the relationship between science and Protestantism in the seventeenth century?
   a. Protestants violently opposed science.
   b. English Protestants supported science, but American Protestants did not.
   c. All early Protestants endorsed the development of science.
   d. In both England and America, Protestants backed science.

_____ 2. After World War II, a major impetus to government-sponsored research was the national government's interest in:
   a. nuclear weapons and nuclear energy.
   b. soil conservation.
   c. the development of synthetic chemicals.
   d. a greater range of cheap, high-quality consumer products.

_____ 3. Scientists' reluctance to accept creationism in the face of archeological evidence supporting the occurrence of evolution in human beings and other animals illustrates which scientific norm?
   a. universalism
   b. communism
   c. organized skepticism
   d. disinterestedness

_____ 4. Which condition does NOT support controversial research?
   a. primacy of the research goal
   b. disinterestedness

      c. governmental support

      d. a policy of secrecy

_____ 5. Illness is:

      a. a condition of biological nonhealth.

      b. an individual's sense that he or she has been affected by disease.

      c. a social status in which an individual is treated as unhealthy.

      d. not effectively defined by sociologists.

_____ 6. Which statement is true?

      a. Younger people are more likely than the old to have developed immunities to illness.

      b. During the first year of life, there is a low death rate.

      c. Acute illnesses occur primarily because of the degeneration of bodily tissues.

      d. The higher the income level, the lower the rate of disease.

_____ 7. In the United States:

      a. the cost of health care decreased in the past decade.

      b. doctors' fees are the principal reason why health care costs are high.

      c. there is the lowest infant mortality rate in the world.

      d. the poor, ethnic minorities, and rural people are often deprived of effective medical care.

_____ 8. Peer review:

      a. is encouraged by some doctors, including a past president of the A.M.A.

      b. is opposed by all modern American physicians.

      c. is supported by all modern American physicians.

      d. is now effectively organized in twenty-five states.

_____ 9. Which statement is true of nurses?

      a. Their career enjoys high status.

      b. The majority of all active health-care professionals are RN's.

      c. Increased salary and promotions are most readily received by nurses working directly with patients.

      d. For women, nursing is a career without vulnerability to antifeminist bias.

_____ 10. The doctor–patient relationship analyzed by Szasz and Hollender that is best for the management of chronic diseases like diabetes and hypertension is:

      a. mutual participation.

      b. guidance–cooperation.

      c. activity–passivity.

      d. Parsons's perception of the sick role.

## Essay test

1. Define science. Discuss the conditions that encouraged the development of science in seventeenth-century England.
2. Why has the United States had such enormous growth in the scientific area during the twentieth century?
3. List and define Merton's four scientific norms. Summarize Mitroff's criticism of Merton's scheme.
4. What conditions encourage the continuance of controversial research? Use DNA and nuclear-weapons research to illustrate the different points made.
5. Define disease, illness, and sickness and summarize males' and females' disease and death patterns.
6. Evaluate American health care, focusing on major problems in the system.
7. Discuss doctors' relations with colleagues and include a summary of the problems involved in peer review.

**4**

8. List and analyze three status problems nurses must face.
9. Summarize the three types of doctor–patient relationships analyzed by Szasz and Hollender. Then discuss in detail two special features of the patient–doctor relationship.

## Suggested Readings

Arditti, Rita, Pat Brennan, and Steve Cavrak (eds.). 1980. *Science and Liberation.* Boston: South End Press. A set of twenty-five articles analyzing significant problems that science and scientists help create and discussing areas in which a more liberated, humane science can develop.

Ben-David, Joseph. 1971. *The Scientist's Role in Society.* Englewood Cliffs, NJ: Prentice-Hall. A concise text on the sociology of science. The book is particularly effective in analyzing the developing role of science in societies from ancient to modern times.

Coe, Rodney M. 1978. *Sociology of Medicine.* New York: McGraw-Hill. Second edition. A nicely written, comprehensive text on the sociology of medicine. Though covering a large, often complicated subject, the book is interesting and easy to read. The author has a flair for clear, thought-provoking sociological conceptualization.

Feuer, Lewis S. 1982. *Einstein and the Generations of Science.* New Brunswick, NJ: Transaction Books. Second edition. An analysis of how the social context in which Einstein and some of his contemporary scientists lived helped determine the substance of their work.

Hingson, Ralph, et al. 1981. *In Sickness and in Health.* St. Louis: C. V. Mosby. A text covering the major issues in medical sociology. Perhaps the most notable contribution is a set of six chapters examining the sequence of major steps that must be taken by patients seeking medical care.

Mechanic, David (ed.). 1983. *Handbook of Health, Health Care, and the Health Professions.* New York: The Free Press. A fine general source for anyone seeking information about disease, health, and the provision of health care in our society.

Merton, Robert K. 1973. *The Sociology of Science.* Chicago: University of Chicago Press. A series of twenty-two scholarly essays by the most prominent investigator of the sociology of science. The papers are divided into five chapters that address the sociology of knowledge, the sociology of scientific knowledge, the normative structure of science, the reward system of science, and the processes of evaluation of science.

Nelkin, Dorothy. 1984. *Science as Intellectual Property: Who Controls Scientific Research?* New York: Macmillan. A thoughtful discussion analyzing troubling issues, including those suggested in this chapter's section on controversial research.

Sidel, Victor W., and Ruth Sidel (eds.). 1984. *Reforming Medicine: Lessons of the Last Quarter Century.* New York: Pantheon. A set of ten interesting essays examining such recent health-care reforms as Medicare and Medicaid, federal funding of community health-care centers, and training programs for physician's assistants and nurse practitioners.

Starr, Paul. 1982. *The Social Transformation of American Medicine.* New York: Basic. A Pulitizer-prize-winning sociological analysis of how American medical practice has become increasingly subjected to corporate control.

## Student Projects

1. We now have scientifically based technologies for both saving lives and artificially prolonging life. We can also alter the production of life through sperm banks, artificial transplants, and embryo transplants. Join with several other members of the class in a "brainstorming" session to develop a list of life–death technologies. Then produce for each technology a set of moral ques-

tions that the members of our society must face in evaluating these technologies and ultimately deciding whether to accept them or reject them.

2. For a week watch a soap opera that at least in part takes place in a medical setting. Keep notes on the interaction patterns of doctors–doctors, doctors–nurses, nurses–nurses, doctors–patients, and nurses–patients. Do the patterns you observed seem consistent with information about these two groups' activities presented in this chapter? If not, what are the primary inconsistencies?

## Answers to Test Questions

### True–false test

| | | | | |
|---|---|---|---|---|
| 1. t | 3. t | 5. f | 7. t | 9. t |
| 2. f | 4. f | 6. t | 8. f | 10. f |

### Multiple-choice test

| | | | | |
|---|---|---|---|---|
| 1. d | 3. c | 5. b | 7. d | 9. b |
| 2. a | 4. b | 6. d | 8. a | 10. a |

# PART FIVE

## The Rapidly Changing World

# 16
# URBANIZATION, POPULATION GROWTH, AND ENVIRONMENTAL PROBLEMS

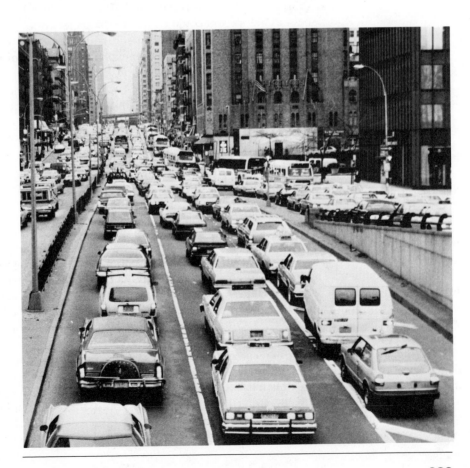

Miners, drillers, and construction workers from across the country streamed into Green River, the modern equivalent of a frontier boom town. " 'This used to be a sleepy little town with nothing but trains coming through,' observe[d] Ann Strand, a state representative for the surrounding Sweetwater County" (*U.S. News and World Report,* 1981: 77).

Trona—a mineral that can be refined into baking soda or used in manufacturing glass, soaps, and a number of other products—has been in abundant supply in Green River, Wyoming.

Between 1970 and 1980, the population shot up from 4000 to almost 13,000 residents. Expansion produced mixed results. Some local people prospered. One car dealer reported a tenfold increase in sales, and her staff jumped from three to twenty-four. Young men from the area suddenly had a new source of employment, making $25,000 a year as miners.

The boom, however, also brought serious problems. One difficulty was a drastic increase in crime. During the 1970s the police force expanded from six to twenty-eight. "The unlocked door is a thing of the past," the former police commissioner said unhappily. "People now line up for safe-deposit boxes."

The town leaders were unprepared for the boom. As one official indicated, "Growth was not mismanaged—it was nonmanaged." A serious housing shortage developed. Clusters of tents and unplanned mobile-home parks sprang up around the city. The trona-processing companies had to construct housing for their employees, but they did not build enough to eliminate the shortage. In 1981 the mayor said, "If we had 500 houses on the market, they'd be sold before you could complete the paperwork."

Longtime residents complained that the new arrivals disrupted their once peaceful life-style. One old-timer explained, "Our favorite fishing areas are full of strangers" (*U.S. News and World Report,* 1981: 77).

Many people came to Green River because of the chance to make a lot of money. The rapid population growth helped produce a disorganized, "nonmanaged" city and, most likely, such environmental problems as air and water pollution and waste-disposal hazards. The Green River experience might be unusual, but the process that has occurred there—the interdependence of cities, population, and the environment—is not.

**Human ecology,** the study of human beings' relationship with the environment, concerns itself with the interdependence of cities, population, and the environment. Human populations build cities and live in them. These cities are located in the natural environment, which develops pollution problems because of human beings' activities within it.

You might not have been especially aware that cities, population, and the environment are interdependent, but certainly you are aware of their independent existence. Many of you live in cities, and those who do not probably visit them frequently. How do you feel about the city you know best? Do you like it, hate it, or have mixed feelings?

Do you feel safe in it all the time, or do your feelings vary with where you are and when you are there? What about population problems? Certainly our society does not have the devastating population problems of many developing nations, but you still can find yourself adversely affected by the situation in the United States. Perhaps you have faced stiff competition for jobs from your age peers, and most likely you will face such a situation in the future. Consider the environmental issue. Twenty years ago most Americans paid little attention to environmental pollution, but now it is a "hot" topic. It should not be difficult to see how you are directly affected. Perhaps there is a river, pond, or bay that was a good place to swim or fish forty years ago but now emits an odor that causes you to hold your breath as you drive by.

This chapter examines three interrelated issues. The next section considers the development of cities. Then the focus shifts to the problem of population growth. The final topic is environmental destruction.

# Urbanization

Let us start with a pair of definitions. A **city** is a large, densely settled concentration of people permanently located within a relatively confined geographical area where nonagricultural occupations are pursued. **Urbanization** is the process by which a city forms and develops.

The earliest cities appeared about 5500 years ago, first along rivers in Mesopotamia (modern-day Iraq) and later in the Nile, Indus, and Yellow River Valleys. The growth of cities was slow until the Industrial Revolution was underway. By 1850 only 2 percent of the world population lived in cities of 100,000 people or more. Currently about 25 percent of people live in such cities, and by the year 2000 about 40 percent of the population will reside in cities of that size. Consequently, from a world perspective, we must recognize that cities are becoming the homes of an increasing percentage of people.

In this section we examine the development of cities, with special attention to the growth of cities in the United States. Then we consider some of the problems and prospects of urban living.

## The Development of Cities

Why was the first city built? Was it because some Mesopotamian leader awoke one morning propelled by a vision that he wanted to transform into reality? More than a mere vision was necessary for the building of the first city.

Early cities developed because three conditions were simultaneously favorable. First, there had to be an environment encouraging a large concentration of people—in particular, a climate and soil supporting an abundant growth of crops, an adequate supply of fresh water, and a location along a trade route, such as a river or a road, favoring contact between people of different cultures. Second, advances in technology were essential: the development and refinement of animal hus-

bandry, irrigation works, metallurgy, the wheel, and especially the domestication of grains. These innovations freed a few members of the populace from the everyday tasks of producing food, clothes, and shelter and permitted them to govern the cities. Finally a well-developed social organization was required. Techniques for the production and distribution of goods had to be developed, and an integration and coordination of the different occupational groups was necessary. An elite group developed to direct these tasks.

Once preindustrial cities evolved, they generally had certain characteristics. As Table 16.1 indi-

**Table 16.1**
**Estimated Populations and Areas of Selected Medieval Cities**

| CITY | DATE | POPULATION | LAND AREA, ACRES |
|------|------|-----------|------------------|
| Venice | 1363 | 77,000 | 810 |
| Paris | 1192 | 59,200 | 945 |
| Florence | 1381 | 54,747 | 268 |
| Milan | 1300 | 52,000 | 415 |
| Genoa | 1500 | 37,788 | 732 |
| Rome | 1198 | 35,000 | 3,450 |
| London | 1377 | 34,971 | 720 |
| Bologna | 1371 | 32,000 | 507 |
| Barcelona | 1359 | 27,056 | 650 |
| Naples | 1278 | 22,000 | 300 |
| Hamburg | 1250 | 22,000 | 510 |
| Brussels | 1496 | 19,058 | 650 |
| Pisa | 1228 | 13,000 | 285 |
| Frankfort | 1410 | 9,844 | 320 |
| Amsterdam | 1470 | 7,476 | 195 |
| Zurich | 1357 | 7,399 | 175 |
| Berlin | 1450 | 6,000 | 218 |
| Geneva | 1404 | 4,204 | 75 |
| Vienna | 1391 | 3,836 | 90 |
| Leipzig | 1474 | 2,076 | 105 |

Source: J.C. Russell. *Late Ancient and Medieval Population.* American Philosophical Society. 1958, pp. 60–62.

*In ancient Athens the center of the city was the Acropolis, a fortified hill containing famous architectual works.*

cates, populations of these cities were small, with some containing no more than 5000 or 10,000 people. In contrast with modern cities, these early settlements lacked the transportation and storage capacities necessary for maintaining large concentrations of people. Another quality of these cities was that the city center served as the focus of government and religious activity as well as the location for elite housing, with lower-status residents pushed toward the outskirts. Thus the privileged people managed to avoid difficult and time-consuming commuting, which had to be accomplished on foot, by boat, on horseback, or in a carriage. In addition, preindustrial cities had a highly restrictive social-class system in which a small privileged group controlled power, wealth, religion, and education, basing their claims to authority on appeal to tradition and religious absolutes. Furthermore, within these early cities, economic growth was slow because of the ruling group's conservative commercial policies, the exclusiveness of the guilds (an early form of unions), the lack of standardized

prices, currency, and measures, and few opportunities for credit and capital development.

In spite of their modest accomplishments, these early cities served a couple of important functions. First, they were founded at key locations along trade routes and so were able to control the most important commerce of their societies. In addition, preindustrial cities were important because they were the places where the elite lived and worked. The elite chose the cities because they could more readily protect themselves in urban areas, which tended to be walled enclosures, than in the open countryside. Another reason members of the elite resided in cities was that, concentrated in the central districts, they could efficiently work together to establish political, economic, and religious policies (Schwab, 1982: 108–109; Sjoberg, 1960: 27–31, 323–328.)

When people took up residence in cities, their outlook and behavior started to change. In 1887 Ferdinand Tönnies wrote a book in which he discussed how urbanized, industrialized living altered people's life-styles. Tönnies suggested that in small, homogeneous, preindustrial communities people generally spend their lives in the same locale. The social structure tends to be simple but rigid. People's position at birth determines where they belong, and few, if any, challenge the situation. Citizens strongly support the moral code and local conventions. In such simple communities, the basic social unit is the family, and an individual's life assumes meaning only in the context of family activity. The community itself, in fact, resembles a large family. Social relationships are personal and supportive. Privacy and individualism are minimal.

In modern urban society, Tönnies contended, self-interest prevails, with the accumulation of property becoming more important than personal ties. The use of a legal device—the contract—becomes the chief means to insure that both parties will fulfill an agreement. The family and the church gradually lose their influence. Individuals are freer to think and act as they please, but the danger exists that they will become isolated and alienated, feeling that life is meaningless and that they are powerless to do anything about it (Tönnies, 1957).

Tönnies's ideas certainly apply to American society. As the United States has urbanized, people's outlooks and social relationships have changed.

## The Growth of American Cities

It seems useful to divide the history of American cities into four eras: the colonial period, the period of westward expansion, the period of metropolitan growth, and the modern period (Spates and Macionis, 1982: Chapter 7). Figure 16.1 shows that over time the United States has become increasingly urbanized.

### COLONIAL PERIOD

During the colonial era, most American cities were small both in physical size and in population. None of the North American urban settlements had as many as 10,000 inhabitants until the eighteenth century, and at the time of the Revolutionary War, Philadelphia, the largest American city, had only 40,000 people. These cities were not only small, but they also had little ethnic and religious diversity; the residents were primarily of northern European ancestry and Protestant. People shared a common life-style and outlook on life, with exten-

**Figure 16.1**
**180 Years of American Urban Growth**

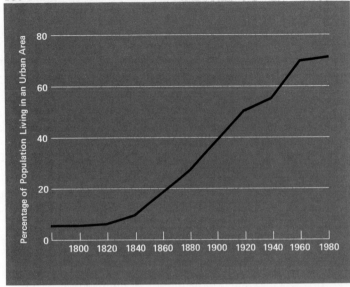

*According to the Bureau of the Census, people live in an urban area if the place is incorporated and contains 2,500 residents or more. By this definition the urban population of the country has been steadily increasing since 1800. (Source: U.S. Bureau of the Census. Current Population Report, Population Characteristics, P–20, No. 374. Table 2–4.)*

sive contacts among neighbors and regular church attendance representing widely accepted patterns.

In spite of the fact that colonial cities seemed to be nothing more than small, intimate villages, they were important trading centers, whose residents sought profit and supported growth. As time passed, American merchants began to resent British directives that they restrict themselves to exporting raw products to the mother country, and they began to compete with the British, establishing their own trade agreements with the West Indies and even with European countries.

### PERIOD OF WESTWARD EXPANSION

Between 1800 and 1880, American cities grew at a faster rate than at any time before or since. It is worth noting that among the fifty largest cities in the United States, only seven were incorporated before 1816. Thirty-nine were incorporated between 1816 and 1876, and only four have been incorporated since then. At the beginning of the nineteenth century, business leaders began to recognize the tremendous economic potential of the rich western lands and started to develop plans to link these new territories with eastern cities. Roads, canals, and later railroads provided the connections. By 1830 New York, Philadelphia, and Baltimore were the most prominent coastal cities, primarily because of their control over commercial relations with the Ohio Valley.

In the course of the nineteenth century, industrialization was also expanding. By the 1830s, in the vicinity of Boston, for example, a proliferation of factory towns contained textile mills, paper mills, shoe factories, and iron foundries.

### PERIOD OF METROPOLITAN GROWTH

Between 1880 and 1940, U.S. cities reached the third phase: the period of metropolitan growth. A **metropolis** is a territorial unit composed of a large central city and the surrounding cities and towns.

During this era cities grew in size — explosively. At the turn of the twentieth century, over fifty cities had populations of 100,000 people or more, with Chicago's growth the most impressive. At the time of its incorporation in 1833, Chicago had a population of 4100, which rose to 1 million in 1890 and then to over 2 million in 1910. Nationally, in the 100-year period from 1790 to 1890, the total population grew sixteenfold, but the urban population increased 139-fold.

Several inventions helped transform the appearance and the size of cities. Buildings containing iron and then steel made it possible to put up taller structures. In 1848 a five-story building with an iron frame was a newsworthy item; less than four decades later, in 1884, a ten-story structure in Chicago initiated the era of the urban skyscraper. The growth of tall buildings was assisted by another invention: the elevator, developed in the 1850s. During this phase of urban growth, cities not only moved upward, but they also pushed outward. New means of transportation made an important contribution here, the electric street trolley in particular. During the 1880s the trolley, which is still in use in Philadelphia, Boston, and New Orleans, helped initiate the use of rapid, cheap, and efficient mass transit between cities and their suburbs. Toward the end of the nineteenth century, real-estate developers quickly understood the implications of improved transportation, and they started to build housing tracts on the outskirts of cities. For instance, between 1870 and 1890, firms constructed over 23,000 new houses in the Boston suburbs.

As we have noted, the entire nineteenth century was a time of extremely rapid urban growth. Between 1880 and 1920, two factors appear to have been largely responsible for the accelerated population increase in cities. First, a movement of people from rural areas into the cities occurred. Between 1880 and 1890, almost 40 percent of the country's more than 25,000 townships actually lost population. Remarkably, thousands of farms were simply abandoned as machinery made handpowered labor obsolete and encouraged people to seek

*Street trolleys were an early response to the need for mass transit in increasingly populated cities.*

more lucrative jobs in the cities. Second, immigration was also an important factor in urban growth. By 1890 New York City had half as many Italians as Naples, as many Germans as Hamburg, twice as many Irish as Dublin, and two-and-a-half the number of Jews as Warsaw. Between just 1901 and 1910, over 9 million immigrants came to the United States. The recent arrivals were packed into slums and offered the lowest-paying, most menial jobs. At the turn of the century, influential native-born Americans, primarily white Anglo-Saxon Protestants (WASPS), tended to blame the immigrants, many of whom were Catholics or Jews, for the sins of the city—slum housing, inferior health conditions, and crime, in particular. It was time, most of these powerful citizens agreed, to cut off immigration. Therefore, in 1924, Congress established a quota system that severely restricted the number of immigrants from the southern and eastern European countries, that had made the heaviest numerical contributions in the late nineteenth and early twentieth centuries.

But this curtailment caused new problems. At that time industrial concerns needed a reliable source of cheap labor, which until then recent immigrants had supplied. Now industrialists started to recruit from within the country, and American cities received a new stream of immigrants, many of them southern blacks. Between 1920 and 1929, over 600,000 blacks migrated to northern cities from the South, and the groundwork for the racial tension that has characterized many American cities in recent years was established. As early as 1925, the rapid influx of blacks created an acute housing shortage and such strong tensions that in Detroit riots broke out.

Toward the end of this period in the history of American cities, another important event occurred. The stock market crash of 1929 threw the country into financial chaos, and most cities were forced to face difficult economic times. In 1932 large numbers of urban residents voted for Franklin Roosevelt in the hope that he could help their cities. The following year the mayors of fifty cities met in Washington, D.C. and founded the U.S. Conference of Mayors, and the members of this organization started to lobby the Roosevelt administration on behalf of the cities. They were very successful. The National Industrial Recovery Act appropriated $3.3 billion for important public works and housing operations, and later bills supplied billions more federal funding for housing, highway construction, and other projects that aided the cities. This policy, whereby cities depend on the federal government for extensive financial assistance, continued until the early 1980s when federal aid to cities was sharply cut.

### THE MODERN PERIOD

From 1940 to the present, two broad trends have dominated U.S. cities: decentralization and the growth of urban centers in the sunbelt. Decentralization means moving out of cities, often into suburbs. A **suburb** is a politically independent municipality that develops next to or in the vicinity of a central city.

Why has the suburban movement occurred? Three reasons stand out. First, by about 1950, an increasing number of businesses, especially manufacturing concerns, were moving away from central city areas. Some assembly-line procedures needed more space than was readily available in the old central business districts. Growing crime rates, high taxes, and traffic congestion were other factors promoting a proliferation of "industrial parks" on the fringe of cities. As factories moved to the suburbs, workers often followed.

Second, technology has played an important part in the growth of suburbs. During the twentieth century, the use of electric power became widespread. Unlike its predecessor, steam power, electricity can be transmitted for long distances, thereby making it possible for both industries and residences to disperse throughout a large area. Automobiles and trucks have had a similar effect, permitting far greater flexibility in movement and location than rail transportation, which had a dominant position during the latter half of the nineteenth and early twentieth centuries.

A third reason for suburban growth is that some people found city living distasteful. For example, at the end of World War II, millions of servicemen returned home to discover various conditions in their residential neighborhoods that they did not like—in particular, extensive physical deterioration because of neglected urban-repair projects during the war years and in some cases (for whites) the proximity of black and other minority-group families. Many veterans took advantage of low-interest loans supplied by the Federal Housing Authority and bought homes outside the center of the city or in the suburbs.

**406**    Looking back, we can easily see how this government policy contributed to urban deterioration. The policy encouraged white, middle-class people to leave cities, and their departure produced a substantial loss of tax revenue. This loss of revenue, in turn, meant the decline of local facilities and services. As police and fire protection, schools, and other facilities and services became more impoverished, people who could afford to leave cities often hastened to do so, further eroding the tax base. In the last several decades, many suburbs have also deteriorated—for instance, some which contain large numbers of elderly citizens. One investigation concluded that since about 1960, the suburban population has been aging more rapidly than the population overall and that elderly suburban citizens tend to be concentrated in denser, poorer suburbs (Fitzpatrick and Logan, 1985). (Figure 16.2 shows Americans' distribution in cities, suburbs, and rural areas.)

In recent years a dramatic urban change has been the growth of the sunbelt cities. During the late 1970s and early 1980s, a shift of population and affluence from the industrial heartland of the Northeast to the fast-growing cities in southern districts has occurred. The population of the fifteen sunbelt states has grown from 61 million in 1970 (about a third of the nation's population) to 85 million in 1976 (nearly 40 percent of the total) and will expand to a projected 112 million inhabitants, representing 43 percent of the population, in the year 2000. We might readily wonder why.

**Figure 16.2**
**Where Americans Live: 1980**

*These figures demonstrate that Americans of various ethnic heritages tend to live in certain areas. Whites are overrepresented in the suburbs, while blacks as well as other less affluent ethnic groups are disproportionaltely located in cities. (Source: U.S. Bureau of the Census. Current Population Reports, Population Characteristics, P–20, No. 374, Table 3–6.)*

The sunbelt cities have had a series of advantages over the historically prominent northern cities. In many cases these southern and southwestern urban centers have industrialized only in recent years, and so they have been able to build modern, efficient plants. In addition, the recent development of the sunbelt cities has meant that their superhighways most efficiently promote access to industrial parks. Furthermore, because their affluence has meant that they have not been pressed for cash, these new cities have been able to offer significant tax incentives to business executives who might want to relocate. Other advantages of the sunbelt cities have included modern services, low energy costs, and limited unionization, which means lower labor costs. The prominent northeastern cities have not fared well in comparison. They contain aging, outmoded plants, superhighways providing limited access to industrial areas, few incentives to entice new business, deteriorating services, high energy costs, and extensive unionization. All in all, it is hardly surprising that businesses have been leaving the North by the thousands and heading for the cities of the South and the Southwest.

On the other hand, a cloudy side to life in the sunbelt has developed. Rapid expansion has led to a massive, disorganized urban pattern, rising air pollution, and an overuse of the water and sewage systems. The influx of more than 10 million illegal aliens from Mexico and a number of other Latin American countries has heightened the problems. In many cases the immigrants are uneducated and unable to speak English, and those who have been able to find employment have taken the lowest-paying, most menial jobs. In a number of southwestern cities, the immigrants' residential areas have begun to resemble the poverty-stricken slums of third-world countries (Palen, 1981: Chapter 3; Spates and Macionis, 1982: Chapter 7). Most recently in the middle 1980s, the loss of affluence in the oil industry has had a negative impact on many sunbelt cities, which have started to suffer the economic woes long experienced in other parts of the country.

We have now briefly examined the history of American urban development, and in the course of this review, we have seen that a number of problems exist. In the following discussion, we focus on some of these problems and on possible solutions to them.

## American Cities: Problems and Prospects

Daniel Boone, the frontiersman, apparently felt that the neighborhood was getting crowded when he could see the smoke from the nearest cabin. Mr. Boone would have had serious difficulty adjusting to modern, urbanized existence.

The massive movement of population and manufacturing from central cities to fringe areas has created "urban sprawl," where one metropolitan area frequently merges with the next. A **megalopolis** is a string of closely bound metropolitan areas (Gottman, 1961). The largest American megalopolis runs from southern New Hampshire to Prince William County, Virginia. It contains part or all of ten states and the cities of Boston, New York, Philadelphia, Baltimore, and Washington, D.C. The population of "Bos Wash" exceeds 44 million people, representing about one fifth of the American population. Megalopolitan growth is presently most rapid in the sunbelt areas: the Southwest, Florida, and southern California.

As metropolitan areas expand and eventually form a megalopolis, serious urban problems often develop.

### Urban Deterioration

Governmental proliferation, the influence of powerful political and economic interests, and financial limitations contribute significantly to the urban crisis.

#### GOVERNMENTAL PROLIFERATION

At present there are about 80,000 governmental units in the United States, averaging nearly 1600 per state. This proliferation of governments makes it extraordinarily difficult to plan rationally. For instance, greater St. Louis is a typically "government-crowded" metropolis, where the participants are the federal government, two states, seven counties, 194 municipalities, and 615 special districts (concerned with such issues as water and sewage). Given such a great number of organizations, it should be clear that coordinated policies will be difficult to achieve (Schwab, 1982).

#### POWERFUL POLITICAL AND ECONOMIC INTERESTS

Lewis Mumford (1971), a well-known city planner, has claimed that throughout human history technological advances have generally been under the control of powerful economic and political groups whose primary goal has been to expand their own wealth and power. Therefore in modern cities, Mumford contended, business people and politicians have cooperated to expand the number of highway miles, automobiles, and retail stores within their communities. As a result their own interests benefit, but the quality of city living for average inhabitants steadily deteriorates.

In the past American cities had "old machines" —corrupt political organizations that ran cities by providing services and favors in exchange for citizens' political support. Modern cities are often controlled by "new machines," such as the departments of health, fire, police, sanitation, water, and public works. These organizations are less corrupt than the old machines, but they can be equally irresponsible. They all help shape important public policies, but the leadership often refuses to accept the control of higher authorities (Lowi, 1981). After decades on the job, some agency heads are able to consolidate considerable power for themselves. Robert Moses, the chief city planner in New York City for over thirty years, was a prominent case in point. Moses controlled the construction and servicing of that city's highway systems, bridges, parks, public housing, and other public works.

#### FINANCIAL LIMITATIONS

American cities have been caught in a powerful financial squeeze. In the early 1980s, the federal government eliminated a range of social and public-works programs that benefit cities. At the same time, strict, local tax-cut measures were legislated in many states and cities. In 1982, in Massachusetts, for example, only .5 percent of the state budget was allotted for maintenance and repair—a policy that one expert on the state's budget called "pennywise and pothole foolish" (Beck, 1982: 12).

It has become impossible for cities to keep up with the deterioration of their public works: roads, bridges, government buildings, sewers, and mass-transit systems. At the current rate of repairs in New York City, for example, it would take 200 years to fix deteriorating streets and water mains and 300 years to replace the sewers (Palen, 1981: 261).

Politics compounds the financial problems. Elected officials seem to believe that they can convince their supporters that they are "doing something'' in Washington if a new office building, dam, or highway is built in the district. The repair of old facilities would often be more beneficial for the local citizens, but such projects lack political appeal. As an official of the Housing and Urban Development Department commented, "Have you ever seen a politician presiding over a ribbon-cutting for an old sewer line that was repaired?" (Beck, 1982: 13).

In the previous pages, it has been apparent that the problems of modern cities often have a profound, intimate impact on urban dwellers' lives. Let us continue to examine that idea.

## The Urban Existence: Is Revitalization Possible?

In March 1983 a young mother of two children entered a bar in New Bedford, Massachusetts. Shortly after the woman arrived, a man ripped off her clothes, threw her on the floor, and raped her. Then the woman was carried to a pool table where she was repeatedly raped by four men for over an hour while the other people in the bar watched. Eventually the woman's screams for help were heard by the occupants of a passing van who called the police, and the woman was rescued. "This woman was treated like a piece of meat," said Debra Robbin, a staff member at a local woman's center (*Newsweek*, 1983: 25). Is this typical behavior in modern cities? In particular, are urban Americans so devoid of a sense of community that they will simply stand by while another citizen is raped or murdered? Sociological analysis has addressed the issue of the extent to which modern cities promote a sense of community.

George Simmel (1950) examined the effect of city living on people's personalities. He observed that each individual encounters a great many people and experiences every day. Cities provide so much stimulation that serious mental disturbance can result. To protect themselves from overstimulation, urban residents must remain psychologically distant from most people. Otherwise they will be unable to cope with the pressures of daily living. Simmel wrote, "As a result of this reserve we frequently do not even know by sight those who have been our neighbors for years. And it is this reserve which in the eyes of the small-town people makes us appear to be cold and heartless" (Simmel, 1950: 415).

Louis Wirth (1938) shared Simmel's outlook on the city. Wirth believed that three factors—the size of cities, their densely populated neighborhoods, and continuous contact with strangers—produce deteriorating interpersonal relations in cities. The social significance of the family declines, neighborhood interaction disappears, and specialized outside agencies, such as the police, health agencies, and welfare organizations, assume tasks once handled by the family or community.

Sociologists like Simmel and Wirth have recognized that the quality of urban life is often low. What are measures that might offer improvement?

### EMPHASIS ON AN ACTIVE NEIGHBORHOOD LIFE

Recent research has concluded that metropolitan residents have definite preferences about their neighborhoods: They tend to prefer them small rather than large and away from the inner city instead of close to it (Dahmann, 1985).

Other factors also affect the quality of neighborhood life. Jane Jacobs, a well-known city planner, has contended that the best way to ensure neighborhood vitality is to combine a variety of land-use patterns in a given area. If neighborhoods contain a mixture of residences, small stores, schools, restaurants, bars, theaters, and parks, then there will be people on the streets from early morning until fairly late at night. Jacobs argued that a busy street life helps create a stimulating neighborhood and also makes it a relatively safe place, as the following account suggests.

One day Jane Jacobs was watching an incident from her second-floor window. A struggle was going on between a little girl of eight or nine years and a man. The man was alternately trying to coax the girl to come with him and then ignoring her. The girl had made herself rigid against the wall of a building. She was determined not to move.

As Jacobs watched from her window and tried to decide whether or not to intervene, she saw that intervention would not be necessary. From the butcher shop, the owner came out with her arms folded and a determined look on her face. The man who ran the delicatessen across the street also emerged. Two men from the bar next to the butcher shop moved to the doorway and waited. On her own side of the street, Jane Jacobs saw that the locksmith, the fruitman, and the laundry owner had all come out of their shops and were standing on the street. Other heads had appeared at windows. The man and the little girl were surrounded. Jacobs wrote, "Nobody was going to allow a little girl to be dragged off, even if nobody knew who she was. I am sorry—sorry purely for dramatic purposes—to have to report that the little girl turned out to be the man's daughter" (Jacobs, 1961: 39).

The protection offered by this city community turned out to be unnecessary. Nonetheless, the incident offered evidence that a vital city neighborhood will help protect people, even strangers.

Neighborhood organizations are a proven means of helping to build strong neighborhoods, and the following Contemporary Issue examines this topic.

---

**CONTEMPORARY ISSUE**

## *Neighborhood Organizations: What Factors Can Make These Structures Active?*

It is the kind of stuff from which American heroic images are created: The people in a local neighborhood or community (the little guys) fight for what they believe to be their undeniable rights against the local political structure or a giant corporation (the big guys). Television news, magazine and newspaper articles, and films sometimes portray this situation. But why are some of these organizations much more active and successful than others? The popular media are not likely to delve into such a topic. Let us consider some of the factors determining active, successful neighborhood organizations.

First, there is the issue of participants' characteristics. Abraham Wandersman and his colleagues studied neighborhood organizations in Nashville. They concluded that people who join such groups are more likely to think highly of their own skills, to believe that their participation can produce change, to place a higher value on their local community, and to have a greater sense of citizen duty than those who do not join. Sociologist Pamela Oliver examined neighborhood organizations in Detroit and found that active members were better educated and, curiously, more pessimistic about their neighbors' willingness to make an active contribution than inactive members. On the last point, Oliver suggested that active participants are people who are convinced that if they do not join and participate actively in these structures, then nobody will; pessimism, in short, seems to encourage involvement.

Like active and inactive individuals, active and inactive neighborhood organizations differ in characteristics. Compared to inactive neighborhood organizations, those which are active tend to have leaders who are more experienced in organizational activity, are more likely to involve their members in the decision-making process, and are more capable of establishing high levels of cohesion and stability within the group. I spent over two years studying the development of neighborhood organizations. It was not difficult to separate those with leaders who had effective organizational skills from those without such leaders. Some relevant questions that will help draw the distinction: Does the leader enter meetings with a well-organized agenda? Does he or she have sufficient respect from members to hold their attention and generate enthusiasm? Do members come to the meetings regularly? What, if any, organizational business is completed between meetings?

I also learned that active neighborhood organizations are more effective at pursuing tactics designed to produce physical and social improvements in the neighborhood area. In what often appears as a David versus Goliath contest, the members of local neighborhood groups can obtain a tremendous morale boost—and with it increased longevity for their organization—if the members know what measures to take to effectively confront the local power structure. Consider the following example.

In an upstate New York city, I was present the day after the leaders of city government agreed to the demands made by three local black-power leaders to tear down some old buildings that were considered dangerous temptations to children playing in the area. Local people spoke admiringly of the way the neighborhood organization leaders had behaved in this situation.

MRS. ALBRIGHT: I think those guys handled themselves perfectly.

MRS. ROCHESTER: Right!

MRS. ALBRIGHT: The politicians won't do anything, because you who are reasonable go down to City Hall and request something. When the three guys from the neighborhood group went down to the mayor's office, they made it clear that if they didn't get what they wanted, they were going to torch those buildings.

MRS. RICHETTE: At City Hall they must have freaked out!

MRS. ALBRIGHT: The threat was there. Certainly appearances helped get their point across. Those politicians took a look at Leroy's Afro, Carl's dashiki (African-style shirt) and beads, and . . .

MRS. ROCHESTER: and Marcus's scar-covered face . . .

MRS. ALBRIGHT: That's right! And then they started thinking of Detroit. (The worst riots of the 1960s occurred there in 1967.)

*(Doob, 1970: 93–94).*

Finally active neighborhood organizations are more capable of accomplishing their goals, particularly their initial ones, than inactive groups. Saul Alinsky, a prominent organizer of community groups, believed that developing active neighborhood organizations is much like training a prize fighter — that like the fighter, the neighborhood organization must be brought along slowly with progressively tougher opponents. Alinsky felt that in the beginning it is often helpful if those in charge set up what he called "a cinch fight," where the accomplishment of the goal is a certainty and thus assures that members' morale can be boosted for future, more difficult tasks. As an example Alinsky described a situation where he organized a demoralized neighborhood in Chicago to obtain infant welfare services. He knew that the services would be supplied the moment they were sought, but he did not tell the members. He wanted their apparent victory to serve as momentum for pursuing more difficult goals. Some people might say that Alinsky was deceptive, even dishonest. Most likely his reply would have been that in the harsh reality of city politics, one must often use harsh methods to accomplish neighborhood organizations' goals.

Sources: Saul D. Alinsky. *Rules for Radicals.* New York: Vintage. 1971; Christopher Bates Doob. *How the War Was Lost.* Unpublished manuscript. 1970; Pamela Oliver. " 'If You Don't Do It, Nobody Else Will': Active and Token Contributors to Local Collective Action." *American Sociological Review.* Vol. 49. October 1984, pp. 601–610; John E. Prestby and Abraham Wandersman. "An Empirical Exploration of a Framework of Organizational Viability: Maintaining Block Organizations." *Journal of Applied Behavioral Science.* Vol. 21. 1985, pp. 287–305; Abraham Wandersman. "Getting Together and Getting Things Done." *Psychology Today.* Vol. 19. November 1985, pp. 64–65+.

### EXPERIMENTS WITH METROPOLITAN SOLUTIONS

As we have noted, a metropolis is composed of a central city and its surrounding cities and towns. The San Francisco Bay area, for instance, has eight counties, seventy-three cities, and eighty planning commissions. Small, local units could often efficiently promote their interests in the past. Today, however, such issues as mass transit, pollution control, civil defense, and water supply defy local solutions.

Many local governments have informally adopted metropolitan solutions to some problems. A survey of 6000 cities and towns indicated that many have joint service agreements that involve either one government purchasing services from another or a collaboration on projects.

Toronto, Canada, has used a two-level approach to the problem of metropolitan government. The first level is a metropolitan or regional government responsible for the issues common to the entire urban area. The second level of government is local, controlling such issues as police work, education, housing codes, and parks and recreation. This two-level approach seems promising. A serious drawback to all metropolitan plans, however, is that in spite of the fact that many urban problems require regional solutions, city and town officials are often unwilling to accept any loss of "home rule" (Campbell and Dollenmayer, 1975; Zimmerman, 1975).

### EFFORTS TO BRING MIDDLE-CLASS PEOPLE BACK INTO CITIES, THEREBY BENEFITING THE AREAS ECONOMICALLY

This trend has become so widespread in recent years that a concept has developed to describe it. **Gentrification** is the move of middle- and upper-middle-class people to formerly deteriorated, inner-city neighborhoods. A recent study concluded that characteristics of cities encouraging gentrification include the existence of a substantial segment of affluent, young adults not interested in having children but wanting to be "where the action is," the presence of corporate wealth that can subsidize redevelopment projects, and real-estate groups that can execute such projects (London et al., 1986). Extensive conversion of apartments to condominiums has already occurred in many American cities. Middle-class people who purchase condominiums have the advantage of owning property that increases steadily in value as well as the tax breaks that go with that ownership. Gentrification has helped transform the deteriorating centers of many American cities, but few of the benefits have spilled over into low-income areas, where a large segment of urban citizens live (Ganz, 1985).

### INCREASED FEDERAL AND STATE ASSISTANCE

As we have noted, since the New Deal, the federal government has provided major financial help to cities. Many financially troubled cities could benefit significantly from federal and state grants.

The recovery plan used in New York City can serve as a useful model. The gist of such a plan is to offer aid in exchange for financial reorganization. In 1975 the nation's largest city faced the threat of bankruptcy. City officials initiated tight management, local investment, and sharp controls on municipal workers' salaries in exchange for federal and state financial assistance. In the middle of 1983, New York City had a substantial budget surplus, one of the few large American cities able to make such a claim. The New York City plan has been far from ideal—fiscal stability has been accompanied by a drastic cutback in local services—and yet this situation shows that if realistic financial reorganization accompanies federal and state aid, impressive fiscal improvement is possible (Alpern, 1981).

To be successful, however, such plans require federal economic support. During the years of the Reagan administration, the two-decade emphasis on substantial federal funding to combat serious urban problems, especially low-income residents' needs, was sharply reduced (Wolman, 1986; Wong and Peterson, 1986).

Poverty is a serious problem in American cities. One specialist on urban affairs noted that

> . . . the poor in cities have increased dramatically, the feminization of poverty has accelerated, the dropout rate in high schools for blacks and hispanics is about 75%, unemployment for black youth is over 50%, teen-age births have reached new highs, infant mortality has increased, and deindustrialization has reduced the number of jobs in large cities.
>
> *(Gittell, 1985: 19)*

*As this scene in Boston suggests, urban revitalization often involves not only the erection of new buildings but also the preservation of old ones.*

One means to halt the deterioration of American cities and the impoverishment of a growing proportion of residents would be a federally funded program ensuring a guaranteed income for all citizens (Gittell, 1985). Such a program would certainly not eliminate all city problems, but it would represent a healthy start.

# The Problem of Population Growth

The crowded, deteriorated sections of American cities illustrate that overpopulation exists in some places within U.S. society. The devastating population growth that many developing nations in Africa, Asia, and Latin America currently face, however, is a considerably more serious situation.

In the pages ahead, we consider the principal factors that affect population size. A **population** is all the people who live within a specified geographic area such as a nation, a region, or a city. **Demography** is the study of human populations. Demographers examine birth, death, and migration rates to understand population changes. This section introduces the basic concepts and theories in demography and then examines the overpopulation issue in the developing and developed nations.

## Basic Demographic Concepts and Theories

Rapid population growth is a new and frightening phenomenon. Since about 1750 the world population started to grow rapidly, and it has continued to do so. It took from the beginning of the Christian era to 1650 for the population to double, but with the current growth rate it will take only thirty-five years for the world's population to double to nearly 10 billion people. Why has this dramatic growth occurred? The central concept has been the death rate.

Before 1750 the primary reason for the low rate of population growth was the high death rate common in almost all societies. The most significant reason for this high death rate was a high infant-mortality rate. In a given year, as many as one half of all infants would die before the age of one. For both adults and children, disease and famine were the major causes of the high death rate. The single most devastating disease in human history has been the bubonic plague, also known as the Black Death. A conservative estimate is that during the fourteenth century, 40 percent of all Europeans died of the disease. While the bubonic plague was the most devastating disease, others were also very destructive during the same period. Typhus, malaria, tuberculosis, and smallpox were at the top of the list. Famine has also helped limit population growth. Through history Asian famines have been more serious than the European ones, primarily because of the less predictable climate and rainfall of that continent. For example, a severe famine occurred in China in 1877–1878. In the course of the devastation, between 9 and 13 million people died of hunger, violence, and disease. Death was so prevalent that bodies were put in mass graves, which sometimes contained as many as 10,000 corpses (Petersen, 1975).

In the nineteenth century, the death rate started to drop in industrial nations, and the population began to rise, first in Western and later in non-Western countries. If we start by understanding a number of demographic concepts, then we can examine theories and problems of population growth.

### The Factors in Population Growth

Demographers focus their attention on birth, death, migration, and growth rates as they attempt to predict population trends around the world.

#### BIRTH RATE

The **crude birth rate** is the number of births per 1000 persons in a society in a given year. This statistical measure is called "crude" because it does not provide specific information about the births. The crude birth rate, for instance, does not indicate the percentages of children born within different ethnic, racial, or class categories. The American crude birth rate of about 14 per thousand per year is scarcely a third the rate in such developing nations as Bangladesh, Biafra, or Zaire.

A crude birth rate gives an indication of the fertility of women in a given society. The **fertility** rate is the number of actual births per 1000 women between the ages of fifteen and forty-four. That thirty-year span is the approximate length of time during which women are capable of giving birth. One must distinguish fertility from fecundity, the biological potential for reproduction. No society has ever approached its reproductive potential.

### DEATH RATE

The **crude death rate** is the number of deaths per 1000 persons in a society in a given year. Once again, the designation "crude" means that the statistical measure provides no specific information, in this instance about death. It does not indicate, for instance, that in the United States the mortality rate (death rate for children during the first year) is 21 per 1000 black infants per year, nearly double the figure of 12 per 1000 white infants per year.

### MIGRATION RATE

**Migration** is the flow of people in and out of a particular territory (city, region, or country). The **in-migration rate** is the number of people per 1000 members of the population moving into an area in a given year, and the **out-migration rate** is the number of people per 1000 members of the population moving out of an area in a given year. The **net migration rate** is the difference between the in-migration rate and the out-migration rate.

For several reasons data on migration are less effective than data on birth and death rates. In the first place, an individual's birth and death are more easily measured, occurring only once, while migration can and often does take place many times during a lifetime. In addition, demographers started to study migration rates much more recently than birth and death rates. Thus less extensive data are available on migration.

Migration can have a significant influence on a nation's population. The United States is certainly a case in point. Between 1819 and 1955, over forty million people immigrated to this country, with the peak years early in the twentieth century. In six of the eleven years from 1905 to 1915, more than a million immigrants per year reached American shores. Although restrictive legislation sharply limited the number of people who could arrive legally after 1920, significant numbers of immigrants have kept coming to the United States, and in recent years estimates indicate that as many illegal as legal migrants have entered the country.

### GROWTH RATE

Immigration can significantly affect population growth, but birth and death tend to be the major influences. The **growth rate** is the crude birth rate minus the crude death rate. Colombia, for instance, has a crude birth rate of about 31 per 1000 people and a crude death rate of about 9 per 1000. Thus the crude growth rate is 22 per thousand or 2.2 percent growth per year. The American growth rate is much lower, about .7 percent per year (United Nations, *Demographic Yearbook, 1980.* Table 7).

A growth rate of 2.2 percent might seem relatively small at first glance, but the long-term result will be an enormous population increase. Consider, for instance, a nation of 10 million that increases 2.2 percent per year. After a year the population will be 10,220,000, and the following year it will total 10,444,840. Each year the population increases by an additional 2.2 percent, and as the population grows, that 2.2 percent represents a larger figure each year. In about thirty-two years, that population of 10 million will double.

**Doubling time** is the time span necessary for a population to double in size. A growth rate of 1 percent produces doubling in seventy years, a growth rate of 2 percent means twice the population in thirty-five years, and a 3.5 percent rate leads to doubling in only twenty years.

The frightening fact is that the developing nations of Africa, Asia, and Latin America currently have a growth rate of about 2.1 percent, which means an average doubling time of only thirty-three years. Starvation and malnutrition are already widespread in many of these countries, and such rapid population growth will only expand these tragic problems.

## Two Significant Demographic Theories

The two theories that we now discuss both consider the disastrous effects that overpopulation can produce.

### MALTHUSIAN THEORY

In 1798 Thomas Robert Malthus published the *First Essay on Population.* In this essay the author, a minister, emphasized that humanity was guilty of original sin and, as a result, was destined to suffer. According to Malthus, God had established two conditions that would operate simultaneously to make continuous suffering inevitable: first, an un-

**414** quenchable passion between the sexes ensuring rapid reproduction and second, a limited capacity to produce food. Malthus contended that population growth occurs at a geometric rate (2, 4, 8, 16, . . . ), whereas the food supply expands at a mere arithmetic rate (2, 3, 4, 5, . . . ). Malthus wrote, "A slight acquaintance with numbers will shew [show] the immensity of the first power in comparison to the second" (Malthus, 1798: 14).

He believed that over time the scarcity of food would become increasingly alarming. While conceding that war, famine, and disease would hold population partially in check, Malthus thought that the future for most of the world population was bleak: bare subsistence at a low level of material existence.

Malthus's first essay was an attack on the contemporary belief that large families among the poor are a blessing to be encouraged. The essay received extensive criticism, and five years later Malthus wrote a revision in which he emphasized that late marriage and fewer children could prevent a population disaster. Malthus advocated financial incentives as a means to restrict the number of children, rejecting birth control and abortion on religious grounds. The second essay was more popular in Malthus's day, but he is much better known for the earlier work.

Certainly Malthus's first essay has shortcomings. In the first place, he did not anticipate significant improvements in agriculture that have made it possible to increase food production more quickly

than he had expected. Second, the industrial societies have not shared Malthus's distaste for birth-control methods. By using a variety of techniques, Westerners have been able to limit population more effectively than the pious minister anticipated.

Yet, in spite of these criticisms, Malthusian theory has turned out to be prophetic. As we see in the pages ahead, the population has outstripped the food supply in most developing countries. In addition, Malthus's theory applies to advanced industrial societies. In the West other resources besides food are rapidly running out — in particular, clean air, clean water, and energy sources. Several years ago a report to the House Committee on Agriculture included the following question: "Will Americans discover too late that Thomas Malthus is a 200-year-old alarmist whose time has finally arrived?" (Committee on Agriculture, 1976: 253).

### DEMOGRAPHIC-TRANSITION THEORY

The demographic-transition theory provides a three-stage analysis of population growth. (See Figure 16.3.) The **preindustrial stage** existed before industrialization, finishing somewhere between 1750 and 1850 for the majority of Western countries. During this stage both the birth and death rates remained high. Overall a slow rate of population growth occurred, and as we have noted, disease or famine sometimes produced a population decline.

The **transition stage** started at the beginning of the industrial age. The birth rate remained high, but because of significant advances in food production, sanitation, and health care, the death rate dropped sharply. The result was a rapid increase in population.

During the **industrial stage,** the death rate settles at a low level, and the birth rate also drops gradually. Eventually the birth and death rates are almost the same, and the population stabilizes.

Some modern demographers have also considered a postindustrial stage, where deaths steadily outnumber births and the population of a society declines, ultimately to the point that the society itself ceases to exist (Bouvier, 1984: 32). While this situation might occur in the future, no modern society presently seems an immediate candidate. Meanwhile, particularly in developing nations, high birth rates are a serious problem.

What conditions encourage a declining birth

**Figure 16.3**
**Demographic Transition Theory**

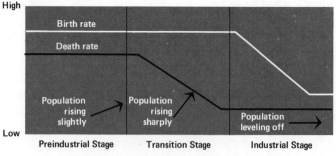

*While the United States and other developed nations are attaining the population stability of the industrial stage, the developing nations are experiencing the rapid population expansion of the transition stage.*

rate? The availability of contraception and family planning information are contributing factors. A more significant factor, however, is the impact of the modern, urban life-style. Children no longer help earn the family living as in preindustrial times. In fact, they represent an economic liability. Furthermore, as women develop careers and other personal interests, they do not want to devote most of their energies to raising a family.

The industrial stage is nearly complete in Europe, the United States, Canada, and Japan. A number of other countries, including Cuba, Taiwan, and Tunisia, have declining birth rates and so are moving into the third stage.

In contrast, developing nations are in the transition stage. The introduction of Western technology—insecticides like DDT, improvements in food transportation and storage, and such modern health practices as inoculations against diseases—has sharply lowered the death rate. The birth rate, however, has remained high because the principal conditions of modern, urban life that would produce a decline in the birth rate do not exist.

A cruel irony is apparent. Western nations have introduced modern technology in order to reduce suffering and death; however, by rapidly expanding the population size of developing nations, those devices have increased suffering.

We will examine the effects of population problems in both developing nations and in the United States and also consider efforts to reduce overpopulation.

## An Overview of World Population Problems

What are some of the results of massive population growth? In the first place, crowding happens. While people's perception of whether or not a situation is crowded varies according to their cultural standards, it seems safe to conclude that the more people, the more probable individuals will perceive a living situation as crowded. Some studies do suggest that as the number of people in a space increases, they are more inclined to experience nervous disorders and to engage in child abuse, incest, and suicide. Certainly the prospect of extreme crowding confronts us when we look at how rapid population expansion in developing nations has been. In 1900 the population of the non-Western nations was about one billion. If present projections hold, the figure will reach about 5.5 billion by the end of the century—nearly a sixfold increase in 100 years.

Shortage of food is another serious problem produced by rapid population growth. In the past many famines were **distribution famines**—food shortages existed in certain provinces or regions of a country, not throughout the nation. Distribution famines usually result from inadequate transportation or the unwillingness of leaders in one region to help starving people in another. In contrast, **deficit famines** are situations in which no food supplies exist elsewhere in a nation sufficient to compensate for local inadequacies. In many developing nations, rapid population growth coupled with limited food supplies makes the occurrence of deficit famines increasingly likely in the future (Sullivan et al., 1980: 111–117).

The future for many developing nations appears frightening. Figure 16.4 shows that a developing nation, such as India, generally has a disproportionately large young population, and therefore its prospect for continuing rapid growth seems excellent. A recent report issued by the National Academy of Sciences has concluded that perhaps the greatest danger of excessive population growth is environmental destruction, particularly the pollution of air, water, and soil and the elimination of forests and various species of plants and animals (Silk, 1986). Developed nations like the United States and Sweden have a much smaller proportion of young people, and so they are unlikely to have rapid growth in the years ahead.

### The American Population Picture

Like other Western societies, the United States has passed through a phase of rapid population growth. Because of a steady flood of immigrants, the national population increased by about 30 percent each decade during the second half of the nineteenth century. Then in the 1920s, restrictions on immigration along with a declining birth rate slowed the rate of population growth. After World War II, the "baby boom" occurred, and in 1955 the birth rate reached its highest postwar figure. From that time the rate dropped steadily until 1975 before increasing slightly. The "baby bust" of the past fifteen years has resulted because young people are having or plan to have fewer children than adults had in the past.

To obtain **zero population growth**—a situation

**Figure 16.4**

**Three Basic Population Pyramids — India, United States, and Sweden: ca. 1980**

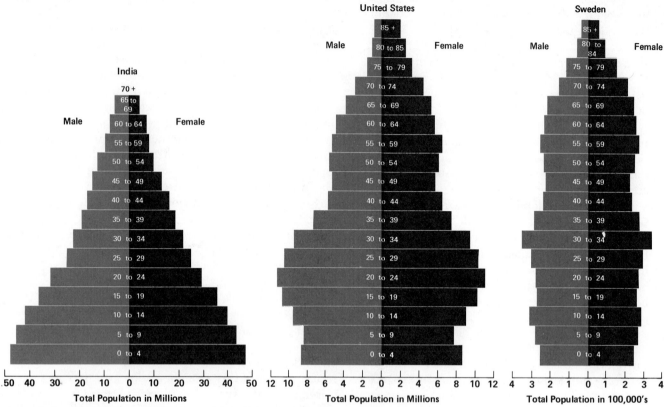

*A population pyramid is a graphic representation of a population's age–sex distribution.
India, with a rapidly growing population, presents a bottom-heavy pyramid typical of
developing nations. A century ago the American population pyramid had a similar shape. At
present our age–sex distribution is gradually moving toward the Swedish pattern. (Sources:
U.S. Bureau of the Census. Current Population Reports, Population Characteristics,
P–20, No. 374. Table 3–1; United Nations Publishing Service. Demographic Yearbook,
1980. Table 7.)*

in which the population size stabilizes — American couples need to average about 2.1 children, slightly more than enough children to replace themselves in order to compensate for offspring who die and people who remain childless. In 1983 lifetime births expected for women aged eighteen to thirty-four was 2.079 children, just about the figure needed for population stabilization (U.S. Bureau of the Census, *Fertility of American Women: June 1983,* 1984. Table 2). It is apparent that unless the birth rate shoots up, the American prospects for zero population growth are good.

Yet the current American population situation contains some serious problems. First, while the overall fertility rate has been dropping, the proportion of births to teenagers out of wedlock has been increasing. In the early 1980s, 18 percent of all births were out of wedlock, more than triple the percentage in 1960, and women under twenty accounted for 40 percent of these births. These children face economic and social disadvantages in the years ahead (Population Reference Bureau, 1984). Second, certain economic strains have developed. Insufficient jobs and housing currently exist to meet the needs of Americans. One of the reasons the crime rate is particularly high among young people seems to be that they are especially prone to unemployment. Third, a number of valuable resources are in increasingly short supply. A shortage of water already exists in the Southwest, and this problem will spread north and east in the years ahead. Food production could become a problem in American society, particularly if there is strict enforcement of the laws regulating the use of pesticides and various chemical fertilizers. With the average American using 450 pounds of wood and wood products each year, there will be continuing deterioration of the nation's lumber supply. Fourth, an increase in the population size will inevitably produce more pollution. In a highly developed country like the United States, the amount of water, air, and soil pollution is considerably greater per capita than in a developing country like India, Zaire, or Peru.

The American population problem is certainly not devastating, but in developing nations, overpopulation is an increasingly serious threat. What can be done to overcome this threat?

## Attempts to Set Limits

How can we visualize the enormous number of people on this planet? In Robert Graves's (1962) historical novel, *Claudius the God,* the Roman Emperor Claudius ordered a census taken of his kingdom, and the total number of Roman citizens was 5,984,072. On a page, Claudius admitted, the figure was not very impressive, but it was impressive if one considered it in human terms. Claudius explained, "If the whole Roman citizenry were to file past me at a brisk walk, toe to heel, it would be two whole years before the last one came in sight" (Graves, 1962: 479). Claudius ruled nearly 6 million people. The current population of the earth is about 4.9 billion people, about 819 times the population of Claudius's Rome, and growing by about 83 million a year. At the current growth rate, the planet gains another million people every four-and-a-half days, about 158 per minute. About 92 percent of the growth is concentrated in the developing nations of Africa, Asia (excluding Japan), and Latin America (*Population Today,* April 1986: 3).

It is easy to feel overwhelmed by the numbers and simply to believe that they are so large that nothing can be done to control overpopulation. Yet some practical measures do exist.

### CONTRACEPTION

Many experts feel that the key to lowering the fertility rate and thus reducing population growth resides in technology: specifically, easy-to-use and effective means of contraception. Certainly the widespread use of contraceptives would curtail the population expansion. Some devices are more effective than others. Oral contraceptives and intrauterine devices (IUDs) are the most effective methods. They are followed by the condom, diaphragm and spermicide, withdrawal, spermicide alone, rhythm, and douche in order of declining effectiveness.

Contraception can reduce the birth rate and curtail population growth, but population control is more than just a technical issue. It requires the motivation to limit one's family size.

### FAMILY PLANNING

**Family planning** is a program that encourages people to decide how many children they want, when they want them, and what contraceptives, if any, they wish to use to achieve their goals. Family-planning programs have helped to reduce the birth rate in such countries as Taiwan, Singapore, South Korea, and Hong Kong. Family planning alone, however, has not been able to halt population growth in any country. One difficulty is that many programs are poorly financed, thus permitting only a small number of people to use their services. The major problem, though, is that the family size a couple wants and the size that will be suitable for the needs of a nation are often not the same. In many cases people turn to family planning after they have had large families, not before. Therefore a major challenge involves incentive, motivating people to accept small families.

### INCENTIVES

The most obvious incentives are financial, and several countries have experimented with paying cash for sterilization or the use of IUDs. Another possibility is to permit tax deductions for only the first two children or to impose a "child tax" on parents with more than a certain number of children. The chief problem with such proposals is that under them large, poor families would only encounter increased suffering. Some incentive plans are more far ranging, emphasizing the development of social and economic policies that would weaken social norms encouraging large families. Whereas couples would be free to decide the number of

*This billboard in Peking, which says "practice birth control to benefit the next generation," is part of the one-child policy which China has been promoting as a means of controlling the size of its already enormous population.*

children, they would encounter pressure from family, friends, and government officials to keep that number low.

### COERCION

If family planning and incentives fail to lower the birth rate, some countries may be forced to impose limits on the number of children people are permitted to have. Such a policy, naturally, would create an uproar in a country like the United States where there has been a strong emphasis on the rights of individuals to conduct their private lives without government interference as long as they do not hurt anyone else. Of course, therein

lies the problem. In many developing nations, if citizens continue to have large families, the current inadequacies of food and other resources will only worsen, and all, or at least many will suffer.

By what measures could a government administer a policy of coercive population control? One approach would be to issue a license to every woman of childbearing age permitting her to have the number of children that would be most suitable for that society's welfare. Another proposal would be to provide a chemical inhibitor for the entire population: some agent that would reduce fertility but not entirely eliminate childbirth. The goal of such an approach would be to regulate the chemical dosage so that the desired number of children would be produced each year. To Americans as well as to citizens of many other countries, such measures seem intolerable. And yet in the future, the governments of nations faced with explosive population growth might decide that no other approach will work.

### A COMBINATION OF TECHNIQUES

It turns out that some developing nations have been remarkably successful in limiting their population growth, and the greatest success seems to have resulted from a combination of techniques.

The People's Republic of China is a particularly significant case in point. In China large families have been a tradition for centuries. Within a ten-year span, however, China has cut its growth rate almost in half, to 1.2 percent a year. To attain this reduction, the government established a family-planning program designed to impress prospective parents with the importance of limiting population growth. Local paramedic teams, which always include at least one woman, pass out free contraceptives. Government officials seek the help of local organizations to establish and maintain birth quotas and to encourage late marriage. In addition, the government has supported strenuous efforts to enlist women in all aspects of local life, not just child-rearing. Finally, in hopes of achieving the goal of zero population growth by the year 2000, the Chinese government is now considering proposals to provide child-care subsidies, priority in housing allocation and school placement, and generous pensions for families with only one child. The system has been remarkably successful, particularly when one realizes that in a society without a pension system, people are motivated to have sons who will support them in their old age. Consider how the system has worked in Maoping, a village where residents have been expected to have just one child in order to maintain a yearly quota of fifteen babies.

> If a couple broke their agreement and the woman conceived again, they were subjected to criticism, and the woman would be persuaded to have an abortion. In Maoping the system was slightly more flexible than in some parts of China. If a couple had produced a girl and the . . . annual baby-quota had not been filled, then the couple could apply to the commune author-

ities to try for another child, and permission might be granted.

*(Clayre, 1984: 153)*

It is clear that the Chinese have used or plan to use several different techniques, and their success demonstrates that developing nations can dramatically limit population growth (Davis, 1967; Nam and Gustavus, 1976; Sullivan et al., 1980).

As the population of a nation grows, its environmental problems are likely to increase. The American case demonstrates, however, that other factors make a more prominent contribution.

## Environmental Problems

A riddle taught to French children asks the following question. If the number of lilies in a pond doubles each day and if the pond is entirely filled with lilies on the thirtieth day, when will the pond be half filled? The answer: On the twenty-ninth day (Brown, 1978). If the lilies represent the human population and the pond stands for the environment, is it reasonable to suspect that humanity is now in the twenty-ninth day?

The subject of this section is the **natural environment,** the combination of land, climate, water, air, mineral resources, and plant and animal life that together compose the physical world where people live. Ecologists point to the existence of a "web of life": an intimate, delicate relationship of plants and animals to each other and to the environment. With the development of mechanical sources of power, we human beings have assumed a dominant role in this community of interdependent living organisms and perhaps have brought ourselves to the eve of "the twenty-ninth day." Ecologists emphasize that many valuable resources are dangerously scarce and that environmental pollution has become increasingly serious.

### Resource Depletion

Food supplies and natural resources are two major areas of resource depletion. Both pose significant difficulties that will become even more significant in the years ahead.

#### Food Supplies

In the developed nations, the average person consumes about 3380 calories per day; in contrast,

in the developing countries, the figure is less than two-thirds as much — 2210 calories. In many cases the level is even lower, especially in the developing African nations, where the majority of the population lives on roots, coarse grains, wild fruits, and vegetables — a diet generally low in both vitamins and proteins.

World hunger is an enormous problem today. An estimated 1.3 billion people are hungry all the time, and about 462 million people, over half of them small children, are starving. From an overall planetary perspective, the problem is not insufficient food. Each year farmers produce enough grain to provide every living person 3000 calories each day. Then why do so many people go hungry? A major problem is that countries where people are starving do not produce enough food or the kind of food they need. At least fifteen such nations grow more acres of food for export than acres of such staples as wheat, corn, rice, vegetables, and fruits that could sustain their own people. As a result they must import these staples, but seldom can they import enough to prevent famine.

Inadequate food supply is the primary problem in developing countries. In developed nations the greatest challenge involves natural resources.

#### Natural Resources

The most publicized concern in this area is energy. Western nations depend on oil for almost half of their energy needs, and at present the world consumption level is awesome: almost 30,000 gallons of oil every second. Estimates suggest that the available supplies of both oil and natural gas will run out within fifty to seventy-five years.

**Figure 16.5**
**Americans' Outlook on Environmental Laws and Regulations**

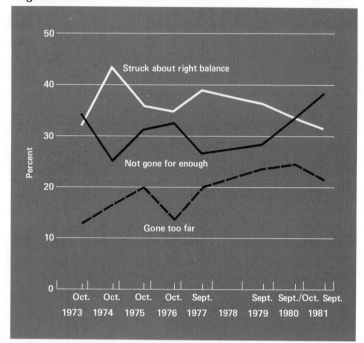

*Question: There are differing opinions about how far we have gone with environmental-protection laws and regulations. At the present time, do you think laws and regulations have gone too far, not far enough, or have struck about the right balance?*

*Over an eight-year period, American public opinion has remained fairly stable on this issue. Americans show the strongest support for the conclusion that environmental-protection laws and regulations have struck the right balance and the least support for the position that those laws and regulations have gone too far. The position that the laws and regulations have not gone far enough has generally fallen in between. (Source: Roper Organization.* Roper Reports. *November 1981.)*

Water is another important, exhaustible resource. American society has required an ever increasing amount of water. In 1900 Americans used 40 billion gallons of water a year. By 1970 the figure had risen to 350 billion gallons. At the end of the century, estimates indicate that consumption will be between 700 and 1000 billion gallons.

Americans also employ a large proportion of various raw materials that are fast running out. We use over 60 percent of the planet's natural gas, more than 40 percent of the aluminum and coal, over 33 percent of the nickel, petroleum, plati-

num, and copper, and about 25 percent of the iron, gold, mercury, silver, tin, lead, zinc, and tungsten.

Technological advances now permit increased extraction of minerals from low-grade ore, but the associated activities—more mining, crushing, treating with chemicals, heating, cooling, and dumping—will greatly expand environmental pollution (Barnet, 1980; Meadows et al., 1972; Ridker and Watson, 1980).

## Environmental Pollution

As we have noted, ecologists indicate that we human beings are a component in the "web of life." The pollution we create also enters this process. Barry Commoner (1972), an ecologist, described several principles of environmental pollution. First, he suggested that within the environment all the parts are interrelated and that a change in one part of the system causes changes in other parts. Second, nothing just disappears. Pollution will simply move from one place to another, or perhaps it will be transformed. Third, nature is enormously complicated. Commoner claimed that the environment is like a watch. If you close your eyes and poke a pencil into the works, the watch might run better, but the chances are it will be seriously damaged. The odds are overwhelming that "poking around" in the environment has been and will continue to be harmful. Commoner concluded that people have ignored these principles and violated the environment for such a long period of time that the current pollution problems literally threaten the survival of humanity.

Americans are becoming increasingly aware of environmental problems. Figure 16.5 indicates that in late 1981 the public was divided on the issue of whether or not to support the extension of environmental-protection laws. In the same year, 39 percent of a national sample believed that air pollution represents a serious threat to future generations, 47 percent visualized a comparable threat from ground and water pollution produced by chemical wastes, and 56 percent contended that atomic wastes pose a major future threat (Roper Organization, *Roper Reports,* March 1981). We will examine some major types of pollution in U.S. society.

In comparison to modern citizens, Native American groups seem to have had a nondestructive, even healthy relationship to the environment. But most of us know little about this subject, and so let us consider it in the following Cross-Cultural Perspective.

## CROSS-CULTURAL PERSPECTIVE

# *Native Americans' Relationship to the Environment*

Frequently Americans have believed that Indians were simply another lower form of animal life, leaving little or no physical impact on the environment. Actually they often had an extensive impact. As we look at Native Americans' interaction with the environment, perhaps we will obtain some insights about our own troubled relationship with it.

As we noted, Indians often left their mark on the land. Many tribes used fire to clear forests and produce grasslands for hunting and fields for planting. Many times they overhunted animals, eliminating or at least greatly limiting the presence of different animal species within a locale. Historian Richard White commented, "One thing that has impressed me about Indians I've known is their realization that this is a harsh planet, that they survive by the deaths of other creatures. There's no attempt to gloss over that or romanticize it" (Cronon and White, 1986: 20).

While the Native Americans' perception of the world should not be romanticized, it should be understood. One critical element in Indians' perception has been their belief that they exist in a social relationship with all other living creatures—something like Commoner's principle that all parts of the environment are related. If Indians killed an animal, for instance, they felt that they were under an obligation that needed to be repaid. This repayment might have taken the form of a prayer or sacrifice to the spirit of the departed animal.

Native Americans also maintained a careful relationship with the land itself. Unlike whites, Indians did not believe that they should seek maximum yield in food supplies but should simply try to obtain security. They tended to have a number of different ways of obtaining food, and these varied with the season. This diversification provided what might be considered "ecological safety nets." If one net failed—for example, a drought made growing corn unproductive in a given year—then the tribe still had other nets on which to rely, such as food gathering or hunting.

Native Americans tended to believe that their cycles of hunting, food gathering, and agriculture were profoundly interdependent. Most Americans failed to appreciate such a linkage. White described a conversation in the 1870s between a Pawnee Indian named Petalesharo and an Indian agent who was trying to persuade Petalesharo to stop hunting buffalo.

Suddenly a cultural chasm . . . [opened] between them, because Petalesharo . . . [was] trying to explain that the corn will not grow without the buffalo hunt. Without buffalo to sacrifice at the ceremonies, corn will not come up and the Pawnee world will cease. You see them talking, but there . . . [was] no communication.

*(Cronan and White, 1986: 21)*

Petalesharo's view makes little sense to modern Americans, but it must be appreciated as typical of Indians' beliefs about their relationship to the environment. Furthermore, whether or not one understands the Native Americans' perception, one can recognize its latent function: to establish a balanced, diversified cycle for obtaining food.

For many Native Americans, the destruction of these cycles, not military conquest, became the chief means by which they were subjected to whites' control. In order to receive such valued items as textiles, alcohol, guns, and other metal goods, Indians had to exchange such products as furs and meat. Eventually these exchanges led to the devastation of beaver, buffalo, and deer. With traditional sources of subsistence destroyed, the Indians had to accept whites' means of obtaining food. These people, who had once been profoundly independent, became almost completely dependent.

There seems to be a lesson to learn from the Native Americans' environmental experiences. While differences exist between our current situation and theirs, we too are compelled to maintain a relationship with the environment, and we too can find our environment sufficiently damaged to destroy our way of life.

Source: William Cronon and Richard White. "Indians in the Land." *American Heritage.* Vol. 37. August/September 1986, pp. 19–25. I am grateful to Shirley Varmette, a member of the Southern Connecticut State University sociology department, for supplying both the idea and source for this box.

## Air Pollution

In 1952, 4000 people died in London when a thick, brownish smog covered the city for four days. On Thanksgiving Day in 1966, a sudden rise in temperature trapped fumes in New York City, and 168 people died.

When we note these dramatic examples, we should not lose sight of the fact that air pollution occurs less dramatically every day. As a result of air pollution, 25 percent of the sunlight headed for New York City is cut off. Some other cities are in an even worse predicament. In Chicago, for example, pollution blocks about 40 percent of the sunlight. The United States ejects about 200 million tons of waste into the air every day—nearly one ton per citizen.

There are four major sources of air pollution: transportation, power generation, industry, and waste incineration. Auto emissions represent the most serious contributor to air pollution. In the United States, 90 million cars release millions of tons of carbon monoxide, sulfur dioxide, hydrocarbons, and nitrogen oxides per year.

## Water Pollution

In the famous 1960s film *Dr. Strangelove,* General Jack D. Ripper never drank water straight from the tap. He believed that only superdistilled $H_2O$ would protect his "precious bodily fluids" from a "Communist plot" to fluoridate U.S. water. While General Ripper's fear of fluoridation was unrealistic, people today are indeed anxious to protect themselves from the pollutants in the American water supply.

Several sources of water pollution exist. One prominent contributor is sewage. As towns and cities have grown, their sewage treatment facilities have often failed to expand accordingly. In many areas septic tanks discharge their refuse into the same underground water supply that people use for drinking. In a public restroom along the upper Mississippi River, a statement scribbled on the wall read, "Flush the toilet. They need the water in St. Louis." This sarcastic bit of humor might contain more truth than St. Louis's citizenry would like to acknowledge. Another significant source of water pollution is industrial waste. Since the beginning of industrialization, American factories have been located near waterways, and manufacturers have long recognized that nothing works as well as a river to make one's own waste problems belong to someone else. As a result the major rivers of the United States contain large quantities of lead, sulfuric acid, hydrofluoric acid, ammonia, and dioxin, one of the most toxic chemicals known. With the current dumping bans, some companies have started to throw their wastes into underground wells. In one section of New Jersey, this practice seems to be contaminating the well water of people living forty miles from dumping sites. Agricultural practices also can create water pollution. Nitrates from fertilizers have become a dangerous contaminant in some midwestern areas. The city of Elgin, Minnesota, had to find a new water supply after its wells were polluted by nitrate runoff.

## Pesticide Residues

In 1981 the Mediterranean fruit fly damaged the fruit and vegetable crops in several sections of California. In order to prevent the further spread of the fruit fly, the governor reluctantly authorized the widespread spraying of insecticides. Shortly afterwards a survey firm asked a national sample of Americans whether they thought spraying the insecticides was the right or wrong thing to do. Seventy-two percent indicated it was the right thing, 8 percent felt it was wrong, and 20 percent had mixed feelings or did not know. However, after the fruit-fly problem started, 41 percent of the

*The pollutants in American waterways are sometimes so potent that they kill the fish inhabiting them.*

respondents—more than two in five—changed their attitudes or behavior about buying California fruits and vegetables or noted that the stores in their area had made a change (Roper Organization, *Roper Reports,* November 1981). These survey results suggest that many Americans have a two-part attitude toward pesticides. Such people feel they are necessary but want to have as little personal contact with them as possible.

One of the most destructive pesticides has been DDT. During the 1960s people in this country used about 100,000 tons of DDT per year. It proved to be both inexpensive and effective, but in the past twenty years, we have become aware of several problems associated with this particular pesticide. First, DDT kills in a nonselective way. Farmers and others have used it to destroy the approximately 1 percent of all insects we consider pests, but this pesticide has been equally effective in killing insects that make significant contributions to the maintenance of a healthy environment. Second, as a result of genetic changes, some insects, including many mosquitos and cockroaches, are developing considerable immunity to DDT. Third, heavy concentrations of DDT accumulate in fish, birds, livestock, and human beings as they feed on animals or plants that have either picked up the DDT from other organisms or absorbed it directly from the water or soil. For example, DDT

will run off an agricultural field and into a stream. It will be carried to a river where water plants will absorb it. Very small animal life in the water (zooplankton) will eat the plants. Minnows, in turn, will feed on the zooplankton. Then larger fish will consume the minnows. Finally waterfowl will eat the large fish. In the course of this sequence, the concentration of DDT has increased 10 million times. The concentration, naturally, will increase even further if human beings eat the waterfowl.

Although the use of DDT has now been restricted, the lethal effects of the pesticide do not just vanish. DDT is a dramatic example of Commoner's contention that nothing simply disappears. Furthermore many of the substitutes for DDT also have dangerous side effects. Yet the production and use of pesticides is still increasing in the United States.

### Radioactivity Effects

Soon after the Three Mile Island accident, a vice-president of the Metropolitan Edison Company, which operated the nuclear-power plant, said, "We didn't injure anybody, we didn't seriously contaminate anybody and we certainly didn't kill anybody . . ." (Matthews: 1979: 25).

It is still much too soon, however, to make such a definite statement. Increasing evidence suggests that soldiers and civilians exposed to nuclear testing in the 1950s took many years, sometimes decades, to show symptoms of cancer or leukemia.

Nuclear-power plants pose several significant dangers. The fallout from a major accident could produce the equivalent of that released by hundreds of Hiroshima-sized atomic bombs. Following the accident at the Chernobyl nuclear plant in the Soviet Union, heavy doses of radioactivity were detected in many European countries. Almost every plant in the United States has been shut down at some time because of an operating problem that could create a hazardous accident.

Another important problem produced by nuclear-power plants is their waste. (See Figure 16.6.) Tiny quantities of this waste can cause cancer or birth defects. Large doses can kill people quickly. The major problem with radioactive waste concerns storage. Unfortunately much of the waste remains radioactive for hundreds, even thousands of years—in some instances as long as 300,000 years. Yet storage tanks are often not sufficiently sturdy to contain the waste for such long periods.

**Figure 16.6**
**Radioactive Waste Disposal, 1962–1980**

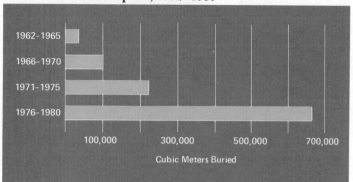

*Because it remains deadly for thousands of years, radioactive waste represents a major pollution problem. This graph shows the growing accumulation of radioactive waste in the last several decades. By 1980 the total accumulation was over one million cubic meters. (Source: Council on Environmental Quality. Environmental Quality, 1981. Table A–61.)*

The most troubling case in point involves the most lethal wastes: the strontium 90 and plutonium buried underground in concrete tanks, primarily in Richmond, Washington. This concentrated radioactive waste, which will remain deadly for thousands of years, has leaked at least sixteen times since 1968, releasing 115,000 gallons of radioactive liquid in 1974. The Nuclear Regulatory Commission is still seeking effective ways to dispose of nuclear wastes. The difficulties are as much political as technical. As one energy department official indicated, the problem is ". . . deciding in which congressional district to put them."

Finally, with the economical working lives of power plants about thirty years in duration, there is the eventual problem of dismantling such units. Unlike other kinds of discarded plants, nuclear facilities cannot just be leveled with a wrecking ball; contaminated parts and equipment must be isolated, sometimes for as long as thousands of years. Around the world more than twenty plants are already shut down; sixty-three more will probably be closed by the turn of the century and another 162 between 2000 and 2010.

It seems reasonable to wonder why the Nuclear Regulatory Commission has continued a program that involves such extreme risks. The answer is that a variety of interests, including recent presidential administrations, major corporations, and many American citizens, believe that the United States must meet its growing energy requirements while decreasing reliance on foreign suppliers, regardless of the environmental impact (Brown, 1980; Ehrlich, Ehrlich, and Holdren, 1977; Pollock, 1986; Robertson, 1980; Sun, 1983).

What will happen in the future? Will we be able to survive the environmental challenge we currently face? Let us consider some measures that could help reduce the current environmental problems.

## Restoration of a Healthy Environment

Law can be an effective instrument to prevent wasted resources and pollution. The National Environmental Policy Act of 1969 indicated that before projects either requiring federal approval and/or involving federal funding can begin, public hearings on the environmental impact must take place. As a result of this requirement, the construction of the Alaskan pipeline did not start until safeguards were established to minimize environmental destruction. The mere passage of legislation, of course, does not ensure its effective implementation. For instance, the Clean Air Act of 1970 established the Environmental Protection Agency (EPA) and empowered it to enforce standards of air quality. In the ensuing years, however, EPA has repeatedly granted extensions of the official deadlines for reducing automobile emissions (Nisbet, 1982).

The influence and resources of the federal government are necessary to make significant steps toward the restoration of a healthy environment. In 1983 President Reagan claimed that under his administration the nation had been growing "more healthy and more beautiful each year" (Weisman, 1983: 1). Yet a thorough analysis has concluded that the Reagan administration has reduced the size, scope, and effectiveness of agencies concerned with environmental protection (Kraft and Vig, 1984).

The federal government might become more actively involved in the years ahead because Americans have been increasingly concerned about environmental issues. Citizen-action groups working to improve environmental health have become widespread (Freudenberg, 1984). Furthermore, "Poll after poll confirms a deep and abiding popular concern for protecting the environment even at a considerable expense" (Reilly, 1982: 473). When asked whether they would make protection of the environment or economic growth the priority, 61 percent of a national sample picked environmental protection, even at the risk of limiting economic growth. Just 28 percent of the sample chose economic growth, and 11 percent had another opin-ion or none at all (George Gallup, *Gallup Poll*, December 1984).

The environmental crisis is now upon us. Will we be able to improve environmental conditions sufficiently to prevent major destruction?

## STUDY GUIDE

## Summary

1. The three topics in this chapter — cities, population growth, and environmental problems — are interdependent. Human ecology concerns itself with all three.

2. A city is a large, densely settled concentration of people permanently located within a relatively confined geographical area where nonagricultural occupations are pursued. Urbanization is the process by which a city forms and develops.

Preindustrial cities generally had certain characteristics: small populations, limited transportation and storage facilities, a center serving as the focus of governmental and religious activity as well as elite housing, and a highly restrictive social-class system. We can distinguish four eras in the development of American cities: the colonial period, the period of westward expansion, the period of metropolitan growth, and the modern period. In the course of their development, American cities have undergone many changes, and in recent years the deterioration of urban facilities and services as well as a steadily eroding tax base have posed serious difficulties.

Central problems of modern cities are governmental proliferation, powerful political and economic interests, and financial limitations. Measures to revitalize American cities include an emphasis on an active neighborhood life, experiments with metropolitan solutions, efforts to bring middle-class people back into cities, and increased federal and state assistance.

3. A population is all the people who live within a specified geographic area such as a nation, a re-gion, or a city. Demography is the statistical study of human populations. To determine population changes, demographers analyze birth, death, and migration rates. Prominent demographic theories include the Malthusian theory and the demographic-transition theory. In the developing nations, population growth now occurs at a rapid rate, and millions of people currently starve to death each year. In the United States, population growth has slowed down. Nonetheless, with the current population size, problems do exist — in particular, insufficient jobs and housing, a strain on the supply of natural resources, and significant levels of pollution. Attempts to set population limits throughout the world involve the use of contraception, family planning, incentives, coercion, and a combination of different techniques.

4. The natural environment is the complex of land, climate, water, air, mineral resources, and plant and animal life that together compose the physical world where people live. Resource depletion is a serious environmental problem. In developing nations the inadequacy of food supplies is the dominant issue related to this topic. In developed nations the chief difficulty is the declining supplies of major natural resources. In recent years Americans have become increasingly concerned about environmental pollution. Serious problems involve air pollution, water pollution, pesticide residues, and radioactivity effects. Laws can help restore a healthy environment, but little significant progress will occur without major governmental support.

## Glossary

**city**  a large, densely settled concentration of people permanently located within a relatively confined geographical area where nonagricultural occupations are pursued.

**crude birth rate**  the number of births per 1000 persons in a society in a given year.

**crude death rate**  the number of deaths per 1000 persons in a society in a given year.

**426**

**deficit famine**   situation in which no food supplies exist elsewhere in a nation sufficient to compensate for local inadequacies.

**demography**   the study of human populations.

**distribution famine**   a food shortage existing in certain provinces or regions of a country, not throughout an entire country.

**doubling time**   the time span necessary for a population to double in size.

**family planning**   a program that encourages people to decide how many children they want, when they want them, and what contraceptives, if any, they wish to use to achieve their goals.

**fertility rate**   the number of actual births per 1000 women between the ages of fifteen and forty-four.

**gentrification**   the move of middle- and upper-middle-class people to formerly deteriorated inner-city neighborhoods.

**growth rate**   the crude birth rate minus the crude death rate.

**human ecology**   the study of human beings' relationship with the environment.

**industrial stage**   (of the demographic-transition theory) the third stage, which occurs as nations stabilize their populations in the course of industrialization.

**in-migration rate**   the number of people per 1000 members of the population moving into an area in a given year.

**megalopolis**   a string of closely bound metropolitan areas.

**metropolis**   a territorial unit composed of a large central city and the surrounding cities and towns.

**migration**   the flow of people in and out of a particular territory (city, region, or country).

**natural environment**   the combination of land, climate, water, air, mineral resources, and plant and animal life that together compose the physical world where people live.

**net migration rate**   the difference between the in-migration rate and the out-migration rate.

**out-migration rate**   the number of people per 1000 members of the population moving out of an area in a given year.

**population**   all the people who live within a specific geographic area such as a nation, a region, or a city.

**preindustrial stage**   (of the demographic-transition theory) the first stage, which existed before industrialization and involved a stable population, with both birth and death rates remaining high.

**suburb**   a politically independent municipality that develops next to or in the vicinity of a central city.

**transition stage**   (of the demographic-transition theory) the second stage, in which a decline in the death rate and a continuing high birth rate produces a rapid growth in population.

**urbanization**   the process by which a city forms and develops.

**zero population growth**   a situation in which the population size stabilizes.

## Learning Objectives

After studying this chapter, you should be able to:

1. Define human ecology and explain its social importance.
2. Define urbanization and describe the conditions encouraging the development of preindustrial cities.
3. List and discuss the four eras in the growth of American cities.
4. Analyze the primary causes of urban deterioration.
5. Discuss measures that could revitalize urban existence.
6. Define demography and discuss factors in population growth: birth rate, death rate, migration rate, and growth rate.
7. Examine in detail Malthusian theory and the demographic transition theory.
8. Identify and explain the population problems of the United States and the world.
9. List and discuss the different measures for limiting population.
10. Discuss major resource-depletion problems.
11. Examine the major types of environmental pollution.

# Tests

## True – false test

_____ 1. In preindustrial cities the city center contained governmental and religious activities and also elite housing.

_____ 2. Ferdinand Tönnies believed that when people took up residence in cities, their outlooks and behavior started to change.

_____ 3. A metropolis is a preindustrial version of a megalopolis.

_____ 4. Recent research has concluded that since 1960 the suburban population has been aging more rapidly than the population overall.

_____ 5. Gentrification is the move of elderly people to inner-city areas.

_____ 6. Fertility refers to the biological potential for reproduction.

_____ 7. In most countries migration is the principal factor affecting population growth.

_____ 8. A recent report issued by the National Academy of Sciences has concluded that perhaps the greatest danger produced by population growth is environmental destruction.

_____ 9. Each year farmers produce enough grain to provide every living person 3000 calories a day.

_____ 10. A variety of powerful interests, including presidential administrations and major corporations, have opposed the development of nuclear-power plants.

## Multiple-choice test

_____ 1. Which of the following qualities was characteristic of preindustrial cities?
   a. an open social-class system
   b. efficient transportation
   c. rapid economic growth
   d. elites' authority based on appeals to tradition and religious absolutes

_____ 2. Which of these factors did NOT contribute significantly to suburban development?
   a. widespread use of electric power
   b. movement of factories out of central cities
   c. unionization of workers in factories
   d. FHA loans to subsidize suburban housing

_____ 3. A recent study found that metropolitan residents prefer their neighborhoods:
   a. small.
   b. close to the inner city.
   c. located in high-rise buildings.
   d. a, b, and c

_____ 4. Jane Jacobs's ideas on improving the quality of urban life by combining land-use patterns in a given area illustrates which measure for improving urban life?
   a. experiments with metropolitan solutions
   b. emphasis on an active neighborhood life
   c. efforts to bring middle-class people back into cities
   d. increased federal and state assistance

_____ 5. The crude death rate:
  a. is determined by the fertility rate.
  b. provides no specific information about deaths.
  c. determines the growth rate.
  d. is the same as the infant-mortality rate.

_____ 6. A limitation of Malthusian population theory is that Malthus did not anticipate:
  a. people's distaste for birth-control methods.
  b. financial incentives as a means to restrict the number of children.
  c. significant improvements in agriculture that have increased the food supply.
  d. that a century after his death people would be more inclined to get divorced.

_____ 7. Which of the following factors contributes to declining birth rates in industrial societies?
  a. famine
  b. availability of medical facilities
  c. an urban life-style in which children are an economic liability
  d. advances in food production

_____ 8. Where no food supplies exist elsewhere in a nation sufficient to compensate for local inadequacies, there is a:
  a. Malthusian famine.
  b. distribution famine.
  c. chronic famine.
  d. deficit famine.

_____ 9. Commoner suggested that all but one of the following statements about the environment is true. Which position was NOT asserted:
  a. All parts of an environment are interrelated, with a change in one part affecting other parts.
  b. Nothing just disappears.
  c. The more things change, the more they stay the same.
  d. Nature is enormously complicated.

_____ 10. Serious problems with nuclear plants include:
  a. the disposal of nuclear wastes.
  b. nuclear fallout.
  c. dismantling of plants at the end of their working lives.
  d. a, b, and c

## Essay test

1. Define human ecology. Analyze the relationship among cities, human populations, and environmental problems. Provide an example that illustrates their interdependence.
2. Discuss major trends of modern urban living, using studies and issues cited in the text to illustrate your conclusions.
3. Will American cities be significantly different in twenty years? What bits of evidence support your conclusion?
4. Discuss the Malthusian theory of population and the demographic-transition theory. What are their similarities and their differences?
5. Do you think rapidly growing developing nations can limit their population increase in the near future? What means will be most productive? Discuss.
6. Summarize the most serious environmental problems in American society.
7. If you were president of the United States, what steps, if any, would you take to combat resource depletion? What about environmental pollution?

# Suggested Readings

Bogue, Donald J. 1985. *The Population of the United States: Historical Trends and Future Projections.* New York: The Free Press. A demographer's view of the American population, examining its primary social and economic characteristics and also its changes over time.

Duncan, E. R. (ed.). 1977. *Dimensions of World Food Problems.* Ames, IA: Iowa State University. A collection of articles that demonstrate the political and economic complexities of eliminating the serious food shortages existing in many developing nations.

Fischer, Claude S. 1984. *The Urban Experience.* San Diego: Harcourt Brace Jovanovich. Second edition. A ten-chapter text effectively covering the basics of urban sociology.

Fuller, R. Buckminster. 1970. *Operating Manual for Spaceship Earth.* New York: Pocket Books. A short book filled with powerful ideas and expressing this well-known inventor's concern about environmental deterioration and his belief that a careful, imaginative use of technology can preserve our "spaceship earth."

Ghosh, Pradip K. (ed.). 1984. *Population, Environment and Resources, and Third World Development.* Westport, CT: Greenwood. Eighteen essays describing and analyzing the troubling, complicated interrelationship among rapid population increase, environmental deterioration, and slow economic growth in third-world nations.

Heer, David M. 1975. *Society and Population.* Englewood Cliffs, NJ: Prentice-Hall. Second edition. A brief introduction to the field of demography, succinctly discussing the basic concepts, theories, and problems of overpopulation.

Humphrey, Craig R., and Frederick R. Buttell. 1982. *Environment, Energy, and Society.* Belmont, CA: Wadsworth. A textbook that effectively examines issues of environment, energy, and population and includes "radical," "liberal," and "conservative" perspectives on most of the topics.

Jacobs, Jane. 1961. *The Death and Life of Great American Cities.* New York: Vintage. An analysis of the different factors that cause cities to be either healthy or unhealthy places to live. Jacobs's writing has been controversial, but whether or not you agree with her, you should find her thinking original and provocative.

Light, Ivan. 1983. *Cities in World Perspective.* New York: Macmillan. A nicely written, carefully documented effort to examine the city historically and cross-culturally in its ecological context.

Palen, J. John (ed.). 1981. *City Scenes: Problems and Prospects.* Boston: Little, Brown. Second edition. A book of readings divided into nine chapters and featuring effective introductions to each section. The heart of the book is the section on critical urban problems, with a chapter on race and ethnicity containing five particularly good articles.

Theodorson, George A. (ed.). 1982. *Urban Patterns: Studies in Human Ecology.* University Park: Pennsylvania State University Press. Revised edition. An updated edition of a well-known reader on the ecological patterns of cities, containing fifty-six articles and including a section devoted to the field of ecology.

Walker, Charles A., Leroy C. Gould, and Edward J. Woodhouse. 1983. *Too Hot to Handle?* New Haven: Yale University Press. A number of specialists writing about the political, economic, technological, and health issues associated with the disposal of radioactive wastes.

Wirth, Louis, 1983. "Urbanism as a Way of Life." *American Journal of Sociology* 44 (July): 3–24. In spite of its age, this widely read sociological article provides a useful introductory analysis of the dominant characteristics of urban life.

# Student Projects

1. Using material from the text and library sources, outline two sets of population proposals, one for the United States and the other for the world. Include a discussion of the following issues:

a. The dilemma of governmental intervention in family decision-making: a limitation on

Chapter 16: Urbanization, Population Growth, and Environmental Problems

**430**

personal freedom versus the need to control population growth. (In addressing world population problems, consider the program initiated in the People's Republic of China.)

b. The most effective/desirable forms of birth control.

c. The prospects for limiting population growth that your programs will produce.

2. Urban areas are centers of high population density. It is a common theme for "disaster" literature and films to contemplate possible harm to large numbers of people. Pick a pollution problem and provide an account describing both the effects on people's lives produced by sudden drastic levels of pollution and the local resources needed to cope with the problem. Think about your own living area. Does it have the service organizations to handle your pollution "disaster"?

# Answers to Test Questions

## True – false test

| | | | | |
|---|---|---|---|---|
| 1. t | 3. f | 5. f | 7. f | 9. t |
| 2. t | 4. t | 6. f | 8. t | 10. f |

## Multiple-choice test

| | | | | |
|---|---|---|---|---|
| 1. d | 3. a | 5. b | 7. c | 9. c |
| 2. c | 4. b | 6. c | 8. d | 10. d |

# 17
# COLLECTIVE BEHAVIOR, SOCIAL MOVEMENTS, AND SOCIAL CHANGE

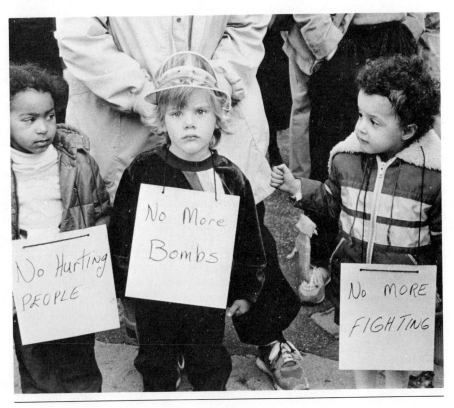

The source of the rumor of Paul McCartney's death remains unknown. Perhaps it originated with an article in the *University of Michigan Daily* or with a Detroit disc jockey's claim. No matter what the source was, in October 1969 thousands of anxious Beatles fans around the country began searching for ominous signs of misfortune. On the jacket of the *Sgt. Pepper* album, a hand raised over McCartney's head suggested an Eastern death symbol, and on the back cover it was troubling to note that Paul was the only Beatle not facing the camera.

The more conscientious fans dug deeper. They carefully studied the Beatles record covers, and they examined all the Beatles records, speeding them up from 33 to 45 rpm, then to 78, slowing them to 16, and finally taping the records and reversing the tapes. An abundance of apparent clues was discovered, and most investigators were convinced that McCartney, indeed, was dead. "I mean, it's all right there," declared Louis Yager, president of the Is Paul McCartney Dead Society at Hofstra University. But McCartney was not dead. He was in a country home with his family. An appearance at a Glasgow airport demonstrated that he was indisputably alive (*Life*, November 7, 1969; *Time*, October 31, 1969).

Eleven years later John Lennon, a former member of the Beatles, did die. He was killed outside his New York City apartment building. Within hours of his death, a crowd of people began to gather near the spot where Lennon had been shot. These people wanted to make a public statement about their mourning for Lennon. In the days and the cold winter nights that followed, the crowd kept growing.

Reporters found that most people were clear about their reasons for being there. Many mourners declared that John Lennon was an important symbol of their youth and idealism. One woman explained that her generation had been robbed of leading heroes—John and Robert Kennedy, Martin Luther King, and now John Lennon. Yet she claimed that people in their thirties and forties passionately cared about freedom and the essential values of human life. She felt ". . . proud and lucky to have grown up in the 60s . . . and grateful that we had John Lennon and the Beatles to express our impatience, our resilience, and our vision of a better world" (Rabinowitz, 1981: 58).

These two situations share more than the fact that they involve former members of the Beatles. Both events are examples of collective behavior. **Collective behavior** is social activity that occurs under conditions that are temporarily unstructured and unstable because of the absence of clearly defined norms. The behavior itself is frequently emotional, often unpredictable, and episodic in occurrence. Collective behavior, in short, falls outside the confines of ordinary social activity. The lack of conventional structure, however, does not prevent the study of forms of collective behavior, although it can make this study difficult. As we will see, analysis reveals definite patterns to these activities.

Most of the time, norms, laws, and customs indicate the actions considered legitimate for the roles people perform. Individuals usually receive rewards for conforming to the conventional expectations, and they normally suffer punishments for failing to conform. Collective behavior occurs when social conditions permit or encourage people to engage in activities that disregard normal expectations. It seems likely that college students would generally ridicule any peers who spent weeks studying Beatles records for obscure clues, but in the fall of 1969, deep concern for Paul McCartney's rumored death eliminated the misgivings the investigators might have had about others' reactions to their tireless search for clues. Mourners standing for hours outside John Lennon's fashionable apartment building clearly felt that behavior that would normally cause curious or disapproving stares and perhaps even a police reprimand was entirely appropriate because of the importance of what they were doing.

All of us occasionally enter collective behavior situations—in particular, when we mingle in crowds. Do crowds stimulate any special feeling? Have you ever considered how you would act if you were in a crowded movie theater and fire broke out? Let us consider another type of collective behavior—rumors. What is your response to rumors that you encounter? Do you willingly believe them and pass them on to others? Or are you careful to confirm information you receive before you transmit it to others? As we discuss the different forms of collective behavior, perhaps you will develop a clearer sense of how you would behave in each case. The difficulty in making such a prediction is that collective-behavior activities take us out of ordinary social situations and put us in relatively unusual, unstructured situations, where much of what happens, including our own behavior, is likely to be quite unpredictable.

Besides collective behavior, we will examine two other topics—social movements and social change. **Social movements** are organized, collective activities undertaken by people to promote or resist social change. Social movements—the women's or civil-rights movements, for instance —involve activities similar to collective behavior in the respect that to some extent they occur outside existing normative guidelines. However, social movements often are more stable and longer lasting than forms of collective behavior, and they can eventually become organizations where the normative standards and members' behavior are quite conventional.

Social movements and collective behavior often occur in situations where social change is taking place and, in turn, they frequently encourage its occurrence. **Social change** involves any modifications in culture, social organization, and social behavior. Generally the topic does not include changes that occur within a small group or organi-

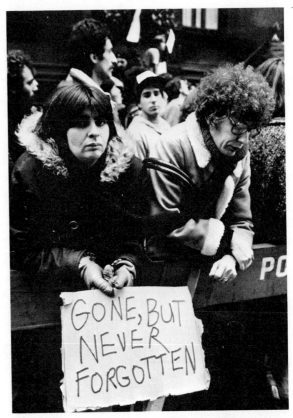

*The murder of John Lennon brought together a broad mix of people in a spontaneous, shared expression of grief.*

zation. The focus of social change is alterations that take place within institutions or societies.

In the following section, we examine the best-known theory of collective behavior and social movements. Next the focus shifts to crowds; the discussion includes an examination of theories of crowd behavior and the analysis of several different kinds of crowd situations. The fourth topic is rumors, the next subject is social movements, and the chapter concludes with an analysis of different sources of social change.

## Smelser's General Theory

A section of George Orwell's *Animal Farm* can serve as an illustration of Neil Smelser's (1963) general theory of collective behavior and social movements.

One day the message filtered among the animals of Manor Farm that Old Major, a prize boar, had had a strange dream the previous night and wanted to communicate it to the other animals. They regarded Old Major with such high regard that as soon as Mr. Jones had stumbled off to bed, drunk as usual, the animals all gathered in the barn to hear what the ancient boar had to say.

With the animals before him, Old Major cleared his throat and started to speak. He indicated that, indeed, he had had a strange dream the previous night, but before he discussed the dream, he needed to speak about something else: the abuse the animals experienced. Old Major spoke about how hard they worked and how little they were fed. He indicated that when each had reached the point where he or she was no longer useful, Mr. Jones would simply put an end to that animal's miserable life. All their problems, Old Major emphasized, were the result of human tryanny. It was clear that the only course of action was to get rid of their human overlords.

Then the old boar described his dream. It involved a time well into the future when humanity would have vanished from the earth. A dominant feature of the dream was a stirring song called "Beasts of England." The song described the glorious future when all animals would be free of human control and would be able to share earth's edible bounty among themselves. Old Major began singing the song, and almost before he had finished the animals joined in.

Three nights after his speech, Old Major died peacefully in his sleep. That was early in March. During the next three months, there was considerable secret activity. Old Major's speech provided the more intelligent animals with an entirely different outlook on life. They did not know when the rebellion would happen—perhaps it would not even take place in their lifetimes—but they all felt that it was their duty to prepare for it. Teaching and organizing were the principal preparatory activities. As the most intelligent animals on the farm, the pigs took a dominant leadership role. Two boars—Snowball and Napoleon—elaborated Major's teachings into a complete system of thought, which they called Animalism. Several nights a week after Mr. Jones had gone to sleep, they held meetings where they discussed principles of Animalism and convinced most of the animals that rebellion was in their interest.

It turned out that the rebellion occurred much sooner than anyone had expected. One Saturday in June, Mr. Jones went into town and got so drunk that he did not return until Sunday afternoon, when he immediately went to sleep on the draw-

ing-room sofa with a newspaper over his face. The farm hands had milked the cows on Sunday morning, but with their boss absent, they went out rabbit hunting, not even bothering to feed the animals. Evening arrived and the animals still had not been fed. Finally they could stand it no longer. One of the cows broke down the shed door with her horns, and all the animals started to help themselves from the bins.

At that point Mr. Jones awoke, and a few moments later he and the farm hands were in the shed with whips in their hands, lashing out wildly at the animals. That was more than the animals could endure. They attacked Jones and his men, butting and kicking them from all sides. The men were shocked. They had never seen animals behaving in this manner before, and this sudden uprising frightened them out of their wits. After no more than a moment of trying to defend themselves, they took to their heels with the animals in hot pursuit. The animals chased the men out of the barn and off the farm, slamming the five-barred gate behind them (Orwell, 1946: 17–22).

Let us suppose that the fleeing men ran into town, and someone asked one of them what had happened. The man might have replied, "It's that new grain we've been feeding the livestock. I told Jones it would bring him nothing but trouble."

People frequently offer one-factor explanations for the occurrence of collective-behavior episodes and social movements. In contrast, Smelser's theory outlines six elements necessary for the development of these activities. These elements develop in sequence, and as each one occurs the likelihood of some alternate activity decreases. By the time the fifth element appears, collective action is inevitable.

1. *Structural conduciveness.* The first point involves basic conditions that permit or allow collective behavior or a social movement to emerge. The animals' ability to speak English, to assemble, and to organize themselves for an expected rebellion were conditions of structural conduciveness. Real farm animals, of course, lack the capacities just mentioned, and so they are unable to rebel.

2. *Structural strain.* Various immediate conditions, such as prejudice and discrimination, economic exploitation, and poor communication between groups or nations, can create a significant amount of tension or pressure for people.

Structural strain can lessen people's willingness to stay within normal behavioral limits. Insufficient food, too much work, and death the moment they proved no longer useful were severe structural strains the animals experienced.

3. *Growth and spread of a generalized belief.* As collective behavior or a social movement develops, an interpretation of the situation and how to respond to it will begin to emerge. The generalized belief supports a break with conventional behavior, emphasizing the current social strain and the rewards collective activity will produce. At the beginning of the account of *Animal Farm*, it is clear that the animals might have simply accepted harsh treatment for the rest of their lives—they could not imagine any other way of living. But then Old Major called them together and explained in painful detail how exploited they were and pointed out that, through rebellion, they could obtain another, much more desirable form of life. The song that he sang them and that they all readily learned summarized these ideas of freedom and equality in a powerful way. After Old Major's death, several pigs developed the doctrine of Animalism, producing an entire system of thought from Old Major's ideas.

4. *Precipitating factor.* Some incident or set of incidents must initiate collective behavior or a social movement. The first three elements of Smelser's theory create a situation that resem-

bles a bone-dry forest vulnerable to devastation by fire. That destruction will not occur, however, unless a match falls unheeded on the forest floor. The precipitating factor is that match. In *Animal Farm* the precipitating factor was the fact that one day the animals were not fed.

5. *Mobilization for action.* At this point all that remains is the occurrence of collective activity. At such a time, people typically find that the rewards and punishments promoting ordinary, everyday behavior are no longer present. The doctrine of Animalism had prepared the animals to understand and want to overthrow the unjust system under which they had been forced to live, and not being fed that Sunday was the outrage that finally produced rebellion against Jones's control.

6. *Social control.* Smelser's final stage concerns the various ways that people in authority act to encourage or discourage a particular incident of collective behavior. After the rebellion no authorities besides the animals remained. They chased Mr. Jones and his men off the farm, and then they slammed the gate, thereby locking out the men and ending the confrontation between beasts and human beings.

Smelser's theory can analyze social movements and all types of collective behavior, including crowds, the topic of the following section.

## Crowds

A **crowd** is a temporary gathering of individuals who share a common concern or interest and find themselves in close physical contact with one another. "Common concern or interest" and "close physical contact" suggest some similarities between crowds and groups. We will see, however, that crowd activity is not as responsive to established norms as group behavior. This section examines crowd characteristics, crowd theories, violent crowds, and frightened crowds.

### Crowd Characteristics

Certainly crowds vary in their qualities and behavior. Some, such as ordinary street crowds, are composed of people sharing little or no common

purpose; others, including the people gathered to hear a popular political candidate, possess a common goal. In many instances crowds are orderly (those attending an opera or a concert of classical music), and in other situations they are not (the participants in a mob or riot). In general, the members of crowds behave in distinct ways.

1. *Suggestibility.* People in crowds do not have the guidelines for behavior that are normally available. They turn to their fellow crowd members for direction, literally "going along with the crowd."

2. *Anonymity and spontaneity.* Individuals in a crowd recognize that they are in a wilderness of strangers—that they are "lost in a crowd." The

**436**

sense of anonymity permits them to act more openly and freely than they normally would. They are likely to lose a sense of responsibility for any misdeeds. "Don't blame me," an individual might say after a riot. "Everyone was breaking things and stealing."

3. *Impersonality.* Since people in crowds are detached from their everyday normative guidelines, they often treat others in a more impersonal, harsh manner than they normally would. When fans at a baseball game yell "Kill the umpire," they are not stopping to consider that the object of their wrath is a human being. For many participants violent crowd activity would be difficult to perform without this element of impersonality.

## Crowd Theories

Perhaps the brief discussion of crowd characteristics seems disturbing. You might have the impression that people in crowds can behave in much the same fashion as a herd of stampeding cattle. One of the crown theories we will consider makes such a claim. The other approach is more sophisticated.

### Contagion Theory

At the end of the nineteenth century, Gustave Le Bon (1952) developed contagion theory. That era was a time of major upheaval characterized by the erosion of traditional religious, political, and social beliefs and their replacement by modern scientific and industrial standards. Le Bon suspected that disorder, even chaos, lay ahead and crowds would become an increasingly destructive force.

**Contagion theory** contends that the presence of a crowd encourages or compels people to think and act in a uniform manner.

Le Bon claimed that, when in a crowd, an individual inevitably becomes less civilized: "Isolated, he may be a cultivated individual; in a crowd, he is a barbarian—that is, a creature acting by instinct. He possesses the spontaneity, the violence, the ferocity, and also the enthusiasm and heroism of primitive beings . . ." (Le Bon, 1952: 32).

Le Bon's work gives the impression that when people enter crowds, something both magical and terrible happens. Herbert Blumer's (1975) analysis of contagion is more systematic. Blumer has

considered contagion a process where crowd members become increasingly preoccupied with each other's behavior, and outlooks and events that would normally concern them become insignificant. Eventually each crowd member becomes so focused on the others' activities that he or she loses self-consciousness, which usually is a "means of barricading oneself against the influence of others." At this point each individual will simply follow the crowd.

It is likely that anonymity also promotes contagion. A study of twenty-one cases in which crowds were present when people threatened to jump off a building, bridge, or tower suggested that certain conditions of anonymity would prompt members of the crowd to encourage individuals to jump: specifically, membership in a large crowd, the protection of nighttime, and a considerable physical distance between the crowd and victim (Mann, 1981).

### Emergent-Norm Theory

Proponents of the emergent-norm theory reject the idea that the members of a crowd think and behave in the same way. Instead they acknowledge the differences in motives, attitudes, and behavior among people in a crowd. Within crowds researchers can find leaders, active members, passive supporters, passers-by, curious observers, disapproving individuals, and dissenters. **Emergent-norm theory** analyzes the process by which a new social standard develops within a crowd—a standard that frequently receives a more enthusiastic acceptance from some crowd members than others, in spite of the fact that both crowd members and observers tend to perceive nearly unanimous support for it.

According to the emergent-norm theory, people in crowds often find themselves in a normative void—no clear standard of behavior exists. At this point some active people are inclined to take the initiative and present a new standard: an emergent norm, which could advocate such diverse activities as starting to throw rocks and bottles at the police or standing and clapping in appreciation at a graduation ceremony when the name of an especially beloved individual has been read off a list of retiring faculty members. Once the norm develops, the more assertive individuals in the crowd are likely to support behavior consistent with it and to oppose behavior against the norm. This helps to develop the impression that the crowd acts in unanimity.

There are important differences between contagion theory and emergent-norm theory. As we have noted, the emergent-norm perspective rejects the idea that crowd members possess a uniform mental state. Accounts of Nazi crowds attacking Jewish merchants often distorted the actual situation in which a few storm troopers harassed and beat the victims while a disapproving crowd afraid to express dissent watched silently.

Another difference is that emergent-norm theory applies to a wider range of emotional situations. Contagion theory cannot effectively analyze crowds in a subdued state, but emergent-norm theory can. For example, there have been situations where late arrivals reaching the site of an automobile accident or airplane crash loudly exclaimed "What happened?" Disapproving looks and gestures from people in the crowd immediately prevented any further loud commentary. In this case the emergent norm required onlookers to speak quietly out of respect for the victims.

Finally, unlike contagion theory, the emergent-norm perspective does not attempt to analyze crowd behavior as separate from the rest of social behavior. In its use of the concept "norm," emergent-norm theory makes a more concerted effort to extend conventional sociological thinking to an unconventional context — collective behavior (Brown and Goldin, 1973; Turner, 1964; Turner and Killian, 1972; Vander Zanden, 1981).

As you read the following Cross-Cultural Perspective, try to determine how the different theories we have discussed apply.

## CROSS-CULTURAL PERSPECTIVE

## *Public Protest in Argentina: The Start of a Tradition*

Can one incident of crowd behavior have a lasting impact on the national political process? Perhaps such a development would not occur in all countries, but it did take place in Argentina about forty years ago.

On October 9, 1945, Juan Perón was dismissed as vice-president, minister of war, and secretary of labor. Then he was arrested and taken to an isolated island near Buenos Aires. The arrest created immediate anger among workers, who strongly supported Perón. The General Confederation of Labor planned a massive strike as a protest, but before that strike could occur, the workers acted on their own. On the morning of October 17th, many thousands of workers in factories, on farms, in the transportation services, and in many other unskilled and semiskilled occupations simply left their jobs and headed toward the center of Buenos Aires. The march into the city was not planned or coordinated. The word simply spread from one work place to another. Jorge Abelardo Ramos, an Argentine historian, described the scene.

The groups of workers, which are separated at first, soon merge into increasingly larger columns. By the end of the afternoon, the center of the city is impossible to recognize. The small businessmen, the students, the lawyers, and the well dressed people, who dominated the streets several hours earlier, have disappeared. On the sidewalks some groups watch perplexed as Buenos Aires is occupied by hundreds of thousands of angry workers. The demonstrators merge in the Plaza de Mayo (May Square). It is a diverse group. Some are shirtless, while others are in shirtsleeves. Some are on horseback, and others are in trucks or in buses, which have been obliged to change their routes and head toward the Plaza de Mayo. There are also women workers with infants in their arms.

*(Ramos, 1981: 79–80)*

This huge demonstration initiated a new chapter in Argentine history. The anti-Perón faction of the army was forced to release Perón from prison. The following February elections took place, and Juan Perón became president.

It seems reasonable to ask why the demonstrations occurred. As secretary of labor, Perón had championed some significant advances for workers, including higher salaries, vacations, and bonuses. But Perón had a greater importance for the Argentine workers. In a nation ruled by a military dictatorship, where workers had no significant political representation, Perón symbolized their only hope for a better life. With Perón removed from office and thrown into prison, the workers felt totally powerless to influence the government. All they could do was initiate a public demonstration.

During recent military dictatorships, Argentine citizens of different classes, denied participation in the political process, have followed the precedent set by workers in 1945. In 1969 workers and students participated in a large and violent demonstration as a means of showing their unhappiness with the current regime. Soon afterwards the president, whose chief goal was the maintenance of order and stability, felt compelled to resign. In March 1982, as the Argentine economy deteriorated, demonstrations happened once more. Then in June 1982, renewed demonstrations broke out when angry citizens packed the Plaza de Mayo demanding the withdrawal of the military regime following defeat by the British in the Malvinas (Falklands) confrontation. After that there were frequent protests against the military dictatorship.

Eventually the military dictatorship was forced out of power, and on October 30, 1983, open national elections were held. It will be interesting to see whether public demonstrations will remain a widely supported public activity now that citizens' participation in the political process has been restored.

Sources: Conversation with Teresa E. M. Carballal, an Argentine political scientist; Jorge Abelardo Ramos. *La era del peronismo— 1943–1976*. Buenos Aires: Ediciones del Mar Dulce. 1981. Seventh edition. Ms. Carballal translated the quotation from the Ramos book.

## Violent Crowds

A typical scene from a cowboy film illustrates a contagion perspective on riots. Standing in front of the seething crowd, the grief-stricken ranch hand shouts, "Hal Smith was a good man who'd give a stranger the shirt off his back. Now he's lyin' dead in his coffin and them stinkin' townspeople are responsible. They ain't gettin' away with it. Let's tear up the town!" And a moment later they mount their horses and gallop down the main street, destroying everything in their path.

Mobs and riots are related phenomena, but we can draw a distinction betweeen them. A **mob** is a crowd whose members engage in destructive and aggressive behavior in the pursuit of a short-term but valued goal. A mob, for instance, might want to catch a certain person and hang him or her or destroy a particular piece of property. A **riot** is aggressive crowd behavior that is less focused or unified than mob activity. A crowd of angry, frustrated people might run through city streets indiscriminately looting and burning buildings.

The most costly racial riots of this century in the United States occurred between 1966 and 1968 in Los Angeles, Newark, Detroit, Washington, D.C., Cleveland, and a host of other American cities. (See Table 17.1.) The bloodiest racial violence happened in Detroit from July 23 to July 28, 1967. Forty-three people were killed and over a thousand injured. The rioters destroyed more than 1300 buildings and sacked more than 700 businesses (Brown and Goldin, 1973).

Riots have also occurred in more recent years. In December 1982 a policeman killed a young black man in Overtown, a black section of Miami. The incident produced violent demonstrations in which nearly 200 enraged protesters ran through the streets throwing rocks and bottles, looting stores, and setting cars ablaze. After three days of rioting, twenty-six people were injured, thirty-eight were arrested, and a second black youth was killed by police, allegedly while trying to break into a store (Beck, 1983).

Smelser's theory can help analyze the development of the 1960s riots. First, there were certain structurally conducive conditions. The mass media played a significant part, spreading the news about the outbreaks of violence. A federal study identified "a chain reaction of racial violence" (National Advisory Commission on Civil Disorders, 1968: 206). Without radio, television, and newspapers, the information that initiated the "chain reaction" would not have been able to speed from city to city.

Structural strain was also apparent. The

## Table 17.1
### Ghetto Riots and Interracial Clashes

| | NUMBER OF EVENTS IDENTIFIED[1] | ESTIMATED NUMBER OF PARTICIPANTS[2] | REPORTED DEATHS | REPORTED INJURIES | REPORTED ARRESTS |
|---|---|---|---|---|---|
| Period I (June 1963–December 1965) | 48 | 100,000 | 56 | 1800 | 12,500 |
| Period II (January 1966–June 1968) | 200 | 150,000 | 140 | 6156 | 37,362 |
| Period III (July 1968–December 1970) | 256 | 100,000 | 42 | 1050 | 4,632 |

[1] The statistics reported here are based on a tally of newspaper accounts.
[2] Only private citizens are counted, not the police, National Guardsmen, and other officials involved in riot suppression.
Source: Adapted from Ted Robert Gurr. "Political Protest and Rebellion in the 1960s," pp. 49–76 in Hugh Davis Graham and Ted Robert Gurr (eds.), *Violence in America: Historical Perspectives.* Beverly Hills: Sage Publications. 1979, p. 54.

*More riots occurred in Period III than in Period II, but participation, casualties, and arrests were much more extensive in the second period.*

"blocked-opportunity" theory, which suggests that "blocked opportunity" represents a significant source of structural strain, claims that blacks who strongly resented racial discrimination were especially likely to join riots. Rioters were more bitter than local nonrioters, were less willing than nonrioters to fight for their country in a major war, and were more likely to express hatred toward whites (Caplan and Paige, 1968). A recent article reached a slightly different conclusion. While this analysis also accepted the blocked-opportunity idea, it did not focus on such emotional topics as bitterness and hatred but emphasized rioters' rationality. According to this argument, the major reason blacks in the 1960s engaged in riots was powerlessness: They clearly perceived their lack of economic and political power and saw no alternative to rioting for asserting their resistance to the devastating impact of racism (Davis, 1986).

During the 1960s there was growth of a generalized belief supporting protests and demonstrations, if not outright rioting. Many black and white civil-rights leaders clearly became more militant, emphasizing that patience was no longer desirable and that the rich and powerful would make necessary political and economic changes only if pressured to do so. The feeling that violence might be a productive course of action was widely discussed and debated during those years.

Local incidents, such as a black man's arrest or shooting by a white policeman, precipitated riots in different cities. One event of national signifi-

cance helped initiate a number of riots in 1968 — the assassination of Martin Luther King.

Mobilization for action occurred because people suffering from "blocked opportunity" were not motivated to abide by conventional norms. Riots offered them a chance to strike out against the system and, more particularly, the groups and individuals that they believed were oppressing them. For instance, following riots in New York City (East Harlem) in 1968, one could observe a number of blocks where stores owned by outsiders had been looted and burned, whereas locally owned stores remained intact.

Eventually police and/or National Guardsmen would occupy a riot area, imposing social control. Many of the deaths and injuries and all the arrests reported in Table 17.1 happened during the process of establishing social control.

The emergent-norm perspective also helps us to understand the riots. One norm that developed during the riots was a standard supporting cooperative looting, with looters working in pairs or in small groups. Many rioters took goods openly while others, including the police in some instances, watched (Quarantelli and Dynes, 1970).

It is noteworthy that while many riots occurred in the United States during the 1960s, other countries have had much more extensive rioting. (See Table 17.2.)

The research section at the end of the chapter examines the topic of prison riots.

**440**

**Table 17.2
Rebellion[1] in Selected Countries, 1961–1970[2]**

| | PERSON DAYS OF REBELLION PER 100,000 CITIZENS | CONFLICT DEATHS PER 10 MILLION CITIZENS |
|---|---|---|
| Largest Western democracies (1970 population 50 million+) | | |
| United States | 250 | 18.3 |
| West Germany | 0 | 0.3 |
| Britain | 20 | 0.5 |
| Italy | 1,300 | 8.0 |
| France | 15,000 | 17.1 |
| Some small Western democracies | | |
| Canada | 700 | 1.5 |
| Australia | 0.1 | 0 |
| Sweden | 0 | 0 |
| Israel | 70 | 11.8 |
| Republic of Ireland | 70 | 0 |
| Northern Ireland | 40,000 | 129.3 |
| Other major nations of the world | | |
| Europe: USSR | 0.3 | 18 |
| Poland | 0 | 118 |
| Spain | 1,900 | 13 |
| Middle East: Turkey | 50 | 14 |
| Egypt | 40 | 9 |
| Iran | 10 | 76 |
| Asia: India | 4,700 | 42 |
| Indonesia | 100,000+ | 30,000+ |
| Japan | 0.5 | 0.1 |
| Africa: Nigeria | 150,000+ | 250,000+ |
| South Africa | 200 | 16 |
| Latin America: Brazil | 150 | 7 |
| Mexico | 9,000 | 26 |
| Argentina | 35,000 | 31 |

[1] An outbreak against those in authority.
[2] Within each group countries are listed by descending population rank. The data are rounded to reflect their imprecision. Estimates of death are more accurate than estimates of person days. Estimates for Western countries are more accurate than those for Communist and third-world countries. Source: Adapted from Ted Robert Gurr. "Political Protest and Rebellion in the 1960s," pp. 49–76 in Hugh Davis Graham and Ted Robert Gurr (eds.), *Violence in America: Historical Perspectives.* Beverly Hills: Sage Publications. 1979, p. 60.

*During the 1960s a number of nations suffered a considerably higher proportion of death produced by rebellion and conflict than the United States did. Nigeria and Indonesia, which had devastating internal wars, were at the extreme.*

## Frightened Crowds

In panics and mass hysteria, the emotional level is high, just as in riots. Members of frightened crowds, however, seek to escape the source of shared concern.

### Panics

A **panic** is a collective flight to safety. Panic occurs under specific circumstances. It takes place only if people believe that escape routes are avail-able but limited or closing. It will not occur if people are convinced that there is no way to escape. In the latter situation—for instance, if people face suffocation in a submerged submarine or death by an approaching fire with all escape routes blocked —they might experience terror or start behaving like children, but they usually will not panic (Smelser, 1963).

One observer of a fire that started in a crowded theater in Chicago in 1903 and killed 602 people offered some evidence for contagion theory when

*Two prominent types of crowds are violent crowds and frightened crowds.*

he indicated that heel prints were apparent on many dead faces. The marks testified ". . . to the cruel fact that human animals stricken by terror are as mad and ruthless as stampeding cattle" (Foy and Harlow, in Turner and Killian, 1957: 96–97).

The same observer further supported the contagion perspective when he noted that if a person screams "Fire!" there are ". . . always hundreds of people who go crazy the moment they hear the word."

Experimental studies involving panic suggest that its occurrence depends primarily on the availability of information about the amount of danger involved, people's perception of opportunities to escape, and their sense of whether or not those present will help each other (Brown and Goldin, 1973). On the last point, the quality of leadership can make a significant difference. In the course of experiments with 144 college-aged males, Klein (1976) offered his subjects financial rewards if they could escape from handcuffs and threatened an electric shock if they could not. Klein found that effective leadership could reduce the likelihood of panic by countering the lack of coordination that "can make a minor crisis a major tragedy." Marshall (1947: 130) has indicated that if an army unit is under attack and the unit leader says, "Let's get out of here!" then panic is quite possible. However, if the leader simply tells his troops to follow him to a nearby destination, then the chances of panic sharply decrease. Both studies suggest that the effectiveness of an emergent norm established by leaders in an anxiety-laden situation will significantly influence the likelihood of panic.

### Mass Hysteria

**Mass hysteria** is a type of panic that occurs when people are scattered over a wide geographical area. Often the mass media play a significant role in promoting these incidents. More than 180 reports have been published describing a variety of ailments for which no medical source can be located. A recent case was the "mysterious gas poisoning" that affected over 900 people, mainly schoolgirls, in the Jordan West Bank region (Hefez, 1985).

A celebrated example of mass hysteria occurred on Halloween, October 30, 1938. Millions of Americans found themselves listening to a broadcast on CBS radio. It was entitled *The War of the Worlds,* an adaptation of H. G. Wells's novel of the same title. At the beginning of the radio play, Orson Welles, the narrator, explained that what followed was, in fact, fiction, but many who tuned in late never heard the statement, and some who listened from the beginning were swept along by the drama and simply forgot what Welles had said.

The play told how Martians had invaded the United States. They landed in New Jersey, then headed north toward New York City, killing hundreds of troops sent to stop them as well as large numbers of civilians. Hadley Cantril (1940), who studied this incident of mass hysteria, wrote:

> Long before the broadcast had ended, people all over the United States were praying, crying, fleeing frantically to escape death from Martians. Some ran to rescue loved ones. Others telephoned farewells or warnings, hurried to inform neighbors, sought information from newspapers or radio stations, summoned ambulances and police cars. At least six million people heard the broadcast. At least a million of them were frightened or disturbed.
>
> (Cantril, 1940: 47)

Cantril conducted 130 detailed interviews soon after the event. He found some people who thought that the invasion had been no more than a story, whereas others were convinced it was true. Several different characteristics, Cantril found, made some people more inclined to believe that an invasion was occurring. In particular, the idea of an invasion fitted better with some people's preconceptions than with those of others. Some respondents had been expecting a foreign invasion from the Germans or the Japanese, and for these people the threat of a Martian attack was a concrete illustration of their war-related dread. Apparently invaders were simply invaders, whether from across the ocean or from outer space. Other people questioned whether they were sufficiently competent to pit their judgment against that of the announcers, scientists, and government authorities supposedly being presented on the program. Uneducated people, in particular, lost confidence in their own judgment (Cantril, 1940).

As this incident suggests, mass hysteria may happen when people suddenly believe that they face serious, rapidly approaching danger. The conventional normative guidelines no longer seem fully

*In the wake of the Tylenol killings of October 1982, steps taken to prevent possible injury to children eating Halloween candy included the use of x-rays to scan candy for razor blades or other metal objects.*

applicable, and terror-stricken people grapple for some way to save themselves. In contrast, if they have an opportunity to prepare for the approaching danger, the conventional norms are likely to remain intact, and mass hysteria is much less likely to occur.

A case in point happened at Halloween time, forty-four years after the War of the Worlds incident. In October 1982 widespread concern developed about the poisoning of Halloween candy following seven nationally publicized deaths involving cyanide-contaminated Extra Strength Tylenol capsules. As the mayor of Vineland, a New Jersey city of 53,000 residents, explained, "I got scared thinking what an opportunity this was for some nut to do something" (Barron, 1982: 81).

That mayor banned trick or treating. In other towns or cities, officials employed a variety of measures. Police chiefs urged parents to limit their children's Halloween visits, school officials promised prizes to children who stayed home, and hospitals offered to scan candy with the same sort of x-ray devices used on luggage at airports. There were no serious injuries that Halloween, nor any panic or mass hysteria.

# Rumors

As part of the breakdown in normative guidelines that occurs in crowd situations, established channels of communication are often either out of order or are unable to supply thorough, explicit, and up-to-date information. Rumors are likely to develop.

A **rumor** is a report transmitted informally (often by word of mouth) and concerned with subject matter difficult to verify. Rumors involve information that is important to people, and in this respect they differ from gossip. Frequently rumors provide false information, but that is not necessarily the case.

Allport and Postman (1947) suggested that rumors are the product of two factors: people's interest in the subject and the extent of ambiguity (the likelihood that two or more interpretations of the situation are possible). It seems likely that both factors are necessary to produce rumors. A group of boys might be fanatically interested in the outcome of the World Series, but normally no rumors would start on that subject because ambiguity would be absent. The boys would be able to watch the Series on television, and they would know the outcome of each game immediately. Rumors might start, on the other hand, if these same boys were deprived of normal contact with the media when a sustained loss of electric power occurred in their area.

## The Development of Rumors

The content of a rumor is likely to change over time, with the amount of change strongly affected by the emotional reaction the rumor creates. The greater the capacity to excite emotion, the more extensive the changes in content are likely to be. Those who transmit the rumor tend to eliminate some details and, in turn, to emphasize others. The changes in detail generally reflect the fears, prejudices, hopes, and other prominent feelings of the people who pass on the rumor.

The transmission of a rumor is a collective process in which individuals can play a number of roles. Some people are messengers, relaying the information. Others act as skeptics, expressing doubt about what they hear. Individuals can also be interpreters, trying to figure out what is happening. Finally there are likely to be decision-makers, who initiate action in response to the news the rumor brings (Shibutani, 1966).

The "shortage" of bathroom tissues was an incident that illustrates how rumors can develop. On December 11, 1973, Harold V. Froehlich, a Wisconsin congressman, issued a statement after many complaints from people in his district about what they perceived as a rapidly developing paper shortage. Mr. Froehlich said, "The United States may face a serious shortage of toilet paper within a few months. . . . I hope we don't have to ration toilet tissue. . . . A toilet paper shortage is no laughing matter. It is a problem that will touch every American" (Malcolm, 1980: 497).

Froehlich and his staff were amazed at how much attention the news release received. This was an era when members of the mass media and the public were becoming increasingly aware of and concerned about shortages. A shortage of toilet tissue seemed no more unlikely than short supplies of gasoline, heating oil, coffee, sugar, and a number of other commodities. As the rumor spread, the message became clear and decisive in line with people's expectations and fears. Qualifying words like "potential" disappeared.

Certain individuals played important roles in the transmission of this rumor. One celebrity became a messenger: "You know, we've got all sorts of shortages these days," Johnny Carson told his faithful late-night television audience. "But have you heard the latest? I'm not kidding. I saw it in the paper. There's a shortage of toilet paper" (Malcolm, 1980: 497). The day after these comments, a toilet-paper-buying binge began nationally. Some shoppers—we can consider them "decision-makers"—went to local stores and bought huge supplies of toilet tissue. Other people remained skeptics, proving correct in their analysis that the rumor of a shortage was false.

Like Carson with the bathroom-tissue rumor, other celebrities sometimes underestimate their impact as messengers. During the "Stupid Pet Tricks" segment of his late-night show, David Letterman presented a poodle that walked upright on its hind legs while balancing a glass of water on an upside-down Frisbee. While the dazzled audience watched, Letterman said, "The only thing that kind of detracts from that [the animal act] is I know that the woman has performed intricate spinal surgery on the dog and that's illegal and she'll end up doing time. But as far as the trick goes it's a 10" (*New Haven Register,* July 26, 1986: 14). Letterman only meant to be humorous. However, there were some immediate negative effects when that segment of his show was rebroadcast at an early evening hour to an audience unused to his off-beat humor. The owner's pet-grooming business rapidly lost customers, and the dog's budding show-business career—modeling, performances at birthday parties, and even some commercials—was seriously damaged. The owner sued Letterman for $1 million.

## Efforts to Stop Rumors

Rumors can be troublesome and persistent. Can individuals or organizations take steps to terminate them?

A number of years ago, the rumor started that McDonald's was selling hamburgers with worms in

them. In some areas sales dropped 30 percent, in spite of the company's advertisements emphasizing that McDonald's sold only "100 percent pure beef" or suggesting that at $5 to $8 a pound for worms, it would be crazy to put them in hamburgers.

Soon after the incident, market researchers at Northwestern University conducted a study. The subjects were sixty-four graduate students, divided into four- to six-member groups. The researchers told the students that they would participate in an experiment evaluating their reaction to violence. Each group watched a typical evening television show containing three commercials for McDonald's. After the third commercial, a young man who, unknown to the students, was working for the researchers casually indicated that the commercials reminded him that McDonald's had worms in their hamburgers.

When the television show was over, the investigators treated various groups in different ways. A couple of groups received no additional information from the research team. In several other groups, a researcher repeated a statement similar to McDonald's own advertisements—that a Food and Drug Administration study had concluded that the company's beef was 100 percent pure and that, besides, worms were simply too expensive to be used in hamburgers. In other groups the researcher asked the students about their own experiences with McDonald's—where and how often they went and whether the franchises they visited had indoor seating. The object of these questions was to stimulate neutral or positive thoughts that would counter the rumors. In a third collection of groups, one of the researchers tried to create a positive attitude toward worms in the students' minds. He told these groups of students that he had taken his mother-in-law to Chez Paul, an expensive Chicago restaurant, where they had eaten a very tasty sauce made out of worms.

At the end of the experiment, the students rated the quality of McDonald's food as well as their likelihood of eating there. The results:

1. The least favorable ratings came from those who heard only the worm rumor and had no follow-up experience. This outcome occurred in spite of the fact that in a separate test most of these students indicated that they did not believe the worm story.

**Table 17.3**
**Some General Comparisons among Violent Crowds, Social Movements, and Organizations**

| | VIOLENT CROWD | SOCIAL MOVEMENT | ORGANIZATION |
|---|---|---|---|
| Leadership | Informal | Increasingly formalized over time | Formal |
| Duration | Minutes or hours | From a few months to many years, depending on the movement | Many years frequently |
| Normative guidelines | Informal and emergent | Increasingly formalized over time | Formal |
| Structural strain on members | Excessive | Considerable when individuals join but generally declining as the movement ages | Variable, depending on the nature of people's tasks |

*With the passage of time, the characteristics of social movements become increasingly like those of organizations.*

2. The ratings from those who heard the worm rumor and the same denials that McDonald's had presented in their own advertisements were almost as low as those of the first group of students.
3. The students who had the opportunity to discuss their own experiences with McDonald's gave significantly higher ratings. Their ratings, in fact, were as high as those that came from people who had not heard any rumors.
4. The students who heard about the worm sauce at Chez Paul gave equally high ratings (Rice, 1981).

The rumor of worms in McDonald's hamburgers created structural strain for the students.

The most effective means to combat the strain was to shift the students' attention to conventional social situations, where structural strain was absent: either their memories of worm-free meals at McDonald's or the situation at Chez Paul, where a worm sauce was considered a delicacy.

Both collective behavior and social movements involve behavior that occurs to some extent outside existing normative guidelines. Social movements, however, are somewhat more conventionally structured, with the possibility that they will eventually become part of established society. (See Table 17.3.)

## Social Movements

As we have noted, a social movement is an organized, collective activity undertaken by people to promote or resist social change. The members of a social movement share:

1. An ideology justifying their actions.
2. A sense of unity.
3. A set of norms prescribing followers' behavior.
4. Some division of labor between leaders and followers and among the different categories of followers (Killian, 1964).

Smelser (1963) outlined a distinction between norm-oriented and value-oriented social movements. The goal of a norm-oriented social movement is to create new norms or occasionally to restore old ones. Examples would be a reform movement agitating for a local park or for more police protection, a group of workers seeking to establish their own independent union, or groups mobilizing at the state or national level for tax reform, nuclear disarmament, or lower gasoline prices. The goal of a value-oriented social movement is to change a society's values, which are the basic principles upon which social behavior is based. Value-oriented social movements often involve efforts to make revolutionary change. They tend to be more demanding of members' time, energy, and emotional commitment than are norm-oriented social movements. Political revolutionaries, religious "cult" members, and people in utopian communities may be considered members of social movements advocating new values.

In the upcoming discussion, we examine two theoretical approaches to social movements.

## Theories of Social Movements

Strain theories dominated the analysis of social movements until the early 1970s. Since then, resource-mobilization theory has assumed a more prominent role. (Hannigan, 1985; Kerbo and Shaffer, 1986; Klandermans, 1984; Nielsen, 1985).

### Strain Theory

As we noted in the discussion of the second stage of Smelser's theory, a number of social conditions

**Figure 17.1**
**The J-curve: Strain and Revolution**

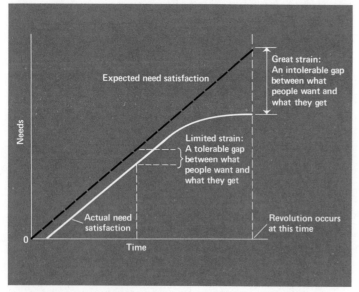

*Davies's theory of revolution suggests that revolutions occur when an intolerable gap develops between people's actual need satisfaction and their expected need satisfaction. (Source: Adapted from James C. Davies. "Toward a Theory of Revolution." American Sociological Review. Vol. 27. February 1962, p. 6.)*

can create structural strain, which is a significant amount of tension or pressure for people, and this strain lessens their willingness to stay within normal behavioral limits.

James Davies (1962) developed a strain theory. He studied historical accounts of the French and Russian revolutions, gathering evidence that revolutions occur when social conditions improve. Davies concluded that during such periods people's expectations inevitably rise, outstripping their capacity to achieve expectations. As long as the gap between expectations and the capacity to achieve expectations remains fairly small, strain will be minimal, and no revolution will occur. The strain, however, becomes great if people's actual capacity to achieve need satisfaction levels off (somewhat like the partially inverted curve of the letter "j" as represented in Figure 17.1), while the expected need satisfaction continues to rise. As Figure 17.1 suggests, an intolerable gap then exists between what people want and what they can get. This gap sets the stage for revolution.

Consider the application of strain theory to the modern women's movement, which we discussed briefly in Chapter 11 ("Emerging Minorities"). In 1963 Betty Friedan published *The Feminine Mystique*, which attempted to analyze the plight of modern women. Friedan was referring to strain when she summarized women's situation as something seldom discussed or understood—"the problem that has no name." In 1966 Friedan and others founded the National Organization for Women (NOW) when the federal government did not take any action to improve women's second-class status. Only a few years later, another large group of women became interested in women's rights. These women, who were generally younger than the members of NOW, had participated in civil-rights and antiwar activities and had begun to feel that they faced the contradiction (a specific type of strain) of working in freedom movements and finding themselves restricted to traditional women's roles that permitted almost no use of creative skills and leadership capacities.

Strain appears to have been a factor in the development of the modern women's movement, and one might argue that it plays a role in the development of other social movements. In recent years, however, many social scientists have become increasingly convinced that the explanatory capacity of strain theories is limited and that the resource-mobilization perspective makes a more valuable contribution to understanding how social movements have developed (Gurney and Tierney, 1982; Kerbo, 1982).

### Resource-Mobilization Theory

**Resource-mobilization theory** focuses on the process by which the members of social movements acquire and use certain resources necessary to accomplish their collective goals. The supporters of this theory agree that strain can encourage people to join social movements but that social movements will not develop until the members have access to such necessary resources as money, goods, power, members' commitment of time and energy, or votes (Gamson, 1975; Tilly, 1978).

Successful social movements do not simply seek to recruit large numbers of people. Their priority is the recruitment of politically experienced and well-adjusted groups and individuals (Oberschall, 1973).

Resource-mobilization theory helps explain the development of the modern women's movement. For instance, one resource that encouraged the creation of NOW was a citizen's advisory council on women's issues established in the early 1960s. This organization provided a communications network through which women could discuss their common grievances and decide what actions to take. Once NOW existed, it broadened and deepened those channels of communications.

The younger segment of the women's movement has acquired its own, informal communications resource: the "rap group." Rap groups engage in a process known as "consciousness-raising." Women come together in groups of five to fifteen members and discuss their feelings, experiences, problems, and concerns. The participants soon realize that what they have considered personal problems are usually the result of limited opportunities imposed on them since birth. They start to understand that the women's movement represents a very effective vehicle for reaching a solution. Jo Freeman, a sociologist, concluded:

> Once women have gone through such a resocialization, their views of themselves and the world are never the same again even if they stop participating actively in the movement. Those who do drop out rarely do so without spreading feminist ideas among their own friends and colleagues. All who undergo consciousness-raising feel compelled themselves to seek out other women with whom to share the experience.
>
> *(Freeman, 1979: 562)*

You should be able to figure out how both the strain theory and the resource-mobilization perspective apply to the nuclear-freeze movement, which is discussed in the following Contemporary Issue.

---

**CONTEMPORARY ISSUE**

## *The Nuclear-Freeze Movement*

A social movement demanding the curtailment of the growth of our nuclear arsenal has developed in the United States and other countries in the last few years. In early 1980 a coalition of about thirty peace groups met to endorse a statement that advocated a mutual, verifiable freeze of American and Soviet nuclear weaponry at their current levels. In August 1980 the Democratic National Convention rejected the proposal. The following year, however, a carefully organized grassroots effort in Vermont led to approval of the freeze proposal in eighteen towns. Within the first four months of 1982, 161 more Vermont towns had passed the proposal, and freeze proposals were starting to appear in towns and cities around the country. Before election day 1982, about 275 city governments, 12 state legislatures, and 446 New England town meetings had passed freeze resolutions. At the polls voters in eight states and several major cities, together comprising about one fourth of the country's population, supported the idea of a freeze. The freeze motion was defeated in Arizona and two small counties in Arkansas and Colorado. The wording of these freeze resolutions varied, but all of them urged that the United States and the Soviet Union begin immediate negotiations toward establishing a mutual verifiable freeze in the production, testing, and deployment of nuclear weapons and also in the bombers, missiles, and submarines that transport them.

In April 1983, 64 percent of the respondents in a nationally conducted survey felt that a nuclear war with the Soviets would be most effectively avoided by a mutual freeze on nuclear weapons while only 25 percent of the sample believed that a military buildup would be the best way to prevent such a war (*CBS News/New York Times Poll,* April 1983). Then in July 1984, a resolution supporting a freeze of American and Soviet nuclear weapons was included as a plank in the platform of the Democratic Party.

An important reason for the growth of the freeze movement has been the increasing concern that both American and Soviet leaders have been belligerently moving toward a confrontation that could produce nuclear war. A particular source of concern in the early 1980s was the Reagan Administration's frequent, vague references to a "limited nuclear war"—an outcome that nuclear opponents consider impossible to ensure and one that they find particularly frightening because of its ability to make political leaders more receptive to nuclear confrontation. Dramatic antinuclear demonstrations in Western Europe have also encouraged the American efforts. Furthermore the supporters of a freeze argue that the finan-

cial cost of a nuclear buildup has been killing important domestic programs.

How does one characterize the movement supporters? One activist in Vermont said, "Someone once criticized the freeze as a mom-and-apple-pie issue. That's exactly what it is" (Alpern, 1982: 22). Supporters include homemakers, clerks, doctors, lawyers, clergymen, teachers, scientists, and even military people. Many, if not most of the antinuclear activists have never participated in public protest before. Whatever their background and current activities, they subscribe to the belief that a continuation of the present arms race would be extremely dangerous and wasteful.

A number of organizations and groups have played a particularly significant part in the mobilization of the freeze movement. Ground Zero was founded in late 1980 by Roger Molander, who served as a nuclear-strategy specialist on the staff of the National Security Council. Ground Zero has a paid staff of ten members and 400 volunteers in 140 cities across the country. The movement has been strictly educational in its approach, taking no stands on various disarmament proposals. Molander has indicated that the organization's goal has been to publicize the precise dangers posed by nuclear war. During Ground Zero Week, the group encouraged communities to organize town meetings and lectures about the threat of nuclear war. Local coordi-

nators received kits from the national headquarters containing Ground Zero markers, directions on where to place the markers, and details of the effects that would be produced if a one megaton bomb were to be dropped on their community.

Physicians for Social Responsibility has been another prominent movement organization. In 1979 the group was small and weak, but then Helen Caldicott, a pediatrician at Children's Hospital Medical Center in Boston, assumed the presidency. Caldicott has traveled around the country tirelessly speaking on behalf of disarmament. She has been so effective that the organization grew from ten doctors to 11,000 while maintaining a twenty-two member staff, eighty-five chapters in forty-five states, and a $600,000 annual budget.

Religious leaders and groups have been playing an increasingly important role in the freeze movement. In 1983, 238 Roman Catholic bishops in the United States publicly supported a freeze, signing a pastoral letter to that effect. The National Council of Churches, which represents 40 million Protestants, has also backed a bilateral nuclear freeze.

It is noteworthy that large numbers of young people, who took such a prominent part in the protests of the 1960s, have been conspicuously absent from the antinuclear movement. On the other hand, a number of college demonstrations, such as a 400-student "die-in" that briefly blocked traffic at the University of Michigan, have suggested that student involvement might be growing.

In the middle 1980s, the majority of the American public supported a nuclear freeze. It seems probable that public support and participation will continue to grow. On the other hand, a substantial number of Americans sincerely believe that the only way to protect the United States effectively is by expanding nuclear might.

Further, a large number of political, military, and business leaders are committed to the latter position. Discussion, debate, and conflict on the nuclear-arms issue seem inevitable in the years ahead.

Sources: David M. Alpern. "A Matter of Life and Death." *Newsweek.* Vol. 99. April 26, 1982, pp. 20–25; John Herbers. "Widespread Vote Urges Nuclear Freeze." *New York Times.* November 4, 1982, p. 22; James Kelly. "Thinking about the Unthinkable." *Time.* Vol. 119. March 29, 1982, pp. 10+. Richard Rhodes. "A Peace Walk." *New York Times Magazine.* December 8, 1985, p. 134.

# Sources of Social Change

Collective behavior and social movements are produced by social change and also cause it to take place. In fact, in the following discussion of the sources of social change, social movements is one of the four factors examined. The others are cultural innovation, population, and environment.

## Cultural Innovation

A **cultural innovation** is the recognition or development of new material or nonmaterial elements in a culture. There are three prominent means by which cultural innovation occurs: discovery, invention, and diffusion.

### Discovery

**Discovery** is the perception of something that already exists but that had not been previously recognized. A discovery can be a material item (another continent or a new "wonder" drug) or a nonmaterial item (the principle of gravity).

A discovery often takes place because of chance. Random strikes of lightning undoubtedly played an important part in the process by which people first learned about fire. It is likely that it took many chance encounters before early humanity began to appreciate the potential contribution that fire could make for cooking food and providing warmth, and it is also probable that efforts to control fire began only after these potentials were recognized and appreciated.

Something that is discovered does not have an effect on social change until it is used widely. In ancient Alexandria, Greece, the residents discovered how to use steam power, and they even employed steam power as a means of hauling firewood to the top of the lighthouse on the nearby island of Pharos (Linton, 1973). However, it was not until about 1700 years later that the use of steam to power boats and trains revolutionized transportation and produced significant social and economic change in Western societies.

### Invention

An **invention** is a combination of existing knowledge to produce something new. The invention of the airplane involved the combination of such elements as the wings of a glider, an internal-combustion engine from an automobile, and the adaptation of a ship's propeller. Though less well known, nonmaterial inventions are also common. The city-manager plan, for instance, represents the transfer of business-management techniques to city government (Murdock, 1956).

It is important to recognize that, like any other cultural element, an invention is a piece in a cultural puzzle, not a disconnected item. Because of this interrelation, the development of an innovation is likely to generate pressure for change in other parts of social life. Thus the invention and production of the automobile, for instance, has stimulated the formation of an entire new body of law. Television led to further innovations in dozens of areas, including advertising, regulatory law, political-campaign styles, family life, and even diet (e.g., TV dinners).

All inventions do not produce an equally strong impetus for change. A new method of painting, for instance, might have no apparent effect beyond a small circle of artists and critics. A new religious

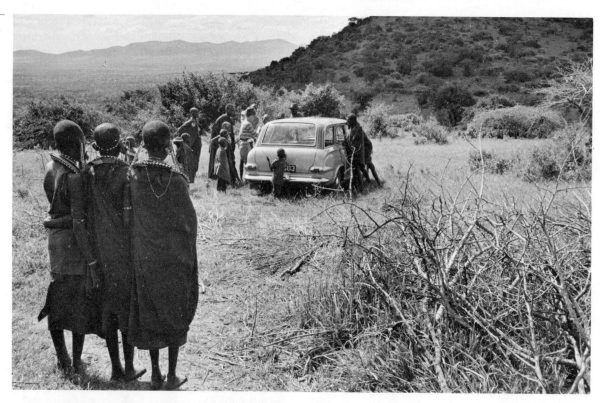

*Achieving modernization involves an abandonment of or, at least, a compromise with old ways.*

doctrine might arouse interest and support only among a highly select group of followers. An invention that affects the way people obtain the material necessities of life, however, will produce extensive changes in a society. The spear, which permitted early hunters to kill animals for food at a much greater distance than had previously been possible, and the automobile, which allowed people to travel distances more quickly and easily than they could before its introduction, are examples Lenski and Lenski, 1982). Without much thought you can probably figure out how the existence of the automobile has affected all five major institutional structures.

## Diffusion

**Diffusion** is the process by which cultural traits move either from one culture to another or from one part of a culture to another. Some scholars believe that about 90 percent of all cultural development results from diffusion. To illustrate this point, Ralph Linton wrote a well-known essay, which with tongue-in-cheek he entitled "One Hundred Percent American." He began, "There can be no question about the average American's Americanism or his desire to preserve this precious heritage at all costs" (Linton, 1982: 58). Then Linton indicated that unfortunately some "insidious foreign ideas" have managed to enter American civilization. He went on to explain that virtually all material objects average Americans encounter in their homes—their pajamas, clocks, toothbrushes, razors, coffee, waffles, newspapers, and so on—are innovations that originated in other cultures.

The diffusion process displays certain definite characteristics. First, some cultural elements diffuse more readily than others. Material objects and technology generally spread more easily than do belief systems and forms of social organization.

Second, innovations that diffuse are often adopted in modified form by the receiving culture. For example, the Africans who were brought to Brazil as slaves carried their religion with them. Whereas their descendants became Catholics, they retained certain modified elements of their tribal religion. These descendants linked particular African gods with different saints, and they developed some interesting mixed beliefs: for example, that a hollow-log drum must receive spiritual control through baptism, or it will fail to call the appropriate deities to a religious ceremony.

A third significant point about diffusion is that it is often a two-way process. Films, novels, history books, and also sociology texts have strongly emphasized the diffusion of culture traits from whites to Native Americans: horses, guns, alcohol, clothing, religion, schooling, and eventually all major elements of the modern American life-style. Much less attention has focused on the cultural contributions that Indians have given to white Americans and also to the members of other countries. A few of the better-known Indian vegetables are corn, beans, squash, sweet potatoes, and the so-called Irish potatoes. Prominent modern drugs well known among Native American cultures include

coca (the source of cocaine and novocaine), curare (an anesthetic), cinchowa bark that produces quinine, and cascara used in laxatives. Furthermore Indian music has had a significant impact on a number of American composers, who borrowed melodies and themes from western Indians (Lauer, 1977). (See Table 17.4.)

**Table 17.4**
**A Variety of Products That Diffused to Modern American Culture**

| FOOD AND DRINK | PLACE OF ORIGIN |
|---|---|
| Alcoholic beverages | Near East (Syria, Lebanon, and Israel) |
| Bananas | South Asia |
| Beans | Eastern United States (Indians) |
| Butter | Near East |
| Chocolate | Mexico |
| Coffee | Abyssinia (Ethiopia)[1] |
| Corn | Eastern United States (Indians) |
| Eggs | Southern Asia |
| Grains | Near East |
| Milk | Asia Minor (Turkey) |
| Squash | Eastern United States (Indians) |
| Sugar | India |
| Sweet potatoes | Eastern United States (Indians) |
| Tea | China |

| OTHER MATERIAL PRODUCTS FOR EVERYDAY USE | PLACE OF ORIGIN |
|---|---|
| Bathtub | Rome (Italy) |
| Bed | Persia (Iran) or Asia Minor (Turkey) |
| Checks | Persia (Iran) |
| Cigar | Brazil |
| Cigarette | Mexico (A.D. 400 to 1400) |
| Clock | Medieval Europe |
| Coins | Lydia (Turkey) |
| Cotton | India |
| Fork | Italy |
| Glass | Egypt |
| Linen | Near East |
| Paper | China |
| Paper money | China |
| Printing | China |
| Shoes | Greece |
| Soap | Gaul (France) |
| Spoon | Rome (Italy) |
| Toilet | Rome (Italy) |

*(continued)*

**Table 17.4 (*continued*)**

| IMPORTANT NONMATERIAL PRODUCTS | PLACE OF ORIGIN |
|---|---|
| Alphabet | Phoenicia (Syria and Lebanon) |
| Banking (credits, loans, discounts, and mortgages) | Babylonia (Iraq) and later influences of Italy and England |
| Family organization | Medieval Europe |
| Language | England |
| Numerical system | India[2] |
| System of real-property ownership[3] | Medieval Europe |

[1] If the product first appeared in a country with an ancient name, the modern name appears in parentheses.
[2] The numerical system originated in India, diffused to the Middle East, and then eventually reached Europe.
[3] Ownership of such fixed, immovable things as land and buildings.
Sources: Ruth Benedict. "The Growth of Culture," pp. 182–195 in Harry L. Shapiro (ed.), *Man, Culture, and Society*. New York: Oxford University Press. 1956; Ralph Linton. "One Hundred Percent American." *American Mercury*. Vol. 40. April 1937, pp. 427–430; George Peter Murdock. "How Culture Changes," pp. 247–260 in Harry L. Shapiro (ed.), *Man, Culture, and Society*.

## Population

At the extremes population size can have a profound effect on a society. If the population becomes small enough, a society will cease to exist. Disease, famine, and annihilation can produce such a result. The Native American population was probably between about 700,000 and one million when Columbus reached the New World. It dropped to about 250,000 at the end of the nineteenth century, and a substantial number of tribes simply disappeared. Most historians agree that more Indians died of white people's diseases than died in warfare. Unlike the whites the Indians had not developed any immunities to smallpox, typhoid, yellow fever, and the other diseases brought over from Europe, and in some areas the effects were devastating, killing 90 percent of the indigenous population (Farley, 1982: 111–112).

On the other hand, rapid population growth can also lead to destructive social change. Many overpopulated developing nations suffer from hunger, poor housing, crowding, poverty, political conflict, and inadequate health services: a complex of conditions producing a deprived life by Western standards (Brown, McGrath, and Stokes, 1982).

A change in the size of particular segments of the population can also promote social change. For instance, the American baby boom of 1946–1965 led to a period of growth for schools and colleges until the early 1970s. However, the past decade, during which the youthful population has declined, has featured teacher layoffs and also the elimination of some schools in many districts. In addition, the baby boom has contributed to intensified job competition and to unemployment in many job areas.

More generally it appears that if prospective parents are part of a large generation, then they will probably find themselves caught in a highly competitive job situation. They will take a fairly long time to establish themselves occupationally, and they will therefore be likely to start having children relatively late in life and to produce a small number of offspring. On the other hand, as members of a small generation, these children will find it somewhat easier to establish themselves occupationally. Thus they will be able to start having children at a younger age and will therefore be likely to produce more of them. Census data indicate that these two patterns have alternated with each other since the 1890s (Ryder, 1980).

## The Environment

At present Americans find themselves confronting two contradictory priorities: one emphasizing a clean environment and the other stressing the significance of low energy costs or other economic issues. National survey data suggest that Americans split evenly on whether they should underscore the development of new energy sources or environmental protection. In September 1981, 39 percent of a national sample indicated that they believed that progress depends on maintaining an adequate supply of energy. On the other hand, 40 percent believed that environmental protection was more important: that it is better to risk not having enough energy than to spoil the environment. Some fluctuations had occurred in these figures since 1973, but they were minor; in that year the respective numbers were 37 and 37 percent (Roper Organization, *Roper Reports*, November 1981).

Controlling and reducing environmental pollution is difficult, even if a consensus exists on the necessity to act. Air pollution is a case in point. What represents a reasonable goal in this area? Is it

*In at least one American town, citizens appear to have made a firm choice about the dangers and benefits of nuclear industrial production. The helmets of the high-school football team (known as The Bombers) are adorned with a mushroom cloud, symbolizing the town's commitment to an industry that employs or supports about three fourths of the area residents.*

enough to remove all pollutants detectable by the human senses, or should we be concerned with impurities identifiable only by scientific instruments? In the late 1940s in Pittsburgh, industrial leaders, politicians, and the public agreed that air pollution was a serious problem, but the different groups could never accept a single comprehensive plan for air-pollution control. The restrictions eventually placed on air pollution were limited, concerned only with solving the immediate, observable problem (Stiefel, 1982).

## Social Movements

As we noted earlier in the chapter, two broad types of social movements exist. Norm-oriented social movements maintain a narrow focus, seeking to change a specific law or practice. Value-oriented social movements, which attempt to alter or replace existing values, are much more ambitious. Effective value-oriented movements can significantly change people's values, beliefs, and behavior.

Four conditions seem to play an especially important role in the development of effective social movements. First, a sense of strain must exist among a large number of people: a clearly shared awareness of the disparity between existing conditions and the ideal state of affairs. Second, developing social movements require close interaction and communication among members. Without such contacts people's perceptions of the strains that they are encountering are apt to be less clear, and they are considerably less likely to develop coherent ideologies. Third, social movements are more likely to grow if the members share prominent statuses—for instance, women, students, blacks, or the elderly—and thus have common outlooks, experiences, and grievances. Fourth, the existence of previous social-movement activity is usually important. Unless the members see actual evidence indicating that large-scale social change is possible, they are unlikely to believe that their own movement will succeed (Morrison; 1973). The more developed these factors, the more successful the social movement is likely to be, at least initially, and successful social movements have the ability to produce significant social change.

What kind of social movements are most likely to succeed? A study of a sample of fifty-three American social movements that developed between 1800 and 1945 found that groups that used violence had a greater likelihood of achieving some of their goals than did social movements that totally rejected forceful means. However, the absolute number of social movements in the sample that did engage in violence was small, and thus all conclusions from this study must be tentative. It does appear that violence is most likely to produce successful change when the protest group is strong and impatient with the pace of change and it directs its wrath against a weak target group. Successful groups, however, do not use violence as their primary tactic (Gamson, 1975).

Social movements can "fail"—cease to exist—and yet still have a long-term effect on society. For instance, twenty years after the Garvey Movement of the 1920s, many scholars had simply dismissed it as an extreme expression of black racial consciousness and pride that flowered temporarily during the social upheaval that occurred in black America during and after World War I. By the 1950s, however, the Black Muslims or Nation of Islam had formed a large social movement that promoted essentially the same goals as Garveyism, and Elijah Muhammed, the founder of the Black Muslims, acknowledged that Marcus Garvey was a spiritual ancestor of his own movement. In American politics "third-party" movements usually fail to put their candidates into office. In some instances, however, they do succeed in making segments of the electorate sympathetic to their positions, ultimately forcing the major parties to adopt modified versions of their own programs (Killian, 1964).

# STUDY GUIDE

## Summary

1. Collective behavior is social activity that occurs under conditions that are temporarily unstructured.

2. Smelser's general theory of collective behavior and social movements contains six stages: structural conduciveness, structural strain, growth and spread of a generalized belief, the precipitating factor, mobilization for action, and social control.

3. A crowd is a temporary gathering of individuals who share a common concern or interest and find themselves in close physical contact with each other. Crowd characteristics include suggestibility, anonymity and spontaneity, and impersonality. Crowd theories include contagion theory and emergent-norm theory.

Mobs and riots occur in violent crowds. A mob is a crowd whose members engage in destructive and aggressive behavior in the pursuit of a short-term but valued goal. A riot is aggressive crowd behavior that is less focused or unified than mob activity. The most costly riots of this century in the United States occurred between 1966 and 1968. Smelser's theory and the emergent-norm perspective are useful in their analysis.

Panics and mass hysteria involve frightened crowds. A panic is a collective flight to safety. Mass hysteria is a type of panic that occurs when people are scattered over a wide geographical area. As "The War of the Worlds" situation demonstrated, some people are more prone to mass hysteria than others. Some measures can be taken to reduce the likelihood of mass hysteria.

4. A rumor is a report transmitted informally (often by word of mouth) and concerns subject matter difficult to verify. Allport and Postman suggested that rumors are the product of people's interest in a subject and the extent of ambiguity. The content of a rumor is likely to change over time, with the elimination of some details and the emphasis of others. The transmission of a rumor is a collective process in which individuals can play a number of roles. A study of a rumor that claimed that McDonald's hamburgers had worms in them examined different ways to limit the impact of this rumor.

5. A social movement is an organized, collective activity undertaken by people to promote or resist social change. Smelser outlined a distinction between norm-oriented and value-oriented social movements.

One theory has indicated that the tension and pressure of structural strain are the chief reasons social movements develop. On the other hand, resource-mobilization theory focuses on the process by which the members of a social movement acquire and use certain resources necessary to accomplish their collective goals.

6. Prominent sources of social change include cultural innovation, population, environment, and social movements. Discovery, invention, and diffusion are three means by which cultural innovation occurs. Some scholars believe that about 90 percent of all cultural development results from diffusion.

A massive increase in population can produce a number of negative changes in societies. In the United States, the size of different age groups will help determine their effect on society.

For Americans two contradictory priorities face them on environmental issues. One places a priority on a clean environment, and the other emphasizes low energy costs and other economic issues. Even where support for the first priority is strong, it is difficult to accomplish substantial social change.

Social movements are another source of social change. A study of fifty-three American social movements has suggested that groups engaged in violence were somewhat more likely to gain advantages than nonusers of violence. The impact of social movements is not always readily apparent. A social movement that "fails" may produce a significant impact years later.

# Glossary

**collective behavior** social activity that occurs under conditions that are temporarily unstructured and unstable because of the absence of clearly defined norms.

**contagion theory** a perspective emphasizing that the presence of a crowd encourages or compels people to think and act in a uniform manner.

**crowd** a temporary gathering of individuals who share a common concern or interest and find themselves in close physical contact with one another.

**cultural innovation** the recognition or development of new material or nonmaterial elements in a culture.

**diffusion** the process by which cultural traits move either from one culture to another or from one part of a culture to another.

**discovery** the perception of something that already exists but that had not been previously recognized.

**emergent-norm theory** a perspective analyzing the process by which a new social standard develops within a crowd—a standard that in reality receives a more enthusiastic acceptance from some crowd members than others.

**invention** a combination of existing knowledge to produce something new.

**mass hysteria** a type of panic that occurs when people are scattered over a wide geographical area.

**mob** a crowd whose members engage in destructive and aggressive behavior in the pursuit of a short-term but valued goal.

**panic** a collective flight to safety.

**resource-mobilization theory** a perspective that focuses on the process by which the members of social movements acquire and use certain resources necessary to accomplish their collective goals.

**riot** aggressive, destructive crowd behavior that is less focused or unified than mob activity.

**rumor** a report transmitted informally (often by word of mouth) and concerned with subject matter difficult to verify.

**social change** modifications in culture, social organization, and social behavior.

**social movement** an organized, collective activity undertaken by people to promote or resist social change.

# Learning Objectives

After studying this chapter, you should be able to:

1. Define collective behavior and social movements and discuss their occurrence in daily life.
2. Discuss and illustrate Smelser's general theory of collective behavior and social movements.
3. Define crowd and discuss its characteristics.
4. Examine the contagion and emergent-norm theories of crowds, defining and illustrating them.
5. Define mob and riot and analyze riots with different crowd theories.
6. Discuss panic and mass hysteria, defining and illustrating them.
7. Define rumor, examine rumors' development, and describe efforts to stop them.
8. Summarize the major conclusions of strain theory and resource-mobilization theory.
9. Discuss prominent sources of social change.

# Tests

## True–false test

_____ 1. Collective behavior is rare in modern societies.

_____ 2. Smelser's general theory can be used to analyze collective-behavior activities but not social movements.

_____ 3. LeBon, who developed contagion theory, believed that when in a crowd, an individual inevitably becomes less civilized.

_____ 4. The emergent-norm theory rejects the idea that crowd members contain a united mental state.

_____ 5. Research has indicated that in potential panic situations, the quality of leadership does not affect the likelihood of such outbreaks.

_____ 6. Mass hysteria is a type of panic that occurs when people are scattered over a wide geographical area.

_____ 7. The rumor of a toilet-paper shortage was a joke that nobody took seriously.

_____ 8. Resource-mobilization theorists would suggest that the "rap group" was an important resource in the development of the modern women's movement.

_____ 9. Discoveries always involve material, not nonmaterial items.

_____ 10. A cultural innovation has a significant impact when people become convinced that its use will provide benefits they previously lacked.

## Multiple-choice test

_____ 1. In Smelser's general theory, basic conditions that permit or allow collective behavior or a social movement to emerge are termed:
   a. structural conduciveness.
   b. structural strain.
   c. growth and spread of a generalized belief.
   d. a precipitating factor.

_____ 2. Blumer suggested that contagion occurs in crowds when:
   a. anonymity decreases.
   b. crowd members lose awareness of each other's activities.
   c. key crowd members establish norms for each other.
   d. crowd members become increasingly preoccupied with each other's activities.

_____ 3. Which of the following statements about crowd theories is true?
   a. Contagion theory is useful for analyzing crowds in subdued states.
   b. Emergent-norm theory applies to a wider range of crowd types than contagion theory.
   c. Emergent-norm theory analyzes collective behavior as separate from the rest of social behavior.
   d. Emergent-norm theory supports the idea that all crowds are destructive forces.

_____ 4. A group of people who oppose the policies of a certain organization overturn a bus belonging to that organization and smash its windows. These people have been participating in:
   a. a mob.
   b. a riot.
   c. mass hysteria.
   d. panic.

_____ 5. The reaction to the radio broadcast of H.G. Wells's *War of the Worlds* was an example of:
   a. a riot.
   b. panic.
   c. a rumor.
   d. mass hysteria.

_____ 6. Which of the following statements is NOT true about the transmission of rumors?
  a. Some people are messengers, relaying the information.
  b. Decision-makers initiate responses to the news a rumor brings.
  c. Some individuals are skeptics, dismissing any possibility that a rumor might be wrong.
  d. There are also interpreters, who try to figure out what is happening.

_____ 7. Compared to violent crowds, social movements:
  a. last longer.
  b. have a more informal leadership.
  c. have more informal normative guidelines.
  d. a, b, and c

_____ 8. Strain theory:
  a. makes the analysis of resource mobilization a priority.
  b. was used by James Davies to analyze the French and Russian revolutions.
  c. cannot analyze such modern social movements as the women's movement.
  d. only examines norm-oriented social movements.

_____ 9. Cultural innovation occurs through all of the following means EXCEPT:
  a. discovery.
  b. invention.
  c. diffusion.
  d. displacement.

_____ 10. Which of the following situations occurs during diffusion?
  a. Belief systems change more rapidly than material elements.
  b. Innovations that diffuse are often adopted in a modified form.
  c. Diffusion is a one-way process.
  d. The process is always easily reversible.

## Essay test

1. Define collective behavior and indicate how it differs from other social behavior.
2. Apply the six-stage Smelser theory to a collective-behavior situation that you choose.
3. Evaluate the effectiveness of the contagion and emergent-norm theories for analyzing crowd behavior, providing examples whenever possible.
4. Use one of the crowd theories to analyze the occurrence of a riot.
5. Define panic and mass hysteria and discuss the conditions encouraging these activities of frightened crowds.
6. Recall a rumor you heard recently or make up a rumor. Then examine the development of the rumor and also possible efforts to stop the rumor.
7. What is a social movement? Choose a prominent modern social movement (not the women's movement) and use both strain theory and resource-mobilization theory to analyze its development.
8. What are four prominent sources of social change? Give an example of each.

## Suggested Readings

Blumberg, Rhoda Louis. 1984. *The 1960s Freedom Struggle*. Boston: Twayne. A well-written, thorough discussion of the 1960s protests, including an appendix on the use of social-movement theories to analyze those protests.

**458**   Chirot, Daniel. 1986. *Social Change in the Modern Era.* San Diego: Harcourt Brace Jovanovich. A broad, effective review of social change in the past, present, and future and in both capitalist and socialist nations.

Cohen, Jean L. (ed.). 1985. *Social Research.* Vol. 52 (Winter). Six somewhat technical but thought-provoking papers on recent developments in theory and analysis of social movements.

Erikson, Kai. 1976. *Everything in Its Path: Destruction of Community in the Buffalo Creek Flood.* New York: Simon and Schuster. Along with the death and physical damage they bring, disasters also destroy social networks, leaving little worthwhile in people's lives. This well-written book provides a painfully detailed account of how a flood devastated a mining community in West Virginia.

Gamson, William. 1975. *The Strategy of Social Protest.* Homewood, IL: Dorsey Press. A study of several hundred protest groups that challenged the American political structure between 1800 and 1945.

Gurr, Ted Robert (ed.). 1983. "Group Protest and Policy Responses: New Cross-National Perspectives." *American Behavioral Scientist* 26 (January/February). A half-dozen articles that examine a variety of cultural settings to determine the effectiveness of political protest as a means of producing the changes that the protesters were seeking.

Levine, Adeline Gordon. 1982. *Love Canal: Science, Politics, and People.* Lexington, MA: Lexington Books. A study of one of the nation's most publicized environmental crises, showing how local people eventually were able to organize a social movement that forced concessions from the federal government and a major chemical company.

Orwell, George. 1946. *Animal Farm.* New York: Harcourt, Brace and World. A short, simply written novel that describes the life of a social movement as it progressed from a pure beginning to complete corruption.

Perry, Joseph B., Jr., and M. D. Pugh. 1978. *Collective Behavior.* St. Paul, MN: West. A clearly written, short overview of collective-behavior theory, disaster research, crowd violence, and social movements. This book has done a particularly good job of blending theoretical analyses with modern and historical illustrations.

Schneider, Louis. 1976. *Classical Theories of Social Change.* Morristown, NJ: General Learning Press. A short summary and analysis of fourteen major theoretical contributions to the topic of social change. With no more than a couple of hours of fairly easy reading, a student can develop a basic understanding of these classical theories of social change.

Smelser, Neil J. 1963. *Collective Behavior.* New York: The Free Press. The broadest theory of collective behavior and social movements. Smelser analyzed a variety of types of collective behavior and social movements, including rumors, panics, mobs and riots, fads, norm-oriented social movements, and value-oriented social movements.

Wood, James L., and Maurice Jackson. 1982. *Social Movements: Development, Participation, and Dynamics.* Belmont, CA: Wadsworth. A textbook that has used a number of sociological theories for analyzing the origin, membership, and activities of social movements. Four categories of theory are presented, and seven articles analyzing different social movements are also included.

## Student Projects

1. Play the following well-known children's game with about a half-dozen classmates. The first person whispers an elaborate story to the next person, who then whispers it to the next in line, and so on. At the end of the game, the last person will tell the story to everyone. What changes in content occurred along the way? With everyone's help, try to reconstruct where information was lost or al-tered. What insights have you obtained about the transmission of rumors? How would a high-stress situation affect the ability to transmit information accurately?

2. Get back issues of newspapers, newsmagazines (such as *Time* or *Newsweek*), or watch the evening network news for a week and list items covered that would be considered either (a) collective

behavior or (b) social movements. Do some activities get more or different coverage than others? Is coverage of some activities more dramatic than of others? What reactions to or commentaries about the different topics are found in the media?

From your observations, what collective activity is "news"? How might an awareness of what serves as "news" affect how people behave collectively to gain their objectives?

## Answers to Test Questions

### True–false test

| | | | | |
|---|---|---|---|---|
| 1. f | 3. t | 5. f | 7. f | 9. f |
| 2. f | 4. t | 6. t | 8. t | 10. t |

### Multiple-choice test

| | | | | |
|---|---|---|---|---|
| 1. a | 3. b | 5. d | 7. a | 9. d |
| 2. d | 4. a | 6. c | 8. b | 10. b |

# Prison Riots: Which Theory Can Explain Them?

If a sociological theory contains clear, thought-provoking statements, has it managed to establish the accuracy of its claims? The answer is a resounding "NO." As we noted in the first two chapters, scientists' work must encounter colleagues' critical review. A sociological theory can be subjected to such a review by determining whether or not it can explain relevant data.

In Chapter 17 we saw that both the strain theory and the resource-mobilization theory can be applied to social movements. They also can be used to analyze prison riots. Does one theory succeed in explaining why prison riots occur while the other one fails? That does not seem to be the case. It appears that in the late 1960s and early 1970s, the causes of prison riots were consistent with resource-mobilization theory, while in the 1980s the factors encouraging riots have fitted better with the strain theory. To illustrate this shift, we will examine a study of the Attica riot, the most devastating prison rebellion of the 1970s, and then analyze research involving the New Mexico riot of 1980. Then we will be able to understand more thoroughly the relationship between theory and research.

## The Attica and New Mexico Riots

Between September 9 and September 13, 1971, forty-three citizens of New York State were killed in the correctional facility at Attica, New York. Thirty-nine of the deaths occurred during the fifteen minutes it took the state police to recapture the prison, which had been controlled by inmates. The total number of deaths was the highest produced in this century from any violent encounter limited to Americans.

Shortly after the Attica riot, the governor of New York asked the five justices of the state's Appellate Division to appoint a citizens' committee — the New York State Special Commission on Attica — to lead an investigation that would try to explain what happened, and why, and also make recommendations to prevent such violence in the future. This nine-person commission hired a staff that then conducted the investigation. These people interviewed most of the inmates who had been at Attica during the riot — about 1,600 men — as well as the majority of the corrections officers and state police who were present during the conflict. It would be helpful to know just what questions were asked or if the researchers had a standard interview for each category of people examined. Unfortunately this information was not made public.

While it is possible to have reservations about how the data for the report were gathered, its presentation is straightforward and clear and its findings consistent with those produced by other investigators of the Attica riot. And what are those findings? Most basically the investigators found that the Attica rioters were products of their social era, a time when protest against inequality and oppression was popular.

Could one argue that conditions in the prison were poor and deteriorating, thus creating strain for inmates? No, the commission concluded. Prison conditions, in fact, were improving under the new state Commissioner of Corrections. The root of the problem was the tone of the times. According to the report, those who participated actively in the riot were

> . . . part of a new breed of younger, more aware inmates, largely black, who came to prison full of deep feelings of alienation and hostility against the established institutions of law and government, enhanced self-esteem, racial pride, and political awareness, and an unwillingness to accept the petty humiliations and racism that characterize prison life.
>
> (New York State Special Commission on Attica, 1972: 105)

Using the resource-mobilization perspective, one can consider these angry young men a potential resource encouraging the development of a riot. "Potential" is an important word here. As we saw in the section on riots, anger and pride are not enough to generate a riot; there must be mobilization. Thus the resource must be developed to contribute to collective action

—in this case a riot. The Attica report indicated that, indeed, this did happen. About a month before the riot occurred, the three major militant organizations among the inmates—the Black Panthers, the Young Lords, and the Black Muslims—reached an accord where they were in sufficient agreement to override their differences and recognize their common grievances against the power structure of the prison. In addition, these common grievances were solidified by the death of George Jackson, a prominent black radical, in a California prison under conditions that made the inmates believe the guards had either cooperated or actually killed the man.

The Attica report concluded that the riot was unplanned, that it began following a confrontation between guards and inmates. Because a central gate failed to function and the communications system within the prison was outmoded, the inmates were able to take over large sections of the prison quickly.

It seems that a resource-mobilization perspective can also be applied to the time period after the takeover. Supporters of this theory would point out that while the inmates lacked the resource of a full-fledged organization at the time of the takeover, they had a somewhat united group of like-minded participants whose common grievances allowed them to be welded into a fairly cohesive unit once the outbreak took place. About an hour after the riot occurred, one of the "inmate lawyers"—a man who, though lacking formal training, was sufficiently knowledgable of the law to help fellow inmates prepare legal petitions—took a bullhorn and spoke. This man was greatly respected, and when he said that they needed to organize themselves effectively, the others listened. A definite tone was set. The report stated:

> Now, inmate after inmate jumped up on the table and took the bullhorn, extolling brotherhood among inmates and calling for the presentation of demands for reform. The speakers were principally those men to whom other inmates naturally turn for guidance and advice: outstanding athletes, leaders of political groups, and, of course, the "inmate lawyers."

> *(New York State Special Commission on Attica, 1972: 297)*

Because of the resource of angry, united inmates, the mobilization of a fairly well-organized group was easily accomplished.

The New Mexico riot of 1980 was a different situation. The political outlook and rhetoric of the 1960s and early 1970s had lessened or disappeared. Within the prison itself, conditions were not improving as at Attica; they were becoming worse. In this era, and particularly within this prison, the strain theory seems to offer a more effective explanation than the resource-mobilization perspective.

The data on the New Mexico riot come from two articles based, in turn, on two sources: the official investigation by the Attorney General's office conducted shortly after the riot and sociologist Bert Useem's interviews in 1985 with the remaining thirty-six inmates who had been present during the riot.

When interviewed, inmates mentioned problems that are compatible with strain theory. Perhaps most significantly they often indicated that the turning point toward worse prison conditions occurred in 1975, when the deputy warden was fired and the warden, named Felix Rodriguez, was transferred. One inmate explained that the new warden

> ". . . came in like a real maniac. People can say what they want about Rodriguez, and maybe he did have his finger in the pie, but all I know, man, all I know empirically, when he was warden here, you didn't have guys stabbing each other in wholesale numbers, you didn't have guys breaking out and running up the fence 15 or 20 at a time because it was too heavy for them to do time here. . . . It was a mellow, laid-back place under Rodriguez."

> *(Useem, 1985: 683)*

According to Useem's data analysis, inmates compared the conditions under different wardens 181 times; 160 of those comparisons favored the Rodriguez administration.

The change in administrations created strain throughout the entire prison system. Inmates related to each other differently after Rodriguez left; robbery and violence were more widespread and trust rarer. Perhaps the new administration's most decisive means of producing strain was its establishment of a system of inmate informants. "Snitching" became the order of day, and most of the inmates despised the snitches.

When the New Mexico riot occurred, it did not resemble the one at Attica. While this outbreak was also unplanned, the inmates behaved differently, reflecting the dissimilar factors behind the violence. The New Mexico riot lacked the resource of inmates capable of being rapidly organized to make demands for reform. Instead these men were wild and uncontrollable, undone by the destructive prison system that had been imposed on them; strain, in short, appears to have been the primary factor igniting this riot. And victims of that strain — the rioters — took out their fury and frustration on those they considered responsible. The twelve guards held as hostages were repeatedly beaten, sodomized, and threatened with death, though none were actually killed. Most of the thirty-three inmates killed were informers, and they were killed with incredible brutality: beaten, raped, mutilated, and tortured to death with acetylene torches.

Perhaps no point indicates the difference between the two riots as sharply as the respective roles played by blacks. At Attica aroused young blacks were the largest group in the prison and at the focus of the riot. In contrast, the New Mexico uprising occurred during a politically more apathetic era, and black inmates represented only 9 percent of the prison population. These men formed a group for their mutual protection and stayed away from the violence. Thus they mobilized themselves for inaction, quite the opposite of what was done by many black inmates at Attica.

## Comment on the Relationship of Theory and Research

As we learned in Chapter 2 ("Doing Research in Sociology"), theory and research need to go hand-in-hand, supporting each other. Effective theory must fit the facts studies provide.

What theoretical contributions will occur in the next few years? While this section strongly implies that it would be difficult to produce a general theory of prison riots, such a theory would be a formidable contribution. Can a theory be developed that more effectively predicts prison outbreaks than intelligent officials or inmates who are on-the-scene? That would be quite an accomplishment. We never know what is ahead. Perhaps at this very moment, some sociologist is preparing to publish a paper or a book that will significantly improve this body of theory.

Sources: Burton M. Atkins and Henry R. Glick (eds.). *Prisons, Protests and Politics*. Englewood Cliffs, NJ: Prentice-Hall. 1972; Mark Colvin. "The 1980 New Mexico Prison Riot." *Social Problems*. Vol. 29. June 1982, pp. 449–463; New York State Special Commission on Attica. *Attica: The Official Report of the New York State Special Commission on Attica*. New York: Bantam Books. 1972; John Pallas and Bob Barker. "From Riot to Revolution." *Issues in Criminology*. Vol. 7. 1972, pp. 1–19; Bert Useem. "Disorganization and the New Mexico Prison Riot." *American Sociological Review*. Vol. 50. October 1985, pp. 677–688.

# GLOSSARY

**absolute wealth**  the cash value of an individual's economic assets.

**abstinence**  total restraint from sex.

**ageism**  an ideology asserting the superiority of the young over the old.

**aggregate**  two or more people who share physical space but lack the interaction maintained by group members.

**androgynous**  possessing a definite blend of both traditionally masculine and traditionally feminine traits.

**anomie**  the confusing situation produced when norms are either absent or conflicting.

**anticipatory socialization**  the acceptance of a group's standards preparatory to becoming a member of the group.

**anti-Semitism**  the complex of prejudicial attitudes toward Jews.

**authoritarian leader**  a leader who controls all aspects of group activity yet stays somewhat aloof from the group.

**authoritarian personality**  a personality pattern where the individual rigidly supports conventional middle-class values, uncritically admires and obeys strong, controlling people, bullies the weak, and exhibits extensive superstitions about and fear of the unknown.

**authority**  power that people generally recognize as rightfully maintained by those who use it.

**backstage**  the region where people construct the illusions and impressions they will use in a performance.

**belief**  a statement about reality that people accept as true.

**biosocial position**  a recently developed perspective that acknowledges the significance of both biology and social experience in the development of gender roles and that emphasizes their interplay, contending that the independent significance of each factor is impossible to assess since they never exist in isolation from one another.

**bourgeoisie**  the class of modern capitalists who own the means of economic production and employ wage labor.

**bureaucracy**  a formal organization's administrative section that has the task of controlling its operation.

**bureaucratic personality**  a personality that emphasizes rule and procedures and tends to lose track of organizational goals.

**capital**  money, goods, or other forms of wealth invested to produce more wealth.

**capitalism**  an economic system where capital is controlled by private citizens who own the means of production and distribution of goods and services.

**causation**  a situation in which one variable can produce the occurrence of another.

**charismatic system of authority**  according to Max Weber, an authority system in which leadership develops because of the personal magnetism of an individual, whose followers believe that he or she possesses supernatural qualities.

**city**  a large, densely settled concentration of people permanently located within a relatively confined geographical area where nonagricultural occupations are pursued.

**civil religion**  a shared, public faith in the nation, a faith linked to people's everyday life through a set of beliefs, symbols, and rituals that contains religious elements and overtones that are not formally affiliated with any particular religion.

**class consciousness**  recognition by the members of a class of the role they play in the production process.

**cognitive ability**  the capacity to use perception, thought, memory, and other mental processes to acquire knowledge.

**collective behavior**  social activity that occurs under conditions that are temporarily unstructured and unstable because of the absence of clearly defined norms.

**commune**  a planned, intentional community, bringing together biologically unrelated people in order to build a large, family-like group.

**communism**  a requirement that the substantive findings of science represent a common heritage, not the exclusive property of individual discoverers and their heirs.

**community**  a settlement of people living in a specific geographical area and maintaining a system of interrelationships that satisfies many of the people's physical and social needs.

**conflict theory**  a theory contending that the

struggle for power and wealth in society should be the central concern of sociology.

**conformity** an individual's behavior in line with the relevant social norms.

**conformity** (Merton's concept) a nondeviant adaptation, where individuals pursue legitimate goals and the culturally accepted means to achieve them, even though it is likely they will not attain those goals.

**contagion theory** a perspective emphasizing that the presence of a crowd encourages or compels people to think and act in a uniform manner.

**corporation** a legally designated organization that has power and responsibilities separate from its workers and owners.

**correlation** a statistical description of the relationship between variables.

**counterculture** a subculture whose members consciously and often proudly reject some of the most important cultural standards of the mainstream society.

**crime** an act that violates criminal law.

**crowd** a temporary gathering of individuals who share a common concern or interest and find themselves in close physical contact with one another.

**crude birth rate** the number of births per 1000 persons in a society in a given year.

**crude death rate** the number of deaths per 1000 persons in a society in a given year.

**cultural innovation** the recognition or development of new material or nonmaterial elements in a culture.

**cultural relativism** the recognition that a culture should be evaluated by its own standards and not by those of any other culture.

**cultural universals** traits believed to exist in all cultures.

**culture** all the human-made products associated with a society.

**deficit famine** situation in which no food supplies exist elsewhere in a nation sufficient to compensate for local inadequacies.

**democracy** a government in which those in power are acting with the consent of the governed.

**democratic leader** a leader who permits group members to determine many policies and takes an active role in discussion.

**demography** the study of human populations.

**dependent variable** the variable that the independent variable influences.

**deviance** any condition or behavior that the more powerful members of a social group consider a reasonably serious violation of their more important values or rules.

**diffusion** the process by which cultural traits move either from one culture to another or from one part of a culture to another.

**discovery** the perception of something that already exists but that had not been previously recognized.

**discrimination** the behavior by which one group prevents or restricts another group's access to scarce resources.

**disease** a condition of biological nonhealth.

**disengagement** a process of mutual withdrawal involving decreasing interaction between an elderly person and others in the social system to which he or she belongs.

**disinterestedness** a standard that scientists avoid the pursuit of work that is self-serving and self-interested.

**distribution famine** a food shortage existing in certain provinces or regions of a country, not throughout an entire country.

**double standard** a position asserting that men may engage in premarital sex but women may not.

**doubling time** the time span necessary for a population to double in size.

**dramaturgic sociology** a theoretical approach that analyzes social interaction as if the participants were actors in a play.

**dysfunction** a disruptive or destabilizing consequence produced by an item, individual, or group and affecting a particular group or society.

**economic institution** the system of norms and roles developed for the production, distribution, and consumption of goods and services.

**education** the transmission of knowledge, skills, and values by either formal or informal means.

**egalitarian** a type of family in which the wife–mother and husband–father share power and also permit their children to participate in the family decisions.

**ego** Freud's conception of the self that must cope with pressures from three often contradictory forces.

**emergent-norm theory** a perpsective analyzing the process by which a new social standard develops within a crowd—a standard that in reality receives a more enthusiastic acceptance from some crowd members than others.

**endogamy** a custom requiring a person to marry within a specific social unit, such as a kinship group, religious organization, or social class.

**ethnicity** a set of cultural or national qualities that distinguishes a particular category of people from other categories.

**ethnocentrism** the tendency to automatically evaluate other cultures by the standards of one's own.

**ethnomethodology** the study of the sometimes recognized, often unrecognized social order, the set of underlying shared norms and expectations that promote harmony in most everyday social interactions.

**exogamy** a custom compelling someone to marry outside a specific social unit.

**experiment** a research technique in which the investigator manipulates conditions so that the effects produced by one independent variable can be isolated and observed.

**explicit norm** a standard out in the open.

**expressive** concerned with emotional or social issues.

**extended family** a family involving two or more generations of people related by blood and living together or close to each other.

**family** traditionally defined as a social unit composed of two or more people who live together and are related by blood, marriage, or adoption.

**family planning** a program that encourages people to decide how many children they want, when they want them, and what contraceptives, if any, they wish to use to achieve their goals.

**fertility rate** the number of actual births per 1000 women between the ages of fifteen and forty-four.

**folkway** a norm that specifies the way things are customarily done; folkways are concerned with standards of behavior that are socially approved but not considered morally significant.

**formal organization** a group characterized by formally stated rules, clearly defined members' roles, and distinct objectives.

**frontstage** the physical area or region where people present a performance.

**function** an adjustive or stabilizing consequence produced by an item, individual, or group and affecting a particular group or society.

**functional equivalent** an organization or activity that serves functions an individual or group

more commonly receives from some other organization or activity.

**game** according to Mead, a group activity in which each participant's role requires interaction with two or more individuals.

**gender** the general behavioral standards that distinguish males from females in a given culture.

**gender role** a set of specific behavioral patterns associated with either the male or female gender.

**generalized other** an image of the role expectations for all the game participants with whom a person must interact.

**gentrification** the move of middle- and upper-middle-class people to formerly deteriorated inner-city neighborhoods.

**grief work** the process by which people attempt to establish a new identity after the death of a loved one.

**group** two or more interacting people who share certain expectations and goals.

**growth rate** the crude birth rate minus the crude death rate.

**health care** the variety of public and private organizations that support an individual's effective physical, mental, and social adaptation to his or her environment.

**hidden curriculum** a set of rules that emphasizes blind obedience and that is seldom made explicit but is recognized as important by students.

**homogamy** marriage with a person having social characteristics similar to one's own.

**human ecology** the study of human beings' relationship with the environment.

**hypothesis** a scientifically researchable suggestion about the relationship between two or more variables.

**id** according to Sigmund Freud, the part of the personality that is unconscious, primitive, and constantly pleasure seeking.

**ideal norm** a standard requiring strict obedience to the guidelines provided.

**ideal type** a simplified description of some phenomenon based on an analysis of concrete examples, emphasizing those characteristics that best help us to understand its essential nature.

**identification** a process by which an individual incorporates another person's values, standards, and expectations into his or her own behavior and sense of self.

**ideology** a system of beliefs and principles that presents an organized explanation of and the justification for a group's outlooks and behavior.

**illness** an individual's sense that he or she has been affected by disease.

**implicit norm** a standard that lies beneath the surface and is not easily stated.

**impression management** the attempt to control others' evaluations by presenting oneself in the most favorable light.

**incest taboo** a rule outlawing sexual relations between certain kin-group members believed to be too closely related as defined by the cultural standards of a given society.

**income** people's earnings obtained through wages, salaries, business profits, stock dividends, and other means.

**independent variable** a variable that influences another variable — the dependent variable.

**industrial stage** (of the demographic-transition theory) the third stage, which occurs as nations stabilize their populations in the course of industrialization.

**informal social control** unofficial pressure intended to convince potential deviants to conform to social norms.

**in-group** any group characterized by a strong sense of identification and loyalty and a feeling of exclusiveness toward nonmembers.

**in-migration rate** the number of people per 1000 members of the population moving into an area in a given year.

**innovation** a deviant adaptation that develops when a person seeks legitimate goals but is blocked from effectively using culturally accepted means to achieve them.

**instincts** unalterable behavioral complexes that parents transmit genetically to their children.

**institution** a system of statuses, roles, groups, and behavioral patterns that satisfies a basic human need and is necessary for the survival of a society.

**instrumental** intended to promote the pursuit of group goals.

**interest group** a group whose members seek to influence elected politicians or government bureaucrats to initiate the legislation or policies they want.

**intergenerational mobility** a comparison of a parent and a child's social-class position.

**internalized** through socialization, social expectations have become part of the personality structure.

**interview** a type of survey composed of questions that are delivered face-to-face or over the telephone.

**intragenerational mobility** an analysis of an individual's occupational changes in the course of a lifetime.

**invention** a combination of existing knowledge to produce something new.

**kinship system** a number of people related by common descent, marriage, or adoption.

**laissez-faire leader** a leader who does not take an active role in group discussions, leaving group members free to reach individual or group decisions.

**language** a system of symbolic communication that uses words, which are sound patterns that have standardized meanings.

**latent function** a function that is not intended and often unrecognized by members of the group producing it.

**leadership** the exercise of influence or authority within a group by one or more members.

**legal-rational system of authority** according to Weber, a system of authority based on laws enacted to produce rational behavior and the achievement of formally designated goals.

**linguistic-relativity hypothesis** the contention that the unique grammatical forms of a language actually shape the thoughts and perceptions of its users.

**lobbying** a face-to-face effort to persuade legislators and other government personnel to support the proposals of an interest group.

**looking-glass self** according to Charles Cooley, our understanding of what sort of person we are is based on how we imagine we appear to other people.

**macro-order** the large-scale structures and activities that exist within societies and even between one society and another.

**manifest function** a function that is intended and openly recognized by members of the group producing it.

**mass hysteria** a type of panic that occurs when people are scattered over a wide geographical area.

**mass media** the instruments of communication that reach a large audience without any personal contact between the senders and the receivers.

**matriarchal** a type of family in which the wife—

mother is the formal head and the absolute or nearly absolute source of power.

**matrilocal** a type of residence that involves settling with or near the wife's parents.

**medical sociology** the study of the social setting in which health, sickness, and health care occur.

**medicine** the scientifically based practice concerned with the prevention and treatment of disease and the treatment of injury.

**megalopolis** a string of closely bound metropolitan areas.

**membership group** a group to which an individual belongs.

**methodology** the set of principles and procedures that guides sociological research.

**metropolis** a territorial unit composed of a large central city and the surrounding cities and towns.

**micro-order** the structure and activity of small groups.

**migration** the flow of people in and out of a particular territory (city, region, or country).

**minority group** any category of people with recognizable racial, religious, or ethnic traits that place it in a position of low esteem and that serve as the basis for unequal treatment.

**mob** a crowd whose members engage in destructive and aggressive behavior in the pursuit of a short-term but valued goal.

**monogamy** a marriage practice in which there is one husband and one wife.

**mores** norms people consider vital.

**mortification process** a series of degradations and humiliations of inhabitants systematically carried out by staff members of total institutions.

**multinational** a large corporation with production plants and distribution centers in many countries.

**natural environment** the combination of land, climate, water, air, mineral resources, and plant and animal life that together compose the physical world where people live.

**natural sciences** older sciences such as astronomy, biology, chemistry, and physics that study the physical world.

**nature** inborn biological characteristics or heredity.

**neolocal** a type of residence that occurs when married people establish an independent place to live.

**net migration rate** the difference between the in-migration rate and the out-migration rate.

**nonparticipant observation** a method of observation in which an investigator examines a group process without taking part in the group activities.

**norm** a standard of desirable behavior. Norms are the rules people are expected to follow in their relations with each other.

**nuclear family** a two-generation family that includes a father, a mother, and their children living separately from other relatives.

**nurture** socialization.

**objective definition of social class** a measuring technique that uses certain quantifiable factors —income, occupational prestige rank, or level of education, for example—as the basis for determining an individual's social-class position.

**objectivity** the ability to evaluate reality without using personal opinions and biases.

**object permanence** according to Jean Piaget, the childhood recognition that specific objects still exist after they are removed from one's line of vision.

**organized skepticism** the conclusion that no scientist's contribution to knowledge can be accepted without careful scrutiny.

**out-group** nonmembers of the in-group who are viewed with hostility and even contempt by in-group members.

**out-migration rate** the number of people per 1000 members of the population moving out of an area in a given year.

**panic** a collective flight to safety.

**participant observation** a method of observation in which an investigator becomes involved in the activities of the group being studied.

**patriarchal** a type of family in which the husband–father is the formal head and the absolute or nearly absolute source of power.

**patrilocal** a type of residence that requires settling with or near the husband's parents.

**patronage** distribution of favors to political supporters.

**permissiveness with affection** a standard arguing that men and women who love each other and have a stable relationship have the right to express their feelings sexually.

**permissiveness without affection** a position contending that men and women should feel free to have sexual relations whether or not there is commitment or affection between them.

**play** according to George Herbert Mead, the process of taking the role of specific individuals and thereby starting to learn the rights and obligations that particular roles entail.

**pluralism** a theory that emphasizes that a dispersion of power exists in American government.

**political institution** the system of norms and roles that concerns the use and distribution of power within a given society.

**political machine** an organization established to control a city, county, or state government.

**polyandry** the form of polygamy in which a wife has two or more husbands.

**polygamy** a marriage practice where one spouse has two or more spouses of the other sex.

**polygyny** the form of polygamy in which a husband has two or more wives.

**population** (for research) the entire category of people possessing the characteristics that interest a researcher.

**population** (people) all the people who live within a specific geographic area, such as a nation, a region, or a city.

**power** the ability of an individual or group to implement wishes or policies, with or without the cooperation of others.

**power-elite perspective** a theory emphasizing that in American society a group of high-status people — well educated, often wealthy, and placed in high occupational positions — control political power.

**preindustrial stage** (of the demographic-transition theory) the first stage, which existed before industrialization and involved a stable population, with both birth and death rates remaining high.

**prejudice** a highly negative judgment toward a group, focusing on one or more negative characteristics that are supposedly uniformly shared by all group members.

**prestige** possession of attributes that elicit recognition, respect, and some degree of deference.

**primary deviance** violation of a social rule but the individuals in question are not labeled and so do not see themselves as deviant.

**primary group** a group in which relationships are usually stable over long periods of time, members are able to expose many facets of their personality, and a strong sense of affection and identity develops.

**principle of verstehen** Max Weber's concept that involves an effort to grasp the relationship between individuals' feelings and thoughts, and their actions.

**privilege system** a framework for inmates' resocialization.

**profane** anything that people consider ordinary and closely linked to practical demands.

**proletariat** the class of modern wage laborers who possess no means of production and thus must sell their own labor in order to survive.

**questionnaire** a type of survey in which a respondent writes the answers to a list of questions.

**race** distinct physical characteristics, such as skin color and certain facial features, used to divide people into broad categories.

**racism** the ideology contending that actual or alleged differences between different racial groups assert the superiority of one racial group. Racism is a rationalization for political, economic, and social discrimination.

**random sample** a sample drawn from a population by a process that assures that every individual in that population has an equal probability of being included.

**real norm** adjustment of a standard to the practical conditions of living.

**rebellion** a deviant adaptation displayed when a person decides that the existing society imposes barriers preventing the achievement of success goals. Therefore that individual strikes out against the society, seeking to change its goals and also the existing means for achieving goals.

**reference group** a group whose standards a person uses to help shape his or her own values, beliefs, and behavior.

**relative wealth** the value of an individual's economic assets compared to the assets possessed by other citizens in that society.

**reliability** consistency in measurement.

**religion** a unified system of beliefs and practices that focuses on sacred things and serves to create a community of worshippers.

**replication** a repetition or near repetition of an earlier study to determine the accuracy of its findings.

**reputational definition of social class** a measuring technique where researchers use batteries of resident experts from the community to assess their neighbors' social-class position.

**resource-mobilization theory** a perspective that focuses on the process by which the members of social movements acquire and use certain resources necessary to accomplish their collective goals.

**retreatism** a deviant adaptation in which an individual pursues neither the culturally prescribed goal of success nor the means for achieving this goal because of limited opportunities or a sense of personal inadequacy.

**riot** aggressive, destructive crowd behavior that is less focused or unified than mob activity.

**ritualism** a behavioral pattern that occurs when culturally prescribed success goals are no longer actively sought, but the legitimate means for achieving those goals are conscientiously pursued.

**role** a set of expected behaviors associated with a particular status.

**role conflict** an incompatibility between two or more roles associated with different statuses.

**role strain** an incompatibility between two or more roles associated with the same status.

**rumor** a report transmitted informally (often by word of mouth) and concerned with subject matter difficult to verify.

**sacred** anything that is superior in power, is set apart from the ordinary and practical, and creates a sense of awe.

**sample** a limited number of individuals chosen from a population for the purpose of conducting research.

**scapegoat theory** an explanation emphasizing that people blocked from achieving a goal will sometimes be unable or unwilling to take out their frustration on its source, and so they direct their aggression against an accessible individual or group.

**science** a systematic effort to develop general principles about a particular subject matter, based on actual observations and stated in a form that can be tested by any competent person.

**secondary deviance** authorities label individuals deviant and the individuals accept the status of deviant.

**secondary group** a group composed of people who cooperate with each other for specific, practical reasons and maintain few, if any, strong emotional ties within the group.

**secondary sources** data banks available to researchers but produced by other individuals and organizations for their own purposes.

**secularization** the process by which religion loses influence within groups and societies.

**self** one's perception of his or her own person, formed as a result of other people's response in the course of socialization.

**self-fulfilling prophecy** an incorrect definition of a situation that comes to pass because people accept the incorrect definition and act on it to make it become true.

**sex** the division of a variety of animal forms, including human beings, into the biological categories of male and female.

**sexism** the ideology emphasizing that actual or alleged differences between males and females establish the superiority of males.

**sickness** a social status in which an individual is treated as unhealthy.

**sign** an object or event that stands for something else.

**social category** a number of people who have one or more social characteristics in common.

**social change** modifications in culture, social organization, and social behavior.

**social class** a large category of people who are similar in income level, educational attainment, and occupational prestige ranking.

**social control** the application of systematic behavioral restraints intended to motivate people to obey social expectations.

**social distance** the feeling of separation between individuals or groups.

**social interaction** the basic process through which two or more people use language and gestures to affect each other's thoughts, expectations, and behavior.

**socialism** an economic system with collective ownership of the means of production and distribution of goods and services.

**socialization** the process by which a person becomes a member of a group or society, learning the necessary cultural content and modes of behavior.

**social mobility** the movement of a person from one social class or status level to another.

**social movement** an organized, collective activity undertaken by people to promote or resist social change.

**social sciences** the sciences that focus on various aspects of human behavior.

**470** **social stratification** structured inequality of access to rewards, resources, and privileges that are scarce and desirable within a society.

**society** the interacting people who share a culture.

**sociobiology** a field in which the proponents contend that through the evolutionary process, human beings have acquired tendencies that determine much of their behavior.

**sociological theory** a combination of observations and insights that offers a systematic explanation about social life.

**sociology** the scientific study of human behavior in groups and of the social forces that influence that behavior.

**status** a position that indicates where a person fits into a group or society and how that person should relate to others in the structure.

**stereotype** an exaggerated image, maintained by prejudiced people, of the characteristics of the group members against whom they are prejudiced.

**structural-functional theory** a theory suggesting that groups in interaction tend to influence and adjust to each other in a fairly stable, conflict-free pattern.

**subculture** the culture of a specific segment of people within a society, differing from the dominant culture in some significant respects.

**subjective definition of social class** a measuring technique that requires people to indicate the social class to which they belong.

**suburb** a politically independent municipality that develops next to or in the vicinity of a central city.

**superego** according to Freud, the part of the personality that has internalized standards of right and wrong, a conscience.

**survey** a research technique that uses carefully constructed questions to obtain a variety of facts about people's thoughts and behavior.

**symbol** an object or event whose meaning is fixed not by the nature of the item to which it is attached but by the agreement of the people who use it in communication.

**symbolic interaction** a theory that emphasizes the importance of symbolic communication—gestures and, above all, language—in the development of the individual, group, and society.

**technology** any repeated operation people use to manipulate the environment to achieve some practical goals.

**total institution** a place of residence where inhabitants experience nearly complete restriction of their physical freedom in order to be effectively resocialized into a radically new identity and behavioral pattern.

**traditional system of authority** according to Weber, an authority system in which the standard of political leadership passes down from one generation to another.

**transition stage** (of the demographic-transition theory) the second stage, in which a decline in the death rate and a continuing high birth rate produces a rapid growth in population.

**universalism** a norm stating that all scientific claims of truth need to be evaluated by impersonal criteria consistent with existing knowledge in that field.

**urbanization** the process by which a city forms and develops.

**validity** the condition where a research item accurately measures what it claims to measure.

**value** a general conviction about what is good or bad, right or wrong, appropriate or inappropriate.

**variable** a factor that has two or more categories or measurable conditions.

**vicious cycle of poverty** a pattern where the parents' minimal income significantly limits the educational and occupational pursuits of the children, thereby keeping them locked into the same economic status.

**victimless crime** the willing (hence "victimless") exchange among adults of strongly desired but illegal goods or services.

**wealth** people's economic assets—their cars, homes, stocks, bonds, and real estate—and individuals can convert these assets into cash.

**white-collar crime** crime committed by members of higher socioeconomic classes in the course of their business activities.

**work alienation** the loss of control over the process of one's labor, with the resulting dissatisfaction primarily caused by overly close supervision, highly routine tasks, and an overall simplicity to one's job.

**zero population growth** a situation in which the population size stabilizes.

# REFERENCES

## Chapter 1

Dahrendorf, Ralf. 1959. *Class and Class Conflict in Industrial Society.* Stanford, CA: Stanford University Press.

Friedrich, Otto. 1983. "The Computer Moves In." *Time* 121 (January 3): 14–18+.

Gans, Herbert J. 1986. "Sociologist's Pride." *New York Times* (October 20): A26.

Kroeber, Theodora. 1963. *Ishi in Two Worlds.* Berkeley and Los Angeles: University of California Press.

Melbin, Murray, 1978. "Night as Frontier." *American Sociological Review* 43 (February): 3–22.

Merton, Robert K. 1968. *Social Theory and Social Structure.* New York: The Free Press. Third edition.

Mills, C. Wright. 1956. *The Power Elite.* New York: Oxford University Press.

Schell, Jonathan. 1982. *The Fate of the Earth.* New York: Knopf.

Toffler, Alvin. 1981. *The Third Wave.* New York: Bantam.

Whyte, William Foote. 1955. *Street Corner Society.* Chicago: University of Chicago Press. Revised edition.

Yin, Peter P. 1980. "Fear of Crime among the Elderly: Some Issues and Suggestions." *Social Problems* 27 (April): 492–504.


## Chapter 2

Bandura, Albert, et al. 1963. "Imitation of Film-Mediated Aggressive Models." *Journal of Abnormal and Social Psychology* 66: 3–11.

Baumrind, Diana. 1964. "Some Thoughts on Ethics of Research: After Reading Milgram's 'Behavioral Study of Obedience.'" *American Psychologist* 19 (June): 421–423.

Berg, Ellen. 1986. "Sociological Perspectives on AIDS." *Footnotes* 14 (December): 8–9.

Cole, Stephen. 1980. *The Sociological Method.* Chicago: Rand McNally. Third edition.

Freudenburg, William R., and Kenneth M. Keating. 1985. "Applying Sociology to Policy: Social Science and the Environmental Impact Statement." *Rural Sociology* 50 (Winter): 578–605.

Gallup, George. 1972. *The Sophisticated Poll Watcher's Guide.* Princeton: Princeton Opinion Press.

Hallowell, Lyle. 1985. "The Outcome of the Brajuha Case: Legal Implications for Sociologists." *Footnotes* 13 (December): 1+.

Hoover, Kenneth R. 1980. *The Elements of Social Scientific Thinking.* New York: St. Martin's. Second edition.

Humphrey, Ronald. 1985. "How Work Roles Influence Perception: Structural-Cognitive Processes and Organizational Behavior." *American Sociological Review* 50 (April): 242–252.

Hunt, Morton. 1974. *Sexual Behavior in the 1970s.* Chicago: Playboy Press.

Milgram, Stanley. 1974. *Obedience to Authority.* New York: Harper & Row.

Sennett, Richard. 1974. *Families against the City.* New York: Vintage.


## Chapter 3

Argyle, Michael. 1979. "The Human Gaze: Silent Language of the Eyes," pp. 59–66 in Phillip Whitten (ed.), *Readings in Sociology: Contemporary Perspectives.* New York: Harper & Row.

Block, Jeanne Humphrey. 1973. "Conceptions of Sex Role: Some Cross-Cultural and Longitudinal Perspectives." *American Psychologist* 28 (June): 512–526.

Bohannon, Laura. 1975. "Hamlet and the Tiv." *Psychology Today* 9 (July): 62–66.

Chagnon, Napolean A. 1977. *Yanamamö: The Fierce People.* New York: Holt, Rinehart and Winston. Second edition.

Devine, John. 1985. "The Versatility of Human Locomotion." *American Anthropologist* 87 (September): 550–574.

Freeman, David M. 1974. *Technology and Society: Issues in Assessment, Conflict, and Choice.* Chicago: Rand McNally.

Gelman, David. 1983. "Making Fun for Profit." *Newsweek* 101 (April 25): 64–68+.

Hall, Edward T. 1981. "How Cultures Collide," pp. 28–33 in *Sociology 81/82.* Guilford, CT: Dushkin.

Harris, Marvin. 1974. *Cows, Pigs, Wars and Witches.* New York: Random House.

Keene, Karlyn, and Daniel Yankelovich. 1984. "American Values: Change and Stability." *Public Opinion* 6 (January): 3–8.

Mead, Margaret. 1963. *Sex and Temperament in Three Primitive Societies.* New York: William Morrow.

Murdock, George P. 1965. *Culture and Society.* Pittsburgh: University of Pittsburgh Press.

Rimer, Sara. 1985. "Poll Sees Landslide for Santa: Of U.S. Children, 87% Believe." *New York Times* (December 24): 1+.

Sapir, Edward. 1921. *Language: An Introduction to the Study of Speech.* New York: Harcourt, Brace and World.

Sapir, Edward. 1929. "The Status of Linguistics as a Science." *Language* 5: 207–214.

Shannon, William V. 1966. *The American Irish.* New York: Macmillan. Revised edition.

Slomczynski, Kazimierz, et al. 1981. "Stratification, Work, and Values: A Polish–American Comparison." *American Sociological Review* 46 (December): 720–744.

Whorf, Benjamin L. 1956. *Language, Thought, and Reality.* New York: Wiley.

Williams, Robin M., Jr. 1970. *American Society.* New York: Knopf. Third edition.

## Chapter 4

Abramovitch, Rona, et al. 1986. "Sibling and Peer Interaction: A Final Follow-up and a Comparison." *Child Development* 57 (February): 217–229.

Applebaum, Herbert A. 1982. "Traditional versus Bureaucratic Methods." *Anthropological Quarterly* 55 (October): 224–234.

Baldassare, Mark. 1986. "Residential Satisfaction and the Community Question." *Sociology and Social Research* 70 (January): 139–142.

Biddle, Bruce J., et al. 1985. "Social Influence, Self-Referent Identity Labels, and Behavior." *Sociological Quarterly* 26 (Summer): 159–185.

Blau, Peter M., and W. Richard Scott. 1963. *Formal Organizations.* London: Routledge & Kegan Paul.

Bluth, B. J. 1985. "Pilots of Outer Space." *Society* 21 (January): 31–36.

Burns, Tom. 1980. "Sovereignty, Interests and Bureaucracy in the Modern State." *British Journal of Sociology* 31 (December): 491–506.

Childe, V. Gordon. 1951. *Man Makes Himself.* New York: Mentor Books.

Clough, S. B., and C. W. Cole. 1941. *Economic History of Europe.* Boston: D. C. Heath.

Cooley, Charles Horton. 1962. *Social Organization.* New York: Schocken Books. Originally published in New York: Charles Scribner's Sons, 1909.

Deane, Phyllis, and W. A. Cole. 1962. *British Growth 1688–1959: Trends and Structure.* London: Cambridge University Press.

Dyer, Gwynne. 1985. *War.* New York: Crown.

Friedl, John. 1981. *The Human Portrait.* Englewood Cliffs, NJ: Prentice-Hall. Second edition.

Gerth, Hans, and C. Wright Mills (eds.). 1946. *From Max Weber: Essays in Sociology.* New York: Oxford University Press.

Granberg, Donald, N. Lyneel Jefferson, Edward E. Brent, Jr., and Michael King. 1981. "Membership Group, Reference Group, and the Attribution of Attitudes to Groups." *Journal of Personality and Social Psychology* 41 (October): 833–842.

Hammond, Thomas H., and Gary J. Miller. 1985. "A Social Choice Perspective on Expertise and Authority in Bureaucracy." *American Journal of Political Science* 29 (February): 1–28.

Janis, Irving L. 1972. *Victims of Groupthink.* Boston: Houghton Mifflin.

Kohn, Melvin L. 1971. "Bureaucratic Man: A Portrait and an Interpretation." *American Sociological Review* 36 (June): 461–474.

Krause, Elliot. 1980. *Why Study Sociology?* New York: Random House.

Langton, John. 1984. "The Ecological Theory of Bureaucracy: The Case of Josiah Wedgwood and the British Pottery Industry." *Administrative Science Quarterly* 29 (September): 330–354.

Lee, Barrett, et al. 1984. "Testing the Decline-of-Neighborhood Thesis: Neighborhood Organizations in Seattle, 1929 and 1979." *American Journal of Sociology* 89 (March): 1161–1188.

Leonard, Wilbert Marcellus. 1980. *A Sociological Perspective of Sport.* Minneapolis: Burgess.

McAuley, William, and Cheri L. Nutty. 1985. "Residential Satisfaction, Community Integration, and Risk across the Family Life Cycle." *Journal of Marriage and the Family* 47 (February): 125–130.

Meindl, James R., and Melvin J. Lerner. 1984. "Exacerbation of Extreme Responses to an Out-Group." *Journal of Personality and Social Psychology* 47 (July): 71–84.

Merton, Robert K. 1968. *Social Theory and Social Structure.* New York: The Free Press. Third edition.

Michener, James A. 1976. *Sports in America.* New York: Random House.

Moore, Wilbert E. 1974. *Social Change.* Englewood Cliffs, NJ: Prentice-Hall. Second edition.

Mowat, Farley. 1965. *Never Cry Wolf.* New York: Dell.

Neill, Alexander Sutherland. 1960. *Summerhill.* New York: Hart.

Newcomb, Theodore M., et al. 1967. *Persistence and Change: Bennington College and Its Students after 25 Years.* New York: Wiley.

O'Bryant, Shirley L. 1985. "Neighbors' Support of Older Widows Who Live Alone in Their Own Homes." *Gerontologist* 25 (June): 305–310.

Patterson, Gerald R., and Thomas J. Dishion. 1985. "Contributions of Families and Peers to Delinquency." *Criminology* 23 (November): 63–79.

Roethlisberger, Fritz J., and William J. Dickson. 1939. *Management and the Worker.* Cambridge, MA: Harvard University Press.

Sahlins, Marshall. 1972. *Stone Age Economics.* Chicago: Aldine.

Scott, William A., and Ruth Scott. 1981. "Intercorrelations among Structural Properties of Primary Groups." *Journal of Personality and Social Psychology* 41 (April): 279–292.

Sherif, Muzafer, and Carolyn W. Sherif. 1956. *An Outline of Social Psychology.* New York: Harper & Brothers. Revised edition.

Sjoberg, Gideon, Ted. R. Vaughan, and Norma Williams. 1984. "Bureaucracy as a Moral Issue." *Journal of Applied Behavioral Science* 20: 441–453.

Slater, Philip. 1976. *The Pursuit of Loneliness.* Boston: Beacon Press. Revised edition.

Stasser, Garold, and William Titus. 1985. "Pooling of Unshared Information in Group Decision Making: Biased Information Sampling during Discussion."

*Journal of Personality and Social Psychology* 48 (June): 1467–1478.

Stouffer, Samuel A., et al. 1949. *The American Soldier: Combat and Its Aftermath.* Volume II. Princeton: Princeton University Press.

Summer, William Graham. 1906. *Folkways.* Boston: Ginn and Company.

Vidich, Arthur, and Joseph E. Bensman. 1968. *Small Town in a Mass Society.* Princeton: Princeton University Press. Revised edition.

Werner, Carol, and Pat Parmelee. 1979. "Similarity of Activity Preferences among Friends: Those Who Play Together Stay Together." *Social Psychology Quarterly* 42 (March): 62–66.

## Chapter 5

Asch, Solomon E. 1963. "Effects of Group Pressure upon the Modification and Distortion of Judgments," pp. 177–190 in Harold Geutzkow (ed.), *Group, Leadership and Men.* New York: Russell and Russell.

Bales, Robert F. 1953. "The Equilibrium Problem in Small Groups," pp. 111–161 in Talcott Parsons, Robert Bales, and Edward A. Shils (eds.), *Working Papers in the Theory of Action.* Glencoe, IL: The Free Press.

Bales, Robert F., and Philip E. Slater. 1955. "Role Differentiation in Small Decision-Making Groups," pp. 259–306 in Talcott Parsons, Robert F. Bales, et al., *Family, Socialization and Interaction Process.* Glencoe, IL: The Free Press.

Bales, Robert F., and Fred L. Strodtbeck. 1968. "Phases in Group Problem-Solving," pp. 389–398 in Dorwin Cartwright and Alvin Zander (eds.), *Group Dynamics.* New York: Harper & Row.

Barnett, Rosalind C., and Grace K. Baruch. 1985. "Women's Involvement in Multiple Roles and Psychological Distress." *Journal of Personality and Social Psychology* 49 (July): 135–145.

Berkowitz, Leonard. 1980. *A Survey of Social Psychology.* New York: Holt, Rinehart and Winston. Second edition.

Bettelheim, Bruno. 1958. "Individual and Mass Behavior in Extreme Situations," pp. 300–310 in Eleanor E. Maccoby, Theodore M. Newcomb, and Eugene L. Hartley (eds.), *Readings in Social Psychology.* New York: Holt, Rinehart and Winston. Third edition.

Bruce, Steve, and Roy Wallis. 1983. "Rescuing Motives." *British Journal of Sociology* 34 (March): 61–70.

Burden, Dianne S. 1986. "Single Parents and Work Setting: The Impact of Multiple Job and Homelife Responsibilities." *Family Relations* 35 (January): 37–43.

Caplow, Theodore. 1984. "Rule Enforcement without Visible Means: Christmas Gift Giving in Middletown." *American Journal of Sociology* 89 (May): 1306–1323.

Caton, Steven C. 1985. "The Poetic Construction of Self." *Anthropological Quarterly* 58 (October): 141–151.

Davis, Leslie L. 1984. "Judgment Ambiguity, Self-Consciousness and Conformity in Judgments of Fashionability." *Psychological Reports* 54 (April): 671–675.

Elman, Margaret R., and Lucia A. Gilbert. 1984. "Coping Strategies for Role Conflict in Married Professional Women with Children." *Family Relations* 33 (April): 317–327.

Erikson, Kai T. 1976. *Everything in Its Path.* New York: Simon & Schuster.

Feldman, Steven P. 1985. "Culture and Conformity: An Essay on Individual Adaptation in a Centralized Bureaucracy." *Human Relations* 38 (April): 341–356.

Fiedler, Fred E. 1967. *A Theory of Leadership Effectiveness.* New York: McGraw-Hill.

Frankl, Viktor E. 1959. *Man's Search for Meaning.* Boston: Beacon Press. Translated by Ilse Lasch.

Frost, Dean E., Fred E. Fiedler, and Jeff W. Anderson. 1983. "The Role of Personal Risk-Taking in Effective Leadership. *Human Relations* 36 (February): 185–202.

Garfinkel, Harold. 1967. *Studies in Ethnomethodology.* Englewood Cliffs, NJ: Prentice-Hall.

Gedye, G. E. 1939. *Fallen Bastions.* London: Victor Gollancz.

Goffman, Erving. 1959. *The Presentation of Self in Everyday Life.* New York: Doubleday.

Goffman, Erving. 1961. *Encounters.* Indianapolis: Bobbs-Merrill.

Hoffman, L. Richard. 1979. "Applying Experimental Research on Group Problem Solving to Organizations." *Journal of Applied Behavioral Science* 15 (3): 375–391.

Houseknecht, Sharon K., Suzanne Vaughan, and Anne S. Macke. 1984. "Marital Disruption among Professional Women: The Timing of Career and Family Events." *Social Problems* 31 (February): 273–284.

Hughes, Everett C. 1968. "Good People and Dirty Work," pp. 596–607 in Robert Perrucci and Marc Pilisuk (eds.), *The Triple Revolution.* Boston: Little, Brown.

Jennings, Luther B., and Stephen G. George. 1984. "Group-Induced Distortion of Visually Perceived Linear Extent: The Asch Effect Revisited." *Psychological Record* 34 (Winter): 133–148.

Kelly, Robert F., and Patricia Voydanoff. 1985. "Work/Family Role Strain among Employed Parents." *Family Relations* 34 (July): 367–374.

McCullough, David. 1983. "Mama's Boys." *Psychology Today* 17 (March): 32–36+.

McGlashan, Charles Fayette. 1879. *History of the Donner Party.* Truckee, CA: Crowley and McGlashan.

Manz, Charles C., and Henry P. Sims, Jr. 1984. "Searching for the 'Unleader': Organizational Member Views on Leading Self-Managed Groups." *Human Relations* 37 (May): 409–424.

Morash, Merry. 1984. "Establishment of a Juvenile Police Record." *Criminology* 22 (February): 97–111.

Murtaugh, Michael. 1984. "A Model of Grocery Shopping Decision Process Based on Verbal Protocol Data." *Human Organization* 43 (Fall): 243–251.

Orwell, George. 1959. *Down and Out in London and Paris.* New York: Berkley Medallion Books. Originally published in 1933.

Regan, Mary C., and Helen E. Roland. 1985. "Rearranging Family and Career Priorities: Professional Women and Men of the Eighties." *Journal of Marriage and the Family* 47 (November): 985–992.

Rochberg-Halton, Eugene. 1982. "Situation, Structure, and the Context of Meaning." *Sociological Quarterly* 23 (August): 455–476.

Schachter, Stanley. 1959. *The Psychology of Affiliation.* Stanford: Stanford University Press.

Schafer, Robert B., and Patricia M. Keith. 1985. "A Causal Model Approach to the Symbolic Interactionist View of the Self-Concept." *Journal of Personality and Social Psychology* 48 (April): 963–969.

Sharrock, W. W., and D. R. Watson. 1984. "What's the Point of 'Rescuing Motives'?" *British Journal of Sociology* 35 (September): 435–451.

Singular, Stephen. 1983. "A Robot and Liking It, Thanks." *Psychology Today* 17 (March): 22.

Sloan, Tod. S. 1983. "The Aura of Projected Personal Futures: A Neglected Aspect of Major Life Decisions." *Personality and Social Psychology Bulletin* 9 (December): 559–566.

Smircich, Linda, and Gareth Morgan. 1982. "Leadership: The Management of Meaning." *Journal of Applied Behavioral Science* 18 (3): 257–273.

Stoner, J. A. F. 1961. "A Comparison of Individual and Group Decisions Involving Risk." Unpublished master's thesis, Massachusetts Institute of Technology.

Vinokur, Amiram, et al. 1985. "Group Decision Making by Experts: Field Study of Panels Evaluating Medical Technologies." *Journal of Personality and Social Psychology* 49 (July): 70–84.

## Chapter 6

Ariès, Phillipe. 1962. *Centuries of Childhood: A Social History of Family Life.* New York: Vintage. Translated by Robert Baldick.

Axline, Virginia M. 1968. *Dibs: In Search of Self.* New York: Ballantine.

Barnes, Grace M. 1986. "Parental Socialization Factors and Adolescent Drinking Behaviors." *Journal of Marriage and the Family* 48 (February): 27–36.

Baron, James N., and Peter C. Reiss. 1985. "Mass Media and Violent Behavior." *American Sociological Review* 50 (June): 347–363.

Baum, Andrew, et al. 1986. "Unemployment Stress: Loss of Control, Reactance and Learned Helplessness." *Social Science and Medicine* 22: 509–516.

Belsky, Jay, and Laurence D. Steinberg. 1978. "The Effects of Day Care: A Critical Review." *Child Development* 49: 929–949.

Berger, Brigitte, and Peter L. Berger. 1984. *The War over the Family.* Garden City, NY: Anchor.

Bohannon, Paul (ed.). 1970. *Divorce and After.* Garden City, NY: Doubleday.

Brofenbrenner, Urie. 1970. *Two Worlds of Childhood.* New York: Russell Sage.

Cherlin, Andrew. 1983. "Remarriage as an Incomplete Institution," pp. 388–402 in Arlene Skolnick and Jerome H. Skolnick (eds.), *Family in Transition.* Boston: Little, Brown. Fourth edition.

Coleman, James. 1961. *The Adolescent Society.* New York: Doubleday.

Cooley, Charles Horton. 1964. *Human Nature and the Social Order.* New York: Schocken. Originally published in 1902.

Costos, Daryl. 1986. "Sex Role Identity in Young Adults: Its Parental Antecedents and Relation to Ego Development." *Journal of Personality and Social Psychology* 50 (March): 602–611.

Counts, Robert M., and Anita Sacks. 1985. "The Need for Crisis Intervention during Marital Separation." *Social Work* 30 (March/April): 151–158.

Davies, Christopher S. 1985. "The Throwaway Culture: Job Detachment and Rejection." *Gerontologist* 25 (June): 228–231.

Davis, Kingsley. 1948. *Human Society.* New York: Macmillan.

Davison, Peter, and Jane Davison. 1979. "Coming of Age in America," pp. 52–55 in Phillip Whitten (ed.), *Readings in Sociology.* New York: Harper & Row.

Flacks, Richard. 1979. "Growing Up Confused," pp. 21–32 in Peter I. Rose (ed.), *Socialization and the Life Cycle.* New York: St. Martin's.

Freud, Sigmund. 1952. *A General Introduction to Psychoanalysis.* New York: Washington Square Press. Originally published in 1920. Translated by Joan Riviere.

Gabrielli, William F., Jr., et al. 1984. "Urban Environment, Genetics, and Crime." *Criminology* 22 (November): 645–652.

Goffman, Erving. 1961. *Asylums.* Garden City, NY: Anchor.

Gracey, Harry L. 1977. "Learning the Student Role: Kindergarten as Academic Boot Camp," pp. 215–226 in Dennis H. Wrong and Harry L. Gracey (eds.), *Readings in Introductory Sociology.* New York: Macmillan. Third edition.

Hardy-Brown, Karen, and Robert Plomin. 1985. "Infant Communicative Development: Evidence from Adoptive and Biological Families for Genetic and Environmental Influences on Rate Differences." *Developmental Psychology* 21 (March): 378–385.

Harlow, Harry F., and Margaret K. Harlow. 1962. "Social Deprivation in Monkeys." *Scientific American* 207 (November): 137–147.

Harlow, Harry F., and R. R. Zimmerman. 1959. "Affectional Responses in the Infant Monkey." *Science* 130: 421–423.

Hiebert, Ray Eldon, Donald F. Ungurait, and Thomas W. Bohn. 1974. *Mass Media.* New York: David McKay.

Hiltz, Starr Roxanne. 1980. "Widowhood: A Roleless Role," pp. 237–253 in Arlene Skolnick and Jerome H. Skolnick (eds.), *Family in Transition.* Boston: Little, Brown. Third edition.

Hoge, Dean R., Gregory H. Petrillo, and Ella I. Smith. 1982. "Transmission of Religious and Social Values from Parents to Teenage Children." *Journal of Marriage and Family* 44 (August): 569–580.

Hultsch, David F., and Francine Deutsch. 1981. *Adult Development and Aging.* New York: McGraw-Hill.

Kagan, Jerome. 1983. "The Psychological Requirements for Human Development," pp. 409–420 in Arlene Skolnick and Jerome H. Skolnick (eds.), *Family in Transition.* Boston: Little, Brown. Fourth edition.

Kinicki, Angelo J. 1985. "Personal Consequences of Plant Closings: A Model and Preliminary Test." *Human Relations* 38 (March): 197–212.

Kirkendall, Lester. 1968. "Understanding the Problems of the Male Virgin," pp. 123–129 in Isadore Rubin and Lester Kirkendall (eds.), *Sex in the Adolescent Years.* New York: Association.

Lewis, Charles E., and Mary Ann Lewis. 1984. "Peer Pressure and Risk-Taking Behaviors in Children." *American Journal of Public Health* 74 (June): 580–584.

Liebert, Robert, and Rita W. Poulos. 1972. "TV for Kiddies — Truth, Goodness, Beauty, and a Little Bit of Brainwash." *Psychology Today* 6 (November): 122–124.

Loether, Herman J. 1975. *Problems of Aging.* Encino, CA: Dickenson. Second edition.

Main, Mary, and Carol George. 1985. "Responses of Abused and Disadvantaged Toddlers to Distress in Agemates: A Study in the Day Care Setting." *Developmental Psychology* 21 (May): 407–412.

Mead, George Herbert. 1930. "Cooley's Contribution to American Social Thought." *American Journal of Sociology* 35 (March): 693–706.

Mead, George Herbert. 1934. *Mind, Self and Society.* Chicago: University of Chicago Press.

Mednick, Sarnoff A., et al. 1984. "Genetic Influences in Criminal Behavior: Evidence from an Adoption Cohort." *Science* 224 (May): 891–894.

Mills, Marlene Christine. 1983. "Adolescents' Self-Disclosure in Individual and Group Theme-Centered Modeling, Reflecting, and Probing Interviews." *Psychological Reports* 53 (December): 691–701.

Montgomery, Reid H., Jr., and Ellis MacDougall. 1986. "Curing Criminals: The High-Tech Prisons of Tomorrow." *Futurist* 20 (January/February): 36–37.

National Commission on the Causes and Prevention of Violence. 1969. *Violence in America: Historical and Comparative Perspectives.* Washington, DC: U.S. Government Printing Office.

Odom, Samuel L., and Phillip S. Strain. 1984. "Peer-Mediated Approaches to Promoting Children's Social Interaction: A Review." *American Journal of Orthopsychiatry* 54 (October): 544–557.

Offer, Daniel. 1969. *The Psychological World of the Teenager.* New York: Basic.

Papirno, Elissa. 1976. "Life on Hectic Fringe Led to Girl's Death Try." *Hartford Courant* (August 25): 1+.

Parker, Seymour. 1984. "Cultural Rules, Rituals, and Behavior Regulation." *American Anthropologist* 86 (September): 584–600.

Phillips, John L., Jr. 1969. *The Origins of Intellect.* San Francisco: Freeman.

Piaget, Jean. 1970. "Piaget's Theory," pp. 707–732 in Paul H. Mussen (ed.), *Carmichael's Manual of Child Psychology.* New York: Wiley. Third edition. Translation of the Piaget article by Guy Gellerier.

Powell, Douglas H., and Paul F. Driscoll. 1979. "Middle-Class Professionals Face Unemployment," pp. 309–319 in Peter I. Rose (ed.), *Socialization and the Life Cycle.* New York: St. Martin's.

Scarr, Sandra, and Richard A. Weinberg. 1977. "Intellectual Similarities within Families of Both Adopted and Biological Children." *Intelligence* 1: 170–191.

Shand, Nancy, and Yorio Kosawa. 1985. "Culture Transmission: Caudill's Model and Alternative Hypotheses." *American Anthropologist* 87 (December): 862–871.

Simmons, Roberta G., Florence Rosenberg, and Morris Rosenberg. 1973. "Disturbance in the Self-Image at Adolescence." *American Sociological Review* 38 (October): 553–568.

Skeels, H. M. 1966. "Adult Status of Children with Contrasting Early Life Experiences: A Follow-up Study." *Monographs of the Society for Research in Child Development* 31: 1–65.

Skinner, B. F. 1972. *Beyond Freedom and Dignity.* New York: Knopf.

Spitz, René. 1945. "Hospitalism." *The Psychoanalytic Study of the Child* 1: 53–72.

Stock, M. B., and P. M. Smythe. 1963. "Does Undernutrition during Infancy Inhibit Brain Growth and Subsequent Intellectual Development?" *Archives of Disorders in Childhood* 38: 546–552.

Thompson, Larry W., et al. 1984. "Effects of Bereavement on Self-Perceptions of Physical Health in Elderly Widows and Widowers." *Journal of Gerontology* 39 (May): 309–314.

*U.S. News and World Report.* 1984. "America: Glued to the Tube." 96 (February 6): 9.

Watson, John B. 1924. *Behavior.* New York: Norton.

Westman, Mina, et al. 1985. "Job Stress, Cigarette Smoking and Cessation: The Conditioning Effects of Peer Support." *Social Science and Medicine* 20: 637–644.

Wilson, Edward O. 1978. *On Human Nature.* Cambridge, MA: Harvard University Press.

Wozniak, Paul R. 1984. "Making Sociobiological Sense out of Sociology." *Sociological Quarterly* 25 (Spring): 191–204.

Yamaguchi, Kazuo, and Denise B. Kandel. 1985. "On the Resolution of Role Incompatibility: A Life Event History Analysis of Family Roles and Marijuana Use." *American Journal of Sociology* 90 (May): 1284–1325.

## Chapter 7

Arnoff, Joel, and William D. Crano. 1975. "A Re-examination of the Cross-Cultural Principles of Task Segregation and Sex Role Differentiation in the Family." *American Sociological Review* 40 (February): 12–20.

Barry, Herbert III, and Alice Schlegel. 1984. "Measurements of Adolescent Sexual Behavior in the Standard Sample of Societies." *Ethnology* 23 (October): 315–329.

Bell, Alan P., and Martin S. Weinberg. 1980. "Homosexualities: A Study of Diversity among Men and Women," pp. 536–545 in Arlene Skolnick and Jerome H. Skolnick (eds.), *Family in Transition*. Boston: Little Brown. Third edition.

Bell, Robert R., and Norman M. Lobsenz. 1977. "Married Sex: How Uninhibited Can a Woman Dare to Be?" pp. 112–118 in John H. Gagnon (ed.), *Human Sexuality in Today's World*. Boston: Little, Brown.

Bem, Sandra L. 1975. "Sex-Role Adaptability: One Consequence of Psychological Androgeny." *Journal of Personality and Social Psychology* 31 (April): 634–643.

Berger, Brigitte, and Peter L. Berger. 1984. *The War over the Family*. New York: Anchor.

Berger, Raymond M. 1983. "What Is a Homosexual? A Definitional Model." *Social Work* 28 (March/April): 132–135.

Block, Jeanne Humphrey. 1973. "Conceptions of Sex Role: Some Cross-Cultural and Longitudinal Perspectives." *American Psychologist* 28 (June): 512–526.

Blumstein, Philip, and Pepper Schwartz. 1983. *American Couples*. New York: William Morrow.

Brodie, H. Keith, et al. 1974. "Plasma Testosterone Levels in Heterosexual and Homosexual Men." *American Journal of Psychiatry* 131 (January): 82–83.

Christopher, F. Scott, and Rodney M. Cate. 1985. "Anticipated Influences on Sexual Decision-Making for First Intercourse." *Family Relations* 34 (April): 265–270.

Collins, Randall. 1971. "A Conflict Theory of Sexual Stratification." *Social Problems* 19 (Summer): 3–21.

Collins, Randall. 1974. *Conflict Sociology: Toward an Explanatory Science*. New York: Academic.

Crano, William D., and Joel Arnoff. 1978. "A Cross-Cultural Study of Expressive and Instrumental Role Complementarity in the Family." *American Sociological Review* 43 (August): 463–471.

Cuber, John F., and Peggy B. Haroff. 1972. "Other Involvements," pp. 115–129 in Robert R. Bell and Michael Gordon (eds.), *The Social Dimension of Sexuality*. Boston: Little, Brown.

Deaux, Kay, and Laurie L. Lewis. 1984. "Structure of Gender Stereotypes: Interrelationships among Components and Gender Label." *Journal of Personality and Social Psychology* 46 (May): 991–1004.

Feldman, Douglas A. 1985. "AIDS and Social Change." *Human Organization* (Winter): 343–348.

Ford, Clellan S., and Frank A. Beach. 1951. *Patterns of Sexual Behavior*. New York: Harper & Row.

Friedan, Betty. 1981. "Feminism's Next Step." *New York Times Magazine* (July 5): 12–15.

Gagnon, John H., and Cathy S. Greenblat. 1978. *Life Designs: Individuals, Marriages, and Families*. Glenview, IL: Scott, Foresman.

Gagnon, John H., and William Simon. 1973. *Sexual Conduct*. Chicago: Aldine.

Goleman, Daniel. 1978. "Special Abilities of the Sexes: Do They Begin in the Brain?" *Psychology Today* 12 (November): 48–49+.

Gonsiorek, John C. 1982. "Results of Psychological Testing on Homosexual Populations." *American Behavioral Scientist* 25 (March/April): 385–396.

Gough, Kathleen. 1983. "The Origin of the Family," pp. 25–42 in Arlene S. Skolnick and Jerome H. Skolnick (eds.), *Family in Transition*. Boston: Little, Brown. Fourth edition.

Green, Richard. 1978. "Sexual Identity of 37 Children Raised by Homosexual or Transsexual Parents." *American Journal of Psychiatry* 135 (June): 692–697.

Hunt, Morton. 1983. "Marital Sex," pp. 219–234 in Arlene Skolnick and Jerome H. Skolnick (eds.), *Family in Transition*. Boston: Little, Brown. Fourth edition.

Kagan, Jerome. 1964. "Acquisition and Significance of Sex Typing and Sex Role Identity," pp. 137–167 in Martin L. Hoffman and Lois W. Hoffman (eds.), *Child Development Research*. Vol. 1. New York: Russell Sage.

Keller, James F., Stephen S. Elliott, and Edwin Gunberg. 1982. "Premarital Sexual Intercourse among Single College Students: A Discriminant Analysis." *Sex Roles* 8 (January): 21–32.

Kohlberg, Lawrence. 1966. "A Cognitive-Development Analysis of Children's Sex-Role Concepts and Attitudes," pp. 82–172 in Eleanor E. Maccoby (ed.), *The Development of Sex Differences*. Palo Alto, CA: Stanford Univeristy Press.

Mead, George Herbert. 1934. *Mind, Self and Society*. Chicago: University of Chicago Press.

Millett, Kate. 1970. *Sexual Politics*. Garden City, NY: Doubleday.

Molm, Linda D. 1986. "Gender, Power, and Legitimation: A Test of Three Theories." *American Journal of Sociology* 91 (May): 1356–1386.

Money, John, and Anke E. Ehrhardt. 1972. *Man and Woman, Boy and Girl*. Baltimore: Johns Hopkins University Press.

Nemy, Enid. 1982. "Does She Phone the Man in '82?" *New York Times* (June 23): C1+.

Parsons, Talcott, and Robert F. Bales. 1955. *Family, Socialization and Interaction Process.* Glencoe, IL: The Free Press.

Peplau, Letitia Anne, Zick Rubin, and Charles T. Hill. 1977. "Sex and Intimacy in Dating Relationships." *Journal of Social Issues* 33 (Spring): 86–109.

Porter, Natalie, et al. 1985. "Androgyny and Leadership in Mixed-Sex Groups." *Journal of Personality and Social Psychology* 49 (September): 808–823.

Rainwater, Lee. 1972. "Marital Sexuality in Four Cultures of Poverty," pp. 79–94 in Robert R. Bell and Michael Gordon (eds.), *The Social Dimension of Human Sexuality.* Boston: Little, Brown.

Reiss, Ira L. 1960. *Premarital Sexual Standards in America.* New York: The Free Press.

Robinson, Bryan E., et al. 1982. "Gay Men's and Women's Perceptions of Early Family Life and Their Relationships with Parents." *Family Relations* 31 (January): 79–83.

Rose, R. M. 1975. "Testosterone, Aggression, and Homosexuality: A Review of the Literature and Implications for Future Research," in E. J. Sachar (ed.), *Topics in Psychoendocrinology.* New York: Grune & Stratton.

Rosen, David H. 1974. *Lesbianism.* Springfield, IL: Charles C Thomas.

Rossi, Alice S. 1984. "American Sociological Association, 1983 Presidential Address." *American Sociological Review* 49 (February): 1–19.

Rubin, Lillian Breslow. 1983. "Blue-Collar Marriage and the Sexual Revolution," pp. 234–250 in Arlene Skolnick and Jerome H. Skolnick (eds.), *Family in Transition.* Boston: Little, Brown. Fourth edition.

Saghir, M. R., and E. Robins. 1971. "Male and Female Homosexuality: Natural History." *Comparative Psychiatry* 12: 503–510.

Saunders, Janice Miller, and John N. Edwards. 1984. "Extramarital Sexuality: A Predictive Model of Permissive Attitudes." *Journal of Marriage and the Family* 46 (November): 825–835.

Siegelman, M. 1974. "Parental Background of Male Homosexuals and Heterosexuals." *Archives of Sexual Behavior* 3: 3–18.

Simon, William, A. S. Berger, and John H. Gagnon. 1972. "Beyond Anxiety and Fantasy: The Coital Experiences of College Youth." *Journal of Youth and Adolescence* 1: 203–222.

Smith, Hendrick. 1976. *The Russians.* New York: Quadrangle.

Stacey, J. 1975. "When Patriarchy Kowtows: The Significance of the Chinese Revolution for Feminist Theory." *Feminist Studies* 2: 64–112.

Terkel, J., and J. S. Rosenblatt. 1972. "Humoral Factors underlying Maternal Behavior at Parturition: Cross Transfusion between Freely Moving Rats." *Journal of Comparative and Physiological Psychology* 80: 365–371.

Weis, David L., and Joan Jurich. 1985. "Size of Community of Residence as a Predictor of Attitudes toward Extramarital Sexual Relations." *Journal of Marriage and the Family* 47 (February): 173–178.

Whitehurst, Robert N. 1972. "Extramarital Sex: Alienation or Extension of Normal Behavior?" pp. 236–248 in John N. Edwards (ed.), *Sex and Society.* Chicago: Markham.

## Chapter 8

Agnew, Robert. 1985. "A Revised Strain Theory of Delinquency." *Social Forces* 64 (September): 151–167.

Alter, Jonathan. 1983. "Sex and Pages on Capitol Hill." *Newsweek* 102 (July 25): 16–17.

Arterton, F. Christopher. 1974. "The Impact of Watergate on Children's Attitudes toward Political Authority." *Political Science Quarterly* 89 (June): 269–288.

Bacon, Donald C. 1979. "Ripoffs: New American Way of Life," pp. 283–290 in Leonard Cargan and Jeanne Ballantine (eds.), *Sociological Footprints.* Boston: Houghton Mifflin.

Bell, Daniel. 1962. *The End of Ideology.* New York: The Free Press.

Benson, Michael L. 1984. "The Fall from Grace." *Criminology* 22 (November): 573–593.

Black, Donald. 1971. "The Social Organization of Arrest." *Stanford Law Review* 23 (June): 1104–1109.

Box, Steven, and Chris Hale. 1984. "Liberation/ Emancipation, Economic Marginalization, or Less Chivalry." *Criminology* 22 (November): 473–497.

Broad, William J. 1983. "Rising Use of Computer Networks Raises Issues of Security and Law." *New York Times* (August 26): 1+.

Chambliss, William J. 1969. *Crime and the Legal Process.* New York: McGraw-Hill.

Chambliss, William J. 1973. "The Saints and the Roughnecks." *Society* 11 (December): 24–31.

Chambliss, William J., and Robert B. Seidman. 1971. *Law, Order, and Power.* Reading, MA: Addison-Wesley.

Clinard, Marshall B. 1974. *Sociology of Deviant Behavior.* New York: Holt, Rinehart and Winston. Fourth edition.

Clinard, Marshall B., and Richard Quinney. 1967. *Criminal Behavior Systems: A Typology.* New York: Holt, Rinehart and Winston. Second edition.

Cohen, Albert K. 1966. *Deviance and Control.* Englewood Cliffs, NJ: Prentice-Hall.

Cohen, Albert K., and James F. Short, Jr. 1976. "Crime and Juvenile Delinquency," pp. 47–100 in Robert K. Merton and Robert Nisbet (eds.), *Contemporary Social Problems.* New York: Harcourt Brace Jovanovich. Fourth edition.

Covington, Jeanette. 1984. "Insulation from Labelling." *Criminology* 22 (November): 619–643.

Dickens, Charles. 1949. *A Tale of Two Cities.* London:

**478**

Oxford University Press. Originally published in 1859.

Durkheim, Émile. 1964. *The Division of Labor in Society*. New York: The Free Press. Translated by George Simpson and originally published in the Simpson translation in 1933.

Easton, David, and Jack Dennis. 1969. *Children in the Political System: The Origins of Political Legitimacy*. New York: McGraw-Hill.

Erikson, Kai T. 1966. *Wayward Puritans*. New York: Wiley.

Feldman, Harvey A. 1968. "Ideological Support in Becoming and Remaining a Heroin Addict." *Journal of Health and Social Behavior* 9 (June): 131–139.

Foote, C. 1954. "Compelling Appearances in Court-Administration of Bail in Philadelphia." *University of Pennsylvania Law Review* 102: 1031–1079.

Gibbons, Don C. 1977. *Society, Crime and Criminal Careers: An Introduction to Criminology*. Englewood Cliffs, NJ: Prentice-Hall.

Giuliani, Rudolph W. 1985. "Organizing Law Enforcement as Well as Organized Crime." *Public Administration Review* 45 (November): 712–717.

Gove, Walter R., et al. 1985. "Are Uniform Crime Reports a Valid Indicator of the Index Crimes? An Affirmative Answer with Minor Qualifications." *Criminology* 23 (August): 451–491.

Green, Mark J., Beverly C. Moore, and Bruce Wasserstein. 1979. "Criminal Law and Corporate Disorder," pp. 527–547 in Jerome H. Skolnick and Elliot Currie (eds.), *Crisis in American Institutions*. Boston: Little, Brown. Fourth edition.

Greenstein, Fred L. 1960. "The Benevolent Leader: Children's Image of Political Authority." *American Political Science Review* 54 (December): 934–954.

Hagan, John, and Celesta Albonetti. 1982. "Race, Class, and the Perception of Criminal Injustice in America." *American Journal of Sociology* 88 (September): 329–355.

Haskell, Martin R., and Lewis Yablonsky. 1974. *Crime and Delinquency*. Chicago: Rand McNally. Second edition.

Hess, Robert D., and David Easton. 1960. "The Child's Changing Image of the President." *Public Opinion Quarterly* 14 (Winter): 632–644.

Hollinger, Richard C., and John P. Clark. 1982. "Formal and Informal Social Controls of Employee Deviance." *Sociological Quarterly* 23 (Summer): 333–343.

Hunt, Morton M. 1961. "How Does It Come to Be So?" *The New Yorker* 36 (January 28): 39–40+.

Jackson, Joan K. 1978. "The Adjustment of the Family to Alcoholism," pp. 335–343 in Saul D. Feldman (ed.), *Deciphering Deviance*. Boston: Little, Brown.

Jensen, Michael C. 1975. "Watergate Donors Still Riding High." *New York Times* (August 24): Section 3(1+).

Lemert, Edwin M. 1951. *Social Pathology*. New York: McGraw-Hill.

McCarthy, Sarah J. 1981. "Pornography, Rape, and the Cult of Macho," pp. 82–90 in *Social Problems 81/82*. Guilford, CT: Dushkin.

Merton, Robert K. 1968. "Social Structure and Anomie," pp. 175–214 in Merton, *Social Theory and Social Structure*. New York: The Free Press. Third edition.

Merton, Robert K. 1976. "Introduction: The Sociology of Social Problems," pp. 3–43 in Robert K. Merton and Robert Nisbet (eds.), *Contemporary Social Problems*. New York: Harcourt Brace Jovanovich. Fourth edition.

Messner, Steven F., and Kenneth Tardiff. 1985. "The Social Ecology of Urban Homicide: An Application of the 'Routine Activities' Approach." *Criminology* 23 (May): 241–267.

Miethe, Terance D., and Charles A. Moore. 1985. "Socioeconomic Disparities under Determinate Sentencing Systems: A Comparison of Preguideline and Postguideline Practices in Minnesota." *Criminology* 23 (May): 337–363.

Nader, Ralph. 1985. "America's Crime without Criminals." *New York Times* (May 19): III:3.

Near, Janet P., and Marcia P. Miceli. 1986. "Retaliation against Whistle Blowers: Predictors and Effects." *Journal of Applied Psychology* 71 (February): 137–145.

Newfield, Jack, and Paul Dubrul. 1979. "The Political Economy of Organized Crime," pp. 414–427 in Jerome H. Skolnick and Elliot Currie (eds.), *Crisis in American Institutions*. Boston: Little, Brown. Fourth edition.

Palamara, Frances. 1986. "The Effect of Police and Mental Health Intervention on Juvenile Deviance: Specifying Contingencies in the Impact of Formal Reaction." *Journal of Health and Social Behavior* 27 (March): 90–105.

Parmerlee, Marcia A., Janet P. Near, and Tamila C. Jensen. 1982. "Correlates of Whistle-Blowers' Perception of Organizational Retaliation." *Administrative Science Quarterly* 27: 17–34.

Pittman, David J., and C. Wayne Gordon. 1968. *Revolving Door*. New York: The Free Press.

Quinney, Richard. 1974. *Critique of Legal Order: Crime Control in Capitalist Society*. Boston: Little, Brown.

Quinney, Richard. 1975. *Criminology*. Boston: Little, Brown.

Reid, Sue Titus. 1982. *Crime and Criminology*. New York: Holt, Rinehart and Winston. Third edition.

Reid, Sue Titus. 1985. *Crime and Criminology*. New York: Holt, Rinehart and Winston. Fourth edition.

Reiman, Jeffrey H. 1979. *The Rich Get Rich and the Poor Get Prison*. New York: Wiley.

Roberts, Steven V. 1983. "House Censures Crane and Studds for Sexual Relations with Pages." *New York Times* (July 21): 1+.

Scully, Diana, and Joseph Marolla. 1985. "'Riding the Bull at Gilley's': Convicted Rapists Describe the Rewards of Rape." *Social Problems* 32 (February): 251–263.

Shapiro, Susan P. 1980. *Thinking about White Collar Crime.* Washington, DC: U. S. Government Printing Office.

Shaw, Clifford R., and Henry D. McKay. 1942. *Juvenile Delinquency and Urban Areas.* Chicago: University of Chicago Press.

Simon, Rita James. 1975. *Women and Crime.* Lexington, MA: D. C. Heath.

Spiegel, Don, and George G. Katz. 1973. "The Whistle-Blower," pp. 503–528 in Don Spiegel and Patricia Keith-Spiegel (eds.), *Outsiders USA.* San Francisco: Rinehart Press.

Stephens, Gene, and William L. Tafoya. 1985. "Crime and Justice: Taking a Futuristic Approach." *Futurist* 19 (February): 18–22.

Sutherland, Edwin H., and Donald R. Cressey. 1978. *Criminology.* Philadelphia: J. B. Lippincott. Tenth edition.

Thio, Alex. 1978. *Deviant Behavior.* Boston: Houghton Mifflin.

Thoits, Peggy A. 1985. "Self-Labeling Process in Mental Illness: The Role of Emotional Deviance." *American Journal of Sociology* 91 (September): 221–249.

Thornberry, Terence P. 1973. "Race, Socioeconomic Status and Sentencing in the Juvenile Justice System." *Journal of Criminal Law and Criminology* 64: 90–98.

Thrasher, Frederic M. 1926. *The Gang.* Chicago: University of Chicago Press.

U. S. Bureau of the Census. 1980. *Statistical Abstract of the United States: 1980.* Washington, DC: U. S. Government Printing Office. 101st edition.

U. S. Bureau of the Census. 1983. *Statistical Abstract of the United States: 1982–83.* Washington DC: U. S. Government Printing Office. 103rd edition.

U. S. Bureau of the Census. 1986. *Statistical Abstract of the United States: 1982–83.* Washington, DC: Government Printing Office. 106th edition.

U. S. Department of Justice. 1981. *Violent Crime in the United States.* Washington, DC: U. S. Government Printing Office.

U. S. Department of Justice. 1983. "Prisoners in 1982." Washington, DC: U. S. Government Printing Office.

U. S. President's Commission on Law Enforcement and Administration of Justice. 1967. *The Challenge of Crime in a Free Society.* Washington, DC: U. S. Government Printing Office.

Wheeler, Stanton, David Weisburd, and Nancy Bode. 1982. "Sentencing the White-Collar Offender: Rhetoric and Reality." *American Sociological Review* 47 (October): 641–659.

Whyte, William H. 1956. *The Organization Man.* New York: Simon & Schuster.

Wilson, James Q. 1981. "Rehabilitating Our Prisons." *Family Weekly* (November 15): 4+.

Wolfgang, Marvin E. 1967. "A Sociological Analysis of Criminal Homicide," pp. 15–28 in Marvin E. Wolfgang (ed.), *Studies in Homicide.* New York: Harper & Row.

Wright, Robin. 1985. *Sacred Rage.* New York: Simon & Schuster.

Zeisel, Hans. 1973. "FBI Statistics: A Detective Story." *American Bar Association Journal* 59 (May): 510.

## Chapter 9

Baltzell, E. Digby. 1971. *Philadelphia Gentlemen: The Making of a National Upper Class.* Chicago: Quadrangle Books. Originally published in New York: The Free Press, 1958.

Beeghley, Leonard. 1978. *Social Stratification in America: A Critical Analysis of Theory and Research.* Santa Monica, CA: Goodyear.

Berelson, Bernard, and Gary A. Steiner. 1964. *Human Behavior.* New York: Harcourt, Brace and World.

Bernstein, Blanche. 1986. "A Way to Break the Welfare Cycle." *New York Times* (October 31): A35.

Blau, Peter M., and Otis Dudley Duncan. 1967. *The American Occupational Structure.* New York: Wiley.

Bluestone, Barry, and Bennett Harrison. 1982. "Plan for People — Not Profits." *Nation* 235 (September 11): 199+.

Breed, Warren. 1963. "Occupational Mobility and Suicide among White Males." *American Sociological Review* 28 (April): 179–188.

Bronfenbrenner, Urie. 1966. "Socialization and Social Class through Time and Space," pp. 362–377 in Reinhard Bendix and Seymour Martin Lipset (eds.), *Class, Status, and Power.* New York: The Free Press. Second edition.

Coleman, Richard P., and Lee Rainwater, with Kent A. McClelland. 1978. *Social Standing in America: New Dimensions of Class.* New York: Basic.

Collins, Sharon M. 1983. "The Making of the Black Middle Class." *Social Problems* 30 (April): 369–382.

Dahl, Robert A. 1967. *Pluralist Democracy in the United States.* Chicago: Rand McNally.

Davis, Fred. 1959. "The Cabdriver and His Fare: Facets of a Fleeting Relationship." *American Journal of Sociology* 65 (September): 158–165.

Davis, Kingsley, and Wilbert E. Moore. 1945. "Some Principles of Stratification." *American Sociological Review* 10 (April): 242–249.

Demo, David H., and Ritch C. Savin-Williams. 1983. "Early Adolescent Self-Esteem as a Function of Social Class: Rosenberg and Pearlin Revisited." *American Journal of Sociology* 88 (January): 763–774.

Duberman, Lucile. 1976. *Social Inequality: Class and Caste in America.* Philadelphia: Lippincott.

Economist. 1986. "America's Underclass." (March 15): 29–32.

Egan, Jack. 1986. "Changing Course." *U. S. News and World Report* 101 (October 6): 46–47.

Ellis, Robert A., and W. Clayton Lane. 1967. "Social

Mobility and Social Isolation." *American Sociological Review* 32 (April): 237–253.

Epstein, Cynthia F. 1970. "Encountering the Male Establishment: Sex-Status Limits on Women's Careers in the Professions." *American Journal of Sociology* 75 (May): 965–982.

Erlanger, Howard S. 1974. "Social Class and Corporal Punishment in Childrearing: A Reassessment." *American Sociological Review* 39: 68–85.

Faris, Robert E. L., and H. Warren Dunham. 1939. *Mental Disorders in Urban Areas.* Chicago: University of Chicago Press.

Featherman, David L., and Robert M. Hauser. 1978. *Opportunity and Change.* New York: Academic.

Gerth, H. H., and C. Wright Mills (eds.). 1946. *From Max Weber: Essays in Sociology.* New York: Oxford University Press.

Gilbert, Dennis, and Joseph A. Kahl. 1982. *The American Class Structure.* Homewood, IL: The Dorsey Press. Revised edition.

Gold, Ray. 1952. "Janitors versus Tenants: A Status-Income Dilemma." *American Journal of Sociology* 57 (March): 486–493.

Grusky, David B., and Robert H. Hauser. 1984. "Comparative Social Mobility Revisited: Models of Convergence and Divergence in 16 Countries." *American Sociological Review* 49 (February): 19–38.

Gurley, John G. 1984. "Marx's Contributions and Their Relevance Today." *American Economic Review* 74 (May): 110–115.

Hall, Wayne. 1986. "Social Class and Survival on the S.S. *Titanic.*" *Social Science and Medicine* 22: 687–690.

Haller, Max, et al. 1985. "Patterns of Career Mobility and Structural Positions in Advanced Capitalist Societies: A Comparison of Men in Austria, France, and the United States." *American Sociological Review* 50 (October): 579–603.

Hodge, Robert W., Paul M. Siegel, and Peter H. Rossi. 1966. "Occupational Prestige in the United States: 1925–1963," pp. 322–334 in Reinhard Bendix and Seymour Martin Lipset (eds.), *Class, Status, and Power.* New York: The Free Press.

Hodges, Harold M. 1964. *Social Stratification.* Cambridge, MA: Schenkman.

Howell, Joseph T. 1973. *Hard Living on Clay Street.* Garden City, NY: Doubleday.

Huckfeldt, R. Robert. 1983. "Social Contexts, Social Networks, and Urban Neighborhoods: Environmental Constraints on Friendship Choice." *American Journal of Sociology* 89 (November): 651–669.

Hurvitz, Nathan. 1964. "Marital Strain in the Blue Collar Family," pp. 92–109 in Arthur B. Shostak and William Gomberg (eds.), *Blue Collar World: Studies of the American Worker.* Englewood Cliffs, NJ: Prentice-Hall.

Isaacson, Walter. 1983. "Searching for the Recovery." *Time* 121 (February 21): 16–17.

Kahl, Joseph A. 1957. *The American Class Structure.* New York: Rinehart Press.

Kerckhoff, Alan C. 1984. "The Current State of Social Mobility Research." *Sociological Quarterly* 25 (Spring): 139–153.

Kessin, Kenneth. 1971. "Social and Psychological Consequences of Intergenerational Occupational Mobility." *American Journal of Sociology* 77 (July): 1–18.

Kessler, Ronald C., and Paul D. Cleary. 1980. "Social Class and Psychological Distress." *American Sociological Review* 45 (June): 463–478.

Koepp, Stephen. 1986. "Playing the New Tax Game." *Time* 128 (October 13): 66–67.

Kohn, Melvin L. 1976. "Interaction of Social Class and Other Factors in the Etiology of Schizophrenia." *American Journal of Psychiatry* 133: 179–180.

Laumann, Edward O. 1966. *Prestige and Association in an Urban Community.* Indianapolis: Bobbs-Merrill.

Lenski, Gerhard E. 1966. *Power and Privilege.* New York: McGraw-Hill.

Lenski, Gerhard E., and Jean Lenski. 1982. *Human Societies.* New York: McGraw-Hill. Fourth edition.

Lerner, Michael A. 1982. "The Elite Meet in Retreat," *Newsweek* 100 (August 2): 21–22.

Logan, John R., and O. Andrew Collver. 1983. "Residents' Perceptions of Suburban Community Differences." *American Sociological Review* 48 (June): 428–433.

McAdoo, Harriette P. 1982. "Stress Absorbing Systems in Black Families." *Family Relations* 31 (October): 479–488.

Maloney, Lawrence. 1981. "America's New Middle Class." *U. S. News and World Report* 90 (March 30): 39–41+.

Marx, Karl, and Friedrich Engels. 1959. "Manifesto of the Communist Party," pp. 6–41 in Lewis S. Feuer (ed.), *Marx and Engels: Basic Writings on Politics and Philosophy.* Garden City, NY: Anchor Books. Translated by N. I. Stone.

Mills, C. Wright. 1956. *The Power Elite.* New York: Oxford University Press.

Moskos, Charles C. 1969. "Why Men Fight." *Transaction* 7 (November): 13–23.

Munroe, Robert L., and Ruth H. Munroe. 1984. "Health and Wealth in Four Societies." *Journal of Social Psychology* 123 (June): 135–136.

New Republic. 1982. "And a Happy New Year." 188 (December 31): 5–6.

Pomeroy, Wardell B. 1972. *Dr. Kinsey and the Institute for Sex Research.* New York: Harper & Row.

Rainwater, Lee. 1964. "Marital Sexuality in Four Cultures of Poverty." *Journal of Marriage and the Family* 26 (November): 457–466.

Reiss, Ira L. 1980. *Family Systems in America.* New York: Holt, Rinehart and Winston. Third edition.

Rossides, Daniel W. 1976. *The American Class System.* Boston: Houghton Mifflin.

Rubin, Lillian Breslow. 1983. "Blue-Collar Marriage and the Sexual Revolution," pp. 234–250 in Arlene Skolnick and Jerome H. Skolnick (eds.), *Family in Transition.* Boston: Little, Brown. Fourth edition.

Schatzman, Leonard, and Anselm Strauss. 1972.

"Social Class and Modes of Communication," pp. 48–60 in Saul D. Feldman and Gerald W. Thiebar (eds.), *Life Styles: Diversity in American Society.* Boston: Little, Brown.

Sennett, Richard, and Jonathan Cobb. 1973. *The Hidden Injuries of Class.* New York: Vintage.

Shiller, Bradley R. 1970. "Stratified Opportunities: The Essence of 'The Vicious Circle.'" *American Journal of Sociology* 76 (November): 426–441.

Simon, William, and John Gagnon. 1972. "Sex, Marriage, and Social Class," pp. 86–88 in Saul D. Feldman and Gerald W. Thielbar (eds.), *Life Styles: Diversity in American Society.* Boston: Little, Brown.

Slater, Philip. 1976. *The Pursuit of Loneliness.* Boston: Beacon Paperbacks. Revised edition.

Slomczynski, Kazimierz M., and Tadeusz Krauze. 1984. "Should the Framework of Structural vs. Circulation Mobility Be Abandoned? If So, Not Because of Faulty Logic." *American Sociological Review* 49 (December): 850–852.

Smith, Kevin B. 1981. "Class Structure and Intergenerational Mobility from a Marxian Perspective." *Sociological Quarterly* 22 (Summer): 385–401.

Snarey, John R., and George E. Vaillant. 1985. "How Lower- and Working-Class Youth Become Middle-Class Adults: The Association between Ego Defense Mechanisms and Upward Social Mobility." *Child Development* 56 (August): 899–910.

Sobel, Michael E. 1984. "'Frameworks' and Frameworks: Reply to Slomczynski and Krauze." *American Sociological Review* 49 (December): 852–853.

Sorokin, Pitrim A. 1927. *Social Mobility.* New York: Harper & Brothers.

Srole, Leo, et al. 1962. *Mental Health in the Metropolis.* New York: McGraw-Hill.

Surrey, Stanley A. 1973. *Pathways to Tax Reform.* Cambridge, MA: Harvard University Press.

Syme, S. Leonard, and Lisa F. Berkman. 1981. "Social Class, Susceptibility, and Sickness," pp. 35–44 in Peter Conrad and Rochelle Kern (eds.), *The Sociology of Health and Illness.* New York: St. Martin's.

Treiman, Donald J. 1977. *Occupational Prestige in Comparative Perspective.* New York: Academic.

Tumin, Melvin M. 1957. "Some Unapplauded Consequences of Social Mobility in a Mass Society." *Social Forces* 36 (October): 32–36.

Tumin, Melvin M. 1967. *Social Stratification.* Englewood Cliffs, NJ: Prentice-Hall.

Turner, Jonathan H., and Charles E. Starnes. 1976. *Inequality: Privilege and Poverty in America.* Pacific Palisades, CA: Goodyear.

U. S. Bureau of the Census. 1984. *Current Population Reports,* Series P–60, *Money Income of Households, Families and Persons in the United States: 1983.* Washington, DC: U. S. Government Printing Office.

U. S. Bureau of the Census. 1986. *Statistical Abstract of the United States: 1986.* Washington, DC: U. S. Government Printing Office. 106th edition.

U. S. Bureau of the Census. 1986. *Current Population Reports,* Series P–70, *Household Wealth and Asset Ownership: 1984.* Washington, DC: U. S. Government Printing Office.

Warner, W. Lloyd, and Paul S. Lunt. 1941. *The Social Life of a Modern Community.* New Haven: Yale University Press.

Whitener, Leslie A. 1985. "The Migrant Farm Work Force: Differences in Attachment to Farmwork." *Rural Sociology* 50 (Summer): 163–180.

Wilson, William J. 1980. *The Declining Significance of Race.* Chicago: University of Chicago Press. Second edition.

Wrong, Dennis H. 1966. "Trends in Class Fertility in Western Nations," pp. 353–361 in Reinhard Bendix and Seymour Martin Lipset (eds.), *Class, Status, and Power.* New York: The Free Press. Second edition.

Zimmerman, L. J. 1965. *Poor Lands, Rich Lands: The Widening Gap.* New York: Random House.

# Chapter 10

Aboud, Frances E. 1984. "Social and Cognitive Bases of Ethnic Identity Constancy." *Journal of Genetic Psychology* 145 (December): 217–230.

Adorno, T. W., et al. 1950. *The Authoritarian Personality.* New York: Harper & Brothers.

Alba, Richard D. 1981. "The Twilight of Ethnicity among American Catholics of European Ancestry." *Annals of the American Academy of Political and Social Science* 454 (March): 86–97.

Aldrich, Howard, et al. 1985. "Ethnic Residential Concentration and the Protected Market Hypothesis." *Social Forces* 63 (June): 996–1009.

Allport, Gordon W. 1954. *The Nature of Prejudice.* Cambridge, MA: Addison-Wesley.

Bahr, Howard M., Bruce A. Chadwick, and Joseph H. Stauss. 1979. *American Ethnicity.* Lexington, MA: D. C. Heath.

Bailyn, Bernard, et al. 1977. *The Great Republic.* Lexington, MA: D. C. Heath.

Berry, Brewton, and Henry L. Tischler. 1978. *Race and Ethnic Relations.* Boston: Houghton Mifflin. Fourth edition.

Blackwell, James E. 1975. *The Black Community: Diversity and Unity.* New York: Harper & Row.

Bogardus, Emory. 1968. "Comparing Racial Distance in Ethiopia, South Africa, and the United States." *Sociology and Social Research* 52 (January): 149–156.

Brantley, Thomas. 1983. "Racism and Its Impact on Psychotherapy." *American Journal of Psychiatry* 140 (December): 1605–1608.

Brown, Dee. 1972. *Bury My Heart at Wounded Knee.* New York: Bantam.

Campbell, Bebe Moore. 1982. "Black Executives and Corporate Stress." *New York Times Magazine* (December 12): 36–39+.

Campbell, Ernest Q., and Thomas Pettigrew. 1959. *Christians in Racial Crisis.* Washington, DC: Public Affairs Press.

Cleaver, Eldridge. 1970. *Soul on Ice.* New York: Dell.

Cohen, Steven M., and Leonard J. Fein. 1985. "From Integration to Survival: American Jewish Anxieties in Transition." *Annals of the American Academy of Political and Social Science* 480 (July): 75–88.

Connor, John W. 1977. *Traditions and Change in Three Generations of Japanese Americans.* Chicago: Nelson-Hall.

Deloria, Vine, Jr. 1981. "Native Americans: The American Indian Today." *Annals of the American Academy of Political and Social Science* 454 (March): 139–149.

Dollard, John. 1937. *Caste and Class in a Southern Town.* New Haven: Yale University Press.

Dollard, John, et al. 1939. *Frustration and Aggression.* New Haven: Yale University Press.

Fallows, Majorie R. 1979. *Irish Americans: Identity and Assimilation.* Englewood Cliffs, NJ: Prentice-Hall.

Farley, Reynolds. 1977. "Trends in Racial Inequalities: Have the Gains of the 1960s Disappeared in the 1970s?" *American Sociological Review* 42 (April): 189–207.

Fitzpatrick, Joseph P. 1975. "Puerto Ricans in Perspective: The Meaning of Migration to the Mainland," pp. 297–304 in Norman R. Yetman and C. Hoy Steele (eds.), *Majority and Minority.* Boston: Allyn and Bacon. Second edition.

Fitzpatrick, Joseph P., and Lourdes Travieso Parker. 1981. "Hispanic-Americans in the Eastern United States." *Annals of the American Academy of Political and Social Science* 454 (March): 98–110.

Fugita, Stephen S., and David J. O'Brien. 1985. "Structural Assimilation, Ethnic Group Membership, and Political Participation among Japanese Americans: A Research Note." *Social Forces* 63 (June): 986–995.

Gordon, Milton M. 1981. "Models of Pluralism: The New American Dilemma." *Annals of the American Academy of Political and Social Science* 454 (March): 178–188.

Greeley, Andrew. 1977. *The American Catholic.* New York: Basic Books.

Greeley, Andrew. 1982. "Is Ethnic Consciousness Good for America?: Yes," pp. 96–101 in Kurt Finsterbusch and George McKenna (eds.), *Taking Sides: Clashing Views on Controversial Social Issues.* Guilford, CT: Dushkin. Second edition.

Green, Constance McLaughlin. 1967. *The Secret City: A History of Race Relations in the Nation's Capital.* Princeton: Princeton University Press.

Heaven, P. C. L. 1985. "Developmental Trends in Authoritarianism: A Research Extension." *Journal of Genetic Psychology* 146 (March): 139–140.

Hodge, William. 1981. *The First Americans: Then and Now.* New York: Holt, Rinehart and Winston.

Ikels, Charlotte. 1985. "Parental Perspectives on the Significance of Marriage." *Journal of Marriage and the Family* 47 (May): 253–264.

Killian, Lewis M. 1975. *The Impossible Revolution, Phase 2: Black Power and the American Dream.* New York: Random House.

Kitano, Harry H. L. 1981. "Asian-Americans: The Chinese, Japanese, Koreans, Philippinos, and Southeast Asians." *Annals of the American Academy of Political and Social Science* 454 (March): 125–138.

Kutner, Bernard, Carol Wilkins, and P. R. Yarrow. 1952. "Verbal Attitudes and Overt Behavior Involving Racial Prejudice." *Journal of Abnormal and Social Psychology* 47 (July): 649–652.

Lacy, Dan. 1972. *The White Use of Blacks in America.* New York: McGraw-Hill.

LaPierce, Richard T. 1934. "Attitudes vs. Actions." *Social Forces* 13 (October): 230–237.

Leighton, Alexander H. 1964. *The Governing of Men.* New York: Octagon Books. Originally published in Princeton: Princeton University Press, 1945.

Lyman, Stanford M. 1977. *The Asian in North America.* Santa Barbara, CA: ABC-Clio.

Moore, John W., and Harry Pachon. 1976. *Mexican Americans.* Englewood Cliffs, NJ: Prentice-Hall. Second edition.

Muraskin, Seth. 1986. "New BSU President Sets Goals for Term." *Southern News* 16 (October 15): 7.

New York Times. 1981. "750 Attend Klan Rally for Fishermen in Texas." (February 26): 36.

Novak, Michael. 1972. *The Rise of the Unmeltable Ethnics.* New York: Macmillan.

Okimoto, Daniel I. 1971. *American in Disguise.* New York: John Weatherhill.

Pachon, Harry P., and John W. Moore. 1981. "Mexican Americans." *Annals of the American Academy of Political and Social Science* 454 (March): 111–124.

Patterson, Orlando. 1982. "Is Ethnic Consciousness Good for America?: No," pp. 102–111 in Kurt Finsterbusch and George McKenna (eds.), *Taking Sides: Clashing Views on Controversial Social Issues.* Guilford, CT: Dushkin. Second edition.

Piliawsky, Monte. 1984. "Racial Equality in the United States: From Institutionalized Racism to 'Respectable' Racism." *Phylon* 45 (June): 135–143.

Prewitt-Diaz, Joseph O. 1984. "Migrant Students' Perceptions of Teachers, School and Self." *Perceptual and Motor Skills* 58 (April): 391–394.

Quigley, Harold E., and Charles Y. Glock. 1979. *Anti-Semitism in America.* New York: The Free Press.

Ray, John J. 1984. "The Effect of Collapsing Response Categories on the Balanced *F* Scale." *Journal of Social Psychology* 123 (August): 279–281.

Robbins, Susan P. 1984. "Anglo Concepts and Indian Reality: A Study of Juvenile Delinquency." *Social Casework* 65 (April): 235–241.

Rosenberg, Morris, and Roberta G. Simmons. 1971. *Black and White Self-Esteem: The Urban School Child.* Washington, DC: American Sociological Association.

Salamon, Sonya. 1985. "Ethnic Communities and the Structure of Agriculture." *Rural Sociology* 50 (Fall): 323–340.

Schaefer, Richard T. 1979. *Racial and Ethnic Groups.* Boston: Little, Brown.

Schmidt, William E. 1981. "Dismissed Workers Call Meat Plant Sale a 'Shame'." *New York Times* (November 7): 7.

Shenon, Philip. 1986. " 'Startling' Surge Is Reported in Illegal Aliens from Mexico." *New York Times* (February 21): A15+.

Simpson, George Eaton, and J. Milton Yinger. 1972. *Racial and Cultural Minorities: An Analysis of Prejudice and Discrimination.* New York: Harper & Row. Fourth edition.

Sklare, Marshall. 1971. *America's Jews.* New York: Random House.

Taylor, Stuart, Jr. 1986. "Justices to Hear Plea on Internment of Japanese-Americans." *New York Times* (November 18): A26.

Ten Broeck, Jacobus, Edward N. Barnhart, and Floyd W. Matson. 1968. *Prejudice, War and the Constitution.* Berkeley and Los Angeles: University of California Press. Originally published by the University of California Press, 1954.

Timberlake, Elizabeth M., and Kim Oanh Cook. 1984. "Social Work and the Vietnamese Refugee." *Social Work* 29 (March/April): 108–113.

Twain, Mark. 1973. *Mark Twain and the Three R's.* Maxwell Geismar (ed.). Indianapolis: Bobbs-Merrill.

Utley, Robert M. 1963. *The Last Days of the Sioux Nation.* New Haven: Yale University Press.

Vander Zanden, James W. 1972. *American Minority Relations.* New York: Ronald Press. Second edition.

Waxman, Chaim I. 1981. "The Fourth Generation Grows Up: The Contemporary American Jewish Community." *Annals of American Political and Social Science* 454 (March): 70–85.

Zaenglein-Senger, M. M., and C. S. Stewart. 1985. "The Parent–Adolescent Power Contest: Rigid Parents, Flexible Adolescents." *Social Casework* 66 (May): 309–313.

## Chapter 11

Atchley, Robert C. 1976. *The Sociology of Retirement.* Cambridge, MA: Schenkman.

Bagshaw, Margaret, and Mary Adams. 1986. "Nursing Home Nurses' Attitudes, Empathy, and Ideologic Orientation." *International Journal of Aging and Human Development* 22: 235–246.

Bourestom, Norman, and Leon Pastalan. 1981. "The Effects of Relocation on the Elderly." *Gerontologist* 21 (February): 4–7.

Bowe, Frank. 1978. *Handicapping America.* New York: Harper & Row.

Butler, Robert N. 1975. *Why Survive? Being Old in America.* New York: Harper & Row.

Chavez, Deborah. 1985. "Perpetuation of Gender Inequality: A Content Analysis of Comic Strips." *Sex Roles* 13 (July): 93–102.

Cohen, Carl I., et al. 1985. "Social Networks, Stress, and Physical Health: A Longitudinal Study of an Inner-City Elderly Population." *Journal of Gerontology* 40 (July): 478–486.

Conway, Katherine. 1985. "Coping with the Stress of Medical Problems among Black and White Elderly." *International Journal of Aging and Human Development* 21: 39–48.

Cox, Sue. 1981. *Female Psychology.* New York: St. Martin's. Second edition.

Creecy, Robert F. 1985. "Loneliness among the Elderly: A Causal Approach." *Journal of Gerontology* 40 (July): 487–493.

Cumming, Elaine, and William Henry. 1961. *Growing Old: The Process of Disengagement.* New York: Basic.

Depner, Charlene E., and Berit Ingersoll-Dayton. 1985. "Conjugal Social Support: Patterns in Later Life." *Journal of Gerontology* 40 (November): 761–766.

Downs, A. Chris, and Sheila K. Harrison. 1985. "Embarrassing Age Spots or Just Plain Ugly? Physical Attractiveness Stereotyping as an Instrument of Sexism on American Television Commercials." *Sex Roles* 13 (July): 9–19.

Duff, Raymond S., and August B. Hollingshead. 1968. *Sickness and Society.* New York: Harper & Row.

Economist. 1985. "The Battle for the Disabled." (December 21): 18.

Ehrenreich, Barbara, and Deirdre English. 1980, "Reflections on the 'Woman Question.' " pp. 217–231 in Arlene Skolnick and Jerome H. Skolnick (eds.), *Family in Transition.* Boston: Little, Brown. Third edition.

Foner, Anne. 1986. *Aging and Old Age.* Englewood Cliffs, NJ: Prentice-Hall.

Freeman, Jo. 1975. *The Politics of Women's Liberation.* New York: David McKay.

Freeman, Jo. 1980. "The Roots of Revolt," pp. 511–524 in Sheila Ruth (ed.), *Issues in Feminism.* Boston: Houghton Mifflin.

Friedan, Betty. 1963. *The Feminine Mystique.* New York: Norton.

Friedan, Betty. 1981. "Feminism's Next Step." *New York Times Magazine* (July 5): 12–15+.

Frieze, Irene Hanson. 1983. "Investigating the Causes and Consequences of Marital Rape." *Signs* 8 (Spring): 532–553.

Gething, Lindsay. 1985. "Perceptions of Disability of Persons with Cerebral Palsy, Their Close Relatives and Able Bodied Persons." *Social Science and Medicine* 20: 561–565.

Gliedman, John. 1979. "The Wheelchair Rebellion." *Psychology Today* 13 (August): 59–60+.

Gubrium, Jaber F. 1975. *Living and Dying at Murray Manor.* New York: St. Martin's.

Gustaitis, Rasa. 1980. "Old vs. Young in Florida: Preview of an Aging America." *Saturday Review* 7 (February 16): 10–12+.

Hacker, Helen Mayer. 1951. "Women as a Minority Group." *Social Forces* 30 (October): 60–69.

Hennig, Margaret, and Anne Jardim. 1977. *The Managerial Woman.* Garden City, NY: Anchor Press.

**484**

Hewlett, Sylvia Ann. 1986. "Feminism's Next Challenge: Support for Motherhood." *New York Times* (June 17): A27.

Horner, Matina. 1969. "Fail: Bright Women." *Psychology Today* 3:36–38.

Howard, Edward F. 1983. "Jobs for Older People." *American Psychologist.* 38 (March): 319–322.

Hultsch, David F., and Francine Deutsch. 1981. *Adult Development and Aging.* New York: McGraw-Hill.

Jowett, Sandra, and Terence Ryan. 1985. "Skin Disease and Handicap: An Analysis of the Impact of Skin Conditions." *Social Science and Medicine* 20: 425–429.

Katz, Elias. 1973. "The Mentally Retarded," pp. 132–153 in Don Spiegel and Patricia Keith-Spiegel (eds.), *Outsiders USA.* San Francisco: Rinehart Press.

Langer, Ellen J., et al. 1985. "Decreasing Prejudice by Increasing Discrimination." *Journal of Personality and Social Psychology* 49 (July): 113–120.

Langway, Lynn. 1982. "A Bad Year for the Disabled." *Newsweek* 99 (February): 82+.

Leidig, Margorie Whittaker. 1981. "Violence against Women: A Feminist-Psychological Analysis," pp. 190–205 in Sue Cox (ed.), *Female Psychology.* New York: St. Martin's. Second edition.

Luszcz, Mary A., and Karen M. Fitzgerald. 1986. "Understanding Cohort Differences in Cross-Generational, Self, and Peer Perceptions." *Journal of Gerontology* 41 (March): 234–240.

Neubeck, G. 1981. "Getting Older in My Family: A Personal Reflection," pp. 313–315 in David F. Hultsch and Francine Deutsch, *Adult Development and Aging.* New York: McGraw-Hill.

Neugarten, Bernice. 1983. "Health Care, Medicare, and Health Policy for Older People." *American Psychologist* 38 (March): 311–315.

Neugarten, Bernice L., Robert J. Havighurst, and Sheldon S. Tobin. 1968. "Personality and Patterns of Aging," pp. 173–177 in Bernice L. Neugarten (ed.), *Middle Age and Aging: A Reader in Social Psychology.* Chicago: University of Chicago Press.

Noble, Kenneth B. 1986. "End of Forced Retirement Means a Lot to a Few." *New York Times* (October 26): E5.

Nuessel, Frank H. 1982. "The Language of Ageism." *Gerontologist* 22 (June): 273–276.

Oakley, Ann. 1974. *The Sociology of Housework.* London: Martin Robertson.

Palmore, Erdman, and C. Luikart. 1974. "Health and Social Factors Related to Life Satisfaction," in Erdman Palmore (ed.), *Normal Aging II: Reports from the Duke Longitudinal Studies 1970–1973.* Durham, NC: Duke University Press.

Pelletier, John R. 1985. "Barriers to the Provision of Mental Health Services to Individuals with Severe Physical Disability." *Journal of Counseling Psychology* 32 (July): 422–430.

Poister, Theodore H. 1982. "Federal Transportation Policy for the Elderly and Handicapped: Responsive to Real Needs?" *Public Administration Review* 42 (January/February): 6–14.

Rotella, Elyce J. 1980. "Women's Roles in Economic Life," pp. 329–340 in Sheila Ruth (ed.), *Issues in Feminism.* Boston: Houghton Mifflin.

Russell, Dan, et al. 1985. "Evaluating the Physically Disabled: An Attributional Analysis." *Personality and Social Psychology Bulletin* 11 (March): 23–31.

Russell, Diana E. H., and Nancy Howell. 1983. "The Prevalence of Rape in the United States Revisited." *Signs* 8 (Summer): 688–695.

Schaffer, Kay F. 1981. *Sex Roles and Human Behavior.* Cambridge, MA: Winthrop.

Schultz, Richard, and G. Brenner. 1977. "Relocation of the Aged: A Review and Theoretical Analysis." *Journal of Gerontology* 32: 323–333.

Shapiro, Bruce. 1982. "Wrinkled Radical." *New Haven Advocate* (July 28): 6–7+.

Shaw, J. I., and P. Skolnick. 1971. "Attribution of Responsibility for a Happy Accident." *Journal of Personality and Social Psychology* 18: 380–383.

Simpson, Michael A. 1976. "Brought in Dead." *Omega* 7: 243–238.

Smith, Richard W. 1973. "The Physically Deviant," pp. 99–115 in Don Spiegel and Patricia Keith-Spiegel (eds.), *Outsiders USA.* San Francisco: Rinehart Press.

Sternglanz, S., and L. Serbin. 1974. "Sex Role Stereotyping in Children's Television Programs." *Developmental Psychology* 10: 710–715.

Streib, Gordon F., and C. J. Schneider. 1971. *Retirement in American Society: Impact and Process.* Ithaca, NY: Cornell University Press.

Sudnow, David. 1967. *Passing On: The Social Organization of Dying.* Englewood Cliffs, NJ: Prentice-Hall.

Wiener, C. 1975. "The Burden of Rheumatoid Arthritis: Tolerating the Uncertainty." *Social Science and Medicine* 9: 97–104.

Williamson, John B., Anne Munley, and Linda Evans. 1980. *Aging and Society.* New York: Holt, Rinehart and Winston.

Wollstonecraft, Mary. 1980. "A Vindication of the Rights of Women," pp. 457–463 in Sheila Ruth (ed.), *Issues in Feminism.* Boston: Houghton Mifflin.

## Chapter 12

Adams, Bert N. 1980. *The American Family.* Chicago: Rand McNally. Third edition.

Albrecht, Stan L. 1979. "Correlates of Marital Happiness among the Remarried." *Journal of Marriage and the Family* 41: 857–867.

Albrecht, Stan L. 1980. "Reactions and Adjustments to Divorce: Differences in the Experiences of Males and Females." *Family Relations* 29 (January): 59–68.

Ariès, Phillipe. 1962. *Centuries of Childhood.* New York: Vintage.

Atkinson, Maxine P., and Becky L. Glass. 1985. "Marital Age Heterogamy and Homogamy, 1900 to 1980." *Journal of Marriage and the Family* 47 (August): 685–691.

Avioli, Paula Smith. 1985. "The Labor-Force Participation of Married Mothers of Infants." *Journal of Marriage and the Family* 47 (August): 739–745.

Berger, Brigitte, and Peter Berger. 1984. *The War over the Family*. Garden City, NY: Anchor.

Bernstein, Barton E., and Sheila K. Collins. 1985. "Remarriage Counseling: Lawyer and Therapist's Help with the Second Time Around." *Family Relations* 34 (July): 387–391.

Bitter, Robert G. 1986. "Late Marriage and Marital Instability: The Effects of Heterogeneity and Inflexibility." *Journal of Marriage and the Family* 48 (August): 631–640.

Bohannon, Paul (ed.). 1970. *Divorce and After*. Garden City, NY: Doubleday.

Booth, Alan, and John N. Edwards. 1985. "Age at Marriage and Marriage Instability." *Journal of Marriage and the Family* 47 (February): 67–75.

Brody, Jane E. 1983. "Divorce's Stress Exacts Long-Term Health Toll." *New York Times* (December 13): C1+.

Buss, David M. 1986. "Human Mate Selection," pp. 60–65 in *Marriage and Family, 86/87*. Guilford, CT: Dushkin.

Cockrum, Janet, and Priscilla White. 1985. "Influences on the Life Satisfaction of Never-Married Men and Women." *Family Relations* 34 (October): 551–556.

Feldman, Harold. 1981. "A Comparison of Intentional Parents and Intentionally Childless Couples." *Journal of Marriage and the Family* 43 (August): 593–600.

Furstenberg, Frank F., Jr., and Christine Winquist Nord. 1985. "Parenting Apart: Patterns of Child-rearing after Marital Disruption." *Journal of Marriage and the Family* 47 (November): 893–904.

Futurist. 1985. "Land Co-op." 19 (April): 62+.

Gagnon, John H., and Cathy S. Greenblat. 1978. *Life Designs: Individuals, Marriages, and Families*. Glenview, IL: Scott, Foresman.

Glenwick, David S., and Joel D. Mowrey. 1986. "When Parent Becomes Peer: Loss of Intergenerational Boundaries in Single Parent Families." *Family Relations* 35 (January): 57–62

Glick, Paul C. 1986. "How American Families Are Changing," pp. 23–26 in *Marriage and Family 86/87*. Guilford, CT: Dushkin.

Goode, William J. 1956. *After Divorce*. New York: The Free Press.

Goode, William J. 1963. *World Revolution and Family Patterns*. New York: The Free Press.

Goode, William J. 1982. *The Family*. Englewood Cliffs, NJ: Prentice-Hall. Second edition.

Green, Ernest J. 1978. *Personal Relationships*. New York: McGraw-Hill.

Gwartney-Gibbs, Patricia A. 1986. "The Institutionalization of Premarital Cohabitation: Estimates from Marriage License Applications, 1970 and 1980." *Journal of Marriage and the Family* 48 (May): 423–434.

Handwerker, W. Penn. 1973. "Technology and Household Configuration in Urban Africa: The Bassa of Monrovia." *American Sociological Review* 38 (April): 182–197.

Hoffman, Lois Wladis, and F. Ivan Nye. 1974. *Working Mothers*. San Francisco: Jossey-Bass.

Holstrom, Lynda Lytle. 1972. *The Two-Career Family*. Cambridge, MA: Schenkman.

Hunt, Morton, and Bernice Hunt. 1980. "Another World, Another Life," pp. 340–354 in Arlene Skolnick and Jerome H. Skolnick (eds.), *Family in Transition*. Boston: Little, Brown. Third edition.

Kamerman, Sheila B., and Alfred J. Kahn. 1981. *Child Care, Family Benefits, and Working Parents*. New York: Columbia University Press.

Kanter, Rosabeth M. 1968. "Commitment and Social Organization: A Study of Commitment Mechanisms in Utopian Communities." *American Sociological Review* 33 (August): 499–517.

Krebs, Albin, and Robert M. Thomas, Jr. 1981. "A Message of Love Travels in High Seas." *New York Times* (August 28): 18.

Kurdek, Lawrence A., Darlene Blisk, and Albert E. Siesky, Jr. 1981. "Correlates of Children's Long-Term Adjustment to Their Parents' Divorce." *Developmental Psychology* 17 (September): 565–578.

Leighton, Alexander H. 1984. "Then and Now: Some Notes on the Interaction of Person and Social Environment." *Human Organization* 43 (Fall): 189–197.

Lein, Laura, and Mary C. Blehar. 1983. "Working Couples as Parents," pp. 420–437 in Arlene S. Skolnick and Jerome H. Skolnick (eds.), *Family in Transition*. Boston: Little, Brown. Fourth edition.

Leslie, Gerald R. 1979. *The Family in Social Context*. New York: Oxford University Press. Fourth edition.

Leslie, Leigh A., and Katherine Grady. 1985. "Changes in Mothers' Social Networks and Social Support Following Divorce." *Journal of Marriage and the Family* 47 (August): 663–673.

Lowery, Carol S., and Shirley A. Settle. 1985. "Effects of Divorce on Children: Differential Impact of Custody and Visitation Patterns." *Family Relations* 34 (October): 455–463.

Luepnitz, Deborah. 1979. "Which Aspects of Divorce Affect Children?" *Family Coordinator* 28 (January): 79–85.

Macklin, Eleanor. 1983. "Nonmarital Heterosexual Cohabitation," pp. 264–285 in Arlene Skolnick and Jerome H. Skolnick (eds.), *Family in Transition*. Boston: Little, Brown. Fourth edition.

Mead, Margaret. 1963. "Children and Ritual in Bali," pp. 40–51 in Margaret Mead and Martha Wolfenstein (eds.), *Childhood in Contemporary Cultures*. Chicago: Phoenix Books. Originally published in Chicago: University of Chicago Press, 1955.

Menaghan, Elizabeth G., and Morton A. Lieberman. 1986. "Changes in Depression Following Divorce: A Panel Study." *Journal of Marriage and the Family* 48 (May): 319–328.

Moffett, Robert K., and Jack F. Scherer. 1976. *Dealing with Divorce*. Boston: Little, Brown.

Murdock, George Peter. 1949. *Social Structure*. New York: Macmillan.

Norton, Arthur J., and Paul C. Glick. 1986. "One Parent Families: A Social and Economic Profile." *Family Relations* 35 (January): 9–17.

Oakley, Deborah. 1985. "Premarital Childbearing Decision-Making." *Family Relations* 34 (October): 561–563.

Ramey, James. 1978. "Experimental Family Forms —the Family of the Future." *Marriage and Family Review* 1 (January/February): 1–9.

Regan, Mary C., and Helen E. Roland. 1985. "Rearranging Family and Career Priorities: Professional Women and Men of the Eighties." *Journal of Marriage and the Family* 47 (November): 985–992.

Reiss, Ira. 1980. *Family Systems in America*. New York: Holt, Rinehart and Winston. Third edition.

Renne, Karen S. 1974. "Correlates of Dissatisfaction in Marriage," in Robert Winch and Graham Spanier (eds.), *Selected Studies in the Family*. New York: Holt, Rinehart and Winston. Fourth edition.

Rosenthal, Carolyn J. 1985. "Kinkeeping in the Familial Division of Labor." *Journal of Marriage and the Family* 47 (November): 965–974.

Sanik, Margaret M., and Teresa Mauldin. 1986. "Single versus Two Parent Families: A Comparison of Mothers' Time." *Family Relations* 35 (January): 53–56.

Saxton, Lloyd. 1980. *The Individual, Marriage, and Family*. New York: Wadsworth. Fourth edition.

Scanzoni, Letha Dawson, and John Scanzoni. 1981. *Men, Women, and Change*. New York: McGraw-Hill. Second edition.

Schultz, Martin. 1984. "Divorce in Early America: Origins and Patterns in Three North Central States." *Sociological Quarterly* 25 (Autumn): 511–526.

Sennett, Richard. 1974. *Families against the City*. New York: Vintage. Originally published in 1970.

Silka, Linda, and Sara Kiesler. 1977. "Couples Who Choose to Remain Childless." *Family Planning Perspectives* 9 (January/February): 16–25.

Singer, Barry. 1982. "Conversation with Robert McGinley." *Alternative Lifestyles* 5 (Winter): 69–77.

Skolnick, Arlene. 1971. "Families Can Be Unhealthy for Children and Other Living Things." *Psychology Today* 5 (August): 18+.

Spanier, Graham B. 1983. "Married and Unmarried Cohabitation in the United States: 1980." *Journal of Marriage and the Family* 45 (May): 277–288.

Spiro, Melford E. 1970. *Kibbutz*. New York: Schocken Books. Second edition.

Stein, Peter J. 1980. "Singlehood: An Alternative to Marriage," pp. 517–536 in Arlene Skolnick and Jerome H. Skolnick (eds.), *Family in Transition*. Boston: Little, Brown. Third edition.

Tanner, Donna. 1978. *The Lesbian Couple*. Lexington, MA: Lexington Books.

Thimberger, Rosemary, and Michael J. MacLean. 1982. "Maternal Employment: The Child's Perspective." *Journal of Marriage and the Family* 44 (May): 469–475.

Turner, Pauline H., and Richard M. Smith. 1983. "Single Parents and Day Care." *Family Relations* 32 (April): 215–226.

U. S. Bureau of the Census. 1982. *Current Population Reports, Series P–20, Population Profile of the United States: 1981*. Washington, DC: U. S. Government Printing Office.

U. S. Bureau of the Census. 1983. *Current Population Reports, Series P–20, Marital Status and Living Arrangements: March 1982*. Washington, DC: U. S. Government Printing Office.

U. S. Bureau of the Census. 1984. *Current Population Reports, Population Characteristics, Series P–20, Fertility of American Women: June 1983*. Washington, DC: U. S. Government Printing Office.

U. S. Bureau of the Census. 1984. *Current Population Reports, Series P–20, Population Characteristics*. Washington, DC: U. S. Government Printing Office.

U. S. Bureau of the Census. 1986. *Statistical Abstract of the United States: 1986*. Washington, DC: U. S. Government Printing Office. 106th edition.

U. S. Department of Labor. 1985. *The United Nations Decade for Women, 1976–1985: Employment in the United States*. Washington, DC: U. S. Government Printing Office.

Veevers, J. E. 1973. "Voluntarily Childless Wives: An Exploratory Study." *Sociology and Social Research* 57 (April): 356–366.

Weitzman, Lenore J., and Ruth B. Dixon. 1983. "The Transformation of Legal Marriage through No-Fault Divorce," pp. 353–366 in Arlene Skolnick and Jerome H. Skolnick (eds.), *Family in Transition*. Fourth edition.

White, Lynn K., and Alan Booth. 1985. "Stepchildren in Remarriages." *American Sociological Reveiw* 50 (October): 689–698.

White, Stephen W., and Bernard L. Bloom. 1981. "Factors Related to the Adjustment of Divorcing Men." *Family Relations* 30 (July): 349–360.

Whiting, Beatrice, and John W. M. Whiting. 1975. *Children of Six Cultures: A Psycho-Cultural Analysis*. Cambridge, MA: Harvard University Press.

Zablocki, Ben. 1977. *Alienation and Investment in the Urban Commune*. New York: Center for Policy Research.

## Chapter 13

Allman, T. D. 1976. "Jesus in Tomorrowland." *New Republic* 177 (November 27): 6–9.

Bailyn, Bernard, et al. 1977. *The Great Republic*. Lexington, MA: D. C. Heath.

Banks, Olive. 1976. *The Sociology of Education*. New York: Schocken Books. Revised edition.

Barr, Browne, 1977. "Finding the Good at Garden Grove." *Christian Century* (May 4): 424–427.

Binzen, Peter. 1970. *Whitetown, USA*. New York: Random House.

Bowles, Samuel, and Herbert Gintis. 1976. *Schooling in Capitalist America: Educational Reform and the Contradictions of Economic Life*. New York: Basic.

Brodinsky, Ben. 1979. "Something Happened: Education in the Seventies." *Phi Delta Kappan* 61 (December): 238–241.

Campbell, Ernest Q., and Thomas Pettigrew. 1959. *Christians in Racial Crisis*. Washington, DC: Public Affairs Press.

Cassidy, Robert. 1972. "The Pros and Cons of Busing." *Parents' Magazine* 47 (April): 46–47+.

Clogg, Clifford C., and James W. Shockey. 1984. "Mismatch between Occupation and Schooling: A Prevalence Measure, Recent Trends and Demographic Analysis." *Demography* 21 (May): 235–257.

Cohen, David K. 1974. "Segregation, Desegregation, and *Brown*." *Society* 12 (November/December): 35–40.

Cohen, Steven M., and Leonard J. Fein. 1985. "From Integration to Survival: American Jewish Anxieties in Transition." *Annals of the American Academy of Political and Social Science* 483 (July): 75–88.

Coleman, James S., et al. 1966. *Equality of Educational Opportunity*. Washington, DC: U. S. Government Printing Office.

Coleman, James S., et al. 1982. *High School Achievement*. New York: Basic.

Collins, Randall. 1979. *The Credential Society*. New York: Academic.

Crossman, Richard (ed.). 1952. *The God That Failed*. New York: Bantam.

Davis, Sharon A., and Emil J. Haller. 1981. "Tracking, Ability, and SES: Further Evidence on the 'Revisionist-Meritocratic Debate.'" *American Journal of Education* 89 (May): 283–304.

Deci, Edward L. 1985. "The Well-Tempered Classroom." *Psychology Today* 19 (March): 52–53.

Demerath, N. J., and Rhys H. Williams. 1985. "Civil Religion in an Uncivil Society." *Annals of the American Academy of Political and Social Science* 477 (July): 154–166.

Douglass, Frederick. 1968. *Narrative of the Life of Frederick Douglass*. New York: Signet Books. Originally published in 1845.

Durkheim, Émile. 1961. *The Elementary Forms of the Religious Life*. New York: Collier Books. Translated by Joseph Ward Swain.

Durkheim, Émile. 1964. *The Division of Labor in Society*. New York: The Free Press. Translated by George Simpson. The Simpson translation originally published in New York: The Macmillan Company, 1933.

Durkheim, Émile. 1975. *Durkheim on Religion*. London: Routledge Kegan Paul. Edited by W. S. F. Pickering and translated by Jacqueline Gedding and W. S. F. Pickering.

Economist. 1985. "Religious Schools: Dividing and Multiplying." 294 (February 23): 25.

Ellerin, Milton, and Alisa Kesten. 1981. "The New Right: What Is It?" *Social Policy* 11 (March/April): 54–62.

Falwell, Jerry. 1981. "The Maligned Moral Majority." *Newsweek* 98 (September 21): 17.

Fiske, Edward B. 1983. "Study Asks Tighter Curriculums." *New York Times* (September 16): A1+.

Fiske, Edward B. 1983. "'Tide of Mediocrity' May Not Be Rising as Fast as It Seems." *New York Times* (September 18): E20.

Goldberg, Milton, and James Harvey. 1983. "A Nation at Risk: The Report of the National Commission on Excellence in Education." *Phi Delta Kappan* 65 (September): 14–18.

Gracey, Harry L. 1977. "Learning the Student Role: Kindergarten as Academic Boot Camp," pp. 215–226 in Dennis H. Wrong and Harry L. Gracey (eds.), *Readings in Introductory Sociology*. New York: Macmillan. Third edition.

Gurley, John G. 1984. "Marx's Contributions and Their Relevance Today." *American Economic Review* 74 (May): 110–123.

Hammond, Phillip E. 1985. "The Curious Path of Conservative Protestantism." *Annals of the American Academy of Political and Social Science* 480 (July): 53–62.

Hanline, Mary Frances, and Carola Murray. 1984. "Integrating Severely Handicapped Children into Regular Public Schools." *Phi Delta Kappan* 66 (December): 273–276.

Hinsberg, Thomas F. 1974. "The Church: Agent of Social Change." *Journal of Applied Behavioral Science* 10 (Summer): 432–437.

Hodgson, Godfrey. 1973. "Do Schools Make a Difference?" *Atlantic* 231 (March): 35–46.

Hurn, Christopher J. 1978. *The Limits and Possibilities of Schooling*. Boston: Allyn and Bacon.

Jackson, Philip. 1968. *Life in Classrooms*. New York: Holt, Rinehart and Winston.

Johnstone, Ronald L. 1975. *Religion and Society in Interaction*. Englewood Cliffs, NJ: Prentice-Hall.

Lewin, Roger. 1986. "Creationism Downed Again in Louisiana." *Science* 231 (January 10): 112.

Lewis, Sinclair. 1970. *Elmer Gantry*. New York: Signet Classics. Originally published in New York: Harcourt, Brace and Company, 1927.

Lichtenstein, Peter M. 1985. "Radical Liberalism and Radical Education: A Synthesis and Critical Evaluation of Illich, Freire, and Dewey." *American Journal of Economics and Sociology* 44 (January): 39–54.

Lienesch, Michael. 1982. "Right-Wing Religion: Christian Conservatism as a Political Movement." *Political Science Quarterly* 97 (Fall): 403–425.

McClendon, McKee J. 1985. "Racism, Rational Choice, and White Opposition to Racial Change: A Case Study of Busing." *Public Opinion Quarterly* 49 (Summer): 214–233.

McNamara, Patrick H. 1985. "American Catholicism in the Mid-Eighties: Pluralism and Conflict in a Changing Church." *Annals of the American Academy of Political and Social Science* 480 (July): 63–74.

Marshall, Eliot. 1986. "Dinosaurs Ruffle Some Feathers in California." *Science* 231 (January 3): 18–19.

Marty, Martin E. 1985. "Transpositions: American Religion in the 1980s." *Annals of the American Academy of Political and Social Science* 480 (July): 11–23.

Marx, Karl. 1970. *Critique of Hegel's "Philosophy of Right"*. Cambridge University Press. Translated by Annette Jolin and Joseph O'Malley.

Miller, Karen A., et al. 1985. "Educational Self-Direction and the Cognitive Functioning of Students." *Social Forces* 63 (June): 923–944.

Niebuhr, Richard H. 1957. *The Social Sources of Denominationalism*. New York: Meridian Books.

Oakes, Jeannie. 1982. "Classroom Social Relationships: Exploring the Bowles and Gintis Hypothesis." *Sociology of Education* 55 (October): 197–212.

O'Dea, Thomas F. 1966. *The Sociology of Religion*. Englewood Cliffs, NJ: Prentice-Hall.

Oestereicher, Emil. 1982. "The Depoliticization of the Liberal Arts." *Social Research* 49 (Winter): 1004–1012.

Parsons, Talcott. 1968. "The School Class as a Social System: Some of Its Functions in American Society," pp. 199–218 in Robert R. Bell and Holger R. Stub (eds.), *The Sociology of Education*. Homewood, IL: Dorsey Press. Revised edition.

Robertson, Roland. 1970. *The Sociological Interpretation of Religion*. Oxford: Basil Blackwell.

Smith, Jonathan Z. 1981. "Liberal Arts for Citizenship." *Center Magazine* 14 (January/February): 63–64.

Sweet, William Warren. 1950. *Story of Religion in America*. New York: Harper & Company.

Theodorson, George A., and Achilles G. Theodorson. 1969. *A Modern Dictionary of Sociology*. New York: Thomas Y. Crowell Company.

Twain, Mark. 1973. "Bible Teaching and Religious Practice," pp. 106–110 in Maxwell Geismar (ed.), *Mark Twain and the Three R's*. Indianapolis: Bobbs-Merrill.

U. S. Bureau of the Census. 1966. *Statistical Abstract of the United States: 1966*. Washington, DC: U. S. Government Printing Office. 87th edition.

U. S. Bureau of the Census. 1986. *Statistical Abstract of the United States: 1986*. Washington, DC: U. S. Government Printing Office. 106th edition.

Weber, Max. 1958. *The Protestant Ethic and the Spirit of Capitalism*. New York: Charles Scribner's Sons. Original Parsons translation published in 1930.

Wilson, John. 1978. *Religion in American Society*. Englewood Cliffs, NJ: Prentice-Hall.

Woodrum, Eric. 1985. "Religion and Economics among Japanese Americans: A Weberian Study." *Social Forces* 64 (September): 191–204.

# Chapter 14

Anderson, Kristine L., and Bruce London. 1985. "Modernization, Elites, and the Distribution of Educational Resources in Thailand." *Social Forces* 63 (March): 775–794.

Arato, Andrew. 1985. "Some Perspectives of Democratization in East Central Europe." *Journal of International Affairs* 38 (Winter): 321–335.

Aziz-al Ahsan, S. 1984. "Economic Policy and Class Structure in Syria: 1958–1980." *International Journal of Middle East Studies* 16 (August): 301–323.

Bailyn, Bernard, et al. 1977. *The Great Republic*. Lexington, MA: D. C. Heath.

Berry, Jeffrey M. 1984. *The Interest Group Society*. Boston: Little, Brown.

Boffey, Philip M. 1985. "Satisfaction on the Job: Autonomy Ranks First." *New York Times* (May 28): 28.

Bradshaw, York W. 1985. "Dependent Development in Black Africa: A Cross-National Study." *American Sociological Review* 50 (April): 195–207.

Burstein, Paul. 1977. "Political Elites and Labor Markets: Selection of American Cabinet Members, 1932–72." *Social Forces* 56 (September): 189–201.

Chirot, Daniel. 1985. "The Rise of the West." *American Sociological Review* 50 (April): 181–195.

Dahl, Robert A. 1967. *Pluralist Democracy in the United States: Conflict and Consent*. Chicago: Rand McNally.

Dahl, Robert A. 1976. *Democracy in the United States: Promise and Performance*. Chicago: Rand McNally. Third edition.

Dahl, Robert A. 1982. *Dilemmas of Pluralist Democracy*. New Haven: Yale University Press.

Dealy, Glen C. 1985. "The Pluralistic Latins." *Foreign Policy* (Winter): 108–127.

de Tocqueville, Alexis. 1966. *Democracy in America*. New York: Harper & Row. Translated by George Lawrence. Originally published in 1835.

Deutsch, R. Eden. 1985. "Tomorrow's Work Force." *Futurist* 19 (December): 8–11.

Domhoff, G. William. 1978. *The Powers That Be*. New York: Random House.

Domhoff, G. William. 1983. *Who Rules America Now?: A View for the Eighties*. Englewood Cliffs, NJ: Prentice-Hall.

Edsall, Thomas Byrne. 1986. "Republican America." *New York Review of Books* 33 (April 24): 3–4+.

Garson, G. David. 1977. *Power and Politics in the United States*. Lexington, MA: D. C. Heath.

Gartner, Alan, and Frank Riessman. 1974. "Is There a Work Ethic?" *American Journal of Orthopsychiatry* 44 (July): 563–567.

Gerth, Hans, and C. Wright Mills (eds.). 1946. *From Max Weber: Essays in Sociology*. New York: Oxford University Press.

Gilpin, Robert. 1975. *U. S. Power and the Multinational Corporation: The Political Economy of Foreign Direct Investment*. New York: Basic.

Grant, Alan R. 1979. *The American Political Process.* London: Heinemann.

Greenberg, Edward S. 1974. *Serving the Few.* New York: Wiley.

Kohn, Melvin L. 1976. "Occupational Structure and Alienation." *American Journal of Sociology* 82 (July): 111–130.

Lemann, Nicholas. 1986. "New Tycoons Reshape Politics." *New York Times Magazine* (June 8): 51+.

Lindblom, Charles E. 1982. "Another State of Mind." *American Political Science Review* 76 (March): 9–21.

Manley, John F. 1983. "Neo-Pluralism: A Class Analysis of Pluralism I and Pluralism II." *American Political Science Review* 77 (June): 368–383.

Marx, Karl. 1932. "Manifesto of the Communist Party," pp. 315–355 in Marx, *Capital, the Communist Manifesto and Other Writings.* New York: The Modern Library. Translated by Stephen L. Trask.

Masters, Marick F., and Gerald D. Keim. 1985. "Determinants of PAC Participation among Large Corporations." *Journal of Politics* 47 (November): 1158–1173.

Merton, Robert K. 1968. "Manifest and Latent Functions," pp. 73–138 in Merton, *Social Theory and Social Structure.* New York: The Free Press. Third edition.

Mills, C. Wright. 1959. *The Power Elite.* New York: Oxford University Press.

Morton, Herbert C. 1977. "A Look at Factors Affecting the Quality of Working Life." *Monthly Labor Review* (October): 64–65.

Mottaz, Clifford J. 1981. "Some Determinants of Work Alienation." *Sociological Quarterly* (Autumn): 515–529.

Ranney, Austin. 1966. *The Governing of Men.* New York: Holt, Rinehart and Winston.

Riegle, Donald W., Jr. 1982. "The Psychological and Social Effects of Unemployment." *American Psychologist* 37 (October): 1113–1115.

Riordan, William L. 1963. *Plunkitt of Tammany Hall.* New York: Dutton.

Roelofs, H. Mark. 1967. *The Language of Modern Politics.* Homewood, IL: The Dorsey Press.

Safran, William. 1985. "The Mitterand Regime and Its Policies of Ethnocultural Accommodation." *Comparative Politics* 18 (October): 41–63.

Salomon, David, and Jules Bernstein. 1982. "The Corporate Thrust in American Politics," pp. 176–179 in Leonard Cargan and Jeanne H. Ballantine (eds.), *Sociological Footprints.* Belmont, CA: Wadsworth. Second edition.

Samuelson, Paul A. 1980. *Economics.* New York: McGraw-Hill. Eleventh edition.

Smith, Adam. 1930. *Inquiry into the Nature and Causes of the Wealth of Nations.* London: Methuen and Company. Originally published in 1776.

Terkel, Studs. 1974. *Working.* New York: Pantheon Books.

Toffler, Alvin. 1981. *The Third Wave.* New York: Bantam.

Tolchin, Martin, and Susan Tolchin. 1972. *To the Victor. . . .* New York: Vintage.

Twain, Mark. 1973. *Mark Twain and the Three R's.* Indianapolis: Bobbs-Merrill.

Weber, Max. 1947. *The Theory of Social and Economic Organization.* New York: The Free Press. Translated by A. M. Henderson and Talcott Parsons.

Wilensky, Harold L. 1966. "Work as a Social Problem" pp. 117–166 in Howard S. Becker (ed.), *Social Problems: A Modern Approach.* New York: Wiley.

Wise, David. 1976. "Cloak and Dagger Operations: An Overview," pp. 88–101 in Jerome H. Skolnick and Elliot Currie (eds.), *Crisis in American Institutions.* Boston: Little, Brown. Third edition.

Wolfe, Alan. 1973. *The Seamy Side of Democracy.* New York: David McKay.

Yankelovich, Daniel. 1974. "The Meaning of Work," pp. 19–47 in J. M. Rosow (ed.), *The Worker and the Job.* Englewood Cliffs, NJ: Prentice-Hall.

## Chapter 15

Addiss, Susan S. 1985. "Setting Goals and Priorities: 1984 Presidential Address." *American Journal of Public Health* 75 (November): 1276–1279.

Anderson, James G., and Stephen J. Jay. 1985. "Computers and Clinical Judgment: The Role of Physician Networks." *Social Science and Medicine* 20: 969–979.

Barnard, David. 1985. "Unsung Questions of Medical Ethics." *Social Science and Medicine* 21: 243–249.

Becker, Howard S., and Blanche Geer. 1958. "The Fate of Idealism in Medical School." *American Sociological Review* 23 (February): 50–56.

Ben-David, Joseph. 1971. *The Scientist's Role in Society.* Englewood Cliffs, NJ: Prentice-Hall.

Betz, Michael, and Lenahan O'Connell. 1983. "Changing Doctor–Patient Relationships and the Rise in Concern for Accountability." *Social Problems* 31 (October): 84–95.

Clymer, Adam. 1986. "Poll Finds Children Remain Enthusiastic on Spaceflight." *New York Times* (February 2): 1+.

Coe, Rodney M. 1978. *Sociology of Medicine.* New York: McGraw-Hill.

Conrad, Peter, and Joseph W. Schneider. 1981. "Professionalization, Monopoly, and the Structure of Medical Practice," pp. 155–164 in Peter Conrad and Rochelle Kern (eds.), *The Sociology of Health and Illness.* New York: St. Martin's.

Feagin, Joe R. 1986. *Social Problems.* Englewood Cliffs, NJ: Prentice-Hall. Second edition.

Fox, Renée C. 1978. "Training for Uncertainty," pp. 189–202 in Howard D. Schwartz and Cary S. Kart (eds.), *Dominant Issues in Medical Sociology.* Reading, MA: Addison-Wesley.

Freidson, Eliot. 1970. *Profession of Medicine.* New York: Harper & Row.

**490**

Freidson, Eliot. 1978. "Colleague Relationships among Physicians," pp. 228–237 in Howard D. Schwartz and Cary S. Kart (eds.), *Dominant Issues in Medical Sociology*. Reading, MA: Addison-Wesley.

Freidson, Eliot. 1981. "Professional Dominance and the Ordering of Health Services: Some Consequences," pp. 184–197 in Peter Conrad and Rochelle Kern (eds.), *The Sociology of Health and Illness*. New York: St. Martin's.

Gray-Toft, Pamela, and James G. Anderson. 1981. "Stress among Hospital Nursing Staff: Its Causes and Effects." *Social Science and Medicine* 15 (September): 639–647.

Honig-Parnass, Tikvah. 1981. "Lay Concepts of the Sick-Role: An Examination of the Professionalist Bias in Parsons' Model." *Social Science and Medicine* 15 (September): 615–623.

Lee, Vicki L. 1985. "Scientific Knowledge as Rules That Guide Behavior." *Psychological Record* 35 (Spring): 183–192.

MacKay, William. 1978. *Salesman Surgeon*. New York: McGraw-Hill.

Markson, Elizabeth. 1971. "A Hiding Place to Die." *Trans-action* 9 (November/December): 48–54.

Mechanic, David. 1978. *Medical Sociology*. New York: The Free Press. Second edition.

Merton, Robert K. 1973. *The Sociology of Science*. Chicago: University of Chicago Press.

Mitroff, Ian I. 1974. "Norms and Counter-Norms in a Select Group of the Apollo Moon Scientists: A Case Study of the Ambivalence of Scientists." *American Sociological Review* 39 (August): 579–595.

Moravcsik, Michael. 1985. "The Ultimate Scientific Plateau." *Futurist* 19 (October): 28–30.

Najman, J. M., D. Klein, and C. Munro. 1982. "Patient Characteristics Negatively Stereotyped by Doctors." *Social Science and Medicine* 16: 1781–1789.

New York Times. 1985. "Tougher Peer Review of Doctors Urged." (June 18): C3.

Parkes, Katherine R. 1985. "Stressful Episodes Reported by First-Year Student Nurses: A Descriptive Account." *Social Science and Medicine*. 20: 945–953.

Parsons, Talcott. 1951. *The Social System*. New York: The Free Press.

Pontell, Henry N., et al. 1982. "Policing Physicians: Practitioner Fraud and Abuse in a Government Medical Program." *Social Problems* 30 (October): 117–125.

Quint, Jeanne C. 1978. "Institutionalized Practices of Information Control," pp. 87–99 in Howard D. Schwartz and Cary S. Kart (eds.), *Dominant Issues in Medical Sociology*. Reading, MA: Addison-Wesley.

Reverby, Susan. 1981. "Re-forming the Hospital Nurse: The Management of American Nursing," pp. 220–233 in Peter Conrad and Rochelle Kern (eds.), *The Sociology of Health and Illness*. New York: St. Martin's.

Rifkin, Jeremy. 1980. "Recombinant DNA," pp. 145–156 in Rita Arditti, Pat Brennan, and Steve Cavrak (eds.), *Science and Liberation*. Boston: South End Press.

Ryan, William. 1976. *Blaming the Victim*. New York: Vintage. Second edition.

Schacht, Paul J., and Alex Pemberton. 1985. "What Is Unnecessary Surgery? Who Shall Decide? Issues of Consumer Sovereignty, Conflict and Self-Regulation." *Social Science and Medicine* 20: 199–206.

Szasz, Thomas S., and Marc H. Hollender. 1956. "A Contribution to the Philosophy of Medicine: The Basic Models of the Doctor–Patient Relationship." *A.M.A. Archives of Internal Medicine* 97 (May): 585–592.

Twaddle, Andrew C., and Richard M. Hessler, 1977. *A Sociology of Health*. St Louis: C. V. Mosby.

U. S. Bureau of the Census. 1984. *Statistical Abstract of the United States: 1984*. Washington, DC: U. S. Government Printing Office. 104th edition.

U. S. Bureau of the Census. *Statistical Abstract of the United States: 1986*. Washington, DC: U. S. Government Printing Office. 106th edition.

University of California Nuclear Weapons Labs Conversion Project. 1980. "Livermore and Los Alamos Scientific Laboratories," pp. 93–112 in Rita Arditti, Pat Brennan, and Steve Cavrak (eds.), *Science and Liberation*. Boston: South End Press.

Williams, Robin M., Jr. 1970. *American Society*. New York: Alfred A. Knopf. Third edition.

Wolinsky, Frederic D. 1980. *The Sociology of Health*. Boston: Little, Brown.

Wolinsky, Frederic D., and Sally R. Wolinsky. 1981. "Expecting Sick-Role Legitimation and Getting It." *Journal of Health and Social Behavior* 22 (September): 229–242.

Wyngaarden, James B. 1984. "Science and Government: A Federal Agency Perspective." *American Psychologist* 9 (September): 1053–1055.

## Chapter 16

Alpern, David M. 1981. "Mr. Fixit for the Cities." *Newsweek* 98 (May 4): 26–30.

Barnet, Richard J. 1980. *The Lean Years: Politics in the Age of Scarcity*. New York: Simon & Schuster.

Beck, Melinda. 1982. "The Decaying of America." *Newsweek* 99 (August 2): 12–17.

Bouvier, Leon F. 1984. "Planet Earth 1984–2034: A Demographic Vision." *Population Bulletin* 39 (February): 3–39.

Brown, Lester R. 1978. *The Twenty-Ninth Day*. New York: Norton.

Brown, M. 1980. *Laying Waste: The Poisoning of America by Toxic Chemicals*. New York: Pantheon.

Campbell, A. K., and J. A. Dollenmayer. 1975. "Governance in a Metropolitan Society," pp. 355–396 in A. H. Hawley and V. P. Rock (eds.), *Metropolitan America in Contemporary Perspective*. New York: Wiley.

Clayre, Alasdair. 1984. *The Heart of the Dragon*. Boston: Houghton Mifflin.

Committee on Agriculture, House of Representatives. 1976. "Malthus and America (1974)," pp. 253–256 in Phillip Appleman (ed.), *Thomas Robert Malthus: An Essay on the Principle of Population*. New York: Norton.

Commoner, Barry. 1972. *The Closing Circle: Nature, Man and Technology*. New York: Bantam.

Dahmann, Donald C. 1985. "Assessments of Neighborhood Quality in Metropolitan America." *Urban Affairs Quarterly* 20 (June): 511–535.

Davis, Kingsley. 1967. "Population Policy: Will Current Programs Succeed?" *Science* 157 (November 10): 730–739.

Ehrlich, Paul R., Anne H. Ehrlich, and John P. Holdren. 1977. *Ecoscience: Population, Resources, Environment*. San Francisco: W. H. Freeman.

Fitzpatrick, Kevin M., and John R. Logan. 1985. "The Aging of the Suburbs: 1960–1980." *American Sociological Review* 50 (February): 106–117.

Freudenberg, Nicholas. 1984. "Citizen Action for Environmental Health: Report on a Survey of Community Organizations." *American Journal of Public Health* 74 (May): 444–448.

Ganz, Alexander. 1985. "Where Has the Urban Crisis Gone? How Boston and Other Large Cities Have Stemmed Economic Decline." *Urban Affairs Quarterly* 20 (June): 449–468.

Gittell, Marilyn. 1985. "The American City: A National Priority or an Expendable Population?" *Urban Affairs Quarterly* 21 (September): 13–19.

Gottman, Jean. 1961. *Megalopolis: The Urbanized Northeastern Seaboard of the United States*. Cambridge, MA: M.I.T. Press.

Graves, Robert. 1962. *Claudius the God*. New York: Vintage. Originally published in New York: Harrison Smith and Robert Haas, 1935.

Jacobs, Jane. 1961. *The Death and Life of Great American Cities*. New York: Vintage.

Kraft, Michael E., and Norman J. Vig. 1984. "Environmental Policy in the Reagan Presidency." *Political Science Quarterly* 99 (Fall): 415–439.

London, Bruce, et al. 1986. "The Determinants of Gentrification in the United States: A City-Level Analysis." *Urban Affairs Quarterly* 21 (March): 369–387.

Lowi, Theodore J. 1981. "Machine Politics—Old and New," pp. 214–217 in J. John Palen (ed.), *City Scenes*. Boston: Little, Brown. Second edition.

Malthus, Thomas Robert. 1798. *First Essay on Population: 1798*. London: Printed for J. Johnson in St. Paul's Churchyard.

Matthews, Tom. 1979. "Nuclear Accident." *Newsweek* 93 (April 9): 24–26+.

Meadows, Donella H., et al. 1972. *The Limits to Growth: A Report on the Club of Rome's Project on the Predicament of Mankind*. New York: Signet Books.

Mumford, Lewis. 1971. "Statement of Lewis Mumford, Author. Hearings before the U. S. Senate,

Subcommittee on Executive Reorganization, Committee on Government Operations, April 21, 1967," pp. 431–456 in Ted Venetoulis and Ward Eisenhauer (eds.), *Up against the Urban Wall*. Englewood Cliffs, NJ: Prentice-Hall.

Nam, Charles B., and Susan O. Gustavus. 1976. *Population: The Dynamics of Demographic Change*. Boston: Houghton Mifflin.

Newsweek. 1983. "The Tavern Rape: Cheers and No Help." 101 (March 21): 25.

Nisbet, Ian C. T. 1982. "Flaws and Failures of the Clean Air Act," pp. 177–178 in John Allen (ed.), *Environment 82/83*. Guilford, CT: Dushkin.

Palen, J. John. 1981. *The Urban World*. New York: McGraw-Hill. Second edition.

Petersen, William. 1975. *Population*. New York: Macmillan. Third edition.

Pollock, Cynthia. 1986. "The Closing Act: Decommissioning Nuclear Power Plants." *Environment* 28 (March): 10–15+.

Population Reference Bureau. 1984. "The American Family Changes and Challenges." Washington, DC: U. S. Government Printing Office.

Population Today. 1986. "Population Momentum Is the Key." 14 (April): 3+.

Reilly, William K. 1982. "Reconciling Mineral Development and Environmental Quality." *Vital Speeches* 48 (May 1): 471–475.

Ridker, Ronald G., and W. D. Watson. 1980. *To Choose a Future: Resources and Environmental Problems of the United States*. Baltimore: Johns Hopkins Press.

Robertson, Ian. 1980. *Social Problems*. New York: Random House. Second edition.

Schwab, William A. 1982. *Urban Sociology*. Reading, MA: Addison-Wesley.

Silk, Leonard. 1986. "Modern Views of Population." *New York Times* (July 9): D2.

Simmel, Georg. 1950. *The Sociology of Georg Simmel*. Glencoe, IL: The Free Press. Translated by Kurt H. Wolff.

Sjoberg, Gideon. 1960. *The Preindustrial City: Past and Present*. Glencoe, IL: The Free Press.

Spates, James L., and John J. Macionis. 1982. *The Sociology of Cities*. New York: St. Martin's.

Sullivan, Thomas, et al. 1980. *Social Problems*. New York: Wiley.

Sun, Marjorie. 1983. "Missouri's Costly Dioxin Lesson." *Science* 219 (January 28): 367–369.

Tönnies, Ferdinand. 1957. *Community and Society*. New York: Harper & Company.

United Nations. 1980. *Demographic Yearbook, 1980*. New York: United Nations Publishing Service.

U. S. Bureau of the Census. 1984. *Current Population Reports, Population Characteristics*, Series P–20, *Fertility of American Women: June 1983*. Washington, DC: U. S. Government Printing Office.

U. S. News and World Report. 1981. "Population Surge Shakes Up Small Towns." 90 (May 18): 76–77.

Weisman, Steven R. 1983. "Reagan, Assailing

Critics, Defends His Environment Policy as 'Sound'." *New York Times* (June 12): 1+.

Wirth, Louis, 1938. "Urbanism as a Way of Life." *American Journal of Sociology* 44 (July): 3–24.

Wolman, Harold. 1986. "The Reagan Urban Policy and Its Impacts." *Urban Affairs Quarterly* 21 (March): 311–335.

Wong, Kenneth K., and Paul E. Peterson. 1986. "Urban Response to Federal Program Flexibility: Politics of Community Development Block Grant." *Urban Affairs Quarterly* 21 (March): 293–309.

Zimmerman, J. F. 1975. "The Patchwork Approach: Adaptive Responses to Increasing Urbanism," pp. 431–473 in A. H. Hawley and V. P. Roch (eds.), *Metropolitan America in Contemporary Perspective.* New York: Wiley.

## Chapter 17

Allport, Gordon, and Leo Postman. 1947. *The Psychology of Rumor.* New York: Henry Holt and Company.

Barron, James. 1982. "Poison Worries Lead to Precautions for Halloween." *New York Times* (October 28): B1.

Beck, Melinda. 1980. "Out of Their League." *Newsweek* 96 (September 8): 21.

Beck, Melinda. 1983. "A Racial Outburst in Miami." *Newsweek* 101 (January 10): 23.

Blumer, Herbert. 1975. "Outline of Collective Behavior," pp. 22–45 in Robert Evans (ed.), *Readings in Collective Behavior.* Chicago: Rand McNally. Second edition.

Brown, Lester R., Patricia L. McGrath, and Bruce Stokes. 1982. "The Population Problem in 22 Dimensions," pp. 262–269 in Leonard Cargan and Jeanne H. Ballantine (eds.), *Sociological Footprints.* Belmont, CA: Wadsworth. Second edition.

Brown, Michael, and Amy Goldin. 1973. *Collective Behavior.* Pacific Palisades, CA: Goodyear.

Cantril, Hadley. 1940. *The Invasion from Mars.* Princeton: Princeton University Press.

Caplan, Nathan S., and Jeffrey M. Paige. 1968. "A Study of Ghetto Rioters." *Scientific American* 219 (August): 15–21.

Davies, James C. 1962. "Toward a Theory of Revolution." *American Sociological Review* 27 (February): 5–19.

Davis, Terry. 1986. "The Forms of Collective Racial Violence." *Political Studies* 34 (March): 40–60.

Farley, John E. 1982. *Majority-Minority Relations.* Englewood Cliffs, NJ: Prentice-Hall.

Foy, Eddie, and Alvin F. Harlow. 1957. *Clowning through Life.* New York: Dutton. 1928, pp. 104–113, excerpted in Ralph H. Turner and Lewis M. Killian, *Collective Behavior.* Englewood Cliffs, NJ: Prentice-Hall.

Freeman, Jo. 1979. "The Woman's Liberation Movement: Its Origins, Organizations, Activities, and Ideas," pp. 557–574 in Jo Freeman (ed.), *Women: A Feminist Perspective.* Palo Alto, CA: Mayfield.

Gamson, William. 1975. *The Strategy of Social Protest.* Homewood, IL: Dorsey Press.

Gurney, Joan Neff, and Kathleen J. Tierney. 1982. "Relative Deprivation and Social Movements: A Critical Look at Twenty Years of Theory and Research." *Sociological Quarterly* 23 (Winter): 33–47.

Hannigan, John A. 1985. "Alain Touraine, Manuel Castells and Social Movement Theory: A Critical Appraisal." *Sociological Quarterly* 26 (Winter): 435–454.

Hefez, Albert. 1985. "The Role of the Press and the Medical Community in the Epidemic of 'Mysterious Gas Poisoning' in the Jordan West Bank." *American Journal of Psychiatry* 142 (July): 833–837.

Kerbo, Harold R. 1982. "Movements of 'Crisis' and Movements of 'Affluence.'" *Journal of Conflict Resolution* 26 (December): 645–663.

Kerbo, Harold R., and Richard A. Shaffer. 1986. "Unemployment and Protest in the United States, 1890–1940: A Methodological Critique and Research Note." *Social Forces* 64 (June): 1046–1056.

Killian, Lewis M. 1964. "Social Movements," pp. 426–455 in Robert E. L. Faris (ed.), *Handbook of Modern Sociology.* Chicago: Rand McNally.

Klandermans, Bert. 1984. "Mobilization and Participation: Social-Psychological Expansion of Resource Mobilization Theory." *American Sociological Review* 49 (October): 583–600.

Klein, Andrew L. 1976. "Changes in Leadership Appraisal as a Function of the Stress of a Simulated Panic Situation." *Journal of Personality and Social Psychology* 34 (December): 1143–1154.

Lauer, Robert H. 1977. *Perspective on Social Change.* Boston: Allyn and Bacon. Second edition.

Le Bon, Gustave. 1952. *The Crowd.* London: Ernest Benn Limited. Originally published in 1896.

Lenski, Gerhard, and Jean Lenski. 1982. *Human Societies.* New York: McGraw-Hill. Fourth edition.

Life. 1969. "The Magical McCartney Mystery." 67 (November 7): 103–105.

Linton, Ralph. 1973. "Discovery, Invention, and Their Cultural Setting," pp. 451–456 in Amitai Etzioni and Eva Etzioni-Halevy (eds.), *Social Change.* New York: Basic. Second edition.

Linton, Ralph. 1982. "One Hundred Percent American," pp. 58–59 in Leonard Cargan and Jeanne H. Ballantine (eds.), *Sociological Footprints.* Belmont, CA: Wadsworth. Second edition.

Malcolm, Andrew H. 1980. "The 'Shortage' of Bathroom Tissue," pp. 497–498 in Reece McGee et al. *Sociology.* New York: Holt, Rinehart and Winston. Second edition.

Mann, Leon. 1981. "The Baiting Crowd in Episodes of Threatened Suicide." *Journal of Personality and Social Psychology* 41 (October): 703–709.

Marshall, S. L. A. 1947. *Men under Fire.* New York: William Morrow.

Morrison, Denton E. 1973. "Some Notes toward Theory on Relative Deprivation, Social Movements, and Social Changes," pp. 103–116 in Robert R. Evans (ed.), *Social Movements.* Chicago: Rand McNally.

Murdock, George Peter. 1956. "How Culture Changes," pp. 247–260 in Harry L. Shapiro (ed.), *Man, Culture, and Society.* New York: Oxford University Press.

National Advisory Commission on Civil Disorders. 1968. *Report of the National Advisory Commission on Civil Disorders.* New York: Bantam.

New Haven Register. 1986. "Letterman's Flip Remark Prompts $1 Million Suit." (July 26): 14.

Nielsen, François. 1985. "Toward a Theory of Ethnic Solidarity in Modern Societies." *American Sociological Review* 50 (April): 133–149.

Oberschall, Anthony. 1973. *Social Conflict and Social Movements.* Englewood Cliffs, NJ: Prentice-Hall.

Orwell, George. 1946. *Animal Farm.* New York: Harcourt, Brace and World.

Quarantelli, E. L., and Russell R. Dynes. 1970. "Property Norms and Looting: Their Patterns in Community Crises." *Phylon* 31 (Summer): 168–182.

Rabinowitz, Dorothy. 1981. "John Lennon's Mourners." *Commentary* 71 (February): 58–61.

Rice, Berkeley. 1981. "Gourmet Worms: Antidote to a Rumor." *Psychology Today* 15 (August): 20+.

Ryder, Norman B. 1980. "The Future of American Fertility," pp. 51–66 in Arlene Skolnick and Jerome H. Skolnick (eds.), *Familiy in Transition.* Boston: Little, Brown. Third edition.

Shibutani, Tamotsu. 1966. *Improvised News: A Sociological Study of Rumor.* Indianapolis: Bobbs-Merrill.

Smelser, Neil J. 1963. *Theory of Collective Behavior.* New York: The Free Press.

Stiefel, Michael. 1982. "Soft and Hard Energy Paths: The Roads Not Taken," pp. 49–50 in John Allen (ed.), *Environment 82/83.* Guilford, CT: Dushkin.

Tilly, Charles. 1978. *From Mobilization to Revolution.* Reading, MA: Addison-Wesley.

Time. 1969. "Of Rumor, Myth and a Beatle." 94 (October 31): 41.

Turner, Ralph H. 1964. "Collective Behavior." pp. 382–426 in Robert E. L. Faris (ed.), *Handbook of Modern Sociology.* Chicago: Rand McNally.

Turner, Ralph H., and Lewis M. Killian. 1972. *Collective Behavior.* Englewood Cliffs, NJ: Prentice-Hall. Second edition.

Vander Zanden. James W. 1981. *Social Psychology.* New York: Random House. Second edition.

# LITERARY CREDITS

Table 16.1. From J. C. Russell, *Late Ancient and Medieval Population.* Philadelphia: American Philosophical Society, 1958, pp. 60–62.

Figures 16.1, 16.2. U.S. Bureau of the Census.

Figure 16.4. U.S. Bureau of the Census; United Nations, *Demographic Yearbook,* 1980. Copyright © 1980 United Nations. Reproduced by permission.

Figure 16.5. From *Roper Reports,* November 1981. Used by permission of the Roper Organization, Inc.

Figure 16.6. Council on Environmental Quality.

Tables 17.1, 17.2. Adapted from Ted Robert Gurr, "Political Protest and Rebellion in the 1960s," in *Violence in America: Historical Perspectives* edited by Hugh Davis Graham and Ted Robert Gurr (Newbury Park, Calif.; Sage Publications, 1979), pp. 54, 60. Used by permission of Ted Robert Gurr.

Figure 17.1. Adapted from James C. Davies, "Toward a Theory of Revolution," *American Sociological Review* 27 (1962), 6: the J-curve.

# Photo Credits

**Chapter 1** Opener: Paul Conklin/Monkmeyer. Page 6, Charles Gatewood/Stock, Boston. Page 12, © 1982, David M. Campione/Taurus. Page 13, © Bettye Lane/Photo Researchers, Inc. **Chapter 2** Opener: © Ellis Herwig/Stock, Boston. Page 25, © Esaias Baitel/Photo Researchers, Inc. Page 26, © Jerry Berndt/Stock, Boston. Page 37, courtesy of Estate of Stanley Milgram. **Chapter 3** Opener: F.B. Grunzeig/Photo Researchers, Inc. Page 27 (top left) © Jean Claude Lejeune/Stock, Boston. Page 47 (top right) Ira Kirschenbaum/Stock Boston. Page 48, © 1983, George E. Jones III/Photo Researchers, Inc. Page 45, Culver Pictures. Page 51, Bettmann Newsphotos. Page 57, P. Spadavecchia/The Image Works, Inc. Page 60, Bettmann Newsphotos. **Chapter 4** Opener: Alice Kandell/Photo Researchers, Inc. Page 71, March St. Gill/Woodfin Camp & Associates. page 73, Jim Anderson/Woodfin Camp & Associates. Page 74, Wide World Photos. Page 78, © Roger Malloch/Magnum. Page 80, © Alan Carey. The Image Works, Inc. **Chapter 5** Opener: Jaye R. Phillips/The Picture Cube. Page 98, © Bohdan Hrynewych/Stock Boston. Page 103 (top), Irene Bayer/Monkmeyer Press Photo. Page 103 (bottom), Alex Webb/Magnum. page 108, © Arthur Tress/Photo Researchers, Inc. **Chapter 6** Opener: © Fred Lyon/Photo Researchers, Inc. Page 110, MOMA/Film Stills Archive. Page 131 © Charles Gatewood/The Image Works, Inc. Page 133, Bettmann Newsphotos. **Chapter 7** Opener: Jan Lukas/Photo Researchers, Inc. Page 147, David Strickler/Monkmeyer. Page 149 (left) Abigail Heyman/Archive Pictures. Page 149 (right) © Jean Claude Lejeune/Stock, Boston. Page 153, Bettmann Newsphotos. Page 154 © Sepp Seitz/Woodfin Camp & Associates. **Chapter 8** Opener: Jan Lukas/Art Resource Center. Page 171, Bettmann Archive. Page 176, Jean Pierre Laffont/Sygma. Page 184, Wide World Photos. **Chapter 9** Opener: © F.B. Grunzweig/Photo Researchers, Inc. Page 204, Bettmann Newsphotos. Page 215, Constantine Manos/Magnum. Page 221, © Elizabeth Hamlin/Stock, Boston. **Chapter 10** Opener: © Alice Kandell/Photo Researchers, Inc. Page 232 (top) © Bob Adelman/Monkmeyer Press Photo. Page 232 (bottom) Dan Wlash/The Picture Cube. Page 237, Wide World Photos. Page 245, © Alex Webb/Magnum. Page 246, © Jason Laure/Woodfin

Camp & Associates. **Chapter 11** Opener: © Jim Anderson/Woodfin Camp & Associates. Page 265, Mark Antman/The Image Works, Inc. Page 266 (left) Culver Pictures. Page 266 (right) © Bettye Lane/Photo Researchers, Inc. Page 269, Alan Carey/The Image Works. Page 270, Martine Frank/Magnum. Page 273, Alan Carey/The Image Works, Inc. Page 279, Ira Wyman/Sygma. **Chapter 12** Opener: © Lynn Eskenazi/Comstock. Page 289, © Marc & Evelyne Bernheim/Woodfin Camp & Associates. Page 291, The Bettmann Archive. Page 298, Christa Armstrong/Photo Researchers, Inc. Page 301, MOMA/Film Stills Archive. **Chapter 13** Opener: © Alan Carey/The Image Works, Inc. Page 314, David S. Strickler/The Picture Cube. Page 315, © Eugene Gordon/Photo Researchers, Inc. Page 318, (top left) © Al Stephenson/Woodfin Camp & Associates. Page 318 (top right) Rick Smolan/Stock, Boston. Page 318, (bottom) Kerwin Roche/Monkmeyer. Page 324, Sybil Shelton/Peter Arnold, Inc. Page 327, George W. Gardner/Stock, Boston. **Chapter 14** Opener: Joan Lifton/Archive Pictures, Inc. Page 342, Tim Gordon/Sygma. Page 343, © Audrey Topping/Photo Researchers, Inc. Pgae 345, © Ellen Shubl/The Picture Cube, Page 348, Wide World Photos. Page 357 (left) © Peter Fougere/The Picture Cube. Page 357 (right) © Frank Siteman/Taurus. Page 359, Mimi Forsyth/Monkmeyer Press Photo. **Chapter 15** Opener: © John Blaustein/Woodfin Camp & Associates. Page 373, (top) © Mary Evans Picture Library/Photo Researchers, Inc. Page 373 (bottom) © Lynn McLaren/Photo Researchers, Inc. Page 377, Sidney Harris. Page 384, © Bruce Roberts/Photo Researchers, Inc. Page 387, Suzie Fitzhugh/Stock Boston. **Chapter 16** Opener: Audry Gottlieb/Monkmeyer Press Photo. Page 402, Grant White/Monkmeyer Press Photo. Page 404, Culver Pictures. Page 411, Alan Carey/The Image Works, Inc. Page 418, Wide World Photos. Page 423, Daniel S. Brody/Stock Boston. **Chapter 17** Opener: © Bettye Lane/Photo Researchers, Inc. Page 433, Diego Goldber/Sygma. Page 441 (top) Owen Franken/Stock, Boston. Page 441 (bottom) Wide World Photos. Page 442, Wide World Photos. Page 449 (top) Marc & Evelyne Bernheim/Woodfin Camp & Associates. Page 449 (bottom) © Robert Azzi/Woodfin Camp & Associates. Page 453, Bettmann Newsphotos.

# NAME INDEX

# SUBJECT INDEX

Abkhasia (Soviet Union), elderly in, 271–272
Abortion, debate about, 320
Abscam scandal, 348
**Absolute wealth,** 206
**Abstinence,** 154
Academic skills, and education, 324,328
Achievement, and success, 60
Acute diseases, 380, 381
Adolescence, 132–133, 135; middle-class, 132
Advance of knowledge, and education, 325, 327
Afrikaners, 238–239
Age, and adjustment to divorce, 302; and crime, 184–185; and death rate, 380; and disease, 380, 381; and divorce, 300
**Ageism,** 269–272, 276; costs, 270–272; process, 269, 276
**Aggregate,** 72
AIDS, 23, 158, 159, 382–383
Air pollution, 422, 452–453
Alienation (*see* Work alienation)
American blacks (*see* Black Americans)
American cities, growth, 403–406
American Controversies, 14–15, 61, 76–77, 208–209, 322–323, 378–379
American family, 291–293
American health care, 383–384
American Indians (*see* Native Americans)
American Jews (*see* Jews)
American minority groups, 242–252
American politics, 344–345, 347–349
American population, 415–417
American science, rise, 373–374
American society, competition, 61; social classes, 210–216; social mobility, 216–222
American values, 61–62
Americanization, of minority groups, 252–253
**Androgynous** person, 160
*Animal Farm,* 433–435

*Année Sociologique,* 9
**Anomie,** 172
Anomie theory, 172–174, 178, 180
Anonymity, in crowds, 435–436
**Anticipatory socialization,** 77–78
**Anti-semitism,** 247
*Apartheid,* 238–239
Arab terrorists, 171
Arapesh (New Guinea), 52, 150–151
Argentina, public protest, 437–438
Arrests, 179–180; of elderly, 270
Asch experiments, 106–107
Asian-Americans, 247–249
Assimilation, 240, 241
Attica riot, 460–461, 462
**Authoritarian leaders,** 104
**Authoritarian personality,** 232–233, 236
**Authority,** 341; in German schools, 326–327; types, 341–343

Baby boom, 415, 452
**Backstage,** 99
Baganda, 55
Bail, 188–189
*Baker vs. Nelson,* 306
Balinese, 290
Bathroom tissue, rumors about, 443–444
Beatles, 432–433
**Beliefs,** 48–49, 54; of civil religion, 317–318
Bennington College, 78
Berkeley (California), and the disabled, 278
Bionic Woman, 263
**Biosocial position,** 149
Birth rate, decrease, 296
Black Americans, 236–237, 242–244, 251; and busing, 330–331; and corporate stress, 357–358; current situation, 243–244; education, 244, 330; housing, 243–244; jobs, 244; migration, 243, 405; protests by, 241–242, 243; and self-esteem, 236–237; slavery, 242; and riots, 438–439, 460, 461, 462; and social mobility, 219

Black Muslims (*see* Nation of Islam)
Black Panthers, 243, 461
Blacks, in South Africa, 238–239
Blind people, accommodations made by, 275
Blocked-opportunity theory, 439
Boers, 238
Bogardus scale, 234–235
**Bourgeoisie,** 203–204
Brazil, 240; and diffusion, 451
"Broken home," 301
*Brown v. the Topeka Board of Education,* 243, 330
Bubonic Plague, 412
**Bureaucracies,** 79–84; ancient bureaucracies, 79; characteristics, 79–80; dysfunctions, 82; informal structure, 80–81
**Bureaucratic personality,** 82, 174
Business, under capitalism, 350–351; in nineteenth-century America, 351; and political machines, 349; and suburban growth, 405
Busing, 330–331

Calvinism, 316
**Capital,** 350
**Capitalism,** 350–351; Marx's analysis, 351; and religion, 316
Carnegie Report, 329
Catholicism, 320; and work, 355
Caucasoid people, 230
**Causation,** 24
Central Intelligence Agency (CIA), 340
Cerebral palsy, 274
*Challenger* disaster, 371
Charisma, research, 367–369
**Charismatic system of authority,** 342–343
Chernobyl nuclear-power plant, 378, 379, 423
Cherokee tribe, 240
Chicago, air pollution, 422; population, 404
Chicago School of Sociology (*see* Sociology, at University of Chicago)
Chicanos, 242, 244–245
Child abuse, 119–120